THE SELF AND SOCIAL LIFE

McGraw-Hill Series in Social Psychology and Personality

CONSULTING EDITOR

Phillip R. Costanzo, *Duke University*

Schlenker: The Self and Social Life

THE SELF AND SOCIAL LIFE

Edited by

Barry R. Schlenker

University of Florida

McGRAW-HILL BOOK COMPANY

New York St. Louis San Francisco Auckland Bogotá
Hamburg Johannesburg London Madrid Mexico Montreal New Delhi
Panama Paris São Paulo Singapore Sydney Tokyo Toronto

This book was set in Times Roman by Black Dot, Inc. (ECU).
The editors were David V. Serbun and James R. Belser;
the production supervisor was Leroy A. Young.
The cover was designed by Mark Wieboldt.
Halliday Lithograph Corporation was printer and binder.

HM 291 .S395 1985 c.1

The Self and social life

THE SELF AND SOCIAL LIFE

Copyright © 1985 by McGraw-Hill, Inc. All rights reserved. Printed in the United States of America. Except as permitted under the United States Copyright Act of 1976, no part of this publication may be reproduced or distributed in any form or by any means, or stored in a data base or retrieval system, without the prior written permission of the publisher.
1234567890HALHAL8987654

ISBN 0-07-055307-6

Library of Congress Cataloging in Publication Data
Main entry under title:

The Self and social life.

    (McGraw-Hill series in social psychology and personality)
    Includes bibliographies and indexes.
    1. Self—Addresses, essays, lectures. 2. Social role—Addresses, essays, lectures. I. Schlenker, Barry R. II. Series.
HM291.S395 1985   302'.15   84-11299
ISBN 0-07-055307-6

To David

CONTENTS

	LIST OF CONTRIBUTORS	ix
	PREFACE	xi
1	Introduction: Foundations of the Self in Social Life—Barry R. Schlenker	1

PART 1   THE INNER AND OUTER SELVES   29

2	Historical Perspectives on the Presented Self—Karl E. Scheibe	33
3	Identity and Self-Identification—Barry R. Schlenker	65
4	The Self as Architect of Social Reality—William B. Swann, Jr.	100
5	To Whom Is the Self Presented?—Anthony G. Greenwald and Steven J. Breckler	126
6	Aspects of Self and the Control of Behavior—Charles S. Carver and Michael F. Scheier	146
7	Socioanalytic Theory: An Alternative to Armadillo Psychology—Robert Hogan, Warren Jones, and Jonathan Cheek	175

PART 2   THE SELF AND THE EXPLANATION OF EVENTS   199

8	Toward an Intuitive Politician Model of Attribution Processes—Philip E. Tetlock	203
9	The Excuse: An Amazing Grace?—C. R. Snyder	235

10 Identity, Self-Presentation, and the Resolution of Moral Dilemmas: Toward a Social Psychological Theory of Moral Behavior—Carl W. Backman 261

PART 3 THE SELF AND SOCIAL POWER 291

11 Social Power, Self-Presentation, and the Self—James T. Tedeschi and Nancy Norman 293

12 Deceiving and Detecting Deceit—Bella M. DePaulo, Julie I. Stone, and G. Daniel Lassiter 323

INDEXES 371
Name Index
Subject Index

LIST OF CONTRIBUTORS

CARL W. BACKMAN
Department of Sociology
University of Nevada

STEVEN J. BRECKLER
Department of Psychology
Ohio State University

CHARLES S. CARVER
Department of Psychology
University of Miami

JONATHAN CHEEK
Department of Psychology
Wellesley College

BELLA M. DEPAULO
Department of Psychology
University of Virginia

ANTHONY G. GREENWALD
Department of Psychology
Ohio State University

ROBERT HOGAN
Department of Psychology
University of Tulsa

WARREN JONES
Department of Psychology
University of Tulsa

G. DANIEL LASSITER
Department of Psychology
University of Virginia

NANCY NORMAN
Department of Psychology
State University of New York at Albany

KARL E. SCHEIBE
Department of Psychology
Wesleyan University

MICHAEL F. SCHEIER
Department of Psychology
Carnegie-Mellon University

BARRY R. SCHLENKER
Department of Psychology
University of Florida

C. R. SNYDER
Psychology Clinic
University of Kansas

JULIE I. STONE
Department of Psychology
University of Virginia

WILLIAM B. SWANN, JR.
Department of Psychology
University of Texas

JAMES T. TEDESCHI
Department of Psychology
State University of New York at Albany

PHILIP E. TETLOCK
Department of Psychology
University of California, Berkeley

PREFACE

A temptation exists to draw a sharp line of demarcation between the "outer" self, or the self as it is projected in our social lives, and the "inner" self, or the self as it exists in our private ruminations. The outer self sometimes evokes the same sort of sentiments as an unwanted, misbehaving offspring. It is an accident of nature that, while understandable when one stops to contemplate the overall picture, one would rather not have had happen. It is regarded by many as chameleon-like; it seems to change from audience to audience, being one thing to friends, another to parents, another to teachers, another to employers, another to employees, and so on. It often permits momentary outcomes to get the better of it; it forgets its heritage and seeks the fleeting regard of associates and mere acquaintances. It may even lie if the price is right (or close). It sometimes seems to be superficial and transparent. In contrast, the inner self is cherished stock. It is steadfast and unyielding. It could not be seduced by the harpies found in social life. It is distinctive, autonomous, proud, consistent, ethical, and true, having a permanence that bestows it with obvious status as the way things should be.

The psychological literature on the self bears a striking and somewhat unfortunate parallel to this metaphor of offspring. At one extreme, a body of literature has developed on self-presentation, which many theorists define as the attempt to influence how audiences, particularly other people with whom a person is momentarily interacting, perceive that person. Self-presentation theorists have often emphasized the strategic aspects of the social self, examining how people vary their presentations of self in order to increase their power in relationships and maximize profitable outcomes. As such, the literature on self-presentation is regarded by some as describing processes that are superficial, fleeting, and nonsubstantive; a topic of interest more to devotees of the advertising game than to scientists who investigate basic processes underlying human behavior. Indeed, some theorists regard self-presentational processes merely as annoying impediments to their research endeavors; they reason that if subjects' attempts to mask the inner self through self-presentation could be minimized or eliminated, their research results would provide a clearer portrait of the nature of the self.

At the other extreme, a large body of literature has developed on the inner self. The inner self is often defined as a theory of oneself that is constructed from experience. It is both a structure, containing the organized, relatively stable contents of our personal experiences, and an active process, which guides and regulates our thoughts, feelings, and actions. It is the core of our inner being; basic, enduring, genuine, and a topic worthy of the noblest of scientific intentions.

This seeming antipathy between the inner and outer self has sparked a variety of controversies. Is there one self, a genuine inner core, or are there many, each representing a public role played largely for the benefit of others? Is the self an inward and active agent, or is it merely a masking device that creates public illusions? Is the public self noble, expressing to others its inner qualities, or is it base, acting like a crass advertising agent that strategically presents qualities that are in its best interests?

This volume brings together current perspectives on the self and social life, focusing particularly on the yin and yang of the inner and outer self. In lieu of the antipathy described above, most of the chapters attempt to provide integrating perspectives, blending the inner and outer selves into a coherent family rather than leaving them a house divided. The chapters examine aspects of how the self is constructed, interpreted, and projected in social life, being both the creator and creature of its own environment. By drawing together into one volume the insights of some of the leading theorists and researchers in the area, the chapters provide a more dynamic portrait of current thought than could a book written by a single individual. Commonalities and controversies can be seen throughout, providing readers with the different emphases and interpretations that mark a vibrant scientific enterprise.

The chapters are divided into three general groupings. Part One deals most directly with the inner and outer self, exploring the structure and motivational properties of the self and its implications for interpersonal relations. Part Two discusses the role of the self in the construction of social reality, especially through the self's effects on the attributions and explanations people employ to describe their own conduct. Part Three deals with the strategic presentation of self in social life. Some of the chapters could have been placed in more than one section, but were located according to their primary emphasis.

Numerous individuals have my thanks for their varied contributions to this project. The chapter contributors are owed a multiple debt. Their enthusiasm, expertise, and helpful suggestions were invaluable in getting the project rolling and guiding the form it ultimately took. In addition, their chapters provide the substance of the volume, giving their readers, myself included, the pleasure of their insights into the nature of the self in social life. I also wish to thank colleagues who reviewed all or part of the manuscript: Robert Arkin, Roy Baumeister, Donelson Forsyth, Svenn Lindskold, and David Schneider. Their comments helped to improve the final product. The series editor, Philip Costanzo, also made numerous helpful suggestions. Colleagues and present and former students have aided me in shaping and refining my own ideas, thus playing an important role. In particular I wish to thank Marvin E. Shaw, Lawrence J. Severy, Mark R. Leary, David Dlugolecki, and John Hallam. Support for my research on self-identification from the National Institute of Mental Health (Research Scientist Development Program, Grant No. 1 K02-MH-00183) has proven invaluable. Finally, my wife, Pat, and son, David, kept me smiling even through the rough spots and provided the best sounding boards of all; I have been fortunate in finding such a supportive environment for my self.

Barry R. Schlenker

THE SELF AND SOCIAL LIFE

CHAPTER 1

INTRODUCTION: FOUNDATIONS OF THE SELF IN SOCIAL LIFE

Barry R. Schlenker
University of Florida

People are, concomitantly, individuals and members of society. As members of society, we are links in a chain that fastens us securely to the associations of people who came before us, who are our contemporaries, and who will be our successors. From this vantage point, we are shaped by the society into which we are born and the people with whom we associate during our lives. As individuals, we are active agents of our own fates, stamping our unique brands on the people and events we encounter. From this vantage point, our actions shape the world around us, leaving in our wakes a series of events that are different from what might have been had each of us never walked the earth. To appreciate the nature of the human experience, one must be cognizant of this yin and yang of the self and the society; both are intrinsic ingredients of what it means to be a human being. The self exists in and through social life, and social life exists through the association of selves.

This volume explores the self in social life: how the self is constructed, interpreted, and presented to audiences, including both other people and oneself as audience for one's own behavior. The chapters, written by prominent theorists and researchers, discuss current theories, research, and controversies about the self, examining such topics as the relationship between the private and public self, the structural and motivational properties of the self, self-regulation and self-evaluation, the ability of the self to create its own social environment, the role of the self in moral behavior, and the implications of the public self for effective social functioning. Together the chapters provide a dynamic portrait of contemporary thought and future directions for research. To pave the way for these explorations, this chapter examines some of the historical streams of thought and central issues that have brought us to our current state of knowledge about the self in social life.

VIEWS OF THE SELF THROUGH THE AGES

Early Views

Self is an elusive concept that has altered over the ages. In ancient Greece, as indicated in the work of Homer, human actions were thought to be determined by the gods, with people pushed and pulled by the whims of powers beyond them. By the fifth century B.C., Hellenistic drama began to show people making personal decisions, indicating human agency. This initial sense of self is "similar to a primitive conception of the soul; this is the self as ego, agency, or will, a sense of self-direction and power" (Hogan, 1976, p. 14). By the time of Plato and Aristotle, the soul was regarded as the legitimate topic of a science of psychology. In his treatise *On the Soul,* Aristotle wrote that the soul was "the principal of animal life," which animated and gave purpose to animals' activities. Humans were distinguished from the lower animals in that they alone possessed a part of the soul called "mind," which is "that whereby the soul thinks and judges." This higher portion of the soul permitted the examination of itself, being both reflective (able to think about things) and reflexive (able to think about oneself).

For Aristotle, body and soul were a single substance comprised of correlative aspects (i.e., bodily organs cannot act except as bodily functions). The human function of thinking, though, was held out as a "probable exception" to this rule, since he did not regard the act of understanding as a function of physical matter. By the fourth century A.D., Augustine added to the concept of the soul by equating it with the immaterial spiritual essence of life; he portrayed humans as acquiring knowledge through both the senses and the inner voice of God. In the thirteenth century, Aquinas developed the view that humans possessed a rational, immaterial soul that could exist independently of matter and continue after death. The idea of separation between mind and body was further developed and elaborated on by Descartes. He noted two meanings of soul that had not been clearly distinguished earlier: (a) soul as the animating force for bodily processes, which is corporeal (bodily) in nature and common to humans and animals, and (b) soul as the rational mind or spirit, which is immaterial, noncorporeal, and possessed by humans alone. He also believed that the existence of the soul (and God) is the most certain of all possible beliefs, following logically from the very act of thought itself ("I think, therefore, I am"). In all of these views, the sense of the unity of self and the continuity of self-experience were provided by the soul. Further, the self became grounded in the process of thinking, or consciousness, which permitted self-examination. Finally, there was at least the hint, if not the explicit recognition, that the self was both a knower and something that could be known, more or less, through reason, revelation, or observation.

An advance in the conception of self can be traced to the Scottish Moral Philosophers of the eighteenth century, including Adam Smith and David Hume (Stryker, 1981). They held that the nature of human association (i.e., the relationships between a person and others in a society) had to be considered if a science of people was to be developed. They discussed the implications of communication, habit, customs, and sympathy and provided a basis for the empirical study of the *self in social life*. For example, the existence of sympathy in humans was said to provide the basis for people to put themselves in the place of others, see the world as others do, and communicate, ultimately reshaping their own views of themselves as they sought the approval of others (Stryker, 1981). This analysis anticipated more recent discussions of role-taking ability (placing oneself in the place of others) and the influence of reflected appraisals (the perceived responses of others to the self) on people's self-conceptions. Further, by linking behavioral habits to the influence of social customs, they emphasized the relative importance of the social over the biological. In anticipation of Cooley's (1902/1922) later concept of the looking-glass self, Adam Smith (1759) wrote that, in contrast to the consequences of the isolation of man, "Bring him into society, and he is immediately provided with a mirror which he wanted before. It is placed in the countenance and behavior of those he lives with. This is the only looking glass by which we can, in some measure, with the eyes of other people, scrutinize the propriety of our own conduct." All of these themes were later taken up by the symbolic interactionists (see below) and have influenced current views of the self. With the Scottish Moral Philosophers, the self became, at least in part, a social phenomenon.

The Pragmatic View

The American Pragmatic Philosophers, including William James, C. S. Pierce, John Dewey, and Joshia Royce, provided another key advance, taking up where the Scottish philosophers had left off. Pragmatists held that ideas and actions must be understood in terms of their functions and usefulness for the actor. They argued that activities must be explained (a) in terms of larger, modulated units that are united by their meaning for the individual (in contrast to the view that perceptions and behaviors represent merely the aggregate of discrete, independent sensations and reflexes, as held by Brittish Associationists such as Locke), and (b) with reference to the social meaning of the activities as affected by customs, norms, and roles. These themes were especially prevalent in the writings of John Dewey, who elaborated on them in his criticisms of the radical stimulus-response behaviorism theories of his day.

The most influential of the Pragmatists for modern social psychology was William James (1890), who provided the first major examination of the nature of the self. Karl Scheibe (Chapter 2) offers a fine discussion of James' views, so only a brief overview will be provided here to serve as an introduction and expose some general themes that appear throughout this volume. James wrote that the constituents of the self could be divided into two classes: the *self-as-knower* or pure ego (the "I") and the *self-as-known* or empirical self (the "me"). The self-as-knower is the "judging thought," which is "passive and subjective." Its existence must be inferred indirectly from the fact that one knows and does things, and it was regarded as a necessary concept to explain the sense of continuity and unity inherent in the sense of self. James contrasted three earlier variants of pure ego theories of the self, including: (a) theories of the soul as immaterial substance (e.g., Descartes), (b) associationist theory (e.g., John Locke and David Hume), which held that the unity of consciousness and self emerged merely from the association of independent, discrete sensations, and (c) transcendental theory (e.g., Kant), which posited an *a priori,* transcendent ego that is a rational, nonempirical, presumed "truth." He totally rejected these positions. In essence, he argued that each passing thought in the "stream of consciousness" (the metaphoric continuous flow of thoughts) *appropriates earlier ones to it* and is *owned by the self as thinker,* thus providing continuity and unity to experience, and that this assertion is a fundamental principle in itself. Nothing more can or should be added to explain the self-as-knower. It is superfluous to look beyond the statement and posit a soul that underlies the process (unless *soul* is stripped of all excess meaning and defined as equivalent to the judging thought and nothing more); it is illogical to regard it merely as an aggregate of sensations (because the latter pretends to explain continuity and unity without ever dealing with the phenomena), and it is ambiguous and ultimately empty to posit an *a priori,* transcendent ego (James asserted that such an ego is either "a cheap and nasty edition of the soul" or "simply *nothing;* as ineffectual and windy an abortion as Philosophy can show").

In contrast, the empirical self, or self-as-known, is the self as an object of self-perception and knowledge, the person as he or she enters into awareness. As an object of knowledge, it can be directly known by the person and represents the contents of self-reflections. James divided the empirical self into the material self, the social self, and the spiritual self. The material self includes one body, clothes, family, friends, home, property, and possessions. The social self is based on the recognition one receives from others based on the impressions one creates. As such, a person can have "as many social selves as there are distinct groups of persons about whose opinion he cares." Finally, the spiritual self is one's "inner or subjective being, his psychic faculties or dispositions, taken concretely"; the ability "to think of ourselves as thinkers." James believed that each of these types of empirical self could arouse different self-feelings or emotions based on self-dissatisfaction or self-complacency (e.g., vanity, pride, guilt) and prompt certain actions based on "self-preservation" and "self-seeking" (e.g., acquisitiveness, the pursuit of honor). James regarded people's overall self-esteem or self-feeling to be based on the ratio of their successes (actual accomplishments) to their pretensions (what they "back" themselves to be, or their perceived potential).

Some Contemporary Domains

Skipping to the present, James' work on the self has proven relevant in at least three domains: (a) sociological views of the nature of the self, (b) traditional psychological views of the self, and (c) current work on social cognition. First,

James had an immediate impact on sociological social psychology by influencing the symbolic interactionists, who in turn shaped much of current microsociological thought. (Karl Scheibe elaborates on James' influence in Chapter 2, and both that chapter and later sections of this chapter discuss the sociological perspective on the self.)

Within academic psychology, however, James' work was quickly discarded in the rush to endorse radical behaviorism, which eschewed concepts that were not directly observable or might seem to be descendants of purely philosophical or metaphysical issues (i.e., the soul). His work entered a period of what might be charitably called hibernation. Interest in the self was kept alive within clinical psychology. Clinicians such as Karen Horney, Harry Stack Sullivan, and Carl Rogers focused on the importance of the self in normal and especially abnormal behavior. (See Chapters 2 and 3 for further discussion.) However, most academicians treated the self as anathema. With the development of the computer, seized upon as the model or analogy for cognitive processes for which psychologists had been searching, the scientific study of cognitive processes became legitimized, and interest in the self reemerged. Scheibe (Chapter 2) notes that this resurgence was felt in the 1960s and comments on some of the views that emerged during that period. At the risk of unfairly generalizing (since there were some notable exceptions; e.g., Carson, 1969), this work fell into two general classes where it concerned the *self in social life*. One class tended to focus on the self-concept and self-esteem as personality variables that are systematically affected by certain social antecedents (e.g., parental upbringing, peer behavior) and that systematically affect certain perceptions and behaviors (e.g., Wylie, 1961). Some of this research has proven very useful over the years in providing a data base for the antecedents and consequences of self-esteem and certain aspects of the self-concept. Nonetheless, much of it tended to treat social life as an afterthought, isolating the self from interpersonal relations. As Scheibe notes, there also was no sense of unity, vividness, or purpose of the self in much of this work. Further, there was virtually no discussion of how people's activities serve to create a public identity to which others can relate and coordinate their own actions. More recent work, falling roughly in the traditions of this line, seems to be redressing some of these problems.

The second class was inspired by E. E. Jones' (1964; Jones & Pittman, 1982; Jones & Wortman, 1973) work on ingratiation and the strategic presentation of self. Jones defines strategic self-presentation as "those features of behavior affected by power augmentation motives designed to elicit or shape others' attributions of the actor's dispositions" (Jones & Pittman, 1982). His initial studies in the area explored ingratiation, examining how people systematically vary their self-descriptions as a function of situational inducements (e.g., the ability to attain rewards mediated by others) in order to increase their attractiveness in the eyes of others. More recently, he and his associates (Jones & Pittman, 1982) explored how self-presentational activities are employed to pursue other goals, such as to intimidate others, to promote one's own competence, to appear in need of help, and to appear morally worthy (cf.

Schlenker, 1980). Tedeschi and Norman (Chapter 11 in this volume) review some of Jones' work in the context of presenting their own theory of strategic and tactical self-presentation.

In general, the focus of Jones' research is on the publicly presented self and how it is influenced by situational and personality determinants. The private or phenomenal self has been given less relative emphasis. For example, Jones suggests that although the phenomenal self is "potentially available" to actors as a basis for disclosing information about themselves, this self (a) "shifts from moment to moment as a function of motivational state and situational cues," and (b) "is constantly evolving in ways that. . . come to terms with one's actions or one's outcomes" (Jones & Pittman, 1982, p. 233). Despite this deemphasis, the private self is regarded as playing some role in the choice of strategies involved in self-presentation. For example, it may influence whether actors who are dependent on other people respond with ingratiatory behaviors, behaviors designed to portray helplessness, or a mixture of both. Jones also has devoted attention to how public self-presentations influence the phenomenal self. People come to internalize a self-presentation when (a) it is approvingly reinforced by others (e.g., Jones, 1964), or (b) emitted under conditions where situational cues indicate it was freely chosen or constructed (e.g., Jones, Rhodewalt, Berglas, & Skelton, 1981).

By virtue of the focus of this line of inquiry, the impression is sometimes left that the private and public self are split off and unintegrated. The private self seems to be an unstable, amorphous entity that must come to grips with a public self that pursues transient objectives (James' "social self" stripped of other properties). Although this characterization does not accurately capture the nuances of Jones' ideas, other researchers have attempted to provide greater theoretical integration of the private and public aspects of the self. As will be seen, the chapters in Part One of this volume are devoted, at least in part, to this task.

One domain with unlimited potential for contributing to such integration is the recent emergence of the area of social cognition as a major force within social psychology. Social psychologists have always been interested in social cognition conceived broadly (e.g., attitudes, values, attribution, person perception). In the 1980s, this interest has taken the form of emphasizing basic cognitive structures and processes (e.g., memory, the encoding and decoding of information) that had previously been the domain primarily of cognitive psychologists. Some of the theories, models, concepts, and research techniques used by cognitive psychologists have been adapted and extended for use in addressing matters of interest to social psychologists. (For example, how is information about other people selected, interpreted, integrated, stored in memory, and recalled?) This development has produced what has been termed the area of *social cognition*. In this context, the self is again flourishing, as researchers address questions such as these: What, in cognitive terms, is the self? How is the self represented in memory? How does the self affect the selection, interpretation, integration, and recall of information?

THE SELF AND SOCIAL COGNITION

The Self as Knower and Known: A Computer Metaphor

Greenwald and Pratkanis (1984) provide an excellent analysis of the self from a social-cognition perspective. They address James' distinction between the self-as-knower (the self as subjective process) and the self-as-known (the self as an object of knowledge) with a computer metaphor. The self-as-knower is identified as being analogous to a computer program, which contains the directions for how information is to be handled by the system, and the self-as-known as analogous to the data, which is the content of the input and output of the system. The program dictates the process (based on particular sets of preprogrammed rules) used to handle the data, while the data itself provides the objective content of the system. The qualities of the self that have long been enigmatic to philosophers and psychologists—the self as subjective versus objective and as process versus content—are thus seen as correlative aspects of the system as a whole.

Greenwald and Pratkanis note that a seeming problem for the metaphor might be that the distinction between program and data is not a sharp one, since both are represented in a computer in the same medium (information in memory). Yet, they feel this is not a real problem, since the difficulty in drawing a sharp distinction between the program and the data appropriately captures the enigma of the subjective and objective "sides" of the self. Further, they note that a related issue is the question of introspective access to mental functioning. It is often held that people have access to ("know") the *products* of cognitive processes but not to the *actual workings* of those processes (e.g., Mandler, 1975; Neisser, 1976; Nisbett & Wilson, 1977). When applied to the self, this position is reminiscent of James' view that people have direct knowledge of the contents of the empirical self, while the self-as-knower must be inferred indirectly on the basis of its functional output. In terms of the computer metaphor, people are viewed as having access to the mental data of input and output, but not having direct access to the "program" (the preprogrammed rules that dictate how the data will be handled) that processes the data (Greenwald & Pratkanis, 1984). The directions given in the "program" must be inferred from the transformations that seem to occur in the data from the input to output stage. (With a computer, of course, there are some people who "know" the particular programs used by it, since they designed these programs and teach them to others. The inner "program" for people, though, is unknown.) Consequently, we cannot definitively "know" the "programs" that guide our own thoughts, emotions, and actions; we cannot definitely answer the question, "Why did I do, say, think, or feel that?" Just as we must make attributions about why others behave as they do, so we must make attributions about the causes of our own activities based on the known data that is at our disposal.

Greenwald and Pratkanis suggest that the computer metaphor is mute on the key aspects of the self-as-knower that occupied much of James' attention—the idea that the continuity and unity of the self arise from the stream of consciousness, as each passing thought appropriates those that came before it and is owned by the thinker. Indeed, Greenwald and Pratkanis do not regard this as a particularly useful idea, suggesting it does not have testable implications and may be in a class with the pure ego theories rejected by James. Scheibe (Chapter 2) tends to express the opposite position, siding with James. We will take up this issue again in a moment. In any event, the social cognition literature usually addresses unity and continuity from a different angle, approaching them in terms of the nature or functions of more clearly specified cognitive components of the self, whose contents are part of what James termed the empirical self but whose processes are reflected in the self-as-knower.

Properties of the Self

Recent work on social cognition has been directed toward specifying the cognitive structure and functions of the self as they relate to perception, judgment, affect, and behavior. (See Greenward & Pratkanis, 1984.) Several theories have been advanced, the most popular and appealing of which is the view of the self as a schema or collection of schemata.

Self as Schema

The current view of the self as a schema, or an organization of knowledge, was anticipated in the analogy of people as scientists. People can be regarded as naive scientists who construct and test theories to aid them in understanding their environments and functioning effectively within them (e.g., Heider, 1958; Kelly, 1955; Lecky, 1945/1969). These theories include those about the self. Seymour Epstein (1973) defined the self-concept as "a theory the individual has unwittingly constructed about himself as an experiencing, functioning individual [and this theory is] part of a broader theory which he holds with respect to his entire range of significant experience" (p. 407). Like a scientific theory, it pertains to a cache of relevant facts, such as those describing one's bodily appearance, possessions, friends, social episodes. It contains constructs that organize and classify the facts, such as handsome, wealthy, friendly, intelligent, independent. It contains hypotheses (or beliefs) that relate aspects of the facts and constructs to each other and to the events that should follow from them, such as, "I am independent and therefore don't conform to the opinions of others." One's aspirations and values also enter into the picture to produce a self-theory that represents a blend of one's actualities and potentialities (Rosenberg, 1979; Turner, 1968).

Like a scientific theory, the self-concept both influences and is influenced by experience. It influences experience in that it affects what its holder does (e.g., the types of "problems" tackled or investigated) and how he or she interprets the world (usually, in accord with the dictates of the theory). It is influenced by experience in that its elements are constantly tested in the crucible of life; these elements often seem to be supported but sometimes must be rejected or modified on the basis of the data.

As an organization of knowledge about the self, the self-concept provides continuity, since its major portions carry over in memory from day to day. It also provides unity, at least to the same extent any (comparably valid) theory provides unity, because it offers a coherent vehicle for integrating and explaining the subject matter it was designed to explain. Consequently, to the extent that it is reasonably valid (consistent with the available evidence and capable of withstanding future tests), it permits relatively effective prediction and control of events that are relevant to the self. The self-concept thereby provides the organization of experience that permits unity and continuity while facilitating the functioning of the individual in everyday life (Epstein, 1973).

This view is really quite compatible with James' discussions. James held that the nature of thought yields products (the components of the empirical self) that emanate unity and continuity. The self-theory view also assumes that it is the nature of the human mind, thought if you will, to construct a theory of self that provides unity and continuity. The language is different, but the bottom line is the same. Each piece of new data (new experience) is integrated with other data that came before it; the new is assimilated to the old or the old is accommodated to the new. This process captures James' sense of thoughts "appropriating" other thoughts. Further, the output or result of this integration is unique to the particular self-concept of the individual, since, as any scientist realizes, alternative theories produce alternative interpretations of data. In James' terms, the self indeed "owns" its products because these products are unique to the particular self-theory. It is not difficult to fit these conclusions to the computer metaphor as well.

Recent work on social cognition has employed the term *schema* to describe something quite similar to the nature of theory. A schema is an organized framework of knowledge about a particular domain (Alba & Hasher, 1983; Neisser, 1976). Although specific uses of the term vary somewhat, it is generally agreed that a schema (a) is an internal structure, sometimes associated with an "active array of physiological structures and processes" (Neisser, 1967, p. 54), (b) is an organized framework of knowledge, (c) is specific to a pertinent domain or area, such as the self or some aspect of self, (d) is modifiable by experience, much like the elements of a theory are modified by new data, (e) guides attention and activity, analogous to how a theoretically derived plan for research on a topic would guide the activities of a scientist, and (f) assimilates appropriate experiences to it such that these experiences are perceived, stored in memory, and recalled in the context of the schema as a whole rather than the experience in isolation. Just as scientists interpret data from the perspective of its theoretical meaning, people interpret experiences in terms of their schemata. Schemata can vary in their inclusiveness, with some pertaining to a large domain (analogous to a grand theory) and some pertaining to a rather specific domain (analogous to a mini-theory).

The self has been regarded as a system of schemata that selects and actively modifies the experiences that are perceived, stored in memory, and recalled by the individual (Markus, 1977; Markus & Sentis, 1982; Markus & Smith, 1981; Taylor & Crocker, 1981). For example, a given person might have self-schemata indicating he is independent, extroverted, and athletic. Each of these schemata contain not just the pertinent construct (e.g., independent), but also specific pertinent experiences (e.g., "I disagreed with the boss today") and implications for action (e.g., "An independent person should be immune to pressures to conform"). In short, self-schemata are *organized* frameworks of knowledge about particular domains that have implications for self-experience.

Research has shown that when a particular self-schema is activated, it affects how information is selected, processed, and retained. People become more likely to:

1 Notice and attend to schema-relevant information in the setting, especially to the degree that information is highly consistent or inconsistent with it (e.g., Alba & Hasher, 1983; Judd & Kulik, 1980).

2 Process schema-relevant information more easily and quickly (e.g., Alba & Hasher, 1983; Markus, 1977).

3 Interpret supporting or ambiguous information, from both the present situation and from memory, in ways that are consistent with the schema (e.g., Alba & Hasher, 1983; Cantor & Mischel, 1979; Judd & Kulik, 1980; Swann & Read, 1981).

4 Polarize attitudes to make them more supportive of the schema (Tesser, 1978).

These results suggest that new experiences are selectively encountered and assimilated to existing self-schemata, causing perceptions and memory to be affected systematically. Schemata thereby represent structure, content, and process (Neisser, 1976).

Script theory (Abelson, 1976; Schank & Abelson, 1977) is an approach that draws heavily on the concept of a schema (also see Minsky, 1975, for a related approach termed *frame theory*). A script is a schema about the structure of an event and is much like a short story that contains specific information about the contents of the event and the sequence in which the components of the event unfold. For instance, a person can acquire a script about events in a fine restaurant: One dresses up beforehand, travels to the restaurant, allows the valet to park the car, walks into the restaurant, is seated by a maitre d', is presented with a menu, orders cocktails, orders the meal, eats and drinks in the appropriate formal manner, receives the check, pays the check, tips the waiter, leaves the restaurant, walks to the parking entrance, gives the valet the claim check, tips the valet, gets in the car, and drives home. Scripts can contain much detail (vastly more than the sketch above) about the contents, meaning, and sequence of events taking the central character through the steps required to complete the activity. Scripts for all types of situations, social and nonsocial, are acquired consciously or unconsciously from experience (Langer, 1978), and once they are activated (cued in memory), again with or without awareness, they provide the holder with a set of expectations and a guide for activities that permit the sequence to be completed and the pertinent goal to be accomplished. According to Abelson (1976, p. 42), "Cognitively mediated social behavior depends on the occurrence of two processes: (a) the selection of a particular script to represent the given situation and (b) the taking of a participant role within the script." The script thus provides a context for action and an indication of the appropriate roles to be played within it, giving the actor, the situation, the other parties, and behavior a meaningful set of interrelationships. Indeed, script theory deals with most of the issues (e.g., meaningful patterns of behavior, role performance, definitions of situations and actors) that were important for the pragmatists and continue to be important for symbolic interactionists (Schlenker, 1980; also see below).

Not surprisingly, given the recency of relevant work, schema theories are still somewhat vague, and their precise implications and mechanisms have yet to be fully explored. Further, schema theories have been criticized for failing to explain the richness and detail of information contained in memory, since they predict perceptual and interpretive biases, in which some details are lost in the process of assimilating new information to existing schemata (Alba & Hasher, 1983). Nonetheless, the bulk of the research is supportive and the scientific utility of these theories is especially high. They provide a heuristic means of designating how the self influences and is influenced by social life.

Other Views

Other positions on how the self is cognitively structured have been advanced (see Greenwald & Pratkanis, 1984). Two of these are compatible with, though not necessarily identical to, schema theory and appear frequently in the literature on the self.

Rogers (1981) has suggested that the self is represented in memory as a hierarchical category structure. Its cognitive components are self-descriptive elements (e.g., traits, values, specific behaviors, or relevant events), and these elements are arranged with the more general, abstract, and inclusive at the top and the more distinctive, concrete, and specific at the bottom. For example, under the abstract concept, "man," a person may subsume being a father and a lawyer; under "lawyer" he may subsume such traits as intelligent, assertive, wealthy, etc.; under "intelligent" he may subsume numerous concrete events pertinent to academic and professional achievements; and so forth. The hierarchical interrelationship of these elements provides an organizational structure for the self, with the higher-order elements having greater importance and centrality for the individual since they subsume lower-order elements (cf. Rosenberg, 1979). Higher-order elements should be more resistant to change than lower-order ones, since the former organize a greater quantity of supportive information in memory.

The self-concept also has been viewed as a system of cognitive prototypes (Kuiper, 1981). A prototype, or exemplar for a category, is a cognitive abstraction that indicates the type of information that can best be classified as a member of the category. If a person's self-conception contains a particular self-categorization (e.g., introverted), he or she also would have a prototype in memory to represent what the category means. New information is compared to existing prototypes to determine how it should be classified, and the speed with which people process information should depend on the degree of similarity between the information and the prototype for the pertinent category. Information that is highly similar to the prototype (e.g., pertinent to the exemplar for being introverted) and information that is highly dissimilar from the prototype on the same dimension (e.g., pertinent to being extroverted), should be processed very quickly when people are called upon to make self-judgments on the dimension, since such information can be readily compared to the prototype. People whose self-conceptions do not contain the particular self-categorization (e.g., they do not usually think of themselves on an introversion-extroversion dimension) should make much slower self-judgments when processing pertinent information. Relevant data on the speed with which people process information about the self is generally supportive of the prototype view (e.g., Kuiper, 1981).

These and other models suggest slight differences in theoretical emphasis and implications. (See Greenwald & Pratkanis, 1984.) However, compatible versions of them can be specified, such as by viewing schemata as being organized hierarchically and/or providing prototype information (e.g., Markus, 1977). For our purposes, the importance of these theories lies in their ability to represent the self in ways that provide opulent implications for how the self influences and is influenced by social life. Many of these implications are discussed in the various chapters of this volume.

BIASES IN SELF-KNOWLEDGE

The biased nature of self-knowledge has been noted by commentators since ancient times and has been the subject of an extensive amount of research in the areas of personality and social psychology. Greenwald (1980) summarized these biases in three general classes, which he termed (a) *egocentricity,* the tendency for perceptions and judgments to revolve around the self; (b) *beneffectance,* the tendency to regard the self as competent and good; and (c) *cognitive conservatism,* the tendency to preserve already established cognitive structures. These biases have implications for the motivational properties of the self and its expression in social life.

Egocentricity

The self occupies a privileged, central position in people's cognitive worlds. As such, perception, memory, and judgment might be expected to reflect his or her centrality, and they do.

Piaget (1955) characterized egocentricity, or the tendency to view objects and events in relation to oneself, as a dominant cognitive tendency in young children. For instance, when preschool children are shown a scene (e.g., a three-dimensional mountain) and asked to describe what an observer who occupies a different perspective sees (i.e., from the opposite side of the mountain), they usually describe objects and events that are salient only from their own perspective (i.e., on their side, rather than the opposite side). As children grow older, they acquire the cognitive ability to take into account alternative perspectives, but egocentrism still lingers. George Herbert Mead noted a comparable tendency. Mead (1934) stated that through play and games, young children try out and master various social roles, including being able to appreciate how others in different roles are likely to respond in various situations (see Chapters 2 and 7 in this volume). Over time, they become less egocentric and able to regard themselves, others, and events from the perspective of others in society. An initial highly egocentric perspective is replaced by a more social perspective, though egocentrism remains, even in adulthood.

Greenwald (1980; Greenwald & Pratkanis, 1984) summarized research on several effects that reliably suggest egocentric judgment in the average adult. He concludes that:

1 One tends to exaggerate the role of the self in explanations of events, thus inserting the self into causal sequences as either an agent who influences other people and events or as a target of the influence of other people and events. (For instance, "it happened because of me.")

2 Information that is actively generated by oneself (e.g., a story one writes) tends to be recalled better than material that is passively encountered (e.g., a story one reads). This has been termed the self-generation effect.

3 Information that is perceived as relevant to oneself (e.g., stories concerning characters whose traits are similar to one's own) is better remembered than is information that is not so perceived (e.g., stories concerning characters whose traits are different). This has been termed the self-reference effect.

4 Information that is pertinent to an ongoing or persisting task is remembered better than information pertinent to a completed task. This has been termed the ego-involvement effect.

In a very real sense, the self is the center of the universe for each of us. Egocentrism appears to be a basic characteristic of human judgment.

Beneffectance

Greenwald (1980) coined the term beneffectance by combining beneficence (doing good) and effectance (being competent), thus designating the proclivity to regard oneself as good, worthwhile, and competent. Throughout the ages, sages have commented on the human tendency to regard oneself favorably. As Seneca said, "Other men's sins are before our eyes; our own are behind our back." James regarded "self-seeking" as a "fundamental instinctual impulse," which prompted people toward vanity, pride, superiority, and so forth. Personologist Gordon Allport (1937) viewed the defense of the ego as "nature's eldest law." Sociologist Morris Rosenberg (1979) regards the self-esteem motive (the motive to protect and enhance self-esteem) as one of two fundamental motives emanating from the self (the second, self-consistency, will be discussed shortly).

In short, people's perceptions, judgments, and memories tend to be biased in ways that benefit the self.

Numerous lines of research reliably support this bias. These include, as a sampling:

1 The tendency to recall successes better than failures. (See Greenwald, 1980.)

2 The tendency to attribute responsibility to self for successes but not for failures on both individual and group tasks (e.g., Schlenker, 1980; Schlenker & Miller, 1977; Snyder, Stephan & Rosenfield, 1978; Weary Bradley, 1978; Weary & Arkin, 1981).

3 The proclivity to regard one's own motives for a behavior as primarily good and the motives of others as less good (Schlenker, Hallam, & McCown, 1983).

4 The tendency to change one's attitudes in a way that justifies negative conduct or provides greater personal acclaim for positive conduct (e.g., Schlenker, 1982; Schlenker & Goldman, 1982; Schlenker & Schlenker, 1975).

5 The tendency to respond positively to favorable evaluations of self and negatively to unfavorable evaluations (e.g., Jones, 1973).

6 The tendency to associate oneself with winners and dissociate oneself from losers (e.g., Richardson & Cialdini, 1981).

These effects, variously termed egotism, self-serving attributions, ego-defensiveness, self-esteem protection, and desirability bias, vary in magnitude from situation to situation and individual to individual. Further, these effects have implications for not only how people regard themselves (e.g., good or bad, competent or incompetent), but for how other people regard them. An interpersonal dimension is thereby added when it comes to explaining such tendencies, and people's private and public tendencies sometimes differ. Many of the chapters in this volume examine the nature of these effects and the conditions under which they are maximized and minimized (Chapters 3, 4, 5, 8, 9, and 11). Beneffectance appears to be a pervasive and reliable general human tendency, perhaps rooted in the evolutionary process of self-preservation.

Cognitive Conservatism

Cognitive conservatism is the proclivity to preserve cognitive structures that have already been established. Such proclivities have been noted in at least three areas. First, people tend to *assimilate* new information by interpreting it via existing cognitive schemata (e.g., Alba & Hasher, 1983; Carson, 1969; Greenwald, 1980). Second, people display *confirmation biases* in their perceptions and judgments of information. They selectively attend to information that confirms rather than refutes their expectations, they give greater weight to confirmatory than refutational information in their judgments, they selectively recall confirmatory information, they selectively generate arguments that confirm their opinions, and they selectively gather confirmatory rather than refutational information (e.g., Greenwald, 1980; Swann, 1983). Third, people tend to *rewrite memory* of prior events in ways to make their cognitions appear to have no change over time, even though they may have changed (Greenwald, 1980). Thus, people remember their prior opinions as being remarkably similar to their present ones even though these objectively differ, they retrospectively believe they predicted the outcome of events better than they actually did, and they believe that new information was actually available to them prior to the time it really was.

When applied to the self, these conservative biases resemble manifestations of what has been termed a self-consistency motive or a unity principle. James commented at length on the properties of the unity and continuity of self. Personality theorist Prescott Lecky (1945/1969) noted that the world would be a chaotic, unmanageable mass of confusion if people did not impose order on it through the construction of a unified conceptual system. He asserted that people's concepts about themselves are organized into a hierarchical, integrated system, much like the theory of a scientist. This cognitive system provides order, unity, and continuity, and people have a stake in its preservation. As such, their behaviors are designed to promote self-consistency.

Lecky's work was the forerunner of an explosion of interest in cognitive consistency theories in the 1960s, including dissonance theory (Festinger, 1957), balance theory (Heider, 1958), and interpersonal-congruity theory (Secord & Backman, 1965). As these and other theories noted, consistency in one sense or another not only serves intrapersonal functions of maintaining the stability and coherence of the individual, it serves interpersonal functions. (See Chapters 2, 4 and 11 in this volume.) For instance, consistency in interpersonal behaviors minimizes strain in social interaction and indicates that the individual is a reliable social participant. For several reasons (that are beyond our purposes to explore here), consistency notions waned in popularity in the 1970s, but they are now reemerging, in part because of research on (a) social cognition and the role of self-schemata in assimilating experiences, and (b) self-verification. (See Swann, Chapter 4 of this volume.) Current work is also attempting to provide a reconciliation of the (sometimes competing) tendencies of beneffectance and self-consistency. Swann (Chapter 4) offers one solution by examining the conditions under which each proclivity predominates; Schlenker (Chapter 3) offers a slightly different approach.

Changing Angles: The Social and the Self

As the blind men discovered when examining the elephant, with each describing the animal differently depending on which part he touched, different perspectives create variations in how objects and events are viewed. Social psychologists who have been trained and work in psychology departments tend to emphasize the individual, with social life being the particular habitat of interest. Social psychologists who have been trained and work in sociology departments tend to emphasize the social, with the individual being a key agent. These somewhat different angles of entry for examining the self in social life generate overlapping perspectives, but with some differences in jargon and concepts, and some disagreements. Symbolic interactionism and the dramaturgical approach have been two of the most heuristic and influential of the sociologically derived theories of the self and social life, and each will be briefly discussed.

Symbolic Interactionism

Symbolic interactionism is a descendant of the socially oriented thought of the Scottish Moral Philosophers by way of the Pragmatists (Stryker, 1981). Three major figures are usually credited with laying its foundations: George Herbert Mead (1934), Charles Horton Cooley (1902/1922), and William I. Thomas (1923). The fundamental premise uniting symbolic interactionists is that they believe the individual and society are "inseparable and interdependent units. Individuals, living together in society [are] viewed as reflective and interactive begins possessing selves" (Meltzer & Petras, 1972, p. 43). In contrast to some of the approaches reviewed thus far, the self is not considered to exist *in* society; the self *and* society mutually interact, with each being fully comprehensible only in the context of the other. Karl Scheibe (Chapter 2 in this volume) elaborates the nature of this relationship in the works of Baldwin, Cooley, and Mead. For the moment we will be content to summarize key themes advanced by symbolic interactionists that provide a foundation for some of the work described in this volume.

Following the Pragmatists, symbolic interactionists emphasize the symbolic meanings attached to objects, activities, and events. They propose that people act toward objects (including one another) and events on the basis of the meanings that these have for them, and that these meanings derive directly from social interaction as mediated by people's cognitive, interpretive processes (Meltzer, Petras, & Reynolds, 1975). Through social interaction, people learn how objects and events are generally interpreted and dealt with by members of their society (McCall & Simmons, 1978; Meltzer et al., 1975; Stryker, 1981). For instance, a Cadillac is not just a car, but can be regarded as either a symbol of status and wealth or a symbol of conspicuous, gas-guzzling wastefulness, depending on the perspective of the viewer. The symbolic interpretation of the object or event can, in turn, effect evaluative reactions toward it and behavior in relation to it.

Symbolic interactionists further propose that objects, activities, and situations are ambiguous until they are defined by the participants who deal with them, that is, until their symbolic meanings are fixed for the occasion (McCall & Simmons, 1978; Meltzer et al., 1975; Stryker, 1981; Thomas, 1923). People must define one another during interactions, that is, fix the characteristics each will have and the roles each will play, and define the nature of the situation in which they are interacting. How much status will each participant be regarded as having? Will each be friendly or hostile, cooperative or competitive? Is the situation formal, calling for certain normative behaviors, or informal, calling for a different set of norms? These and numerous other questions are answered, usually automatically and unwittingly, by the participants before their interaction can proceed smoothly in a coordinated, expected fashion. These expectations, in turn, derive from years of socialization, during which we learn the appropriate roles, rules, and rituals pertinent to particular types of people in particular types of situations. As Stryker (1981) put it, "Social interaction is constructed by the participants" (p. 8), and the significant symbols employed in this construction "'make possible the anticipation of responses, one's own and others, and adjustment of those responses on the basis of anticipation" (p. 7).

The concepts of cognitive schemata and cognitive scripts were introduced in psychology in part to handle phenomena such as symbolic meaning, the contextual nature of knowledge (i.e., the meaning of an object or event depends on the context in which it is viewed), the definition of persons and situations, and anticipated sequences of events. These topics, once the concern primarily of symbolic interactionists, have now been incorporated into mainstream psychology. Schemata and cognitive scripts, as organized frameworks of knowledge, give meaning to new information, place it in a coherent context of previously acquired information, and provide anticipated sequences of events based on social experience. From one perspective, the construction of reality through the definition of persons and situations can be regarded as the conscious or unconscious "selection" of a cognitive script from among alternative possible scripts. Once selected, these constructions rather than alternative ones define the context and influence subsequent activities.

For symbolic interactionists, people are not just passive reactors to situations, programmed by society with fixed action patterns. Instead, they are active agents who develop plans out of the bits and pieces supplied by culture and who attempt to execute these plans in social encounters (McCall & Simmons, 1978). As active agents, they can be said to "make" the roles they enact and not simply "play" roles handed to them (Stryker, 1981). Given that disagreements can occur between individuals about how the participants and situation are to be defined (e.g., a male may want to play the traditional male role and cast a female into the traditional female role, a position she does not favor), these definitions are often *negotiated* by the participants, as they attempt to influence the views of one another and reach mutually acceptable definitions (Weinstein, 1969). The sometimes subtle, sometimes obvious, process of negotiation can produce a solution that represents a true interaction of the participants, in that the final product can be significantly different from what the participants each may have initially envisioned.

The self, as both an internal cognitive representation and a set of public characteristics and roles presented in interaction, is presumed to develop through the *social interaction process*. It must be defined, constructed, and negotiated with others in interaction, becoming a "social structure existing in the activity of viewing oneself reflexively" (Stryker, 1981, p. 7). Cooley (1902/1922) placed the genesis of the self in the child's perceptions and feelings about how significant others' treat him or her, as an appreciation develops of the relationship of the child's own actions and characteristics and the reactions of others to these actions. Children learn that others' actions are directed toward them and reveal something about them, and that others' actions can be influenced or controlled by their own appearance and behavior. The realization that the actions of others toward oneself reveals information about oneself provided the basis for Cooley's concept of the looking glass self:

> Each to each a looking-glass
> Reflects the other that doth pass (p. 184).

Through these reflected appraisals from significant others, children develop a "self-idea" that has three major elements: "the imagination of our appearance to the other person; the imagination of his judgment of that appearance; and some sort of self-feeling, such as pride or mortification" (p. 184). The potency of reflected appraisals from significant others in shaping one's self-conception has been supported in a variety of studies. (See Schlenker, 1980; Secord & Backman, 1974; Shrauger & Schoeneman, 1979.) Cooley also anticipated later work on the presentation of self when he noted that children quickly learn to control the appearance they give to others in order to capitalize on others' tendencies: "The young performer soon learns to be different things to different people. . . . If the mother or nurse is more tender than just, she will almost certainly be 'worked' by systematic weeping" (p. 197).

Mead (1934) extended Cooley's ideas by emphasizing cognitive skills acquired through role playing and leaning the rules of societal interactions. He stressed the importance of play and games, as children try out different roles (e.g., being mommy, daddy, a teacher, a hero), and gain an appreciation of them. (See Chapter 7 in this volume.)

Through socialization, each person becomes a "society in miniature" (Meltzer, 1972, p. 11). As such, each person can interact with himself just as he can interact with other people. The process of thought itself was regarded as interactive in nature, as when people talk to themselves, alternating roles of speaker and audience (Mead, 1934). This is private dialogue, not monologue. Only through social activities can people be expected to develop coherent views of themselves and others. The embedment of the self and the social is presumed to be complete enough for Mead to state that "selves can only exist in definite relations to other selves. No hard-and-fast line can be drawn between our own selves and the selves of others, since our own selves exist and enter into our experience only insofar as the selves of others exist and enter as such into our experience also" (1934, p. 196).

Symbolic interactionism influenced the development of role theory (e.g., Biddle & Thomas, 1966; Sarbin & Allen, 1968). Its central premise is that people's perceptions and behaviors in social interactions are shaped by the roles they occupy and enact. A role is usually defined in terms of the functions or parts a person performs when occupying a particular position within a particular social context. Roles are interdependent, and each participant's role is partially defined by the roles of others (e.g., the role of high status person depends in part on the specification of the role of a low status one). Each role carries with it certain anticipated behavior patterns that the role occupant should perform. These expectations partially guide and regulate the participants' actions in the particular social context, much like a stage script would guide and constrain an actor's portrayal of a character. From the perspective of role theory, the self-concept is usually regarded as comprising the internalization of the accumulated roles played by the person.

A related approach is situated identity theory, developed by C. N. Alexander (e.g., Alexander & Wiley, 1981). Situated identities (the identities formed for each participant in a given situation) reside not in the person or in the environment; instead, they define the relationship between the actor and the environment at a given point, representing the interaction of the person with the other participants and the social situation. In any given situation for a particular type of person, a particular situated identity emerges that maximizes the normative appropriateness of his or her conduct, the regard in which he or she will be held by others, and the extent to which the other participants can coordinate their behavior to his or hers.

One of the most influential approaches developing from symbolic interactionism has been the dramaturgical perspective on social life, as promulgated and popularized by Erving Goffman. We will now turn to this descendant.

The Dramaturgical Perspective

The theater is an expression of human life. At its best, it poignantly captures the full range of experience, from drama to comedy, that crystallizes and inspires our thoughts, emotions, and actions. Many people view theater primarily as a artful expression of life, yet the tables can be turned. In a truly meaningful sense, life is an expression of theater.

The analogy of life as theater has been drawn throughout the ages. Plato spoke of the "great stage of human life." In his *Laws*, he "developed the stage imagery in the moral fable of the human puppets, whose strings . . . are manipulated by the gods" (Burns, 1973, p. 8). Common words in the English language derived from terms associated with the theater. The word *person* derives from the Latin term *persona,* which was a mask used by a character in a play. The word *role* derived from the Latin word *rotula,* which was a sheet of parchment wrapped around a wooden roller that contained the part that an actor recited on stage (a primitive "idiot card"). The word *attitude,* as one of its first English uses in 1725, denoted a theatrical performer's expressions of the character he was playing; the images projected by the actor were said to convey a certain attitude on the part of the character.

By the seventeenth century, sages noted and endorsed the theatrical analogy in vivid terms. The English philosopher Thomas Hobbes (1952, p. 96) stated, "[A] person is the same as an actor is, both on the stage and in common conversation." The Globe Theatre in London, stage for Shakespeare's plays, had atop its entrance the phrase, *Totus Mundus Agit Histrionem* ("all the world is a theater"). In *As You Like It,* Shakespeare's character, Jaques, elaborated the notion:

All the world's a stage,
And all the men and women merely players.
They have their exits and their entrances;
And one man in his time plays many parts.

Miguel de Cervantes, a Spanish dramatist and contemporary of Shakespeare, also noted the analogy. In *The History of Don Quixote de la Mancha,* Don Quixote expounded on life as theater. Sancho Panza replied, "It is a fine comparison . . . though not so new but that I have heard it many times before." The dramaturgical analogy cannot be said to be a recent conception or one that is applicable only in our supposedly plastic, superficial era.

The twentieth century, though, has provided the climate for a more meticulous delivery of the pregnant idea. Nicholas Evreinoff, a Russian dramatist, introduced the concept of *theatrocracy:* Human actions are governed by rules of the theater. In his book, *The Theatre in Life* (1927), he wrote, "Examine any . . . branch of human activity and you will see that kings, statesmen, politicians, warriors, bankers, business men, priests, doctors, all pay daily tributes to theatricality, all comply with the principles ruling on the stage." Kenneth Burke, dramatist and literary critic, dissected the psychological question of what is involved when one asks what someone is doing and why he or she is doing it (1945/1962). He found the answer in *dramatism,* a dramaturgical examination of the basic forms of human thought that underlie our explanations of people's conduct. To explain human conduct, he posited five "generating principles." One must know the *act* (the specification of what took place), the *scene* (the background of the act; i.e., the situation in which it occurs), the *agent* (the type of actor who performed the act), the *agency* (the means or instruments used to perform the act), and the *purpose* (the actor's motive or reasons for performing the act). Burke's analysis, couched in stage terms, has influenced sociologists' views of events having meaning only in context.

The analogy is not lost in modern daily life. Politicians have, of the necessity demanded by television, become performers; products are sold based on the appearance clever advertisers can create; people are marketed and market themselves much like a product created by a Madison Avenue advertiser (simply contemplate dating behavior, job interviews, and so forth). As Sammy Davis, Jr., once remarked, "As soon as I go out the front door of my house in the morning, I'm on daddy, I'm on."

This seeming obsession with appearance as substance was described by Erich Fromm (1947) as the "marketing personality." Fromm rooted its development in a sociohistorical phenomenon: the shift from a highly competitive capitalist society to a more technologically based, marketing society. Fromm argued that in the early days of capitalism, success derived from the competitive advantage of producing a superior product for less money; those who could do so prospered, those who couldn't failed. With the advent of modern technology, products and prices became more interchangeable, with numerous producers capable of delivering roughly equivalent goods. The result was not competition for superior products at attractive prices, but for superior effect on the consumer based on marketing skill; the salespersons sold themselves and the images of their products. Substance gave way to skill at managing appearances. The presentation of self was regarded by Fromm as dominating social life. Of course, one can ask whether the change described by Fromm represents (a) a major shift in people's personalities, (b) merely a shift in emphasis or salience due in part to modern communication media and awareness of a greater array of events, or (c) no real shift at all. (See Chapter 2 for further discussion.)

At any rate, the full impact of the life-as-theater analogy was not felt until Erving Goffman, a sociologist, devoted his critical powers to its examination. While a graduate student at the University of Chicago, Goffman was influenced by the symbolic interactionists and, while accepting most of the major premises of the movement, gave the study of social life a twist by accentuating the theatrical elements of even the most inconspicuous social gestures. He began his most influential work, *The Presentation of Self in Everyday Life* (1959), by noting the basic differences between life and theater: The stage is make believe, while life is real; and the stage contains at least three parties (i.e., performers who are each momentarily actors and then audiences for each other and a real audience who watches the performance), while in real life there are only actor and audience, with one person capable of playing both parts (as when people talk to themselves, alternating the roles of actor and audience). That these are the only differences noted by Goffman perhaps reflected his belief in the power of the analogy.

No brief summary of Goffman's ideas can do him justice, nonetheless, a general outline of his approach may be instructive. Goffman argued that social interactions, real or imagined, consist of *performances* by the parties involved. A performance is, "All the activity of a given participant on a given occasion which serves to influence in any way any of the other participants" (Goffman, 1959, p. 15). Following the thought of symbolic interactionists, Goffman contended that whenever people confront audiences, in real life or their own imaginations, their actions carry symbolic meanings that convey what they are like and have a promissory character, implying that the actors will behave in a fashion consistent with the type of "face" they are creating for those audiences. It is the very nature of interaction that when in the presence of others "the individual will have to act so that he intentionally or unintentionally expresses himself, and the other will in turn have to be impressed in some way by him" (p. 2). Consequently, "[w]hen an individual appears in the presence of others, there will usually be some reason for him to mobilize his activity so that it will convey an impression to others which is in his interests to convey" (p. 4). People's activities are thus transformed into performances that present images of self for the social world to see and evaluate. People serve as the authors, stage directors, actors, audiences, commentators, and critics for their own performances.

The "face," or "image of self delineated in terms of approved social attributes" (p. 2), that an actor projects varies, according to Goffman, from audience to audience. People present themselves somewhat differently before their parents, coworkers, employers, subordinates, spouses, children, etc. Each face conveys a partial slice of the individual's "social self." Faces also carry both opportunities and constraints. People are entitled to be regarded and treated commensurate with the type of face they project. "Society is organized on the principle that any individual who possesses certain characteristics has a moral right to expect that others will value and treat him in an appropriate way" (p. 13). Concomitantly, claiming a particular face obligates the actor to live up to the expectations of others regarding how such a person should act. Failure to do so produces a violation of the social contract and generates embarrassment and possible negative sanctions for the charlatan. Performances, then, define the participants' faces or situated identities for the interaction, casting each into certain roles and allowing each to know what to expect from one another.

In constructing and maintaining these situated identities, people establish *fronts,* which Goffman defined as "that part of the individual's performance which regularly functions in a general and fixed fashion to define the situation of those who observe the performance" (p. 22). A front is comprised of the actor's appearance, manner, and setting; judiciously controlling these facets projects the sorts of images desired by the actor.

Goffman applied numerous other theatrical terms in his analysis. He discussed the implications of a *front stage,* where people are "on" for audiences, and a *back stage,* such as alone at home, where people can relax out of sight of audiences and critics. He discussed *performance teams* that function to put on coordinated shows before audiences, such as a husband and wife or an employer and secretary. He considered *dramatized performances,* which are calculated efforts designed to convince fully an audience of the authenticity of one's claims (e.g., a student who spends so much time in class appearing attentive and interested that she actually loses track of what the lecturer is saying), and *idealized performances,* which fulfill and often exceed the stereotypes or standards of the audience for what a particular type of actor should be like (e.g., a priest who acts more devout, humble, and moral than he really believes himself to be). In short, he embued social life with the characteristics and trappings of a theatrical endeavor.

Goffman's work has been criticized by symbolic interactionists, other social psychologists, and the public at large, and many of these criticisms contain significant merit. Nonetheless, most criticisms are aimed less at the utility of the perspective itself than at some of the particular directions in which Goffman took it. First, it has been charged that he left too much of the person and psychological processes out of the interaction; for example, he did not view people's private self-conceptions as playing major roles in influencing behavior. Indeed, Goffman (1959, p. 252) contended that "a correctly staged and performed scene leads the audience to impute a self to a performed character, but this imputation—this self—is a *product* of the scene that comes off, it is not a *cause* of it." The self of interest to Goffman was the social self, not the private self of the actor, and this social self shifted from scene to scene.

Second, following closely from the first point, Goffman placed excessive weight on the power of social rules and rituals in determining behavior. He devoted considerable attention to interaction rituals, which are normatively prescribed patterns of coordinated actions, and believed that these social scripts determine how the participants will behave, constraining their actions much like the script handed to a professional actor. The extremity of his arguments is typified by the following: "Universal human nature is not a very human thing. By acquiring it, the person becomes a kind of construct, built up not from inner psychic propensities but from moral rules that are impressed upon him from without" (Goffman, 1967, p. 45). Society and normative patterns of action gain superiority over the individual, who seems to be left at the mercy of forces and scripts beyond his or her control. These themes represent a departure from Mead, Cooley, and other symbolic interactionists, who refused to grant priority to the individual or society and stressed the reciprocal interaction of each.

Third, Goffman has been criticized for overemphasizing the conscious, calculated use of impression management tactics, as people perform for an immediate audience and try to gain advantages. However, it should be acknowledged that while many of his examples indeed suggest deliberation and manipulation, he noted that impression management is not solely conscious in nature. Performances often flow routinely, based on nonconscious, modulated patterns of behavior that develop through years of socialization. Further, he made frequent mention of the impact of real and imagined audiences, thus not limiting himself to what people try to do to immediate others.

The above criticisms partially underlie the common view of Goffman—insightful but amoral, more concerned with appearance than substance. Karl Scheibe (Chapter 2) examines this view, placing Goffman's work in context. For the moment, it is enough to note that Goffman's work has had a significant impact on how the self is regarded. Current thought and research appears to have moved in the direction of capitalizing on Goffman's insights while expanding them, thus restoring inner substance to the self. This will be seen throughout most of the chapters in this volume.

CONFLICTS AND INTEGRATIONS

At the risk of oversimplifying, it can be said that two parallel bodies of thought and research on the self have developed within social psychology (Backman, 1983). The first has its traditions largely within American academic psychology and tends to look first at the nature of the individual and then toward the interaction process. It has tended to seek explanations that have a universal character, usually emphasizing social cognition and exploring how the structure and processes of the self influence self-relevant thoughts, affect, and actions. Individual differences on such personality dimensions as self-consciousness, social anxiety, self-esteem, self-monitoring, etc., have been the focus of much research. Social information pertinent to roles, rules, and rituals can be handled by treating it as a type of information that, along with other experiential information, is integrated and held in memory in the form of cognitive schemata and scripts. These cognitive structures in turn affect perceptions of new information and guide behavior. Social interaction is generally viewed in terms of the reciprocal influence each participant has on the other.

The second approach has its traditions within academic sociology, drawing especially from symbolic interactionism and dramaturgy. It tends to look first at the nature of society in general and social interaction in particular, and then looks at the individuals who are involved. People's scripts for social interaction are generally viewed as more "social" in nature than the ones mentioned above, emphasizing societally based information such as normatively sequenced action patterns and situated identities. A high priority is given to discovering what these socially scripted rules and identities are since they are presumed to exist independently of particular individuals and guide the course of interactions. Emphasis is also placed on the joint construction and negotiation of reality, as people define the roles each will have and the type of situation in which their activities will be embedded. Once the meaning of the interaction is jointly constructed, appropriate scripts can guide the participants' actions. As compared to the first approach, this approach ties the self somewhat more directly into the social interaction process and stresses the interactive nature of social participation. These emphases have led some theorists to contend that social behavior is, in large part, historically bound and relevant to a particular locale, since the meanings and hence interpretation of social activities will change over time and places as the prevailing cultural context changes (thus affecting the pertinent rules, roles, etc. that guide these activities).

Each approach (or, more properly, some of the more popular variants of each approach) has been criticized. The first has been criticized for (a) a tendency to adopt a view of people that is more passive than active, such as by seeing people as organisms that "react" to stimuli or as computers that mechanistically rather than creatively deal with information; (b) being overly analytical and so concerned with methodological precision as to lose sight of important issues and produce research results that are trivial when applied to everyday life; (c) overemphasizing the individual to the extent that the interactional and structural aspects of social participation are neglected; (d) neglecting the *joint* construction and negotiation of reality, including the negotiation of self; and (e) failing to appreciate that actions are set in a particular historical and local context which, if changed, can drastically alter the entire meaning and interpretation of an event. The second approach has been criticized for (a) being vague and inexact, and employing concepts that are minimally useful for scientific explanation because they are fuzzy, inconsistently employed, and not adequately interrelated; (b) demoting or ignoring the personality and psychological processes of the individual; (c) overemphasizing the social situation and the potency of social norms instead of recognizing that social information must be transformed by the individual for entry, along with much other information, in cognitive schemata and scripts; (d) overemphasizing the transient aspects of social customs and conventions rather than placing greater emphasis on universals; and (e) overemphasizing the construction of social reality to the point that the existence of an independent reality outside the mind of the individual is ignored.

These conflicts, sometimes representing differences in emphases and jargon rather than qualitative matters, have existed for years and still exist to some extent. However, as Carl Backman (1983) has noted, we seem to be moving toward a more interdisciplinary social psychology. Previously, advocates of each approach tended to ignore the others. Now, cross-referencing is increasing and key ideas from each approach are appearing in the literature of the other, albeit sometimes in slightly modified form, sometimes under different labels or terms, and sometimes embedded in the particular theoretical contexts that have dominated each approach. Each approach has moved toward the other, in the direction of rectifying the criticisms made about each other.

By design, the chapters in this volume tend to draw more heavily from the psychological tradition than the sociological one (Backman, Chapter 10, is a major exception). Nonetheless, the influence of symbolic interactionism and dramaturgy can be seen in many places. As compared to the past, a more interdisciplinary, multifaceted, yet integrative view of the self in social life is emerging, and it provides a more enlightening portrait than has previously existed.

REFERENCES

Abelson, R. P. (1976). Script processing in attitude formation and decision making. In J. S. Carroll & J. W. Payne (Eds.), *Cognition and social behavior.* Hillsdale, NJ: Erlbaum.

Alba, J. W., & Hasher, L. (1983). Is memory schematic? *Psychological Bulletin, 93,* 203–231.

Alexander, C. N., Jr., & Wiley, M. G. (1981). Situated activity and identity formation. In M. Rosenberg & R. H. Turner (Eds.), *Social psychology: Sociological perspectives.* New York: Basic Books.

Allport, G. W. (1937). *Personality: A psychological interpretation.* New York: Holt.

Backman, C. W. (1983). Toward an interdisciplinary social psychology. In L. Berkowitz (Ed.), *Advances in experimental social psychology* (Vol. 16). New York: Academic Press.

Biddle, B. J., & Thomas, E. J. (Eds.). (1966). *Role theory: Concepts and research.* New York: Wiley.

Burke, K. (1969). *A grammar of motives.* Berkeley: University of California Press. (Original work published 1945).

Burns, F. (1973). *Theatricality: A study of convention in the theatre and in social life.* New York: Harper & Row.

Cantor, N., & Mischel, W. (1979). Prototypes in person perception. In L. Berkowitz (Ed.), *Advances in experimental social psychology* (Vol. 12). New York: Academic Press.

Carson, R. C. (1969). *Interaction concepts of personality.* Chicago: Aldine.

Cooley, C. H. (1922). *Human nature and the social order* (Rev. ed.). New York: Charles Scribner's Sons. (Original work published in 1902)

Epstein, S. (1973). The self-concept revisited: Or a theory of a theory. *American Psychologist, 28,* 404–416.

Epstein, S. (1981). The unity principle versus the reality and pleasure principles, or the tale of the scorpion and the frog. In M. D. Lynch, A. A. Norem-Hebeisen, & K. J. Gergen (Eds.), *Self-concept: Advances in theory and research.* Cambridge, MA: Ballinger.

Evreinoff, N. (1927). *The theatre in life.* New York: Benjamin Bloom.

Festinger, L. (1957). *A theory of cognitive dissonance.* Evanston, IL: Row, Peterson.

Fromm, E. (1947). *Man for himself.* New York: Rinehart.

Goffman, E. (1959). *The presentation of self in everyday life.* Garden City, NY: Doubleday Anchor.

Goffman, E. (1967). *Interaction ritual.* Garden City, NY: Doubleday Anchor.

Greenwald, A. G. (1980). The totalitarian ego: Fabrication and revision of personal history. *American Psychologist, 35,* 603–618.

Greenwald, A. G. & Pratkanis, A. R. (1984). The self. In R. S. Wyer & T. K. Srull (Eds.), *Handbook of social cognition* (Vol. 3). Hillsdale, NJ: Erlbaum.

Heider, F. (1958). *The psychology of interpersonal relations.* New York: Wiley.

Hobbes, T. (1952). *Leviathan.* Chicago: Encyclopaedia Britannica. (Original work published 1651)

Hogan, R. (1976). *Personality theory: The personological tradition.* Englewood Cliffs, NJ: Prentice-Hall.

James, W. (1890). *The principles of psychology.* New York: Holt.

Jones, E. E. (1964). *Ingratiation: A social psychological analysis.* New York: Appleton-Century-Crofts.

Jones, E. E., & Pittman, T. S. (1982). Toward a general theory of strategic self-presentation. In J. Suls (Ed.), *Psychological perspectives on the self* (Vol. 1). Hillsdale, NJ: Erlbaum.

Jones, E. E., Rhodewalt, F., Berglas, S., & Skelton, J. A. (1981). Effects of strategic self-presentation on subsequent self-esteem. *Journal of Personality and Social Psychology, 41,* 407–421.

Jones, E. E., & Wortman, C. (1973). *Ingratiation: An attributional approach.* Morristown, NJ: General Learning Press.

Jones, S. C. (1973). Self and interpersonal evaluations: Esteem theories versus consistency theories. *Psychological Bulletin, 79,* 185–199.

Judd, C. M., & Kulik, J. A. (1980). Schematic effects of social attitudes on information processing and recall. *Journal of Personality and Social Psychology, 38,* 569–578.

Kelly, G. A. (1955). *The psychology of personal constructs* (2 Vols.). New York: Norton.

Kuiper, N. A. (1981). Convergent evidence for the self as a prototype: The inverted-U RT effect for self and other judgments. *Personality and Social Psychology Bulletin, 7,* 438–443.

Langer, E. J. (1978). Rethinking the role of thought in social interaction. In J. H. Harvey, W. Ickes, & R. F. Kidd (Eds.), *New directions in attribution research* (Vol. 2). Hillsdale, NJ: Erlbaum.

Lecky, P. (1969). *Self-consistency: A theory of personality.* Garden City, NY: Doubleday Anchor. (Original work published 1945)

Mandler, G. (1975). Consciousness: Respectable, useful and probably necessary. In R. Solso (Ed.), *Information processing and cognition: The Loyola Symposium.* Hillsdale, NJ: Erlbaum.

Markus, H. (1977). Self-schemata and processing information about the self. *Journal of Personality and Social Psychology, 35,* 63–78.

Markus, H., & Sentis, K. (1982). The self in information processing. In J. Suls (Ed.), *Psychological perspectives on the self* (Vol. 1). Hillsdale, NJ: Erlbaum.

Markus, H., & Smith, J. (1981). The influence of self-schema on the perception of others.

In N. Cantor & J. Kihlstrom (Eds.), *Personality, cognition and social interaction.* Hillsdale, NJ: Erlbaum.
McCall, G. J., & Simmons, J. E. (1978). *Identities and interactions* (2nd ed.). New York: Free Press.
Mead, G. H. (1934). *Mind, self, and society.* Chicago: University of Chicago Press.
Meltzer, B. N. (1972). Mead's social psychology. In J. G. Manis & B. N. Meltzer (Eds.), *Symbolic interaction* (2d ed.). Boston: Allyn & Bacon.
Meltzer, B. N., & Petras, J. W. (1972). The Chicago and Iowa schools of symbolic interactionism. In J. G. Manis & B. N. Meltzer (Eds.), *Symbolic interaction* (2nd ed.). Boston: Allyn & Bacon.
Meltzer, B. N., Petras, J. W., & Reynolds, L. T. (1975). *Symbolic interactionism: Genesis, varieties and criticism.* Boston: Routledge & Kegan Paul.
Minsky, M. (1975). A framework of representing knowledge. In P. H. Winston (Ed.), *The psychology of computer vision.* New York: McGraw-Hill.
Neisser, U. (1976). *Cognition and reality.* San Francisco: Freeman.
Nisbett, R. E., & Wilson, T. D. (1977). Telling more than we can know: Verbal reports and mental processes. *Psychological Review, 84,* 231–259.
Piaget, J. (1955). *The child's construction of reality.* London: Routledge & Kegan Paul.
Richardson, K. D., & Cialdini, R. B. (1981). Basking and blasting: Tactics of indirect self-presentation. In J. T. Tedeschi (Ed.), *Impression management theory and social psychological research.* New York: Academic Press.
Rogers, T. B. (1981). A model of the self as an aspect of the human information processing system. In N. Cantor & J. Kihlstrom (Eds.), *Personality, cognition, and social interaction.* Hillsdale, NJ: Erlbaum.
Rosenberg, M. (1979). *Conceiving the self.* New York: Basic Books.
Sarbin, T. R., & Allen, V. L. (1968). Role theory. In G. Lindzey & E. Aronson (Eds.), *The handbook of social psychology* (2d ed., Vol. 1). Reading, MA: Addison-Wesley.
Schank, R., & Abelson, R. (1977). *Scripts, plans, goals and understanding.* Hillsdale, NJ: Erlbaum.
Schlenker, B. R. (1980). *Impression management: The self-concept, social identity, and interpersonal relations.* Monterey, CA: Brooks/Cole.
Schlenker, B. R. (1982). Translating actions into attitudes: An identity-analytic approach to the explanation of social conduct. In L. Berkowitz (Ed.), *Advances in experimental social psychology* (Vol. 15). New York: Academic Press.
Schlenker, B. R., & Goldman, H. J. (1982). Attitude change as a self-presentation tactic following attitude-consistent behavior: Effects of choice and role. *Social Psychology Quarterly, 45,* 92–99.
Schlenker, B. R., & Hallam, J. R., & McCown, N. E. (1983). Motives and social evaluation: Actor-observer differences in the delineation of motives for a beneficial act. *Journal of Experimental Social Psychology, 19,* 254–273.
Schlenker, B. R., & Miller, R. S. (1977). Egocentrism in groups: Self-serving biases or logical information processing? *Journal of Personality and Social Psychology, 35,* 755–764.
Schlenker, B. R., & Schlenker, P. A. (1975). Reactions following counterattitudinal behavior which produces positive consequences. *Journal of Personality and Social Psychology, 31,* 962–971.
Secord, P. F., & Backman, C. W. (1965). Interpersonal approach to personality. In B. H. Maher (Ed.), *Progress in experimental personality research* (Vol. 2). New York: Academic Press.

Secord, P. F., & Backman, C. W. (1974). *Social Psychology* (2nd ed.). New York: McGraw-Hill.

Shrauger, J. S., & Schoeneman, T. J. (1979). Symbolic interactionist view of self-concept: Through the looking glass darkly. *Psychological Bulletin, 86,* 549–573.

Smith, A. (1759). *A theory of moral sentiments.* London: A. Miller.

Snyder, M. L., Stephan, W. G., & Rosenfield, D. (1978). Attributional egotism. In J. H. Harvey, W. Ickes, & R. F. Kidd (Eds.), *New directions in attribution research* (Vol. 2). Hillsdale, NJ: Erlbaum.

Stryker, S. (1979). Symbolic interactionism: Themes and variations. In M. Rosenberg & R. H. Turner (Eds.), *Social psychology: Sociological perspectives.* New York: Basic Books.

Swann, W. B., Jr. (1983). Self-verification: Bringing reality into harmony with the self. In J. Suls & A. G. Greenwald (Eds.), *Psychological perspectives on the self* (Vol. 2). Hillsdale, NJ: Erlbaum.

Swann, W. B., Jr., & Read, S. J. (1981). Self-verification processes: How we sustain our self-conceptions. *Journal of Experimental Social Psychology, 17,* 351–372.

Taylor, S. E., & Crocker, J. (1981). Schematic bases of social information processing. In E. T. Higgins, C. P. Herman, & M. P. Zanna (Eds.), *Social cognition: The Ontario Symposium* (Vol. 1). Hillsdale, NJ: Erlbaum.

Tesser A. (1978). Self-generated attitude change. In L. Berkowitz (Ed.), *Advances in experimental social psychology* (Vol. 11). New York: Academic Press.

Thomas, W. I. (1923). *The unadjusted girl.* Boston: Little, Brown.

Turner, R. H. (1968). The self-conception in social interaction. In C. Gordon & K. J. Gergen (Eds.), *The self in social interaction.* New York: Wiley.

Weary Bradley, G. (1978). Self-serving biases in the attribution process: A reexamination of the fact or fiction question. *Journal of Personality and Social Psychology, 36,* 56–71.

Weary, G., & Arkin, R. M. (1981). Attributional self-presentation and the regulation of self-evaluation. In J. H. Harvey, W. C. Ickes, & R. F. Kidd (Eds.), *New directions in attribution research* (Vol. 3). Hillsdale, NJ: Erlbaum.

Weinstein, E. A. (1969). The development of interpersonal competence. In D. A. Goslin (Ed.), *Handbook of socialization theory and research.* Chicago: Rand McNally.

Wylie, R. C. (1961). *The self-concept.* Lincoln: University of Nebraska Press.

PART ONE

THE INNER AND OUTER SELF

The first section contains six chapters that focus on the yin and yang of the self as both a private and public entity. As Jacob Bronowski remarked, "Man alone desires to be both in one, a social solitary." The self is represented in the inner life of the person and in the public forum. The inherently human balance between these aspects of self, and how these aspects influence and are influenced by social life, is a theme that runs throughout the section. The intellectual debt that contemporary work owes to William James, George Herbert Mead, Erving Goffman, and other pioneering luminaries whose ideas were described in the introduction, is evident in the chapters. Many of the same themes and issues first addressed by these pioneers continually reappear. At the same time, the chapters clearly reveal the increased sophistication of inquiry, advances in knowledge, and controversies that have occurred in the area in recent years.

In Chapter 2, Karl Scheibe examines historical perspectives on the presented self. He focuses on the shifts of content and method that have occurred in writings about the presented self over the last hundred years in American psychology. Scheibe suggests that a real shift has occurred in the direction of portraying the self as a fragmented, discontinuous collection of expedient social images. Along the way, something important has been lost that was dominant in the writings of James, Mead, and others—the more complete view of the self as an inward and active agent. Scheibe's analysis attempts to restore the unity of the private and public sides of self. He also comments on the historical transformation in values, both in society at large and within psychology, that seems to have accompanied this shift over time, and he explores the moral issues raised by Goffman's analysis of the self as a public presentation.

In Chapter 3, Barry Schlenker presents an identity-analytic theory of self-identification that draws from both the psychological and sociological traditions in addressing the nature and motivational implications of the self. The identification process consists of fixing and specifying our identities, both privately through self-reflection and publicly through self-disclosure and self-presentation. The theory rests on the fundamental principles that (a) people constantly attempt to achieve goals, (b) people formulate (or evoke from memory) plans and scripts for goal accomplishment, and (c) these plans or scripts contain desired images of self that act as prototypes and guides for self-identification. Desired identity images represent what the person believes he or she *could and should be* in the particular situation, blending wishes and reality. The theory explores, among other topics, how people attempt to create environments that support desired identities, progress smoothly in relationships or experience social anxiety based on their expectations of establishing desired identities, and are more or less satisfied in particular relationships depending on the extent to which desired identities are supported. By focusing on the nature of the self-identification process, the theory also attempts to place public self-presentation and private self-referent activities under a common theoretical rubric. This contrasts with some prior approaches that have regarded public self-presentation as more of a unique but superficial curiosity than a genuinely interesting phenomenon that reveals much about the nature of the self.

In Chapter 4, William Swann examines the self and its motivational properties. Drawing on the ideas of Lecky (1945/1969) and Secord and Backman (1965), he explores the implications of the self-sustaining nature of the self, proposing that people attempt to verify their self-conceptions. Such self-verification is achieved through cognitive biases (e.g., the tendency to see more self-confirmatory information than actually exists) and through actions, as people display for others the signs and symbols of who they are (e.g., clothes, diplomas, cars), seek out others whose appraisals are likely to confirm their self-conceptions, and employ interaction strategies that elicit from others self-confirmatory reactions (e.g., trying to shape the opinions of others about oneself in ways that increase the likelihood of receiving self-confirming feedback). A self-sustaining cycle is created in which people's self-conceptions guide their interpersonal behaviors which, in turn, influence the type of information they receive about themselves. Swann suggests that the motives of self-consistency and self-esteem enhancement coexist, with the former being most relevant to cognitive processes and the latter most relevant to affective reactions, and examines the conditions under which each is most likely to influence behavior. Both Schlenker (Chapter 3) and Swann propose that people attempt to construct environments that support the self, but their emphases differ, with the former focusing on desired images of self and the latter focusing on existing images of self.

In Chapter 5, Anthony Greenwald and Steven Breckler document the case that a primary audience for the presented self is oneself and not just other people. Focusing on the cognitive bias of beneffectance, they propose that the presented self is usually "too good to be true," yet is genuinely regarded as true by the actor. Their emphasis on beneffectance (self-esteem enhancement) contrasts somewhat with Swann's emphasis on self-consistency. After establishing the importance of oneself as well as others as audiences for self-presentations, they examine how different types of ego tasks, or goals for the self, affect self-presentations and self-evaluations. Their analysis permits specific predictions about how personality and situational factors affect the type of ego task selected by actors, the basis for self-evaluation, and the self-presentational strategies associated with the ego task. Their view of the self as an active, complex agent who strives to achieve diverse goals is compatible with Schlenker's propositions about self-identification.

In Chapter 6, Charles Carver and Michael Scheier analyze the nature of self-attention and its implications for the private and public aspects of self. The reflective and reflexive capacities of the human mind have been acknowledged by philosophers for centuries, and both James and Mead expounded on the importance of self-consciousness in influencing social activities. Only recently, however, have these concepts been systematically researched. Carver and Scheier expand on the idea that the self is a major determinant of cognition, affect, and behavior primarily when the self-system is activated by taking the self as an object of attention (Argyle, 1969; Buss, 1980; Duval & Wicklund, 1972; Fenigstein, Scheier, & Buss, 1975). They distinguish between (a) private self-attention, which is a focus of attention on personal standards, thoughts, feelings, and behaviors, and (b) public self-attention, which is a focus of attention on the perceived standards, thoughts, feelings, and behaviors of others as they pertain to the self. These different attentional states appear to be reliably associated with different patterns of self-relevant cognitions and behaviors, thus affecting the type of self that is projected. To explain these patterns, they present a model of self-regulation based on control-theory principles. They also discuss some differences deriving from the distinction between a *focus of attention,* as represented in their approach, and an *evaluative orientation,* as represented in the approach of Greenwald and Breckler (Chapter 5).

Finally, in Chapter 7, Robert Hogan, Warren Jones, and Jonathan Cheek present a socioanalytic theory of personality and social behavior. The theory draws from some of the major ideas of personality theorists, symbolic interactionists, and dramaturgists, integrating and extending those ideas to embed the person in the socius while maintaining the uniqueness of the individual as an active agent. The theory starts with the proposition that people have a number of biologically based dispositions, the most important of which are dispositions to seek attention and approval, to seek status, and to seek structure and order. These dispositions combine to make people seek ritualized social interaction in which roles and rules provide order while people go about the business of acquiring status and approval. The self-conception, as both privately conceived and publicly projected, arises as people "choose" and perfect the roles they will perform in social life. In this context, research on the development of the self-concept is reviewed. In melding the biological and social aspects of our nature, the chapters provides a return to some of the things that Scheibe noted have been misplaced over the years.

REFERENCES

Argyle, M. (1969). *Social interaction.* Chicago: Aldine.

Buss, A. H. (1980). *Self-consciousness and social anxiety.* San Francisco: W. H. Freeman.

Duval, S., & Wicklund, R. A. (1972). *A theory of objective self-awareness.* New York: Academic Press.

Fenigstein, A., Scheier, M. F., & Buss, A. H. (1975). Public and private self-consciousness: Assessment and theory. *Journal of Consulting and Clinical Psychology, 43,* 522–527.

Lecky, P. (1969). *Self-consistency: A theory of personality.* Garden City, NY: Doubleday Anchor. (Original work published 1945)

Secord, P. F., & Backman, C. W. (1965). Interpersonal approach to personality, In B. H. Maher (Ed.), *Progress in experimental personality research* (Vol. 2). New York: Academic Press.

CHAPTER 2

HISTORICAL PERSPECTIVES ON THE PRESENTED SELF

Karl E. Scheibe
Wesleyan University

For if anything in the world is worth wishing for . . . it is that a ray of light should fall on the obscurity of our being.

Arthur Schopenhauer

This chapter is a willfully partial slice through the history of theory and research on the self in psychology. The design is to describe such rays of light as have fallen along the way and to retrieve them from the obscurity of temporal remoteness. This implies immediately what this chapter is not; namely, it is not a complete or even fair history of theory and research on the self in modern psychology. Such an order would be too large for a chapter. The reader may find facets of such a general history in recent works by Gergen (1984), Lynch, Norem-Hebeisen, and Gergen (1981), Schlenker (1980), Mischel (1977), and Sarbin and Scheibe (1983). However, no comprehensive history of the self within psychology has been written. Perhaps the recent surge of interest in the topic will encourage the preparation of just such a work. For the present, we shall have to be content with partial, incomplete, and highly selective historical reviews, of which the present chapter is simply another example.

The selectivity of the present treatment is determined by several problematic issues. The first concerns the obvious shift in the dominant method and content of writings about the self over the last hundred years in American psychology. Are the questions William James found to be central different from those that attract the attention of current researchers on the self? And how are we to understand the tremendous change in preferred methodology over this hundred-year span? The second issue is related to the first, for it is the question of the historical conditionality of the self. Is it possible that the self as an object of inquiry has undergone an historical transformation over the last hundred years? One extention of contemporary narrative theories of the self suggests the possibility that selves are not constant but are evolving products of history. (See Mancusco & Sarbin, 1983; Gergen & Gergen, 1983; Boswell, 1983.) It is difficult either to comment on the massive changes that have occurred in the way psychologists have gone about their study of the self or to consider the question of the historical conditionality of self without encountering strongly charged questions of value. This suggests a third issue for this chapter. Something in the modern spate of work on impression management seems to cause offense, even moral outrage. Modern research on the self touches upon issues of deceit, of hypocrisy, of manipulation, of a cynical denucleation of human material. These issues deserve attention in historical context. In the present chapter these questions are not discussed in serial order; rather, they pervade and inform the entire discussion.

An additional caveat must be mentioned before we begin to trace a particular line of theory and research on the self in psychology. This book is about the self in social context. Thus, little attention will be given in this history to theories which concentrate on the psychology of the individual in isolation from social context. One such tradition is psychoanalysis, which Freud developed as a psychological theory out of his practice of treating individuals with neurotic problems. Another is the Dasein tradition, again a preeminently individual theory of self of continental European origin. This work is a veritable lake of writing about the self, from which only a minor tributary has found its way into the main currents of contemporary theory and research in North America (cf. Heidegger, 1962). In addition, Jung's analytic psychology, as distinguished from traditional Freudian theory, is preeminently about the self, and is concerned with the development and integration of self throughout the lifespan. Yet Jung's is also an individual psychology, and it is not prominent in major current writings on the self in psychology.

We may say, with just arbitration, that the line of development within the psychology of the self begins with William James. This line includes also James Mark Baldwin, whose exile from the United States for the latter part of his career seems to have cost him the high regard which is his due. It leads through Charles Horton Cooley and George Herbert Mead, seminal figures in American sociology. As this line is absorbed into sociology, it becomes lost to behavioral psychology, which had no use for it in any event. Symbolic interactionism is the culmination of this line in contemporary sociology (cf. Manis & Meltzer, 1978), but here again we encounter a body of writings on the self which is largely isolated from corresponding treatments within psychology. The contact between the sociological and psychological lines of theory and research on the self has been achieved principally through the work of Erving Goffman, whose brilliance and whose productivity has commanded the attention of social psychologists, even though he has been the maverick of mavericks in sociology. Another major contribution to the reconnection of the James, Cooley, and Mead line to the mainstream of social psychology is provided by the introduction of role theory into psychology, mainly through the writings of Theodore Sarbin (Sarbin, 1954; Sarbin, 1976; Sarbin & Allen, 1968; Allen & Scheibe, 1982).

CURRENT RESEARCH ON THE SELF AND A CONSTRUCTION OF HOW IT AROSE

The self is a hot topic in contemporary psychology. Current journals and newly published books, of which this work is an example, manifest a new centrality for self and social identity in theory and research. For example, Schlenker's (1980) monograph on *Impression Management* has over 500 references in its bibliography, 58 percent of which were published in the preceding decade. Including the previous two decades, 93 percent of the references are included. The 600-plus references in Sarbin and Scheibe's (1983) edited collection, *Studies in Social Identity,* show a similar profile for date of publication. Additional evidence of this new centrality of interest in self and identity is provided by a quantity of current research on self-awareness theory, as inspired by the original work of Duval and Wicklund (1972; see also Buss, 1980). Bandura (1977) has turned his attention to self-efficacy, which he considers to be a ". . . unifying theory of behavioral change." Similarly, Greenwald (1980), in writing of "the totalitarian ego," urges consideration of a "self-centered" theory as the best means of integrating the cognitive and behavioral perspectives of current psychology.

As suggested previously, it was not always thus. Twenty years ago in psychology, references to self were relatively rare. Wylie's (1961) book surveying research on *The Self Concept* was a landmark. In this book, Wylie notes the hiatus of research and theory on the self during the period of major domination of American behaviorism, for most of the twentieth century. Prescott Lecky's (1945) *Self Consistency: A theory of Personality* is a genuine exception to the norm. Lecky argued that the key to psychological development is provided by "self-consistency," both in terms of the person's self perception and in terms of perception by others. This book proved to be an anticipation, if not the direct antecedent, of the later development of balance theories within social psychology (Heider, 1958), and, later, of attribution theory, which has been an especially fertile ground for empirical studies on self-perception (Kelley, 1967). Similarly, Erikson's (1950) *Childhood and Society,* while deriving from the psychoanalytic tradition, provided at least one current reference in the 1950s and 1960s for anyone seeking to understand the psychological significance of human identity.

One must return to the very beginnings of American psychology to encounter another period of strong interest in self and identity. The pragmatist-functionalist school, of which William James was the foremost representative, gave central importance to the self. In this, as in much else, James must be regarded as a pivotal figure in the history of American psychology. He devoted a single chapter of his famous *Principles of Psychology* (1890) to "The consciousness of self." Thereafter, he never wrote with direct focus on this topic again. With this remarkable chapter, James not only provided a critical synthesis of previous philosophical writings on the self, but he also endowed succeeding generations of scholars with a fixed point of reference for their inquiries. James' chapter is the single most common reference in modern writings on the self. The next section of this chapter examines the method and content of James' chapter in some detail, for it is almost of monograph length (111 pages), and its contents merit more than the customary passing bow.

It is the generative importance of James' chapter that deserves emphasis at this point. Within psychology, it provided a recapitulation of the philosophically based views of self that proceeded it. It stands as intellectual parent to the work of Baldwin, and Cooley and Mead. But the death of James in 1910 was proceeded by a general waning of his influential position in American psychology. His student, G. Stanley Hall, wrote an obituary notice for *The American Journal of Psychology,* which praised James for his style, his humanity, his generosity of spirit, but also predicted that his substantive contributions to psychology would soon be eclipsed and forgotten with the gathering momentum of a more specialized and scientific, altogether less philosophical psychology. Hall proved in the short run to be prescient, for within three years of James' death, behaviorism was to be launched. At the same time, the Gestalt school was founded by Kohler, Koffka, and Wertheimer in Germany, and psychoanalysis emerged as a major intellectual force. The decade surrounding the death of James must be regarded as the period of the most profound creativity and change in the history of psychology. The general direction of these changes was very much in keeping with Hall's prediction. However, if one looks at psychology since 1965, it appears that there is a return to a more Jamesian pattern. With the emergence of modern cognitive psychology and with the growing recognition of the artificiality of the separation of psychological and philosophical questions, James is very much in the ascendancy. (See Sarason, 1975 and Adelson, 1982.) Recently Harvard University Press published a three-volume, new edition of *Principles of Psychology,* complete with scholarly commentary, a description of the twelve-year period of composition, and facsimiles of manuscript pages. Many contemporary psychologists would claim that *Principles* is still the single most important psychology book ever published, not only for its vivid style and generous spirit, but, also, *pace* Hall, for its substantive contribution to current problems in psychology, including the problem of the self.

This is in no sense a historical regression. In fact, if the reader has patience to listen to James and to Baldwin, Cooley, and Mead, the thought will occur that we have lost something, and that the mountains of accumulated empirical studies are in some ways not as instructive as were the frankly more meditative reflections of these earlier writers, whose main materials by way of data seem to have consisted of literature, drama, poetry, and philosophical writings. We now have data on the self in God's plenty, and most of it is recent. But it is an open question as to whether our understanding of this topic is significantly advanced. It is worth examining what that earlier understanding was.

WILLIAM JAMES' CHAPTER ON "THE CONSCIOUSNESS OF SELF"

Perhaps because James' chapter on "The Consciousness of Self" is so frequently cited in modern writings on the self, it is a surprise to return to the actual source. Its contents are not what one would expect from the customary brief reference, and the context within which that content appears is further occasion for refreshing our understanding.

The passage that is most often quoted from James' chapter (1890) is this one:

> Properly speaking, a man has as many social selves as there are individuals who recognize him and carry an image of him in their head. But as the individuals who carry the images fall naturally into classes, we may practically say that he has as many different social selves as there are distinct *groups* of persons about whose opinion he cares. (p. 294)

This passage is certainly consistent with James' general view of the self. It is also a clear anticipation of the entire domain of work in social psychology known as reference group theory, wherein the individual is considered to derive an identity by association, affiliation, and identification with a particular set of social reference groups. (See Hyman & Singer, 1968, and Miller, 1963.) But taken by itself, as it usually is, the passage is entirely misleading as to the most general significance James attaches to the self. The preference of modern writers for this passage as a way of typing James' position on the self is both unfair to James and revealing of a preference to have a conception of self that is consistent with division, fragmentation, and pluralism. Perhaps the "me generation" of the 1980s wants just such a psychological reflection.

The full title of James' chapter is "The Consciousness of Self." It directly follows the famous chapter on "The Stream of Thought," itself 65 pages long. It is evident that these two chapters are, for James, closely connected conceptually. The consciousness of self is taken to be a particular but most significant portion of the stream of thought. James notes at the beginning of the stream of thought chapter that, "The universal conscious fact is not 'feelings and thoughts exist,' but 'I think' and 'I feel'" (p. 226). The difference in these two ways of conceiving of consciousness is twofold. Thoughts and feelings are not passive occurrences, but active processes—processes directed by the individual to perceive and remember events selectively, in accord with what is meaningful and useful. Moreover, they are not just disembodied processes, but are appropriated or owned by the I, the self. Skipping now to the conclusion of the same chapter, we find an elaboration of the sense of connection between consciousness and self:

> One great splitting of the whole universe into two halves is made by each of us: and for each of us almost all of the interest attaches to one of the halves; but we all draw the line of division between them in a different place. When I say that we all call the two halves by the same names, and that those names are 'me' and 'not-me' respectively, it will at once be seen what I mean. (p. 289)

Here James makes an observation not about his own consciousness but about "our" consciousness. The use of the first person plural pronoun is significant, for it presumes communality. It was only later (say around 1912) that the psychologist would rise above his subject matter—studying objects that are called *Ss* (subjects) by means of an intelligence called *E* (experimenter)—thus gaining "the psychologist's advantage" (see Scheibe, 1978). James' method of achieving assent to an assertion could be called phenomenological, although there is no systematic observation of phenomena. It is certainly not introspective, for the entire effect of the stream-of-thought metaphor is to show that thought cannot be systematically analyzed by the methods of introspection, for thought is a complex and continuous flow which cannot in principle be exteriorized by the crude and slow representational means available to the observer. The assertion also provides us with a major contextual feature for James' discussion of the self, for he is saying here that the self is a goodly portion of the stream of thought. The word *consciousness* in the title deserves as much emphasis as the word *self*, for self is seen as a specially significant portion of that consciousness. Interest in the self is simply taken as a common-sense given. "The altogether unique kind of interest which each human mind feels in these parts of creation which it can call *me* or *mine* may be a moral riddle, but it is a fundamental psychological fact" (James, 1890, p. 289).

Proceeding to an examination of that special domain of thought for which the referent is *me* or *mine*, James presents a protracted and systematic exploration of the territory. He recognizes at the outset a major distinction between the empirical self (the "me")—that which can be observed—and the pure ego (the "I")—that which by implication provides a sort of nucleus of the self and performs the observations of various constituents of the empirical self. James' discussion of the constituents of the empirical self is based on a tripartite division—the material self, the social self, and the spiritual self. Each of these receives discussion in turn, and it is from a segment of the discussion of the second of these constituents that the famous statement is taken about the multiplicity of social selves. In his discussion of all these constituents, the emphasis on the self as thought content is constant. While the spiritual self represents a different sort of thought than the material self, this distinction is really not so great as it might appear. The material self concerns thoughts about possessions, gains and losses, economic affairs, investments, places, objects, and tangible things, which are in some sense *me* or *mine*. The spiritual self concerns thoughts and feelings about God, the cosmos, the mystery of one's inner life, curiosity about origins and destinies. It is only the referents for these thoughts which differ in their tangible qualities. As types of thought, they are equally thoughts. So, too, with the social selves, by which James means only that we have specific kinds of self-thoughts in relation to distinct social groups. While in this empirical sense the selves are discontinuous, James does not intend to say that the self as a whole is discontinuous. His discussion of pure ego makes this plain. Pure ego is a concept defined only by functional implication, not by empirical necessity. James makes no claim for a substantial pure ego. His claim is for the functional interpretation of pure ego as providing the sense and conviction of continuity over time for the entire stream of self. The *me* is an empirical aggregate which is objectively knowable.

> The I which knows them cannot itself be an aggregate. Neither for psychological purposes need it be considered to be an unchanging metaphysical entity like the Soul, or a principle like the pure Ego, viewed 'out of time.' It is a *Thought* at each moment different from that of the last moment, but appropriative of the latter, together with all that the latter called its own. (1890, p. 401)

Perhaps the second most famous quotation from James' chapter on the self is one that describes the function of maintaining continuity of self, which James attributes not to any entity or empirical constituent of self, but to Thought itself:

> ... Peter, awakening in the same bed with Paul, and recalling what both had in mind before they went to sleep, reidentifies and appropriates the 'warm' ideas as his, and is never tempted to confuse them with those cold and pale-appearing ones which he ascribes to Paul. As well might he confound Paul's body, which he only sees, with his own body, which he sees but also feels. Each of us when he awakens says, Here's the same old self again, just he says, Here's the same old bed, the same old room, the same old world. (1890, p. 334)

It is possible to regard James as contradicting himself when he argues first for a plurality of selves and then argues with equal conviction for the continuity and unity of self. This might seem a personological version of the mystery of the Trinity. But the real point about James' view of self is that he does insist on having it both ways.

> If from the one point of view they are one self, from others they are truly not one but many selves. And similarly of the attribute of continuity; it gives its own kind of unity to the self—that of mere connectedness, or unbrokenness, a perfectly definite phenomenal thing—but it gives not a jot or tittle more. And this unbrokenness in the stream of selves, like the unbrokenness in an exhibition of 'dissolving views,' in no wise implies any farther unity or contradicts any amount of plurality in other respects. (1890, p. 335)

The metaphor of 'dissolving views' is significant, for it seems that James is referring to the "flip-picture" predecessors of the motion picture. In motion pictures we have phenomenal continuity laid over what is a series of discreet images, if viewed at a slower rate. It is consistent with James' conception of the unity and plurality of selves to employ a cinema metaphor which he could not have known—that of the montage. In making a motion picture scene, the camera or cameras operate in ways that are unrepresentative of the process of ordinary visual perception and would be totally impossible for an actual human observer. The camera moves back and forth, up and around its subject in impossible ways, or cuts are made from one perspective to a totally different perspective, and yet the viewer knows when the montage remains within the same scene and knows when the scene shifts to another scene, near or distant in space and time. All of this is accomplished with a minimum of strain. The view of a modern football game on television, with perhaps six different perspectives on the same play repeated in sequence, is visually unrepresentative and impossible. And yet this disjoint experience is easily assimilated and accepted as a unified event. The visual sequence represented on film or television is normally experienced as having unity, despite the jerkings about, the discontinuities, the lack of realistic presentation.

The self is similar. James makes the claim that despite our many social roles and the masks they require, despite our combining dreaming with planning and hoping, and loafing, and loving, and feeling both secure and afraid at the same time—despite all of these discontinuities in the empirical constituents of our selves, we retain an overall conviction of unity and continuity. Just as shifting one's attention from the montage to the *making* of the montage somewhat spoils the illusion, so the focusing of attention on that which creates the montage "me" tends to threaten that unity which once seemed natural. Thus, it seems reasonable to expect behavioral and emotional consequences of enforced self-awareness. (See Buss, 1980, and Duval & Wicklund, 1972.) The stream of thought is never in the same condition twice, but even so, it is the same continuous stream. If this assertion is true when literally applied to an actual stream, then it is at least not a logical absurdity for it also to be true for the stream of thought.

I have noted above that James does not view this continuous and knowing I as some sort of metaphysical entity. Of course, James is insinuating, as a fundamental premise for this argument about the constituents and continuity of self, something that he has not demonstrated and something that is in principle not empirically demonstrable. The premise is that no thinker would deny the reality of his own thought. The premise is revealed again in an emphasized sentence at the conclusion of James' chapter: *"If the passing thought be the directly verifiable existent which no school has hitherto doubted it to be, then that thought is itself the thinker"* (1890, p. 401). But this was written before the advent of radical behaviorism in psychology or of radical empiricism in philosophy, and these schools make a point of showing their lack of sympathy for the premise which James considers unrefuted, for the simple reason that nobody had yet bothered to deny it. Today it cannot be said that no school has hitherto denied the existence of thought. The sequel to this denial, as shall be shown in later sections of this chapter, is the denial of that portion of the self which James considered to be unified and enduring.

Suppose for now that the denial of this nonempirical and functional "I" did, in fact, occur when a more rigorously scientific psychology took hold in the twentieth century. Suppose also that this denial of thought and of self is not just a trend for a set of academic psychologists, but in some way manifests a more pervasive historical transformation in cultural modes of self-regard. It is then possible to understand current assertions, which seem to insist upon a reintroduction of the conception of continuous self that James urged upon us over 90 years ago. Witness the following characterization of personality as a phenomenon akin to hypnotic trance. It is at once an assertion that subjective life can lose its sense of continuity and connection with reality, and at the same time it is a plea for the restoration of continuity and reality.

> There are times when having a personality seems to me like a vastly elaborate defense erected against the mystery of living. It's as though the cultural, familial, and individual trances we are all in contribute to one large personal dream—a world view. It's as though we were all amnesiacs, having forgotten our truer identities; seeing, like the underside of a weaving, only a fraction of what's before us, unconscious to the ground of our own being, the unregarded river of our life. (Condon, 1982)

There is, of course, no stream of thought, no unregarded river of our life. But these metaphors are not merely sentimental or gratuitous, for they express something about the human condition which can be expressed in no other way. The positing of the knowing "I" seems a generous act of social grace, a grant to all of more than can be demonstrated in any. For James, who was later to write "The Will to Believe" as an apologia for the legitimacy of all sorts of beliefs on nonscientific but humanly significant questions, such a position is entirely in character. But a later and more skeptical age of psychologists would come to regard such wispy claims as an embarrassment to scientific integrity.

What is the motivational significance of the self for James? It is implicit in the preceding discussion that the care and grooming of the various components of the self constitute a major focus of human activity. James considered the impulse to enhance, expand, and integrate the self to be fundamental—a motivational given. In the language of his time, James considered social self-seeking to be instinctual. But while the self is at the center of human purposes and actions, the motives to which James refers are not hedonistic in the sense of either gratifying bodily needs or maximizing some rational expectation of gain. Several of James' own comments on this subject will help to clarify his sense of the importance of the impulse to social self-seeking.

> "The noteworthy thing about the desire to be 'recognized' by others is that its strength has so little to do with the worth of the recognition computed in sensational or rational terms" (1890, p. 308).

> "Not only the people but the places and things I know enlarge my Self in a sort of metaphoric social way" (1890, p. 308).

> "In the more positive and refined view of heaven many of its goods, the fellowship of the saints and of our dead ones, and the presence of God, are but social goods of the most exalted kind. It is only the search of the redeemed inward nature, the spotlessness from sin, whether here or hereafter, that can count as spiritual self-seeking pure and undefiled" (1890, p. 309).

Thus, for James, the evaluative significance of others, of places and things, and of heaven itself must be understood in terms of strivings of the self.

DEVELOPING CONCEPTIONS OF THE SOCIAL SELF: BALDWIN, COOLEY, AND MEAD

James Mark Baldwin (1861–1934), like many nineteenth century American psychologists, was drawn to psychology from an earlier interest in religion. As a student at Princeton in the 1880s, Baldwin studied with President James McCosh, a philosopher who was newly converted to the empirical psychology of Wilhelm Wundt. Upon graduation, Baldwin departed for a year's study abroad, including a period with Wundt in Leipzig. On his return to the United States, Baldwin accepted a teaching post at Princeton Theological Seminary, and then a position in psychology at Lake Forest College in Illinois. In his peregrinations, he founded psychological laboratories at Toronto and at Princeton, was President of the American Psychological Association in 1897, and with James McKeen Cattell founded *The Psychological Review*. His last academic appointment in the United States was at Johns Hopkins University. He was dismissed from this position after an alleged incident of unprofessional conduct, for which he protested his innocence. (See Evans & Scott, 1978.) After 1908, the year he left Johns Hopkins, Baldwin spent his career abroad, first in Mexico and later in Paris. It is important to know that Baldwin left the stage of American psychology, for his prodigious writing has had very little direct impact on the subsequent development of psychology, save in two respects, both of which are in their way remarkable.

Although Baldwin admired Wundt and himself did a number of experiments, his contributions are not chiefly experimental, nor were his beliefs about psychology consistent with the hard materialism that came to dominate American psychology. He was easily dismissed by Boring (1950) in his magisterial *History of Experimental Psychology* as being of essentially no importance to psychology—for Boring noted that his real interests and strengths were "philosophical," a telling reproach.

But Baldwin's importance to the history of psychology must necessarily be revised because of two of his contributions, one of which is somewhat tangential for this essay, the other of prime importance. The tangential issue has to do with Jean Piaget, whose impact upon developmental psychology and on psychological theory in general has been enormous. Baldwin was in Paris at the beginnings of Piaget's career, knew him, and must be regarded as a clear influence upon Piaget, both in method of research and in theoretical content. When his first child was born, Baldwin began to study "genetic psychology," i.e., the psychology of mental development, based on close observations of the development of his own children. He described stages of mental development—prelogical thinking, logical thinking, hyperlogical thinking—and described the movement of the child through these stages of development as a function of a dialectical exchange of assimilation and accommodation. In his autobiographical assessment of his career, Baldwin makes some predictions about important future developments in psychology. He chooses for special emphasis, ". . . the child study movement in Switzerland centered in the J. J. Rousseau Institute and in the work of the group led by Piaget" (Baldwin, 1930, p. 28). After saying this, he went on to excoriate the movements of psychoanalysis ("unreal" and "extravagant") and American behaviorism ("an intellectual fad"). Small wonder that Baldwin was written off by Boring and until recently has been quite out of favor.

Baldwin's importance for our present purpose lies in his elaboration and reworking of James' notion of the social self. This reworking is presented in the second of Baldwin's studies of mental development, *Social and Ethical Interpretations* (1897), which was meant as a general text in social psychology. In this book, Baldwin describes the process of development of the self out of social interaction. While such a process is implicit in James' conception of the empirical selves, it remained for Baldwin to work out and illustrate how the social genesis of self might occur. The general drift of his thesis is captured in the following statement:

> The "ego" and the "alter" are thus born together. Both are crude and unreflective, largely organic. And the two get purified and clarified together by this twofold reaction. . . . My sense of myself grows by imitation of you, and my sense of yourself grows in terms of my sense of myself. Both *ego* and *alter* are thus essentially social, each is a *socius* and each is an imitative creation. (1897, p. 9)

The self develops, according to Baldwin, as a function of the dialectic between the child and the socius. Baldwin relies heavily on the conception of imitation proposed by the French sociologist, M. Tarde.

> The development of the child's personality could not go on at all without the constant modification of his sense of himself by suggestions from others. So he himself, at every stage, is really in part someone else, even in his own thought of himself. . . . He thinks of the . . . alter as his socius, just as he thinks of himself as the other's socius: and the only thing that remains more or less stable, throughout the whole growth, is the fact that there is a growing sense of self which includes both terms, the ego and the alter. (1897, p. 24)

Baldwin sees both a habitual self and an accommodating self. The habitual self is a product of imitative assimilation—the self that is established and is resistant to change. The accommodating self, on the other hand, is an active agent of change, constantly seeking modifications in response to new experiences. Throughout the developmental span, the dialectic continues; the challenges to the habitual self are posed by continued interaction with the socius. Much of Baldwin's discussion concerns the way in which the child acquires a moral and ethical sense through the unfolding of this interactive process. This is the same problem and very similar terminology to Kohlberg's (1963) research on moral development. That Baldwin's conceptions and very language should resemble Kohlberg's is not a surprise if we remember that Piaget stands as the mediating link between them.

Just as Baldwin elaborated certain ideas of James about the self, so he influenced in turn the thinking of Charles Horton Cooley (1864–1929). Like Baldwin, Cooley found it impossible to consider the self as existing in isolation.

> Persons are not separable and mutually exclusive . . . they interpenetrate one another, the same element pertaining to different persons at different times, or even at the same time. (Cooley, 1902, p. 90)

To this assertion Cooley appends a footnote acknowledging his indebtedness to Baldwin's conception of the social self in the *Social and Ethical Interpretations,* and as well to James.

Cooley's life seems to have been one of smooth academic tranquility. Son of a law professor at the University of Michigan, his academic work was done entirely at that institution; moreover, he served on Michigan's faculty for his entire academic career. His writing is meditative, contemplative, laced with references to Goethe, the Bible, Darwin, and to James and Baldwin. His empirical work is very limited—really unimportant in relation to the corpus of his writings. But he did, like Baldwin before him and Piaget after him, take advantage of his own children as a source of observations about social and personal development.

Cooley is widely identified in modern secondary sources as the author of conception of the "looking glass self"—the idea that the raw empirical material for the formation of self consists of reflections provided by others. That Cooley is so closely identified with this conception is testimony to the power of metaphor as the vehicle of memory. While this identification is certainly correct, it seems a particular injustice to Cooley's life work to be so summarily captured in a snippet of a phrase. Philip Rieff states the matter well:

> Cooley is best taken slowly; the student should linger long enough in his presence to appreciate some of his nobility of mind and rare gift for analyzing society as a whole, yet without oversimplification. . . . Cooley is not the only sociologist whose works communicate a nobility, a magnanimity of mind. But there are not so many that students can be permitted, without cost to their development as sociologists, to spare themselves the experience of confronting him. (1968, p. 33)

Cooley's solution to the problem of the relation between the individual and society is radical for all its gentility. For he considered self and society to be coterminus. Society is in the mind of each of us and everyone has a self that is product of the particular others with whom he has had contact in the course of development. Cooley considered human life to have two aspects—the individual and the social.

> But [it] is always, as a matter of fact, both individual and general. In other words, "society" and "individual" do not denote separable phenomena, but are simply collective and distributive aspects of the same thing, the relation between them being like that between other expressions, one of which denotes a group as a whole and the other the members of the group, such as the army and the soldiers, the class and the students, and so on. (1902, pp. 1–2)

Samples of Cooley's writing will have to suffice for this presentation, for they can convey the flavor of his work if not its texture and substance. "It is worth noting here that there is no separation between real and imaginary persons:

indeed, to be imagined is to become real, in a social sense" (1902, p. 60); and, "The life of the mind is essentially the life of intercourse" (1902, p. 62). Like James, his psychological mentor, Cooley rejects the notion of a substantive or metaphysical discussion of pure ego, ". . . whatever that may be." But he considers analysis of the empirical self to be no more difficult a matter than the analysis of any object of thought at all. His analysis of the empirical self begins along lines that we should now find similar to "ordinary language analysis" in philosophy. He inquires into what is meant in common speech by first-person singular pronouns. From this he concludes that the empirical self is essentially social, for the major portion of uses of first person pronouns have a social sense. Cooley does not follow James in including separate discussions of material and spiritual constituents of the empirical self. He prefers to think of the empirical self as social, " . . . not as implying the existence of a self that is not social—for I think that 'I' of common language always has more or less distinct reference to other people as well as to the speaker, but because I wish to dwell upon the social aspect of it" (1902, pp. 136–7).

The reader senses in Cooley a quality of moral loftiness, of gentle humanism, of tolerance and catholicity of mind. Perhaps the frequent quotations from Emerson, Shakespeare and other classical sources have their effect in this way. But Cooley is overtly and decidedly a political moralist. He advocates democracy as the form of social organization that is most compatible with human nature. Like Mead after him, he proclaims himself to be an internationalist and lays claim to a vision of universalism.

George Herbert Mead (1863–1931) was educated at Oberlin and at Harvard, where he studied for a time with William James. He served briefly on the faculty at the University of Michigan, where he was contemporary with Cooley. In 1894, Mead joined John Dewey at the University of Chicago, where he remained and taught until his death. While the dates of Mead's work are practically identical to Cooley's, he seems logically to come after him. This is due, in part, to the peculiar pattern of the publication of Mead's scholarly work. He wrote no book during his lifetime, and published very few articles. His major work was pulled together by students after his death and published in several volumes, the most important of which is *Mind, Self and Society* (1934). For this reason, Mead's major publication dates succeed those of his more prolific contemporary, Cooley.

In other ways as well, Mead's work is successor to the line extending from James to Baldwin to Cooley. While all of these figures were defenders and advocates of Darwinian thinking in science, it was Mead who worked out a new way to conceptualize the social nature of man in Darwinian terms. As product of this conceptualization, he articulated a radically new set of relationships for mind, self, and society. This conceptual work was conducted under the disciplinary aegis of sociology and the philosophy of pragmatism. As such, it comprised a seminal achievement that had very little or no immediate impact upon psychology. Anselm Strauss (1956) notes in his introduction to *The Social*

Psychology of George Herbert Mead that the individualistic psychology of Mead's day had little use for a social psychology based on the primacy of the socius. Strauss states that:

> The recently awakened interest of psychologists in problems of self and ego has not been affected greatly by Mead's discussion of these problems, perhaps because his assumptions differ from theirs. His I and Me. . . . represent quite a different formulation of the relations of man to society and man to biological natures; and there is in Mead no trace of speculation about basic human drives toward self-consistency or self-realization. (1956, p. xvi)

The particularly evolutionary understanding that Mead developed of the social origins of self is succinctly described in a note in his chapter on the self:

> Man's behavior is such in his social group that he is able to become an object to himself, a fact which constitutes him a more advanced product of evolutionary development than are the lower animals. Fundamentally it is this social fact—and not his alleged possession of a soul or mind with which he, as an individual, has been mysteriously and supernaturally endowed and with which the lower animals have not been endowed—that differentiates him from them. (In Strauss, 1956, p. 214.)

This position differs from that of James in that James' psychology of self was fundamentally an individual psychology, where part of the constituents of the self is considered to be social in nature. It differs from Baldwin in that it proposes the terms of the dialectic between self and alter to be initially asymmetrical, and in favor of the socius. In Mead's view, the self simply does not exist at birth, but arises as a result of social commerce. Mead's affinity to Cooley is obvious, but there is an important difference there, too.[1] Cooley defends a kind of social mentalism, where the socius essentially exists in the minds of individuals. Mead styles himself a social behaviorist and places emphasis on social actions, particularly the symbolic social actions mediated by language. These actions are the essential means by which selves and societies are both created and sustained. Fundamental to Mead's view is the concept of "taking the role of the other," and this again is a distinctive contribution to the line of theory to which he was heir:

> The individual experiences himself as such, not directly, but only indirectly, from the particular standpoints of other individual members of the same social group, or from the generalized standpoint of the social group as a whole to which he belongs. . . . He becomes an object to himself only by taking the attitudes of other individuals toward

---

[1] Mead's assessment of Cooley's social psychology is carried in a footnote in the chapter on Self, and bears repeating here in part:
[H]is psychological method carried with it the implication of complete solipsism; society really has no existence except in the individual's mind, and the concept of the self as in any sense intrinsically social is a product of imagination. Even for Cooley the self presupposes experience, and experience is a process within which selves arise; but since that process is for him primarily internal and individual rather than external and social, he is committed in his psychology to a subjectivistic and idealistic, rather than objectivistic and naturalistic metaphysical position. (in Strauss, 1956, p. 258)

himself within a social environment or context of experience and behavior in which both they and he are involved. (Mead, 1934, p. 140)

Mead's self is not of the "looking glass" variety proposed by Cooley. Cooley's metaphor implies a self looking at its own reflection in the passive mirror provided by alter. Mead suggests that we can take the position of alter and see ourselves, as it were, nonreversed and three-dimensional. By taking the role of the other, we can see ourselves "objectively." Moreover, the very development of an inward self is dependent first on gaining the outward perspective provided by the socius.

The form of behavior in which Mead is interested is certainly not bodily movement or physicalistic change. He is interested in the communicative acts among individuals, conducted by means of significant symbols. He further posits that social communication leads to the capacity of the individual to be a companion to himself, to think of himself—indeed, to think. Mead insists that one cannot converse with oneself without first conversing with others. Thought is itself social in origin and interactive in its nature, with the thinker taking alternatively the roles of actor and audience.

As social and self-development proceed, the child is considered by Mead to be morally fragmented in a way that reflects the differing interests or values of the social entities to which the child has been exposed. But gradually, the child learns to take toward him or herself the attitude of the generalized other. "The organized community or social group which gives the individual his unity of self may be called 'the generalized other'" (in Strauss, 1956, p. 231). This generalized other can consist of abstractions or nonexistent groups. In a functional sense, it provides the individual both with a consistent way of thinking about oneself and with a generally useful perspective from which to decide the rightness of any contemplated course of action. The play of the child is the serious business of internalizing the generalized other and at the same time developing skill in role playing.

Mead is as much a pragmatist as any of the thinkers in his line, and he applies his pragmatism to the recurrent problem of the self as knower (the I) and the self as known (the me) in a way that is reminiscent of James, but with a special Meadian touch:

> The simplest way of handling the problem would be in terms of memory. I talk to myself, and I remember what I said and perhaps the emotional content that went with it. The "I" of this moment is present in the "me" of the next moment. There again I cannot turn around quick enough to catch myself. (in Strauss, 1956, p. 242)

So as the "I" moves along, it leaves "me" in its wake and provides for the self a way of thinking about the self. Like James, Baldwin, and Cooley, Mead has no use for a metaphysical or essential "I" but uses the term to describe the activity that takes place in the specious present, including the contemplation of memories and the acts of past "I"'s. This point is extended by Mead to an implication about the limitations of self-knowledge. Since the I cannot know itself in the present, it never knows exactly what it is going to do in advance. The I is in this sense free and imparts a sense of initiative. "Exactly how we will act never gets into experience until after the action takes place" (in Strauss, 1956, p. 246). The adverb *exactly* deserves emphasis here, for Mead is not asserting that actions are unaffected by prior intentions and anticipations.

Mead also takes pains to account for originality and uniqueness in at least two other senses. Even though individual selves are of common social origin, still each self is unique in that the actual character of the social interactions experienced by any one person is unique. Also, society itself is not constant, for continual changes are introduced through the accretion throughout history of the consequences of gestures made by social actors. Of course, there are great gestures and small, great changes and small. "Profound changes which take place through the action of individual minds are only the extreme expression of the sort of changes that take place steadily through reactions which are not simply those of a 'me' but of an 'I' " (in Strauss, 1956, p. 249). Historical changes are due to the reactions of individuals to the social situations in which they find themselves. For Mead history is undetermined in the same way that the active "I"s are undetermined. The future is always to a degree unpredictable. In this, Mead would agree with Ortega y Gassett, who said:

> I believe that all life, and consequently the life of history, is made up of simple moments, each of them relatively undetermined in respect of the previous one, so that in it reality hesitates, walks up and down, and is uncertain whether to decide for one or another of various possibilities. (1930, p. 78)

It is, therefore, a mistake to think of Mead as the same sort of behaviorist as those who dominated psychology in his time, for they would admit no reflections either about self-consciousness nor about the indeterminacy of movement from the present to the future. In another sense as well, Mead is more similar to James than to his psychological contemporaries. Mead's discourse is full of the incorporative "we," as in, "We know that as we pass from one historical period to another . . . ." And, of course, Mead did not do experiments, did not rely upon empirical evidence to document his assertions. He may have styled himself a behaviorist to distinguish himself from what he considered to be the mentalism of Cooley, but he never thought of "self" or "mind" as predictive variables in a behavioral equation.

FREUD AND SULLIVAN: ANTITHESIS AND SYNTHESIS WITH THE PRAGMATIST'S LINE

With Mead, the line of theory which originated with James becomes completely submerged within sociology. There it would prove to be the germinal material for the development of symbolic interactionism (see Manis and Meltzer, 1978) and of role theory (see Sarbin and Allen, 1968). Within behavioral psychology at the time of Mead's active influence in the 1920s and 1930s the self had just about disappeared as an object of concern. To be sure, behavioral psychology included many empirical studies on the description of self and the use of those descriptions for behavioral prediction. We shall examine some of this work in the next section of this chapter. But it is instructive to look first at the general conception of self that was emerging within the psychoanalytic tradition—particularly in the later work of Freud and in that of one of the deviationist American analysts, Harry Stack Sullivan.

Charles Morris notes in his introduction to *Mind, Self and Society* that at the headwaters of social psychology are to be found Darwinism and democracy. Indeed, the question of the fit between human nature and the optimal form of human governance is never far in the background for any of the four thinkers we have considered. It is more than a matter of coincidence that all considered democracy to be that ideal form. Their participation in the American form of democracy was at a time and in a condition that allowed patriotism, optimism, and internationalism to coexist without painful contradiction.

While Darwinism is also at the headwaters of psychoanalysis, democracy most assuredly is not. This is not the place to labor an explanation of the major directions taken by psychoanalytic thinking in terms of the political and social ambiance of authoritarian rule characteristic of late nineteenth-century Europe (see Ellenberger, 1970). However, it is descriptively correct to note a similarity between the brash optimism of the young American republic between 1880 and 1930 and the sorts of theories of self produced by James, Baldwin, Cooley, and Mead. On the other hand, the relation between the person and the socius conceived by Freud in the same period would seem to correspond to a political environment characterized by the traditional rule of authority, the acceptance of class divisions as given, and—by the time of Freud's later writings—a profound political pessimism engendered by World War I.

Psychoanalysis is preeminently a psychology of the individual. The individual psyche is the prime entity for analysis; its nature, genetic laws, mechanisms, disorders, and restorative properties are the chief features of psychoanalytic theory. The socius is not ignored, for it is by means of the conflict resulting from the contact of the developing psyche with the agents of society, usually the parents, that ego begins to deploy its defenses, producing the development of personality. The id is supposed to be the repository of instinctual impulses and the superego is supposed to represent the tyrannical demands of society; the ego is sandwiched in between. Defense mechanisms are aptly named in psychoanalytic theory, for the ego is considered to be under a more or less constant state of seige.

In this brief discussion of a major and highly elaborate theoretical and interpretive structure, I must risk vast oversimplification. I am willing to do so for reasons of didactic clarity, in the belief that the fundamental contrast here being proposed is sound. Briefly, it is this: In *Civilization and Its Discontents*, Freud (1930) suggested that the basic and most fundamental relation between the individual and civilization is one of enmity. As a consequence of the basic incompatibility of the interests of the individual and the pressures of society, the individual is literally forced to adapt by sublimating basic instinctual energies.

The cost of this forced adaptation is repression, anxiety, and neurosis. Civilization demands a renunciation of individual sexual and aggressive impulses. As a consequence the person is made everlastingly guilty. Through the working off of this guilt, the individual paradoxically makes a contribution to the development of civilization, with the result that the distance between the protean psyche and civilization becomes ever greater. "The two processes of individual and of cultural development must stand in hostile opposition to each other and mutually dispute the ground" (Freud, 1930, p. 88).

The contrast of this view of the relation of the self to society to that described in the last section for Mead's psychology is great and pointed. If one position is understood, then both are, for they are diametrically opposed. For Freud, the individual is primary; for Mead, the socius is primary. For Freud, the relation between the individual and the society is one of enmity; for Mead, it is one of mutual dependence. (See Pfeutze, 1954.) For Freud, the consequence of identification with the culture is self-renunciation; for Mead, the achievement of the perspective of the generalized other is coincident with the highest level of self-development and integration. Freud's is a psychology of mental pathology, in which normality is regarded as a special case. The opposite is true for Mead, where the dissociation of personality is viewed as an ordinary and nonneurotic phenomenon, resulting from role conflicts. For example, the role of "son" and the role of "fraternity brother" might be behaviorally incompatible for a college student—a garden-variety role conflict. Only in the most extreme cases is such dissociation to be regarded as pathological, and then the pathology is not absolute but is socially relative and contextual.

If it is correct to say that Freud and Mead represent antithetical views on the relation between self and society, then we might identify the Interpersonal Psychiatry of Sullivan as a synthesis, or at least a middle ground. It is of interest to note that Sullivan became the guide for a generation of dynamic psychiatrists in the 1940s and 1950s, but was subsequently replaced by guides who looked to Freud for their inspiration.

Harry Stack Sullivan (1892–1949) was the son of Irish-American parents in rural New York state. He earned a M.D. degree at the Chicago College of Medicine and Surgery in 1917, entering the specialty of psychiatry after completing his military service during World War I. His early career was spent in service to the Federal Government, in several government-run mental hospitals in Washington, D.C. From 1931 to 1938, he had a private practice in New York, returning to Washington and government service just before World War II. Like Mead, Sullivan never published a book in his lifetime, though he did publish many papers in psychiatric journals and helped to found *Psychiatry* (see Mullahy, 1970). Several volumes of Sullivan's work were published after his death.

Sullivan's theoretical orientation was initially that of classical Freudian psychoanalysis. However, his early professional responsibilities required attention to therapy with schizophrenics, and Freudian psychoanalysis was intended principally for neurotics, not psychotics. Through a combination of his early experience in devising therapeutic programs for schizophrenics and through his reading in the social sciences, Sullivan developed a variant of psychoanalytic theory which came to be called Interpersonal Psychiatry. The major differentiating feature of Sullivan's theory is the central importance it gives to interpersonal processes rather than intrapsychic processes. Mental disorders for Sullivan are seen to be social in origin and nature. As a consequence, therapy demands attention to the total social surroundings of the patient, not merely a talking out of intrapsychic tensions.

Sullivan's affinity to the line we have described from James to Mead is very clear. "For all I know every human being has as many personalities as he has interpersonal relations" (quoted in Perry, 1982, p. 108). Further, "Mead demonstrated very clearly that the individual person was a complex derivative of many others" (Sullivan, 1953, p. 17). Sullivan considered the self to be essentially social in origin. The relations established between the person and others enable the self to achieve some definition. Because the others with whom the self relates are many and diverse, the self will have many and diverse facets, and its precariousness or fragility derives from the precariousness or fragility of the communicative links established with others.

Two developments in popular psychology in the last twenty years are properly seen as products of the Sullivanian view on the nature of personal adjustment. One is represented by the book, *I'm OK, You're OK* by Harris (1973). Therapy is seen as a process of providing for the person a secure and unconditional recognition of the basic validity of one's being. This reassurance takes place "on the level," with the therapist first asserting his own self-acceptance and then the acceptance of the other. Sullivan has a view of human fulfillment and happiness that is represented not by the mutual orgasm, as the Reichian variant of the psychoanalytic line might have it, but by mutual intimacy, consisting of an entire and unqualified acceptance of ego and alter by each other.

Sullivan's psychology also is a direct antecedent to the book popularized by Berne (1978), *Games People Play*. Games, for Berne, are not trivial or superficial exercises whereby one individual tries to gain mastery over another. Rather, Berne used the metaphor in a general way to characterize the ritualized or improvised series of moves and countermoves that take place in all social interactions—interactions which comprise not only the very stuff of social life, but also the unique means by which individuals can come to have self-knowledge.

In order to understand the significance of Sullivan's thought in the tradition of research and theory on the social aspects of self, it is worth quoting his views on the social nature of anxiety at some length:

> Anxiety is what keeps us from noticing things which would lead us to correct our faults. Anxiety is the thing that makes us hesitate before we spoil our standing with the stranger. Anxiety when it does not work so suavely becomes a psychiatric problem, because then it hashes our most polite utterances to the prospective boss, and causes

us to tremble at the most inopportune times. So you see it is only reasonable and very much in keeping with an enormously capable organization, such as the human being, that anxiety becomes a problem only when it doesn't work smoothly, and that the anxiety which has had to be grasped as a fundamental factor in understanding interpersonal relations is by no means an anxiety attack, a hollow feeling in the stomach, and so on. Much more frequently it manifests as what I have called selective inattention, by which I mean you must miss all sorts of things which would cause you embarassment, or in many cases, great profit to notice. It is the means by which you stay as you are, in spite of the efforts of worthy psychiatrists, clergymen, and others to help you mend your ways. You don't hear, you don't see, you don't feel, you don't observe, you don't think, all by the very suave manipulation of the contents of consciousness by anxiety—or, if you must . . . by the threat of anxiety, which still is anxiety. This very great extent of the effects of disapproval and the disturbance of euphoria by the significant people in early life—the people who are tremendously interested in getting you socialized—is what makes the concept of anxiety so crucially important in understanding all sorts of things. (Sullivan, 1950, pp. 216–17)

This quotation is taken from an article published in *Psychiatry* in 1950, shortly after Sullivan's death, called "The Illusion of Personal Individuality." The title is worth pondering, for it provides some warrant for thinking of Sullivan as a pivotal figure in a progression from Mead to Goffman. With anxiety making us deaf and blind to much of what is going on around us, the self survives only as an illusion, the more secure illusion when anxiety is functioning well. On this view, James' well-trained social anxiety allowed him to maintain confidence in the continuity of thought and of that self which is the thinker. But with Mead and now with Sullivan, the self is moved out of the body and into social space, where its vulnerability is measured by the potential inconstancies of our associates. It is all very well for the psychiatrist to say, "I'm OK, you're OK," but will he continue so to regard me after I have broken off my temporary game with him by no longer paying him? Sullivan envisages a terror of the person's entire self-system—an immanent collapse. Therapy in such a case consists not in explaining that fears are groundless or that conditions are really neutral. Therapy consists in the careful provision of social reassurance to the patient, which allows the reassertion of the illusion of personal individuality. Sullivan does not try to eliminate anxiety; he tries to get the patient to use his anxiety well, in a way that is socially and personally functional.

Sullivan's writings contain a disordered and dangerous kind of richness. They are disordered because he never systematized his ideas of personality in a coherent or complete fashion, and also because he attempted a synthesis of views about the self—the Freudian and the Meadian—which are essentially contradictory. They are dangerous because he seems ever ready to risk giving away the psychologist's advantage—his or her maintenance of a superior and invulnerable role vis-a-vis his or her patient or subject. The Sullivanian therapist, indeed Sullivan himself, must admit to the same sorts of anxieties and vulnerabilities which characterize the patient; the risk of the evaporation or fragmentation of self is fully shared. At least one biographer of Sullivan has suggested that he succumbed to a schizophrenic breakdown for two years, thus manifesting in this most direct way his shared vulnerability and lack of consistent advantage in relation to his patients (Perry, 1982).

Sullivan is a borderline character for the mainstream of personality theory and research. He does merit brief inclusion in Hall and Lindzey's (1957) influential textbook. I will presently argue that social psychology has moved to appreciate Sullivan, or better, has become Sullivanian because of the prominence and importance of Erving Goffman, who wrote the book for us on impression management. But first we must pause for a brief interlude featuring research and theory on the self within psychology proper at midcentury, as represented by Ruth Wylie.

THE SURPRISING GUISE IN WHICH SELF REEMERGED IN PSYCHOLOGY

All of the approaches to self mentioned thus far have been responsive to the problem of understanding, as represented in the plaintive note from Schopenhauer, the epigraph for this chapter. From James through Sullivan, all writers on the problem of the self have taken it as their task to aid in casting a ray of light on the "obscurity of our being." All in the set we have surveyed have also been in some ways pragmatists and functionalists; they have been interested in what the self does, where it comes from, how it works, and not in what it *is*. None has been interested in the task of providing an operational definition of self, for none has found it possible to believe that the self is an entity, an existent. The empirical self does, of course, lend itself to description, but the description is always circumstantial, relational, contextual. None of the writers we have surveyed has made a claim that the empirical self could be described in a way that is fixed and general across all kinds of social conditions and contexts of action.

The view of self that emerges in Ruth Wylie's (1961) survey, *The Self-Concept,* is something entirely different. This book is a survey of research on the self within psychology proper—most of it not initially titled as research on the self, but rather on personality or personality assessment. *The Self-Concept* was revised in 1974 to include material published through 1972. I shall rely on this later edition for the characterizations which follow.[2]

Wylie's book contains a three-page introduction given to the historical background of interest in the self in psychology. James and Mead are mentioned, but only in passing. Cooley is not included, and Sullivan registers only in

---

[2]In 1979, Wylie published a second volume on the self-concept, subtitled, "Theory and Research on Selected Topics." It consists of 825 pages, including over 4500 citations. The tenor and conclusions of the second volume are entirely consistent with those presented in the first volume, though the survey of research is much more extensive and recent. (See Wylie, 1979).

a single reference. Wylie correctly notes that, "During the second, third, and fourth decades of the twentieth century, constructs concerning the self did not receive much attention from the behaviorist and functionist psychologies which were dominating the American scene" (1974, p. 2). It is also obvious from examining the contents of Wylie's book that the dominant concerns of American psychology during this period fed into the way in which the self problem was conceptualized when it did reemerge. The major theme to be found in Wylie's book is a concern over the methodology of self-assessment and the extent to which those assessments could be used as a means of generating predictions of behavior. Chapter 2 is a survey of "self-concept theories and problems of research methodology." It is followed by chapters on description, on measurement, on operational definitions, and on actual attempts to use self-concept studies in a predictive fashion. The conclusion of all this is as laconic as it is sober, for Wylie suggests the even possibility that the entire area ought to be abandoned. She suggests that the reasons for this state of affairs are two: that self concept theories are at present vague and incomplete, and that research methodology in this area has been very loose, inprecise, and generally not up to the level of control required for science.

Much of the argument that leads to these conclusions comes from a critical examination of methodological and substantive problems encountered in the tasks of self-assessment and the prediction of behavior from personality studies. Projective tests are notoriously unreliable. Response sets are vexing. Predictive indices are weak and do not replicate. Mischel's (1968) challenge to personality theories is strongly featured. The notion that assessed personality traits (components of the self-described self-concept) can be used as general predictors of behavior received a severe blow from Mischel's empirical and theoretical argument that situations determine much more behavioral variance than do fixed dispositions. There is no point in reviewing here the vast controversy produced by this challenge. (See Mischel & Peake, 1982, for a recent statement on the problem.) In the present perspective, the argument about whether personality has predictive utility is tantamount to an argument about whether personality exists, or whether there exists a stable self. In the theoretical tradition we have been surveying, the answer is, "Of course not." It is curious that the enormous emphasis placed on methodological rigor and theoretical definition in American psychology during the twentieth century should have produced such simplistic thinking as to have loaded the import of Mischel's book, or a somewhat different challenge presented in the work of Crowne and Marlowe (1964) on "social desirability" as a contaminant in the process of self-assessment.

The subtitle of Wylie's book is, "A review of Methodological Considerations and Measuring Instruments." The suggestion is that the legacy of psychology's visitation to the problem of self over the past 70 years has been a plethora of paper-and-pencil tools for self-assessment, plus an intricate set of arguments, pro and con, as to why such instruments should or should not work in the prediction of behavior. An outside observer would have to agree that paper-

and-pencil self-assessments have a limited range of predictive utility. An outside observer would also be forced to conclude that the very quantity of trait names that have been suggested for enduring psychological dispositions is strong evidence that the contents of self are not unequivocally describable.[3]

The hegemony of behaviorism has evidently come to an end in psychology. Cognition has emerged again as the psychological counterpart of the philosophical problem of epistemology and the preeminent topic for experimental research. Mind is beginning to reappear in our discourse; as it becomes evident that in a functional sense machines can think, so it is no longer considered to be absurd to allow people the same functional capacity. And the self has emerged again. If it emerges in the Wylie volume and in succeeding literature on the "self-concept" as a reified grotesque, more recent thinking has been less guilty of ontological error. The methodological strictures accompanying behaviorism succeeded in producing just the sort of homunculus they were meant to exorcise—the elusive "self" of Wylie's books. Now that the arbitrariness of those strictures is more evident, inquiry into the problem of self can enjoy liberation.

This suggests one additional feature of contrast between the self-concept research presented by Wylie and the earlier theory of self we have reviewed: It is the contrast of literacy. Psychologists coming upon the problem of the self have acted as if they were discovering the problem for the first time—that nothing any poet, dramatist, historian, philosopher, or social critic might have said could have value or interest. Gone are the references to Shakespeare, to Carlyle, to Goethe, to John Donne, to Kant or Mill or Nietzsche. As Philip Rieff has said in an essay on Cooley, "Ours is a discipline suffering from a widespread belief in its own radical contemporaneity" (1968). If one finds references to literature on self from outside of psychology in modern writings, they usually have the character and depth of the cartoon illustrations that seem to have become a permanent and ubiquitous feature of our undergraduate textbooks. One might quote a segment of description from *The Double* by Dostoyevsky in order to illustrate some principle of impression management, but one really doesn't rely upon Dostoyevsky to provide any real light of his own upon the problem of self. These observations might easily be taken as a mark of sentimentality or nostalgia for a more picturesque literature in psychology. But I think it seriously worth considering that psychology might look to explore the fields of literature, theater, and philosophy for such insights as might there be found. If our topic is the self, we should be ready to welcome insights from any quarter.

---

[3]Observers from inside psychology, however, will often be convinced that they have succeeded in identifying *the* universals of human personality. Hogan (1982; see also Hogan and Cheek, 1983) has identified a core group of traits as consistently emerging within the personality literature, and these he has incorporated into his own socioanalytic theory. He may, of course, be right. However, the main features of Hogan's theory deal with the processes of achieving and maintaining a social identity, not with static features of personality.

ERVING GOFFMAN: A COLD NEW LIGHT ON THE SELF IN INTERACTION

The preparation of a historical perspective is itself an activity embedded in historical context, a context which exercises its influence on the way history is told. I note that Erving Goffman died during the time of composition of this chapter. (He died on November 20, 1982, in his sixtieth year.) Thus was closed a career, a life, a self; so now it is possible to talk about Goffman's work as contained, defined, finished.

Goffman's importance to contemporary thinking about the self can scarcely be overestimated. While he, like Mead and Cooley, was a sociologist, his productivity and genius were such as to make him a conspicuous—even unavoidable—presence in the social sciences generally; indeed, he influenced the world of ideas generally.

> He was one of the very few sociologists whose work was known beyond the field—and his influence on the world, as well as within the disciplines of social science, has already been so great that he stands as a giant among the social thinkers of his day. (from "A Tribute to Erving Goffman," ASA Footnotes, January, 1983, A. K. Daniels)

Goffman's principle writings are contained in 11 books written over a period of 25 years. The first is *The Presentation of Self in Everyday Life* (first published in 1956 in Scotland; American edition published in 1959), and the last is *Forms of Talk* (1981). While the specific topical reference in his works covers a wide range (mental hospitals, stigmatized individuals, gambling casinos, uses of gender in advertising, etc.), his work employs a singular methodology, has consistency of tone, and possesses thematic unity.

Goffman's special talent is that of the observer and commentator. If our earlier contributors to the study of self have been long on theory and short on empiricism, Goffman is quintessentially the empiricist. His first work is based on a period of his life with a village of crofters in the Shetland Isles of Scotland. His last work is based in large part on recordings and texts of "talk," including lectures, radio shows, public speeches, and informal discourse. Because of Goffman's observational power, it has been hard for critics to trace his origins in the history of social thought. Indeed, he never engages in extended discussion of somebody else's ideas, but refers to them as side supports to his own conceptions, which grow right out of his own observations (or "microanalysis") of the social life around him. Goffman did no experiments, and never, to my knowledge, devised a paper-and-pencil assessment of anything. He swam, in fact, in the same social sea as the rest of us, with the difference being that he had the capacity to make the most familiar observation a source of strange and fascinating insight. He identified himself quite insistently as a sociologist, allowed himself to be affiliated with anthropology, but was more wary of psychology. Psychology seems to want to carry its empiricism into the depths of the person, and this is territory Goffman was content to ignore. It is revealing to note the epigraph Goffman chose for his first work, from George Santayana. In part:

> Living things in contact with the air must acquire a cuticle, and it is not urged against cuticles that they are not hearts; yet some philosophers seem to be angry with images for not being things, and with words for not being feelings. Words and images are like shells, no less integral parts of nature than are the substances they cover, but better addressed to the eye and more open to observation. (Goffman, 1959)

It has often been urged against Goffman that his concern with cuticles and shells make him a mere chronicler of human superficiality. One finds little that is spiritually warm or morally uplifting in Goffman's writings. His obituary in the New York Times noted that he argued, "People are essentially performers whose main business is fabricating an identity." In fabricating his own identity, Goffman did little to dispel this impression. His regard for self is that of its presentation, its management, its outward interactions. Some would say that he denied inwardness. I would say that as a sociologist he considered that he could and should ignore it, for the methodological reason suggested by the Santayana aphorism.

Goffman's tone of commentary, as well as the content of what he said, conveys the impression of waspishness, or a certain lack of sympathy for the material of his microanalysis. Goffman, as an observer, seems to be "on the level" with the people he observed. But, unlike James, he concentrates only on the surface. He chooses not to wake people up, but to note "how they snore"; not to interfere with or perturb his material, but to note carefully how it acts. Goffman observes that actors expect others to take their performance seriously, to credit them with being sincere and genuine. "When the audience is convinced in this way about the show he puts on—and this seems to be the typical case—then for the moment at least, only the sociologist or the socially disgruntled will have any doubts about the 'realness of what is presented'" (1959, p. 17). It follows that one must be concerned with the fronts and faces that people manage to show to their audiences, in ways that are more or less igenuous. Goffman's methodological ignoring of the inward self appears in his writing to be also a refusal to grant that inward self any sort of moral legitimacy; so that one's honesty becomes a matter of appearing to be honest or generating the impression of honesty, integrity becomes a matter of not being caught out. Thus the sociologist in Goffman is perpetually disgruntled; this puts him in a position to doubt the legitimacy of all puttings on and givings off.

No one should have wished Goffman to be more charitable; for his very coolness enables his perspicacity. Examples of the power of his posture are to be found throughout his writings. I chose an example from *Relations in Public:*

> This analysis began on the most magisterial note I can attempt: moral rules and their function as the link between self and society. This led, with little loss of abstractness, to a consideration of deviations from the rules and the ritual dialogue that provides a remedy. But now it has been argued that moral claims are made with respect to a

multitude of minor territories of the self, and that correctives for infraction are to be found in body gloss—the indignities of overacted gesticulation. This brings the study of remedial activity into the street, into the little interactions that are forgotten about as soon as they occur, into what serious students of society never collect, into the slop of social life. (1971, p. 138)

Of course, when Goffman analyzes the slop of social life, it becomes highly meaningful material—essential to our understanding of the intricacies of the interactions of persons. Just as the analysis of coprolites yields essential information to the archeologist about the diets and living habits of prehistoric peoples, so Goffman is able to show how the waste material in social life can lead us to a fuller understanding of the functioning of selves in society. Now we see body gloss, "withs," tucks, cants, filler gestures, and eye play in a way that fits analytic needs.

Goffman's vision is often taken to be cynical, but it is better described as wry. As a final example of his tone, I cite a passage from *Forms of Talk*, wherein he discusses the use of little jokes and wisecracks interpolated into discourse:

Thus the same little plum can be inserted at the beginning or end of quite different speakers' quite different talks with easy aptness. Stage plays provide similar opportunities in allowing for the performance of 'memorable' exchanges, that is, sprightly bits of dialogue that bear repeating and can be repeated apart from the play in which they occurred. (1981, pp. 31–32).

The thematic unity in Goffman's work is obvious. He remained consistently interested in the topic that formed the theme of his first book—the management of impressions. His interest in the self is only in its empirical manifestations, and in this he is consistent with James, Baldwin, Cooley, Mead, and Sullivan. However, he eschewed an interest in thoughts about the self—that sort of empiricism—in favor of a meticulous cataloging and analysis of the self's cuticle—the air-hardened, outward surface of the self in interaction. Given his stubborn aloofness, it is perhaps inevitable that Goffman himself should have become a mystery, an enigma. And that he was.

Goffman appears not to have capitalized on his knowledge of the intricacies of impression management, for the impression he managed to convey of himself, particularly to reference groups that would seem to matter greatly—sociologists and other social scientists—was not entirely favorable. While all show a grudging respect for his style and his care for the quotidian detail, he has been charged with being preoccupied with the trivial, with dehumanizing and degrading human material, and with political and social amorality. (See Gouldner, 1970; Young, 1971; Hall, 1977.) His sociology does not start with recognition of the primacy of class stratification: While he does acknowledge and comment on dominance orderings in society, he often does not seem to take sides—with the weak against the powerful—and this appears to be a fault from the standpoint of conventional sociological morality.

Sociology has accorded Goffman its admiration principally for *The Presentation of Self in Everyday Life* and *Asylums*. As his later works received more favorable notice in the world of academic and intellectual life, they received from within sociology proportionally less praise. The view within sociology is that Goffman's later work is increasingly self-indulgent, increasingly careless or perhaps heedless of the impression he was conveying. Indeed, his later works show very brief bibliographies and refer mostly to his own work and that of his seminar students. His methodology seemed increasingly haphazard, his observations an odd collection of whatever came to hand.

In all of this we are led to examine again the difficult question of the relationship between the social scientist and his material. The traditional role of the experimental psychologist is one of temporary dominance and control over subject matter. (See Scheibe, 1979.) The psychoanalyst is in a position of unique advantage in relation to the patient—controlling, regulating, advising, seeing, but not being seen. What of Goffman? Published photographs are hard to find. Interviews are rarer still. And yet Goffman has somehow managed to place himself on the same level as that of his material. We end up concluding that he is no better than the rest of us in any moral sense, while we might concede that he is decidedly more clever than any of us.

The thought occurs that Goffman's great moral triumph was precisely his refusal to contrive an image of moral superiority for himself. Certainly no one knew better than Goffman how to do this. And yet surely no one was more aware than Goffman of the pervasiveness of falseness—of contrived images, converting the self-love of the clever into a magnified adulation by the crowd. It may easily be supposed that Goffman simply found it morally preferable to walk away from such a prize—and in this he is like Kierkegaard. He seemed content to convey the impression that he was himself all cuticle, all the way down to his heart. I expect he allowed only a very close circle to know that this was not true.

THE CURRENT PLEA FOR SELF AS INWARD AND ACTIVE AGENT

Perhaps the spirit of an age selects for special prominence the voice which happens to respond most directly to the particular needs of that age. Ours is an era in which change seems more powerful than stability, when identities seem hollow, commitments tentative and fragile—an age of skepticism, a cosmetic age, an age of press agentry and the manufacturing of public image, an age in which a former Hollywood actor can be groomed up to become President of the United States, where appearance seems to matter for all, substance and essence for very little. I am not here characterizing our era, but merely referring to a rather common—even hackneyed—way in which it has been characterized. Goffman happens to be the voice within the social sciences that resonates most closely with these features of description. For this reason, a consummate student of the management of impression is taken to be some sort of advocate or apologist for human hollowness. It is a moot point as to whether Goffman changed the history of the self as was merely someone who wrote about changes in the history of the self that had already taken place.

The involvement of moral and ethical issues with one's conception of the nature of self cannot be avoided. In a recent philosophical treatise on ethics, Alisdair MacIntyre makes this challenging assertion:

> ... I am not merely contending that morality is not what it once was, but also and more importantly that what once was morality has to some large degree disappeared—and that this marks a degeneration, a grave cultural loss. (1981, p. 31)

MacIntyre takes Goffman to be almost an architect of this cultural decay: "Erving Goffman . . . has liquidated the self into its role-playing, arguing that the self is no more than 'a peg' on which the clothes of the role are hung" (1981, p. 31). Jean-Paul Sartre is seen as performing the complementary task of characterizing the self in a way that is completely removed from transitory social roles. MacIntyre sees these moves as amounting to fundamentally the same thing:

> Both see the self as entirely set over against the social world. For Goffman, for whom the social world is everything, the self is therefore nothing at all, it occupies no social space. For Sartre, whatever social space it occupies it does so only accidentally, and therefore he too sees the self as in no way an actuality. (1981, p. 31)

This argument supposes that selves are products of historical manufacture and that the mode of their manufacture depends in some profound way on the ideas which philosophers and social scientists manage to make prevail by whatever special powers they may command. Since our ideas about the self are products of specific historical and ideological conditions, great power is attributed to those who shape those conditions and thus modify our sense of self, as well as our moral sense.

MacIntyre suggests that the Aristotelian conception of life, with its concern for the *telos* of a person's being, provided ground for morality and at the same time a morally constraining definition of selfhood. When the hold of the Aristotelian view was broken by the Enlightenment, it was no longer possible to align the virtue of the self with reason, for the overarching *telos* of human life is now rejected. In its place we have the elevation of reason—as a way of finding out truth, as a means of settling questions of fact. But this led immediately to "emotivist" doctrines on the origin and nature of values, morals, and goodness. Since questions of value are not resolvable by the enlightened methods of applied reason, their origins are not considered to have either consistency or coherence. Values and morals thus divorced from reason are quite ungrounded. MacIntyre argues that both Kant and Kierkegaard tried desperately to restore some ground for morality—the first through positing the criterion of "universalizability" as a means for determining the moral legitimacy of any action. If for Kant moral choices are product of a categorical imperative, for Kierkegaard the emphasis is on the agency of choice itself. Faced with the competing values of aesthetic self-indulgence and ethical self-restraint, the individual for Kierkegaard is compelled to choose—but it is not a choice compelled by reason. In different ways, then, Kant and Kierkegaard attempt to rescue morality for the self—the self which as product of the Enlightenment was found stripped of its a priori purpose for being, and thus immersed in anomie and liberty at the same time. But these attempts, says MacIntyre, were failures. It was Neitzsche who most powerfully and cogently showed these attempts to ground morality to be a sham. In *The Geneology of Morals,* he characterized *all* previous attempts at human moralizing to be based on a profound immorality. It was Nietzsche, MacIntyre argues, who showed the abject moral nakedness of post-Enlightenment philosophy. Nietzsche mocks our ethical pretensions—and he mocks truly and with great effect, for there is nothing in the emotivist soul to make any serious claim to a grounded virtue. The psychological sequel to this moral surrender, which Nietzsche seems to demand, is cynicism, lack of will (what James referred to as *abulia*), a sense of lack of meaning or purpose in life. Thus the way is prepared for the existential anarchy of Jean-Paul Sartre as well as the hollow-selved impression managers of Erving Goffman.

MacIntyre argues that this new emptiness was made inevitable by the determination of those who survived the brutal human extermination of the spirit in the trenches of World War I that ". . . nothing was ever going to matter to them again" (1981, p. 40). There may be a similar sequence of psycho-logic between the massive genocidal horrors of World War II and a self-indulgent, self-complacent, consumer-oriented, narcissistic "me generation" of the 1970s and 1980s. Nietzsche had shown that all moralistic responses to answer seriously the pervasive question, "Why not?" were false pieties. And it is Erving Goffman, says MacIntyre, who is the modern apostle of Nietzsche's brilliant but caustic criticism of conventional morality.

Since MacIntyre claims that the distinctively modern self was a product of social and historical invention, he considers it to be possible, at least in principle, to invent a postmodern self to which some *telos* is restored. His book is intended as a move in this direction.

This is not the place to decide how much of this sort of argument is intellectual pretension and how much is worthy of claiming our belief and assent. I note only that many voices are now claiming that our view of self should in fact be rescued from the sociologists, and thereby be made to have a place for inwardness and perhaps even for purpose. Many examples of this sort of plea can be cited. Gergen (1982) suggests that the new view of the self is that of the active agent, to be contrasted with the traditional conception of passivity or reactivity. The self, for Gergen, is a moment-to-moment improvisation, with an independence of and even mastery over the impinging stimuli of the environment. Tyler concludes a review of modern theories of the self by suggesting, "Each individual represents a different sequence of selective acts by means of which only some of the developmental possibilities are chosen and organized" (1978, p. 233). Sarbin (1976) has developed an extensive contextualist view of human conduct, in which both self and role combine in the context of meaning—a view which departs radically from the dominant, mechanistic world view of traditional psychology. Juhasz (1983) has provided a brilliant sketch of how our conceptions of identity are at once personal, social, and human, participating necessarily in timeless requirements of our nature. Juhasz argues that no matter what history does to our social identity, the requirements for human identity are the same as they were for Aristotle and will always be the same. Thus, there may be no need for the restoration of a *telos,* only a recognition of it.

Psychologists are becoming literate again—in the sense in which I have earlier used that term. Some of the more challenging and fresh views of self to have emerged in the recent literature suggest that the self is author of its own story—an active, participating agent in the process of prospective construction. (See Boswell, 1983; Mancuso & Sarbin, 1983; Gergen & Gergen, 1983.) This line of thinking is in some ways an extension of Goffman's perspective, though it certainly is more upbeat. The narrative view of self also makes extensive use, perforce, of human stories as they are found and displayed in novel, drama, and poem. The literary critic and drama theorist, Kenneth Burke, was an influence in Goffman's thinking, and his influence is increasingly evident in recent writings on the self.

To return full circle, I note a conspicuous resurgence of interest in William James, not just as a historical point of reference, but for the substance of his ideas about self. The metaphor of the stream and the notion of self as active agent are elements enjoying renewed favor. In this sense, psychology has rediscovered its self. In the period of its disappearance from psychology, the self was somehow preserved within sociology, leading to the work of Erving Goffman. Upon its return to psychology, the self seemed to want some restoration of balance—between the social selves that comprised only a part of the Jamesian stream and the thinker's active core. This restoration of balance is now occurring, and the remaining chapters in this volume are testimony to the vitality of this synthesis.

The self in psychology is alive. And getting better.

REFERENCES

Adelson, J. (1982). Still vital after all these years. *Psychology Today, 16,* 52–59.
Allen, V. L., & Scheibe, K. E. (1982). *The social context of conduct: Psychological writings of T. R. Sarbin.* New York: Praeger.
Baldwin, J. M. (1897). *Social and ethical interpretations.* New York: Macmillan.
Baldwin, J. M. (1930). Autobiographical statements. In C. Murchison (Ed.), *History of psychology in autobiography* (Vol. 1). Worcester, MA: Clark University Press.
Bandura, A. (1977). Self-efficacy: Toward a unifying theory of behavioral change. *Psychological Review, 84,* 191–215.
Berne, E. (1978). *Games people play.* New York: Ballantine.
Boring, E. G. (1950). *A history of experimental psychology,* 2nd edition. New York: Appleton-Century-Crofts.
Boswell, D. A. (1983, March 7). *The construction of self as a textual process.* Lecture delivered at the Center for the Humanities, Wesleyan University.
Buss, A. H. (1980). *Self-consciousness and social anxiety.* San Francisco: W. H. Freeman.

Condon, T. R. (1982). *Trance personality: Language and hypnosis in everyday life.* Paper presented Southwestern Anthropological Association.

Cooley, C. H. (1902). *Human nature and the social order.* New York: Scribners.

Crowne, D. P., & Marlowe, D. (1964). *The approval motive: Studies in evaluative dependence.* New York: Wiley.

Duval, S., & Wicklund, R. A. (1972). *A theory of objective self-awareness.* New York: Academic Press.

Ellenberger, H. (1970). *The discovery of the unconscious.* New York: Basic Books.

Erikson, E. H. (1950). *Childhood and society.* New York: W. W. Norton & Co.

Evans, R. B., & Scott, F. J. D. (1978). The 1913 International Congress of Psychology: The American congress that wasn't. *American Psychologist, 33,* 711–722.

Freud, S. (1962). *Civilization and its discontents.* New York: Norton, 1962. (Original work published 1930)

Gergen, K. J. (1982). *Toward transformation in social knowledge.* New York: Springer-Verlag.

Gergen, K. J. (1984). Self theory: Impasse and evolution. In L. Berkowitz (Ed.), *Advances in experimental social psychology.* New York: Academic Press.

Gergen, K. J., & Gergen, M. M. (1983). Narratives of the self. In T. R. Sarbin & K. E. Scheibe (Eds.), *Studies in social identity.* New York: Praeger.

Goffman, E. (1971). *Relations in public.* New York: Basic Books.

Goffman, E. (1959). *The presentation of self in everyday life.* Garden City, NY: Doubleday Publishers.

Goffman, E. (1981). *Forms of talk.* Philadelphia: Univ. of Pennsylvania Press.

Gouldner, A. W. (1970). *The coming crisis of western sociology.* New York: Basic Books.

Greenwald, A. G. (1980). The totalitarian ego. *American Psychologist, 35,* 603–618.

Hall, C. S., & Lindzey, G. (1957). *Theories of personality.* New York: Wiley.

Hall, J. A. (1977). Sincerity and politics: "Existentialists" vs. Goffman and Proust. *Sociological Review, 25,* 535–550.

Harris, T. (1973). *I'm OK, you're OK.* New York: Avon.

Heidegger, M. (1962). *Being and time.* New York: Harper & Row.

Heider, F. (1958). *The psychology of interpersonal relations.* New York: Wiley.

Hogan, R. (1982). A socioanalytic theory of personality. In M. Page & R. Dienstbier (Eds.), *The Nebraska symposium on motivation: 1982.* Lincoln, NE: University of Nebraska Press.

Hogan, R., & Cheek, J. M. (1983). Identity, authenticity and maturity. In T. R. Sarbin and K. E. Scheibe (Eds.), *Studies in Social Identity.* New York: Praeger.

Hyman, H. H., & Singer, E. (Eds.). (1968). *Readings in reference group theory and research.* New York: Free Press.

James, W. (1890). *The principles of psychology* (Vol. 1). New York: Henry Holt & Co.

Juhasz, J. B. (1983). Social identity in the context of human and personal identity. In T. R. Sarbin & K. E. Scheibe (Eds.), *Studies in social identity.* New York: Praeger.

Kelley, H. H. (1967). Attribution theory in social psychology. In D. Levine (Ed.), *Nebraska symposium on motivation* (Vol. 15). Lincoln, NE: University of Nebraska Press.

Kohlberg, L. (1963). The development of children's orientation towards a moral order. *Vita Humana, 6,* 11–33.

Lecky, P. (1945). *Self-consistency: A theory of personality.* New York: Island Press.

Lynch, M. D., Norem-Hebeison, A. A., & Gergen, K. J. (Eds.). (1981). *Self-concept: Advances in theory and research.* Cambridge, MA: Ballinger.

MacIntyre, A. (1981). *After virtue.* Notre Dame, IN: University of Notre Dame Press.
Mancuso, J. C., & Sarbin, T. R. (1983). The self-narrative in the enactment of rules. In T. R. Sarbin & K. E. Scheibe (Eds.), *Studies in social identity.* New York: Praeger.
Manis, J. G., & Meltzer, B. N. (Eds.). (1978). *Symbolic interactionism: A reader in social psychology.* Boston: Allyn and Bacon.
Mead, G. H. (1934). *Mind, self and society from the standpoint of a social behaviorist.* Chicago: University of Chicago Press.
Miller, D. R. (1963). The study of social relationships: Situation, identity and social interaction. In S. Koch (Ed.), *Psychology: A study of a science.* New York: McGraw-Hill.
Mischel, T. (Ed.). (1977). *The self: Psychological and philosophical issues.* Totowa, NJ: Rowman and Littlefield.
Mischel, W. (1968). *Personality and assessment.* New York: Wiley.
Mischel, W., & Peake, P. K. (1982). Beyond deja vu in the search for cross-situational consistency. *Psychological Review, 89,* 730–755.
Ortega y Gassett, J. (1932). *The revolt of the masses.* New York: Norton. (Original work published 1930)
Perry, H. S. (1982). *Psychiatrist of America: The life of Harry Stack Sullivan.* Cambridge, MA: Belknap Press.
Pfuetze, P. E. (1954). *Self, society, and existence.* New York: Harper.
Rieff, P. (1968). Cooley and culture. In A. J. Reiss, Jr. (Ed.), *Cooley and sociological analysis.* Ann Arbor: Univ. of Michigan Press.
Sarason, S. (1975). Psychology to the Finland station in the heavenly city of the eighteenth century philosophers. *American Psychologist, 30,* 1072–1080.
Sarbin, T. R. (1954). Role theory. In G. Lindzey (Ed.), *Handbook of social psychology* (Vol. 1). Cambridge, MA: Addison-Wesley.
Sarbin, T. R. (1976). Contextualism: A world view for modern psychology. In J. K. Cole (Ed.), *Nebraska Symposium on Motivation* (Vol. 24). Lincoln: University of Nebraska Press.
Sarbin, T. R., & Allen, V. I. (1968). Role theory. In G. Lindzey & E. Aronson (Eds.), *Handbook of social psychology* (Vol. 1). Reading, MA: Addison-Wesley.
Sarbin, T. R., & Scheibe, K. E. (Eds.). (1983). *Studies in social identity.* New York: Praeger.
Scheibe, K. E. (1978). The psychologist's advantage and its nullification: Limits of human predictability. *American Psychologist, 33,* 869–881.
Scheibe, K. E. (1979). *Mirrors, masks, lies and secrets.* New York: Praeger.
Schlenker, B. R. (1980). *Impression management.* Monterey, CA: Brooks/Cole.
Strauss, A. (1956). *The social psychology of George Herbert Mead.* Chicago: Univ. of Chicago Press.
Sullivan, H. S. (1950). The illusion of personal individuality. *Psychiatry, 13,* 317–332.
Sullivan, H. S. (1953). *The interpersonal theory of psychiatry.* New York: Norton.
Tyler, L. E. (1978). *Individuality.* San Francisco: Jossey-Bass.
Wylie, R. (1974). *The self-concept, Vol. 1: A review of methodological considerations and measuring instruments.* Rev. Ed. Lincoln: Univ. of Nebraska Press.
Wylie, R. C. (1979). *The self-concept, Vol. 2: Theory and research on selected topics.* Rev. Ed. Lincoln: Univ. of Nebraska Press.
Young, T. R. (1971). The politics of sociology: Gouldner, Goffman, and Garfinkel. *American Sociologist, 6,* 276–281.

CHAPTER 3

IDENTITY AND SELF-IDENTIFICATION

Barry R. Schlenker
University of Florida

To think about ourselves requires that the self be viewed as an object ("me") that is defined and appraised (James, 1890; Mead, 1934). Identifying the self's qualities is an inherent aspect of the self-regulation of conduct as we select goals, work out plans for accomplishing the goals, engage in self-observation to determine how we are doing, make self-judgments (e.g., "Am I living up to the appropriate standards for accomplishment?"), and experience self-reactions (e.g., "I did well") (e.g., Bandura, 1982; Carson, 1969; Miller, Galanter, & Pribram, 1960). Similarly, to interact with other people requires that each party be viewed as a social object, with each person's identity specified in a way that permits the participants to relate to one another and regulate their conduct accordingly (e.g., Alexander & Wiley, 1981; Backman, 1983; Foote, 1951; McCall & Simmons, 1978; Schlenker, 1980, 1984; Stone, 1962; Stryker, 1981). The participants project images of self and define and appraise one another to allow them to select goals and develop plans for their joint activities. Once identities are fixed in terms that are understandable and potentially agreeable to the parties involved, all other dealings can follow. Without these personal and social specifications, done consciously or unconsciously, confusion and tentativeness result because the nature and meaning of the person would be unclear.

Identification is the process, means, or result of showing something to be a particular type of person or thing, thereby specifying its identity through definition, description, evidence, inference, interpretation, analogy, or treatment (Schlenker, 1984). This definition is much broader than the traditional psychoanalytic use of the term, which refers to a person emulating (identifying with) someone else and seemingly taking over the other's perceived personality

---

Thanks are extended to Patricia Schlenker and Ruth Allis for their valuable comments and assistance in the preparation of the chapter. This chapter was supported by a Research Scientists Development Award (K02-MH00183) from the National Institute of Mental Health.

characteristics. Emulation is certainly one means of identifying oneself, because "I am like him" fixes one's identity through analogy. However, it is only one of the many ways people specify who and what they are. My use of the term derives from its proper English usage, and is in the spirit of McCall and Simmons' (1978) use of identification as "placing things in terms of systematically related categories" (p. 62). Self-identification involves fixing and expressing one's own identity, privately through reflection about oneself and publicly through self-disclosures, self-presentations, and other activities that serve to project one's identity to audiences. The complementary process is identification of the other, wherein a person attempts to specify, in thoughts and through actions, what the other is like. Cognitive or behavioral activities that serve to establish, maintain, clarify, or modify identities are identifications.

By its nature, self-identification requires a context in which the self is specified for some purpose to some audience. Three general types of audiences can be distinguished. First, there are other people with whom we interact; they might be present at the time or their presence can be imagined, as when we contemplate an upcoming meeting. Some people are significant or important to the actor (e.g., others who are attractive, powerful, or esteemed), prompting the actor to care about the others' expectations and judgments; and some are not, prompting relative indifference. Second, there are imagined audiences who serve as internalized referents for conduct. Internalized referents are significant to the actor and are privately evoked across a wide range of situations to serve as exemplars and evaluators for self, e.g., one's parents, best friends, spouse. Also included are fantasized others who might not even exist but who have an impact on self-regulation, as in the case of the child who tries to emulate Superman or considers Santa Claus' reactions as Christmas approaches, or the adult who emulates James Bond after departing from a theater. The idea of an imagined referrent is nicely illustrated by Steve Garvey's (a baseball star) comment: "I walk around as if a little boy or a little girl were following me, and I don't do anything physically or mentally to take away the ideal they might have for Steve Garvey." Finally, people serve as their own audiences, employing internalized knowledge and standards for self-regulation.

Different audiences are salient on different occasions, and attention can even alternate between them during the course of an interaction, as when we compare our expectations to others' expectations and attempt to integrate them (Schlenker, 1980, 1982; Snyder, Higgins, & Stucky, 1983; Chapters 5, 6, and 9 in this volume). As will shortly be considered more fully, when particular audiences are salient, they influence people's goals, plans, and desired images of self, thereby affecting self-identification. For example, a member of a street gang that values toughness and censures emotional sensitivity expresses the "warm" side of his identity when alone with a girl he likes who is sincere, sweet, and conventional. When the couple is in the presence of other gang members, though, he reverts to more insensitive, "cold" behavior toward her. (Visions of John Travolta's character in the movie *Grease* come to mind.) Or, a housewife may do an unusually thorough job of housecleaning when her mother, a vanguard of traditional values, comes to visit.

The purpose or goal of self-identification can vary, but it usually falls into one or more of three broad categories: (a) attempting to answer a personal question about the self posed by oneself or others (e.g., "Do I have sufficient skill, desire, and money to attend college?"), (b) attempting to express and validate desired images of self that provide a sense of self-worth and offer a definition of self to audiences (e.g., affirming that one is honorable, respected, wise), and (c) attempting to present images of self that serve some strategic interpersonal objective (e.g., trying to obtain approval, power, nurturance, autonomy). These categories are not distinct, but fade into one another, varying from the attempt to gain or convey useful information about the self to the attempt to control the reactions of other people. At one extreme, we can talk about self-inquiry (attempting to gain self-knowledge), or self-disclosure (attempting to express personal information to others); at the other extreme, we can talk about self-presentation (attempting to control images of self to audiences). Attempts have been made to define and distinguish among these terms, and there are differences in emphasis and criteria (e.g., Baumeister, 1982; Jones & Pittman, 1982; Schlenker, 1980, 1984; Tedeschi, 1981). For our immediate purposes, though, these types of self-identifications share common properties that permit us to group them: They (a) are purposive, or goal-directed, activities that specify the properties of the self, (b) occur in a particular context consisting of a social situation and one or more salient audiences for whom the self is specified, and (c) involve standards for goal-completion that people attempt to satisfy through their cognitive or behavioral activities.

The remainder of this chapter presents a framework for a theory of self-identification. We'll first address the nature of identity, briefly defining it, considering its functions, and discussing desired identity images. Then we'll turn to a set of propositions about self-identification that begin to elaborate the theoretical approach.

THE SELF AND IDENTITY

Erik Erikson (1959) reintroduced the term identity to the social sciences, stating that "the conscious feeling of having a personal identity is based on two simultaneous observations: the immediate perception of one's self-sameness and continuity in time; and the simultaneous perception that others recognize one's self-sameness and continuity" (p. 23). Although Erikson did not put it in these terms, identity can be regarded as a *theory of self* (cf. Epstein, 1973; see Chapter 1) that is formed and maintained through actual or imagined interpersonal agreement about what the self is like. Analogous to a scientific theory, its contents must withstand the process of consensual validation by informed, significant observers. As the philosopher Rom Harré (1983) put it, "[T]he sense of personal identity depends on a socially enforced theory of self by which a human being conceives a continuous coordination of point of view and point of action" (p. 41). Gregory Stone (1962) addressed the same consensual process from a sociological perspective, stating, "One's identity is established when others place him as a social object by assigning him the same words of identity that he appropriates for himself" (p. 93). Stone and other sociologists focus on the social construction of identities in interactions, in which people socially categorize and act in a certain way toward one another on the basis of their more or less shared understandings of social roles, rules, and symbols (Alexander & Wiley, 1981; Backman, 1983; McCall & Simmons, 1978). The key theme that emerges from these slightly different perspectives is that a person's identity is forged, expressed, maintained, and modified in the crucible of social life, as its contents undergo the continual process of actual or imagined observation, judgment, and reaction by audiences (oneself and others).

Identity can be most succinctly defined as *a theory (or schema) of an individual that describes, interrelates, and explains his or her relevant features, characteristics, and experiences.* As a theory of self, it has two properties that correspond to the distinction between the self-as-known and the self-as-knower (James, 1890). First, identity specifies the *contents* of what we are like in terms that are understandable by and potentially agreeable to audiences. These contents consist of numerous interrelated images (or schemata) that specify the constructs that are pertinent to us (e.g., man, extroverted, lawyer, athletic) and fix our standing on construct dimensions relative to others (e.g., higher status than John Doe, lower than James Smith). These images, in turn, subsume and interrelate numerous relevant facts and experiences (e.g., he received an award from the State Bar Association, he wins 85 percent of his court cases, he lost his last big case). Second, it *guides and regulates* subsequent experience by affecting our thoughts, affect, behaviors, and outcomes. It thus permits the self-regulation of conduct, as people observe, judge, and react to themselves in different contexts. Our conception of another person's identity provides comparable properties, specifying for us (a) the contents of what the other is like as a person and (b) guiding and regulating our interpersonal conduct by influencing our thoughts, affect, and behaviors toward the other. These functions will be examined more fully below.

When identity refers to a person's cumulative, generalized theory of self, it appears to be identical to how the term self-concept is usually used, especially by theorists who have been influenced by James (1890) and Mead (1934). A distinction can be drawn between identity qua self-concept and identity as it is situated or conceived in relation to particular other people in social settings (e.g., at home with one's spouse, at the office with coworkers) (cf. Hewitt, 1976). A situated identity is, from the actor's perspective, a theory of self that is wittingly or unwittingly constructed in a particular social situation or relationship. As such, its contents can differ from those contained in the self-concept. The difference can arise because (a) the actor attempts to "package" or fit information about the self to the appropriate context, making it more understandable or agreeable to particular others, (b) the actor attempts to distort or fabricate information about the self to achieve particular interpersonal objectives, and (c) other people attempt to influence the actor to adopt particular characteristics and roles that the others feel are appropriate or beneficial given their plans. An actor's situated identity in a particular relationship, as a *joint construction* of the participants, can thus differ qualitatively and quantitatively from the actor's self-concept as it is evoked in the context of the self-as-audience across various classes of situations.

Functions of Identity Images

When particular identity images are formed of an actor, they can function in five ways to influence social interaction. They (a) provide an organizational structure for relevant information about the person; (b) influence how information is selected, interpreted, stored, and recalled from memory; (c) provide scripts for conduct based on behavioral-prototype or response-specifying information and standards; (d) affect the evaluation of characteristics and conduct through comparisons with relevant standards; and (f) provide information about the relationship between images and outcomes.

Identity as an Organizational Structure Identity provides an organizational structure for the relevant features and experiences of the person. It is analogous to a sophisticated filing system in memory containing numerous facts, constructs, and cross-indices (beliefs and hypotheses) that provide references for interrelating, storing, and retrieving information about the person. Like any theory, identity transforms what might otherwise be a mass of confusing, unrelated bits of information into a structure that is understandable and usable. Its contents include information about the person's roles (e.g., husband, father, lawyer), appearance (e.g., physical features, health, style of dress), background (e.g., ancestral lineage, schools attended), associates, friends, and relatives (people are judged by the company they keep), accomplishments (e.g., caliber of job performance, awards), aspirations (e.g., hopes and dreams), motives and personal qualities (e.g., sociability, intelligence, accommodativeness), performance settings (e.g., frequenting bars or church socials), and pursuits (e.g., hobbies). Identity-images serve as frameworks for accumulating and recalling knowledge about the person, and they provide the direct or inferential basis for statements to be made about him or her. The sense of distinctiveness provided by personal identity (e.g., Apter, 1983; Breakwell, 1983) is due in part to the unique contents and combinations of information that pertain to the self; no two people have exactly the same life histories, accumulations of self-knowledge, and organizations of self-knowledge.

The images that comprise identity vary in their *centrality,* or the extent to which they subsume other images and experiences (e.g., the image of being intelligent can subsume being a good student, chess player, puzzle solver), and also vary in their *importance,* or the extent to which they are associated with the satisfaction of significant needs and values (e.g., getting a college degree might fulfill numerous values, while solving the crossword puzzle in the newspaper provides less satisfaction). Images of self that are more central and important have usually been formed and stabilized over years of personality development through their continual use and subsequent validation by significant others; they form the core of the individual's personality (cf. Hogan, 1982). These images also are generally more resistant to change; more central ones are resistant because they subsume a vast backlog of prior information about the person that is unlikely to be significantly altered by a single contrary bit of data (Carson, 1969), and more important ones are resistant because they are associated with significant values that are difficult to abandon (Carson, 1969; Rosenberg, 1979). Images that are more rather than less central and important also are more likely to be retrieved from memory in any particular situation, and are therefore more likely to be represented in people's thoughts, self-presentations, and self-disclosures across a wider range of situations and audiences (cf. Cheek & Hogan, 1983; Hogan, 1982; Markus, 1980; Schlenker, 1980, 1984). Indeed, the sense of continuity provided by identity seems partly due to the salience and influence of these central and important images across a variety of contexts. These factors (and others described below) partially account for findings that show the relative stability of the major elements of the self-concept from late adolescence throughout the life span (Hogan, 1982; McCrae & Costa, 1982).

Identity Images as Interpretational Filters Identity also regulates how information is perceived and recalled. When particular identity images are salient they act to channel thoughts, feelings, and actions (e.g., Cantor & Mischel, 1979; Greenwald & Pratkanis, 1984; Markus, 1980; Wyer, 1981). Like a template or filter, they screen out some types of information and transform other types to provide the best possible fit to existing images, selectively coloring interpretation and recall. People are more likely to notice and attend to image-relevant information, process such information more quickly and easily, and organize and interpret supporting or ambiguous information in image-consistent ways (Cantor & Mischel, 1979; Carson, 1969; Greenwald & Pratkanis, 1984; Judd & Kulik, 1980; Markus, 1977, 1980; Neisser, 1976; Swann, 1983; also Chapters 1 and 4 in this volume). As examples, people with low self-regard on a particular dimension are likely to interpret an ambiguously positive comment from another person as criticism, thereby assimilating the information to the existing image. Or, people who have a self-image of being "independent" are more likely to notice when others are placing pressure on them to conform, and if they do find themselves conforming, be more likely to interpret the behavior as "tact" rather than "conformity." People's conceptions of another person have similar guiding effects. For instance, people reconstruct the biographies of friends to make them more consistent with their images of them, interpret others' behaviors in terms of the images they have assigned to them, and expect others to behave in ways that are consistent with these images (Backman, 1983; Cantor & Mischel, 1979; Schlenker, 1980). These interpretational properties promote cognitive conservatism—the resistance to change of existing cognitive structures (Greenwald, 1980; also Chapters 1 and 5). Information is assimilated to existing images, and people tend to see more confirmatory information for those images than may actually exist. The result is the consistency over time of these structures, generating the feeling of continuity and sameness about oneself.

Identity Images as Prototypes Images also contain behavioral-prototype or response-specifying information and standards that influence expectations and activities. To illustrate, if asked how an honest person behaves, you could describe the sorts of things such an individual should and should not do. The definition of the concept of honesty (e.g., being sincere, trustworthy, upright) provides criteria that someone should fulfill in order to be accorded the image. An image contains information about how it should be symbolically expressed through actions, when it is most likely to be relevant (e.g., the types of conditions to which it is pertinent), and the types of reactions that are appropriate to a person who is or is not accorded the image (e.g., positive or negative reactions). Images of abilities provide comparable information, as suggested by Bandura's (1977, 1982) work on self-efficacy. Self-efficacy expectations are beliefs "that one can successfully execute the behavior required to produce" particular outcomes (Bandura, 1977, p. 193). They derive from the relationship between one's perceptions of self-competence on a particular dimension and the relevance of the dimension to the particular task being confronted. People with high rather than low self-efficacy expectations begin to cope sooner with a particular task, especially when it is unpleasant, expend greater effort on the task, and persist longer on it in the face of obstacles until the task is completed (Bandura, 1977, 1982).

When a particular image of an individual is salient, it channels activities in ways that are consistent with it (cf. Backman, 1983; Harré, 1980; McCall & Simmons, 1978; Schlenker, 1980, 1984). It thereby serves as a miniscript or plan that guides expectations and behavior in the setting. People who regard themselves as inordinately honest, for example, should be more likely than those who do not to evidence signs of honesty and resist temptations to lie, cheat, or steal. Or, people who regard themselves as especially athletic should be more likely than those who do not to try to evidence signs of the ability, embrace the opportunity to compete, and persevere in the face of setbacks. In a complementary fashion, people who regard another person as inordinately honest expect they can place their trust in him and can act accordingly, such as by believing his statements or lending him money with confidence that it will be repaid; or, people who regard another person as especially athletic expect her to do well at such endeavors and will probably act accordingly, such as by choosing her as a partner for tennis.

Identity Images and Evaluative Judgment Images also influence evaluative judgments. An evaluation depends on the comparison between a perceived object or event and the standards that are applied to that object or event. These standards vary idiosyncratically (e.g., some people have loftier standards for honesty or ability than others), and can be influenced by the particular environment (e.g., some teachers impose loftier standards on their students than do others). Since images contain standards that the possessor of the image should fulfill, they directly influence evaluation when perceived characteristics or performances are compared to them. Characteristics or performances that meet or exceed the standards produce positive evaluations, while those that fall short generate negative evaluations; both types of reactions are intensified as the relevant images and standards increase in centrality and importance (Carver, 1979; Duval & Wicklund, 1972; Schlenker & Leary, 1982a). For example, people who have no pretensions of being an intellectual should be relatively unaffected if they are not so regarded, while those who have lofty pretensions should be greatly upset to discover they appear to be simpletons. In any particular situation, evaluative judgments of self are equatable to situated self-esteem; cumulative judgments of self are equatable to general self-esteem (cf. James, 1890).

Identity Images and Goal Achievement Finally, identity images can facilitate or impede goal achievement. Images contain information about the values and outcomes that are associated with them. Given a particular goal (e.g., being regarded by a professor as a good student), certain images will be perceived as facilitating goal attainment (e.g., appearing to be intelligent, attentive, diligent) and others will be perceived as impeding it (e.g., appearing to be insipid, lazy, disinterested). Knowledge employed to understand image-outcome relationships can be used during social interaction to obtain goals. To be regarded and treated in a particular way requires that a particular combination of images "exist" that would mediate the regard or treatment (e.g., Blau, 1964; Goffman, 1959; Jones & Pittman, 1982; Schlenker, 1980; Tedeschi, 1981). For example, if one wants to be respected, one must have, or be seen as having, the types of attributes that others admire, such as intelligence or status. If people can construct, for themselves and significant others, identity images that permit them to achieve valued goals in life, their self-satisfaction and interpersonal rewards should be high. If they cannot do so, they are likely to be continually frustrated and dissatisfied. It follows that there are usually reasons for people to attempt to control the images of self that are presented to particular audiences, for by controlling the images, people control the regard and treatment they receive.

Desirable Identity Images

People can create in their own imaginations idealized images of the type of person they would truly prefer to be, the ultimate person who could satisfy their values and achieve their goals. The concept of an idealized image has occupied an important place in the literature on the self (Hall & Lindzey, 1978; Rosenberg, 1979). Karen Horney (1945), whose writings primarily addressed the behavior of neurotics, introduced the concept to the psychoanalytic literature. She held that in the face of unfavorable childhood conditions, neurotics attempt to place themselves above others by developing an idealized image of self, thereby affirming their significance and worth. This idealized image represents the ultimate sort of person who could be everything they want to be, beautiful, strong, popular, successful, etc. This idealization is the neurotic's solution to the problems of feeling unworthy or inferior, and soon comes to replace the real self as the individual's self-view. Unfortunately, while seeming to solve one problem, it exacerbates the difficulty, because its standards are too high, prompting neurotics to feel driven to succeed at unrealistic levels (e.g., to make the most money, to be the best student), to be insatiable in their quests (however much they succeed is never enough), to be indiscriminate in their attempts to be liked and admired (by not just some people but by everyone), and to become excessively anxious, depressed, and panicked when facing failure. In his analysis of personality, Carl Rogers (1959) similarly distinguished between the real self, or self as it is perceived to be, and the ideal self, which is what the person would ultimately like to be. Rogers suggested that larger discrepancies between the real and ideal selves produce feelings of lower self-worth.

When asked to do so, people are able to articulate a distinction between the real and ideal self, describing the way they actually are and the way they would ideally like to be (Hall & Lindzey, 1978; Wylie, 1974, 1979). Turner (1968), however, suggested that people normally do not make such a distinction when thinking about themselves, divorcing their ideas of what they want to be from what they are and permitting their ideal self to provide an unvarying anchor, or set of standards, that is untouched by the experiences of reality. Turner held that while such reality-divorced standards may be present in certain psychopathological cases, the self-concept normally represents a blend of the real and ideal that is "reality edited" to permit the retention of self-respect. Rosenberg (1979) similarly described such an edited version of the ideal self, which he termed the *committed image.* It is a desired self that represents how the person would like to see himself, taking into account his limitations. Unlike Turner, Rosenberg distinguished between the committed image and the actual self as separate portions of the self-concept.

I prefer to come at the issue from a slightly different angle, by examining the usefulness of particular images of self. Pragmatic philosophers (e.g., Charles Sanders Peirce, William James, John Dewey; see Rorty, 1966) linked the truth of an idea with its usefulness to the holder. For an idea (a belief, an interpretation) to be regarded as true, it should be useful in permitting those who hold it to function effectively in the world. Although the pragmatists did not discuss usefulness in precisely these terms, it would not be an unfair extension to say that a "good" idea should allow those who hold it to understand, predict, and control events more satisfactorily than they could with alternative ideas. When an idea is acted on, does it produce mistakes, errors, and the inability to accomplish one's goals? If so, its utility, and hence truth, is low and it should be abandoned. For instance, a scientific theory whose hypotheses are continually disconfirmed impedes one's understanding, leads to incorrect predictions, and cannot be applied to control events or benefit humanity. If an idea minimizes errors, increases the domain of things that can be understood and predicted, and permits one to control events and accomplish one's goals, then it should be used until an even more useful alternative can be found to replace it.

Pragmatic themes can be extended to the nature of identity images, which are ideas about a person. When are identity images useful, and hence true, to the holder? They are useful to the extent that they maximize the product of being *believable* (being reasonably accurate construals of the salient evidence) and *personally beneficial* (being able to interpret the person in a way that serves the holder's values and goals). These can be termed *desirable identity images* because they would facilitate the holder's ability to function effectively in the world (Schlenker, 1980, 1982, 1984). Elsewhere (Schlenker, 1980) I've offered an expectancy-value formulation for measuring desirable images. Instead of repeating it here, I'll use this space to explore further their nature and implications.

Desirable identity images represent what the person would *like to be* and thinks he or she *really can be,* at least at his or her "best." Phrased differently, they are what the person thinks he or she *could and should* be. Desirable images speak to potential, or more accurately perceived potential; they contrast with ideals, which speak to unreachable heights. Unlike ideals, they are affected by reality, which provides constraints and influences aspirations. Desirable images must take into account our skills, abilities, appearance, history, and other available evidence about what we are like. If the evidence does not converge to provide a reasonable basis for the belief, it is unlikely to prove useful and will not be particularly effective in managing oneself or one's environment (e.g., Kelley, 1967, 1971; Rosenberg, 1979; Schlenker, 1980). For example, excessively idealistic self-images that are not matched by people's abilities prompt them to tackle tasks on which they are doomed to failure, exposing them to personal disappointment, social ridicule, and the beginning of the neurotic behavior pattern described by Horney. At the opposite extreme, people who underestimate their ability are likely to avoid tasks at which they could succeed, thereby unnecessarily limiting their accomplishments. A large quantity of research indicates that people raise their standards (or levels of aspiration) after success and lower them following failure, both in individual and group situations (e.g., Lewin et al., 1944; Rosenberg, 1979; Zander, 1971). Interestingly, people raise their standards following success by a greater amount than they lower them following failure, suggesting a reluctance to abandon desirable images and a willingness to embrace even more desirable ones.

Because of the personal and social repercussions of unrealistic self-identifications, people do not prefer to view themselves or have others view them as Supermen or Superwomen; the fall to the ground would be quick and painful. People even reject excessive praise if it appears to commit them to live up to standards that they believe they cannot fulfill (cf. Carson, 1969; Jones, 1973). Nonetheless, our values and goals prompt us to fly as high as we reasonably can. People's goals and values channel self-identifications in the direction of ones that are personally beneficial, permitting the construction of images of self that are potentially manageable, justifiable, but glorified (Schlenker, 1980, 1982, 1984). These images represent a construal of the available evidence (the believability component) in a way that serves the person's goals and values (the beneficiality component).

This description of desirable images seems to be in the spirit of James' (1890) use of the term *pretensions,* or what we "back ourselves to be," Rosenberg's (1979) description of the committed image, and Turner's (1968) description of the self-conception comprising "reality-edited" ideals. McCall and Simmons

(1978) advanced a similar view in their analysis of role identities, suggesting that a role identity is a person's "imaginative view of himself as he likes to think of himself being and acting as an occupant of that position" (p. 65). They proposed that these role identities are reality bound but glorified, and are what people attempt to express in social life.

As will be elaborated shortly, I propose that desirable identity images mediate self-presentations and self-disclosures to others, as well as private thoughts about the self. Desirable images function in the five ways described earlier to influence cognitions, affect, and behavior. Like Turner, I propose that the self-conception is normally comprised of desirable images, including self-knowledge and standards that portray a somewhat glorified but reality-bound portrait of self. In any particular social situation, however, the actor's desired identity images can differ from either (a) the desired images in his or her self-concept, or (b) his or her perceptions of the identity images that have actually been created in the situation. In the first case, situational pressures and significant others, such as being on an important date or having a job interview, can prompt people to package or fabricate information about the self in ways designed to create a desired situated identity that is not coextensive with the self-concept as it is evoked in the context of the self-as-audience. In the second case, the process of interacting with the environment, including other people, can produce perceptions of a situated identity that differs qualitatively and quantitatively from the one that was desired. Unanticipated good or bad fortune (e.g., successes or failures, mistakes or accidents) and the behaviors of others can cast people into identities that are better or worse than the ones they desired. When such a discrepancy goes against the actor, creating a situated identity that is worse than the desired one, and pertains to recurring situations (e.g., place of employment) or enduring relationships (e.g., marriage), it produces serious personal and interpersonal problems, including negative self-reactions and feelings of rejection by others (Schlenker, 1984). The line then begins to blur between situated identity and the self-concept because the relative frequency of occurrence and importance of the situated identity begins to threaten the desired images comprising the self-concept. These cases justify the counselor or clinician's distinction between the real and ideal self. Thus, while the self-conception consists of desirable identity images, there are occasions and image dimensions on which it is important to distinguish between one's desired identity images and one's perceived identity images.

SELF-IDENTIFICATION IN CONTEXT

Goals, Scripts and Plans, and Desired Identity-Images

The following propositions describe the initial basis for self-identification in a given context.

Proposition 1 *Self-identification occurs in a particular context that reflects the interaction of the person (e.g., the actor's self-concept and values), the situation (e.g., opportunities for and constraints on the satisfaction of values; social rules* and rituals that provide information about normatively structured patterns of behavior), and one or more salient audiences for the activity (other people, imagined referents, and the self).

Proposition 2   *An initial assessment and evaluation of self, the situation, and the audience evokes for the actor or prompts the actor to formulate: (a) a goal or set of goals that might satisfy needs and values, (b) a script or plan for goal accomplishment, and (c) a set of desired identity images.*

Proposition 3   *These desired identity images mediate self-identification on the occasion, acting like subscripts or subplans embedded within the overall script or plan.* These images organize and regulate self-identifications via the five functions described earlier, and may or may not be coextensive with the desired images comprising the self-concept.

The propositions assume a basic principle about human behavior: People are purposive, planning creatures who are always thinking, always acting, and always trying to achieve particular objectives in life (e.g., Carson, 1969; Harré, 1980; McCall & Simmons, 1978; Miller et al., 1960). The goals (or objectives) we want to achieve at a particular time can be mundane or important, specific or vague, obvious or camouflaged. Nonetheless, we always have them, and they always provide purpose to our activities, even if the goal is simply to lie down on the sofa and relax.

In order to achieve goals, people construct (or access from memory previously constructed) scripts or plans (Miller et al., 1960; Schank & Abelson, 1977). Scripts and plans are related concepts that describe the operations (steps and procedures) taken to achieve a goal. They specify appropriate sequences of events and conditions that, if the sequences unfold as expected, lead to the appropriate results. They can be regarded as analogous to a computer program that contains a hierarchically ordered sequence of operations (for the person, a sequence of thoughts and behaviors) that have a purpose. As such, they are an organization of knowledge that permits understanding of means-end relationships, and they contain numerous feedback loops that permit responsiveness to unfolding and changing circumstances. Schank and Abelson (1977) distinguish between scripts and plans based on their specificity versus generality. Scripts are relatively specific, prepackaged (previously acquired and used), and available in memory as a reasonably complete representation of the procedure in the particular context. When a script is triggered consciously or unconsciously by cues, it provides a definition of the situation being encountered, a set of expectations about events, and a set of operations for thoughts and behaviors in the situation. For instance, we have scripts for how to worship in church, to be served dinner at a restaurant, to establish friendly relationships with new coworkers. Plans, in constrast, are constructed when existing scripts are unavailable or unacceptable. This is done by interweaving general information about how people achieve goals with specific information pertinent to the situation and audience. The ability to construct plans in a creative, sometimes scheming, fashion permits people to deal with situations they may never have previously encountered and to obtain goals they may never have pursued in the situation before. Scripts and plans can be conscious or unconscious (Langer, 1978; Miller et al., 1960), and once they are evoked or constructed, they direct the individual's thoughts and actions on the occasion, analogous to the way a program directs the operations of the computer, providing the processes and sequenced structure needed to obtain results.

The concepts of goals, scripts and plans, and desirable identity images are the foundation for the theory of self-identification. Self-identification always occurs in a background that reflects the interaction of the person, situation, and audience (Proposition 1), the assessment of which generates a set of goals, a script or plan, and a set of desired situated identity images for the occasion (Proposition 2); these images mediate self-identifications on the occasion (Proposition 3). Phrased differently, given a particular setting, we assess its possibilities (consciously or unconsciously) and work out our objectives, strategies and tactics, and a pertinent portrait of self that permits us to take advantage of its opportunities and constraints. This sequencing of events is somewhat arbitrary, because goals often exist first (arising from our needs and values) and prompt us to fashion scripts and plans to accommodate them, which we do by imagining and constructing environments that provide opportunities for goal achievement. The more creative process of constructing environments to accommodate goals will be postponed until we consider Proposition 9. Nonetheless, goals and the environmental contexts for their satisfaction go hand in hand.

Personality enters via the actor's (a) self-conception, especially those self-images that are more central and important to the actor and hence more likely to be salient in many contexts (e.g., Hogan, 1982; Schlenker, 1980, 1984) and those self-images that seem especially pertinent to the particular context; (b) needs and values (desired end states for self) that underlie the selection of goals, e.g., bodily maintenance, spiritual fulfillment, self-respect, social recognition, dominance, true friendship, beauty, personal comfort (e.g., Rokeach, 1973); and (c) dispositional tendencies, such as the proclivity to be inner directed, or focused on personal beliefs and standards, versus outer directed, or focused on the perceived expectations and standards of immediate others (e.g., Hogan & Cheek, 1982; see Chapters 5 and 6 in this volume). The situation enters via (a) its capacity to satisfy or thwart specific values, such as by presenting particular opportunities or constraints and reward-cost contingencies (e.g., envision the different possibilities for value satisfaction on a job interview, important date, in an army barracks, at a party, at home), and (b) its capacity to cue particular goals, scripts or plans, and identity images that include information about appropriate social roles, rules, rituals, and standards (e.g., contemplate the differences in goals and scripts at a wedding, in the classroom, on a date, in the office, at home). The audience enters comparably to the situation, through (a) their capacity to satisfy or thwart particular needs and values (e.g., friendship, wisdom, approval, respect), and (b) their capacity to cue particular goals, scripts or plans, and identity images (e.g., contemplate differences in conduct in relation to one's parents, fiancé, employer, friends).

Any of the three factors (self, situation, audience) can predominate and account for the greatest proportional influence on self-identifications on given occasions. For example, at an informal party among close friends, people are relatively unconstrained by particular situational and audience pressures and their self-identifications can be guided largely by their self-conceptions (Hogan, 1982; Schlenker, 1984). At the opposite extreme, during a job interview, the situational and audience pressures can be intense and prompt people to present themselves in ways they expect will gain the approval of the interviewer (Jones & Pittman, 1982; Schlenker, 1980, 1984; Tedeschi, 1981). Even in these two extreme cases, however, all of the factors are involved to some extent. For instance, at the party, people's scripts and plans still take into account pertinent social rules and rituals, such as those calling for civility, reciprocity, taking turns during conversations. Scripts and plans also take into account the particular person with whom they are talking, such as by packaging self-identifications and subjects of conversations in ways that are expected to be most clear to the other. At the job interview, people still have considerable latitude in how they express (or even fabricate) information they believe will most impress the interviewer, thus permitting personality to be evidenced. On most occasions, the interaction of all three of the factors must be considered in order to explain self-identifications. Thus, Proposition 1 adopts an interactionist view of the relationship between personality, situations, and audiences (Bandura, 1978, 1982). The interaction of the person and the environment (including other people) influences behavior, which in turn can change the environment and the person (e.g., thoughts, reactions).

Orienting to the Context

On the vast majority of occasions on which self-identifications occur, they arise automatically, without prior thought or planning. The confluence of the situation, audience, and person generates a routine goal, script, and set of desired identity images that flow freely without conscious monitoring or control. These comprise the habits of social life, sets of well-practiced, modulated units of behavior expressed to the broad classes of audiences and situations we frequently encounter (e.g., Hogan, 1982; James, 1890; Schlenker, 1980). As James (1890, p. 79) eloquently put it, "Already at the age of twenty-five you see the professional mannerism settling down on the young commercial traveller, or the young counsellor-at-law. You see the little lines of cleavage running through the character, the tricks of thought, the prejudices, the ways of the 'shop,' . . . from which the man can by-and-by no more escape than his coat-sleeve can suddenly fall into a new set of folds. On the whole, it is best he should not escape. It is well for the world that in most of us, by the age of thirty, the character has set like plaster, and will never soften again."

There are occasions, of course, when we expend considerable thought and planning on our performances, such as before an important date or giving a speech, and are especially alert during the performance itself, monitoring and controlling our activities and vigilantly searching out information about how we are doing. Proposition 2a addresses when such consideration is likely to occur:

The extent or thoroughness of the initial assessment of the self, situation, and audience increases as a function of (a) the importance of the goals that might be achieved on the occasion, (b) the magnitude of any perceived conflicts in values that are relevant to the goals, and (c) the existence and magnitude of any anticipated impediments that might thwart goal achievement (e.g., tenuous or incomplete scripts or plans, a novel situation or unfamiliar audience, doubts about one's skills, a hostile audience).

As goals (or the values and needs that underlie them) increase in importance, so does the extent to which the occasion marshals the individual's mental resources. The importance of the goal depends on (a) the subjective worth of the outcomes that are associated with it, that is, the worth of the associated rewards and costs (e.g., being liked by the other, being respected, getting the job), (b) the centrality of the goal, that is, the degree to which it subsumes or satisfies other important goals (e.g., gaining love from another might satisfy numerous other objectives in life), and (c) the extent to which the goal can be satisfied in other situations or with other audiences (e.g., if one has several equally attractive job interviews, each can be regarded as less crucial than if only one job prospect is on the horizon). Research on attribution (e.g., Berscheid, Graziano, Monson, & Dermer, 1976), self-attention (Carver, 1979), decision making (e.g., Janis & Mann, 1977), social anxiety (Schlenker & Leary, 1982a), and self-presentation (e.g., Schlenker, 1980; Tedeschi, 1981) suggests that important goals focus and channel people's thoughts and activities.

Assessment should also increase when situations present value conflicts. These conflicts can involve the clash of personal values (e.g., "I need the job; I'll probably get it only if I lie about my credentials, but I am an honest person; lying is against my principles") or the clash between personal values and social values and expectations (e.g., "I feel that using drugs is wrong, but my friends say it's great and want me to try it"). Such value conflicts demand increased assessment of oneself, the situation, and the audience to compare the importance of the values that are involved, gather information that may be useful, and reach some decision about one's goals, script or plan, and desired identity.

Finally, assessment is increased when impediments are anticipated that might thwart goal achievement. These impediments can derive from a variety of sources. The person's script or plan may be tenuous or incomplete, providing only a partial specification of what should be done in the situation (Langer, 1978). The person may doubt his or her skills in executing the script or plan appropriately, as in the case of the individual who lacks confidence in his or her conversational ability on a date (Schlenker & Leary, 1982a). The situation may be novel or the audience may be unfamiliar, such as at one's first school dance (Carson, 1969; Schlenker & Leary, 1982a). The audience may be viewed as especially critical, hostile, irrational, or otherwise difficult to get along with and plan accordingly (Schlenker & Leary, 1982a). All of these cases should increase thought, concern, and assessment.

Proposition 2b addresses the consequences of increased assessment. *Increased assessment produces: (a) greater attention to and consciousness of pertinent information about the self, situation, or audience, (b) a search for information (in memory or in the environment) that might clarify any ambiguous, missing, or conflicting information, (c) greater examination and comparison of alternative goals, scripts or plans, and desired identity images, (d) greater rehearsal of the contemplated performance, (e) increased salience of the pertinent standards for the performance and greater monitoring and control of one's activities in the effort to match the standards, and (f) increased sensitivity and responsiveness to information that pertains to how well or poorly the standards are being met.* Space does not permit these many consequences to be examined in detail, but a few select comments should help to illustrate the implications. Take the case of people who have the goal of creating a particular impression on another person, say on an important first date. These conditions have been found to increase people's sensitivities to the characteristics, values, and opinions of the other, as they search for, attend to, and attempt to recall information to achieve as clear an image as possible of what he or she is like and how he or she might act (Berscheid et al., 1976). The conditions cause the other's perceived characteristics, opinions, and standards to play a larger role than they otherwise would in guiding and regulating the actors' self-presentations; that is, the actors perform more for *this* audience than other possible audiences (Schlenker, 1980, 1984). The conditions increase the actors' self-attention and self-assessment, focusing them on relevant abilities, attributes, and other information that might facilitate or impede their goals (Carver, 1979; Schlenker & Leary, 1982a). The conditions increase the actors' self-monitoring and control of their performances in order to meet the standards (e.g., Bandura, 1982; Carver, 1979). The conditions intensify the actors' sensitivities to the other's reactions to self, prompting them to interpret feedback in terms of its implications for their own identities (Fenigstein, 1979; Schlenker & Leary, 1982a). The conditions also intensify actors' affective reactions to the desired or undesired quality of the other's reactions (Fenigstein, 1979; Schlenker & Leary, 1982a), and they generate nervousness to the extent their assessment prompts the actors to question whether their goals will be achieved (Schlenker & Leary, 1982a).

To illustrate more vividly, picture a person conversing at a party with a rather uninteresting, unappealing female who he is hardly motivated to impress positively. Although he tries to maneuver away, he becomes cornered. He asks few or no questions, barely manages to keep up his end of the conversation, couldn't care less about her thoughts on any topic, and doesn't even notice what she is wearing. His attention is elsewhere and, when she subtly hints that she finds him attractive, he misses the point. When she later makes her attraction to him clearer, it is met with affective indifference. Self-monitoring and control are minimal, and his actions are guided by habit, not concern. His behaviors may coincidentally impress her, but he makes no concerted effort to do so. In contrast, he seeks out the classmate he has admired from afar. Prior to the party he planned what he would do and say if she were there, considered several possible introductory scripts and sides of self to present (e.g., his dashing, athletic side, or his pensive, sensitive side), put on his best outfit in anticipation, and even borrowed his roommate's more expensive car so he might be seen arriving in style. He is enthralled by her every word and phrase, tries to infer the personal implications of each verbal and nonverbal nuance, and even notices the attractive ankle bracelet she is wearing. He monitors his actions to insure they are creating the "right" impression and takes the available opportunities to tell her about himself and his achievements. He especially stresses self-relevant information that he thinks she'll find appealing, trying to introduce it in ways that avoid stepping over the line that might make him appear egotistical. He asks questions about her interests to find out more about her, and packages his self-identifications in ways designed to suit her interests. (Packaging includes arranging, interpreting, and weighting information about oneself in a fashion that is designed to create a desired impact on others, even though one might not normally arrange, interpret, or weight the information in the same way. Thus, the packaged information is basically "true," but better facilitates one's immediate goals.) For example, although he likes to read but loves to hunt, he emphasizes his intellectual pursuits and plays down hunting when he finds she is a Phi Beta Kappa and member of the Audubon Society. When hunting is mentioned, he places it in the context of his love of nature rather than enjoyment of the sport, and he notes the benefits of thinning herds to accommodate the available food supply. Earlier in the day he had been talking to his roommate about their planned hunting trip that weekend and had exchanged tales of their exploits, trophies, and relish for the hunt, but these aspects don't come up in his present conversation. At one point, he even goes beyond packaging and misrepresents the number of classic books he's read, doubling the actual count. When she subtly hints she finds him attractive, his pulse quickens. Up until that point he had noticed how nervous he felt; now he feels more self-confident.

The nature and implications of the initial assessment (and its impact on goals, scripts and plans, and desired identity images) clearly influences people's orientation toward the situation or audience. Greater initial assessment should increase the likelihood that people's activities are better fitted to the opportunities and constraints that exist (Schlenker, 1980). When particular goals, scripts, and desired identity images are cued without thought, it conserves our energies and permits us to concentrate on more important matters; but this freedom, gained through the acquisition of habits, has a price—the self, situation, and audience may not be sufficiently assessed to maximize personal benefits or minimize costs. For example, a hasty reading of a party invitation may evoke the wrong script and prompt one to show up at a black-tie-and-tails affair dressed in a regular suit. As another example, a common complaint heard by marriage counselors is, "My spouse is taking me for granted." The spouse doesn't appear to notice what the neglected party does or says and no longer seems to show concern. Concomitantly, the offenders allow their own appearances and actions to depart dramatically from what they once were when they were on their "best" behavior during courtship and initial married life. The extreme case is, say, a man who after 10 years of marriage sits around in his underwear all weekend watching television, drinking beer, and building up a growth of stubble on his face. His motivation to impress his wife has obviously slipped to the point of neglect as his routines have settled over the years.

Self-Presentation

When the goal (or one of the goals) of a performance is to create a particular impression of self on an audience, we can say the actor is *motivated to impress* the audience (Schlenker, 1984, Schlenker & Leary, 1982a). The desired impression can be positive or negative (e.g., trying to show an opponent during a conflict that one is tough, irrational, and likely to inflict severe harm, thus creating a "negative" impression of self that is in one's best interests at the time) and can include attributes that are not a normal part of one's self-concept as evoked in the context of the self-as-audience in a different class of situations. As the goal increases in importance, the actor's goals, scripts and plans, and desired identity images become increasingly interrelated, marshalling self-identifications in a manner that may appear to be more strategic in nature, especially when the performance is directed toward another person. The audience's perceived or anticipated reactions to the performance then become the primary criterion determining whether satisfactory progress has been (or is being) made toward that goal. To take a range of examples involving an immediate other, imagined referent, and self-as-audience, respectively, consider (a) a job applicant who plans and regulates his self-identifications in ways designed to achieve a favorable reaction from the interviewer, (b) a medical student who is motivated in her attempts to be a doctor by the thought of how much her desired identity would have pleased her deceased father, and (c) a priest who is guided in his conduct by the recognition that his moral integrity is a central, priceless identity image that must be kept beyond reproach even when confronted with temptations. These cases illustrate how the anticipated reactions of audiences, self included, serve to guide and regulate self-identification when the goal involves creating or maintaining a particular identity image.

The above examples were chosen to emphasize the commonalities among self-identifications that occur privately and publicly, with an immediate other, imagined referent, or the self as a primary audience for the activity. The important distinction is not whether the behavior is public or private, but what context (audience and situation) is salient to the actor at the time. As the contexts change, so can the desirability of particular identity images, because the context can influence (a) the range of potentially believable self-identifications (e.g., the standards and pertinent evidence can seem more or less ambiguous or confining), and (b) the beneficiality of self-identifications (e.g., the importance of the images can become greater or less) (Schlenker, 1980). This analysis does suggest, however, that when people are motivated to impress a particular other person, the line blurs between what *one can and should be* and what *one can reasonably get away with*. Given the motivation to impress particular others, others who are perceived as uninformed, naive, undiscriminating, or supportive provide greater latitude for exaggeration about the self than do others who are perceived as discriminating, hostile, and aware of evidence that could contradict otherwise beneficial self-presentations.

People's reactions to the self-presentations of another person are influenced by the fit between the self-presentation and the audience's independent knowledge about the actor. Schlenker and Leary (1982b) found that people regarded an actor less favorably when the actor's self-presentations departed from information that was believed to be true of the actor; the greater the discrepancy, the less positive was the evaluation of the actor. We are expected to be what we present ourselves to be in social life (Gergen, 1968; Goffman, 1959; Schlenker, 1980; Tedeschi et al., 1971). If we are not, it is difficult for others to rely on us, or to plan and coordinate their activities with ours. People who are discovered to be unlike what they claim to be are regarded as incompetent (e.g., uninsightful, ignorant), weak (e.g., insecure, defensive), egotistical (e.g., braggarts), or deceptive (e.g., liars), depending on the type and extent of the perceived inaccuracy (e.g., Was it a gross distortion intended for personal gain or a silly error in judgment?) (Schlenker & Leary, 1982b). Interpersonal pressures thus place a premium on knowing oneself and honestly conveying this information to others, or at least being perceived as doing so.

Schlenker and Leary (1982b) also found that when people were unaware of information about an actor, the actor was evaluated more favorably the more positively he presented himself. In the absence of contradictory information, people appear to assume that an actor's words are at least generally truthful. As Goffman (1959) noted, we tend to give others the benefit of the doubt when it comes to accepting their self-presentations. The advantages of modesty appear to come into play when people are already aware of or give the actor credit for superior attributes or accomplishments. Schlenker and Leary (1982b) found that an actor who was self-effacingly modest about an accomplishment was evaluated most favorably only when people were aware of the actor's achievement; they then preferred such an actor to one who was pompously accurate about it. If people are unaware of the accomplishment, modest self-presentations were apparently mistaken for less-than-superior performance.

These patterns of reactions to particular types of self-presentations are undoubtedly anticipated by most people during their face-to-face interactions. Research has shown that people whose failures can be hidden from public view tend to present themselves more favorably on the relevant dimension than people who believe others will know of their failure (Baumeister & Jones, 1978; Schlenker, 1975). Further, the more certain people are of displaying negative qualities to others, the less favorably they present themselves, thus maintaining a general consistency between their self-identifications and other publicly known information about them (e.g., Maracek & Mettee, 1972; Ungar, 1980). The believability of particular self-identifications acts as a constraint. In contrast, people tend to display modesty when they believe that others know they performed at a superior level, but exaggerate the favorableness of their qualities when others are unaware of the performance (Baumeister & Jones, 1978; Schlenker, Miller, & Leary, 1983).

Such results indicate that people's self-identifications change as the context changes. However, one should not jump to the conclusion that all people are liars at heart, or that self-presentations are transient, momentary displays divorced from self-conceptions. There is a difference between an exaggeration (be it self-aggrandizing or self-effacing) and a lie. People's self-identifications can be stretched to fit the available context, a process that probably occurs unconsciously much of the time, without them representing falsehoods (Jones & Pittman, 1982; Schlenker, 1980). Further, earlier portions of this chapter documented the case that people's self-images, values, and personality proclivities influence their self-identifications. These personality factors act as additional constraints on self-identification through the anticipation of self-reactions. Hoffman (1977), for example, distinguished between moral orientations characterized by fear of external detection and punishment from others versus those characterized by independence from external sanctions and the self-imposition of punishment for failures to live up to one's moral standards. The latter orientation corresponds with what is traditionally regarded as having a conscience: The existence of internal moral principles, represented in one's self-images and values, that regulate behavior and generate self-punishment for misbehavior through self-condemnation and feelings of guilt (cf. Bandura, 1982). In contrast, the former orientation is typified by the cynic H. L. Mencken's comment that "conscience is the inner voice that warns us someone may be watching." Although the evidence is scarce, we can speculate that people who have outer- as compared to inner-directed moral orientations are more likely to lie and misrepresent themselves in situations where deceit is otherwise to their short-term advantage, and the possibility of external detection is low.

MOVING TOWARD GOALS

Once a set of goals, a script or plan, and set of desired identity images have been evoked or formulated, these guide the actor's self-identifications and other activities on the occasion. They function analogously to a template or roadmap to steer behavior from a starting point to a desired destination. They do not account for all possible contingencies that could arise, but they permit the actor to fill in the gaps along the way (Schank & Abelson, 1977). They contain the type of general and specific information needed to handle most events that are likely to occur, such as by answering questions posed by the other with responses that are "in character" (i.e., consistent with the goals, script or plan, and desired identity). This capacity to fill in the gaps is consistent with sociological analyses of role performances being "made," and not simply "played out" in rote form (cf. Stryker, 1981). On perhaps most occasions, no serious problems arise in the execution of scripts or plans, and the occasion eventually ends with goals being achieved. Occasionally, however, difficulties arise during execution. Although these difficulties may pertain to any facet of the script or plan, we will concentrate on ones related to self-identifying activities. (It should be noted that the same general propositions could be advanced about any sort of problem to script or plan completion.)

Proposition 4 *If the self-identifying activity is interrupted or impeded during the performance, an assessment process occurs in which the self, situation, and audience are reexamined. This assessment generates (a) an expectancy about the likelihood of satisfying the standards for self-identification, and (b) an explana-*

tion of the difficulties. Interruptions or impediments to self-identifying activities mean that something has gone wrong and desired identity images are not being properly constructed or maintained. The obstacle can arise because of events related to the person's own behaviors (e.g., ineptness, mistakes, accidents, transgressions) or events in the environment (e.g., chance events, questions or threats posed by others) and generates a threat to desired identity (Schlenker, 1980, 1982). When such obstacles occur, a reassessment takes place, refocusing the actor's attention in ways that might alleviate the problem and restore activities to their preplanned course. This reassessment follows the same general form outlined in Propositions 2, 2a, and 2b. Occasionally, reassessment prompts people to change goals, scripts and plans, or desired identity images in midstream, but I suspect that such drastic shifts are rare, probably occurring only when a new set of alternatives seems so attractive compared to the old, and when the costs of abandoning the old are so minimal that there is little recourse but to switch. Usually, the reassessment provides the opportunity to fine tune the original set of goals, scripts/plans, and desired identity-images in ways that address the obstacle.

Explanations

Proposition 5 *Explanations of events occur during assessment (initially or after confronting impediments) that function to reconcile, as best as possible, undesired events with the actor's desired identity images.* The undesired event evokes an explanation. According to proper English usage, an explanation gives an interpretation or meaning to something that is not known or clearly understood. Day-to-day events do not require explanations. Their meaning is clear to anyone who has been properly socialized in the particular culture and has the appropriate background of knowledge. People's existing scripts and schemata about themselves, other people, the world, and causal events permit them to interpret such events automatically, without conscious attention or public discussion (cf. Kelley, 1972; Langer, 1978; Schlenker, 1980, 1982). This economy of effort frees people to concentrate on more important matters. Questions arise or are anticipated about events for a reason, and only when reasons exist will explanations be consciously proffered (Goffman, 1971; Mills, 1940). In an earlier paper (Schlenker, 1982), I proposed that *identity-relevant explanations occur when events appear to (a) violate standards in ways that threaten desired identity images (e.g., Was the actor responsible for "bad" conduct? Was the event really condemnable and unjustifiable?), or (b) meet commendable standards, but ambiguity exists about the relevance of the event for desired identity images (e.g., Was the actor responsible for "meritorious" conduct? Was the conduct really commendable?).* Both these conditions present obstacles to desired identity images and evoke explanations during the assessment process. The objective of these explanations is to reconcile the event with desired identity images as best as possible, given the available information. The so-called *egotistical biases* in attributions and perceptions that have been extensively documented in research, with people attempting to associate themselves with positive objects and events and dissociating themselves from negative objects and events, can be regarded as types of explanations that fall under the rubric of the above proposition. (Chapters 8, 9, and 10 in this volume review the relevant literature.)

Although space does not permit a complete analysis of the implications and hypotheses that can be derived from this proposition (see Schlenker, 1982), a few general comments may clarify the types of explanations. When events violate standards in identity-threatening ways, people's remedial explanations generally take the form of accounts or apologies (Goffman, 1971; Schlenker, 1980, 1982). Two general classes of *accounts* for the event exist: *excuses,* which attempt to eliminate or minimize the actor's personal responsibility for the event (e.g., denying one did it, denying foreseeability or intent, or citing mitigating circumstances), and *justifications,* which attempt to change the appearance of the event and minimize its apparent negativity (e.g., by minimizing harm done, such as "It was a white lie," or appealing to higher values such as "I did it for your own good"). *Apologies* permit actors to accept blame for the event and split the self into two parts, a "good" self that admits error, won't repeat the error, and should be forgiven; and a "bad" self that is villified and left behind (e.g., Darby & Schlenker, 1982; Goffman, 1971; Schlenker, 1980; Schlenker & Darby, 1981). Through apologies, actors reaffirm the value of the standards and inform audiences that despite the one "problem," they will continue to recognize and strive to achieve the standards, thereby reaffirming their desired identities.

When people might be denied the desired implications of events that meet or exceed standards because ambiguity exists about the event, their explanations take the form of *acclamations* (Schlenker, 1980, 1982). These comprise *entitlements,* which attempt to increase personal responsibility for the event, and *enhancements,* which attempt to characterize the event in desirable ways. Acclamations permit the event to be clarified for audiences (self included) so that it is interpreted in a manner that is congruent with desired identity images.

Finally, it should be noted that identity-relevant explanations occur prior to as well as after the occurrence of obstacles. People often anticipate obstacles at the stage of the initial assessment (Proposition 2). They then either (a) modify their goals, scripts and plans, and desired identity images in ways that avoid the obstacle, such as the abandoning contemplated activities for which no acceptable explanation can be found (Mills, 1940), or (b) proffer explanations in advance, such that the path to the event can be smoothed and it can be placed in the "proper light" when it occurs (Backman, 1983; Hewitt & Stokes, 1975; Schlenker, 1980, 1982).

Expectations

In addition to explanations of obstacles, the reassessment process yields expectations of the likelihood that the standards for self-identification can be achieved.

Proposition 6 *To the extent that the assessment yields expectations of meeting the relevant standards, the actor will continue the activity and experience positive affect.* Reassessment can produce the expectation that the self-identification is on the right track (perhaps after minor readjustment of scripts or plans) and that the desired identity images will be achieved. People then continue their activities and experience positive affect, feeling good about themselves, their performance, and the environment. (These same affective feelings also should accompany the initial assessment if expectations indicate a reasonable likelihood of success, and the final outcome of goal accomplishment.) The picture is that of the person proceeding reassuredly toward goals after an unexpected momentary interruption. The amount of positive affect should be a direct function of (a) the importance of the relevant goals and standards (Carver, 1979; Schlenker & Leary, 1982a), and (b) the extent to which the success can be attributed to desired characteristics of self (e.g., ability, effort) rather than to situational supports or luck, which detract from personal responsibility and feelings of accomplishment (e.g., Frieze, 1976).

Since the assessment process increases the salience of relevant standards and produces greater behavior-standard matching than might otherwise occur (see Proposition 2b), such assessment can actually facilitate performance, provided that the individual emerges with a reasonable expectation of success (Carver, 1979; Schlenker & Leary, 1982a). The assessment reduces or eliminates any temporary mental wanderings and promotes concentration on the task at hand. In sports, coaches often try to reemphasize the standards and point out impediments to teams who have grown too self-assured, thus rededicating them to the task so that they don't take their next victory for granted. Similarly, an occasional interruption or impediment serves to channel cognition and behavior back on course, and can actually improve performance over what it might have been if the assessment had not taken place. Whether it is before a big game, speech, date, class, or whatever, such "psyching" is more effective than taking the situation for granted.

Assessment does not always generate such beneficial effects, because the individual may reach the conclusion that the goal and standards cannot be achieved. When this expectation occurs, the consequences are malignant.

Proposition 7 *To the extent that the assessment yields expectations of being unable to meet the relevant standards, the actor will experience negative affect.*

Proposition 8 *The expectation that the standards cannot be met also produces physical or psychological withdrawal from the situation and audience. If physical withdrawal is impractical, the actor becomes trapped in self-assessment, and performance is debilitated.*

People who have low expectations of achieving a goal usually avoid the task if possible and, if they cannot, readily abandon it in the face of obstacles (Bandura, 1977, 1982; Carver, 1979). Similarly, people who anticipate failure in constructing or maintaining desired identity images experience negative affect and attempt to withdraw, physically or psychologically, from the setting (Schlenker & Leary, 1982a). (If the initial assessment generates expectations of failure and no satisfactory goal or desired identity could be achieved, the actor will avoid the situation if at all possible. If the situation is unavoidable, then the negative consequences discussed here should begin at the stage of the initial assessment.) The amount of negative affect and withdrawal should be a direct function of (a) the importance of the relevant goals and standards (Carver, 1979; Schlenker & Leary, 1982a), (b) the anticipated or perceived discrepancy between the images created by the performance and desired identity images (Schlenker & Leary, 1982a), and (c) the extent to which the anticipated or perceived failure is attributed to undesired characteristics of the self (e.g., poor ability) rather than to uncontrollable situational obstacles, bad luck, or transitory personal conditions (e.g., a bad mood, tiredness) that minimize personal responsibility for the failure (e.g., Frieze, 1976).

Physical withdrawal from such identity-threatening circumstances appears to be the preferred course of action, as people avoid affiliating with others under such conditions and prematurely leave such situations as soon as feasible (Schlenker, 1984; Schlenker & Leary, 1982a). For the sake of illustration, picture the individual who is socially mortified by a faux pas at a party (e.g., her wig falls off, she slips picking it up and falls in the pool, and is the object of considerable laughter); a hasty exit is the normal routine. Avoiding or withdrawing from such circumstances is not always practical, however, since coexisting pressures (e.g., job demands, social responsibilities) may make the situation unavoidable and physical withdrawal impractical. When actual withdrawal is blocked, people become frozen or locked in assessments of self, situation, audience, and the problem (Carver, 1979; Schlenker & Leary, 1982a). Their minds race with thoughts about the unreachable goal and their inability to attain it; they become self-preoccupied and self-focused, continually reexamining their limitations. The combination of cognitive withdrawal from the difficult situation (e.g., fantasizing about more preferred activities, outcomes, and being anywhere but where one is at the moment) and self-preoccupation produces distraction and further debilitates social performance. Information processing declines in effectiveness, reducing sensitivity to ongoing events, and self-monitoring and self-control worsen. The products are the types of behaviors that are associated with high social anxiety. These include nervousness (e.g., twitching hands and feet, nervous habits such as twirling one's hair), hesitant and awkward words and acts (e.g., stuttering, frequent use of "ahs" and "uhs," failure to complete one's sentences, clumsiness), reticence, slower and less frequent speech filled with long pauses, head nodding and other signs of acquiescence to others, and minimal self-disclosure (Schlenker & Leary, 1982a).

Propositions 7 and 8 thus address the aversive aspects of self-identification and social interaction, when seemingly insurmountable problems occur in the pursuit of identity-relevant goals and produce virulent cognitions, negative affective reactions, and debilitated behaviors. People whose personality characteristics and life situations continually expose them to problems in constructing and maintaining desired identities become chronically anxious, fearing the worst in any particular situation and avoiding interpersonal interactions as much as possible, producing a spiral into loneliness (Schlenker, 1984; Schlenker & Leary, 1982a).

THE QUEST FOR DESIRABLE IDENTITIES

Creating Environments

Desirable identities represent what people would like to be, *and* believe they can be, given particular contexts for self-identification. These contexts can be confronted in the real world, as when people interact with particular others in particular social situations, or they can exist in imagination, as when people contemplate themselves while evoking particular imagined audiences (self included) and situations. Our discussion up until now has focused primarily on what transpires when people find themselves "in" a particular environment, which they may or may not have actively chosen. Now we'll examine self-identification a bit more broadly and consider how people construct their own environments, actively attempting to create and maintain ones that facilitate desirable identities.

Proposition 9 *As active agents, people strive to create environments, in both their own minds and the real world, that support, validate, and elicit desirable identity images. They thus selectively encounter, perceive, and influence the situations and audiences with which they deal.* The identification process is an active one, not a passive one in which people find themselves in a particular environment and then merely react to the context that exists. People attempt to create environments that facilitate their values and desired identity images as conceived in the context of the self-as-audience across particular classes of imagined situations and other people. We do so, both mentally and in actuality, in at least four general ways (cf. Rosenberg, 1979; Schlenker, 1980, 1984; Secord & Backman, 1965; Swann, 1983):[1] (a) through selective attention, interpretation, and recall, (b) through selective valuation and the setting of standards, (c) through selective exposure of the self to particular types of other people and situations, and (d) through the selective expression of self-identifying information and the selective use of influence to change other people and situations.

---

[1]The process of creating environments that support the self has been emphasized by Secord & Backman (1965) and Swann (in press; see Chapter 4 in this volume). These positions suggest that people attempt to create environments that maintain congruence with the self-concept. As such, they can be distinguished from the position advanced here, which emphasizes the attempt to construct support for desired identity images; the latter are not always coextensive with the images contained in the self-concept as that term is usually defined. For example, Backman (1983) has rejected the exclusive emphasis on consistency that was taken in the earlier version of congruency theory and now emphasizes the importance of attempting to create support for more glorified images of self. His more recent position appears to be very close to the one described in Proposition 9, emphasizing the attempt to construct and maintain desired identity images.

Selective Attention, Interpretation, and Recall Selective attention, interpretation, and recall permits people to entertain and express, for themselves and to others, desired identity images. Prior sections of this chapter (the discussions of the functions of identity images, and Proposition 5, dealing with the construction of explanations) have already considered research bearing on these selective tendencies. The following examples illustrate:

1 People attend to and recall information in ways that support desired identity images, such as by noticing information that validates existing images, recalling successes better than failures, and searching through memory in ways that support desired conclusions (e.g., Greenwald, 1980; Rosenberg, 1979).

2 People tend to perceive and recall more consensual agreement for their identity images than actually exists, thereby overestimating the extent to which others actually validate their self-identifications (e.g., Rosenberg, 1979; Secord & Backman, 1965; Swann, 1983).

3 People tend to take personal responsibility for "good" outcomes (e.g., their successes) and minimize personal responsibility for "bad" outcomes (e.g., their failures) (e.g., Riess et al., 1981; Snyder et al., 1978; Weary Bradley, 1978; Weary & Arkin, 1981). Two exceptions to this tendency arise when (a) people have established a widely known negative reputation or exhibited an unmistakable pattern of prior failure on a particular dimension, in which case they accept, admit, and even initiate negative attributions about the self (e.g., Dutton, 1972; Frey, 1978; Schlenker, 1980, 1982; Tetlock & Levi, 1982; Weary Bradley, 1978); and (b) others already give them credit for superior achievements or expect modesty from a person in their position, in which case more modest attributions prevail (e.g., Baumeister & Jones, 1978; Schlenker & Leary, 1982b; Tetlock & Levi, 1982). These conditions either limit the believability of self-serving atrributions or enhance the worth of modesty, and we've already discussed how these factors alter the desirability of identity images. These self-serving attributions take the form of excuses and entitlements (Proposition 5).

4 People ascribe their conduct to "good" motives (e.g., to procure meritorious goals) and minimize or deny "bad" motives (e.g., to procure crass personal gains) (Schlenker, Hallam, & McCown, 1983). These explanations justify or enhance desired identity images (Proposition 5).

5 People interpret their qualities in ways that maximize the desirable implications for self, as when the garbage collector calls himself a "sanitation engineer" or the terrorist regards herself as a "freedom fighter" (Rosenberg, 1979; Schlenker, 1980, 1982).

6 People tend to denigrate sources of information that threaten desired identity images and affirm the value of sources that validate desired identity images. Thus, people who deliver negative interpersonal evaluations to subjects are liked less and regarded as less discerning and credible than are those who deliver positive interpersonal evaluations (e.g., Jones, 1973; Rosenberg, 1979), and tests or tasks that generate negative feedback are regarded as less reliable, valid, and useful than those that generate positive feedback (e.g., Schlenker & Miller, 1977).

Selectivity in Values and Standards People tend to set their standards for self high enough to represent what they could be but not too high as to be unrealistic, adjusting standards upward after success and slightly downward after failure (e.g., Lewin et al., 1944; Rosenberg, 1979; Zander, 1971). In addition, people adjust their values to enhance the worth of attributes or abilities at which they consider themselves good and devalue those at which they consider themselves poor (Rosenberg, 1979). People also tend to focus on and overvalue those aspects of their jobs that are superior to some other line of work, such as in the case of telephone operators who boost the attractiveness of their job by elevating it against manual labor and citing its superior cleanliness, better manners, and superior dress (Rosenberg, 1979; Seidman, 1962). Finally, people tend to compare themselves to others who permit them to maintain or elevate their desired identities, and when comparing self to people in general, regard themselves as "above average" or better on most dimensions and at worst "average" on a few (Rosenberg, 1979). These proclivities for selective valuation and the setting of standards permit people to construct and maintain desired identity images in their own minds and in their conversations with others.

Selective Exposure People selectively expose themselves to particular tasks and other people that permit the creation and maintenance of desired identities. As examples, people tend to gravitate toward careers, hobbies, and friendships that they expect will support or elicit desired identities and values (cf. Cheek & Hogan, 1983; Rosenberg, 1979; Secord & Backman, 1965; Swann, 1983). By selectively affiliating with supportive others and avoiding critical others, selectively picking hobbies and jobs, selectively joining particular groups or clubs and disparaging those opposed to one's principles, and selectively frequenting particular places (e.g., singles bars, church socials), people are able to increase the likelihood that they can fulfill their values, project desired identities, and receive validating feedback.

Selective Expression and Influence Finally, people can attempt to create supportive environments through (a) the display of the symbols of their desired identities, and (b) the exercise of influence to try to change other people and situations to bring about greater compatibility than may initially exist (cf. Backman, 1983; Rosenberg, 1979; Schlenker, 1980; Secord & Backman, 1965; Swann, 1983). The symbols of identity include personal appearance (e.g., physical features, makeup, wardrobe), props (e.g., briefcases, pipes, furniture, trophies, cars, pets, wall hangings, books, records, sports equipment) and "style" of behavior (e.g., type of walk, mannerisms, accent) (Schlenker, 1980; Swann, 1983). Displays of symbols not only express personal values and desired images of self, but influence how others react. People also can attempt to influence other people and situations directly through the use of verbal and nonverbal behaviors that can modify the opinions, values, standards, and rules of their environment. In conjunction, expressions of identity and the exercise of influence can alter existing environments. For example, people can try to change the regard in which they are held by coworkers, redecorate their offices to express their personal tastes, and try to change the rules of the company to make work environments more enjoyable and supportive. Organized social movements (e.g., Women's Liberation) frequently involve attempts to change the opinions, values, standards, and laws of society to make them more conducive to the types of identities desired by the movement's members.

Evolving Identities

These cognitive and behavioral activities can be more or less successful in constructing supportive environments. They sometimes result in the construction of real environments that are even better than people may have hoped. For example, some people are fortunate enough to find the "right" person and enter into a life-long relationship that produces mutual satisfaction. The partners seem to "bring out the best" in each other, eliciting and supporting the style of life and desired identity each prefers (Schlenker, 1984). Each can be largely what he or she desires to be, and has a nearly prototypic partner for continued support. No one is perfectly satisfied and no one can create the perfect environment, but some people manage to get much closer than others.

Situations and relationships that do not support or elicit desirable identities are usually avoided if possible, but sometimes people become trapped in them (e.g., an unhappy marriage, a disliked job with no good alternatives). The identities that evolve in such environments represent scaled-down versions of what people initially desired to be, full of compromises and lowered aspirations.

Proposition 10 *Over time, the identities that evolve for people in particular situations and relationships reflect the accumulation of experiences in the situations or relationships, resulting in perceived identities that can be qualitatively and quantitatively different from their desired identity images in the context.* Given the variety of techniques at our disposal for creating facilitative environments, it might seem surprising that identities ever fall short of desired ones. Yet we know they do. There are at least three general reasons. First, information accumulates over time and reputations become fixed in particular relationships and settings, locking the individual into patterns of social interaction and feedback that are less than desirable. Accidents, mistakes, failures, ineptness, off-guard moments, insults or pressures from others all add up; although any one or even several of these patterns can be discounted, their cumulative effect takes its toll. In marriages, for example, people are often surprised to discover how different they and their spouses look after a few years of such accumulation.

Second, people are not totally free to select their own values and standards (Rosenberg, 1979). Some values and standards are so well established in particular societies and groups that while they might be modified somewhat in the person's mind, they still remain important and perhaps difficult for the person to achieve. Also, people's values change over time, as in cases where the ideals of one's youth appear trivial by middle age, being replaced with alternate values. When values change faster than extant identities, as in the case of a burned-out professional who remains in his old job with new values and desires, discrepancies arise.

Third, some situations and audiences are difficult to avoid, however unpleasant, and people are thereby exposed to the feedback they generate. Other people, including friends and relatives, have their own desired images for us to fulfill, and attempt to impose them on us in the pursuit of their own values (e.g., Backman, 1983; Schlenker, 1984). An example is the person who vows in her own mind that after marriage, she will eliminate all of her husband's faults and make him into the type of mate she desires; of course these attempts are usually met with frustration and dissatisfaction on the parts of both (Schlenker, 1984). Such feedback, especially when it comes from a significant other such as a friend or relative, can be discounted only up to a point.

The result is that people become trapped in particular identities in specific relationships and settings. Patterns of behavior accumulate over time and leave people with habitually enacted identities that are perceived to fall short of desired ones. Thus, married people sometimes complain of being locked in relationships that do not let them fulfill themselves, yet they "know" they could be a "better" person in a different sort of relationship. Midlife crises over careers are similar, with people feeling that their present occupations are too unsatisfying and confining to permit them to be what they think they can and should be. Privately (to self and imagined referents) they yearn for escape and fantasize about what they could be like in a different relationship or occupation. These fantasies may remain and fester, be temporarily enacted (e.g., through extramarital affairs), or result in a decision to find a new spouse or career. It is a rare person who has not at one time or another desired to start over, fresh, with no entanglements, no prior reputation, no constraints—only opportunities to start from scratch to build a desired identity in full form. For some people, these fantasies involve only minor adjustments in their perceived identities; for others, wholesale changes are envisioned.

Satisfaction

Proposition 11 *People are more satisfied in particular relationships and situations to the extent that their desired identity images are supported, validated, or elicited.* More precisely, people's satisfaction with their own identities in a particular relationship or situation is an inverse function of the perceived discrepancy between desired identity images in the relationship or situation across image dimensions and their perceived identity images in the relationship or situation on those dimensions, weighted by the importance of the images to them in the relationship or situation (Schlenker, 1984). As support decreases, typified by criticism, complaints, and nagging from others, people become increasingly dissatisfied with the relationship or situation. Indeed, individuals who exhibit the greatest amounts of stress in their interpersonal relationships also have been found to have the greatest discrepancies between their views of self and the perceived or actual appraisals of themselves by others (Lundgren, 1978).

Some Parting Words on Consistency and Esteem

It is worth noting that the self-identification approach described here differs in emphasis from approaches that propose that people are primarily motivated by either a need to maintain self-esteem or a need to make their thoughts and behaviors consistent with existing self-images. Each of these basic needs has been assumed by some theorists to be a central motivator for self-identification. Proponents of each typically cite data that supports their position and then introduce qualifiers to allow them to account for data that are more readily handled by the other position (Schlenker, 1984). From the present perspective, it appears that each position approaches the relevant phenomena from a different angle and addresses different aspects of the self-identification process. Esteem proponents focus largely on the extent to which self-identifications are *personally beneficial;* consistency proponents focus largely on the extent to which information is *believable* by virtue of its congruity with existing beliefs. As consistency proponents emphasize, the esteem motive is not without bounds; it is held in check by the believability of the self-identification. As esteem proponents emphasize, the consistency motive is not a driving force that compels people to remain in a steady state; people act to maximize their esteem as much as possible. In lieu of such supposedly sharp contrasts, the present theory refocuses the issue on the nature of desirable identity images and thereby provides an integrating theme. Desirable identity images exist in context and comprise what people believe they can and should be in the context. These images then guide people's self-identifications, reactions to others, and creation of environments. We've seen that desired identity images are not always coextensive with existing self-images, as when people attempt to package and exaggerate information about the self in order to impress particular others or fantasize about what they can and should be after being trapped in less-than-desired indentities in particular relationships or situations. Similarly, people do not act merely to maximize their self-esteem without bounds, but act within the confines of the identities they think they can reasonably maintain. Desirable identity images refocus the discussion and provide people with the basis for self-reflection and self-regulation.

SUMMARY

The identification process of fixing and expressing one's own and others' identities is at the core of social life. The approach to self-identification presented here can be summarized best via its major propositions.

1 Self-identification occurs in a particular context that reflects the interaction of the person, the situation, and one or more salient audiences.

2 An initial assessment and evaluation of self, the situation, and the audience evokes for the actor or prompts the actor to formulate (a) a goal or set of goals, (b) a script or plan for goal accomplishment, and (c) a set of desired identity images.

3 These desired identity images mediate self-identification on the occasion, acting like subscripts or subplans embedded within the overall script or plan.

4 If the self-identifying activity is interrupted or impeded during the performance, an assessment process occurs in which the self, situation, and audience are reexamined. This assessment generates (a) an expectancy about the likelihood of satisfying the standards for self-identification, and (b) an explanation of the event.

5 Explanations of events occur during assessment (initially or after confronting impediments) that function to reconcile, as best as possible, undesired events with the actor's desired identity images.

6 To the extent the assessment yields expectations of meeting the relevant standards, the actor will continue the activity and experience positive affect.

7 To the extent the assessment yields expectations of being unable to meet the relevant standards, the actor will experience negative affect.

8 The expectation that the standards cannot be met also produces physical or psychological withdrawal from the situation and audience. If physical withdrawal is impractical, the actor becomes trapped in self-assessment, and performance is debilitated.

9 As active agents, people strive to create environments, in both their own minds and the real world, that support, validate, and elicit desirable identity images. They thus selectively encounter, perceive, and influence the situations and audiences with which they deal.

10 Over time, the identities that evolve for people in particular situations and relationships reflect the accumulation of experiences in the situations or relationships, resulting in perceived identities that can be qualitatively and quantitatively different from their desired identity images in the context.

11 People are more satisfied in particular relationships and situations to the extent that their desired identity images are supported, validated, or elicited.

REFERENCES

Alexander, C. N., Jr., & Wiley, M. G. (1981). Situated activity and identity formation. In M. Rosenberg & R. H. Turner (Eds.), *Social psychology: Sociological perspectives*. New York: Basic Books.

Apter, M. J. (1983). Negativism and the sense of identity. In G. M. Breakwell (Ed.), *Threatened identities*. New York: Wiley.

Backman, C. W. (1983). Toward an interdisciplinary social psychology (Vol. 16). In L. Berkowitz (Ed.), *Advances in experimental social psychology*. New York: Academic Press.

Bandura, A. (1977). Self-efficacy: Toward a unifying theory of behavioral change. *Psychological Review, 84*, 191–215.

Bandura, A. (1978). The self system in reciprocal determinism. *American Psychologist, 33,* 344–358.
Bandura, A. (1982). The self and mechanisms of agency. In J. Suls (Ed.), *Psychological perspectives on the self* (Vol. 1). Hillsdale, NJ: Erlbaum.
Baumeister, R. F. (1982). A self-presentational view of social phenomena. *Psychological Bulletin, 91,* 3–26.
Baumeister, R. F., & Jones, E. E. (1978). When self-presentation is constrained by the target's prior knowledge: Consistency and compensation. *Journal of Personality and Social Psychology, 36,* 608–618.
Berscheid, E., Graziano, W., Monson, T., & Dermer, M. (1976). Outcome dependency: Attention, attribution, and attraction. *Journal of Personality and Social Psychology, 34,* 978–989.
Blau, P. M. (1964). *Exchange and power in social life.* New York: Wiley.
Breakwell, G. M. (1983). Formulations and searches. In G. M. Breakwell (Ed.), *Threatened identities.* New York: Wiley.
Cantor, N., & Mischel, W. (1979). Prototypes in person perception. In L. Berkowitz (Ed.), *Advances in experimental social psychology* (Vol. 12). New York: Academic Press.
Carson, R. C. (1969). *Interaction concepts of personality.* Chicago: Aldine.
Carver, C. S. (1979). A cybernetic model of self-attention processes. *Journal of Personality and Social Psychology, 37,* 1251–1281.
Cheek, J. M., & Hogan, R. (1983). Self-concepts, self-presentations, and moral judgments. In J. Suls & A. G. Greenwald (Eds.), *Psychological perspectives on the self* (Vol. 2). Hillsdale: NJ: Erlbaum.
Darby, B. W., & Schlenker, B. R. (1982). Children's reactions to apologies. *Journal of Personality and Social Psychology, 43,* 742–753.
Dutton, D. G. (1972). Effect of feedback parameters on congruency versus positivity effects in reactions to personal evaluations. *Journal of Personality and Social Psychology, 24,* 366–371.
Duval, S., & Wicklund, R. A. (1972). *A theory of objective self-awareness.* New York: Academic Press.
Epstein, S. (1973). The self-concept revisited: Or a theory of a theory. *American Psychologist, 28,* 404–416.
Erikson, E. H. (1959). Identity and the life cycle. In G. S. Klein (Ed.), *Psychological issues.* New York: International Universities Press.
Fenigstein, A. (1979). Self-consciousness, self-attention, and social interaction. *Journal of Personality and Social Psychology, 37,* 75–86.
Foote, N. N. (1951). Identification as a basis for a theory of motivation. *American Sociological Review, 16,* 14–21.
Frey, D. (1978). Reactions to success and failure in public and in private conditions. *Journal of Experimental Social Psychology, 14,* 172–179.
Frieze, I. H. (1976). Role of information processing in making causal attributions for success and failure. In J. C. Carroll & J. W. Payne (Eds.), *Cognition and social behavior.* Hillsdale, NJ: Erlbaum.
Gergen, K. J. (1968). Personal consistency and the presentation of self. In C. Gordon & K. J. Gergen (Eds.), *The self in social interaction.* New York: Wiley.
Goffman, E. (1959). *The presentation of self in everyday life.* Garden City, NY: Doubleday.
Goffman, E. (1971). *Relations in public.* New York: Basic Books.

Greenwald, A. G. (1980). The totalitarian ego: Fabrication and revision of personal history. *American Psychologist, 35,* 603–618.
Greenwald, A. G., & Pratkanis, A. R. (1984). The self. In R. S. Wyer & T. K. Srull (Eds.), *Handbook of social cognition* (Vol. 3). Hillsdale, NJ: Erlbaum.
Hall, C. S., & Lindzey, G. (1978). *Theories of personality* (3rd ed.). New York: Wiley.
Harré, R. (1980). *Social being: A theory for social psychology.* Totowa, NJ: Littlefield, Adams.
Harré, R. (1983). Identity projects. In G. M. Breakwell (Ed.), *Threatened identities.* New York: Wiley.
Hewitt, J. P., & Stokes, R. (1975). Disclaimers. *American Sociological Review, 40,* 1–11.
Hoffman, M. L. (1977). Moral internalization: Current theory and research. In L. Berkowitz (Ed.), *Advances in experimental social psychology* (Vol. 10). New York: Academic Press.
Hogan, R. (1982). A socioanalytic theory of personality. In M. Page & R. Dienstbier (Eds.), *Nebraska symposium on motivation.* Lincoln: University of Nebraska Press.
Hogan, R., & Cheek, J. (1982). Identity, authenticity, and maturity. In T. R. Sarbin & K. E. Scheibe (Eds.), *Studies in social identity.* New York: Praeger.
Horney, K. (1945). *Our inner conflicts.* New York: Norton.
James, W. (1890). *The principles of psychology.* New York: Holt.
Janis, I. L., & Mann, L. (1977). *Decision making: A psychological analysis of conflict, choice, and commitment.* New York: Free Press.
Jones, E. E., & Pittman, T. S. (1982). Toward a general theory of strategic self-presentation. In J. Suls (Ed.), *Psychological perspectives on the self* (Vol. 1). Hillsdale, NJ: Erlbaum.
Jones, S. C. (1973). Self- and interpersonal evaluations: Esteem theories vs. consistency theories. *Psychological Bulletin, 79,* 185–199.
Judd, C. M., & Kulik, J. A. (1980). Schematic effects of social attitudes on information processing and recall. *Journal of Personality and Social Psychology, 38,* 569–578.
Kelley, H. H. (1967). Attribution theory in social psychology. In D. Levine (Ed.), *Nebraska symposium on motivation.* Lincoln: University of Nebraska Press.
Kelley, H. H. (1971). *Attribution in social interaction.* Morristown, NJ: General Learning Press.
Kelley, H. H. (1972). *Causal schemata and the attribution process.* Morristown, NJ: General Learning Press.
Langer, E. J. (1978). Rethinking the role of thought in social interaction. In J. H. Harvey, W. Ickes, & R. F. Kidd (Eds.), *New directions in attribution research* (Vol. 2). Hillsdale, NJ: Erlbaum.
Lewin, K., Dembo, T., Festinger, L., & Sears, P. S. (1944). Level of aspiration. In J. McV. Hunt (Ed.), *Personality and the behavior disorders* (Vol. 1). New York: Ronald Press.
Lundgren, D. C. (1978). Public esteem, self-esteem, and interpersonal stress. *Social Psychology, 41,* 68–73.
Maracek, J., & Mettee, D. R. (1972). Avoidance of continued success as a function of self-esteem, level of esteem certainty, and responsibility for success. *Journal of Personality and Social Psychology, 22,* 98–107.
Markus, H. (1977). Self-schemata and processing information about the self. *Journal of Personality and Social Psychology, 35,* 63–78.
Markus, H. (1980). The self in thought and memory. In D. M. Wegner & R. R. Vallacher (Eds.), *The self in social psychology.* New York: Oxford University Press.

McCall, G. J., & Simmons, J. E. (1978). *Identities and interactions* (2nd ed.). New York: Free Press.

McCrae, R. R., & Costa, P. T., Jr. (1982). Self-concept and the stability of personality: Cross-sectional comparisons of self-reports and ratings. *Journal of Personality and Social Psychology, 43,* 1282–1292.

Mead, G. H. (1934). *Mind, self, and society.* Chicago: University of Chicago Press.

Miller, G. A., Galanter, E., & Pribram, K. H. (1960). *Plans and the structure of behavior.* New York: Holt, Rinehart & Winston.

Mills, C. W. (1940). Situated actions and vocabularies of motives. *American Sociological Review, 5,* 904–913.

Neisser, U. (1976). *Cognition and reality.* San Francisco: W. H. Freeman.

Riess, M., Rosenfeld, P., Melburg, V., & Tedeschi, J. T. (1981). Self-serving attributions: Biased private perceptions and distorted public descriptions. *Journal of Personality and Social Psychology, 41,* 224–231.

Rogers, C. R. (1959). A theory of therapy, personality, and interpersonal relationships, as developed in the client-centered framework. In S. Koch (Ed.), *Psychology: A study of a science* (Vol. 3). New York: McGraw-Hill.

Rokeach, M. (1973). *The nature of human values.* New York: Free Press.

Rorty, A. (1966). *Pragmatic philosophy: An anthology.* Garden City, NY: Doubleday.

Rosenberg, M. (1979). *Conceiving the self.* New York: Basic Books.

Schank, R., & Albelson, R. (1977). *Scripts, plans, goals and understanding.* Hillsdale, NJ: Erlbaum.

Schlenker, B. R. (1975). Self-presentation: Managing the impression of consistency when reality interferes with self-enhancement. *Journal of Personality and Social Psychology, 32,* 1030–1037.

Schlenker, B. R. (1980). *Impression management: The self-concept, social identity, and interpersonal relations.* Monterey, CA: Brooks/Cole.

Schlenker, B. R. (1982). Translating actions into attitudes: An identity-analytic approach to the explanation of social conduct. In L. Berkowitz (Ed.), *Advances in experimental social psychology* (Vol. 15). New York: Academic Press.

Schlenker, B. R. (1984). Identities, identifications, and relationships. In V. Derlega (Ed.), *Communication, intimacy, and close relationships.* New York: Academic Press.

Schlenker, B. R., & Darby, B. W. (1981). The use of apologies in social predicaments. *Social Psychology Quarterly, 44,* 271–278.

Schlenker, B. R., Hallam, J. R., & McCown, N. E. (1983). Motives and social evaluation: Actor-observer differences in the delineating of motives for a beneficial act. *Journal of Experimental Social Psychology, 19,* 254–273.

Schlenker, B. R., & Leary, M. R. (1982a). Social anxiety and self-presentation: A conceptualization and model. *Psychological Bulletin, 92,* 641–669.

Schlenker, B. R., & Leary, M. R. (1982b). Audience's reactions to self-enhancing, self-denigrating, and accurate self-presentations. *Journal of Experimental Social Psychology, 18,* 89–104.

Schlenker, B. R., & Miller, R. S. (1977). Egocentrism in groups: Self-serving biases or logical information processing? *Journal of Personality and Social Psychology, 35,* 755–764.

Schlenker, B. R., Miller, R. S., & Leary, M. R. (1983). Self-presentation as a function of the validity and quality of past performance. *Representative Research in Social Psychology, 13,* 2–14.

Secord, P. F., & Backman, C. W. (1965). Interpersonal approach to personality. In B. H. Maher (Ed.), *Progress in experimental personality research* (Vol. 2). New York: Academic Press.

Seidman, J. (1962). Telephone workers. In S. Nosow & W. Form (Eds.), *Man, work and society*. New York: Basic Books.

Snyder, C. R., Higgins, R. L., & Stucky, R. J. (1983). *Excuses: The masquerade solution*. New York: Wiley.

Snyder, M. L., Stephan, W. G., & Rosenfield, D. (1978). Attributional egotism. In J. H. Harvey, W. Ickes, & R. F. Kidd (Eds.), *New directions in attribution research* (Vol. 2). Hillsdale, NJ: Erlbaum.

Stone, G. P. (1962). Appearance and the self. In A. M. Rose (Ed.), *Human behavior and social processes*. Boston: Houghton Mifflin.

Stryker, S. (1979). Symbolic interactionism: Themes and variations. In M. Rosenberg & R. H. Turner (Eds.), *Social psychology: Sociological perspectives*. New York: Basic Books.

Swann, W. B., Jr. (1983). Self-verification: Bringing social reality into harmony with the self. In J. Suls & A. G. Greenwald (Eds.), *Psychological perspectives on the self* (Vol. 2). Hillsdale, NJ: Erlbaum.

Tedeschi, J. T. (1981). *Impression management theory and social psychological research*. New York: Academic Press.

Tedeschi, J. T., Schlenker, B. R., & Bonoma, T. V. (1971). Cognitive dissonance: Private ratiocination or public spectacle? *American Psychologist, 26,* 685–695.

Tetlock, P. E., & Levi, A. (1982). Attribution bias: On the inconclusiveness of the cognition-motivation debate. *Journal of Experimental Social Psychology, 18,* 68–88.

Turner, R. H. (1968). The self-conception in social interaction. In C. Gordon & K. J. Gergen (Eds.), *The self in social interaction*. New York: Wiley.

Ungar, S. (1980). The effects of the certainty of self-perceptions on self-presentation behaviors: A test of the strength of self-enhancement motives. *Social Psychology Quarterly, 43,* 165–172.

Weary Bradley, G. (1978). Self-serving biases in the attribution process: A reexamination of the fact or fiction question. *Journal of Personality and Social Psychology, 36,* 56–71.

Weary, G., & Arkin, R. M. (1981). Attributional self-presentation. In J. H. Harvey, W. Ickes, & R. F. Kidd (Eds.), *New directions in attribution research* (Vol. 3). Hillsdale, NJ: Erlbaum.

Wyer, R. S. (1981). An information-processing perspective on social attribution. In J. H. Harvey, W. Ickes, & R. F. Kidd (Eds.), *New directions in attribution research* (Vol. 3). Hillsdale, NJ: Erlbaum.

Wylie, R. C. (1974, 1979). *The self-concept* (2 Vols.). Lincoln: University of Nebraska Press.

Zander, A. (1971). *Motives and goals in groups*. New York: Academic Press.

CHAPTER 4

THE SELF AS ARCHITECT OF SOCIAL REALITY

William B. Swann, Jr.
University of Texas at Austin

Tommy was seven years old when I met him. At first blush, he seemed no different than the other economically deprived children at the summer camp. It was not until I watched him remove his shirt prior to taking a shower that he really stood out. To my horror, I saw that his back was covered with scars and bite marks. The next day the caseworker confirmed my suspicions. Tommy was a battered child.

Neither I nor any of the other counselors were surprised at Tommy's incredibly negative self-concept. After all, according to the case worker, Tommy had been the target of a steady stream of verbal and physical abuse since the age of two. Tommy must have simply decided that his parents were abusing him for a reason, that he was indeed the stupid, dishonest, ugly, little boy that they made him out to be. What *was* remarkable about Tommy was that so many of his activities seemed designed to perpetuate his negative self-view. His choice of interaction partners (his favorite was "Crazy Louis," who loved to inflict pain on those around him, especially Tommy), his style of interaction (Tommy had a penchant for inspiring hatred by taunting the other children and disrupting their games) even his memory (Tommy never remembered the good things that had happened to him, only the bad)—all of these activities seemed structured in ways that tended to validate and sustain his negative self-concept.

In this chapter, I will argue that all of us have a bit of Tommy in us. In particular, I contend that once people form self-concepts, they engage in a variety of behavioral and cognitive activities that tend to verify and confirm

---

I am grateful to Toni Giuliano, John Griffin, Nancy Hazen, Barry Schlenker, Sid Shrauger, and Rich Wenzlaff for their helpful comments on an earlier version of this manuscript.

these conceptions. Some of these activities ensure that people's friends, colleagues, and intimates see them as they see themselves. Others make the social environment seem more compatible with their self-concepts than it really is. Together, these *self-verification* processes enable people to create—both in their social environments and their own minds—a social reality that verifies, validates, and sustains their self-concepts (cf. Lecky, 1945; Secord & Backman, 1961, 1965).

One of my objectives in this chapter will be to identify the strategies through which people verify their self-views. Another goal will be to reconcile arguments concerning the existence of a "self-enhancement" motive with the self-verification formulation. Still another concern will be to show how self-verification processes are woven into people's ongoing social relationships. Finally, in the last section, I will consider self-concept change, the opposite side of the self-verification coin. I begin with a discussion of the antecedents of the self and self-verification processes.

THE ORIGINS OF THE SELF AND SELF-VERIFICATION

A world that is devoid of security, comfort, and a sense of solace is incomprehensible. Undoubtedly, a major reason that children are motivated to make sense of their worlds is to gain security, comfort, and solace. Towards this end, they develop an elaborate set of theories about the world, theories that allow them to predict the behavior of the people and entities around them. At the heart of this theoretical system are their beliefs about themselves (e.g., Epstein, 1973; 1983).

In forming their self-concepts, children have at least three sources of information available (e.g., Schoeneman, Tabor, & Nash, 1982; Wegner & Vallacher, 1977). First, they may take note of how others react to them, then translate these reactions into corresponding self-views (e.g., Cooley, 1902; Mead, 1934). Second, they may observe their own behaviors and use these behaviors as a basis for inferring what sorts of individuals they are (e.g., Bem, 1972). Third, they may notice how well they perform relative to others and judge themselves accordingly (e.g., Festinger, 1954; Suls & Mullen, 1982).

As children begin to gather more and more evidence on which to base their self-concepts, these conceptions begin to serve an increasingly important role in their efforts to predict and control their worlds (e.g., Mead, 1934). They will consequently invest in seeing to it that their self-concepts do not change in any radical way. Lecky (1945), for example, has argued that because an individual's self-concept "is his only guarantee of security, its preservation soon becomes a goal in itself. He seeks the type of experience which confirms and supports the unified attitude, and rejects experiences which seem to promise a disturbance of this attitude" (p. 123).

In the spirit of Lecky's contentions, there is evidence that people do indeed prefer phenomena that are predictable and consistent with expectation. Research on the effects of "mere exposure" (Harrison, 1977; Zajonc, 1968), for example, has offered convincing evidence that humans and animals alike grow to love that which is familiar and predictable to them. Furthermore, recent research on hypothesis testing has shown that in testing the validity of either propositions about other individuals (e.g., Mary is an extrovert) or physical objects (e.g., all chairs have four legs), people preferentially search for evidence that will confirm rather than disconfirm the propositions they are testing (e.g., Snyder & Swann, 1978; Swann & Giuliano, 1983; Wason & Johnson-Laird, 1972). Even the curiosity that people display when confronted with unfamiliar stimuli apparently reflects a desire to render such stimuli more predictable by identifying their underlying properties (e.g., Berlyne, 1961).

One implication of this analysis is that as soon as people form reasonably certain self-views, they should strive to confirm and verify these views. This should occur even if these views happen to be negative. Admittedly, soliciting negative feedback at first seems maladaptive. However, consider the incapacitating confusion that might result if someone who had experienced a lifetime of negative feedback were suddenly forced to completely revise his or her self-view. For such individuals, the cognitive disorganization associated with developing a more positive self-view might simply be too great a price to pay for the benefits that might accompany such a shift.

Recent research by Swann and Read (1981a: Investigation 1) has provided direct support for the notion that people prefer self-confirmatory feedback. In this research, each participant first completed a series of questionnaires, including a personality inventory and measures of self-perceived assertiveness and self-perceived emotionality. The experimenter then secured the participant's consent to show his or her responses on the personality inventory to another individual. Several minutes later, the experimenter returned and announced that the other individual had read over the participant's responses on the personality inventory and answered some questions about the participant. She then displayed two lists of questions that the other person had ostensibly answered. On one list, some questions probed for evidence of assertiveness, for example, "What makes you think that this is the type of person who will complain in a restaurant if the service is bad?"; other questions probed for evidence of unassertiveness, for example, "Why would this person not be likely to complain if someone cuts into line in front of him or her at a movie?" On the second list, some questions probed for instances of emotional behavior, for example, "What about this person makes you think that he or she would go to pieces if a friend died?" Other questions probed for evidence of unemotional behavior, for example, "Why do you think this person doesn't get angry, even when provoked?" The experimenter told the participant to read each list of questions and select from each list the five questions whose answers he or she was most interested in scrutinizing.

The results showed that participants sought information that would confirm their self-conceptions. Just as those who saw themselves as assertive asked to examine more questions that probed for evidence of assertive feedback than unassertive feedback, those who saw themselves as unassertive asked to examine more questions that probed for evidence of unassertive feedback than assertive feedback. Similarly, those who perceived themselves as emotional preferentially solicited emotional feedback, and those who saw themselves as unemotional preferentially solicited unemotional feedback.

Swann and Read (1981a) conducted two followup investigations to assess the generality and nature of this preference for self-confirmatory feedback. One study showed that males and females were equally likely to manifest a desire for self-confirmatory feedback, and that participants were even willing to relinquish their private funds to acquire such feedback. Another study indicated that participants regarded self-confirmatory feedback as especially informative and diagnostic with respect to the type of persons they were.

The message emerging from this research is simple and clear cut: People not only prefer information that confirms their self-conceptions, they translate this preference into active efforts to acquire such information. The next section of this paper identifies some specific strategies people utilize in their quest for self-confirmatory feedback.

THE SELF-SUSTAINING SELF

In the tradition of several theorists within both other perception (e.g., Bruner, 1951; Darley & Fazio, 1980; Hogarth, 1981), and nonsocial perception (e.g., Gregory, 1970, 1973; Levine, 1975; Neisser, 1976), I assume here that the self-perception process is continuous and cyclical. In this cycle, the relationship between people's self-perceptions and behavior is a symbiotic one; just as their behavior allows them to determine the validity of their perceptions, their perceptions provide them with guides to behavior. As Powers (1973) has noted, "What an organism does affects what it senses and what it senses affects what it does" (see also Carver & Scheier, 1982; Wiener, 1948). From this perspective, the self-perception process constitutes a feedback loop, in which people's self-conceptions influence their actions, which channel the reactions of others, which in turn serve as a basis for people's subsequent inferences about themselves, and so on.

The nature of the self-perception process can be even more clearly understood by noting that it is akin to a *negative* feedback loop. In cybernetic theory, a negative feedback loop is one that serves to negate or minimize perceived deviations from a comparison value (e.g., Powers, 1973). The comparison value in self-perception is the self-concept. Hence, each successive cycle of the self-perception process will tend to minimize discrepancies between the self-concept and the social realities that sustain it. (For related discussions, see Heise, 1979; Stryker & Gottlieb, 1981; Watzlawick, Beavin, & Jackson, 1967.)

As can be seen in Figure 4-1, I assume that there are two major links in the chain of events by which people sustain their self-views: the behavioral activities through which people develop a self-confirmatory opportunity structure and the

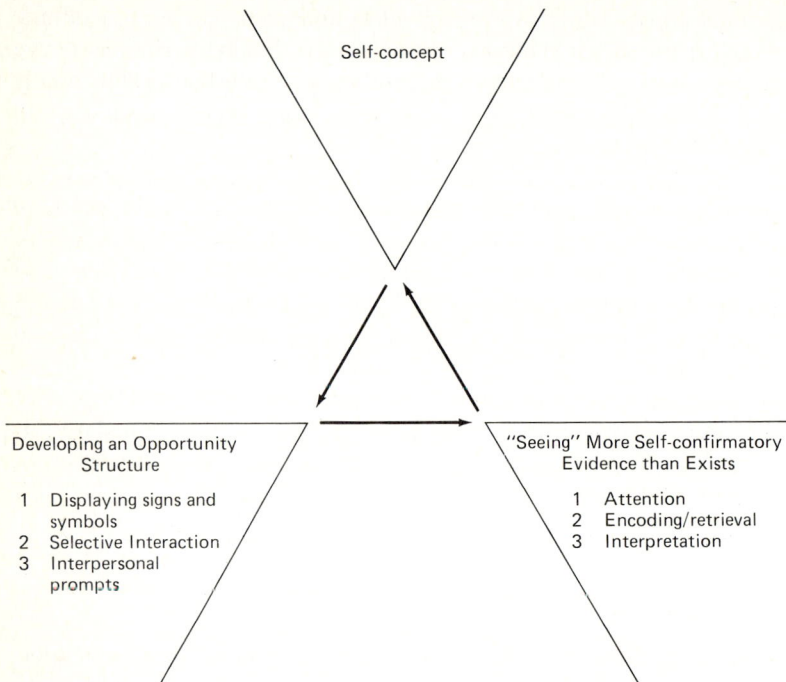

FIGURE 4-1
Self-Verification Processes. This figure is taken from Swann, W. B., Jr., Self-verification: Bringing social reality into harmony with self, which appeared in J. Suls & A. G. Greenwald (Eds.), *Psychological Perspectives on the Self,* Vol. 2, Hillsdale, N.J.: Erlbaum.

cognitive activities whereby people process the information they receive. In this section I will first discuss the strategies through which people develop an opportunity structure.

Developing a Self-Confirmatory Opportunity Structure

Sociologists have long assumed that people tend to inhabit social environments that offer support for their self-concepts. One of the first to articulate this viewpoint was Goffman (1955):

> Whatever his position in society, the person insulates himself by blindnesses, half-truths, illusions and rationalizations. He makes an "adjustment" by convincing himself, with the tactful support of his intimate circle, that he is what he wants to be . . . he need only be careful about the expressed judgments he places himself in a position to witness. Some situations and acts and persons will have to be avoided . . . (p. 230).

More recently, McCall and Simons (1966) have elaborated Goffman's (1955) position by drawing an analogy between the social environments people inhabit and the "ecological niches" (e.g., Clarke, 1954; Odum, 1963) in which animals live. They propose that both human and nonhuman organisms gravitate toward environments that routinely satisfy their needs. Humans, of course, differ from nonhumans in that they are motivated to confirm their self-concepts. Toward this end, they try to develop social environments that nurture their self-views. McCall and Simons have used the term "opportunity structure" to refer to such environments.

People can employ a number of strategies in their efforts to develop a self-confirmatory opportunity structure. Consider, for example, a self-conceived macho man who decides to attend a beach party. In the weeks prior to the party, he takes steps to ensure that when he arrives, everyone will recognize him for the brute that he is. Through hours of feverish weight lifting, the purchase of tight-fitting clothes, and the loan of a friend's machomobile, he takes on highly visible signs and symbols of his machismo. In this way, he makes certain that when he makes his appearance at the party, most are quick to notice his masculine virtues. But he does not stop there. As he begins to circulate, he is careful to seek out and mingle with the "right" people. He is drawn to bicep worshipers like a magnet; at the same time, he avoids these who appear unappreciative of bulging muscles. And even if this strategy fails to ensure that he receives the reactions he craves, he may still acquire such reactions through his style of interaction. By striking his weight-lifter's pose and grunting his most ferocious grunt, he may induce even the most myopic or inebriated guest to marvel at his uncanny resemblance to the Incredible Hulk.

This hypothetical example suggests that there are three distinct strategies through which people may develop a self-confirmatory opportunity structure: They may display signs and symbols of who they are, they may seek out individuals whose appraisals confirm their self-views, and they may adopt interaction strategies that elicit self-confirmatory reactions. For a more detailed account of each of these strategies as well as relevant empirical evidence, see Swann (1983).

"Seeing" More Self-Confirmatory Evidence Than Actually Exists

As effective as the strategies through which people develop self-confirmatory opportunity structures may be, there are surely times when such strategies run aground. Does this mean the end of the line for the self-concept in question? Perhaps not. Consider the contentions of Prescott Lecky (1945):

> ... All of an individual's values are organized into a single system the preservation of whose integrity is essential. The nucleus of the system, around which the rest of the system revolves, is the individual's valuation of himself. ... *Any value entering the*

system which is inconsistent with the individual's valuation of himself cannot be assimilated; it meets with resistance and is likely, unless a general reorganization occurs, to be rejected (pp. 152–153, my italics).

In more contemporary language, Lecky believed that people's information-processing activities are structured in ways that foster the survival of their self-views. In support of this viewpoint, recent research suggests that self-concepts do indeed exert a powerful channeling influence on people's information-processing activities (e.g., Greenwald, 1982). Take, for example, a business executive who thinks of herself as shrewd, astute and hardworking—all in all, a force to be reckoned with. If she is to maintain her self-concept, her coworkers and subordinates must confirm her view of self by treating her with deference and respect. But even if they occasionally greet her suggestions with snickers and jeers, she may still cling to her self-view by engaging in several distinct activities. For one, she may attend closely when her coworkers display signs of admiration but look the other way when she fears that a less favorable reaction is headed her way. Also, in thinking back to past interactions with her employees, she may remember successful transactions in perfect detail but completely forget the worker revolt she once confronted. Finally, even if she does faithfully recall an ugly encounter with an insubordinate employee, she may soften the blow by interpreting it in ways that make it compatible with her belief that she is an effective administrator.

This business executive's experiences suggest that people's selective attention, encoding, retrieval, and interpretation processes may work to ensure that their self-concepts will survive even in the face of a mountain of discrepant evidence. (For a review of relevant research, see Swann [1983].) In the following section, I will attempt to reconcile the existence of these and other strategies of self-verification with recent contentions that people strive to enhance their self-esteem.

SELF-ENHANCEMENT VERSUS SELF-VERIFICATION

My position in this chapter is that people are highly motivated to maintain their self-concepts. So, for example, people with positive self-views act so as to maintain favorable self-views and those with negative self-views act so as to maintain unfavorable self-views. As such, the self-verification formulation is rooted in the self-consistency theories of Lecky (1945) and Secord and Backman (1961, 1965).

An equally influential school of thought within social psychology argues that people are motivated to acquire self-enhancing feedback. Self-enhancement theorists begin by assuming that all people are motivated to bolster their feelings of personal worth and value. This need is believed to be especially strong among people with negative self-concepts, because the need for positive feedback is frequently frustrated among such individuals (e.g., Jones, 1973; Kaplan, 1975).

Both self-consistency and self-enhancement formulations predict that people with positive self-views will prefer positive feedback. The reasons underlying this prediction differ for the two theories, however. Whereas self-consistency theory assumes that positive feedback is preferred by people with favorable self-views because it fulfills a desire for information that *confirms* their self-views, self-enhancement theory assumes that positive feedback is preferred because it fulfills a desire for information that *bolsters* people's self-views. The two theories make competing predictions when it comes to individuals with negative self-views. Whereas the self-consistency approach argues that low self-esteem individuals should prefer negative feedback, the self-enhancement approach suggests that such individuals should prefer positive feedback. This has led researchers and theorists to ask which theoretical viewpoint offers a better characterization of the way people actually think and behave.

One of the most popular reactions to the impasse between these competing theoretical positions has been to assert that both self-consistency and self-enhancement motives exist and that each will manifest itself under the proper conditions (e.g., Epstein, 1982). One problem with this approach is that its advocates have generally failed to provide a means of specifying when one motive will predominate over the other. Without such specifications, it is impossible to know which motive will control behavior, thereby defeating the purpose of postulating the motives in the first place.

Shrauger (1975) has made one of the few attempts to specify the conditions under which each motive will control behavior. He has reviewed evidence indicating that "cognitive" measures such as recall tend to yield consistency effects, whereas "affective" measures such as participants' liking of individuals who have evaluated them yield enhancement effects. Although Shrauger's (1975) argument fits the data reasonably well, it is not without drawbacks. One is that even in those studies that have focused on cognitive measures, people with positive self-views have typically displayed stronger consistency effects than those with negative self-views. A second problem is that Shrauger failed to explain *why* the consistency motive should control cognitive responses and the enhancement motive should control affective responses. In what follows I shall attend to both of these problems in turn.

Low Self-Esteem, Self-Uncertainty, and the Cognitive-Affective Crossfire

As mentioned above, a nagging problem for advocates of the self-consistency position has been that the preference for unfavorable feedback displayed by people with negative self-concepts is generally weaker than the preference for favorable feedback displayed by those with positive self-concepts. (For just two examples, see Experiments 2 and 3 in Swann & Read, 1981b.) One reason for this may be that people in our society typically have rather positive self-views. Hence, when researchers divide people in their samples into relatively high and low self-esteem individuals, the "lows" are only low in a *relative* sense; on an absolute scale, the lows often think rather favorably of themselves (e.g., Swann, Griffin, & Ely, 1983).

The prevalence of favorable self-views in our society probably reflects the fact that children generally receive positive feedback from their caretakers (e.g., Fagot, 1978; Langlois & Downs, 1980). In addition, there appears to be a powerful norm in our society against conveying negative information to others (e.g., Blumberg, 1972; Tesser & Rosen, 1975). This means that whether people are children or adults, they usually receive positive feedback. It is consequently little wonder that people with truly negative self-concepts are rather rare in our society.

Social sanctions against delivering negative feedback may also ensure that when people do encounter negative feedback, they will receive it in small, intermittent doses. As a result, of those who do develop negative self-views, most will typically base these views on weak and inconsistent evidence. This should make them highly uncertain of their negative self-views. In fact, we (Swann, Griffin, & Ely, 1983) have recently collected data that supports this hypothesis. In our sample of University of Texas undergraduates, we found that of the few individuals who had truly negative self-views, most were very uncertain of these views. These data are important because theoretically people should verify a self-concept only after they become at least somewhat certain that it is correct, since only then will the self-concept be useful in predicting and controlling their social worlds (cf. Lecky, 1945). Therefore, insofar as most people with low self-esteem are highly uncertain of their negative self-views, these individuals should not systematically verify these views.

Although there is no evidence that bears directly on the links between self-esteem, self-certainty, and self-verification, Maracek and Mettee (1972) have reported some suggestive evidence. These investigators recruited a group of individuals who thought poorly of themselves and were either high or low in self-certainty. The experimenter provided both of these groups with success feedback and induced them to attribute it to either luck or skill. He then monitored their subsequent performance. Among individuals who were low in self-certainty, there was no evidence of self-verification: In both the luck and skill conditions they sought to elicit highly positive evaluations. Among the highly self-certain individuals, those who attributed their success to luck made no efforts to verify their negative self-concepts. Presumably, because they could attribute their performance to luck, the positive feedback did little to threaten their belief in their own incompetence. It was a different story for highly self-certains who attributed their success to skill. These individuals apparently regarded their successes as a threat to their self-concept and responded by going out of their way to perform poorly, thereby bolstering their conviction that they were incompetent.

Together with the results of the Swann, Griffin, and Ely (1983) study, the Maracek and Mettee (1972) data make it easy to understand why researchers have encountered so much difficulty documenting self-verification phenomena among college students low in self-esteem. For people to prefer highly negative feedback, they must possess self-views that are relatively certain as well as highly negative. Although these conditions are undoubtedly present in some clinical populations, they are usually not present in college-student populations.

And if people verify negative self-views only when they are somewhat certain of them, then it is impossible to equate *manipulated* low self-esteem with *chronic* low self-esteem. That is, in some studies the investigators have attempted to induce low self-esteem by having participants perform some task and then giving them bogus negative feedback. Manipulating self-esteem in this manner is very different from measuring people's self-concepts because a dose (or even four doses, as in Jones & Schneider, 1968) of negative feedback should not put individuals into the same psychological state as those whose self-reports indicate that they have experienced a lifetime of negative feedback. This will be especially true if recipients of the bogus feedback happen to have chronic high self-esteem. At the very most, such manipulations might make individuals with high self-esteem wonder if their positive self-view is really accurate—a state of high uncertainty. It is therefore not surprising that most studies in which self-esteem has been manipulated rather than measured seem to support self-enhancement theory. (For reviews, see Jones, 1973; Shrauger, 1975.)

But if the neglect of the self-certainty variable can explain why self-consistency effects have been more difficult to demonstrate among low as compared to high self-esteem individuals, it cannot explain why measures of cognition are apt to yield consistency effects, whereas measures of affect yield enhancement effects (e.g., Shrauger, 1975). The answer to this puzzle may emerge from considering recent evidence indicating that cognitive and affective responses are controlled by independent mental systems that are centered in different areas of the brain. Zajonc (1980) has recently argued that whereas people's cognitive responses are controlled by higher-order mental processes and goal systems that involve fairly sophisticated learning processes, their affective responses are driven by lower order, relatively primitive neural mechanisms. This suggests that only people's cognitive responses will be influenced by the desire for predictability and control, because a great deal of learned information is required to differentiate predictable and unpredictable phenomena. Meanwhile, people's affective responses will vary according to more basic characteristics of the stimulus, such as whether it seems likely to benefit or harm them. One result of the distinct priorities associated with the two systems might be that low self-esteem individuals would appear to find unfavorable feedback cognitively pleasing but affectively abhorrent. This is, of course, the picture that Shrauger (1975) painted of the low self-esteem individual in his review of the literature.

In the final analysis, I suspect that the only way to resolve the consistency-enhancement debate once and for all will be to carefully analyze the activities of individuals in clinical populations, since these individuals should have self-views that are both highly certain and highly negative. If my analysis is correct, these individuals should appear rather ambivalent because they are caught in a crossfire between their cognitive and affective responses. That is, even as their cognitions urge them to maintain the status quo, their feelings demand that they take steps to improve their situation. In fact, the anecdotal and experimental evidence reviewed in the next section supports this characterization of the negative self-concept individual.

Self-Verification in Psychopathological Populations

Whether one reads Adler (1927), Jung (1952), Horney (1950), Rogers (1961), or Sullivan (1953), one discovers that changing self-concepts is a central goal of the therapeutic process. However, despite the importance that many therapists attribute to self-concept change, the research literature suggests that therapy often has little lasting impact on people's self-concepts. (For a recent review, see Wylie, 1979.) One of the first to discuss the difficulties involved in reshaping people's modes of construing themselves and social reality was Sigmund Freud (1921):

> When we undertake to cure a patient, to free him from the symptoms of his malady, he confronts us with a vigorous, tenacious resistance that lasts during the whole time of the treatment. This is so peculiar a fact that we cannot expect much credence for it. . . . Just consider, this patient suffers from his symptoms and causes those about him to suffer with him. . . . And yet he struggles, in the very interests of his malady, against one who would help him. How improbable this assertion must sound! (p. 248).

As improbable as such resistance phenomena may seem, they are precisely what one would expect from the perspective of the self-verification formulation. Recent experimental research has in fact shown that depressed persons engage in several specific cognitive and behavioral processes that could be construed as evidence of resistance. Several studies have indicated that depressives process information in ways that tend to perpetuate their negative self-views. Roth and Rehm (1980), for example, have reported that depressed patients in a Veterans Administration hospital asked to scrutinize evidence chose that evidence that was relevant to failure experiences more often than nondepressed patients. In a similar vein, several researchers have found that relative to nondepressed controls, depressives recall negative information more quickly (e.g., Lloyd & Lishman, 1975) and more thoroughly (e.g., Buchwald, 1977; Derry & Kuiper, 1981; Nelson & Craighead, 1977; Wener & Rehm, 1975).

Other aspects of depressives' information-processing activities may also play a part in the verification of their negative self-concepts. Kuiper and McDonald (1982), for instance, have discovered that depressives offer higher estimates of the frequency of negative situations and outcomes than normals. Similarly, several researchers (Abramson, Alloy & Rosoff, in press; Alloy & Abramson,

1979, 1982) have discovered that depressed people have much less faith in their ability to control personally relevant events than do those who are not depressed. Finally, still others (Seligman, Abramson, Seinmel, & von Baeyer, 1979) have shown that depressives are especially inclined to attribute negative outcomes to internal, stable, and global causes and positive outcomes to external, unstable, causes.

At least part of the pessimism displayed by depressives may be well-founded. Coyne and his colleagues (e.g., Coyne, 1976a; 1976b; Strack & Coyne, 1982) have reported that depressives may behave in ways that turn the individuals in their opportunity structures against them. After even the briefest of interactions, depressed people are able to generate anxiety and hostility in their interaction partners. Not surprisingly, the negative mood states that depressives evoke in others make them prime candidates for rejection.

To make matters worse, it is probably the case that people who reject depressed persons do so in ways that exacerbate one of the depressives' major symptoms—an excessive need for social support. (For evidence of a link between depression and need for support, see Coyne, Aldwin, & Lazarus, in press; Schaefer, Coyne, & Lazarus, in press.) The unhappy chain of events may proceed as follows. Driven by an affectively based desire for positive feedback, depressed individuals attempt to elicit support from their interaction partners. Unfortunately, they fail to elicit genuine support, because their interaction partners are generally rejecting or because their social ineptness gets in the way (e.g., Youngren & Lewinsohn, 1980). They are not rejected outright, however, because most people feel compelled to follow social norms that discourage them from giving others direct negative feedback (e.g., Blumberg, 1972; Tesser & Rosen, 1975). Instead, others provide them with positive verbal responses but negative nonverbal responses (e.g., Gottlieb & Robinson, 1982). These mixed messages then serve to further increase their feelings of ambivalence (cf. Bateson, Jackson, Haley, & Weakland's [1956] analysis of the role of the "double bind" in the etiology of schizophrenia).

Perhaps the most ironic aspect of the depressive's plight is that efforts to release such individuals from the self-perpetuating cycles in which they are trapped may produce just the opposite of the effect intended. Shrauger (1983), for example, has noted that therapy sessions typically focus on what is "wrong" with the client. By forcing clients to dwell on their inadequacies and problems, therapists may inadvertently fuel the negative self-conceptions that their clients had hoped to improve.

But even if therapists employed highly effective strategies in their efforts to bolster the self-esteem of individuals who seek therapy, properties of their clients' opportunity structures may militate against *permanent* self-concept change. In particular, people may often surround themselves with individuals who act to undermine any lasting changes in their self-views. This process can be seen most readily in the case of intimate relationships as well as those between parents and children.

SELF-VERIFICATION IN INTIMATE AND PARENT-CHILD RELATIONSHIPS

Some of the most important mechanisms through which people sustain their self-concepts are those by which they develop self-confirmatory opportunity structures. Their intimates and family members are among the most important figures in their opportunity structures because such individuals are apt to command high levels of credibility and affective involvement.

In the case of intimate relationships, the processes whereby people bring their partners to treat them in a self-confirmatory manner are usually initiated very early. In fact, the initial months of such relationships can be understood as training periods during which both persons let one another know who they are and how they expect to be treated. If both parties communicate their desires clearly and each finds the terms of the relationship acceptable, an arrangement or "working consensus" will emerge that will be relatively difficult to modify thereafter (cf. Goffman, 1955). Jackson (1965) has put it this way:

> Couples . . . who may engage in wondrously varied behavioral plays during courtship, undoubtedly achieve considerable economy after a while in terms of what is open to dispute and how it is to be disputed. Consequently they seem . . . to have mutually excluded wide areas of behavior from their interactional repertoire and never quibble further about them (p. 13).

By establishing such implicit agreements as to one another's mutual identities, people may insure that they more or less automatically receive self-confirmatory feedback. Consider the case of Tommy, the battered child introduced in the opening pages of this chapter. One thing I noticed about Tommy was the rather bizarre relationship he had with another boy whom the counselors referred to as "Crazy Louis." We called Louis "crazy" because he had a disturbing habit of brutalizing the other children. Most everyone learned very quickly that it was best to stay clear of Louis. Not Tommy. Time and again, Tommy sought him out and Louis would oblige by subjecting Tommy to all sorts of verbal and physical abuse.

It was strange enough that Tommy made Louis his most frequent companion. What was really paradoxical to me was the soothing effect that Tommy's interactions with Louis sometimes seemed to have on Tommy. For example, if Tommy won at a game and received a compliment, he would often seem very confused and agitated. The only thing that settled Tommy down was to interact with Louis for a while. It seemed that being browbeaten by Louis reaffirmed Tommy's negative self-concept, thereby buffering him against any threatening self-discrepant feedback he might receive.

Among many of us, a similar buffering function may be performed by our intimates. For example, consider the person who comes home and cries out, "Is it true? Am I getting fat?" The perceptive spouse will know exactly what to say, "Be serious, honey, your body is in great shape. What are you worrying about?" Of course, not all of us are so lucky. Some may find that their spouses enhance their anxiety by saying something such as, "Well, you know, you *could* stand to lose a couple hundred pounds. But don't worry about it; people stopped looking at that old body of yours years ago."

Although most of us would certainly prefer the first, highly supportive loved one, it unfortunately does not always work out that way. And which type of intimate we wind up with will have important consequences for the stability of our self-concept. An intimate who has a congruent view of us will help us sustain our self-view, just as Crazy Louis sustained Tommy's self-view. However, an intimate who has an incongruent view of us will tend to undermine our self-view.

Toni Giuliano and I (Swann & Giuliano, 1982) tested these notions in our research. All participants had completed a measure of self-perceived dominance at the beginning of the semester and had been in an intimate relationship for an average period of 15 months. Each participant reported to the experiment with his or her intimate. Upon arrival, the participant and intimate were separated and the subject played a game with a confederate. There was a break between the games during which the confederate delivered discrepant feedback to the participant. Thus, confederates delivered submissive feedback to participants who rated themselves as dominant during the pretest. "You really don't seem to be the forceful, dominant type." In contrast, confederates delivered dominant feedback to participants who rated themselves as submissive during the pretest. "You really seem to be the forceful, dominant type."

After the feedback manipulation, there was an interruption and either the participants' intimate or an opposite-sexed stranger entered the room for a 4-minute, unstructured interaction. Finally, the experimenter assessed the participant's self-view.

We were interested in whether having an opportunity to interact with their intimates after receiving self-discrepant feedback would diminish the amount of self-rating change participants experienced. The answer was yes and no. If there was a relatively small discrepancy between the participant's self-view and the participant's estimate of the intimate's view of the participant, then interacting with the intimate served to buffer the participant against the discrepant feedback. That is, participants who interacted with a congruent intimate displayed virtually no self-rating change. In contrast, if there was a relatively large discrepancy between the participant's self-view and the participant's estimate of the intimate's view of the participant, interacting with the intimate resulted in a great deal of self-rating change, much more change than occurred if the participant interacted with a complete stranger. In sum, participants who interacted with a congruent intimate tended to display the least amount of self-rating change of all participants in the study, participants who interacted with a noncongruent intimate evidenced the most amount of change of all participants in the study, and those who interacted with strangers displayed moderate amounts of change.

An especially interesting implication of these data is that they suggest that if people arrange their lives properly, they can acquire self-confirmatory feedback without having to seek it actively each time. That is, once people manage to locate someone who sees them in a congruent manner, all they need do is keep the relationship alive, and they will be guaranteed self-confirmatory feedback to protect them in their hour of need. Of course, if they fail to locate such a person, they will probably be upset about it and look for a replacement. In fact, Laing, Phillipson, & Lee (1966) have reported that relationships characterized by noncongruency are unhappy ones. (See also Harvey, Wells, & Alvarez, 1978; Knudson, Summers, & Golding, 1980; Orvis, Kelley, & Butler, 1976; Sillars, 1981.)

It is noteworthy that intimates may be instrumental in verifying unhealthy as well as healthy self-concepts. Fry (1962), for example, has noted that husbands and wives who enter therapy have often established implicit agreements that allow the husband to verify his belief that he is the healthier, more competent individual in the relationship and the wife to verify her belief that she is the sick, dependent individual. Once the agreement has been reached, both parties actively work to honor it, even if it requires that the wife bear the responsibility for a debilitating pathology that is as much her husband's as her own:

> The spouses reveal, upon careful study, a history of symptoms closely resembling, if not identical to, the symptoms of the patient. Usually they are reluctant to reveal this history. For example, a wife was not only unable to go out alone, but even in company she would panic if she entered a brightly lighted and/or crowded place or had to stand in line. Her husband disclaimed any emotional problems of his own at first, but then revealed he experienced occasional episodes of anxiety and so avoided certain situations. The situations he avoided were: being in crowds, standing in line, and entering brightly lighted public places. However, both marriage partners insisted the wife should be considered the patient because she was *more* afraid of these situations than he was.
>
> In another case the wife was labeled the patient because she was afraid of enclosed places and could not ride in elevators. Therefore, the couple could not visit a cocktail lounge on the top of a tall building. However, it was later revealed that the husband had a fear of high places which he never needed to face because of the marital agreement that they never went to the tops of buildings because of the wife's fear of elevators. (p. 248).

The underlying dependency of the "dominant partner" on the "dependent partner" in such relationships often becomes manifest when the dependent partner attempts to break the contract. A case in point is the relationship between a mother, "Mrs. Field," and her daughter "June," described by Laing and Esterson (1960). June was born with a dislocation of her hip which severely curtailed her activities. Surprisingly, her mother recalled June's predicament in a lighthearted manner:

Mother: Oh yes, she was *always* with me, always. Well, naturally I wouldn't leave her because of her irons in case she fell on anything. She did fall as a matter of fact, she knocked her front teeth out . . . she had good leather straps

on because she's always been a very strong child and I had a dog lead here and a dog lead there, then June could move freely up and down. . . . As I say, she was always a boisterous child, she's always been such a happy little girl, haven't you June?
June: Mmm.
Mother: Yes you have dear. (p. 135–6).

From Mrs. Field's perspective, all went well with June until, at age 14, she went to a girl's camp organized by the church. This was the first time that her mother and June had been separated since June was hospitalized for surgery at the age of two. In this radically different opportunity structure, June began to realize that she was not as helpless and dependent as her mother believed her to be. When she returned home, June began to tentatively assert herself as an individual. Almost everyone, including her sister, father, and teacher, regarded the change in June as the normal manifestations of an individual who had finally come to realize that she could function on her own. Mrs. Field, however, decided that June's emerging independence was a sign of mental illness. Any efforts June made to assert her emergent autonomy were greeted with vehement resistance by her mother. The whole situation grew quite volatile and culminated with June being hospitalized for catatonia. When she finally left therapy, June was still locked in a vicious struggle with her mother over her right to independence.

Just as the spouses described by Fry (1962) were dependent on the survival of their partner's self-view, Mrs. Field was quite dependent on the continued existence of her daughter's view of self. In the instance of Mrs. Field, it was probably the case that her daughter's self-conceived dependence allowed her to verify the belief that she was a caring mother. In any event, it is clear that any attempts to redefine such symbiotic relationships can be extremely disruptive. In fact, in some instances intervention can lead to the termination of the relationship. As Watzlawick, Beavin, & Jackson (1967) have noted, this often creates an awkward position for therapists who are asked to treat individuals involved in such relationships. That is, therapists may fear that the relationship will end if they succeed in altering the self-views of one of the clients, leaving them with a "successful operation" but a "dead patient."

Together, the Swann and Giuliano (1982) research and the case studies described in this section suggest that the self-verifying properties of people's interaction partners may have positive as well as negative consequences. For adults who are satisfied with their existing self-views, a self-verifying intimate can be quite handy. After all, it is probably quite adaptive for people to have someone around who will serve to stabilize their self-concepts, especially because people's self-concepts may figure so importantly in their efforts to predict and control their worlds. However, for individuals like June, who began to develop a new self-concept after exposure to a different opportunity structure, an interaction partner who is unwilling to be flexible may seriously impede the change process. This raises a separate issue: If people are generally motivated to verify their self-views, why should they ever want to change them? This issue will be addressed next.

CHANGES IN SELF-CONCEPTS

As Nigel Dennis's (1955) *Cards of Identity* opens, the lead character, a caretaker, goes to look in on some tenants. He is drugged and when he awakens, he finds everyone responding to him as if he were the house butler. Then something remarkable happens. After a brief period of confusion, the caretaker comes to accept the idea that he is a butler. For the remainder of the book, he takes on this new identity and behaves accordingly.

The central thesis of Dennis' book is that people will modify their self-views in response to changing inputs from the social environment. The idea that the self is rooted in the social environment is certainly a familiar one to social psychologists, having won acceptance long ago with the publication of Cooley (1962) and Mead's (1934) seminal monographs. In the context of this chapter, this notion is important because it suggests that people's self-views will change only if a corresponding shift occurs in their social environment.

The process of self-concept change may be set in motion in either of two ways. As in Dennis's novel, one or more outside agents may begin treating the person in a self-discrepant manner. Alternatively, individuals may themselves decide that their self-definition or some other factor requires that they modify some aspect of their behavior or lifestyle. Later, such modifications may produce a shift in their self-view. I will consider self-concept changes that are produced by outside agents first.

Self-Concept Change Induced by Outside Agents

Outside agents may take steps to change a person's self-concept if they believe that it is somehow deficient, dysfunctional or inappropriate. A good example of this is the therapy situation wherein the therapist tries to induce the client to adopt a more positive self-view. Such self-concept changes are apt to be extremely difficult to effect, because individuals suffering from various pathological conditions may count on their negative self-concept as a means of predicting and controlling their social environments. The trick is to somehow bring people to see themselves in a more favorable light without posing a serious threat to the integrity of their self-concept. One way to do this is to structure their environment so that they have success experiences that they can attribute to chance. Although people should theoretically attribute such random success to chance, they may eventually come to view themselves more positively—the "lucky me" phenomenon (cf. Maracek & Mettee, 1972).

Change attempts may also occur in the context of parent-child relations. Parents, for example, may sometimes encourage their children to develop new, more mature, images of themselves ("You are a big girl now. Stop behaving like a 2-year old"). Such parent-assisted identity changes are just one example of a more general phenomenon: Whenever it becomes necessary or appropriate for someone to take on a new role or status, the socialization community will see to it that the target individual adopts a suitable identity. In fact, the identity transformation process may be construed as a key aspect of role change and status passage (cf. Secord & Backman, 1965).

Whether outside agents actually succeed in their efforts to modify an individual's self-view depends on a number of factors. One important variable is the potency of the feedback that the agents utilize. Feedback will be potent to the extent that it is (a) delivered by a source who is credible (e.g., Webster & Sobieszek, 1974), (b) not so farfetched that it is dismissed as ridiculous or absurd (e.g., Eagly, 1967), (c) directly related to the self-concept (Maehr, Mensing, & Nafzger, 1962; Videbeck, 1960), and (d) delivered by a large rather than small number of people (e.g., Backman, Secord, & Pierce, 1963).

Even highly potent feedback may fail to modify a self-concept if the individual is highly certain of that self-concept, because people should theoretically be quite invested in, and hence motivated to verify, highly certain self-concepts. A study by Swann & Ely (1984) supports this viewpoint. In this investigation, some participants ("perceivers") were first led to form erroneous beliefs about other participants ("targets"). That is, perceivers interacting with targets who viewed themselves as extroverts were led to believe that targets were introverted. Perceivers interacting with targets who viewed themselves as introverts were informed that targets were extroverts. Perceivers then interviewed targets in a series of three sessions.

After all the individuals in this study had participated, a team of undergraduate judges rated audiotapes of the interviews between perceivers and targets. The results indicated that targets who were certain of their self-concepts steadfastly refused to provide behavioral support for perceivers' erroneous expectancies. Even targets who were uncertain of their self-concepts offered only modest behavioral evidence to buttress perceivers' expectancies. Furthermore, when perceivers rated targets after the three sessions, the vast majority had brought their expectancies into line with targets' actual characteristics. Therefore, few targets in their study—especially those who were certain of their self-concepts—fell victim to the well-known "self-fulfilling prophecy" effect (e.g., Kelley & Stahelski, 1971; Rosenthal, 1976; Snyder, 1981). That is, only rarely were perceivers able to constrain the actions of targets in ways that caused their initial expectancies to come true. In light of these data, it is perhaps not surprising that some of the most compelling demonstrations of such self-fulfilling prophecies used targets with relatively uncertain self-concepts—that is, children (e.g., Rosenthal & Jacobson, 1968).

To the extent that people are able to resist erroneous characterizations of themselves as Swann and Ely's (1984) participants were, they should experience little self-rating change. For example, the self-conceived macho man who overhears himself referred to as "that wimp" may subsequently reassure himself by showing just how tough and ferocious he can be. By engaging in such activity, he may convince himself (and perhaps others as well) that he is the man he thought he was; consequently, he should display little self-rating change. In contrast, if individuals receive self-discrepant feedback and are then given no opportunity to refute that feedback, they will be at a relative disadvantage in generating highly salient evidence with which to dismiss the feedback. They may therefore align their subsequent self-ratings to the feedback. In such instances, self-rating change should be substantial.

Craig Hill and I tested this reasoning (Swann & Hill, 1982). We first collected a measure of participants' self-perceived dominance during a pretesting session at the beginning of the semester. We chose this dimension of the self-concept because other research (Swann, Griffin, & Ely, 1983) indicated that most individuals are fairly certain of their position on this dimension. The actual experimental sessions began with participants playing a game in which each player alternately assumed the dominant "leader" role or the submissive "assistant" role. There was a break between the games, and the experimenter asked the two players who would like to be the leader for the next set of games. This was the cue for the confederate to deliver the feedback manipulation. Within some conditions she indicated that the participant seemed dominant: ". . . You really seem to be the forceful, dominant type. . . ." Within the other conditions, she asserted that the participant seemed rather nondominant: ". . . You really don't seem to be the forceful, dominant type. . . ."

How did participants react to this feedback? The key was whether the feedback confirmed or disconfirmed their self-conceptions. If the feedback confirmed their self-conceptions, they did not do much of anything; they more or less passively accepted the confederate's appraisal. In contrast, if the feedback disconfirmed their self-conceptions, they reacted quite vehemently, resisting the feedback and bending over backwards to demonstrate that they were not the persons the confederate made them out to be. That is, self-conceived dominants who were labeled nondominant became all the more dominant, and self-conceived submissives displayed just the opposite reactions.

But this is just half the story. In this study we were also interested in the psychological consequences of allowing participants to resist the feedback they received. And so, after they interacted with the confederate, we asked participants to complete the same self-conceived dominance scale that they completed earlier in the semester. This allowed us to assess whether or not the self-discrepant feedback caused participants to change their self-conceptions. We compared their scores with those of participants in a control group who had also received self-discrepant feedback but did not have an opportunity to interact with the confederate.

The results were clear cut. For individuals who received self-discrepant feedback and then had no opportunity to interact with the confederate who delivered the feedback, self-concept change was considerable. However, for those who received self-discrepant feedback and then *did* have an opportunity to interact with the source of feedback, self-conception change was minimal.

These data point to three conclusions. First, when people receive self-discrepant feedback, their standard reaction may be to stand up and refute it.

Second, people will reject any feedback that is *inconsistent* with their self-conceptions; feedback does not need to be negative for people to reject it, as many investigators have assumed (e.g., Dutton & Lake, 1973; Farina, Allen, & Saul, 1968; Sherman & Gorkin, 1980; Steele, 1975). Third, when people have occasion to resist self-discrepant feedback, they will not be inclined to change their self-concepts.

An interesting feature of the Swann and Hill (1982) study was that individuals who had an opportunity to resist the discrepant feedback displayed little self-rating change even though they did not believe that they had succeeded in modifying the confederates' appraisal of them. Apparently, simply being able to observe themselves act in a self-consistent manner was enough to reaffirm participants' self-concepts (cf. Bem, 1972; Schlenker, 1982).

The results of this study suggest that people will change fairly certain self-concepts only when they receive self-discrepant feedback in social environments in which they have little opportunity to influence or resist the treatment they receive. Moreover, other research has shown that even if people are trapped in environments that are hostile to their existing self-views, once they escape these environments their self-concepts will revert back to their initial status (e.g., Swann & Hill, 1983). In light of this evidence, it is not surprising that clinicians and field researchers alike have reported that it is extremely difficult to produce lasting and substantial changes in people's self-concepts, at least among adults. (For reviews, see Shrauger & Shoeneman, 1979; Wylie, 1979.)

Self-Initiated Self-Concept Change

If outside agents often experience difficulty changing the self-views of individuals, this does not mean that self-concept change is exceedingly rare. Instead, self-concept changes are often brought about by the actions of individuals themselves. Many of these changes can be understood by considering the processes whereby people formulate and execute self-relevant plans. My basic assumption here is that people often structure their plans so as to insure the continued availability of self-confirmatory feedback. For example, just as the woman who construes herself as dedicated to helping others may plan to earn a medical degree, the man who thinks of himself as a superior scientist may set out to win a Nobel prize.

Once people formulate a given plan, there are at least three pathways that they could follow that would ultimately lead them to change their self-concept. Consider a fledgling tennis player who has set his sights on winning the yearly tournament at Wimbledon. One chain of events that might lead him to change his self-concept would be if his plans were thwarted. For example, if after years of trying it became clear that he would never win *any* tournament, let alone Wimbledon, he might rechannel his energies into becoming a businessman or dentist. Such a shift would be apt to produce substantial self-concept change, since his new aspirational identity would bring him into contact with a new group of people who would treat him differently, demand that he behave differently, and provide a new set of standards against which to evaluate himself.

Even if he achieved his goal of winning at Wimbledon, he would still be at risk of self-concept change. As George Bernard Shaw has noted, "There are two great tragedies in life. One is not to get your heart's desire. The other is to get it." For the triumphant tennis player "tragedy" would strike when he recognizes that he cannot go on winning tournaments forever. And so, he may eventually decide to become a sports commentator or tennis instructor or tennis coach. Although these new endeavors would not promote as radical a shift in his self-concept as would becoming a dentist, they would alter his self-concept somewhat by influencing his behavior, reference group, and the treatment he receives from others. (See also Schlenker, this volume.)

Another mechanism underlying self-concept change may be set in motion when people pursue a goal that is compatible with one component of their self-concept but not another. Low self-esteem individuals who are low in self-certainty, for example, may strive to eliminate the discrepancy between their cognitively based belief that they are incompetent and their affectively based desire to be respected. Towards this end, they may consciously set out to become a proficient artist, lawyer, or racketball player. They may then pursue such goals by attempting to develop the requisite abilities. If they become more proficient at the task they have designated for themselves, they may gradually modify their self-view accordingly. The artistically inclined individual may come to regard herself as a recognized artist; the verbally facile individual may realize that he has become an accomplished lawyer; the gifted athlete may acknowledge that at this point she is a racketball star.

Of course, it is not always possible for people to improve their self-concepts in this manner. At the very least, target persons must have some native ability in the endeavor in question—extremely short persons will never become basketball stars. Also, individuals must be sufficiently uncertain of the negative self-concept that they do not categorically dismiss contradictory evidence. This means that it will be difficult to modify the self-concepts of people who are highly certain of their negative qualities. Finally, self-concept changes must be accompanied by corresponding shifts in the individual's social environment or opportunity structure. No matter how convinced individuals become of their personal worth, they will have difficulty sustaining positive self-views if their friends and acquaintances constantly greet them with ridicule and abuse.

Lest it seem that I believe that the process of self-concept change is always orderly and planful, let me hasten to add that *some* self-concept changes probably occur quite inadvertently. Consider Becker's (1960, 1964) and Hormuth's (1983) contentions that in pursuing various goals people often become involved in activities that ultimately alter their self-concepts. For example, in striving to become a competent oceanographer, an individual may become enamored with scuba diving. As Vallacher and Wegner (in press) have noted, in such instances a new "action identity" may emerge that overshadows the identity that was initially prepotent; the would-be oceanographer may shift from identifying her activities as "becoming an oceanographer" to "enjoying the life of a scuba diver." If she then dismisses her former career plans in favor of a life devoted to teaching scuba diving on an island in the Caribbean Sea, her new action identity may eventually lead to major revisions in her self-concept.

These examples clearly illustrate that the notion of self-concept change is quite compatible with the self-verification formulation. As long as people remain in touch with the social world around them and are attentive to their capacity for future development, their self-concepts will undergo change. Nevertheless, the self-verification formulation suggests that such changes will not occur rapidly, nor will they take place without substantial reorganization of the person's knowledge system and interpersonal environment. But this is surely for the best. If it were the case that our self-concepts changed at the drop of a hat, the world would be an unpredictable and frightening place indeed.

REFERENCES

Abramson, L. Y., Alloy, L. B., & Rosoff, R. (in press). Depression and the generation of complex hypotheses in the judgment of contingency. *Behavior Research and Therapy*.

Adler, A. (1927). *The practice and theory of individual psychology*. New York: Harcourt, Brace, & World.

Alloy, L. B., & Abramson, L. Y. (1979). Judgment of contingency in depressed and nondepressed students: Sadder but wiser? *Journal of Experimental Psychology: General, 108*, 441–485.

Alloy, L. B., & Abramson, L. Y. (1982). Learned helplessness, depression, and the illusion of control. *Journal of Personality and Social Psychology, 42*, 1114–1126.

Backman, C., Secord, P., & Pierce, J. (1963). Resistance to change in the self-concept as a function of consensus among significant others. *Sociometry, 26*, 102–111.

Bateson, G., Jackson, D. D., Haley, J., & Weakland, J. (1956). Toward a theory of schizophrenia. *Behavioral Science, 1*, 251–264.

Becker, H. S. (1964). Personal change in adult life, *Sociometry, 27*, 40–53.

Becker, H. S. (1960). Notes on concept of commitment. *American Journal of Sociology, 66*, 32–40.

Bem, D. J. (1972). Self-perception theory. In L. Berkowitz (Ed.), *Advances in experimental social psychology* (Vol. 6). New York: Academic Press.

Blumberg, H. H. (1972). Communication of interpersonal evaluations. *Journal of Personality and Social Psychology, 23*, 157–162.

Bruner, J. S. (1951). Personality dynamics and the process of perceiving. In R. R. Blake & G. V. Ramsey (Eds.), *Perception—an approach to personality*. New York: Ronald Press.

Buchwald, A. M. (1977). Depressive mood and estimates of reinforcement frequency. *Journal of Abnormal Psychology, 86*, 443–446.

Carver, C. S., & Scheier, M. F. (1982). Control theory: A useful conceptual framework for personality, clinical and health psychology. *Psychological Bulletin, 92*, 111–135.

Clarke, G. L. (1954). *Elements of ecology*. New York: Wiley.

Cooley, C. H. (1902). *Human nature and the social order*. New York: G. Scribner's Sons.

Coyne, J. C. (1976a). Depression and the response of others. *Journal of Abnormal Psychology, 85,* 186–196.

Coyne, J. C. (1976b). Toward an interactional description of depression. *Psychiatry, 39,* 28–40.

Coyne, J. C., Aldwin, C., & Lazarus, R. S. (in press). Depression and coping in stressful episodes. *Journal of Abnormal Psychology.*

Darley, J. M., & Fazio, R. H. (1980). Expectancy confirmation processes arising in the interaction sequence. *American Psychologist, 35,* 867–881.

Dennis, N. F. (1955). *Cards of identity.* London: Weidenfeld Nicholson.

Derry, P. A., & Kuiper, N. A. (1981). Schematic processing and self-reference in clinical depression. *Journal of Abnormal Psychology, 90,* 286–297.

Dutton, D. G., & Lake, R. A. (1973). Threat of own prejudice and reverse discrimination in interracial situations. *Journal of Personality and Social Psychology, 28,* 94–100.

Eagly, A. H. (1967). Involvement as a determinant of response to favorable and unfavorable information. *Journal of Personality and Social Psychology Monograph, 7* (3, Pt. 2).

Epstein, S. (1973). The self-concept revisited: Or a theory of a theory. *American Psychologist, 28,* 404–416.

Epstein, S. (1983). The role of the unconscious in an individual's self-system. In J. Suls & A. G. Greenwald (Eds.), *Psychological perspectives on the self* (Vol. 2). Hillsdale, NJ: Erlbaum.

Fagot, B. I. (1978). The influence of the child on parental reactions to toddler children. *Child Development, 49,* 459–465.

Farina, A., Allen, J. G., & Saul, B. (1968). The role of the stigmatized person in affecting social relationships. *Journal of Personality, 36,* 169–182.

Festinger, L. (1954). A theory of social comparison processes. *Human Relations, 7,* 117–140.

Freud, S. (1921). *A general introduction to psychoanalysis.* New York: Boni & Liverwright.

Fry, W. F., Jr. (1962). The marital context of the anxiety syndrome. *Family Process, 1,* 245–252.

Goffman, E. (1955). On face work: An analysis of ritual elements in social interaction. *Psychiatry, 18,* 213–221.

Gottlieb, I. H., & Robinson (1982). Responses to depressed individuals: Discrepancies between self-report and observer-rated behavior. *Journal of Abnormal Psychology, 91,* 231–240.

Greenwald, A. G. (1982). Self and memory. In G. H. Bower (Ed.), *Psychology of learning and motivation* (Vol. 15). New York: Academic Press.

Gregory, R. L. (1970). *The intelligent eye.* New York: McGraw-Hill.

Gregory, R. L. (1973). The confounded eye. In R. L. Gregory & E. H. Gombrinch (Eds.), *Illusion in nature and art.* London: Duckworth.

Harvey, J. H., Wells, G., & Alvarez, M. (1978). Attribution in context of conflict and separation in close relationships. In J. H. Harvey, W. Ickes, and R. F. Kidd (Eds.), *New directions in attribution research* (Vol. 2). Hillsdale, NJ: Erlbaum.

Heise, D. R. (1979). *Understanding events: Affect and the construction of social action.* Cambridge: Cambridge University Press.

Hogarth, R. M. (1981). Beyond discrete biases: Functional and dysfunctional aspects of judgmental heuristics. *Psychological Bulletin, 90,* 197–217.

Hormuth, S. E. (1983). Transitions in commitments to roles and self-concept change:

Relocation as a paradigm. In V. Allen & E. van de Vliert (Eds.), *Role transitions*. New York: Plenum.

Horney, K. (1953). *Neurosis and human growth*. New York: Norton.

Hovland, C. I., & Weiss, W. (1953). Transmission of information concerning concepts through positive and negative instances. *Journal of Experimental Psychology, 45*, 175–182.

Jackson, D. D. (1965). The study of the family. *Family Process, 4*, 1–20.

Jones, S. C. (1973). Self and interpersonal evaluation: Esteem theories versus consistency theories. *Psychological Bulletin, 79*, 185–199.

Jones, S. C. & Schneider, D. J. (1968). Certainty of self-appraisal and reactions to evaluations from others. *Sociometry, 31*, 395–403.

Jung, C. G. (1953). *Collected Works*. H. Read, M. Fordham, & G. Adler (Eds.), Princeton: Princeton University Press.

Kaplan, H. B. (1975). Prevalence of the self-esteem motive. In H. B. Kaplan (Ed.), *Self-attitudes and deviant behavior*. Pacific Palisades, CA: Goodyear.

Kelley, H. H., & Stahelski, A. J. (1970). The social interaction basis of cooperators' and competitors' beliefs about others. *Journal of Personality and Social Psychology, 16*, 66–91.

Knudsen, R. M., Summers, A. A., & Golding, S. L. (1980). Interpersonal perception and mode of resolution in marital conflict. *Journal of Personality and Social Psychology, 38*, 751–763.

Koriat, A., Lichenstein, S., & Fischoff, B. (1980). Reasons for confidence. *Journal of Experimental Psychology: Human Learning and Memory, 6*, 107–118.

Kuiper, N. A., & MacDonald, M. R. (1982). Self and other perception in mild depressives. *Social Cognition, 1*, 223–239.

Laing, R. D., & Esterson, A. (1964). *Sanity, madness, and the family* (Vol. 1). London: Tavistock Publications.

Laing, R. D., Phillipson, H., & Lee, A. R. (1966). *Interpersonal perception: A theory and a method of research*. New York: Springer.

Langlois, J. H., & Downs, A. C. (1980). Mothers, fathers, and peers as socialization agents of sex typed play behaviors in young children. *Child Development, 51*, 1217–1247.

Lecky, P. (1945). *Self-consistency: A theory of personality*. New York: Island Press.

Levine, M. (1975). *A cognitive theory of learning: Research on hypothesis testing*. Hillsdale, NJ: Erlbaum.

Lloyd, C. G., & Lishman, W. A. (1977). Effect of depression on the speed of recall of pleasant and unpleasant experiences. *Psychological Medicine, 5*, 173–180.

Maehr, M. L., Mensing, J., & Nafzager, S. (1962). Concept of self and the reaction of others. *Sociometry, 25*, 353–357.

Marecek, J., & Mettee, D. R. (1972). Avoidance of continued success as a function of self-esteem, level of esteem certainty, and responsibility for success. *Journal of Personality and Social Psychology, 22*, 98–107.

Mead, G. H. (1934). *Mind, self and society*. Chicago: University of Chicago Press.

McCall, G. J., & Simmons, J. L. (1966). *Identities and interactions: An examination of human associations in everyday life*. New York: The Free Press.

Neisser, U. (1976). *Cognition and reality*. San Francisco: Freeman.

Nelson, R. E., & Craighead, W. E. (1977). Selective recall of positive and negative feedback, self-control behavior and depression. *Journal of Abnormal Psychology, 86*, 379–388.

Odum, E. P. (1963). *Ecology*. New York: Holt, Rinehart, & Winston.

Orvis, B. K., Kelley, H. H., & Butler, D. (1976). Attributional conflict in young couples. In J. H. Harvey, W. Ickes, & R. F. Kidd (Eds.), *New directions in attribution research* (Vol. 1). Hillsdale, NJ: Erlbaum.

Powers, W. T. (1973). *Behavior: The control of perception.* Chicago: Aldine.

Rogers, C. R. (1961). *On becoming a person: A therapists' view of psychotherapy.* Boston: Houghton Mifflin Co.

Rosenthal, R. (1976). *Experimenter effects in behavioral research.* New York: Irvington.

Rosenthal, R., & Jacobson, L. (1968). *Pygmalion in the classroom: Teacher expectations and pupils' intellectual development.* New York: Holt, Rinehart, & Winston.

Roth, D., & Rehm, L. P. (1980). Relationships among self monitoring processes, memory, and depression. *Cognitive Therapy and Research, 4,* 149–157.

Schaefer, C., Coyne, J. C., & Lazarus, R. S. (in press). The health-related functions of social support. *Journal of Behavioral Medicine.*

Schlenker, B. R. (1982). Translating actions into attitudes: An identity-analytic approach to the explanation of social conduct. In L. Berkowitz (Ed.), *Advances in experimental social psychology (Vol. 15).* New York: Academic Press.

Schoeneman, T. J., Tabor, L. E., & Nash, D. L. (1981). Children's perceptions of the sources of self-knowledge. Paper presented at the meeting of the American Psychological Association, August.

Secord, P. F., & Backman, C. W. (1961). Personality theory and the problems of stability and change in individual behavior: An interpersonal approach. *Psychological Review, 68,* 21–32.

Secord, P. F., & Backman, C. W. (1965). An interpersonal approach to personality. In B. A. Maher (Ed.), *Progress in Experimental Personality Research,* (Vol. 2). New York: Academic Press.

Secord, P. F., & Backman, C. W. (1966). *Social psychology.* New York: McGraw-Hill.

Seligman, M. E. P., Abramson, L. Y., Semmel, A., & von Baeyer, C. (1979). Depressive attributional style. *Journal of Abnormal Psychology, 88,* 242–247.

Sherman, S. J., & Gorkin, L. (1980). Attitude bolstering when behavior is inconsistent with central attitudes. *Journal of Experimental Social Psychology, 16,* 388–403.

Shrauger, J. S. (1975). Responses to evaluation as a function of initial self-perceptions. *Psychological Bulletin, 82,* 581–596.

Shrauger, J. S. (1982). Selection and processing of self-evaluative information: Experimental evidence and clinical implications. In C. Bradeley & H. Mirels (Eds.), *Integrations of clinical and social psychology,* New York: Oxford.

Shrauger, J. S., & Schoeneman, T. J. (1979). Symbolic interactionist view of self-concept: Through the looking glass darkly. *Psychological Bulletin, 86,* 549–573.

Sillars, A. L. (1981). Attributions and interpersonal conflict resolution. In J. H. Harvey, W. Ickes, & R. F. Kidd (Eds.), *New directions in attribution research* (Vol. 3). Hillsdale, NJ: Erlbaum.

Snyder, M. (in press). On the self-perpetuating nature of social stereotypes. In P. L. Hamilton (Ed.), *Cognitive processes in stereotyping and intergroup behavior.* Hillsdale, NJ: Erlbaum.

Steele, C. M. (1975). Name calling and compliance. *Journal of Personality and Social Psychology, 31,* 361–369.

Strack, S., & Coyne, J. C. (1982). Social confirmation of dysphoria: Shared and private reactions. Unpublished manuscript, University of California at Berkeley.

Stryker, S., & Gottlieb, A. (1981). Attribution theory and symbolic interactionism: A comparison. In J. Harvey, W. Ickes, and R. Kidd, (Eds.), *New Directions in Attribution Research* (Vol. 3). Hillsdale, NJ: Lawrence Erlbaum Associates.

Sullivan, H. S. (1953). *The interpersonal theory of psychiatry.* New York: Norton.
Suls, J., & Mullen, B. (1982). From the cradle to the grave: Comparison and self-evaluation across the life-span. In J. Suls (Ed.), *Psychological perspectives on the self.* Hillsdale, NJ: Erlbaum.
Swann, W. B., Jr. (1983). Self-verification: Bringing social reality into harmony with the self. In J. Suls & A. G. Greenwald (Eds.), *Psychological perspectives on the self* (Vol. 2). Hillsdale, NJ: Erlbaum.
Swann, W. B., Jr., & Ely, R. (1984). A battle of wills: Self-verification versus behavioral confirmation. *Journal of Personality and Social Psychology.*
Swann, W. B., Jr., & Giuliano, T. (1982). How our intimates stabilize our self-views. Paper presented at the annual meetings of the American Psychological Association, Washington, D.C.
Swann, W. B., Jr., & Giuliano, T. (1983). Confirmatory search strategies in social interaction: Why, how and with what consequences. Unpublished manuscript, University of Texas at Austin.
Swann, W. B., Jr., Griffin, J. J., & Ely, R. (1983). Self-certainty and self-regard. Unpublished manuscript, University of Texas at Austin.
Swann, W. B., Jr., & Hill, C. A. (1982). When our identities are mistaken: Reaffirming self-conceptions through social interaction. *Journal of Personality and Social Psychology, 43,* 59–66.
Swann, W. B., Jr., & Hill, C. A. (1983). The temporal stability of changes in self-ratings. Unpublished manuscript, University of Texas at Austin.
Swann, W. B., Jr., & Read, S. J. (1981a). Acquiring self-knowledge: The search for feedback that fits. *Journal of Personality and Social Psychology, 1,* 39–44.
Swann, W. B., Jr., & Read, S. J. (1981b). Self-verification processes: How we sustain our self-conceptions. *Journal of Experimental Social Psychology, 17,* 351–372.
Tesser, A., & Rosen, S. (1975). The reluctance to transmit bad news. In L. Berkowitz (Ed.), *Advances in experimental social psychology* (Vol. 8). New York: Academic Press.
Vallacher, R. R., & Wegner, D. M. (in press). *A theory of action identification.* Hillsdale, NJ: Erlbaum.
Videbeck, R. (1960). Self-conception and the reaction of others. *Sociometry, 23,* 351–359.
Watzlawick, P., Beavin, J. H., & Jackson, D. D. (1967). *Pragmatics of human communication: A study of interactional patterns, pathologies & paradoxes.* New York: Norton.
Webster, M., & Sobieszek, B. I. (1974). *Sources of self-evaluation: A formal theory of significant others and social influence.* New York: Wiley.
Wegner, D. M., & Vallacher, R. R. (1977). *Implicit psychology: An introduction to social cognition.* New York: Oxford University Press.
Wener, A., & Rehm, L. P. (1975). Depressional affect: A test of behavioral hypothesis. *Journal of Abnormal Psychology, 84,* 221–227.
Wiener, N. *Cybernetics.* (1948). New York: Wiley.
Wylie, R. (1961). *The self-concept.* Lincoln, NE: University of Nebraska Press.
Youngren, M. A., & Lewinsohn, P. M. (1980). The functional relation between depression and problematic interpersonal behavior. *Journal of Abnormal Psychology, 89,* 333–341.
Zajonc, R. B. (1980). Feeling and thinking: Preferences need no inferences. *American Psychologist, 35,* 151–175.

CHAPTER 5

TO WHOM IS THE SELF PRESENTED?

Anthony G. Greenwald and Steven J. Breckler
Ohio State University

Many psychologists have answered the question posed in this chapter's title by saying that the audience for self-presentation is an outer audience, an audience of *other persons*. Goffman (1959) states that "when an individual appears in presence of *others*, there will usually be some reason for him to mobilize his activity so that it will convey an impression to *others* which it is in his interests to convey" (p. 4, emphasis added). Similarly, Jones and Pittman (1982) define strategic self-presentation as "those features of behavior . . . designed to elicit or shape *others*' attributions of the actor's dispositions" (p. 233, emphasis added). And Baumeister (1982) considers self-presentation to be "aimed at establishing . . . an image of the individual in the minds of *others*" (p. 3, emphasis added).

In this chapter we make the case for an alternative view in which a primary audience for self-presentation is oneself. We refer to this as the inner-audience hypothesis. The presented self is, in terms of the inner-audience hypothesis, a true, privately accepted self—not one that is harboring, deep down, a less worthy being that it hopes to prevent others from discovering. (The idea of an inner audience for self-presentation has also been discussed by Schlenker, 1980, and by Snyder, Higgins, & Stucky, 1983.)

Our argument starts by first establishing that the presented self is (usually) too good to be true. We then show that the (too) good self is often genuinely believed, by showing that self-descriptions are self-enhancing in private (and also under other conditions that should yield honest reporting). We do not intend, however, for the inner-audience hypothesis to replace the prior outer-audience view. Rather, we regard both audiences—as well as one more that we introduce below—as important. Our major aim is to show this multiply oriented character of the presented self, to which end we show that self-presentations are variably directed to different audiences, as a function of both situational and personal variables.

THE PRESENTED SELF IS (USUALLY) TOO GOOD TO BE TRUE

Beneffectance

In a recent review, Greenwald (1980) interprets the self (or ego) as an organization of knowledge that is characterized by three information-control strategies. The three strategies, or cognitive biases, are (1) *beneffectance,* the tendency for self to be perceived as effective in achieving desired ends while avoiding undesired ones, (2) *cognitive conservatism,* the tendency to resist cognitive change, and (3) *egocentricity,* the tendency for judgment and memory to be focused on self. The constellation of these three biases was labeled the "totalitarian ego," acknowledging that the biases match ones that are considered to be characteristic of the information-control strategies of a totalitarian dictatorship. Perhaps the most important of these three cognitive biases is *beneffectance* (a term fabricated from *benefi*cence [doing good] and ef*fectance* [competence]). Beneffectance is the cognitive bias of perceiving oneself as selectively responsible for desired or successful outcomes. The beneffectance bias is manifest in self-descriptions that are typically more favorable than can be justified by objective information—in other words, a self that is too good to be true.

Four lines of research indicate the pervasiveness of this beneffectance bias in the normal personality. These are (1) the tendency to recall successes more readily than failures (Glixman, 1949; Rosenzweig, 1943), (2) the acceptance of responsibility for successes but not for failures on individual or group tasks (Johnston, 1967; Miller & Ross, 1975; Schlenker & Miller, 1977; Snyder, Higgins, & Stucky, 1983; Weary Bradley, 1978; Wortman, 1976); (3) denial of responsibility for harming others (Harvey, Harris, & Barnes, 1975), and (4) the tendency to identify with victors and disaffiliate with losers ("basking in reflected glory") (Cialdini et al., 1976; Tesser & Campbell, 1983).

Absence of Beneffectance in Depressives

Although manifestations of beneffectance are frequently observed in research, it is not always so. An interesting set of exceptions occurs in research with depressed subjects. Lewinsohn et al. (1980) compared depressed and normal subjects' self-ratings with similar ratings of them made by observers. Normals rated themselves more favorably than did observers, consistent with the usual beneffectance pattern. It was expected that depressed subjects would rate themselves less favorably than would observers. However, the obtained finding was that depressed subjects rated themselves *objectively,* in the sense of judging themselves no more nor less favorably, on average, than did observers. Alloy and Abramson (1979) found similarly that, after succeeding on a probabilistic experimental task over which they objectively had little control, normal subjects overestimated the extent of their control. In contrast, depressed subjects perceived their relatively low level of control more accurately, and (unlike normals) did not perceive greater control for successful than unsuccessful performances. The contrast with the "realism" of depressed subjects quite strikingly highlights the self-enhancing bias of normals.

THE (TOO) GOOD SELF IS OFTEN GENUINELY BELIEVED

We here develop four predictions based on the proposition that subjects genuinely believe the favorable self-presentations that they typically make. First, when self-reports are made in private and are believed to be anonymous, subjects should have little reason to mispresent themselves. Therefore, if favorable presentations occur even in the absence of any public audience, it would appear that they are honest. Second, if the experimenter is believed to have accurate data on characteristics for which self-reports are requested, subjects should be specially motivated to be honest. If favorable self-presentations are undiminished by such an honesty constraint, it would then appear that these presentations are genuinely believed. Third, judgments that are intentionally falsified should take longer to make than ones that are truthfully reported. Therefore, if subjects routinely give favorable reports more rapidly than other self-judgments, it would seem likely that these reports are truthful. Finally, although it may make a good appearance to present oneself as having control over an experimental task, it is neither impressive to others nor personally satisfying to persevere at a task at which one truly expects to fail. Therefore, if subjects who report that they have control over a task also work persistently at that task, it would appear that they believe in their control. We now proceed to review evidence that confirms *all* four of these predictions.

Self-Attributions Are Favorable in Private as well as in Public

Weary (Weary Bradley, 1978) reviewed the literature on self-serving biases in attribution. A self-serving bias is typically manifest in subjects' taking personal credit for favorable outcomes, while blaming unfavorable outcomes on external forces (e.g., bad luck, task difficulty, or interference by others). In all the studies reviewed by Weary Bradley, subjects made causal attributions for favorable and unfavorable outcomes only under conditions of experimenter or other observation. It was therefore plausible that observed self-enhancing self-reports were intended to impress others. More recently, however, several studies have examined attributions for success and failure made under private as well as public conditions. In a study by Weary Bradley et al. (1982), subjects showed self-enhancing biases, surprisingly, *only* when their attributions were made in private. Public self-presentations were apparently distorted, not in the direction of self-enhancement, but in the direction of modesty. In another study, Schlenker, Hallam, and McCown (1983) investigated actor-observer differences in attributions made for the positive act of helping another. Self-enhancement occurred about equally under public and private conditions. Findings of self-enhancement under private reporting conditions have also been obtained by Arkin, Appleman, Burger (1980), Frey (1978), and Greenberg, Pyszczynski, & Solomon (1982). From all these studies it appears that beneffectance is at least as much in the service of maintaining private self-regard as it is in the service of one's public image.

Favorable Self-Attributions Occur under Strong Constraint to be Honest

Whether or not lie detectors work they can be powerful elicitors of honesty simply because many people assume that they do (or may) work. This phenomenon provides the basis for the laboratory device known as the "bogus pipeline," which is little more than a set of electrodes that appear to be attaching a subject to some recording equipment. (Jones & Sigall, 1971, originally described the bogus pipeline; Quigly-Fernandez & Tedeschi, 1978, have provided evidence for its effectiveness in creating a powerful constraint toward honest self-reporting.) The bogus pipeline was used in a study of self-enhancing attributions by Riess, Rosenfeld, Melburg, and Tedeschi (1981). In that study, half of the college student subjects were led to believe that they had done well on a supposed social intelligence test, and the remainder were informed that they had done poorly. In the "reliable bogus pipeline" condition, subjects were persuaded that the response apparatus could detect false responses. In the "unreliable bogus pipeline" condition, subjects were told that the apparatus was unreliable. In a third condition, subjects learned nothing about the apparatus. After being connected to the apparatus, subjects were asked questions that elicited attributions regarding their performance on the social intelligence test. The reliable bogus pipeline condition was the one that should have eliminated any dishonest responding. Thus, if beneffectance is due to falsified self-presentations, a self-enhancing bias should have been observed in only the other two conditions. However, a beneffectance pattern—in the form of both attributing successes more to internal factors (ability and effort) than to external ones (easy task or good luck), and attributing failures more to external than internal factors—was obtained in *all three* conditions. Riess et al. concluded "that so-called self-serving attributions are not merely misrepresentations . . . in the service of self-presentation. Instead, this attributional asymmetry seems to reflect actual bias in *private* perceptions of objective causality" (p. 229, emphasis added).

Favorable Self-Referent Judgments Are Made Rapidly

Markus (1977) and Rogers, Kuiper, and Kirker (1977) have demonstrated that information central to one's self-concept is processed rapidly. A similar finding reported by Breckler and Greenwald (1981) relates directly to the inner-audience hypothesis. They found that favorable self-referent judgments are made faster than unfavorable ones. This latency effect is in agreement with the assumption that favorable self-referent information is (usually) central to the self-concept. If favorable self-referent judgments were falsified, then one would expect that the latencies of those judgments would be slowed by the cognitive demands of fabricating. An interesting contrast with Breckler and Greenwald's findings comes from research on the self-referent judgments of depressed subjects. Derry and Kuiper (1981) have shown that depressives are most efficient in processing *un*favorable self-relevant information. They concluded that, for depressives, negative information is central to the self-concept.

Self-Enhancing Judgments Are Acted Upon

Subjects who expect to succeed at a task will work persistently at it (Bandura, 1982; Brown & Inouye, 1982; Feather, 1961), suggesting that they truly believe that they will eventually succeed. Similarly, high self-esteem subjects—who presumably have a high expectation of success—persevere longer at difficult tasks (McFarlin & Blascovich, 1981; Shrauger & Sormon, 1977) and actually do better than their low self-esteem counterparts (Shrauger & Rosenberg, 1970). Individuals high in achievement motivation (McClelland et al., 1953), compared to those low in achievement motivation, spend more time attempting to solve difficult problems (Feather, 1962). Also, Weiner (1965) reported that subjects high in need for achievement continued to persevere at difficult problems after failing to solve earlier ones, whereas those low in need for achievement gave up following their initial failure. Weiner and Kukla (1970) have observed that such performance differences are associated with divergent causal attributions. Persons who ordinarily expect to succeed (such as those high in achievement motivation) attribute their poor performance to lack of effort, whereas those who ordinarily expect to fail most often attribute their poor performance to lack of ability. (See also Diener & Dweck, 1978, 1980; Dweck & Repucci, 1973.) In sum, the research evidence indicates that people who report personal responsibility for success (those high in self-esteem and high in achievement motivation) persevere as if they genuinely believe in their self-efficacy.

EGO TASK ANALYSIS—FOUR FACETS OF THE SELF

The preceding sections have developed the distinction between inner and outer audiences for self-presentations. This distinction was recently associated (by Greenwald, 1982a) with two meanings of ego involvement that could be identified in research done between the mid-1930s and the early 1960s.

Ego Involvement$_1$ Concern about public impression, or evaluation by outer audiences; similar to evaluation apprehension, need for approval.

Ego Involvement$_2$ Concern about self-evaluation, private self-image, or evaluation by the inner audience; similar to self-esteem maintenance, need for achievement.

Greenwald also noted a third use of ego involvement, but he did not (at the time) associate it with a specific evaluative audience. This third sense of ego involvement originated in the work of Sherif and Cantril (1947), and has been used in subsequent work that was influenced by their treatment, especially in research on persuasive communication (e.g., Sherif, Sherif, & Nebergall, 1965).

Ego Involvement$_3$ Personal importance, linkage to central values.

In this section we extend the analysis of audiences for self-presentations to accommodate the third type of ego involvement. We do this by identifying a third type of audience, one that contains both inner and outer components—the reference group. Reference groups serve as the source of the central values that are mentioned in the definition of ego involvement. Having identified this third audience, we proceed to relate the three audiences to an analysis of facets of the self[1]—one directed to the outer audience (the public facet of the self), one directed to the inner audience (the private facet), and one directed to the reference-group audience (the collective facet). (There is also a fourth, more primitive, facet—the diffuse self—that has no identifiable audience.) The analysis of audiences for self-presentation and their associated facets of the self is rooted in the concept of an *ego task,* which is the persisting task of earning the approval of a significant audience (Greenwald, 1982a).

Ego Task Analysis—A Framework for Describing Person-Situation Interaction

Task Analysis Figure 5-1 presents basic concepts of *task analysis,* which offers a model of the interaction of situation and personality in determining behavior. Figure 5-1 shows behavior as a direct function of two cognitive task components, *goals* and *strategies.* The goal component is determined jointly by incentives in the situation and by the person's goal preferences. Similarly, the strategy component is influenced both by situational influences (instructions, the behavior of others) and by personal preferences among strategies.

Greenwald (1982a) used the game of golf as an illustration of the way in which goals and strategies are jointly determined by situation variables and person variables. In golf, *goals* are *situation*ally determined by the rules of the game, the layout of the course, and the performance of other players. Goals can also be determined by *person*al preferences, such as expectations based on past performance, and relative concerns about hitting for distance, hitting with good form, and minimizing score. Similarly, *strategies* are determined *situation*ally (by design of the course, lie of the ball, and instructions from teachers or playing companions) and *person*ally (by previous practice and ability to hit various strokes).

---

[1] We refer, in this discussion, to *the self* without having said just what we mean by that term. In the conception that guides the present analysis, the self is a complex entity that has cognitive, affective, and conative components. Ego-task analysis is concerned just with the conative, or motivational, aspect of the self. For a treatment that places ego-task analysis in the context of the self's other components, see Greenwald and Pratkanis (1984).

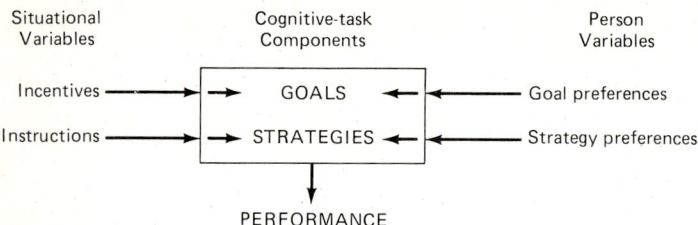

FIGURE 5-1
Basic concepts of task analysis (after Greenwald, 1982a).

Ego Tasks An ego task is an important, persisting task that provides a basis for self-evaluation. It is an important task in the sense that the goal of an ego task will take precedence over the goals of most other tasks. It is a persisting task in the sense that obtaining the goal does not end the task—the goal continues to be important. Greenwald initially identified three types of ego tasks, one based on each type of ego involvement. In the present extension of ego task analysis, we introduce new designations for the three major ego tasks and we analyze each ego task as a distinct (motivational) facet of the self.

Four (Motivational) Facets of the Self

Table 5-1 summarizes our extension of ego-task analysis. This analysis is based on the identification of four ego tasks, or *facets* of the self, which we believe to develop in the left-to-right order of the table.[2] The *diffuse self* is, in some senses, a preself, a condition of not distinguishing sharply between self and others, with behavior hedonically guided toward positive affective states. The *public self* is sensitive to the evaluations of others and seeks to win the approval of significant outer audiences of parents, peers, and authorities. Developmentally, the public self depends on achievement of a cognitive discrimination between self and others, and an ability to attend to those aspects of one's behavior that are also noticed by others. The ego task of the public self can be described, in part, as social accreditation—that is, earning credit in exchange relationships with others. However, another important aspect of the public self's task is to internalize the evaluative standards of significant others. This self-definition aspect of the public self's task leads to development of the *private self*. By providing an inner audience for behavior, the private self permits self-evaluation to be effected in the absence of others. We designate the private self's ego task as individual achievement, with "achievement" being used, in the sense of

---

[2]It should be noted that our speculation that the four facets of the self develop in the left-to-right order of Table 5-1 is partly at odds with others' suggestions that the private self developmentally precedes the public self (Buss, 1980; Cheek & Hogan, 1983). (See Loevinger, 1976, for a broad review of theories of ego development.)

McClelland et al. (1953), to indicate guidance by internal standards. As a further developmental step, the goals of groups with which the person is identified (reference groups) become internalized, yielding the *collective self*. The collective self is a *we* facet of the self, in contrast to the *I* facet of the private self and the *you-they* facet of the public self. The collective self's task is a collective-achievement task, the task of achieving a reference group's attainment of its goals.

Strategies in the Service of Ego Tasks

Winning a Nobel Prize or an Olympic gold medal are, we would guess, strongly satisfying experiences. Perhaps they are so satisfying because they simultaneously serve the interests of a public self, a private self, and a collective self. That is, they simultaneously earn the approval of others, achieve success by personal standards, and signify fulfillment of a reference group's goal. Many everyday achievements, similarly, serve two or more ego tasks simultaneously. Examples are being promoted in one's job, earning a college degree, winning in competitive sports, and raising children. If all human endeavors simultaneously pleased inner and outer audiences and achieved group goals, we could be sure that the ego task analysis of Table 5-1 would be useless. But that is not the case.

Interestingly, some of the everyday activities that focus on one ego task correspond well to tasks that have been cultivated for use in the social psychological laboratory. In particular, the procedures of experiments on conformity, obedience, and persuasion characteristically put the subject in a dilemma that pits the public self against the private self. That is, concern about approval by an outer audience pulls behavior in the direction of conformity, obedience, and opinion moderation. At the same time, the attempt to adhere to the private standards of the inner audience pulls in the opposite direction of independence, defiance, and opinion resistance.

The Diffuse and Collective Selves

The pattern of entries in Table 5-1 indicates that the facets identified as diffuse and collective selves have been relatively neglected in social-psychological research. Nevertheless, there is sufficient evidence to justify their inclusion in Table 5-1 and to encourage further research efforts.

The diffuse self has been investigated in research on *deindividuation*, which is a condition in which one's individual identifiability is decreased, and internal constraints against various types of action tend to be reduced. Previous reviewers' observations about paradoxical aspects of deindividuation (Diener, 1977, 1980; Dipboye, 1977) were summarized by Greenwald (1982b):

> Deindividuation is sometimes associated with loss of identity but other times with acquisition of identity via a distinctive group (of which one is an indistinguishable member); it is sometimes sought but other times avoided; and it is sometimes

TABLE 5-1
INTERRELATION OF FACETS OF THE SELF, EGO TASKS, PERSONALITY MEASURES, EXPERIMENTAL PROCEDURES, AND PERFORMANCE STRATEGIES

Facets of Self	Diffuse Self	Public Self	Private Self	Collective Self
Ego task designation	Hedonic satisfaction	Social accreditation; Self-definition	Individual achievement	Collective achievement
Basis for self-evaluation	Attainment of positive affect	Approval of others (outer audience)	Internal standards (inner audience)	Internalized goals of reference group
Individual difference measures of task orientation		Public self-consciousness; Need for approval; High self-monitoring	Private self-consciousness; Need for achievement; Low self-monitoring	
Situation inducers of task orientation	Anonymity in group; Drug intoxication	Minority status in group; Solo before audience; Camera; Public failure	Privacy; Exposure to performance replay; Mirror; Private failure	Reference group salience; Cohesive group; Superordinate goals
Strategies in service of task	Norm violation	Conformity; Obedience; Opinion moderation; Basking in reflected glory	Independence; Defiance; Opinion resistance	

associated with chaotic, norm-violating behavior but other times with conforming, uniform behavior (p. 172).

This paradox can be resolved with the aid of the distinction between the diffuse and the collective selves. All deindividuating conditions, including anonymity, alcohol intoxication, and strong stimulation, reduce the salience of internal standards. However, some of these situations can make the subject's participation in a reference group salient—for example, being amidst a shouting crowd of home-team supporters at a football game, or wearing a uniform that hides one's individual features, while making one's group affiliation apparent. Deindividuation procedures that make a reference group salient can engage the collective self, leading to coordinated or norm-adhering behavior. This is in contrast to nonsocial conditions—for example, alcohol intoxication or being in a darkened room—which can engage the diffuse self, leading to social chaos or norm-violating behavior. Greenwald suggested that the term "deindividuation" be restricted to the effects of nonsocial procedures that elicit norm-violating behavior—ones that (in present terms) invoke the diffuse self.

In contrast to the modest amount of (deindividuation) research on the diffuse self, the collective self has received almost no research attention from social psychologists, apart from the contributions of Muzafer Sherif and his coworkers. Sherif and Cantril's (1947) description of ego involvement stressed participation in the causes of reference groups, causes that give the individual "some relative role with respect to other individuals, groups, or institutions" (p. 96). And the famous Robbers' Cave experiment of Sherif et al. (1961) stands as a relatively isolated, but nevertheless convincing, plea for the usefulness of superordinate, collective goals in overcoming intergroup hostility.

An Illustration of Ego-Task Analysis— the Conformity Experiment

The usefulness of ego-task analysis can be suggested by applying it to a classic social psychology experiment, Asch's (1951) conformity experiment. In the conformity experiment, the subject's explicit task is to judge line lengths. However, there are also some implicit tasks, such as completing requirements for a psychology course, or learning about laboratory research in psychology, or trying to achieve a favorable evaluation by the experimenter. The last of these is, of course, part of the public self's social accreditation ego task. The frequent presence of this ego task in experiments helps to explain the importance that subjects often attach to their participation in laboratory experiments (cf. Weber & Cook, 1972).

Neither the explicit task nor any of the implicit tasks of the conformity experiment pose any problem to the subject until the first critical trial—that is, the first trial on which each of the experimenter's confederates gives a blatantly incorrect response, and it then becomes the subject's turn to respond. It is then apparent that, in addition to the experimenter, there are two other important audiences present, and the subject cannot choose a strategy that will please all three. One audience is the group of which the subject is a part; to achieve the goal of this group (a reference group of sorts), there should be consensus among all group members, and to have consensus the subject would have to go along with the others' already-stated incorrect judgments. The remaining audience is the inner audience, which can be pleased only by independence—in other words, by the subject's rejecting the obviously incorrect majority judgment. The power of the conformity experiment, in ego task analysis terms, is (a) its simultaneous evocation of the three major ego tasks—social accreditation (pleasing the experimenter), individual achievement (pleasing oneself), and collective achievement (achieving the group goal of consensus)—and (b) putting at least the last two of these into direct conflict with one another. In the face of this conflict, it is left to the subject's relative predispositions to please one or another audience to determine whether to conform or to act independently.

The Concept of Ego-Task Orientation

Almost every adolescent or adult should have some tendency to display each of the four facets of the self—in other words, to perform each of Table 5-1's four ego tasks. The importance of any ego task can be referred to as the strength of *orientation* toward that task. Consistent with the framework of task analysis, as presented in Figure 5-1, ego-task orientations can vary as a function of both situational influences and personality differences. We proceed to consider research that demonstrates these sources of influence, particularly for the ego-task orientations of the public and private selves.

Situational Determinants of Ego-Task Orientation

Situations vary in the opportunity they provide to evoke the various ego-task orientations. Concern over one's public self is likely to be engaged when admired or socially powerful others are present. On the other hand, the individual achievement task may be engaged most readily when the subject is alone. Collective achievement should be engaged by the presence of members of an important reference group, or by participation in a group task that requires cooperation. The diffuse self can be engaged by drug intoxication, by isolation, or by anonymity in a group.

Because the actual presence of others considerably complicates a laboratory situation, it is useful to be able to establish ego-task orientations without having others actually present. Toward this end, the ego task of the public self should be engaged by having a camera prominently present. Consistent with this interpretation, the presence of a camera has been shown to increase susceptibility to conformity pressure (Duval, 1976). The individual achievement task of the private self can be engaged by confronting subjects with feedback from performance, such as by allowing self-observation in a mirror or by providing subjects with audio or video playbacks of their performance. For example, the presence of a small mirror increases resistance to persuasion (Carver, 1977), which can be regarded as a strategy in the service of the private self. The procedures just noted for inducing the ego tasks of the public and private self correspond to ones suggested by Buss (1980) for inducing public and private self-awareness, respectively. The collective achievement task should be evoked by symbolic presence of reference groups—for example, by suggesting to subjects that their performances will be compared with those of other racial, religious, or ethnic groups, or with students from rival schools.

Some common laboratory procedures have not been included in Table 5-1 because they evoke more than one ego task. For example, having the subject perform in the presence of a one-way mirror makes salient both the private and public selves, by providing self-feedback at the same time as indicating the presence of an audience of others. Similarly, having the subject take a test that measures an important skill or personality attribute can evoke inner and outer audiences simultaneously. These compound ego-task procedures, despite their apparent motivational impurity, can be useful precisely because they may succeed in motivating more subjects than do procedures that engage only one ego task.

Individual Differences in Orientation toward the Public and Private Selves

Public and Private Self-Consciousness   Fenigstein, Scheier, and Buss (1975) developed a scale that provides separate measures of consciousness of the public and private facets of self.[3] Fenigstein et al. define the public self as consisting of observable, self-produced stimuli, such as physique, clothing, grooming, facial expression, and speech; the private self consists of self-produced stimuli that are not publicly observable, such as internal bodily sensations, emotional feelings, thoughts, and self-evaluations. (See also Buss, 1980.) Fenigstein et al. interpret public vs. private self-consciousness as a difference in *focus of attention*, which can be directed toward the public or private self. In contrast, ego-task analysis makes *evaluative orientation* toward outer versus inner audiences central to the public vs. private contrast. Despite this difference in interpretation of the public vs. private contrast, these two analyses nevertheless overlap substantially in their empirical implications. This is because persons concerned about evaluations of others should be attentive to the signals that they transmit to others. In other words, they may focus attention on the public self. Similarly, persons guided by internalized evaluative standards should be relatively attentive to their private thoughts and feelings. Because of this conceptual overlap, the measures that Fenigstein et al. (1975) developed to assess individual differences in focus of attention—that is, their Public and Private Self-Consciousness Scales[4]—may serve also to measure predispositions to seek evaluation from outer and inner audiences, respectively.

Studies in which subjects have been put in situations of social pressure indicate the usefulness of the Public and Private Self-Consciousness Scales as measures of ego-task orientations. Scheier (1980) found that opinion moderation in anticipation of a discussion (that is, anticipatory change in the direction of possible opposition) was greater for subjects high in Public Self-consciousness than for ones low in Public Self-consciousness. Scheier and Carver (1980) found that resistance to the opinion change effects of a counterattitudinal role-playing procedure was associated with high scores on Private Self-consciousness; in contrast, expression of opinion change in this situation (interpreted as an

---

[3]The present formulation has been strongly influenced by the analyses of Buss (1980), Carver and Scheier (1981), Fenigstein, Scheier, and Buss (1975), and Scheier and Carver (1983), which, in turn, evolved from important earlier work by Duval and Wicklund (1972).

[4]The self-awareness theorists have clearly distinguished the situationally induced *state*, of focusing attention on the public or private self, from the *trait*, or personality predisposition, of focusing on one or the other self. They refer to the state as (public or private) self-*awareness*, and the trait as (public or private) self-*consciousness*.

impression management strategy of maintaining consistency) was associated with high scores on Public Self-consciousness. Froming and Carver (1981) found that subjects high in Private Self-consciousness were more likely to resist group pressure than were those low in Private Self-consciousness. In an experiment in which women subjects were deliberately ignored by two peers holding a conversation, Fenigstein (1979) found that those high in Public Self-consciousness were most sensitive to this rejection.

Self-Monitoring The conceptual analysis underlying Snyder's (1974) Self-Monitoring Scale suggests its relation to the motivational orientations of the public and private facets of the self. In Snyder's concept, the high self-monitoring person is one who is sensitive to cues transmitted in interpersonal interaction. Snyder (1979) asserts that the self-presentations of low self-monitors are "controlled from within by their affective states and attitudes (they express it as they feel it) rather than molded and tailored to fit the situation" (p. 89). This suggests that the low self-monitor's concern is primarily with the private facet of the self, consistent with Snyder and Campbell's (1982) description of the low self-monitor as a "principled self." At the same time, the high self-monitoring person is "particularly sensitive to the expression and self-presentation of relevant others in social situations and uses these cues as guidelines for monitoring (that is, regulating and controlling) . . . verbal and nonverbal self-presentation" (Snyder, 1979, p. 89). This description is suggestive of the outer-audience orientation of the public self.

Need for Achievement McClelland et al. (1953) developed the concept of achievement motivation to describe individual variations in motivation to succeed in intellectual and social endeavors. Because McClelland et al. defined success in such endeavors as the surpassing of *internal* standards of excellence, their concept of need for achievement is similar to the ego task that we have labeled individual achievement. (Indeed, we chose this label in consideration of the McClelland et al. definition of achievement motivation.) If need for achievement is indicative of a general orientation toward an inner audience, then subjects high in need for achievement should, like ones high in private self-consciousness, be resistant to group pressure. McClelland et al. did report such a finding (1953, p. 287).

Need for Approval Crowne and Marlowe (1964) formulated their Social Desirability Scale as a measure of need for approval, defined as concern about evaluation by others. Strickland and Crowne (1962) reported that subjects scoring high on the Social Desirability Scale (that is, those classified as high in need for approval) were more responsive to a social-influence attempt. This is consistent with an interpretation of the Social Desirability Scale as a measure of the ego-task orientation of the public self.

All of the personality measures discussed in this section were developed in theoretical contexts unrelated to the analysis of ego tasks as facets of the self.

Nevertheless, until measures based directly on the concepts of ego-task analysis are developed, these various related measures will be useful for assessing ego-task orientations. The Public and Private Self-Consciousness Scales are especially close, conceptually, to measures of the public and private facets of the self. However, there are no existing measures that tap the predisposition to engage in the collective achievement ego task of the collective self, or the hedonic satisfaction task of the diffuse self.

Self-Esteem: Measures of Expected Success at Ego Tasks

Ordinarily, we assume, one expects to succeed at personally important tasks. But it is not necessarily so. A person may, for example, strongly wish to impress others, but may nevertheless expect to make a poor impression. This person can be described as oriented toward the social-accreditation ego task of the public self, but as having a low expectation of success. Variations in expected success are important in predicting behavior, because persons who expect to succeed should often act differently from those who expect to fail. (As noted previously, one important difference is that those who expect to succeed should persevere at a task more than those who expect to fail.)

Ambiguity of Self-Esteem Measures The concept of self-esteem, if taken literally, implies evaluation of self by the inner audience—or, in present terms, evaluation of success at the individual-achievement ego task. However, examination of the items in most self-esteem scales (and there are many—see Wylie, 1974) suggests that they measure expected success *also* at the ego tasks of the public self. For example, the well-known and widely used Janis-Field scale (Hovland & Janis, 1959) includes several items that refer to expected evaluation by outer audiences (e.g., "How often are you troubled with shyness?" and "Do you find it hard to make talk when you meet new people?"), as well as items that refer to evaluation by the inner audience (e.g., "Do you ever feel so discouraged with yourself that you wonder whether anything is worth while?"). (See Berger, 1968, for a factor analysis of the Janis-Field scale.)

Public Self-Esteem vs. Private Self-Esteem Ego-task analysis indicates the desirability of having separate measures for public self-esteem (expected success at social accreditation) and private self-esteem (expected success at individual achievement). Ordinarily, these two varieties of self-esteem may be mutually dependent and therefore correlated. Nevertheless, they are conceptually distinguishable as varieties of self-esteem, and it should be useful to have separate measures of them. Among existing measures, Rosenberg's (1965) scale is one that appears to include almost exclusively items that measure private self-esteem (e.g., "I feel I have a number of good qualities"), and Fenigstein et al.'s (1975) Measure of Social Anxiety appears to focus well on public self-esteem (e.g., "I don't find it hard to talk to strangers"). We are aware of no existing measures that focus on expected success in achieving reference-group goals—that is, there are no measures of what might be referred to as collective self-esteem.

CONCLUSIONS—REMAINING TASKS FOR EGO-TASK ANALYSIS

The results reviewed in the preceding section are generally consistent with expectations based on the concepts of task analysis applied to the classification of ego tasks in Table 5-1. Nevertheless, the claim that ego-task analysis provides a satisfactory framework for analyzing person-situation interactions is far from established. Perhaps the main usefulness of our review has been to make clear the substantial gaps in present knowledge.

Collective Achievement Ego Tasks

One major general gap is the lack of empirical knowledge concerning the type of ego task that we have identified as collective achievement. By and large, social psychologists have failed to follow the lead of Sherif and Cantril (1947), who defined ego-involvement as concern with the goals of reference groups, or of Sherif et al. (1961) who induced cooperation among initially hostile factions in a boys' camp by providing them with collective goals. One might interpret the limited study of collective tasks as an indication that few persons attach importance to collective endeavors (a point that receives some support from the findings of Latané, Williams, & Harkins, 1979). Alternatively, one might fault the psychological establishment for undervaluing the study of collective tasks—perhaps a symptom of individualistic biases in our contemporary culture (a point made by Sampson, 1977). Our ignorance notwithstanding, collective efforts are undeniably important in political, industrial, scientific, and even recreational endeavors. This importance justifies much new effort in developing procedures and measures needed to investigate collective performance.

Esteem Measures

Another apparent deficiency is the lack of standardization among measures of self-esteem—or what we have referred to as expected success at ego tasks. Although many measures of "self-esteem" exist, it is apparent that these measures assess mixtures of expected favorable evaluation from outer and inner audiences, and none measures expected success at the collective efforts of reference groups.

Other Audiences, Other Objects of Evaluation

Table 5-1 can be regarded as a portion of a larger classification that potentially includes other evaluative audiences and other objects of evaluation. For example, the goal of being evaluated favorably by a sexual partner may be sufficiently different from the other goals in Table 5-1 to be worthy of separate treatment. A second possible extension is to go beyond the single person as the evaluated object to a collective entity. Such an extension might be needed, for example, to accommodate intentional acts of risk-taking or self-sacrifice in the defense of friends, family, or nation. Another possible extension would be to differentiate among the various groups of others toward whom social accreditation efforts are directed, or among reference groups that have different collective goals. Such additional distinctions may be useful to the extent that the favorable regard of each subgroup requires a different strategic approach. These speculations are reminiscent of William James's (1890) well-known observation, which effectively captures a central point of this chapter—that there is an intimate connection between audiences for self-presentation and facets of the self.

> Properly speaking, a man has as many social selves as there are individuals who recognize him and carry an image of him in their mind. . . . But as the individuals who carry the images fall naturally into classes, we may practically say that he has as many different social selves as there are distinct groups of persons about whose opinion he cares (p. 294).

Conclusion

In answer to the question asked in this chapter's title: *The self is presented to multiple audiences.* The prevalent assumption heretofore has been that self-presentations are targeted at audiences of others. We have reviewed evidence establishing that there is also an important inner audience, oneself. Reference groups provide yet a third type of audience, one that is composed of others—but these are others with whom one is a coparticipant. We have associated each of the three audiences for self-presentation with a distinct motivational facet of the self—the public self, the private self, and the collective self, respectively. Each of these facets of the self corresponds to an orientation toward an ego task—that is, toward the persisting task of establishing one's self-worth by achieving a significant audience's favorable evaluation.

REFERENCES

Alloy, L. B., & Abramson, L. Y. (1979). Judgment of contingency in depressed and nondepressed students: Sadder but wiser? *Journal of Experimental Psychology: General, 108,* 441–485.

Arkin, R. M., Appelman, A. J., & Burger, J. M. (1980). Social anxiety, self-presentation, and the self-serving bias in causal attribution. *Journal of Personality and Social Psychology, 38,* 23–35.

Asch, S. E. (1951). Effects of group pressure on the modification and distortion of judgments. In H. Guetzkow (Ed.), *Groups, leadership, and men.* Pittsburgh, PA: Carnegie Press.

Bandura, A. (1982). Self-efficacy mechanism in human agency. *American Psychologist, 37,* 122–147.

Baumeister, R. F. (1982). A self-presentational view of social phenomena. *Psychological Bulletin, 91,* 3–26.

Berger, C. R. (1968). Sex differences related to self-esteem factor structure. *Journal of Consulting and Clinical Psychology, 32,* 442–446.

Bradley, G. (1978). Self-serving biases in the attribution process: A reexamination of the fact or fiction question. *Journal of Personality and Social Psychology, 36,* 56–71.

Breckler, S. J., & Greenwald, A. G. (May, 1981). Favorable self-referent judgments are made faster than nonfavorable ones. Paper read at 53rd meetings of the Midwestern Psychological Association, Detroit.

Brown, I., & Inouye, D. K. (1978). Learned helplessness through modeling: The role of perceived similarity in competence. *Journal of Personality and Social Psychology, 36,* 900–908.

Buss, A. H. (1980). *Self-consciousness and social anxiety.* San Francisco, CA: Freeman.

Carver, C. S. (1977). Self-awareness, perception of threat, and the expression of reactance through attitude change. *Journal of Personality, 45,* 501–512.

Carver, C. S., & Scheier, M. F. (1981). *Attention and self-regulation: A control-theory approach to human behavior.* New York: Springer-Verlag.

Cheek, J. M., & Hogan, R. (1983). Self-concepts, self-presentations, and moral judgments. In J. Suls & A. G. Greenwald (Eds.), *Psychological perspectives on the self* (Vol. 2). Hillsdale, NJ: Erlbaum.

Cialdini, R. B., Borden, R. J., Thorne, A., Walker, M. R., Freeman, S., & Sloan, L. R. (1976). Basking in reflected glory: Three (football) field studies. *Journal of Personality and Social Psychology, 34,* 366–375.

Crowne, D., & Marlowe, D. (1964). *The approval motive.* New York: Wiley.

Derry, P. A., & Kuiper, N. A. (1981). Schematic processing and self-reference in clinical depression. *Journal of Abnormal Psychology, 90,* 286–297.

Diener, C. I., & Dweck, C. S. (1978). An analysis of learned helplessness: Continuous changes in performance, strategy, and achievement cognitions following failure. *Journal of Personality and Social Psychology, 36,* 451–462.

Diener, C. I., & Dweck, C. S. (1980). An analysis of learned helplessness: II. The processing of success. *Journal of Personality and Social Psychology, 39,* 940–952.

Diener, E. (1977). Deindividuation: Causes and consequences. *Social Behavior and Personality, 5,* 143–155.

Diener, E. (1980). Deindividuation: The absence of self-awareness and self-regulation in group members. In P. Paulus (Ed.), *The psychology of group influence.* Hillsdale, NJ: Erlbaum, 1980.

Dipboye, R. L. (1977). Alternative approaches to deindividuation. *Psychological Bulletin, 84,* 1057–1075.

Duval, S. (1976). Conformity on a visual task as a function of personal novelty on attitudinal dimensions and being reminded of the object status of self. *Journal of Experimental Social Psychology, 12,* 87–98.

Duval, S., & Wicklund, R. A. (1972). *A theory of objective self-awareness.* New York: Academic Press, 1972.

Dweck, C. S. (1975). The role of expectations and attributions in the alleviation of learned helplessness. *Journal of Personality and Social Psychology, 31,* 674–685.

Dweck, C. S., & Repucci, N. D. (1973). Learned helplessness and reinforcement responsibility in children. *Journal of Personality and Social Psychology, 25,* 109–116.

Feather, N. T. (1961). The relationship of persistence at a task to expectation of success and achievement-related motives. *Journal of Abnormal and Social Psychology, 63,* 552–561.

Feather, N. T. (1962). The study of persistence. *Psychological Bulletin, 59,* 94–115.

Fenigstein, A. (1979). Self-consciousness, self-attention, and social interaction. *Journal of Personality and Social Psychology, 37,* 75–86.

Fenigstein, A., Scheier, M. F., & Buss, A. H. (1975). Public and private self-consciousness: Assessment and theory. *Journal of Consulting and Clinical Psychology, 43,* 522–527.

Frey, D. (1978). Reactions to success and failure in public and private conditions. *Journal of Experimental Social Psychology, 14,* 172–179.

Glixman, A. F. (1949). Recall of completed and uncompleted activities under varying degrees of stress. *Journal of Experimental Psychology, 39,* 281–296.

Goffman, E. (1959). *The presentation of self in everyday life.* New York: Doubleday.

Greenberg, G., Pyszczynski, T., & Solomon, S. (1982). The self-serving attributional bias: Beyond self-presentation. *Journal of Experimental Social Psychology, 18,* 56–67.

Greenwald, A. G. (1980). The totalitarian ego: Fabrication and revision of personal history. *American Psychologist, 35,* 603–618.

Greenwald, A. G. (1982a). Ego-task analysis: An integration of research on ego-involvement and self-awareness. In A. H. Hastorf and A. M. Isen (Eds.), *Cognitive social psychology.* New York: Elsevier North Holland.

Greenwald, A. G. (1982b). Is any*one* in charge: Personalysis versus the principle of personal unity. In J. Suls (Ed.), *Psychological perspectives on the self* (Vol. 1). Hillsdale, NJ: Erlbaum.

Greenwald, A. G., & Pratkanis, A. R. (1984). The self. In R. S. Wyer & T. K. Srull (Eds.), *Handbook of social cognition* (Vol. 3). Hillsdale, NJ: Erlbaum.

Harvey, J. H., Harris, B., & Barnes, R. D. (1975). Actor-observer differences in perceptions of responsibility and freedom. *Journal of Personality and Social Psychology, 32,* 22–28.

Hovland, C., & Janis, I. (Eds.) (1959). *Personality and persuasibility,* New Haven, CT: Yale University Press.

James, W. (1890). *The principles of psychology* (Vol. 1). New York: Holt.

Johnston, W. A. (1967). Individual performance and self-evaluation in a simulated team. *Organizational Behavior and Human Performance, 2,* 309–328.

Jones, E. E., & Pittman, T. S. (1982). Toward a general theory of strategic self-presentation. In J. Suls (Ed.), *Psychological perspectives on the self* (Vol. 1). Hillsdale, NJ: Erlbaum.

Jones, E. E., & Sigall, H. (1971). The bogus pipeline: A new paradigm for measuring affect and attitudes. *Psychological Bulletin, 76,* 349–364.

Latané, B., Williams, K., & Harkins, S. (1979). Many hands make light the work: The causes and consequences of social loafing. *Journal of Personality and Social Psychology, 37,* 822–832.

Lewinsohn, P. M., Mischel, W., Chaplin, W., & Barton R. (1980). Social competence and depression: The role of illusory self-perceptions. *Journal of Abnormal Psychology, 89,* 203–212.

Loevinger, J. (1976). *Ego development.* San Francisco: Jossey-Bass.

Markus, H. (1977). Self-schemata and processing information about the self. *Journal of Personality and Social Psychology, 35,* 63–78.

McClelland, D. C., Atkinson, J. W., Clark, R. A., & Lowell, E. L. (1953). *The achievement motive.* New York: Appleton-Century-Crofts.

McFarlin, D. B., & Blascovich, J. (August, 1982). Affective, behavioral, and cognitive consequences of self-esteem. Paper read at a symposium on Functioning and

Measurement of Self-Esteem, 90th annual meetings of the American Psychological Association, Washington, D.C.

Miller, D. T., & Ross, M. (1975). Self-serving biases in the attribution of causality: Fact or fiction? *Psychological Bulletin, 82,* 213–225.

Quigley-Fernandez, B., & Tedeschi, J. T. (1978). The bogus pipeline as lie detector: Two validity studies. *Journal of Personality and Social Psychology, 36,* 247–256.

Riess, M., Rosenfeld, P., Melburg, B., & Tedeschi, J. T. (1981). Self-serving attributions: Biased private perceptions and distorted public descriptions. *Journal of Personality and Social Psychology, 41,* 224–231.

Rogers, T. B., Kuiper, N. A., & Kirker, W. S. (1977). Self-reference and the encoding of personal information. *Journal of Personality and Social Psychology, 35,* 677–688.

Rosenberg, M. (1965). *Society and the adolescent self-image.* Princeton, NJ: Princeton University Press.

Rosenzweig, S. (1943). An experimental study of "repression" with special reference to need-persistive and ego-defensive reactions to frustration. *Journal of Experimental Psychology, 32,* 64–74.

Sampson, E. E. (1977). Psychology and the American ideal. *Journal of Personality and Social Psychology, 35,* 767–782.

Scheier, M. F. (1980). The effects of public and private self-consciousness on the public expression of personal beliefs. *Journal of Personality and Social Psychology, 39,* 514–521.

Scheier, M. F., & Carver, C. S. (1980). Private and public self-attention, resistance to change, and dissonance reduction. *Journal of Personality and Social Psychology, 39,* 390–405.

Scheier, M. F., & Carver, C. S. (1983). Two sides of the self: One for you and one for me. In J. Suls, & A. G. Greenwald (Eds.), *Psychological perspectives on the self* (Vol. 2). Hillsdale, NJ: Erlbaum.

Schlenker, B. R. (1980). *Impression management.* Monterey, CA: Brooks-Cole.

Schlenker, B. R., Hallam, J. R., & McCown, N. E. (1983). Motives and social evaluation: Actor-observer differences in the delineation of motives for a beneficial act. *Journal of Experimental Social Psychology, 19,* 254–273.

Schlenker, B. R., & Miller, R. S. (1977). Egocentrism in groups: Self-serving biases or logical information processing? *Journal of Personality and Social Psychology, 35,* 755–764.

Sherif, M., & Cantril, H. (1947). *The psychology of ego-involvements.* New York: Wiley.

Sherif, M., Harvey, O. J., White, B. J., Hood, W. R., & Sherif, C. W. (1961). *Intergroup cooperation and competition: The robbers cave experiment.* Norman, Oklahoma: University Book Exchange.

Sherif, M., Sherif, C. W., & Nebergall, R. (1965). *Attitude and attitude change: The social judgment-involvement approach.* Philadelphia: Saunders.

Shrauger, J. S., & Rosenberg, S. E. (1970). Self-esteem and the effects of success and failure feedback on performance. *Journal of Personality, 38,* 404–417.

Shrauger, J. S., & Sorman, P. B. (1977). Self-evaluations, initial success and failure, and improvement as determinants of persistence. *Journal of Consulting and Clinical Psychology, 45,* 784–795.

Sigall, H., & Gould, R. (1977). The effects of self-esteem and evaluator demandingness on effort expenditure. *Journal of Personality and Social Psychology, 35,* 12–20.

Snyder, C. R., Higgins, R. L., & Stucky, R. J., (1983). *Excuses: The masquerade solution.* New York: Wiley.

Snyder, M. (1974). Self-monitoring of expressive behavior. *Journal of Personality and Social Psychology, 30,* 526–537.

Snyder, M. (1979). Self-monitoring processes. In L. Berkowitz (Ed.), *Advances in Experimental Social Psychology* (Vol. 12). New York: Academic Press.

Snyder, M., & Campbell, B. H. (1982). Self-monitoring: The self in action. In J. Suls (Ed.), *Psychological perspectives on the self* (Vol. 1). Hillsdale, NJ: Erlbaum.

Strickland, B. R., & Crowne, D. P. (1962). Conformity under conditions of simulated group pressure as a function of the need for social approval. *Journal of Social Psychology, 58,* 171–181.

Tesser, A., & Campbell, J. (1983). Self-definition and self-evaluation maintenance. In J. Suls, & A. G. Greenwald (Eds.), *Psychological perspectives on the self* (Vol. 2). Hillsdale, NJ: Erlbaum.

Weary, G., Harvey, J. H., Schwieger, P., Olson, C. T., Perloff, R., & Pritchard, S. (1982). Self-presentation and the moderation of self-serving attributional biases. *Social Cognition, 1,* 140–159.

Weber, S. J., & Cook, T. D. (1972). Subject effects in laboratory research: An examination of subject roles, demand characteristics, and valid inference. *Psychological Bulletin, 77,* 273–295.

Weiner, B. (1965). The effects of unsatisfied achievement motivation on persistence and subsequent performance. *Journal of Personality, 33,* 428–442.

Weiner, B., & Kukla, A. (1970). An attributional analysis of achievement motivation. *Journal of Personality and Social Psychology, 15,* 1–20.

Wortman, C. B. (1976). Causal attributions and personal control. In J. H. Harvey, W. J. Ickes, & R. F. Kidd (Eds.), *New directions in attribution research* (Vol. 1). Hillsdale, NJ: Erlbaum, 1976.

Wylie, R. C. (1974). *The self-concept* (Vol. 1). Lincoln, NB: University of Nebraska Press.

CHAPTER 6

ASPECTS OF SELF, AND THE CONTROL OF BEHAVIOR

Charles S. Carver
University of Miami

Michael F. Scheier
Carnegie-Mellon University

Against her better judgment, Susan has let herself be coaxed into a blind date. Her suite-mates at school all agreed that Harry (one of the girl's cousins) was good looking and likeable, and that Susan should feel lucky she had been free on the weekend he was coming to visit. Nevertheless, Susan faces the initial encounter with some trepidation. The weekend has already been planned—a football game and parties. But Susan has never much liked football, and the parties that her friends throw always seem too loud and raucous to her. Susan wants everyone to have a good time—including herself—and thus confronts a dilemma. What will be the best way to approach the weekend's events? Will Susan indicate her true feelings to Harry when he arrives? Or will she pretend she enjoys the activities that are in store?

Ned's fraternity brothers are discussing the rumor that tuition will be increased again for next year, despite the student government's announced opposition. Several of them are arguing that students should publicly demonstrate against any increase. Though no one else in the room opposes the idea, Ned thinks it's foolish. In fact, Ned privately feels that the college must really need the money, or else it wouldn't be asking for it. Someone turns to Ned and looks at him as if to ask "What do you think?" What will Ned do? Will he voice his opinion? Remain silent? Go along with the others?

As these illustrations make plain, we are often confronted with situations in which we must choose among several possible ways of presenting and portraying ourselves. These situations can be difficult to deal with, because they typically involve conflicting pressures from a variety of different sources. The sources include our own personal values, desires, and preferences; the wishes of specific other persons whom we judge to be important to ourselves ("significant

Preparation of this chapter was facilitated by grants BNS 80-21859 and BNS 81-07236 from the National Science Foundation.

others"); and a vague sense of the values held by "people in general." When the pressures that emanate from these various sources of guidance contradict each other, we must decide how to respond to them. Sometimes we attempt to steer a middle course, hoping to satisfy everyone at once. But often enough one influence or another dominates our thinking, and is reflected in our self-presentations.

How do people decide among the behavioral alternatives that are open to them? A deceptively simple answer to this question is that the qualities displayed in action are often greatly influenced by where the actors are focusing their attention. More specifically, focusing on your own personal values and attitudes makes you more likely to act in ways that reflect those values and attitudes (all other things being equal). In the same manner, focusing on the existence of a reference group, or on the more general need to get along with others, makes you more likely to act in ways that are calculated to facilitate social interchange (all other things, once again, being equal). This set of assertions is quite simple. But we think that there is a good deal of truth to them. Amplifying upon these assertions is the purpose of this chapter.

We begin the chapter by briefly outlining the way in which we came to study these variations in behavior. In that context we also describe the research strategy that we (and others) have used in attempting to map the pattern of these variations. We then turn to the research itself, emphasizing studies in which two contradictory pressures on behavior were brought to bear simultaneously. Finally we explore some conceptual issues, which concern how best to think about the evidence emerging from this body of research, and indeed how best to think about human behavior more generally.

BACKGROUND

The roots of the ideas under discussion in this chapter go deep into the fabric of the history of psychology. William James (1890), who touched upon many themes that would be developed into fertile research areas decades later, pointed out that the self has a unique capacity termed *reflexivity*. That is, the self is somehow able to turn back and take itself as the object of its own view. Thus we have both self as process (the knower or perceiver) and self as content (that which is known or perceived). This self-reflective capability is one that we have come to view as crucial in effective self-regulation of behavior.

An echo of this conceptualization resounds in the writings, years later, of Cooley and Mead. The term "looking glass self" (Cooley, 1902) conveys a strong and striking image of the tendency to reflect upon oneself and one's characteristics. Similarly, the distinction between the "I" and the "me" (Mead, 1934) seems to embody the distinction between self as knower and self as known.

Even as they echoed James, of course, these theorists added ideas and emphases of their own. Of greatest relevance to present concerns is Mead's emphasis on what might be regarded as the social quality of this self-reflective property of the self. Mead believed that the self is created from social interaction. As we deal with others, we develop a sense of how others react to us—how others have a point of view on us. This gradually becomes internalized as what Mead termed the "residue of the generalized other." When people reflect upon themselves, in Mead's view, they do so from the perspective of that generalized other. Thus self-reflection (to Mead) implies a consideration of social values of some sort or other.

Mead was certainly not alone in taking the point of view that the self is intimately bound up in the social matrix. (See, e.g., Baumeister, 1982; Goffman, 1959.) On the other hand, this point of view has by no means been universally accepted. A very different perspective, drawing from a different philosophical position on human nature, holds that the self is not socially defined, that people can and should define their identities for themselves. What would seem to be important in this view is the attempt to gain an understanding of what constitutes the self as it exists independent of societal pressures and the socially defined roles that the self must take on from time to time.

What emerges from this brief historical overview are two issues. With regard to one of them, there has been little disagreement: The self has the property of reflexivity, of looking back at itself. With regard to the second issue, however, argument has been strenuous. The self is seen either as being social in nature or as being autonomous and separate. The reflexive property of the self thus is viewed either as incorporating the perspective of the social matrix or instead as reflecting a perspective that is independent of that matrix.

As is indicated by this brief review, these various concepts have been a source of interest for decades. But for the most part they have been matters of theory and philosophical argumentation, until relatively recently. In 1971 Wicklund and Duval (see also Duval & Wicklund, 1972) undertook an experimental investigation of the notion that self-reflection has an important influence on people's actions. More specifically, what Wicklund and Duval proposed—and found—was that when subjects were induced to focus their attention inward, they displayed enhanced conformity to salient behavioral standards. This relationship—that higher levels of self-focus produce increased responsiveness to salient standards or reference values for behavior—has subsequently been replicated many times (e.g., Carver, 1974, 1975; Scheier, Fenigstein, & Buss, 1974). (See Carver & Scheier, 1981a, for a more comprehensive review.)

Shortly after Wicklund and Duval began the experimental investigation of these processes, Fenigstein, Scheier, and Buss (1975) pointed out that it was useful and desirable to distinguish between two aspects of the self. Drawing on the historical precedents cited just above, Fenigstein et al. proposed that some self-aspects are covert, hidden, and inaccessible to others, whereas other self-aspects are social, overtly displayed to others, and indeed intimately tied to relationships with others. The former component of self they termed "private" self; the latter component they termed "public" self. As was noted above, there had been ample historical precedents for treating each of these conceptual entities as if it were the entirety of the self. But what Fenigstein et al.

emphasized was that *both* conceptualizations were valid—that the two self-aspects always coexisted, to a greater or lesser degree, within the same person.

This point of view suggested the following corollary: It is too simple—too ambiguous—to talk about the "self" being involved in the determination of one's behavior. In order to speak precisely about such involvement, it is necessary to consider which facet of self—public or private—is salient, or is taken as the focus of the person's attention. That is, there are many circumstances where attending to private self-aspects should influence behavior in one way, but attending to public self-aspects should influence behavior in a very different way. Thus it is not simply "self" that becomes involved in behavior when attention is directed inward, but rather some *side* of the self.

These arguments regarding two facets of the self, both of which contribute to one's overall identity, seem interesting and plausible. But interesting and plausible arguments are not always correct. Researchers interested in these ideas needed ways to assess their accuracy. Two converging techniques have been developed to examine these ideas. The first technique involves measuring personality differences; the second involves experimental manipulations. We address these methods in turn, in the following paragraphs.

Individual Differences

At the same time that they were advancing their argument about the two facets of self, Fenigstein et al. (1975) were also proposing a way to assess individual differences in the tendency to take each of the self-aspects as the object of awareness. More specifically, they had developed a self-report instrument called the Self-Consciousness Scale (SCS) to measure these dispositional qualities. We should perhaps note explicitly at this point that the term self-consciousness as used here does not have the connotations of embarassment or nervousness that everyday use of the term implies. Self-consciousness as used here refers simply to the disposition to be aware of the self.

The SCS has two separate dimensions, each bearing on one of the facets of self now under discussion.[1] *Private* self-consciousness is the tendency to be aware of self-aspects that are personal, autonomous, and covert. It is measured by items such as "I reflect about myself a lot" and "I'm generally attentive to my inner feelings." People who tend to agree with these statements are relatively high on this dimension. *Public* self-consciousness is the tendency to be aware of the self as a social object to which other people react. It is measured by items such as "I'm very concerned about the way I present myself" and "I'm concerned about what other people think of me." The tendency to agree with these statements reflects a relatively high standing on this dimension.

---

[1]The SCS has a third subscale, as well, which measures social anxiety. This subscale reflects a reaction to one's self-presentations, rather than reflecting a simple awareness of some self-aspect. Because this portion of the SCS has received relatively little research attention, it will not be discussed further here.

Both private and public self-consciousness scales have been shown to be factorially sound and stable across time (see Fenigstein et al., 1975). Furthermore, the two dimensions of self-consciousness are relatively independent of each other. They inevitably are positively related when measured across large samples of people, but the correlation usually is rather low.

This finding has two implications, one theoretical, the other methodological. First, the absence of any hint of an inverse relationship between scales may be taken as support for the theoretical position that the two tendencies do not represent opposite ends of a bipolar dimension of variability. Rather, both facets of awareness are there to play a potential role in the personal experience and behavioral guidance of any particular individual (cf. Tesser & Paulhus, 1983). To put it more plainly, this finding implies that being high on one dimension of awareness does not by any means imply being low on the other dimension.

Nevertheless, it is true that people do vary in their balance of sensitivity to their private vs. public self-aspects. Methodologically, the relative independence of the two dimensions means that it is relatively easy to find people who are particularly attentive to one self-aspect exclusively, particularly attentive to both self-aspects, or particularly attentive to neither self-aspect. This, in turn, means that it is relatively easy to create independent tests of hypotheses concerning focus on the private versus public aspects of the self, without having the two dimensions confounded with each other.

Once the scale was developed, the next step was to obtain evidence concerning its validity. Efforts to validate the SCS have been quite fruitful. For example, the tendency to respond with "self-focused" material in a sentence-completion task has been found to be correlated with private self-consciousness (Carver & Scheier, 1978).[2] Persons high in private self-consciousness have also been shown to be more aware of relatively strong emotions than are persons lower in private self-consciousness (Scheier, 1976; Scheier & Carver, 1977). In fact, persons high on this dimension are even particularly aware of the *absence* of a sensation that they had been led erroneously to expect (Scheier, Carver, & Gibbons, 1979).

There is also validational evidence with respect to the other dimension of the SCS. For example, public self-consciousness has been found to be associated with sensitivity to interpersonal rejection (Fenigstein, 1979). Other research has found that people high in public self-consciousness are particularly prone to be fashion conscious, to report using clothing to influence their self-portrayals to other persons, and to value having a range of clothing to work with (Solomon & Schopler, 1982). Similarly, women who are high in public self-consciousness wear more makeup than do those lower on this dimension, in a (self-reported) attempt to facilitate and optimize their social interactions (Miller & Cox, 1981). Finally, public self-consciousness has been shown to be related to people's

---

[2]As an illustration of the kind of material under discussion, respond yourself to the sentence "I think that . . . ." Responses such as "I have a lot of work to do" or "I am hungry" reflect self-focus. Responses such as "it might rain today" or "the international political situation is a terrible mess" reflect focus on the external world.

accuracy in predicting the impressions that they would convey to an audience of people who did not know them (Tobey & Tunnell, 1981).

These studies provide a good deal of information concerning the construct validity of each dimension of self-consciousness. An equally important part of the validation process, however, is obtaining evidence that the scale is not related to other psychological dimensions that might render its meaning ambiguous (discriminant validation). If self-consciousness were highly correlated with intelligence, for example, it would be hard to be confident that a research finding based on the measure of self-consciousness did not actually reflect differences in intelligence.

This is not the case, however. Several studies have been conducted in which the SCS was correlated with measures of other psychological and behavioral characteristics. These studies indicate that neither dimension of self-consciousness is appreciably correlated with dimensions such as intelligence, need for approval, or achievement motivation (Carver & Glass, 1976; Turner, Scheier, Carver, & Ickes, 1978). Thus it is difficult to make a strong case that any of these alternative psychological characteristics underlie the effects of self-consciousness that are documented in research discussed throughout this chapter.

Experimental Manipulations

The second way in which researchers have studied the effects of variations in attentional focus is by experimentally manipulating subjects' attention. For the most part, this has been done by confronting subjects with some stimulus that reminds them of themselves, thus increasing self-focus. The manipulations that have been used most frequently are a small mirror propped before the chair that the subject sits in, a TV or videotape camera placed prominently near subjects and aimed at them, or an audience of observers.

Evidence of the construct validity of these manipulations comes from several sources. For example, in the research discussed above, examining subjects' responses on a sentence-completion task, more "self-focused" responses were made if the subject was seated before a mirror or an observer than if the room was empty. Perhaps the most compelling source of evidence concerning the validity of these manipulations, however, is the large number of cases in which manipulations of self-awareness have been shown to create effects that are practically identical to effects associated with individual differences in self-consciousness. For example, being seated before a mirror makes people more aware of salient emotional states (Scheier, 1976; Scheier & Carver, 1977), and more aware of the absence of an expected internal state (Gibbons, Carver, Scheier, & Hormuth, 1979). These effects are conceptually the same as those discussed earlier that were a function of variations in private self-consciousness.

Evidence of discriminant validity for experimental manipulations is usually rarer than for personality measures, and this is probably almost as true of manipulations of self-focus as it is of other manipulations. There is, however, evidence that self-focus is not necessarily associated with arousal states (Carver & Scheier, 1981b), which represents one important discrimination to be made. And by the logic of "converging operations" (Garner, Hake, & Eriksen, 1956), if manipulations and dispositions are associated with the same behavioral effects, evidence of discriminant validity for the one (in this case, the disposition) implicitly generalizes to the other (the manipulation). Thus we have a good deal of confidence in the validity of these manipulations.

Indeed, the converging operations allow us to make even a more specific point. The existing evidence appears to indicate a parallel between two categories of experimental manipulations and the two dimensions of self-consciousness. Small mirrors, positioned in locations that do not suggest the presence of external observers, have on many occasions created effects that are quite similar to those associated with dispositional private self-consciousness. Other manipulations—audiences, TV cameras, one-way mirrors, and the like—appear to create states that are more similar to the disposition of public self-consciousness. It thus seems reasonable to suggest that certain experimental manipulations make people selectively aware of their private self-aspects, and that other manipulations make people selectively aware of their public self-aspects.

RESEARCH

In the previous section we described the conceptual antecedents of research on the effects of focusing on various aspects of oneself. And we discussed the two ways in which researchers have most often studied those effects. Now let us turn to some of the research itself. In this section we examine how people's actions and self-portrayals are influenced by their attentional focus in a variety of behavioral circumstances. These studies will provide a sense of the diversity of situations in which attending to some aspect of self predictably influences behavior.

Here we will emphasize studies in which *both* self-aspects may potentially play an important role in guiding behavior. That is, in the majority of the cases discussed in the following paragraphs, focusing on the private self should promote one kind of self-presentation; focusing on the public self should promote a very different kind of self-presentation. These studies thus provide a very clear test of the thesis that people's actions are heavily influenced by which aspect of themselves they are focusing their attention on.

Anticipating Interaction

The process of social interaction often really begins before the other people involved are even encountered. That is, simply anticipating that one will be interacting in a casual, nonadversarial way with people who are unfamiliar often evokes concerns about making a good impression. One strategy that people sometimes use when preparing to interact with people they don't know is to "moderate," or make more neutral, the opinions they will be projecting to those people. (See, e.g., Cialdini, Levy, Herman, Kozlowski, & Petty, 1976; Newtson & Czerlinsky, 1974.) This strategy—which may be thought of as "smoothing the edges" off one's public display—minimizes the chances of offending the other person by taking what may appear to be an extreme or deviant position. It thereby is useful in making a good impression.

Use of this tactic clearly reflects the taking into account of other people's sensibilities. This, in turn, suggests that such a tactic should be associated with focus on the public aspects of self, that is, with focus on one's existence as a social object to which other people react. It seems likely, on the other hand, that focus on private self-aspects will not induce a person to be sensitive to these particular considerations. Indeed, people who are being especially attentive to their private self-aspects may be especially likely to attempt to portray themselves precisely as they see themselves.

This reasoning has been tested (Scheier, 1980) in a study in which subjects reported their attitudes on a particular issue at two different times. The first report was made during a large questionnaire-completion session at the beginning of the semester. The self-presentational considerations operating in this circumstance should have been minimal. The second report was made during an experimental session (conducted separately for each person). Subjects were told that the research was part of a social opinion survey, and that they would be describing their opinions in two separate ways during the session. First they would write a brief essay; later on they would be talking about the same opinion issue with another participant. In reality this discussion never took place. But this description should have planted the idea in subjects' minds that they would have to orchestrate a self-presentation a bit later. It was expected that if moderation of opinions were induced by the anticipation of the interaction, it would be displayed in the essays that subjects wrote.

Ratings of the essays revealed a pattern that was consistent with predictions. Public self-consciousness was associated with a reliable tendency to express more moderated (i.e., more neutral) opinions in the essay than had been expressed during the earlier questionnaire session. In contrast, private self-consciousness was associated with a tendency to report opinions that were very similar to those that had been expressed during the earlier session. This latter effect was eliminated, however, if the subjects were high in public as well as private self-consciousness. Apparently the tendency to moderate opinions in this situation is a very strong one, influencing self-presentations to a greater degree than do the competing tendencies that are associated with focus on the private self.

Behavioral Intentions

The process of anticipating a social interaction is conceptually similar to the process of formulating a behavioral intention (whether that intention bears on other people or not). One might therefore ask whether focusing on various self-aspects can play an important role in determining what behavioral intention is formulated in a given situation. A particularly useful framework for addressing this question is a theory proposed by Ajzen and Fishbein (1970, 1974). They have argued that intentions are a joint product of personal attitudes toward whatever act is being contemplated, and perceptions of the operative social norms with respect to that act. One decides how to act by weighing these two influences and combining them as a function of their relative weights. It seems reasonable to suggest the possibility that this process is influenced by predispositions to attend either to one's private self-aspects (which includes one's attitudes) or to one's public self-aspects (which should include a sense of the norms of one's reference groups).

Precisely this line of reasoning was developed by Davis, Holtgraves, Kasmer, and Ginsburg (1982). They tested their ideas by assessing subjects' behavioral intentions on several different issues, their personal attitudes on the same issues, and their subjective norms (i.e., the norms that they ascribe to the people whom they think of as their reference groups). Beta weights were then computed to indicate the strength of the predictive relationships (for each subject) from personal attitudes and subjective norms, respectively, to behavioral intentions. Davis et al.'s reasoning predicts that private self-consciousness should be positively correlated with the tendency to weight personal attitudes heavily in formulating behavioral intentions. Similarly, public self-consciousness should be correlated with the tendency to weight subjective norms heavily in formulating intentions. Examination of the data yielded support for both of these predictions.

Thus behavioral intentions, as well as anticipatory orientations toward an unfamiliar other, can vary as a function of people's levels of private and public self-consciousness. But what of behavior itself? What actually happens when the other people are present, or when the intention must be translated into action?

Conformity

The effects of attending to public and private self-aspects while engaged in overt behavior have been assessed in several studies. This research covers a substantial range of behavioral contexts and widely varying qualities of action. Consider, for example, what may be the most basic self-presentational dilemma of all: the problem faced by the person who confronts a unanimous group, which has taken a position that the person feels is wrong. The literature has shown quite consistently that people often bend to the implicit pressure of such a group, even to the point of disregarding the evidence provided to them by their own senses (cf. Asch, 1951, 1956; Crutchfield, 1955). Presumably this conformity reflects self-presentational concerns. People want to avoid "making waves," or being disagreeable, and therefore go along with the majority, even when they are convinced the majority is incorrect.

This description sounds very much like the sort of effect that one would expect to be associated with a sensitivity to one's public display. The more conscious of that display one is, the more likely one is to be concerned about the possibility of appearing deviant. What, on the other hand, would be the effect of attending to private self-aspects in such a situation? We noted earlier that focus on the private self is associated with enhanced awareness of internal states, and in some cases, an enhanced awareness of the absence of expected states (Gibbons et al., 1979; Scheier & Carver, 1977; Scheier et al., 1979). It seems plausible to suggest that focusing on the private self when confronted with an incorrect group would lead one's own personal impression to be more salient, and thus to be relied on to a greater degree than would otherwise be the case. Note that these are entirely separate predictions, congruent with the fact that focusing on public and private self-aspects are separate and distinct tendencies.

These two possibilities were assessed (Froming & Carver, 1981) in a study in which subjects participating in group sessions were asked to count sets of metronome clicks. After each set of stimuli, each person in the group was to report aloud how many clicks had been presented. In reality, all of the reports (heard over headphones) came from a pre-recorded tape. Everyone in the session made his or her own reports simultaneously, but was prevented from hearing each other by the arrangement of the experimental apparatus. On some of the trials, the voices reported the correct number of clicks. But on the trials that were the focus of the study, all of the supposed group members reported a number that was incorrect. The dependent measure was the frequency with which the subjects went along with the group and reported the wrong answer themselves.

As expected, conformity to the incorrect majority was positively associated with level of public self-consciousness (though there are some qualifications on this finding—see Froming & Carver, 1981, for details). Independent of this, but also in line with predictions, private self-consciousness was associated with disregarding the majority, with subjects responding instead by reporting the values that their own ears had told them were correct. Thus focusing on the public self appears to promote a tendency to go along with the group (even when the group is in error), whereas focusing on the private self appears to promote a tendency to ignore the group and go one's own way. Similar findings have also been reported more recently by Santee and Maslach (1982).

Attitudes, Subjective Norms, and Behavior

The Froming and Carver study drew directly from a literature on responses to social pressure. Its findings bear on the question of whether to go along with one's own perceptions or to accept the judgments of other people. But that is surely not the only context in which the processes now under discussion are important. Another example was addressed by implication a bit earlier in the chapter. Specifically, situations often arise in which people must decide whether to depend on their personal attitudes about issues to guide their actions, or to rely instead on social norms that are held by salient reference groups. Our earlier discussion of this point revolved around these two categories as determinants of intentions. But now let us consider the question as it applies to overt behavior.

The research that bears on this point was conducted by Froming, Walker, and Lopyan (1982). They selected as subjects people who satisfied two criteria. First, they had a specific personal opinion about the use of punishment as a technique to promote learning (i.e., they either favored or opposed its use). Second, they also reported the belief that "most people" hold the opposite opinion (subjective norm). These subjects later came to experimental sessions (individually) in which they were instructed to teach a concept to an ostensible cosubject via an experimental apparatus. The apparatus was to be used to present stimuli, determine the correctness of responses, and to deliver punishments. More specifically, every time the learner made an incorrect response, the subject was to administer an electric shock, choosing from among ten graded intensities. Unbeknownst to the subject, the ostensible cosubject was actually delivering a preprogrammed series of correct and incorrect responses, and was reading shock-intensity numbers from a panel, rather than actually receiving the shocks.

Instead of examining the effects of individual differences in dispositional self-consciousness in this research, Froming et al. varied the direction of their subjects' attentional focus by means of experimental manipulations. In one experimental condition, a small mirror was suspended from the apparatus before the subject, above the control panel. In another experimental condition, an audience of evaluative observers was standing next to the apparatus while the subject was attempting to teach the concept. These two manipulations were expected to direct subjects' attention toward themselves, but toward different aspects of themselves—private and public, respectively. The consequence of this difference should have been heightened responsiveness to personal attitudes and subjective norms, in the respective groups.

The results of this study were quite consistent with Froming et al.'s reasoning. Compared to a control condition, the presence of the mirror caused subjects to behave in a fashion that was more consistent with their personal attitudes. That is, subjects who opposed the use of punishment as a teaching tool used lower shock levels if the mirror was there than if it was not; subjects who favored the use of punishment used higher shock levels if the mirror was there than if it was not.

The presence of an evaluative audience had precisely the opposite influence on behavior. Rather than promoting conformity to personal attitudes, the presence of the audience promoted conformity to subjective norms. Subjects who thought that "most people" favored punishment became more punitive when the audience was present; those who thought that most people opposed punishment became less punitive when the audience was present. These effects occurred despite the fact that the audience members never voiced an opinion on the use of punishment, and the fact that the audience was not constituted in such a way as to suggest an opinion on their part.

Thus once again overt action was greatly influenced by which self-aspect was focal in subjects' minds. When their attention was directed to the private self, personal attitudes were manifested in behavior. When attention was directed to the public self, entirely different qualities emerged, qualities reflective of salient norms.

Reference-Group Behavior

The behavior of subjects in the audience condition of the Froming et al. (1982) research is very reminiscent of what is often discussed as reference-group behavior (e.g., Newcomb, 1950, 1958). Reference groups are groups that we use as points of comparison, as beacons for guiding our opinions and our actions. Positive reference groups are those we accept as desirable; negative reference groups are those we see as undesirable. We often behave in ways that make us seem more similar to our positive reference groups. And we sometimes act in ways that are calculated to make us appear dissimilar to groups that we view as negative reference groups.

The research discussed above suggests that reference-group behavior may be mediated by focus on the public aspects of self. There are at least two research projects that bear on this question. In the earlier of the two (Wicklund & Duval, 1971, Experiment 1), subjects completed an extensive opinion questionnaire in large group sessions. Later on (in individual sessions) they were asked to respond to nine items drawn from the larger set. Each item was followed by a rating scale on which a mark had been placed, corresponding to the response ostensibly made most often among the pretest sample of undergraduates. In the positive reference group condition, these points were accurately described as the average responses of a group of students at the university where the study was being conducted.

Half the subjects completed this questionnaire just after listening to a tape recording of their own voice (made under a guise). The other subjects completed the questionnaire after listening to another person's tape-recorded voice. Subjects whose attention had been self-focused by their own voices proved to be more likely than the other subjects to shift their opinions (from their pretest values) toward closer conformity with the positive reference group. This study was conducted before much thought had been given to the possibility that experimental manipulations could be viewed as focusing attention selectively on one or the other self-aspect. But we have suggested elsewhere (e.g., Carver & Scheier, 1981a; Scheier & Carver, 1981, 1983a) that the sound of one's voice, a highly public stimulus that is very unfamiliar to most people, is likely to focus attention on the public self.

This reasoning is plausible, but remained somewhat speculative until additional research had been conducted. Gaining additional information on this question was one purpose of studies conducted several years later by Carver and Humphries (1981). These studies also expanded on a point that had been a secondary focus of the Wicklund and Duval experiment. This point was the use of a reference group that subjects disliked: a negative reference group.

Subjects in this research were Cuban-American students at the University of Miami. There is a large community of Cuban exiles in Miami, who maintain an intense and active dislike for the Castro government in Cuba and anything related to that government. Thus, the Castro government would seem to be functioning as a negative reference group for these people. Subjects were asked to give their opinions on a series of issues bearing on relations between Cuba and the United States. In a preliminary study, these issues either were or were not introduced by a brief statement—attributed to a representative of the Castro government—claiming an official position on the issue. Consistent with the negative reference-group notion, these attitudinal positions were renounced to a greater degree if the Castro position had been stated than if it had not. Of greater interest in the present context, a second study determined that this renunciation was correlated with subjects' levels of public self-consciousness. Private self-consciousness, in contrast, was unrelated to this phenomenon.

The nature of this particular finding foreshadows a more complex issue that is addressed in greater detail later in the chapter. Specifically, the fact that public self-consciousness was associated with renouncing the position of a negative reference group is open to multiple interpretations. On the one hand, it might be argued that such behavior is an attempt to create a particular public image, which may or may not fit with subjects' own personal opinions. Solidarity with other Cuban Americans presumably has in the past led to social rewards for these persons, and image manipulation of this type would seem to be a useful strategy for ensuring continued rewards.

On the other hand, it might also be argued quite reasonably that because reference group behavior is an intrinsically "social" phenomenon, it is only natural that the social side of the self is implicated in the behavior, rather than the personal and autonomous side of the self. This argument would not imply image manipulation, but only the use of social comparison information in defining one's opinions. These interpretations are quite different from each other in important respects. They imply very different concerns and motivations on the part of the actors involved. At present, however, we have no evidence to indicate which of the two characterizations is the more accurate.

Distributive Justice

Another area of behavior that we would like to address in concrete research terms is sometimes referred to with the term *distributive justice*. Work in this area focuses on the manner in which people allocate rewards in situations where more than one person has contributed to the outcome on which the reward depended. Allocations tend to follow one of two principles, depending on the circumstances surrounding the decision. The first is the principle of equity: the idea that people should be rewarded as a direct function of their contributions. The second is the principle of parity or equality: the notion that people should share evenly in rewards, without regard to their relative contributions. Much of the research on resource allocation examines variables that influence which of these rules people adopt.

One very general perspective on the distributive justice process holds that people are inclined to allocate rewards in ways that are calculated to gain social approval from others. (See Reis, 1981, for a summary of this point of view.) Thus this area of behavior is one in which the issue of self-presentation is quite salient. It is also an area in which researchers have begun to investigate the effects of focusing one's attention on various aspects of the self.

One project bearing on this question (Greenberg, 1982, Experiment 2) studied allocation of resources in a situation where the subject was to distribute rewards to two other persons for an outcome in which the subject was not personally involved. The target persons were depicted as workers competing against each other in a profit-making venture. Each was attempting to be as productive as possible, but one was portrayed as having done substantially better than the other. Competition and productivity were highlighted in this description because previous research suggests that emphasizing these qualities in a work situation tends to make the *equity* principle salient as a *personal* distribution standard (Deutsch, 1975; Greenberg, 1982, Experiment 1; Leventhal, 1976).

Previous findings also suggest some variables that are likely to create concerns over impression management in this kind of situation. For example, expecting to have future interaction with a person whose production has been low leads people to adopt equality as an allocation rule. Presumably this is done as a means of creating a good impression in that person's eyes (e.g., Reis & Gruzen, 1976; Shapiro, 1975; Von Grumbkow, Deen, Steensma, & Wilke, 1965). Accordingly, in order to create a salient *social* standard of *equality,* Greenberg (1982) told subjects that they themselves would have to pay the low-input worker at the end of the experimental session and explain the basis for the allocation policy chosen.

The dilemma facing these subjects, then, was the following. They could act on the basis of their own convictions about what was just in the situation, and allocate the reward on the basis of equity. Or they could allocate on the basis of equality, thereby creating a more favorable impression on the low-input recipient. As Greenberg had predicted, how subjects resolved this conflict proved to be heavily influenced by their levels of private and public self-consciousness. Persons who were dispositionally focused on their private self-aspects tended to allocate on the basis of the privately held principle of equity. Persons who were dispositionally focused on their public self-aspects tended to act on the basis of the social standard, allocating according to the principle of equality.

It will be noted that this finding is conceptually quite similar to that of Froming et al. (1982), described earlier, despite the use of dispositional differences instead of experimental manipulations, and despite the fact that the projects focused on very different qualities of behavior. This provides a nice illustration of the convergence among research findings in the literature under discussion. That is, some of the data come from studies of individual differences, some from studies with manipulations. Furthermore, the data come from studies with widely varying behavioral content. Yet they make a very consistent case conceptually.

An additional illustration of this point comes from yet another study of the effects of self-consciousness on choice of allocation principle. This project focused on a situation that had been set up in a somewhat different manner than the situation discussed earlier. In this research (Kernis & Reis, 1982), subjects arrived at the laboratory in pairs for what was portrayed as an investigation of familiar objects. Subjects were told they would be paid for their participation, but the exact amount of pay would be determined by the pair's combined performance. The orientation to the experimental situation that was given to subjects emphasized cooperation among participants and the joint status of their contributions. This was expected to evoke a private sense that allocation should be equal between partners (cf. Deutsch, 1975; Reis & Gruzen, 1976). The experimenter also suggested, however, that the person who allocated the payment between them might want to take into account how much each person had contributed to the performance of the pair. This was intended to make equity salient as a socially sanctioned value.

The events of the session were rigged in such a way that both subjects believed that they had contributed slightly more than half to the group's production. And both subjects were named to be reward allocators (without the other's knowledge, of course). In accord with the reasoning outlined in the preceding paragraph, private self-consciousness in this study was associated with a tendency to allocate payment equally between partners. Public self-consciousness was associated with allocation based upon the equity principle.

Note that in terms of the behavioral quality that was associated with a particular focus of attention, the Greensberg (1982) study and the Kernis and Reis (1982) study yielded diametrically opposing results. Equity was associated with private self-consciousness in one case, and with public self-consciousness in the other. Yet conceptually the two sets of results are very consistent with each other. The allocation rule that had been established as *socially* appropriate was used in each case when public self-consciousness was high; and the rule that had been made salient as a *privately* held principle was used when private self-consciousness was high.

This interesting pattern allows us to emphasize a more general theme that characterizes accurate prediction on the basis of the two aspects of self-consciousness. Specifically, private and public self-consciousness should not be thought of as being inevitably associated with specific concrete behavioral qualities (in this case equity- vs. equality-based allocation). Rather, what these dimensions define is the tendency to be concerned with, and focus attention on, whatever behavioral qualities are situationally associated with the two aspects of the self. If the situation is such that social constraints suggest equity as desirable, then focusing on the public self should lead to self-presentations reflective of the equity principle. If the situation is such that equality is salient as a socially appropriate value, then focus on the public self should cause equality to be expressed in behavior.

Difficulties and Disengagement

We would like to mention one final aspect of research on the effects of self-directed attention before closing this section. This area of work involves phenomena with clear implications for social life, but phenomena that have been studied in somewhat less breadth than those addressed thus far. In particular, this work examines what happens when difficulties are encountered in the course of carrying out desired actions.

Throughout the chapter thus far we have limited ourselves to discussing situations in which people are able to carry out their behavioral intentions without impediments. But it is important to recognize that this is not always the case. In social interaction as well as in task directed behavior, difficulties are sometimes encountered in attaining the goals to which we aspire. If these difficulties lead to expectations of failure, the result may be a behavioral withdrawal or mental disengagement from the attempt (cf. Klinger, 1975). This disengagement is enhanced by self-focus, just as is the attempt to attain the goals when expectancies are more favorable. (See Carver & Scheier, 1981a, 1983, for more elaborate discussions of this set of processes.)

Sometimes people's difficulties in carrying out intended actions derive from doubts that they can overcome anxiety or fear that the actions happen to entail. Sometimes the difficulties are tied to frustrations inherent in the activity itself. And sometimes the difficulties seem based in a personal sense of inadequacy, which suggests that one is incapable of carrying out the desired behavior successfully. In each of these cases, the result appears to be the same. If expectancies of overcoming the obstacle and attaining the goal are favorable, self-focus promotes perseverance. If expectancies are sufficiently unfavorable, self-focus enhances the tendency to disengage.

These processes have been examined in some detail, but the studies are largely restricted to cases in which subjects are attempting to attain personal or instrumental goals rather than social or self-presentational goals. For example, Carver, Blaney, and Scheier (1979a) asked persons who were afraid of nonpoisonous snakes to do their best to approach and pick up a boa constrictor. Enhanced attention to the self (created via a mirror) caused subjects who were not convinced that they had the ability to cope with their fear—doubtful subjects—to disengage and withdraw earlier in the approach sequence (compared to similar subjects in whom self-focus was lower). But (very much in line with prediction) enhanced self-focus had the opposite effect among fearful but more confident subjects. Despite personal discomfort, they tended to exert even stronger effort toward carrying out their assignment when self-focus was high than when it was lower.

Additional research (Carver, Blaney, & Scheier, 1979b) applied the same reasoning to the effects of task frustration. All subjects in this research were caused to fail badly on an initial task. Their expectancies of potentially being able to redress this failure on a second task were then manipulated experimentally. Subjects led to have a degree of confidence toward the second task proved to be more persistent (at what actually was an insoluble puzzle) when self-focus was high than when it was lower. Subjects led to be doubtful about doing well on the second task disengaged sooner (i.e., were less persistent) when self-focus was high than when it was lower.

Nor are these the only studies that make this point about continuing to attempt versus disengaging from goals. For example, Brockner (e.g., 1979) has used much the same reasoning in an analysis of the debilitating effects of low self-esteem. And we have elsewhere (Carver, Peterson, Follansbee, & Scheier, 1983) provided evidence that similar processes are involved in the impairments associated with test anxiety.

By implication, at least, the studies outlined just above involved cases in which subjects took performing well at some task to represent a personal goal. But what of social goals? Though direct evidence on the involvement of self-attention in such phenomena is somewhat more sketchy, the theoretical analysis presented here appears to be easily applied to this behavioral domain. In particular, the category of phenomena given the term *social anxiety* would seem to represent cases in which people have severe doubts about being able to make adequate self-presentations, to create desired impressions in others, or to obtain desired social goals. Indeed, Schlenker and Leary (1982; see also Leary & Schlenker, 1981) have made precisely this argument.

The doubts of socially anxious persons presumably become especially salient to them when they are anticipating or are engaged in social interaction. And these doubts, particularly when taken together with high levels of self-attention, presumably produce a desire to withdraw or disengage from the situational context. The result, then, is the sort of flustered, disorganized, unhappy, and not altogether adequate display that often characterizes the person who is high in social anxiety. These effects presumably should be mediated by attention to the public self. Preliminary evidence that this is so has been obtained in at least one study thus far (Burgio, Merluzzi, & Pryor, 1982), and we expect the issue to receive additional scrutiny in future research.

SELF-REGULATION AND SELF-PRESENTATION

Let us step away from the domain of research activity, now, and take stock of where we have been and what we have seen. Thus far in the chapter we have focused primarily on behavioral demonstrations of the fact that attentional focus can have a pronounced impact on how people act and how they present themselves to others. We began with situations in which there are fairly obvious and concrete consequences of focusing on one's public self-aspects, in particular. And we gradually moved into situations in which the behavioral qualities that are associated with the two sides of the self as guidelines for action vary quite substantially with the behavioral context. In these latter situations it became clearer that in studying the effects of these two kinds of self-focus we are dealing with a difference in the *channeling of the flow of information related to behavior,* rather than with differences in concrete behavioral qualities per se.

Given this transition in the focus of the research presented, it is perhaps appropriate at this point to consider some broader questions bearing on the self-regulation of behavior. In this portion of the chapter we address three such questions. The first is how to conceptualize the public-private distinction within the purview of a broader model of behavior. The second stems from the fact that there are several shades of meaning that can be inferred from the term self-presentation, and indeed from the self-regulatory concomitants of focusing on private and public self-aspects. The question, then, is which shades of meaning are most appropriate? The final question is how best to conceptualize the relationship between attention and action. Is the shifting of attention itself an initiator of behavior, or is it more typically a consequence of prior intentions to act? These questions are addressed in turn in the following sections.

Hierarchical Feedback Systems as a Model of Behavior

We have proposed elsewhere (e.g., Carver & Scheier, 1981a, 1982, 1983) that it is useful to conceptualize the self-regulatory activities of the human being as reflecting the principles of closed-loop, cybernetic control. The control-process point of view is consistent with the notion that human behavior is purposive and goal oriented. It assumes a picture of the human nervous system as a vast information-processing device, with elaborate capabilities and flexibility, though not without biases in the way in which information is handled.

In discussing this perspective on behavior, we have tentatively adopted the framework suggested by Powers (1973a, 1973b), who developed his ideas by studying the nature of cybernetic self-regulatory systems in the abstract and by considering how the logic that underlies them might also underlie functioning in the nervous system. Powers' ideas are detailed and elaborate, and we will not go into them in much depth here. But there are several aspects of the Powers model, taken together with the more general notions of control theory, that are relevant to the ideas discussed earlier in the chapter.

First consider the basic idea of cybernetic control itself. Cybernetic models emphasize the flow of particular kinds of information as critical determinants of various kinds of self-regulatory activity. Indeed, the word *control* refers to the fact that information of a certain type, arriving at a certain place, serves the function of turning on or off another process. When control involves a closed loop of processes, a very interesting picture results. As applied to a behaving system, this model of self-regulation implies that behavior is not a reflexive response to a stimulus, nor is behavior simply "emitted." Rather, self-regulation incorporates a feedback process in which the effects of behavior are monitored, with this information being used to guide subsequent behavior (Figure 6-1). The result is a continuous loop of feedback and control, causing behavioral adjustments (when necessary) so that the resulting state or condition closely approximates the reference value that has been taken up as a guide, or standard of comparison.

We see this abstract model of self-regulatory activity as being very much related to the human behaviors discussed throughout this chapter. In particular, we have argued that directing attention inward to the self promotes the comparison process that lies at the heart of this feedback system (Carver & Scheier, 1981a, 1982, 1983). As we said earlier, attending to one or the other facet of the self causes behavior to become more responsive to whatever behavioral standards and values are associated with that self-aspect in the present circumstance. Being "more responsive" typically means "maintaining closer conformity to." And this is precisely what happens in a feedback system such as that shown in Figure 6-1.

The feedback loop as a model of self-regulatory activity is intriguing, but taken alone it is somewhat limited. Powers responded to some of these limitations by proposing that overt, physical behavior incorporates a hierarchy of feedback systems, each controlling self-regulation of qualities at a particular level of abstraction. In the hierarchical organization that he argued for, a superordinate feedback loop "behaves" by specifying reference values to a subordinate system. Said differently, the behavioral output of the higher-order system *is* the setting and resetting of the reference values of the lower-order system. In the three-level hierarchy shown in Figure 6-2, for example, the behavioral output of the level 3 system constitutes the setting of the reference value for the level 2 system; the behavioral output at level 2 constitutes the setting of the reference value for level 1.

Though discussion of many of the implications of this sort of arrangement are beyond the scope of this chapter, there are points at which these ideas are quite relevant to present concerns. In order to illustrate this relevance, we return to the example with which we began the chapter. A girl named Susan has accepted a blind date for a football weekend, but she is less than overjoyed at the specific activities to be engaged in. She is unsure about how best to present herself—how to act and how open to be about her feelings.

Susan has a vague, but important (to her) image of the kind of person she thinks she ought to be—an idealized image of herself as a person. The coherent sense of personal unity that constitutes Susan's ideal self-image is an illustration of what Powers (1973a) called a "system concept." System concepts represent

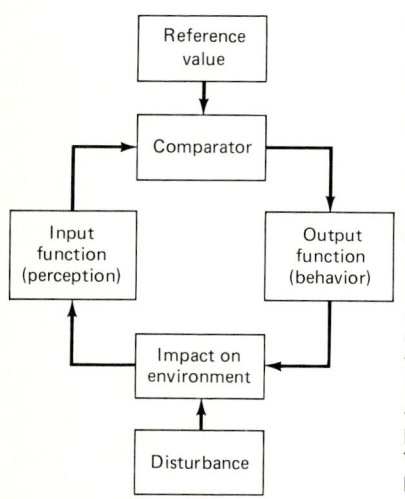

FIGURE 6-1
The (negative, or discrepancy reducing) feedback loop, the basic unit of cybernetic control. The "reference value" is the standard of comparison for the system's present action or state (an air temperature in a room if the system is a thermostat; a behavioral quality manifested in one's actions, such as "altruism" or "successful problem solution," if the system is a person). The "comparator" is the subsystem in which the presently existing state (present air temperature; behavioral quality now being displayed by the person) is compared with the reference value. "Disturbance" is anything outside the system that may influence the degree of discrepancy between the present state and the reference value (e.g., a gust of cold wind or a blazing sun; a hint or a misleading suggestion from another person concerning how to approach the problem that one is attempting). The overall function of the feedback loop is to create and maintain close proximity between reference value and present state.

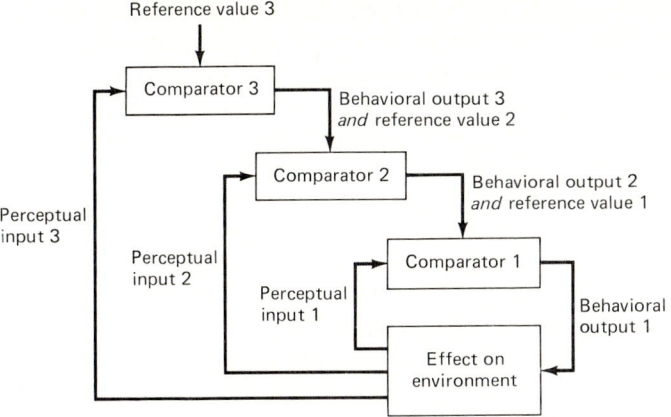

FIGURE 6-2
A three-level hierarchy of control systems, in which the behavioral output of a superordinate feedback loop constitutes the providing of a reference value to the next lower level feedback loop.

reference values at the highest level of abstraction that Powers postulated as being reflected in human behavior. According to the logic of control theory, this reference value serves as a very general guide for behavior, whenever a comparison is made between this value and one's present perception of the kind of person one is. In more familiar language, people try to build or enhance their self-esteem by attempting to be more like who they think they ought to be (cf. Tesser, 1980).

But how do people "be" the kind of people that represent their idealized selves? The answer suggested by Powers is that self-regulation at the level of system concepts involves (as its behavioral output) the specifying of reference values at the next lower level of abstraction (see Figure 6-2)—what Powers termed "principles." Principles in this hierarchy are essentially the same as what that word conveys in ordinary English. Principles are generalized guides for action (and thus somewhat more concrete than system concepts). Among the principles that Susan's idealized self specifies are (a) that one should always make the best possible use of one's time, and (b) that one should go out of one's way to make other people feel welcome and at ease. Susan often buttresses her own positive sense of self-worth by seeing that her behavior conforms to these values (and to other principles she holds) as closely as possible.[3]

---

[3] Note another very general point here: what actions are used to promote self-enhancement depends entirely upon the nature of the principles specified by the particular idealized self to which one aspires. If one's idealized self incorporates a sense of authority and command, the principles one holds (and the programs of action one undertakes) will tend to reflect issues involved in exerting control over other persons' actions. If one's idealized self incorporates a sense of nurturance and feeling needed by others, the principles one holds (and the programs of action one undertakes) will tend to reflect issues involved in noticing and dealing with the needs felt by others.

We should point out in passing that one implication of this sort of model is that self-esteem enhancement does not follow from a specific behavioral act. Rather, it can accrue from behaviors of diverse types, in many different domains of action. Difficulties for one's self-esteem in one domain can be partially compensated for by conforming to important principles in other domains (cf. Wicklund & Gollwitzer, 1982). And yet the overall sense of living up to one's self-image requires that one's actions reflect the multiple principles by which one has chosen to live.

A principle is more specific than a system concept, but it is still quite abstract. Principles do not specify behavior, but rather some quality that can be manifested in many different kinds of behavior. In Powers' view, we conform to principles by choosing plans of action, called "programs." Programs are much more concrete streams of behavior that are partially specified ahead of time and partially made up along the way. As an illustration, the principle of friendliness could specify a letter-writing program. But whether the letter is written at a typewriter, with a fountain pen, or with a pencil may depend upon the circumstances that confront the behaving person at the moment the letter is begun. Similarly, Susan's principle that other people should be made to feel welcomed and comfortable has led her to resolve to go to the football game and try to make the best of it. But how she and Harry will get to the game, and what actions will be entailed in "making the best of it," will be determined only as events unfold.

At the level below program control, the qualities suggested by Powers as the constituents of behavioral self-regulation begin to fall outside the domain of present interest. (These constituents have to do with the question of how a given activity—for instance, writing a letter—is physically created by means of an elaborate set of muscle movements.) For this reason we will refrain from describing them. On the other hand, it would seem to be useful to go backward a bit, to return to one of the levels discussed a few paragraphs earlier. By doing this we will be able to indicate what (in our view) this hierarchy has to say about the self-presentational issues that we addressed much earlier in the chapter.

Levels of Abstraction and the Public-Private Distinction

In particular, let us reexamine the notion of principle control. There is certainly a wide range of principles that could be utilized for behavioral self-regulation. But we would suggest that many of the principles that people use form two broad groups. One set of principles—and the programs of action that stem from them—reflect private, autonomous, egocentric goals. These are goals that do not necessarily involve considering, or even recognizing, the opinions or desires of other people. These reference values—e.g., personal attitudes, or privately held moral values—can be thought of as reflecting the private side of the self. These are the principles that are salient, we believe, when attention is directed to that facet of the self. For Susan, who finds sports events boring, a "private" principle is that it is a good idea to avoid such events.

Another set of principles—and the programs that they specify—describe qualities of action in which the needs or desires of other people are acknowledged and taken into account, either explicitly or by implication. These reference values can be thought of as reflecting the public side of the self. These are the principles that are often salient when attention is directed to public self-aspects. This set of principles is colored by the need to get a social consensus, or to consider the effects that an action may have on other people or on the impressions that other people have of oneself, before acting. One of Susan's principles that fits this category is the notion that people should be made to feel comfortable.

The public-private distinction appears to have little impact at levels of abstraction lower than principle control. Programs of action (e.g., going to the football game) are pretty much the same whether done for private reasons (because one likes such events) or socially-relevant reasons (because one wants to make a friend who likes football feel comfortable). Similarly, the distinction becomes less pronounced at the level of system concepts. That is, an idealized self-image is in a sense holistic. It combines and integrates both private values and goals and those that are social and self-presentational (cf. Tesser & Paulhus, 1983). At this level, a success or failure is fully as "personal" if the domain of action involves a social relationship or the creation of a public image as if it involves private achievement considerations. To conclude our example, it would make Susan feel good to have spent the afternoon doing something productive rather than waste the time at the game; but it will also make her feel good to know that she played a part in helping someone else from out of town feel welcome and at home.

In sum, it seems to be primarily at the level of principle control where the distinction between public and private self-aspects exerts its influence, as the person adopts one or the other of these two general orientations to behavior. Each of these orientations can satisfy concerns at the higher level, and each is ultimately expressed via control of very concrete action qualities at lower levels. Yet at this particular level, the public-private distinction can be seen to be nicely embedded within a far broader framework for discussing the self-regulation of behavior.

Self-Presentation, Image Manipulation, and the Issue of Purpose

The above discussion provides a way of addressing the public-private distinction in the context of a more general model of motivation. But by no means does it answer all of the questions that arise in talking about the role of the public-private distinction in understanding the kinds of self-presentational phenomena that comprise much of social behavior. As one considers how best to construe the behavioral effects documented in the research literature that we have been addressing, several additional questions easily suggest themselves. Let us phrase some of these questions in rather extreme terms. When people are focused on their public self-aspects, are they simply more conscious of and responsive to the social contingencies surrounding their behavior? Or are they instead engaged in an attempt to create false images in the minds of those others with whom they are dealing? When people are focused on their private self-aspects, are they engaged in active attempts to portray themselves as they think they really are to whoever else happens to be nearby? Are they engaged in acts of self-portrayal directed toward themselves? Or are they not really engaged in acts of self-presentation at all?

Our answers to these questions are partial answers at best, and quite frankly they are speculations as much as they are answers. Consider first public self-consciousness and its meaning for social behavior. There is indirect evidence from several sources that people high in public self-consciousness are motivated to avoid appearing deviant. As we noted earlier, they moderate their opinions when anticipating a social interaction (Scheier, 1980), they conform to an incorrect majority when there is risk of standing out (see Froming & Carver, 1981, for greater detail), and they make use of reference-group positions to help determine what opinions to state (Carver & Humphries, 1981). There is also evidence that this disposition is associated with a tendency to avoid overreaction to coercive communications, in a circumstance where overreaction might interfere with one's image maintenance (Carver & Scheier, 1981c).

We have suggested that these various effects represent a desire to facilitate social exchange, to get along. Presumably this is accomplished by presenting oneself in ways that tend to ease pressures that might otherwise be generated by conflict between one's actions and the expectations of relevant other persons. It is unclear from the available data, however, whether the effect of focusing on the public self is limited to this sort of facilitative self-presentation, or whether it also shades over into a cynical attempt to manipulate.

This question—whether self-presentations to others in a given situation are well meaning or manipulative—may be posed with regard to virtually all analyses of self-presentational phenomena, of course, and it is a question for which it is hard to provide a definitive answer. In all probability these two qualities (the well meaning and the manipulative) are present to varying degrees whenever people portray themselves to each other (or, indeed, even when people present themselves to themselves; see Schlenker, this volume). The issue should probably be recast in terms of what factors influence the balance between them at any given time.

The effects of private self-consciousness present us with a slightly more elaborate kind of puzzle. When people focus on the private aspect of self, do they simply "tune out" the social matrix? Are they instead aware of that matrix and of attempting to convey an image of what they see as their true selves to others around them (cf. Cheek, 1982; Cheek & Hogan, 1983; Swann, 1983)? Are they perhaps attempting to make acceptable self-presentations to themselves as audiences? (See Greenwald and Breckler, this volume, or Schlenker, 1980, for broader treatments of this position.)

Though all of these possibilities clearly exist, and all presumably do occur at one time or another, once again we know of no data that unequivocally address these questions as they pertain to the effects of focusing on the private self. To the various positions advanced by other theorists who have addressed the issue, however, we add one speculation: that different things may be occurring in people who are highly focused on the private self, depending upon how much they are also attentive to the public self. We assume that a restrictive focus on private self-aspects results in egocentric behavior that leaves aside any concern regarding self-presentation to other persons (though it may well involve presentations of self to the self as audience). The person in this state is behaving, but not portraying (unless to self). When this focus is tempered by an awareness of public self-aspects, however, there may occur instead an effort to present or portray that private self to others, to demonstrate as accurately as possible that inner sense of who one is.[4]

Attention and Behavior Reconsidered

In this chapter we have emphasized a distinction between private and public self-aspects. In so doing, however, we have simultaneously painted a picture of behavioral self-regulation in which inward focus of attention is an important determinant of action. In this final section we examine this picture from a slightly different perspective.

Attention has always been a difficult concept to pin down, though it is also a concept that most of us take for granted most of the time. Attentional processes are usually discussed in terms of a set of properties that they embody. Most relevant to the present discussion is the "selective" property of attention: Things attended to are selected out from the proliferation of things that are available to be attended to. But is attention selective because it is *directed* to certain attributes? Or is it selective because it is *drawn* to those attributes? The answer appears to be a little of both, or perhaps the one under some circumstances and the other under different circumstances.

An analogous issue occurs in trying to decide on the role of attentional processes (i.e., self-directed attention) in behavioral self-regulation. There are two rather different points of view that might be taken in that regard. One might assume that people wish to evaluate themselves in terms of either private goals or social-comparison goals (see Greenwald & Breckler, this volume), and then proceed to act by directing attention to those aspects of self-information that are relevant to such evaluations. Alternatively, one might assume that people focus on some aspect of self (out of dispositional habit, or because something has induced such a focus) and evaluate what they are seeing in terms of the

---

[4]Our emphasis in this discussion is on the motivational structure underlying the person's behavior. We should note, however, that success in an attempt to portray oneself very definitely has additional determinants, e.g., the degree to which the person has the communication skills necessary to create a coherent self-presentation.

associated reference values. These characterizations are distinguished from each other (in part, at least) by the fact that the one portrays attention to the self as merely an intermediate step between intention and action, whereas the other portrays attention to the self as a process that initiates action.

Which, then, is correct? The answer that springs most easily to the lips (or word processor) is that reality incorporates a little of both. Experimental research (discussed earlier in this chapter) makes it clear that shifts in attentional focus are capable of causing shifts in behavior. The logic of the experimental method dictates that this is a cause-effect relation. But here we encounter one of the potential dangers of overreliance on experiments and the data that they yield. Specifically, the fact that a manipulation of attentional focus (or any other manipulation) is *capable* of causing an effect in the laboratory does not necessarily mean that that variable is inevitably the beginning of the causal chain outside the laboratory. Nevertheless, our intuitions join these data in telling us that we are sometimes induced by circumstances to direct our attention to particular dimensions of ourselves, and that subsequent events follow directly from those shifts in focus.

Data recently gathered by Cheek and Briggs (1982) appear at first glance to help in resolving this issue. Yet ultimately they do not. Cheek and Briggs (1982) found that there are strong correlations between the two dimensions of self-consciousness and the importance with which people weight various aspects of their identities. More specifically, private self-consciousness was associated with a tendency to rate nonsocial or personal self-aspects as highly important to the sense of identity. Public self-consciousness was associated with a tendency to rate social self-aspects as highly important to the sense of identity. One is tempted to conclude from these findings that people develop a tendency to focus on certain aspects of self precisely *because* they value those self-aspects highly. Because other self-aspects are regarded as less important, they receive less of the person's attention over time.

Unfortunately, however, such a conclusion is too facile. It runs afoul of a problem inherent in all research involving the measurement of personality differences: One can never be sure of what is cause and what is effect. It is fully as reasonable to argue from the Cheek and Briggs data that the tendency to focus on a particular self-aspect is causal, and induces one to come to view that self-aspect as fundamentally important to one's identity, perhaps merely by virtue of its phenomenological prominence. We simply cannot be sure which of the two portrayals is the more accurate. And thus we cannot be sure whether behavioral effects associated with variations in self-consciousness are initiated by attentional processes, or are initiated instead by the sense of where and how one's identity is defined, and the desire to evaluate one's present status regarding that identity definition.

In the broader view, however, we wonder if these perspectives are not perhaps two sides of the same coin. When people are considering the values that are important to them and are preparing to seek information that will help in evaluating themselves, are they not thereby being self-reflective? We have already seen that self-consciousness is implicated in the process of formulating behavioral intentions (Davis et al., 1982). And there is also evidence that self-focus causes people to seek out concrete information that would facilitate a mental evaluation of their behavior at a more abstract level (Scheier & Carver, 1983b). Perhaps the intent to evaluate oneself, or the more general intent to behave, becomes formulated by the very process of attending to the information that suggests a need for such evaluation or behavior. Perhaps neither has primacy, but rather—like public and private aspects of self—are two facets of what is in reality a single process.

REFERENCES

Ajzen, I., & Fishbein, M. (1970). The prediction of behavior from attitudinal and normative variables. *Journal of Experimental Social Psychology, 6,* 466–487.

Ajzen, I., & Fishbein, M. (1974). Factors influencing intentions and the intention-behavior relation. *Human Relations, 27,* 1–15.

Asch, S. E. (1951). Effects of group pressure upon the modification and distortion of judgments. In H. Guetzkow (Ed.), *Group, leadership, and man.* Pittsburgh, PA: Carnegie Press.

Asch, S. E. (1956). Studies of independence and conformity: I. A minority of one against a unanimous majority. *Psychological Monographs, 70,* 9 Whole No. 416.

Baumeister, R. F. (1982). A self-presentational view of social phenomena. *Psychological Bulletin, 91,* 3–26.

Brockner, J. (1979). The effects of self-esteem, success-failure, and self-consciousness on task performance. *Journal of Personality and Social Psychology, 37,* 1732–1741.

Burgio, K. L., Merluzzi, T. V., & Pryor, J. B. (1982). The effects of self-focused attention and performance expectancies on social interaction. Paper presented at the meeting of the Eastern Psychological Association, Baltimore.

Carver, C. S. (1974). Facilitation of physical aggression through objective self-awareness. *Journal of Experimental Social Psychology, 10,* 365–370.

Carver, C. S. (1975). Physical aggression as a function of objective self-awareness and attitudes toward punishment. *Journal of Experimental Social Psychology, 11,* 510–519.

Carver, C. S., Blaney, P. H., & Scheier, M. F. (1979a). Focus of attention, chronic expectancy, and responses to a feared stimulus. *Journal of Personality and Social Psychology, 37,* 1186–1195.

Carver, C. S., Blaney, P. H., & Scheier, M. F. (1979b). Reassertion and giving up: The interactive role of self-directed attention and outcome expectancy. *Journal of Personality and Social Psychology, 37,* 1859–1870.

Carver, C. S., & Glass, D. C. (1976). The self-consciousness scale: A discriminant validity study. *Journal of Personality Assessment, 40,* 169–172.

Carver, C. S., & Humphries, C. (1981). Havana daydreaming: A study of self-consciousness and the negative reference group among Cuban Americans. *Journal of Personality and Social Psychology, 40,* 545–552.

Carver, C. S., Peterson, L. M., Follansbee, D. J., & Scheier, M. F. (1983). Effects of self-directed attention on performance and persistence among persons high and low in test anxiety. *Cognitive Therapy and Research, 7,* 333–354.

Carver, C. S., & Scheier, M. F. (1978). Self-focusing effects of dispositional self-consciousness, mirror presence, and audience presence. *Journal of Personality and Social Psychology, 36,* 324–332.

Carver, C. S., & Scheier, M. F. (1981a). *Attention and self-regulation: A control-theory approach to human behavior.* New York: Springer-Verlag.

Carver, C. S., & Scheier, M. F. (1981b). The self-attention-induced feedback loop and social facilitation. *Journal of Experimental Social Psychology, 17,* 545–568.

Carver, C. S., & Scheier, M. F. (1981c). Self-consciousness and reactance. *Journal of Research in Personality, 15,* 16–29.

Carver, C. S., & Scheier, M. F. (1982). Control theory: A useful conceptual framework for personality-social, clinical, and health psychology. *Psychological Bulletin, 92,* 111–135.

Carver, C. S., & Scheier, M. F. (1983). A control-theory model of normal behavior, and implications for problems in self-management. In P. C. Kendall (Ed.), *Advances in cognitive-behavioral research and therapy* (Vol. 2). New York: Academic Press.

Cheek, J. M. (1982). Aggregation, moderator variables, and the validity of personality tests: A peer-rating study. *Journal of Personality and Social Psychology, 43,* 1254–1269.

Cheek, J. M., & Briggs, S. R. 1982). Self-consciousness and aspects of identity. *Journal of Research in Personality, 16,* 401–408.

Cheek, J. M., & Hogan, R. (1983). Self-concepts, self-presentations, and moral judgments. In J. Suls & A. G. Greenwald (Eds.), *Psychological perspectives on the self* (Vol. 2). Hillsdale, NJ: Erlbaum.

Cialdini, R. B., Levy, A., Herman, C. P., Kozlowski, L. T., & Petty, R. E. (1976). Elastic shifts of opinion: Determinants of direction and durability. *Journal of Personality and Social Psychology, 34,* 663–672.

Cooley, C. H. (1902). *Human nature and the social order.* New York: Scribners.

Crutchfield, R. A. (1955). Conformity and character. *American Psychologist, 10,* 191–198.

Davis, D., Holtgraves, T., Kasmer, J., & Ginsburg, G. (1982). Self-consciousness, attitudes, subjective norms, and behavioral intentions. Paper presented at the annual meeting of the American Psychological Association, Washington, D.C.

Deutsch, M. (1975). Equity, equality, and need: What determines which value will be used as the basis of distributive justice? *Journal of Social Issues, 31,* 137–149.

Duval, S., & Wicklund, R. A. (1972). *A theory of objective self-awareness.* New York: Academic Press.

Fenigstein, A. (1979). Self-consciousness, self-attention, and social interaction. *Journal of Personality and Social Psychology, 37,* 75–86.

Fenigstein, A., Scheier, M. F., & Buss, A. H. (1975). Public and private self-consciousness: Assessment and theory. *Journal of Consulting and Clinical Psychology, 43,* 522–527.

Froming, W. J., & Carver, C. S. (1981). Divergent influences of private and public self-consciousness in a compliance paradigm. *Journal of Research in Personality, 15,* 159–171.

Froming, W. J., Walker, G. R., & Lopyan, K. J. (1982). Public and private self-awareness: When personal attitudes conflict with societal expectations. *Journal of Experimental Social Psychology, 18,* 476–487.

Garner, W. R., Hake, H. W., & Eriksen, C. W. (1956). Operationalism and the concept of perception. *Psychological Review, 63,* 149–159.

Gibbons, F. X., Carver, C. S., Scheier, M. F., & Hormuth, S. E. (1979). Self-focused attention and the placebo effect: Fooling some of the people some of the time. *Journal of Experimental Social Psychology, 15,* 263–274.

Goffman, E. (1959). *The presentation of self in everyday life.* Garden City, NY: Doubleday.

Greenberg, J. (1982). Self-image versus impression management in adherence to distributive justice standards: The influence of self-awareness and self-consciousness. *Journal of Personality and Social Psychology, 44,* 5–19.

James, W. (1890). *The principles of psychology.* New York: Holt.

Kernis, M., & Reis, H. T. (1982). The role of attentional focus in choosing between allocation standards. Unpublished manuscript.

Klinger, E. (1975). Consequences of commitment to and disengagement from incentives. *Psychological Review, 82,* 1–25.

Leary, M. R., & Schlenker, B. R. (1981). The social psychology of shyness: A self-presentational model. In J. T. Tedeschi (Ed.), *Impression management theory and social psychological research.* New York: Academic Press.

Leventhal, G. S. (1976). The distribution of rewards and resources in groups and organizations. In L. Berkowitz & E. Walster (Eds.), *Advances in experimental social psychology* (Vol. 9). New York: Academic Press.

Mead, G. H. (1934). *Mind, self, and society.* Chicago: University of Chicago Press.

Miller, L. C., & Cox, C. L. (1981). Public self-consciousness and makeup use: Individual differences in preparational tactics. Paper presented at the annual meeting of the American Psychological Association, Los Angeles.

Newcomb, T. M. (1950). *Social psychology.* New York: Dryden Press.

Newcomb, T. M. (1958). Attitude development as a function of reference groups: The Bennington study. In E. E. Maccoby, T. M. Newcomb, & E. L. Hartley (Eds.), *Readings in social psychology* (3rd ed.). New York: Holt, Rinehart, & Winston.

Newtson, D., & Czerlinsky, T. (1974). Adjustments of attitude communications for contrasts by extreme audiences. *Journal of Personality and Social Psychology, 30,* 829–837.

Powers, W. T. (1973a). *Behavior: The control of perception.* Chicago: Aldine.

Powers, W. T. (1973b). Feedback: Beyond behaviorism. *Science, 179,* 351–356.

Reis, H. T. (1981). Self-presentation and distributive justice. In J. T. Tedeschi (Ed.), *Impression management theory and social psychological research.* New York: Academic Press.

Reis, H. T., & Gruzen, J. (1976). On mediating equity, equality, and self-interest: The role of self-presentation in social exchange. *Journal of Experimental Social Psychology, 12,* 487–503.

Santee, R. T., & Maslach, C. (1982). To agree or not to agree: Personal dissent amid social pressure to conform. *Journal of Personality and Social Psychology, 42,* 690–700.

Scheier, M. F. (1976). Self-awareness, self-consciousness, and angry aggression. *Journal of Personality, 44,* 627–644.

Scheier, M. F. (1980). Effects of public and private self-consciousness on the public expression of personal beliefs. *Journal of Personality and Social Psychology, 39,* 514–521.

Scheier, M. F., & Carver, C. S. (1977). Self-focused attention and the experience of emotion: Attraction, repulsion, elation, and depression. *Journal of Personality and Social Psychology, 35,* 625–636.

Scheier, M. F., & Carver, C. S. (1981). Private and public aspects of the self. In L.

Wheeler (Ed.), *Review of personality and social psychology* (Vol. 2). Beverly Hills CA: Sage.

Scheier, M. F., & Carver, C. S. (1983a). Two sides of the self: One for you and one for me. In J. Suls & A. G. Greenwald (Eds.), *Psychological perspectives on the self* (Vol. 2). Hillsdale, NJ: Erlbaum.

Scheier, M. F., & Carver, C. S. (1983b). Self-directed attention and the comparison of self with standards. *Journal of Experimental Social Psychology, 19,* 205–222.

Scheier, M. F., Carver, C. S., & Gibbons, F. X. (1979). Self-directed attention, awareness of bodily states, and suggestibility. *Journal of Personality and Social Psychology, 37,* 1576–1588.

Scheier, M. F., Fenigstein, A., & Buss, A. H. (1974). Self-awareness and physical aggression. *Journal of Experimental Social Psychology, 10,* 264–273.

Schlenker, B. R. (1980). *Impression management: The self-concept, social identity, and interpersonal relations.* Monterey, CA: Brooks/Cole.

Schlenker, B. R., & Leary, M. R. (1982). Social anxiety and self-presentation: A conceptualization and model. *Psychological Bulletin, 92,* 641–669.

Shapiro, E. G. (1975). Effect of expectation of future interaction on reward allocation in dyads: Equity and equality. *Journal of Personality and Social Psychology, 31,* 873–880.

Solomon, M. R., & Schopler, J. (1982). Self-consciousness and clothing. *Personality and Social Psychology Bulletin, 8,* 508–514.

Swann, W. B., Jr. (1983). Self-verification: Bringing social reality into harmony with the self. In J. Suls & A. G. Greenwald (Eds.), *Psychological perspectives on the self* (Vol. 2). Hillsdale, NJ: Erlbaum.

Tesser, A. (1980). A self-evaluation maintenance model of social behavior. University of Georgia, Unpublished manuscript.

Tesser, A., & Paulhus, D. (1983). The definition of self: Private and public self-evaluation management strategies. *Journal of Personality and Social Psychology, 44,* 672–682.

Tobey, E. L., & Tunnell, G. (1981). Predicting our impressions on others: Effects of public self-consciousness and acting, a self-monitoring subscale. *Personality and Social Psychology Bulletin, 7,* 661–669.

Turner, R. G., Scheier, M. F., Carver, C. S., & Ickes, W. (1978). Correlates of self-consciousness. *Journal of Personality Assessment, 42,* 285–289.

Von Grumbkow, J., Deen, E., Steensma, H., & Wilke, H. (1965). The effect of future interaction on the distribution on rewards. *European Journal of Social Psychology, 1,* 282–293.

Wicklund, R. A., & Duval, S. (1971). Opinion change and performance facilitation as a result of objective self-awareness. *Journal of Experimental Social Psychology, 7,* 319–342.

Wicklund, R. A., & Gollwitzer, P. M. (1982). *Symbolic self-completion.* Hillsdale, NJ: Erlbaum.

CHAPTER 7

SOCIOANALYTIC THEORY: AN ALTERNATIVE TO ARMADILLO PSYCHOLOGY

Robert Hogan
Warren H. Jones
University of Tulsa

Jonathan M. Cheek
Wellesley College

INTRODUCTION

Among the many animals that die along the highways of the American Southwest, the armadillo may be the most pathetic. Shuffling along, nose to the ground, looking for food, utterly absorbed in the smaller details of life, the armadillo never sees the truck bearing down on it. Modern psychology, with its passion for little theories, is in many ways like the armadillo. Utterly absorbed in the small details of research, obsessed by the requirements of pure experimental design, psychology has wandered onto a highway that is likely to lead to futility and obsolescence.

In a thoughtful analysis of this trend, Maddi (1982) points out that our commitment to minitheories has spawned a lot of empirical research but few advances in fundamental understanding. Hundreds of studies of attributions and depression, androgyny, and intrinsic motivation have not revealed the core dynamics of self-esteem, sex-role acquisition, or motivation because, he observes, the research in these areas has been placed in such narrow theoretical contexts.

Twenty-five years of little theories have brought little progress: we believe that it may be time to try developing broader theoretical perspectives which could themselves be used to choose topics for research. The purpose of this chapter, therefore, is to present a viewpoint on the psychology of self-presentation that comes from a larger theoretical context—in this case socioanalytic theory, which is a synthesis of evolutionary biology, depth psychology, and symbolic interactionism (Hogan, (1982). The argument in a nutshell is that in order to take part in the life of one's social or cultural group, one must have a part to play. Once that part—one's social identity—has been established—it must be maintained. One maintains the credibility of one's social identity through self-presentation. The way we do self-presentation at any time may reflect changeable environmental circumstances, but the tendency to do self-presentation is archaic, unconscious, a distinctive feature of our species, and fundamentally related to one's opportunities for reproductive success.

SOCIAL, PSYCHOLOGICAL, AND SOCIOANALYTIC THEORIES OF IMPRESSION MANAGEMENT

Perhaps the best known and most influential modern analysis of impression management is Goffman's (1959) book, *The Presentation of Self in Everyday Life*. Goffman was a sociologist and from his perspective roles are defined by society and are external to people. A role is a typified set of responses or a script; persons who occupy specific roles (e.g., son, daughter, student) use the script to respond to social expectations. According to Goffman, people use impression management to signify the kinds of roles they are playing (and their attitudes toward them). Nonetheless, for Goffman a person's behavior is defined by the roles he or she plays (see also, Berger, 1963). Social psychologists (e.g., Jones & Thibaut, 1958) have also used role theoretical analyses for some time, and their views on impression management are similar to Goffman's. The writings of Jones and his colleagues represent a major point of view regarding impression management; we call this the traditional social-psychological view, and it is quite distinctive.

These writers assume, for example, that there is no stable core to personality. Personality is defined in terms of peoples' self-presentations; the external surface is the essence of a person and there is nothing of importance underneath (cf. Arkin, 1980). Moreover, the primary determinants of self-presentational behavior are in the environment (Baumeister & Jones, 1978). Environmental or situational demands elicit or pull out self-presentational actions, whatever they may be. When the environment changes, the self-presentational behaviors change as well.

Our actions depend on environmental demands and pressures; so, however, do our self-images. According to Gergen (1981), for example, peoples' self-concepts change whenever they adopt different social roles, and he concludes that the self is nothing more than a highly malleable reflection of the ongoing processes of social interaction. His position is quite consistent with Goffman's (1959) dramaturgical metaphor, which views a person's self as a "product of a scene that comes off, and not a cause of it" (p. 252). Finally, in traditional social-psychological theories, the motives for doing impression management are conscious and goal directed (Athay & Darley, 1981). It is always in our best interest to control the impressions that others form of us; controlling these impressions is a primary means by which we achieve our other goals in life (cf. Snyder, 1981).

In contrast with traditional social-psychological views of impression management, traditional personality theory tends to ignore these issues altogether. Freudian and Jungian theory, for example, are concerned almost entirely with understanding and explaining what goes on inside each person's mind, independent of his or her social circumstances. They regard impression management as a topic too superficial to be given serious attention. In the case of Carl Jung, a tendency toward self-presentation is something to be overcome.

Our view is somewhere between the traditional views of personality and social psychology. We believe, for example, that there *is* a stable core to personality; there are "structures' within each person that give a stylistic coherence and a distinctive flavor to everything he or she does. These structures are both biological and social in origin. On the biological side, they include species-typical instincts or programs for behavior and the individual's unique complement of temperaments (cf. Buss & Plomin, 1975). On the social side, these stable structures include each person's self-image, life goals and plans, interactional strategies, and theories about the social world.

These stable structures tend largely to undercut the influence of situational factors on everyday behavior. For example, in order to persuade others that we are reasonable, we normally must do different things in different situations. Our behavior may change; nonetheless, the image that guided the behavior and the impressions that we convey will remain the same.

Although the structures underlying overt behavior may be stable, this doesn't mean that self-presentation is typically conscious and goal directed. In our view the process of self-presentation is rooted in human nature and is therefore largely unconscious. In fact, it takes unusual concentration and introspection to become aware of one's self-presentational habits and tendencies. As Archer and Akert (1980) point out, the sheer volume of meaningful information exchanged in social interaction would overwhelm conscious processing; this suggests that effective social interaction depends on un-self-conscious habits and considerable unconscious monitoring of communication channels. Conversely, to the degree that one is self-conscious about his or her self-presentations, he or she will appear stilted, mannered, artificial, and unconvincing.

Finally, some peoples' actions do reflect "situational influences" rather closely. But Barron's (1953) research on the Asch conformity situation shows that this is largely a matter of individual differences. Socially self-confident individuals with a strong sense of personal identity tend to resist group pressure; individuals who are anxious about their social identity and fear negative social evaluations tend to conform to group pressure (Hogan & Cheek, 1983). On further analysis, however, we see that the question is not one of conformity versus nonconformity, but rather one of which reference group one conforms to. As we have argued elsewhere (Cheek & Hogan, 1983), autonomy is conformity to the expectations of an internalized reference group rather than resistance to persons present in a particular social situation. Moreover, from a socioanalytic perspective, craven conformity and clinch-jawed autonomy are both extreme forms of behavior; psychological maturity is a function of integrating both the inner and the outer determinants of one's actions. But in most normal cases the crucial determinants of those actions are in the person rather than in the social situation.

AN OUTLINE OF SOCIOANALYTIC THEORY

Most traditional personality theories come from psychiatry and are based on the study of neurotic patients. These theories imply that the major generalization we can make about people is that everyone is somewhat neurotic, and that the most important problem in life is to overcome that neurosis. Although these generalizations nicely serve the financial interests of the psychiatric community, they just *may* be empirically false, and in any case they contain a very peculiar image of human nature. Moreover, other perspectives are equally defensible. Consider, for example, the implications of our history as a biological species. We appear to have evolved about two million years ago (more or less) as a pack-hunting primate on the East African plains. Our social organization and talent for tool use allowed us first to supplant other close competitors (e.g., australopithecus, chimpanzee), and then to leave East Africa and literally populate the earth. We should note that, at a level perhaps even more fundamental than tool use, people have always lived in groups, every group is organized in terms of a status hierarchy, and everyone knows his or her place in that hierarchy.

Think for a moment about what this implies. In order for group living and status hierarchies to be human universals (and they are), tendencies toward social living and status attainment must be innate and must confer an adaptive advantage on those who effectively exploit these tendencies. Predators (lions, tigers, hunting dogs) quickly take advantage of solitary primates but avoid primate troops, so there is a clear benefit to being able to live in a group. At the same time, having status in one's group confers powerful advantages on the person who has it; one gets one's choice of food, romantic partners, living space, and other desirable commodities. We conclude, therefore, that getting along and getting ahead are two great problems in life that each person must solve.

We are literally driven to socialize, to interact with others. At the same time, we are driven to compete with those same people for status. Our strivings for status and for interaction are largely unconscious, and they insure that a measure of conflict is inherent in group living at every level. Conflict is not a matter of misunderstanding among people that open communication will resolve; it is part of what it means to live with other people. There is also a biogrammar for human social interaction; social interaction from the most informal (morning coffee) to the most elaborate (a presidential inauguration) is rule governed (Hogan & Henley, 1970) and surprisingly ritualistic. Evidence of systematic burial practices 50,000 years ago suggests that we have always needed our rituals and that they give form and meaning to our lives.

We seek status and attention, but always in the context of ritualized social interaction. Follow another person around for a day and observe what goes on. What you will see is that person moving from one interaction to another. Although the players and the game will change across interactions, each will have its own particular flavor, and the actions will be ritualized and repetitious. Moreover, people become quite upset when the rituals are disturbed: Consider what happens when a fan runs on the field during a baseball game, or when another person constantly interrupts during a conversation.

To say that people seek attention and status in the context of ritualized interactions is not to say that (a) everyone is equally driven to pursue attention and status, or (b) everyone is equally competent at pursuing them. At the genetic level some people will be more affiliative than others, and some will be more dominant than others. Conversely, through experience and modeling, some people will be more pleasant to deal with than others, and some will be more skilled at enhancing their status. Consequently, one's level of status and popularity is a joint function of inheritance and experience. Obviously, status and popularity must be defined with regard to the people with whom one interacts, either directly or symbolically.

Our evolutionary heritage as group-living animals suggests the presence of a number of biologically based behavioral dispositions. Most important among these are the dispositions to seek attention and approval, to seek status, and to seek structure and order in our everyday lives. Positive attention, high status, and predictability are rewarding; criticism, low status, and unpredictability are quite unpleasant. Taken together, these dispositions are the reason we seek ritualized social interaction. Interaction organized in terms of rituals, no matter how trivial or informal, is the primary means by which we obtain attention, status, and predictability in our lives. Consequently, most of us spend our days preparing for, doing, and occasionally reflecting on our interactions.

As Goffman (1967) pointed out, interaction is literally where the action is. But more important, personality exists primarily during interaction. Personality is a by-product of interaction in much the same way that light is a by-product of electric current passing through the filaments of a light bulb.

The word *personality* actually has two referents, two meanings which refer to the two sides of every interaction. That is, personality must be defined from the perspectives of the observer *and* the actor. From the perspective of the observer, personality refers to an actor's reputation, to the distinctive impact he or she makes on others. Personality from an observer's perspective is encoded and expressed in trait words, terms such as "honest," "assertive," and "imaginative." Although the total number of trait words in English is quite large, present evidence suggests they can be sorted or organized in terms of six broad categories: These can be labelled intelligence, adjustment, ambition, self-control, sociability, and likeability (e.g., Digman & Takemoto-Chock, 1981). This much is reasonably well-established. We would like to make a further and more radical claim; namely, that trait words express observers' evaluations of actors as potential contributors to the observers' group. Language evolved in conjunction with social living. In small groups each person's actions have consequences for the entire group. Through praise and censure, language serves as a means of social control. Trait terms are used to construct and evaluate actors' reputations; consequently, they serve in subtle ways to regulate social action.

Personality from the perspective of the actor is made up of the structures that explain why actors create the kinds of reputations that are uniquely theirs. These reputations are immensely consequential because they bear on individual fitness. Fitness is a key concept in evolutionary theory, and is defined as the number of *viable* progeny an individual leaves behind. Reproduction is a major goal in life, but there are some major preliminaries that must be dealt with before one can get on with it. At the very least, one must have a role to play in one's social group or community; i.e., one must establish a social and occupational identity. Moreover, once that identity is established, it must be maintained. We establish and maintain our identities through self-presentation, through actions designed (often unconsciously) to tell others who we are and how we want to be regarded.

Actually, we have to know who we are before we can decide who we want to be. Social identity is in fact built upon and arises out of a private sense of identity, which is a complex amalgam of self-images and self-esteem that reflects each person's developmental history. Inner or private identity is logically and causally prior to social identity—the former is the foundation on which the latter rests. From a phenomenological perspective, one's self-esteem and feelings of self worth are more important than one's social identity, but social identity is more consequential—outer or social identity is directly tied to fitness. The two forms of identity exist in a kind of dialectical relationship; one's social and occupational successes and failures feed back into and influence one's feelings of self regard which, in turn, influence occupational success.

Self-presentations are actions designed for two very different audiences: one's self and other people. We put on performances for ourselves, watch ourselves, and carry out interior monologues as a way of maintaining and enhancing our private or inner identities. The maintenance of one's internal image, once again, is prior to and normally takes precedence over, the maintenance of one's social identity, although the two processes are related.

A good or positive internal image makes hope and striving possible; a bad internal image is associated with despair, and, in extreme cases, with illness and even death. To the degree that one must invest energy maintaining and repairing one's internal image, one uses up energy necessary to pursue one's social and occupational goals. The blessed, the charmed, and the lucky need spend little time on inner work.

But a positive private identity doesn't necessarily guarantee occupational success. Social and occupational success, which ultimately are tied to fitness, are related to one's social identity and its maintenance. The assessment, repair, and maintenance of a person's feelings of self-regard is the province of clinical psychology. This paper, however, focuses on those aspects of personality associated with developing and maintaining a social identity, i.e., factors associated with social and occupational success. Nor does this paper deal with the implications of dissociation between the two forms of identity; we will dismiss that crucial topic by simply noting that when there is too much incongruity between the two forms of identity, that inevitably causes problems for the person involved.

People differ from one another largely in terms of the groups whose approval they value, and their success in achieving status and popularity within those groups. Sheer technical competence is not sufficient for these purposes. Abrasive, self-defeating nerds will not maximize their talents no matter how great they may be; charming, tactful, and engaging people tend, conversely, to be overachievers (Hobert, & Dunnette, 1968). And this is the sense in which neurosis is an important issue—people who are neurotic are underachievers. This is also the sense in which neurosis is irrelevant—people who are well adjusted may still lack the positive skills necessary to achieve their life's goals.

It seems to us, therefore, that the crucial subject matter for personality psychology concerns the determinants of individual differences in interpersonal competence rather than psychological adjustment. One can best learn about the game of tennis by studying accomplished players rather than incompetent amateurs. Personality psychologists who study neurotics are like tennis coaches who study hackers; they are looking at the wrong group.

The foregoing sketch of socioanalytic theory is deceptively simple. We will close this section by pointing out some not-so-obvious consequences that it entails. There are six of these that we would like to emphasize. The first is that self-presentation and impression management are not trivial party games. They are fundamental processes, rooted in our history as group-living animals. They are archaic, powerful, compulsive tendencies that are closely tied to our chances for survival and reproductive success.

Second, *all* social action has a symbolic component; everything we do can be interpreted in self-presentational terms. The clothes we wear, the books we have on our shelves, the music on our radios, our jobs, our friends, and our enemies—all of these tell others how we want to be regarded. Others, noting these external signs, appraise us and construct our reputations accordingly.

Third, this model means that it is, in principle, impossible to simply "be oneself." How, for example, are others to know that you are being yourself? Does "being yourself" mean doing that which is "natural," defecating on a public sidewalk perhaps? If not, why not? To "be yourself" requires a very careful performance—it may mean wearing old clothes and worn shoes, using colloquial expressions, perhaps cursing, and maintaining a slouched posture, but always being careful not to go too far in intruding on the sensibilities of others—avoiding flatulence in an elevator, for example.

Fourth, the point of our model is to *explain* social action (cf., Athay & Darley, 1981). The problem of explanation raises issues in the philosophy of science that psychologists seem to want to avoid. For example, many psychologists treat prediction and explanation as synonymous, when in fact they are not. Rather than going into that technical literature here, we will simply state, without justification, that this model is intended to provide an explanation for social action.

A fifth point is that adult personality is frequently the crystallization of childhood defenses. We don't always act so as to tell others how we want to be regarded; sometimes we act to tell others how we do *not* want to be regarded. Self-presentation often has a defensive intent (Arkin, 1980); conversely, the traditional defense mechanisms can be seen in terms of self-presentation.

Finally, individual differences in role-taking and role-playing skill are the major variables underlying the attainment of status and popularity. George

Herbert Mead (1934) suggested that role-taking ability is the "g" factor in human abilities and we concur. Moreover, there is a substantial body of literature to support this claim (cf. Hogan & Briggs, 1983; Snyder, 1981).

PERSONALITY DEVELOPMENT

Perhaps as a result of its concern with "situational variables," traditional social psychology has little to say about social development. In contrast, traditional personality psychology from Freud to Erikson is organized around a developmental perspective. In Freud's mature view, adult personality reflects the manner in which people accommodate to authority in early childhood (i.e., adult personality reflects the manner in which each person has resolved his or her Oedipal crisis). According to George Herbert Mead, however, adult personality reflects the manner in which people accommodate to peer expectations in later childhood, and this directly contradicts Freud. Both views are partially correct, but both require further extension and modification. Our notions about development represent one form that this extension and modification might take. Before we present these views, however, we need to say something about self-consciousness, and about our units of analysis.

Units of Analysis

The superordinate function of personality theory is to explain human actions (Athay & Darley, 1981). The success of this explanatory process crucially depends on choosing the correct units of analysis (Allport, 1958). There are as many units as there are writers, but some units are more natural than others. The life cycle, for example, has a certain biological reality to it; but as a practical unit it is terribly cumbersome. A more manageable unit is an interaction sequence.

Our days (and our time) are organized in terms of interactions. Each interaction has an assumed or conventionally agreed-on goal. In each interaction the participants deal with one another in terms of their roles. Associated with each role is a set of norms—rules that define the parameters of performance when one is in a particular role. Correlated with these norms are individual expectations: When we know someone is in the role of the bride at a wedding ceremony, we know the *norms* associated with the bride's performance and we *expect* the bride to act in accordance with them. The roles that we play in interactions vary along a continuum from informal to formal; informal roles are the ones we invent for ourselves (or others invent for us—e.g., Mother's boy, Daddy's girl); formal roles are socially ordained—e.g., president, teacher, bride at a wedding. The norms that operate in an interaction vary along a continuum from implicit to explicit; implicit norms regulate interactions among good friends; explicit norms regulate wedding ceremonies. The expectations that we have about other people's behavior during an interaction vary from conscious to unconscious; the expectations for interactions among old friends are largely unconscious; the expectations that prevail in a classroom are usually conscious.

Why is our social behavior organized in terms of ritualized interaction sequences and roles? Because, as we noted above, people need social attention, and they need structure and predictability. Ritualized interaction gives them both. At the same time, outside our roles we have very little to say to one another; for example, go to a class reunion and try to talk to your former friends about something other than the old days. Even more importantly, we may have little to say to ourselves outside our roles. Our sense of self, our sense of identity, is largely a function of the social positions we have negotiated through the various roles that we play.

Concerning units of analysis, social action can be structured in terms of interaction sequences. These interactions can be further decomposed into the roles that are involved, the norms associated with these roles, and the expectations that are correlated with the norms. Because our terminology is similar to the social-psychological model called "rule-role theory" (Gergen & Gergen, 1981), we might point out two ways in which our approach differs from the Gergens'. First, although we agree that roles are the natural units of human behavior, we don't believe people's actions are caused or explained by their roles. In our view a person's self-concept determines the roles he or she is willing to play, rather than the roles determining the self-concept. (However, the consequences of a person's role performances may modify his or her self-concepts.) Second, a person's self-concept is the result of a process of identity negotiation that begins at birth and culminates in an internalized character structure that is relatively stable throughout adulthood. (For the Gergens, the self-concept constantly changes.) This process is a transactional one, involving the mutual influences of person's biological temperament, early family experiences, peer interactions, and cultural environment. We emphasize role playing in our account of personality development because it is the arena in which the crucial process of identity negotiation is carried out.

Self-Consciousness

The social behavior of many animals is structured in terms of roles. Chickens, for example, have pecking orders; a single chicken's position in this order defines its role and its behavior vis-à-vis other chickens. The social lives of wasps, bees, ants, and termites are also organized in terms of roles. Similarly, there is a definite role structure underlying the social behavior of wolves. What, then, is the need for or the place of self-consciousness in human social behavior given that complex and integrated social orders are possible in creatures that certainly don't seem self-conscious?

As always, the larger question concerns the organization of behavior. Among infrahumans, behavior is organized in terms of genetically controlled, fixed-action patterns that can be more or less modified by experience. People have few innate fixed-action patterns. Something, therefore, must have evolved to take their place; otherwise, there would be no structure to social action. That something is self-consciousness (cf. Barkow, 1978).

Mead's early analysis of this issue is quite perceptive. He notes that the behavior of young children is impulsive, dissociated, and not in conformance with social norms. In contrast, the behavior of most adults is self-controlled, integrated, and socially conforming. He suggests that the mechanism for this transformation is self-consciousness, and that self-consciousness emerges from playing games. Self-consciousness (in Mead's terms, role-taking ability) does two things simultaneously. On the one hand, it makes one aware of and responsive to the expectations of others; a person who is self-conscious can perceive others' expectations and is usually disposed to comply with them. On the other hand, self-awareness allows us to see ourselves in a role and use that perception to correct, modify, or moderate our role performance. In short, self-awareness simultaneously promotes conformity to social norms and provides flexibility in role performance—and a viable social system requires that people have both capacities.

Role Playing in Infancy

At any given time, the structure of personality reflects the kinds of relationships in which one is involved. In the course of development, three kinds of relationships are especially important. Each presents unique problems, and each leaves a distinctive mark on adult personality. During early childhood we must learn to live with adults; during later childhood, we must learn to live with peers; in early adulthood, we must learn to live in bureaucracies.

In our view, people from birth need interaction in structured and predictable terms. Building on this, competent adults can construct interactions with very young infants—as young as two weeks, for example (Meltzoff & Moore, 1983). The technique is simple; place the infant in a comfortable position, then repeat a gesture—a tickle in the stomach, a hand over the eyes—taking care to pace the gesture so that the infant can track it. This will produce wriggles, chortles, and diffuse excitement. Why? Because the infant is getting attention in a predictable format. Stern (1977) and Rattner and Bruner (1978) provide detailed descriptions of rule-bound interactions between infants and their caretakers beginning shortly after the child's birth.

By 11 months a more complicated interaction is possible: Hold a child on your lap and open a book, point to a picture and say "what's that;" then turn the page and repeat the sequence. Children love such interactions because, once again, they are receiving predictable attention. But there is an important difference between this and the previous game. Here one is not interacting face to face with the child; rather, the interaction is structured around an external focus—the book—and the child can participate by, for example, banging the book, tearing the pages, and saying "what's that" too. But more importantly, with an external focus, and mutual parts to play, we have the essential ingredients of any interaction.

By 20 months children can actually do role playing; this is usually in the form of "mother-baby" games, where mothers use a particular language and tone of voice to signify that the game is on, and children respond in their way—usually by being whiney and demanding. By 36 to 40 months children are sufficiently sophisticated that they will deliberately initiate the sequence by saying something like: "Pretend you are the mommy and I was the baby." Our guess is that such deliberate playing of actual roles is one way in which children acquire role distance and self-consciousness. This is consistent with Mead's views on development and with data presented by Lewis and Brooks (1975) showing that children acquire the concepts of object—and person—permanence before they acquire the capacity for self-recognition. The problem, as Mead (1934) phrased it, is to learn to adopt a perspective outside oneself from which it is possible to regard oneself as a social object. The process of deliberately "playing at" playing a familiar role may be a major means by which we develop the capacity for self-objectification, and therefore self-recognition.

There are three final points about this early period of social interaction that we would like to emphasize. The first concerns the consequences of being in a prolonged series of interactions largely organized and initiated by adults. The major outcome of this period of development is the manner in which a child typically responds to authority. A child's parents are the prototypical authority figures in his or her life, and they are subsequently replaced by teachers, coaches, police, and so forth; the quality of that original set of interactions will shape a person's attitudes toward authority for life. This, in turn, has implications for everything from academic performance to tax evasion. That is to say, persons with positive attitudes toward authority do better at everything; they are the popular and high-status members of their groups. The evidence on this point is quite clear. Consider, for example, research associated with the socialization scale of the California Psychological Inventory (Gough, 1975). This is quite possibly the most thoroughly validated scale in the history of personality measurement. It is a powerful measure of attitudes toward authority, and the behavioral consequences of scores on this scale involve the entire range of achievement, status attainment, and adjustment to one's social groups. The central cluster of items on this empirically derived scale concerns the quality of one's interactions with one's parents in childhood. The foregoing observation regarding the link between parent-child interaction and attitudes toward authority is, of course, commonplace in traditional psychoanalytic theory.

Our second point concerns what children bring to the early socialization process. Children are not blank tablets on which adult authority writes a social script; rather, the innate characteristics of an infant interact with its ingoing social environment in complex ways (cf. Bell, 1968). For example, a child's basic level of affiliativeness will determine the amount of interaction he or she needs and how rewarding he or she will be to deal with. Similarly, Buss (1981) shows that a child's temperament-based activity level at age 3 predicts the vigor with which he or she is disciplined at age five. Thus,". . . in the ontogenesis of social behavior a child's instinctual tendencies come together with arbitrary social requirements and both are transformed" (Hogan, 1976, p. 204). In the case of a very active child, for example, the child will curb its energies, and its parents will become more tolerant.

Our third point here is that a child's attitudes toward authority are reflected in its self-image (good girl, bad boy) and self-presentational behaviors (conformance, defiance) in interactions with adults. During this early phase of life, children develop their unique ways of responding to the expectations of parents, adult relatives, teachers, coaches, scout masters, and in an impersonal sense, the rules and values of their culture.

Role Playing in Childhood

As children leave the exclusive care of their parents and spend more time in their peer groups (as found in their extended family, neighborhood, and nursery school), social interaction depends on their ability to initiate and participate in play sequences with peers. There is substantial evidence that role play occurs spontaneously in the free-play episodes of children, beginning around 36 months. The structure of these interactions should be familiar by now: Young children in dyads will mill about randomly until one (typically a girl) says something like "Pretend you were the mommy and I was the baby and we were having dinner." At that point the children begin moving about purposefully, their actions become synchronized, and they talk until they have exhausted their repertoires and the possibility of the situation. There will be a pause in the action until they invent another set of roles and a pretext for interaction.

It appears that children are able to construct interactions at about the time they need to—as defined by their social ecology. Moreover, even by 36 months there are individual differences in children's ability to interact. Specifically, Lieberman (1977) shows that children classified earlier as having solid attachment relationships with their parents are the most skilled in social interaction in nursery school. Individual differences in shyness and in sociability will also influence the vigor of these early interactions.

An interesting side light of this research on early role playing is that children's conceptions of the mommy role is more complete than their conceptions of the baby role. There are two explanations for this. On the one hand, children understand very early that there are status differences among roles (e.g., that the male role is preferable to the female role), and that mommies have more status than babies. They may therefore think and talk more about the mommy than the baby role. On the other hand, this may reflect the fact that awareness of others precedes self-awareness (Lewis & Brooks, 1975).

By 36 months children understand the mechanics of social interaction (roles, context, etc.) so well that they can engage in a kind of metaplay. For example, girls, in an effort to tease little boys, will say "Pretend you were the mommy and

I was the daddy." This conversational gambit typically elicits howls of protest. But it also reveals a remarkably subtle knowledge of the interaction process as early as 36 months. It shows, for example, that the girl knows (a) how to initiate an interaction, (b) that there are status differences associated with various roles, (c) that the boy recognizes these status differences, and (d) that the boy will resent a loss of status.

These role-play interactions among three year olds are the prototypes of *all* adult interaction. Children need to interact; at the same time, they understand that interactions must proceed in terms of roles organized around assumed or stated agendas; they understand there are norms associated with roles, that others *expect* these norms to be observed; and they sense that their self-conceptions determine the kinds of roles they are willing (or allowed) to play. As adults we spend our days moving from one interaction to another; in each interaction the formal elements described above are the same.

The evidence is clear that preschool children engage in surprisingly complex role play in which they demonstrate an impressive understanding of sex and status appropriate norms. A remaining question concerns what this sociodramatic play contributes to personality and social development. One view is that this play merely reflects a child's social knowledge as expressed in a primarily egocentric fantasy world. In a recent view Rubin (1980) notes that ". . . while fantasy play serves a consolidating and practice role . . . the major moving/guiding force (in the development of social skills) is the peer interaction itself and *not* the dramatic activity per se" (p. 81).

In contrast, Vandenberg (1978), in a recent review of the *animal* literature, remarks that:

> [T]hrough *play,* the animal masters the mature social behaviors that it then later *applies* in a "serious" context. The previously reviewed evidence substantiates the fact that extensive social play is necessary for later successful social intercourse (p. 736).

Vygotsky, Bruner, and Mead also regard play as serious. Curiously, all of the studies Rubin (1980) reviews report that fantasy play is important in the stimulation of social skill development in humans. He criticizes the methodologies of these studies, but his own conclusion regarding the importance of play (or unimportance) is not supported by a single piece of evidence.

Several logical arguments also suggest that play stimulates social development. For example, interacting in a variety of pretend roles may allow children to see roles in perspective, to understand their conventional and arbitrary nature; in short, such play may lead to role distance and to mastery of the *concept* of role itself, all of which is essential for *competent* subsequent social development. This idea originated with Bateson and contrasts sharply with the view that role play is mere practice of previously acquired knowledge (cited by Fein, 1979). In later childhood, playing team games replaces dramatic play as the major stimulant of a child's growing understanding of the requirements of and the mutual expectations involved in role performances (Mead, 1934). As Mead noted, pretend play gives way to play in organized games, but the effects on social development should be the same—i.e., practice at role playing within a socially agreed on context, the capacity to see roles in perspective, and the ability to see oneself as a social object, the occupant of a particular, arbitrary role whose performance in that role will usually be evaluated.

A child can experiment with more roles in an hour of play than he or she could perform in years of actual social behavior. In addition to developing social skills, sociodramatic play stimulates the entire range of symbolic functioning (i.e., thinking in terms of analytical units that are purely hypothetical), but this is an issue that goes beyond the present paper's focus on social interaction. (See, however, Fein, 1979.)

Perhaps some psychologists underemphasize the importance of role play in personality development because they underestimate the complexity of role playing in everyday life. The social world is substantially more complex than a grade-school Christmas pageant; great skill is necessary competently to play the "game of games"—i.e., to live with other people. As Cicourel (1974) notes:

> The dramaturgical metaphor of the stage is defective in explaining how actors are capable of imitation and innovation with little or no prior rehearsal, just as a child is capable of producing grammatically correct utterances that he has never heard, and of understanding utterances that have never been heard before (p. 30).

The point is that children must learn general interpretive procedures for negotiating novel interpersonal encounters and situations. An ideal way to gain experience in generating and responding to novel variations in basic social roles is through sociodramatic play, and such play would be much more than mere "practice" (Vandenberg, 1978). An observational study by Rubin (1982) found that socially withdrawn children engage in less dramatic play and are judged to play in ways that are cognitively less mature than that of their age mates. This shows the consequences of individual differences in role-playing skill in young children and provides logical support for the developmental importance of fantasy role play.

Young children, in their play, flit from role to role. As they move toward adolescence, they begin to develop more habitual ways of reacting to others; this probably parallels their developing sense of identity and core levels of self-esteem. In adolescence, peer play turns serious as youngsters begin to compete in earnest for status and popularity. Drawing on their surprisingly extensive past experience, they try out various public identities or roles on their peers. These are in reality fairly stereotyped—athlete, scholar, deviant, *femme fatale*, etc. These public roles are thematically organized self-presentations designed to gain or protect status and popularity. The lucky few are able to play the roles they choose. Some withdraw and refuse to participate—to no avail, of course, because the others simply assume that *that* is the role they have chosen. Still others have (usually undesirable) roles thrust upon them. By adolescence, everyone must join in the game; some do it successfully, using the roles of their choice, and others do it defensively, in an effort mainly to minimize unpopularity.

And so it goes until these early forms of self-presentation harden, become habitual and un-self-conscious, and turn into a person's social identity in adulthood. The way we appear to others in adulthood has clear developmental antecedents. Fantasy role play in childhood gives way to play in organized games. Those lessons are incorporated into the increasingly serious social interactions of adolescence, where the themes of status and popularity become important for the first time. As the game turns serious, self-presentations become more habitual, fixed, and unconscious—and they begin to seal our fate.

Role Playing in Adulthood

Individual differences in the self-presentational skills and social competencies developed in childhood and adolescence have fateful consequences for status and popularity in adulthood. This is seen most clearly in the areas of family life and career development, where successful outcomes depend on competency in social interaction. High-status people in every field appreciate and understand the interpersonal dynamics we have been discussing, although they rarely can describe what they are doing—and the same is true for athletes; the great ones all have the same skills but typically can't analyze what they are doing. As one rather homey example of the importance of self-presentational skill, consider the presidential career of Jimmy Carter. He was "in reality" a very bright, well-organized, and highly principled man—exactly the sort of person one would want for a president. At the same time, however, he had only modest talents for self-presentation and was perceived by the public and his critics as weak, indecisive, and ultimately inappropriate for the job. His successor, Ronald Reagan, on the other hand, has masterful self-presentational skills and is apparently a popular president.

One's self-images and typified self-presentational behaviors, in conjunction with one's opportunities, produce career choices and careers. The key problems in adulthood concern having a family and a career, and these goals must typically be pursued through bureaucratic channels. Schooling is excellent training for adult life in a bureaucracy. In school as well as in later organizations, one must accommodate the demands of authority while maintaining good relations with one's peers. In this process, one must rely on all the lessons of development. And one's failures can be traced to early lessons poorly mastered.

We would like to close this section by pointing out that the traditional emphasis in personality psychology on psychopathology is misplaced. Our model stresses the role of social competency and self-presentational skill in the attainment of one's life goals. The absence of psychopathology does not entail the presence of social competency, and the presence of interpsychic afflictions does not entail the absence of competency. This is not to say that psychopathology is irrelevant to the social process; it is to say, however, that personality psychology should focus on competency rather than psychopathology if it wishes to explain and understand social action.

SOCIOANALYTIC THEORY AND ADJUSTMENT

As noted above, we believe that the major problems in life concern achieving interpersonal status and acceptance from others. Attaining status and acceptance is inherently problematic, however, and will be so independent of one's level of adjustment. Disappointment and failure are inevitable concomitants of an active life in society because no parent can ever be sufficiently appreciative, no spouse sufficiently attentive, no subordinate sufficiently grateful, no employer sufficiently supportive.

We disagree with traditional clinical theories regarding the problems in life. But we also disagree with traditional accounts of adjustment, because these accounts (a) are ahistorical, decontextualized, and treat human behavior as if it emerged only yesterday and occurs in a vacuum; (b) emphasize, almost exclusively, individualistic and self-contained models of human action that misconstrue the nature and consequences of deviance; (c) ignore the fact that one can be seriously deviant without manifesting any of the symptoms of neurosis (e.g. certain criminal groups); (d) imply that the absence of neurosis is equivalent to social competence, whereas it is clear that one need not be neurotic to be a failure; and (e) emphasize exotic, but statistically infrequent clinical syndromes (anorexia, sexual dysfunction) and deemphasize problems of enormous social consequence (shyness, loneliness).

The sociologists have always maintained that the determinants, the appropriate definition, and most of the negative consequences of psychopathology are to be found in the social groups from which these phenomena emerge. What, after all, is wrong with being maladjusted? There is of course the distress experienced by those who are so afflicted. But beyond that, psychopathology mainly disrupts the functioning of the social units (e.g., marriages, families, communities) in which it occurs. In large and geographically mobile societies such as ours, deviant persons are abandoned or isolated in institutions. Consequently, even though the economic impact of psychopathology (e.g., reduced productivity, taxes to underwrite hospital costs) is substantial, its pernicious social consequences are not always apparent. By contrast, in a relationship (a family, or small, interdependent societies), the consequences of psychopathology are enormous; maladjustment not only degrades the quality of life for the disturbed individual, it threatens the welfare and survival of the group as well. A group can't rely on someone whose behavior is unpredictable and bizarre. The Shamen of nonliterate societies are therefore quite right to treat both psychological and medical ailments so as to restore the social order that they threaten (Howells, 1963). In our judgment, then, an adequate account of adjustment requires placing it in the context of relationships, and that is the topic to which we now turn.

SOCIOANALYTIC THEORY OF RELATIONSHIPS

Quickly reprising our earlier argument, socioanalytic theory (Hogan, 1982) starts with three assumptions: (1) the distinctive feature of human evolution is a capacity for social organization, (2) people therefore live in groups, and (3) human groups are always organized according to status. These assumptions imply that our social nature is biologically driven; our need for others apparently arose as a function of primate morphology—isolated hominids were vulnerable to the larger carnivores, but there is safety in numbers—and thus an evolutionary advantage accrues to beasts who live in groups. Language and ritual appeared very early in human evolution, and these are major ingredients in the recipe for interpersonal relationships. Finally, group living and social organization make personal relationships both possible and necessary. In fact, that which we recognize as most uniquely human (e.g., culture, art, law, religion) is predicated on and facilitated by the roles and rules of social interchange. We are gregarious, group-living creatures, and relevant illustrations of this fact stretch beyond the dawn of civilization and across every imaginable cultural radiation. A second implication of our biologically based social nature is that interpersonal failures (e.g., ostracism, social isolation, lost or dissolving personal relationships) entail more than reduced social rewards; they signal an inability to satisfy the fundamental human need for companionship.

These core assumptions also imply that there are two ways by which the need for others is expressed: (1) the need for acceptance and approval (popularity); and (2) the need for power and control (status). A moment's reflection will reveal, however, that there is a dilemma here: to the extent that one achieves status, one runs the risk of engendering jealousy and resentment in others. (Try bragging about your accomplishments to your colleagues.) On the other hand, popularity is often bought at the price of foregoing personal achievement. The tension between popularity and status means that relationships are inherently problematical; consequently, it is perhaps surprising that anyone ever avoids persistent alienation and loneliness. On the other hand, it is clear that some people are more successful in the interpersonal sphere than others. This suggests that there are important individual differences in the capacity to achieve interpersonal satisfaction, and self-presentational skill is part of this. Moreover, as noted earlier, most self-presentations are habitual and mainly unconscious. This means that persons who are relatively unsuccessful at achieving status and popularity will also, for the most part, be unaware of those features of their own behavior that defeat their interpersonal goals. It becomes important, therefore, to identify those aspects of interpersonal functioning that disrupt relationships.

We can summarize the foregoing as follows: (a) human beings are fundamentally, perhaps innately, oriented to doing social interaction; (b) beyond survival, people, regardless of cultural or historical settings, mostly seek status and acceptance from their social groups; (c) personal relationships are inherently problematical; (d) interpersonal success requires maintaining a balance between egocentric drives for status and sociocentric drives for popularity; (e) individual differences in social competence determine, in part, social success; and (f) the reasons for interpersonal failure are largely unavailable to those persons who chronically fail.

THE PSYCHOPATHOLOGIES OF EVERYDAY LIFE

Considerable research has recently focused on the role of relations and social-support systems in individual adjustment and health. For example, measures of the quality of one's social network and intimate relationships predict the frequency, severity, and prognosis of both psychological and medical complaints; they also mediate the connection between environmental stressors and their effects (Cobb, 1976; Heller, 1979; Sarason et al., 1980). Similarly, vulnerability to life-threatening illness is, in many cases, as strongly related to marital status (and hence the experiences entailed by marital status) as it is to the physiological conditions presumed to cause such ailments (Lynch, 1977). Social competency is therefore related to health because it minimizes disruptions in interpersonal functioning. From our earlier discussion of relationships, we can derive several hypotheses regarding social failure. For example, because relationships are both fundamentally necessary and inherently problematical, social failure should be relatively common but highly aversive. We would expect social failure to be related to individual differences in the skill and confidence necessary for effective interpersonal functioning as well as to self-defeating self-presentations. Finally, self-defeating persons should lack insight regarding their interpersonal behavior generally, and specifically be unaware of the impact of their own behavior on others.

Shyness

The shyness literature provides one way of testing these hypotheses. Shyness can be defined as a form of social impairment in which one acts in a reticent, timid, and inhibited manner in unfamiliar or threatening social situations (Buss, 1980). As we would predict, shyness is both common and aversive. One survey indicated that 73 percent of a large sample of American college students reported having experienced shyness and 42 percent labelled themselves as characteristically and chronically shy (Zimbardo, 1977). Shyness is also strongly associated with such aversive emotional and cognitive states as fearfulness, self-consciousness, and low self-esteem (Cheek & Buss, 1981; Jones & Russell, 1982; Pilkonis, 1977a). Although virtually anyone may feel shy in certain circumstances (e.g., those involving novelty, ambiguity, or formality; cf. Buss, 1980), there is growing evidence that shyness is also a stable disposition that is manifested consistently across situations (Jones & Russell, 1983) and for which there may be a genetic predisposition (Cheek, 1983; Plomin & Rowe, 1979). Finally, it is important to note that shyness is not just a self-label for experience—instead it has concrete and recognizable behavioral manifestations (e.g., avoidance of gaze, low speaking voice).

Shyness involves more than social incompetence. On the one hand, shy persons report that they lack the confidence and skill necessary to perform well in social situations (Zimbardo, 1977), and there is evidence that these deficits translate into specific interpersonal inadequacies (Cheek & Buss, 1981; Jones &

Russell, 1982). On the other hand, these deficits are judged by others to be more than they are: Shy persons are seen as untalented, unfriendly, aloof, snobbish, and lacking in leadership, in addition to being socially reticent (Cheek & Buss, 1981; Jones, Cavert, & Indart, 1983; Pilkonis, 1977b). Thus, the implications of a shy person's awkward self-presentations for his or her status and popularity (Schlenker & Leary, 1982) are probably more important than the discomfort he or she experiences. It is one thing to feel uncomfortable in social interactions, but quite another to be denied social opportunities because of the erroneous but highly probable impressions of others. Finally, we should note that, in an important sense, shy persons are unaware of how they are perceived by others (Jones et al., 1983).

To argue that shyness involves self-presentations, the nature and effects of which a shy person is at least partially unaware, is not to suggest that shyness is never strategic. Anyone may be deliberately quiet in order not to appear foolish, or perhaps to appear unassuming and cooperative, and to gain the approval of others. No doubt this strategy is effective in some situations. On the other hand, it is likely that dispositionally shy people are often unable to tell when reticence is appropriate and when it is not; it is also apparent that shy people are unable to project a warm and friendly image when it is obviously to their benefit to do so.

Loneliness

Another example of the psychopathology of everyday life is loneliness, a situation that occurs when one is without close personal relationships or is dissatisfied with the relationships one has. As socioanalytic theory predicts, loneliness is a common problem. One large national survey found that 26 percent of the respondents reported having felt lonely during the previous two weeks (Bradburn, 1969). Loneliness is the most common psychological complaint among widows (Lopata, 1969), but is also particularly high among adolescents and young adults (Brennan, 1982). Surprisingly, given the typical conceptualization of loneliness as transitory, there is evidence that, once experienced, loneliness is a relatively persistent state (Cutrona, 1982). In addition, there is considerable evidence that loneliness is always aversive and involves extensive self-derogation, anxiety, depression, poor self-esteem, alienation, and hostility (Jones, Freeman & Goswick, 1981; Russell, Peplau & Ferguson, 1978; Russell, Peplau & Cutrona, 1980).

Moreover, laboratory and naturalistic studies show that lonelier people tend to present themselves in ways that seem to reduce their attractiveness to others and to reduce the probability that any given interaction will lead to a mutually satisfying relationship. For example, studies involving group and dyadic conversations show that lonely people interact (at least with strangers) in a self-absorbed and unresponsive manner. One study (Jones, Hobbs, & Hockenbury, 1982) found that lonely people asked fewer questions of their partners, talked relatively more about themselves, and arbitrarily changed the topic of conversation more frequently. Not surprisingly then, lonely people are judged by others as more difficult to get to know (Jones, Sansone & Helm, 1983; Solano, Batten, & Parish, 1982).

Two experiments reported by Hansson and Jones (1982) are particularly interesting in this regard. Participants were exposed either to an extremely altruistic model or to an extreme solution to a personal problem. As compared with the not-lonely men and women, lonely men conformed and modelled significantly less (a pattern associated with dominance and status but also with less acceptance from others), whereas lonely women conformed and modelled significantly more (suggesting greater acceptance from others, but lower status). Thus, loneliness seems specifically associated with the failure to balance status and popularity needs.

Finally, as is the case of shyness, lonely persons are generally unaware of their interpersonal style and their impact on others. In one series of experiments, lonely people indicated that their partner's and fellow group member's view of them was more negative and rejecting than was actually the case (Jones et al., 1981; Jones, 1982; Jones et al., 1983); they were also less accurate at predicting the self-ratings of their fellow participants. In another study, lonely college students underestimated the average number of conversations in which they engaged daily (Jones, 1981).

CONCLUSION

In this chapter we have outlined an account of self-presentational processes that differs from the traditional social-psychological versions (e.g., Goffman, 1958; Snyder, 1981). In our view, self-presentation can best be understood in the broader context of personality theory. From this perspective, self-presentational behavior is, as it were, the tip of the iceberg; it is behavior that itself requires interpretation and analysis.

The first level of analysis shows that self-presentational behavior is highly symbolic—it reflects efforts on the part of an actor to tell us how he or she would like to be regarded (or not regarded)—and therefore it ought not be taken at face value. Self-presentations are the means by which actors convey information regarding their self-images.

The second level of analysis reveals that each person's self-concepts and modes of self-presentation have a developmental history. As a consequence of this history, actors (a) are often unaware of how other people react to them, and (b) typically can't modify their behavior even if they realize they are, for example, annoying others. Self-presentational behaviors are largely unconscious and often defensive in their intent.

At the third level of analysis, we see that there is a rather precise structure underlying self-presentations—which are, of course, normally embedded in social interaction. There is always an assumed or conventional reason for the interaction ("We need to discuss this problem." "Let's get together for a drink."), and there are roles for the participants to play. Self-presentations are, therefore, constrained and circumscribed in a number of ways: They are constrained by the actor's social skill and self-image, by the goals of the interaction, and by the roles that the actor must play.

The fourth level of analysis concerns the dynamics of social interaction, self-presentation, and therefore social conduct. Self-presentational strategies and interactional goals provide the *reasons* for social behavior but not the *causes*. The reasons for social action are quite varied; the causes, however, are always the same. People need approbative attention, people need status, and people need structure and predictability. There are, of course, a variety of biologically programmed impuses to action (hunger, thirst, etc.), but attention, status, and predictability are the master motives under which these are organized. For our present purposes, however, we would like to emphasize the point that these master motives cause and explain social action—why we do it and why it takes its prototypical forms. They testify to the essential validity of the lyrics of the song in the movie *Casablanca*: "It's still the same old story, a fight for love and glory, a case of do or die. . . ." That the search for love and glory is fundamental comes as no surprise; in a plastic culture devoted to superficial trends, the need for predictability and stability is sometimes overlooked.

REFERENCES

Allport, G. W. (1958). What units shall we employ? In G. Lindsey (Ed.), *Assessment of human motives*. New York: Rinehart.

Archer, D., & Akert, R. M. (1980). The encoding of meaning: A test of three theories of social interaction. *Sociological Inquiry, 50,* [3–4], 393–419.

Arkin, R. M. (1980). Self-presentation. In D. M. Wegner & R. R. Vallacher (Eds.), *The self in social psychology*. New York: Oxford University Press.

Athay, M., & Darley, J. M. (1981). Toward an interaction-centered theory of personality. In N. Cantor & J. K. Kihlstrom (Eds.), *Personality, cognition, and social interaction*. Hillsdale, NJ: Erlbaum.

Barkow, J. H. (1978). Social norms, self, and sociobiology. *Current Anthropology, 19,* 99–118.

Barron, F. (1953). Some personality correlates of independence of judgment. *Journal of Personality, 21,* 287–297.

Baumeister, R. F., & Jones, E. E. (1978). When self-presentation is constrained by the target's knowledge: Consistency and compensation. *Journal of Personality and Social Psychology, 36,* 608–618.

Bell, R. Q. (1968). A reinterpretation of the direction of effects in studies of socialization. *Psychological Review, 75,* 81–95.

Berger, P. (1963). *An invitation to sociology*. New York: Doubleday.

Bradburn, N. (1969). *The structure of psychological well-being*. Chicago: Aldine.

Brennan, T. (1982). Loneliness at adolescence. In L. A. Peplau & D. Perlman (Eds.), *Loneliness: A sourcebook of current theory, research and therapy*. New York: Wiley-Interscience.

Buss, A. H. (1980). *Self-consciousness and social anxiety*. New York: W. H. Freeman.

Buss, A. H., & Plomin, R. (1975). *A temperament theory of personality development.* New York: Wiley.

Buss, D. M. (1981). Predicting parent-child interactions from children's activity level. *Developmental Psychology, 17,* 59–65.

Cheek, J. M. (1983). William James and the fourth force in personality psychology. *Personality Forum, 1* (No. 2), 21–24.

Cheek, J. M., & Buss, A. H. (1981). Shyness and sociability. *Journal of Personality and Social Psychology, 41,* 330–337.

Cheek, J. M., & Hogan, R. (1983). Self-concepts, self-presentation, and moral judgments. In J. Suls & A. G. Greenwald (Eds.), *Psychological Perspectives on the Self* (Vol. 2). Hillsdale, NJ: Erlbaum.

Cicourel, A. V. (1974). *Cognitive Sociology.* New York: Free Press.

Cobb, S. (1976). Social support as a moderator of life stress. *Psychosomatic Medicine, 38,* 300–314.

Cutrona, C. E. (1982). Transition to college: Loneliness and the process of social adjustment. In L. A. Peplau & D. Perlman (Eds.), *Loneliness: A sourcebook of current theory, research and therapy.* New York: Wiley-Interscience.

Digman, J. M., & Takemoto-Chock, N. R. (1981). Factors in the natural language of personality: Re-analysis, comparison, and interpretation of six major studies. *Multivariate Behavioral Research, 16,* 149–170.

Fein, G. G. (1979). Play and the acquisition of symbols. In L. Katz (Ed.), *Current topics in early education* (Vol. 2). Norwood, NY: Albex.

Gergen, K. J. (1981). The function and foibles of negotiating self-conception. In M. D. Lynch, A. A. Norem-Hebersin, & K. J. Gergen (Eds.), *Self-concept: Advances in theory and research.* Cambridge, MA: Ballinger.

Gergen, K. J., & Gergen, M. M. (1981). *Social psychology.* New York: Harcourt, Brace, Jovanovich.

Goffman, E. (1959). *The presentation of self in everyday life.* New York: Doubleday.

Goffman, E. (1967). *Interaction ritual.* New York: Doubleday.

Gough, H. G. (1975). *Manual: The California psychological inventory* (rev. ed.). Palo Alto, CA: Consulting Psychologist Press.

Hansson, R. O., & Jones, W. H. (1981). Loneliness, cooperation and conformity among American undergraduates. *Journal of Social Psychology, 115,* 103–108.

Heller, K. (1979). The effects of social support: Prevention and treatment implications. In A. P. Goldstein & F. H. Kanfer (Eds.), *Maximizing treatment gains: Transfer enhancement in psychotherapy.* New York: Academic Press.

Hobert, R., & Dunnette, M. D. (1968). Development of moderator variables to enhance the prediction of managerial effectiveness. *Journal of Applied Psychology, 51,* 50–64.

Hogan, R. (1982). A socioanalytic theory of personality. In M. Page (Ed.), *Nebraska Symposium on Motivation.* Lincoln, NE: University of Nebraska Press, 55–89.

Hogan, R. (1976). *Personality theory: The personological tradition.* Englewood Cliffs, NJ: Prentice-Hall.

Hogan, R., & Briggs, S. (1983). Noncognitive measures of social intelligence. Paper presented at the meeting of the American Psychological Association, Anaheim, CA.

Hogan, R., & Cheek, J. M. (1983). Identity, authenticity, and maturity. In T. R. Sarbin & K. E. Schiebe (Eds.), *Studies in social identity.* New York: Praeger.

Hogan, R., & Henley, N. (1970). Nomotics: The science of human rule systems. *Law and Society Review, 51,* 135–146.

Howells, W. (1962). *The heathens: Primitive man and his religion.* Garden City, New York: Doubleday.

Jones, E. E., & Thibaut, J. W. (1958). Interaction goals as bases of inference in interpersonal perception. In R. Tagivri & L. Petrullo (Eds.), *Person perception and interpersonal behavior.* Stanford, CA: Stanford University Press.

Jones, W. H. (1981). Loneliness and social contact. *Journal of Social Psychology, 113,* 295–296.

Jones, W. H. (1982). Loneliness and social behavior. In L. A. Peplau & D. Perlman (Eds.), *Loneliness: A sourcebook of current theory, research and theory.* New York: Wiley-Interscience.

Jones, W. H., Cavert, C. W., & Indart, M. (1983). Impressions of shyness. Paper presented at the 1982 meeting of the American Psychological Association, Anaheim, CA.

Jones, W. H., Freeman, J. A., & Goswick, R. A. (1981). The persistence of loneliness: Self and other determinants. *Journal of Personality, 49,* 27–48.

Jones, W. H., Hobbs, S. A., & Hockenbury, D. (1982). Loneliness and social skill defects. *Journal of Personality and Social Psychology, 42,* 682–689.

Jones, W. H., & Russell, D. (1982). The social reticence scale: An objective measure of shyness. *Journal of Personality Assessment, 46,* 629–631.

Jones, W. H., & Russell, D. (1983). A personality congruent analysis of situations. Unpublished manuscript, University of Tulsa.

Jones, W. H., Sansone, C., & Helm, B. (1983). Loneliness and interpersonal judgments. *Personality and Social Psychology Bulletin, 9,* 437–444.

Lewis, M., & Brooks, J. (1975). Infants' social perception: A constructionist view. In L. B. Cohen & P. Solapatek (Eds.), *Infant perception: From sensation to cognition* (Vol. 2). New York: Academic Press.

Liberman, A. F. (1977). Preschooler's competence with a peer: Relations with attachment and peer experience. *Child Development, 48,* 1277–1287.

Lopata, H. Z. (1969). Loneliness: Forms and components. *Social Problems, 17,* 248–261.

Lynch, J. (1977). *The broken heart: The medical consequences of loneliness in America.* New York: Basic Books.

Maddi, S. R. (1982). Personality for the 1980s. Henry A. Murray lectures in personality. East Lansing, Michigan.

Mead, G. H. (1934). *Mind, self, and society.* Chicago: University of Chicago Press.

Meltzoff, A. N., & Moore, M. K. (1983). Newborn infants imitate adult facial gestures. *Child Development, 54,* 702–709.

Pilkonis, P. A. (1977a). Shyness, public and private, and its relationship to other measures of social behavior. *Journal of Personality, 45,* 585–595.

Pilkonis, P. A. (1977b). The behavioral consequence of shyness. *Journal of Personality, 45,* 596–611.

Plomin, R., & Rowe, D. (1979). Genetic and environmental etiology of social behavior in infancy. *Developmental Psychology, 15,* 62–72.

Rattner, M., & Bruner, J. (1978). Games, social exchange, and the acquisition of language. *Journal of Child Language, 5,* 391–1.

Rubin, K. H. (1980). Fantasy play: Its role in the development of social skills and social cognition. *New Directions for Child Development, 9,* 69–84.

Russell, D., Peplau, L. A., & Cutrona, C. E. (1980). The revised UCLA loneliness scale: Concurrent and discriminant validity evidence. *Journal of Personality and Social Psychology, 39,* 472–480.

Russell, D., Peplau, L. A., & Ferguson, M. (1978). Developing a measure of loneliness. *Journal of Personality Assessment, 42,* 290–294.

Sarason, I. G., Levine, H. M., Basham, R. B., & Sarason, B. R. (1983). Assessing social support: The social support questionnaire. *Journal of Personality and Social Psychology, 44,* 127–139.

Schlenker, B. R., & Leary, M. R. (1982). Social anxiety and self-presentation: A conceptualization and model. *Psychological Bulletin, 92,* 641–669.

Snyder, M. (1981). Impression management: The self in social interaction. In L. S. Wrightsman, & K. Deaux, *Social psychology in the eighties* (3rd ed). Monterey, CA: Brooks/Cole Publishing Co.

Solano, C. H., Batten, P. G., & Parish, E. A. (1982). Loneliness and patterns of self-disclosure. *Journal of Personality and Social Psychology, 43,* 524–531.

Stern, D. (1977). *The first relationship.* Cambridge, MA: Harvard University Press.

Vandenberg, B. (1978). Play and development from on ethological perspective. *American Psychologist, 33,* 724–738.

Zimbardo, P. G. (1977). *Shyness: What it is, what to do about it.* Reading, MA: Addison Wesley.

PART **TWO**

THE SELF AND THE EXPLANATION OF EVENTS

The properties of the self are often revealed indirectly through the ways in which the self intrudes on people's judgments and explanations of events. When events are relevant to the self, they contain implications for how the self is perceived and regarded by oneself and others. For example, consider the personal implications of succeeding vs. failing a test, thereby exposing information about one's competence or motivation, or the implications of committing a transgression vs. exhibiting exemplary conduct, thereby exposing information about one's moral values. In a similar fashion, people's explanations of events have implications for how the self is perceived and regarded. For example, failing a test may not be so bad if the test was excessively difficult and most people failed, or breaking the rules might be acceptable if it was done for the right reasons. Through the explanations they construct, people attribute the causal origins of events, assign responsibility, and ultimately reach conclusions about what the actors (themselves included) involved in the event are like.

As such, explanations of events are not simply *descriptive* of what happened, being either true or false in a logical sense. They are what Austin (1970) called *performative,* being actions with their own ends and effects. They are behavioral problems in their own right, demanding analysis to determine the personal and interpersonal functions they serve. The examination of the kinds of explanations people use and the conditions under which particular types of explanations occur shed considerable light on our understanding of the self in social life because it is partially through such explanations that people build and maintain their views of self.

Part Two contains three chapters that examine the implications of the self for how people construct and negotiate the meaning of events. In Chapter 8, Philip

Tetlock presents the merits of an intuitive politician model of attribution. He begins by describing another model that has been dominant in the attribution area: the model of people as intuitive scientists, a view that regards the primary goal of attribution to be gaining understanding of the environment. Tetlock suggests that this model, while quite heuristic, is too restrictive to be considered the only appropriate perspective. He suggests that an intuitive politician model of attribution handles much material that would otherwise be ignored. Just as politicians must reconcile many competing demands from special interests and constituencies, so must people reconcile competing pressures when making attributions in ways that allow them to maintain or enhance their self-esteem, their social esteem, and their strategic or material positions in the social world. On the basis of this proposition, he examines some of the major directions taken by theory and research that provides a rounded view of the model and its implications for attribution.

In Chapter 9, C. R. Snyder explores the functions and types of excuses people employ to ward off intrusions of negative information on the self. He proposes that excuses arise from motives to maintain self-esteem and the esteem in which one is held by others. When an event occurs that might jeopardize esteem, people tend to construct explanations that (a) disconnect the self from the event (e.g., "I didn't do it"), (b) lessen personal responsibility for the event (e.g., "I didn't mean to do it"), (c) reinterpret the event in a way that makes it seem less negative (e.g., "It wasn't so bad"), or (d) combines several of these. (As Snyder notes, he uses the term *excuses* to signify all of these types of explanations, while most other writers use the term only for explanations that effect responsibility but not the apparent consequences or nature of the event; see Chapters 8 and 10.) Within each of these categories, Snyder dissects the impressive array of excuses that people can marshal, examines why excuses serve protective functions, and discusses relevant research. He also examines some of the personal and social implications of excuses for preserving the status of self and producing beneficial consequences.

In Chapter 10, Carl Backman presents a sociological perspective on moral judgment and conduct (i.e., pertaining to questions of right and wrong). When conduct occurs or is anticipated that violates the shared norms and values of the members of a group, the perpetrator faces the dilemma of constructing a definition of the situation that would, as much as possible, reconcile the conduct with those values while preserving a favorable situated identity. Moreover, this construction must be negotiated with other people (publicly or in imagination), thereby generating a joint construction that must take into consideration all of the participants' goals and identity claims in the situation. Backman examines the types of constructions people use to account for potentially questionable conduct, considers the personal, situational, and cultural factors that influence such accounts, and reviews evidence pertaining to the ideas he advances. It should be noted that while he considers many of the same types of issues addressed by Tetlock and Snyder, the perspective, while compatible with theirs, sheds new light on the explanation of conduct by shifting the angle from a psychological to a sociological one.

REFERENCE

Austin, J. L. (1970). *Philosophical papers* (2nd ed.). New York: Oxford University Press. (Original Work published 1961.)

CHAPTER 8

TOWARD AN INTUITIVE POLITICIAN MODEL OF ATTRIBUTION PROCESSES*

Philip E. Tetlock
University of California, Berkeley

The last fifteen years have witnessed an explosion of social-psychological interest in attribution theory. Broadly construed, the domain of attribution theory is that of common-sense psychology or lay epistemology (Heider, 1958). Attribution theory deals with the rules and standards of evidence that ordinary people rely upon in explaining and drawing causal inferences (attributions) from behavior. How, in other words, do people answer questions of the form: Why did person X do that?

Most attribution theorists work from the premise that people are active information processors—intuitive scientists—whose primary goal in explaining behavior is to "attain cognitive mastery of the causal structure of the environment" (Kelley, 1967, p. 193; see also Heider, 1958; Jones & Davis, 1965; Nisbett & Ross, 1980; Ross, 1977). People make causal inferences or attributions for the purpose of developing an organized and coherent view of the social world that enables them to anticipate future events. A natural focus for research is on the data-analysis strategies of intuitive scientists. What information-processing rules do people use to infer the causes of behavior? To what extent do these strategies resemble formal procedures of statistical inference (Bayes' theorem, analysis of variance) as opposed to more informal judgmental heuristics (cf. Kelley, 1967; Nisbett & Ross, 1980; Taylor & Fiske, 1978)?

The intuitive scientist framework is not, however, the only possible way of thinking about attribution processes. People may not always explain behavior with the cold, emotionless objectivity of intuitive scientists. As many writers

---

*I appreciate the helpful comments of Barry Schlenker, Tony Manstead, and Don Forsyth on an earlier version of this chapter. Preparation of this chapter was assisted by NIMH Grant RO3 MH35907. Correspondence address: Philip E. Tetlock, Department of Psychology, 3210 Tolman Hall, University of California, Berkeley, CA, 94720.

have noted, the attributions people offer for behavior may serve important psychological and social functions in addition to establishing cognitive mastery of the environment. For instance, people often explain events that have major implications for how they think of themselves (their self-images) and for how others see them (their public or social images). Why did you fail at that task? Why did your competitor succeed? Why did you act that way toward your wife? Why did she act that way toward you? In such cases, people may frequently offer explanations for behavior designed to protect or enhance their sense of self-worth (Stephan & Gollwitzer, 1981; Zuckerman, 1979) or to protect or enhance their social images (Bradley, 1978; Orvis, Kelley, & Butler, 1976; Scott & Lyman, 1968; Schlenker, 1980, 1982; Tetlock, 1981; Weary & Arkin, 1981). Attributions, like attitudes, may serve multiple, interrelated functions (Forsyth, 1980; Katz, 1960).

I shall argue in this chapter that the intuitive scientist framework is, indeed, too restrictive. The vast majority of theoretical and empirical work has been directed toward developing increasingly sophisticated models of how people (intuitive scientists) analyze stimulus information in arriving at causal attributions. To be sure, this work has yielded very important insights into the nature of human social judgment. However, social psychologists should not allow their commitment to the intuitive-scientist image of human nature to obscure the insights that can be gained from pursuing the research implications of alternative images of human nature.

The chapter is divided into two sections. In the first section, I propose an alternative to the intuitive-scientist image of human nature: that of the person as intuitive politician who seeks to convince both real and imaginary audiences that he or she possesses desired characteristics. I argue that, just as the intuitive-scientist image has stimulated and guided a dynamic research program on the cognitive processes underlying attributional judgments, the intuitive-politician image has the potential to stimulate a similarly dynamic research program on the interpersonal determinants and consequences of attributional judgments. In the second section, I explore specific research implications of the intuitive-politician image of human nature. Within this conceptual framework, the key theoretical question becomes: What type of politician is the average person? I examine theory and research relevant to this question and point to gaps in our understanding that advocates of the intuitive-politician research program need to resolve. I conclude by considering some fundamental conceptual issues that the proposed research program raises.

THE LOGIC OF RESEARCH PROGRAMS ON ATTRIBUTION PROCESSES

Implicit or explicit assumptions about human nature underlie virtually all empirical work in social psychology. These assumptions exert a profound impact on how we design, execute, and interpret research (c.f. Deutsch & Krauss, 1965; Kendler, 1981; Shaw & Costanzo, 1982).

Imré Lakatos, a philosopher of science, has offered an insightful analysis of how underlying assumptions influence the actual conduct of scientific research. According to Lakatos (1970), the "most natural" unit for describing scientific progress is not the isolated hypothesis or even theory, but the research program. Research programs can extend over decades (even centuries) and inspire enormous numbers of hypotheses and empirical studies. Underlying all of the activity inspired by a research program is, however, a "hard core" of basic, unmodifiable assumptions about the subject matter. This hard core gives coherence, impetus, and direction to the research program. It specifies the ground rules for theory formulation and empirical work. The primary objective of the scientific community is to develop and test theories compatible with the hard core. And the defining characteristic of a "mature" research program is the emergence of consensus among investigators on the most effective theoretical and methodological strategies for achieving that objective (cf. Kuhn, 1970; Royce, 1978).

Viewed in the above light, the dominant research program on attribution processes has clearly been the cognitive or information-processing approach. The hard core of this now fairly well-established program is the earlier-mentioned assumption that people are intuitive scientists whose sole motive in explaining behavior is to achieve a better understanding of the "causal structure" of the social world. This assumption provides the conceptual starting point for most social-psychological theory and research on everyday explanations of behavior. It directs investigators to develop theories that take for granted the veridicality of the intuitive scientist image of human nature. The central question for empirical inquiry is: What type of intuitive scientist is the average person? How well does the average person perform the information-processing tasks widely associated with making reasonable causal inferences (e.g., detecting relationships among events, recalling evidence, explaining why events occur, adjusting prior beliefs in response to new evidence)?

An enormous body of theory and research has addressed these challenging issues. It is very important to note, however, that advocates of the cognitive research program by no means agree on all issues. The cognitive research program contains a potentially infinite number of specific models and theories. Different theorists have painted markedly different portraits of the intuitive scientist. For instance, theorists have proposed that people employ a wide variety of inferential rules in their search for causal understanding. At one extreme are models that posit complex and rather sophisticated rules of social data analysis—for example, correspondent inference (Jones & Davis, 1965; Jones & McGillis, 1976), the discounting and augmentation principles (Kelley, 1971, 1972), the covariation principle (Kelley, 1967) and Bayes' theorem (Ajzen & Fishbein, 1975). Here the intuitive-scientist metaphor is taken literally. Perceivers use informal versions of basic logical and statistical principles to make sense of behavior. Confronted by an event they wish to explain, people carefully assess the plausibility of each potential explanation and methodically eliminate those explanations that are inconsistent with the evidence. At the other extreme are models that identify less rigorous and normatively acceptable rules of inference. These models depict sloppy intuitive scientists who rely heavily on the most salient information in the situation and settle for the first adequate (satisficing) explanation that comes to mind (e.g., the availability and representativeness heuristics—Nisbett & Ross, 1980). In short, theoretical diversity within a research program is not at all uncommon. To belong to the same research program it is necessary only that the diverse formulations share a common cluster of hard-core assumptions.

If the cognitive research program does contain a potentially infinite variety of portraits of the intuitive scientist, some important conclusions follow. It becomes possible to explain virtually any conceivable event in terms of the hard-core principles of the research program. And it becomes impossible to achieve decisive empirical tests of the adequacy of the program. These conclusions are consistent with Lakatos' (1970) position. In his historical case studies of scientific progress, Lakatos argues that research programs are not falsifiable. Advocates of a program are often willing to cling tenaciously to hard core assumptions in the face of difficult-to-assimilate evidence (cf. Kuhn, 1970).

For instance, what evidence would it take to convince a committed advocate of the cognitive research program that the intuitive scientist image of the attribution process is flawed or incomplete—that the explanations people offer for behavior serve important noncognitive or motivational functions such as protecting people's self-images or social images? In their review of the controversy over cognitive versus motivational explanations of attribution processes, Tetlock and Levi (1982) conclude that a committed advocate of the cognitive research program can reconcile virtually any "inconsistent" evidence with the intuitive-scientist hard core of the program. They note that specific portraits (theories) of the intuitive scientist may be shown to be incorrect. People in everyday life are not, for example, "perfect" scientists. They are too slow to revise beliefs in response to disconfirming evidence. They often attach too much importance to logically irrelevant information and too little importance to logically relevant information in drawing conclusions about other people or groups. However, the intuitive-scientist hard core lives on. All that need be conceded is that we are imperfect or biased intuitive scientists. The overall research program is extraordinarily flexible and resilient. As Tetlock and Levi (1982, p. 74), state:

> As it now stands, the cognitive research program requires no more than that people offer what seem to them to be the most plausible explanations for behavior, where plausibility is some unspecified combination of formal and informal rules of judgment and relevant knowledge structures.

From this perspective, the frequently ingenious search for crucial experiments to distinguish cognitive and motivational explanations is misguided. The cognitive research program has reached a stage in its development at which it can mimic the predictions of any viable motivational theory.

What, then, is to be done? Should social psychologists be content with working primarily, or even exclusively, within the guidelines of the cognitive research program? For many, this option possesses considerable appeal; the cognitive research program has stimulated many of the most important advances in the field in the last 15 years (cf. Kelley & Michela, 1979; Nisbett & Ross, 1980). However, the successes of the cognitive research program should not blind social psychologists to the insights that can be gained by exploring alternative images of human nature. Although the intuitive-scientist image has provoked much theory and research, it also severely constrains the types of theories and research that social psychologists pursue.[1] Following Feyerabend (1970), I see "theoretical pluralism" (not crucial experiments) as the best means of overcoming the severe constraints that hard-core assumptions place on our theories and research. Specifically, we must be willing to study the attribution process from more than one (the intuitive scientist) underlying point of view. We must be prepared to entertain seriously the possibility that alternative hard-core images of human nature will illuminate aspects of the attribution process that would have been neglected or ignored had we confined our attention to a single, dominant hard-core image. In essence, the argument for theoretical pluralism is an argument for open-mindedness, or—as Feyerabend puts it—"a plea for tolerance in matters epistemological." To my mind, it is a compelling plea.[2]

On what image of human nature should this alternative research program be built? My nomination is the "intuitive politician." Just as politicians must deal with many, sometimes contradictory, demands from special interests and constituencies, so people in their everyday lives must deal with many, sometimes contradictory, demands from other people in their psychological environment. Some of these demands are internal ("I feel I should say no to this illegitimate request" or "The people whose opinion I value most would want me to say no"); other demands are external ("The person or group I am dealing with right now wants me to say yes"). Occasionally, the cross pressures are extremely intense and complex (various internal and external audiences arguing both for and against complying with the request). At other times, the decision process may be

---

[1] As Tompkins (1981) warns, we should beware of "cognitive imperialism"—the temptation to reduce all psychological events to information-processing terms.

[2] The position that I have taken here is similar to McGuire's (1983) recent advocacy of a "contextualist" philosophy of science for social psychology. McGuire notes that social psychology has "for the last generation been dominated by a Logical Empiricist epistemology which takes for granted that our field progresses by our having a theory from which we derive testable hypotheses which are then put in jeopardy by an empirical test, and the hypothesis or theory from which it is derived are accepted or rejected depending on the outcome of this test" (p. 20). He argues that the shortcomings of this view are "with increasing uniformity distorting the way we think about and describe our work" (p. 21) and proposes an alternative "contextualist" epistemology. "In contrast to Logical Empiricism's contention that some theories are right and others wrong and that the function of the empirical work is to test which of several different theories is right, contextualism asserts that each of the several different theories is right and that the empirical work is conducted in order to reveal the conditions under which each of the complementary theories obtain" (p. 21). I have little doubt that both the intuitive-scientist and politician research programs capture important aspects of psychological functioning. I do, though, have serious reservations about the usefulness of portraying our research efforts as if they were means of identifying the "true theory."

much less conflict-ridden, all pressures pointing to one line of action. The essence of the analogy is that, like politicians, people try to strike viable compromises between the demands of these various constituencies: compromises that permit them to maintain or enhance their self-esteem (their self-images as morally worthy and competent beings), their social-esteem (their social images as morally worthy and competent beings) and, finally, their strategic or material positions in the world. (Because other people control desired resources such as money, promotions, sexual favors, etc., people often have strong ulterior motives in seeking to impress them in particular ways.)

The intuitive-scientist and intuitive-politician images highlight very different aspects of how human beings function in and cope with a complex social world. Whereas the central motive for intuitive scientists is the quest to achieve causal understanding and reduce uncertainty, the central motive for intuitive politicians is the quest to convince both themselves and others that they possess desired traits or characteristics. I shall refer to these twin objectives as personal-identity motives (What type of person do I seek to be?) and social-identity motives (What type of person do I want specific others to believe me to be?). The intuitive politician image thus subsumes two types of motivational determinants of attributions that theorists often prefer to distinguish: ego-defensive or self-esteem needs and social-esteem or impression-management needs. No doubt, there are important distinctions to be drawn here—to which I shall return later. But the differences should not be allowed to obscure a fundamental similarity in the logic of the two types of motivational explanations (cf., Carson, 1969; Mead, 1934; Sullivan, 1953). In both cases, theorists posit that people "use" explanations of behavior to establish or maintain desired images in the eyes of an audience, which may exist either "in the head" of the individuals advancing the explanations (an internalized or imaginary audience) or in the external world (the actual presence of other persons). Attributions serve, in the most general sense, identity maintenance and enhancement functions (Schlenker, 1980, 1982; Scott & Lyman, 1968). They assist us in living with both ourselves and others.[3]

The intuitive-politician hard core of the incipient research program provides a valuable starting point for understanding motivational determinants of how people explain and interpret behavior. The central questions for empirical

---

[3]In emphasizing the similarities between self- and social-esteem needs, I am taking a position compatible with that of symbolic interactionists (Blumer, 1969; Stryker & Gottlieb, 1981). From this standpoint, people cannot become aware of themselves as objects of evaluation without social experience. In the words of Schlenker (1982, p. 199):

> Social experience, in conjunction with inherent mental capacities, allows people to view themselves as specific others or others in general might, to anticipate and apply the appropriate evidence, views, and inclinations in such judgments, and to regulate their conduct in ways that permit them to fit into the social matrix of relationships between members of society. Indeed, Mead (1934) argued that the process of thought itself is interactive in nature, as when people privately talk to themselves. . . . Personal feelings of self-satisfaction/dissatisfaction, worthiness/unworthiness and so forth, following the personal evaluation of one's own conduct are the internalized residue of a socialization process that once focused on the reactions of significant immediate others.

inquiry now become: What type of politician is the average person? What types of personal or social identities do people seek to create and maintain? Why? In what ways do the processes of creating and maintaining personal identities differ from those of creating and maintaining social identities? What attributional strategies do people use to achieve desired personal or social identities? In short, the intuitive-politician image raises an enormous array of issues that would simply have gone unnoticed if speculation had been confined to the intuitive-scientist image.

In comparison to the empirical base for cognitive theories of attribution, the amount of research on the impact of personal and social identity needs on attributions is modest indeed. I shall refer to some of this literature in the next section of this chapter. Now, however, it is important to recognize that just as advocates of the cognitive research program disagree on exactly what types of intuitive scientists people are, so advocates of the motivational research program do not have to agree on exactly what types of politicians people are. (If anything, the smaller data base means that there are even fewer constraints on advocates of a motivational research program.) We should expect healthy disagreements to arise on such issues as the relative importance of personal versus social-identity motives (When are people more concerned with maintaining or furthering their personal as opposed to their social identities?), the nature of personal and social identity motives (What types of personal or social identities do people try to create? What types of audiences do they seek to impress?), and the degree to which people are aware of the impact of personal- and social-identity motives on the attributions they offer for behavior (When are people deceptive as opposed to honest intuitive politicians?). There is no limit, in principle, to the range of portraits of the intuitive politician that theorists may sketch.

Finally, and as a corollary to the last point, it should be emphasized that the intuitive-politician research program is no more falsifiable than the intuitive-scientist research program. It is not at all clear what evidence would be needed to convince a committed advocate of the intuitive-politician program that the politician image of human nature is flawed or incomplete. In moving from one research program to another, we substitute one all-embracing set of philosophical assumptions ("blinders") for another. The key point to bear in mind is that these assumptions, although not directly empirically testable, sensitize us to very different types of research questions and issues. It is not particularly useful to think of one research program as more correct or in tune with reality than the other (at least in our current state of knowledge). The real test of the merit of the politician research program will lie in its ability to stimulate the discovery of facts and relationships that otherwise would have gone undiscovered.

BUILDING AN INTUITIVE POLITICIAN RESEARCH PROGRAM

Research programs appear to have life cycles. In the beginning, there is only the hard core: basic philosophical assumptions about the nature of the subject matter. Over time, the program matures out of this speculative or philosophical phase into an empirical or descriptive phase of development (Royce, 1978). Investigators undertake exploratory studies designed to refine methodology, demonstrate the existence of phenomena, and test and develop initial hypotheses and theories. The culmination of the descriptive phase is marked by the emergence of a relatively solid empirical base (a body of well-demonstrated effects) and well-articulated and testable "theories of the middle range" (Merton, 1957). Finally, the program enters into an "explanatory" phase characterized by a high degree of formalization and theoretical unity.

By these standards, the intuitive-politician research program is only starting to emerge from its initial speculative phase of development. It is possible, though, to discern some of the major directions in which the research program appears to be developing and some of the major empirical and theoretical issues that need to be resolved as the program enters more fully into the descriptive phase. In this section, I shall focus on key issues that advocates of the intuitive-politician research program need to address. I raise these issues not to provide definitive answers to them, but to point to the rich network of unexplored issues that the intuitive-politician research program raises.

What Types of Identities Do People Seek?

It is tempting to assume that people seek "socially desirable" identities—that is, to convince target audiences that they possess culturally valued traits or characteristics (e.g., likeable, friendly, honest, compassionate, intelligent, mature). The intuitive-politician metaphor superficially seems to support this assumption. The term "politician" (at least to an American audience) evokes images of the electioneering role in which every act appears carefully calculated to persuade others to ascribe culturally valued traits to the candidate.

Without question, people do often seek culturally valued identities (Alexander & Rudd, 1981; Schlenker, 1980; Tedeschi, 1981). This statement is, however, too sweeping and simplistic. For one thing, what counts as a desirable identity varies sharply from one cultural-historical setting to another. One need only think of a Red Guard revolutionary in China during the "Cultural Revolution," a Nazi party official in Hitler's Germany, and an aspiring presidential candidate in contemporary America to realize that the types of images politicians attempt to project depend profoundly on the prevailing social system and values. Second, even if we restrict discussion to one social system at a given time, we will find that politicians may not always find it advantageous to claim culturally valued identities. On occasion, one may wish to intimidate rivals or opponents by emphasizing one's rigidity, toughness, and perhaps even irrationality (cf. Jones & Pittman, 1981; Schelling, 1966; Schlenker, 1980). On other occasions, one may wish to emphasize one's weakness and dependency, such as when one seeks the protection of another more powerful individual or group (cf. Jones & Pittman, 1981; Schlenker, 1980). In brief, there seems to be little, if any, limit to the range of identities people may try to establish and maintain.

This wide variety of identity objectives reflects the wide variety of underlying "needs" that may motivate intuitive politicians. Do people seek the approval and respect of others as an end in itself or as a means of satisfying "deeper" motives such as gaining public validation for their self-concepts (Swann & Read, 1981), increasing their bargaining power in interpersonal relationships (Jones & Pittman, 1981) or even acquiring material possessions (Jellison & Gentry, 1978)? When does one or another motive become "dominant"? Different theorists may well choose to sketch different motivational portraits of the intuitive politician.

Whom Do People Seek to Impress?

We have seen that the intuitive-politician metaphor places virtually no constraints on the types of identities people may wish to claim. The politician metaphor also places virtually no constraints on the types of audiences (constituencies) people may wish to impress or on the relative importance people attach to impressing different audiences.

For instance, intuitive politicians may be principled (primarily concerned with adhering to the standards of internalized audiences) or pragmatic (primarily concerned with establishing and maintaining good working relationships with whomever they are dealing at the moment). Both personality and situational variables seem to exert an important influence on the degree to which people are pragmatic as opposed to principled in a given context. Thus, investigators have discovered that people who are above average in their concern for how they are perceived and evaluated by others (as indicated by high scores on measures of social anxiety, public self-consciousness, need for approval or self-monitoring) are more likely to tailor their conduct to audiences of the moment than are people less concerned with the reactions of others (e.g., Arkin, Appelman, & Burger, 1980; Buss, 1980; Crowne & Marlowe, 1964; Schlenker, 1982; Snyder, 1979).

Situational factors can also have an important effect. The relative importance of internal versus external audiences depends, for example, on whether people believe their behavior will be anonymous (only subjects themselves will know how they acted) or public (other people will know about subjects' behavior). Investigators often ascribe differences in private and public behavior to the activation of social-esteem or impression-management needs in public (Baumeister, 1982). Much also depends on subjects' beliefs concerning the importance or status of the audience, or the values of the audience (Gergen & Taylor, 1969; Schlenker, 1980; Tetlock & Fleisher, 1981). It may well be harder to "ignore" the views of an important or high-status audience with well-defined preferences or opinions.

People vary not only in the importance they attach to internal and external audiences, but also in the importance they attach to specific internal or external audiences. One individual may highly value living up to religious standards (What would my minister say if I did that?), another may value familial standards (What would my mother say?), another, peer standards (What would the guys at the bar say?), and still another, occupational or professional standards (What would my co-workers or colleagues think?). Which reference individuals or groups people seek to impress depends on relatively stable value priorities anchored in our life experiences and histories (Jackson, 1981), as well as momentary situational factors which serve to make one or another reference group more salient or significant (Kelley, 1952).

What Attributional Tactics Do People Use to Achieve Personal or Social-Identity Goals?

The use of attributions to claim desired identities, or to avoid undesired ones, is no where more obvious than in the political arena. The outcomes of political conflicts (elections, revolutions, diplomatic confrontations) often hinge on how the participants define or interpret key actions. Debate over what constitutes an adequate explanation for conduct is a ubiquitous feature of the political scene. The labor leader charges that the businessman refuses to give his workers a raise because he is greedy; the businessman responds that he needs the money to pay off debts and invest in plant equipment in order to remain competitive. The government official condemns attacks by an antigovernment organization as bloodthirsty terrorism; the antigovernment organization portrays the same attacks as valiant attempts to secure basic human rights and justice. Antiabortionists view proabortionists as morally callous and insensitive to the unborn infant's right to life; proabortionists view themselves as defenders of womens' rights and freedom of choice. As C. Wright Mills (1940, p. 905) pointed out, "What is reason for one man is rationalization for another." Success in politics often depends on persuading others to accept one's attributional definition of the situation.

In both politics and everyday life, people use attributions defensively (to protect their claims to desired identities) and offensively (to claim even more desirable identities). People use attributions defensively to extricate themselves from what Schlenker (1980) has called predicaments. A predicament, in essence, is any event that casts unwanted aspersions on the character of an actor. As such, predicaments can take diverse forms. Predicaments can be private affairs (only the actor is aware of the identity-threatening event) or public affairs (others are aware of the identity-threatening event). Predicaments can also cast aspersions on a wide array of traits or characteristics that people may wish to claim. For instance, telling a lie casts doubt on one's trustworthiness or honesty, failure to complete an ability-demanding task casts doubt on one's competence or industriousness; harming another individual casts doubt on one's self-control or concern for the well-being of others.

We are all familiar with the types of predicaments from which politicians often struggle to extricate themselves. Many journalists try to formulate the questions they pose to politicians to make this task as difficult as possible: "Why did you claim that the government should do X at time 1 and Y at time 2?"

"Why did individuals acting under your authority perform this act?" "How can you defend the 'immoral' conduct of some other individual, group or government?" A classic example of a political predicament was the Watergate crisis during the Nixon administration. Suspicion mounted throughout 1973 that President Nixon had attempted in 1972 to cover up connections between his administration and a burglary of Democratic party offices. As calls for public release of secret tape recordings of confidential Nixon conversations grew, Nixon needed a politically powerful explanation for refusing to release the tapes. The explanation he offered was "executive privilege." Nixon could argue that he was not stonewalling investigation of illegal activity; he was upholding the Constitutional doctrine governing the confidentiality of presidential communications and, in the process, preserving the separation of powers between the legislative and executive branches of government. Ultimately, Nixon's attribution for refusing to release the tapes failed because it was simply not sufficiently persuasive. The Supreme Court ordered Nixon to release the tapes, and the evidence contained in the tapes was so difficult to explain away that Nixon's political position became untenable and he was forced to resign to avoid impeachment.

Less well-known are the predicaments that social psychologists have ingeniously created for their experimental subjects. One common method of creating predicaments is the "forced-compliance paradigm." Forced-compliance experiments are studies in which experimenters persuade subjects to behave in ways that contradict subjects' beliefs or preferences, such as lying to others, advocating unpopular positions (protuition increase, antitoothbrushing) or working on tedious tasks (Wicklund & Brehm, 1976). These experiments can cast aspersions on such typically desired identity characteristics as honesty, good sense, intelligence, and maturity (Alexander & Rudd, 1981). Another common method of creating predicaments is by providing false feedback to subjects about their performance on ability-demanding tasks. For instance, experimenters have led subjects to believe that they are poor or excellent teachers of a young pupil, competent or incompetent psychotherapists, socially sensitive or insensitive, and skillful or inept problem solvers. (For reviews, see Bradley, 1978; Tetlock & Levi, 1982; Zuckerman, 1979.) Still other types of experimentally induced predicaments are discussed in Schlenker (1980) and Tedeschi and Riordan (1981).

In general, the more severe a predicament, the greater is the need to use attributions to protect one's personal or social identity. I shall emphasize three key determinants of the severity of predicaments: (1) the undesirability of the event that triggered the predicament, (2) the actor's apparent responsibility for the event, and (3) the importance the actor attaches to creating desired impressions on real or imaginary observers of the predicament. For instance, consider the predicament created for a subject (call him John) in a forced-compliance experiment. John has agreed to a request to deliver an antitoothbrushing speech which the experimenter will record. In itself, this act may create a modest predicament. John may feel that most people he knows would disapprove of the position he has taken in the speech. However, the experimenter can increase the severity of the predicament by manipulating a variety of specific features of the experimental situation and instructions. Thus, the predicament will be more severe to the degree that the situation suggests that John freely chose to make the antitoothbrushing speech (e.g., if the experimenter had emphasized that, while he wanted John to make the speech, John was free to choose). Freedom of choice increases responsibility for the identity-threatening event. The predicament will also be more severe if foreseeable negative consequences follow from John's making the speech (e.g., if John believes the speech is to be used to encourage junior high school students not to brush their teeth). Foreseeable negative consequences increase the undesirability of the event. Finally, the predicament will be more severe to the degree John believes other people will associate him with the speech and to the degree that John values the good opinion of those particular people.

Previous writers have identified a variety of attributional tactics that people use to defend themselves in predicaments (Austin, 1961; Schlenker, 1980, 1982; Scott & Lyman, 1968; Tedeschi & Riess, 1981). Perhaps the simplest defense is that of innocence. The person maintains that the identity-threatening event did not occur ("I don't believe there was any attempt to cover up connections between key figures in my administration and the Watergate burglary."), or that, if the event did occur, that he or she was in no way causally linked to it. ("If there was a so-called cover up, I certainly knew nothing of it.") Unfortunately—at least for perpetrators of predicaments—the defense of innocence is often not credible and therefore likely to be ineffective. To return to the predicament that John faced in the forced compliance experiment, he can hardly deny having delivered the antitoothbrushing speech if he did so in front of several witnesses.

People, can, however, turn to more sophisticated attributional defenses. The best known of these are justifications and excuses. Justifications are explanations in which individuals accept responsibility for their conduct, but deny that the act in question provides grounds for ascribing negative traits or characteristics to them. (See Schonbach, 1980; Tedeschi & Riess, 1981, for detailed taxonomies of justifications.) Usually, justifications refer to some salient norm or standard (e.g., self-defense, equity, equality, reciprocity, honesty) that is widely shared in the culture and that explains the conduct in question so as to minimize its negative connotations. Examples of justifications abound in political discourse. Indeed, dispassionate observers often feel politicians "overjustify" or engage in "belief system overkill" (Jervis, 1976). It is not enough to say that, "On balance, my policy is better than my opponent's policy"; many politicians insist (publicly and sometimes privately) that their policy is superior to rival policies in *all* possible respects: "Not only will my policy save the world from nuclear war, it will reduce defense spending, increase international cooperation, and promote human rights abroad." "Not only will my policy reduce taxes, it will eliminate government budget deficits and inefficiency, lower interest rates, cut unemployment and inflation, and stimulate productivity." In the words of Merelman (1966, p. 559),

Most major political conflicts within any policy area can be seen as the attempt by partisans to attach the available legitimacy (justificatory) symbols to policies they advocate and to sever the relationship between these symbols and the policies of their opponents.

Social psychologists have studied justifications most intensely in the context of the forced-compliance paradigm. In these experiments, subjects often appear concerned with justifying their counterattitudinal behavior by shifting their attitudes in the direction of the behavior (e.g., our hypothetical subject John might assert that he really does doubt the wisdom of regular toothbrushing). Subjects are especially likely to engage in "justificatory attitude change" when (a) they believe they freely chose (or that others think they freely chose) to perform the counterattitudinal behavior, (b) they believe their counterattitudinal behavior will have negative consequences for themselves or others, (c) the negative consequences were—at least in hindsight—foreseeable (e.g., Calder, Ross, & Insko, 1973; Collins & Hoyt, 1972; Goethals, Cooper, & Nafficy, 1979; Schlenker, 1982; Wicklund & Brehm, 1976). Such results make good sense from a theoretical perspective that emphasizes the impact of personal- and social-identity needs on attributions. Subjects who feel personally or socially responsible for conduct with foreseeable, negative consequences have few options other than to try to justify their conduct—to argue that the behavior was "really not so bad after all."

Excuses are another important attributional line of defense. Excuses are explanations in which individuals acknowledge that their conduct was somehow bad, wrong, or inappropriate, but attempt to minimize their personal responsibility or culpability for it. Excuses occur frequently in political discourse: "I have not been able to fulfill that campaign promise because I didn't realize how badly my opponents had messed up the economy, because the Congress was uncooperative, and because several unforeseeable events occurred."

The most infamous political excuses were, perhaps, those that Nazi war criminals offered to explain why they organized or participated in mass murders of millions of Jewish and other European civilians. The standard excuse was, "I was just obeying orders." Individuals attempted to deflect blame by denying that they were "free agents" and depicting themselves as mere cogs in a complex social machine. Many more everyday examples exist of people offering excuses to dissociate themselves from identity-threatening events. According to both self-esteem and impression management interpretations of attitude shifts in forced compliance experiments, subjects feel little need to justify their counterattitudinal behavior (via attitude change) when they have had little or no choice about performing the behavior. This is because subjects in the "low choice" condition can plausibly deny responsibility for the counterattitudinal act (i.e., offer an excuse). Subjects who appear to have freely chosen to perform the counterattitudinal act do not have a plausible excuse and must therefore justify their behavior. Subjects also frequently try to excuse poor performance on ability-demanding tasks (Bradley, 1978; Darley & Goethals, 1980; Zuckerman, 1979). These excuses take diverse forms: "The task was too difficult," "I was too tired to give the task my full attention and effort," "I am feeling 'under the weather,'" "I was distracted by family problems," and "I was just plain unlucky" (Darley & Goethals, 1980). They appear well designed to forestall or prevent attributions of lack of ability.

All of the attributional tactics considered up to this point—protests of innocence, justifications, excuses—are defensive attempts to minimize damage to one's personal or social identity. Intuitive politicians are not, however, always on the defensive. They may also use attributions "offensively" by offering identity-enhancing explanations for positive events and behavior (Schlenker, 1982). Thus, people try not only to de-emphasize their responsibility for negative events (excuses), but also to emphasize their responsibility for positive events (entitlements). Similarly, people try not only to minimize the negative implications of undesirable events linked to them (justifications), but to maximize the positive implications of desirable events linked to them (enhancements). Political debates often focus on entitlement and enhancement claims. Politicians in power stress their role in bringing about positive events (e.g., the end of wars, improvements in the national economy) as well as the importance and significance of these accomplishments ("Let's consider the wonderful consequences that flow from my having solved this problem"). Politicians in opposition attempt to refute these claims. Entitlement and enhancement claims also occur with some frequency in everyday life (e.g., "I volunteered to help this charitable cause because I thought it the right thing to do—not because of social pressure—and because I get a lot of satisfaction out of giving happiness to desperate and needy persons").

In sum, people have invented an impressive array of attributional tactics to protect or promote their claims to desired personal or social identities. I have only skimmed the surface of this complex topic. It is not enough, though, simply to say that people are inventive intuitive politicians. We need to know what criteria or decision rules people employ in selecting attributional tactics to achieve personal or social identity objectives.

Our understanding of how people choose attributional tactics is highly incomplete. We do know, though, that one important constraint on the selection process is the plausibility of the explanation or attribution advanced for behavior. If people are to use attributions effectively in achieving identity goals, they should not offer attributions that are implausible or incredible to the target audience. There are many ways in which attributions can be implausible. One requirement is that an attribution should be consistent with widely accepted cultural assumptions concerning the causes of behavior (what C. Wright Mills termed the prevailing "vocabulary of motives" in a culture). An explanation that is plausible in one societal or historical context (e.g., witchcraft, demonic possession) may be mocked in other societal or historical contexts. A second requirement is that an attribution should be consistent with available information on the social situation in which the behavior in question occurred. Who was involved in the incident? What types of people are they? What circumstances exist that mitigate or exacerbate the severity of the predicament? For instance, a student may be tempted to attribute her poor performance on an exam to the unfairness of the exam and to the ineptitude of the instructor. The plausibility of this explanation may, however, be undercut by the large number of other students who performed well on the exam. In Kelley's (1967) terms, consensus information points to a dispositional, not a situational, cause of the student's poor performance. Or, consider another example. A husband attributes his failure to help with household chores to the particularly stressful demands that his job has recently placed on him. The plausibility of this explanation is, however, undercut by his unwillingness to help with chores at virtually all other times and on virtually all other occasions in his relationship with his wife. Again in Kelley's (1967) terms, consistency and distinctiveness information point to a dispositional, not a situational cause.

This discussion highlights an important connection between the intuitive-scientist and intuitive-politician research programs. The intuitive-scientist program focuses exclusively on the cognitive processes by which people assess the plausibility of possible explanations and interpretations of behavior. The intuitive-politician program begins, in a sense, where the intuitive-scientist program ends. People use attributions to protect and reinforce their claims to desired personal or social identities, within plausibility or cognitive constraints. In a nutshell, the key distinction between the two research programs seems to boil down to whether people seek only plausible explanations for behavior (intuitive scientists whose objective is causal understanding) or seek both plausible and identity-satisfying explanations for behavior (intuitive politicians whose objective is to lay credible claim to desired personal or social identities).

A largely unmet challenge for the intuitive-politician research program is to clarify how people cope with the tension between the conflicting goals of explaining conduct in both plausible and identity-satisfying ways. Schlenker (1980) has offered an interesting expectancy-value analysis of this issue. He proposes that people choose attributional tactics that they believe will maximize their "reward/cost ratios" in the situation. Reward/cost ratios are a function of both the desirability of the identity one claims through one's attributions and the likelihood of the explanation being accepted by a salient audience (self included). For instance, consider again the example of a student—call her Mary—who feels a need to explain her poor performance on an exam. The most self-flattering explanation might be to attribute her failure to the unfairness of the exam and the ineptitude of the instructor. If believed, Mary would be totally successful in protecting her social identity as both intelligent and hardworking. Let's assume Mary rates these consequences highly positively (+3 on a −3 to +3 scale). However, the probability (P) of the explanation being accepted is rather low (say, only .20). Moreover, the social consequences of the explanation being rejected (an event with probability .80) are very unpleasant. Others will view Mary as defensive, brittle, and immature. Let's assume Mary rates these consequences highly negatively (−3 on a +3 to −3 scale). According to Schlenker's model, the expected value (EV) of the account can be computed using the following formula:

EV = (probability that identity claim is accepted) (desirability of consequences of acceptance)
  + (probability that identity claim is rejected) (undesirability of consequences of rejection)

In this case, EV = (.2) (3) + (.8) (−3) = −1.8.

The expected value of advancing a highly favorable, but implausible, identity claim is quite negative. The expected value of advancing a more plausible, but self-critical, explanation may well be substantially higher. (E.g., "I have been having family problems and had trouble concentrating; I just couldn't get motivated to study.")

Schlenker's model leads us to expect that people will offer largely self-flattering explanations when they perceive little or no danger of such explanations being rejected. However, people will become more self-critical when they have reason to suspect that others will not honor or accept self-flattering attributions. A substantial amount of evidence appears consistent with this hypothesis. For instance, a number of personality and situational variables play a role in determining how self-critical or counterdefensive people become in a given context. Thus, persons with low self-esteem (who presumably view self-critical explanations as more plausible than self-flattering ones) tend to attribute their failures on experimental tasks to lack of ability (Fitch, 1970) and to deny credit for success (Maracek & Mettee, 1972). Persons high in social anxiety (who presumably are especially concerned with loss of social approval and rejection) are prone to be self-critical, especially when they believe that their task performance and the explanations they advance for it will be scrutinized and evaluated by a high-status audience (Arkin, Appelman, & Burger, 1980). Situational factors also exert an important influence. Thus, persons offer more self-critical explanations for performance on ability-demanding tasks when they believe they will be subjected to further testing (Wortman, Costanzo, & Witt, 1973) or that the attributions they make for their performance may be invalidated by others' present or future assessments of the same performance (Beckman, 1973; Bradley, 1978; Feather & Simon, 1971; Ross, Bierbrauer, & Polly, 1974).

Overall, Schlenker's expectancy-value model of how people choose attributional tactics depicts people as highly rational, intuitive politicians who carefully assess the relative plausibility and favorableness of possible explanations and then advance the explanation with the largest expected value. Sometimes this explanation will be self-flattering; sometimes it will be self-critical. The validity of the expectancy-value model is still, however, to be established. The model may, for example, exaggerate the rationality of the tactic selection process. People may rely on simple "satisficing" rules (offer the first explanation that comes to mind, that is believable, and that is at least minimally compatible with personal- and social-identity objectives). There may also be personality and situational variations in the importance or emphasis people place on different components for calculating the expected value of an attribution. Some people may be oblivious to the possibility that their attributional claims will be rejected; others may be obsessed with this possibility. Different types of situations may have the same effect. In some situations, we may never even think of the possibility of our claims being rejected; in other situations, we may be extremely self-conscious and concerned with rejection.

Are People Successful Intuitive Politicians?

The expectancy-value model of the intuitive politician asserts that people try to claim personal or social identities with the highest expected values. The model does not, however, assert that people are always successful. Do people typically select attributional tactics well designed to achieve important personal- or social-identity goals? Or, are people prone to certain characteristic errors and biases in selecting attributional tactics?

It is important to distinguish here between effectiveness in achieving personal-identity objectives (gaining the approval and respect of internalized audiences: "Most people whose opinion I value would approve of how I acted today") and achieving social identity objectives (gaining the approval and respect of other individuals with whom one is currently dealing). Our understanding of how effective people are in using attributions to satisfy both motives is very limited. Moreover, what little evidence exists is relevant to impressing external, not internal audiences.

Results from early studies suggest that, by and large, people do a pretty good job at using attributions to protect and even enhance their images in the eyes of others. For instance, Tetlock (1981) focused on the social impact of the ordinary-language (as opposed to rating-scale) attributions that people offer for behavior. He adopted two approaches to assessing the social impact of attributions:

1 Measuring the degree to which the attribution, when taken at face value, is flattering to the person who performed the behavior—the identity-favorableness of the attribution. To illustrate this concept, consider the behavior "John does not help his wife with tedious household chores," and the attribution that "this is because he has an extremely demanding job that completely exhausts him." The attribution is identity-favorable to the extent that other people evaluate the actor (John) more positively when they believe the attribution is the true explanation for the actor's behavior than they do when they are aware only of the behavior. In general, self-flattering attributions are identity-favorable; self-critical attributions are identity-unfavorable.

2 Measuring the actual impression that other people form of the actor when they know that the actor was the source of a particular attribution for his or her behavior—the impression management value of the attribution. It is not sufficient simply to claim to be a good or competent person; it is necessary to avoid sounding implausible, conceited, or defensive. In the context of the previous example, John's attributing his failure to help to his demanding job will have positive impression-management value to the extent that others evaluate

John more positively when they learn of his attribution than when they know of his behavior. Impression management value, in other words, is the source-discounted persuasive impact of attributions.[4]

To assess the identity-favorableness and the impression-management values of attributions, Tetlock asked a group of subjects to report events from their everyday lives in which they or acquaintances had behaved in desirable or undesirable (identity-threatening) ways. Subjects then explained their own or their acquaintances' behavior under the expectation that their explanations would be completely confidential (creating only internal audiences) or topics for public discussion (creating both internal and external audiences). Another group of subjects was asked to explain their own behavior as if they were trying to create the most favorable possible impression on others. Finally, Tetlock instructed an independent group of observer subjects to form impressions of the subjects in the original sample. These observers had information about only the subjects' behavior or about both the subjects' behavior and the attributions the subjects expressed. Some observers were told to assume the explanations described the true causes of the behavior (to measure identity favorableness); others were told the explanations were offered by the person who performed the behavior (to measure the impression-management values of attributions).

The results were clear-cut. Subjects reported public attributions for their own behavior that were well designed to create positive impressions on others. Subjects' public attributions for their own behavior were significantly more self-flattering (as indicated by their higher identity-favorableness values) than their private attributions for their own behavior or for their private or public attributions for others' behavior. However, subjects did not go "overboard" and offer implausibly self-serving public attributions. Subjects' public attributions for their own behavior were significantly more effective than their private attributions in impressing others who were aware that the actor was the source of the explanation (as indicated by the impression-management values of attributions). Overall, the attributions that subjects publicly expressed for their own behavior most closely resembled those expressed by subjects who had been explicitly instructed to explain their behavior in order to impress others.

Tetlock also found that subjects in the public condition used attributions to protect those aspects of their social identities most directly threatened by the behavior they were called upon to explain. Thus, in explaining their worst

---

[4]It is important to note that the impression-management value of an attribution will depend on the relationship between the individual offering the explanation and the "target audience." Different audiences may have different thresholds for accepting or rejecting accounts. Some audiences will be predisposed to be sympathetic (e.g., many Republicans were willing for a long time to give President Nixon the benefit of the doubt during the Watergate crisis); other audiences will be predisposed to be unsympathetic (e.g., many Democrats disbelieved Nixon's accounts for the Watergate events from the outset). In everyday life, as in politics, we have our supporters and detractors—some strongly committed, others weakly committed. In the words of Scott and Lyman (1968, p. 58): "Every account is a manifestation of an underlying negotiation of identities." Through the explanations we advance for behavior, we claim certain identities for ourselves. Through their reactions to our explanations, others indicate their willingness or unwillingness to recognize those claims.

performance in a course, subjects offered attributions that actually led others to think of them as more ambitious and intelligent (but not as more likeable, honest, or mature); in explaining dubious interpersonal acts (e.g., giving someone reason to be angry with you, failing to act in accord with principles), subjects offered attributions that led others to think of them as more likeable, honest, and mature (but not as more ambitious or intelligent). Attributions appeared targeted to eliminate threats to particular aspects of the identities that people sought to protect. All in all, the patterning of the evidence is highly suggestive: When people explained undesirable behavior in public (antecedent variables), they offered attributions that eliminated specific threats to their social identities (consequence variables).

One is not, however, always well advised to offer self-serving identity-favorable) attributions for one's behavior. Tetlock (1980) found that schoolteacher subjects in an experiment by Ross, Bierbrauer, & Polly (1974) created the best possible social identities for themselves by being self-critical or modest. In the original Ross et al. (1974) experiment, teachers were led to believe that they had been successful or unsuccessful in teaching a spelling lesson to an 11-year-old pupil in a special laboratory environment. Ross et al. then asked the teachers to rate the importance of several possible causes of their successful or unsuccessful performance. Some causes related to the student (e.g., ability, aptitude), others to the teacher (e.g., overall teaching ability, techniques and strategies employed). Teachers generally advanced self-critical attributions: They attributed primary (although not sole) causal responsibility for failure to themselves and primary (although, not sole) causal responsibility for success to the pupil. Tetlock (1980) constructed a simulation of the Ross et al. study in which he asked observers to form impressions of a hypothetical teacher who had been either successful or unsuccessful and who had offered either no explanation or one of four explanations that ranged from highly self-serving to highly self-critical. The explanations were scaled so that moderately self-critical attributions corresponded to the mean "importance of cause" ratings given by the actual teachers. Tetlock found that observers evaluated the moderately self-critical teacher more positively than any of the other types of teacher. This was true, moreover, on both social-moral traits or characteristics (likable, honest, mature) as well as achievement-related traits or characteristics (smart, dynamic). Moderate self-criticism was clearly the optimal social response in this situation. (See also Carlston & Shovar, 1983.)

The previous studies depict people as shrewd intuitive politicians who adroitly employ attributional tactics that protect or advance their claims to desired identities. Everyday experience suggests, though, that we are not that skillful and that we often miscalculate how others will react to the attributions we express. As Scott and Lyman (1968) point out, the accounts people offer are not always "honored." People may be as imperfect at being intuitive politicians as they are at being intuitive scientists—prone to numerous errors and biases. Indeed, many of our shortcomings as intuitive politicians may directly derive from our shortcomings as intuitive scientists. For instance, people may exaggerate how receptive observers are to "situational" attributions for their behavior. Social psychologists have known for some time that actors (persons behaving in specific ways) tend to explain their own behavior in situational terms, whereas observers tend to explain the same behavior in trait or dispositional terms (Jones & Nisbett, 1971). Since people tend to assume that others view events in much the same way as they do (the false consensus effect—Ross, Greene, & House, 1977), they may often be surprised to discover that others take a more "dispositional" perspective toward their conduct. Actors may also overestimate the willingness of observers to revise their initial opinions of actors' behavior. Work on belief-perseverance effects on judgment suggests that people are often slow to revise their first impressions of events (Nisbett & Ross, 1980). If actors want to maximize the persuasive impact of their attributional claims, they should advance those claims before, rather than after, the target audience has had an opportunity to judge their behavior (Jones, Riggs, & Quattrone, 1979; Zillmann & Cantor, 1976). Prebehavioral disclaimers (Hewitt & Stokes, 1975) may be much more effective than postbehavioral accounts.

How Sincere Are Intuitive Politicians?

For many, politicians are individuals who are willing to say almost anything in order to gain public support. To call people intuitive politicians is, in effect, to call them liars: to imply that people typically make attributional claims they themselves do not believe. No doubt, people do sometimes advance explanations that they do not fully believe to be true—or that they simply disbelieve. However, deliberate or self-conscious deception is neither a necessary nor an integral part of the intuitive-politician research program. There is no compelling psychological reason why people might not, under certain conditions, be completely convinced of the truthfulness of explanations that serve to support their claims to desired personal or social identities.

One distinction that many researchers implicitly or explicitly accept is that people need to believe attributions designed to protect their sense of self-worth (otherwise the attributions do not serve their "intended" motivational function), but people do not need to believe attributions designed to protect their public or social identities (we can offer explanations for conduct that impress others favorably, but that we do not really believe to be true). On its surface, this argument seems valid. Two important caveats do, however, need to be introduced. First, as Sackeim (1981) argues on the basis of considerable experimental evidence, people engage on occasion in self-deception and may not even believe all the claims they make to protect their self-images. People seem capable of simultaneously holding contradictory beliefs, but keeping one of the beliefs out of awareness. Second, people may sometimes sincerely believe attributions designed to protect their public images (Hass, 1981; Schlenker, 1980; Tedeschi & Riess, 1981; Weary & Arkin, 1981). Many factors promote internalization of opinions originally expressed simply to gain the approval of others. People are more likely to believe their attributional claims if the claims are plausible (Hass, 1981), if they receive social encouragement or reinforcement for the claims (Jones, Gergen, & Davis, 1962), and if they are in settings in which the social pressures for making the claims are subtle and low-key (Bem, 1972; Wicklund & Brehm, 1976).

The challenge is then to identify when intuitive politicians are being sincere or insincere. Tedeschi and his colleagues are responsible for the largest body of work on this topic. (For a review, see Tedeschi & Rosenfeld, 1981.) They have argued that the "justificatory attitude-change" effects observed in many forced-compliance experiments are not real. Subjects do not actually change their attitudes in the direction of their counterattitudinal behavior (e.g., subjects who freely choose to deliver antitoothbrushing speeches do not actually develop more antitoothbrushing attitudes). The attitude change reported in such studies is spurious: It represents an "uninternalized, temporary, feigned shift in attitudes that has the purpose of mending a spoiled social identity" (Tedeschi & Rosenfeld, 1981, p. 158). As support for this hypothesis, they point to the results of a series of "bogus-pipeline" experiments. In a typical bogus-pipeline experiment, some subjects are led to believe that the attitudes they express are being monitored by an extremely accurate lie detector (the bogus pipeline), whereas other subjects express their attitudes on traditional paper-and-pencil questionnaires. If subjects in forced-compliance studies are simply pretending to change their attitudes in order to be consistent with their behavior, they should be much less likely to do so when responding to the bogus pipeline (where they think there is a good chance of their deception being revealed) than when responding to paper-and-pencil questionnaires (where they think there is no danger of their deception being revealed).

The bogus-pipeline experiments suggest that attitude change effects in forced-compliance studies are "not real" (Gaes, Kalle, & Tedeschi, 1978; Malkis, Kalle, & Tedeschi, 1981). For instance, Gaes et al. (1978) induced subjects to write antitoothbrushing essays that would allegedly be read by impressionable junior high school students. The postbehavior attitudes of half of the subjects were assessed on standard paper-and-pencil attitude scales; the remaining half responded to the same attitude questions while connected to the bogus pipeline. Gaes et al. found that subjects shifted toward a more antitoothbrushing position only when they responded to the paper-and-pencil measures, not when they responded to the bogus pipeline. Gaes et al. also found that subjects in the paper-and-pencil condition only shifted their attitudes when they felt "publicly identified" with the antitoothbrushing speech, not when they felt their anonymity was guaranteed. In short, the data indicate that intuitive politicians in this study engaged in largely deceptive impression management aimed at external audiences.

Although the bogus-pipeline experiments suggest that some (many?) attitude-change effects observed in forced-compliance studies may not be "real," they do not demonstrate that *all* such effects are feigned. Arkin (1981), Scheier and Carver (1980) and Schlenker (1982) have identified several problems with drawing strong theoretical conclusions from a research procedure as complex and potentially reactive as the bogus pipeline. It is, moreover, unclear how representative a portrait of the intuitive politician emerges from forced compliance studies. These studies create novel situations that may elicit unusually self-conscious tactics of impression management. More routine situations probably elicit more well-ingrained, habitual tactics (cf. Langer, 1978).

Attributions and Deeds

In discussing how people use attributions to achieve desired personal or social identities, I have treated the attribution process—the search for plausible and satisfying explanations for conduct—as something that occurs only after people have acted or committed themselves to act. First people behave, then they worry about constructing acceptable rationalizations for their conduct.

The intuitive-politician image of the average person suggests that the attributions people offer for behavior are more than afterthoughts. People—like politicians—may consider the justifiability or excusability of behavioral options before they commit themselves to action. The social necessity of defending one's conduct can serve as an important constraint on how people make behavioral decisions. In the words of C. Wright Mills (1940, p. 906):

> Often anticipations of acceptable justifications will control conduct. ("If I did this, what could I say? What would they say?") Decisions may be, wholly or in part, delimited by answers to such queries.

This intimate relationship between attributional and behavioral decision making is probably most obvious in high-level policy making. As the political scientists Snyder, Bruck, & Sapin (1962) have observed: "The decision to perform or not to perform a given act may be taken on the basis of available answers to the question 'what will be said?'" Historical accounts of important decisions abound with references to policy makers assessing possible attributional lines of defense against critics and opponents (Anderson, 1981; Bennett, 1980; Graber, 1976). For instance, after Egypt nationalized the Suez canal in 1956, British leaders tried to avoid open collusion with Israel because they thought it could not be justified to their constituents. The British therefore delayed the Franco-British invasion until after the initial Israeli strike into Egypt when they thought (in this case, erroneously) they could assume the role of peacemaker. In Goldman's (1971) words: "In a sense, the British searched for an acceptable justification. Having found one, actions were modified accordingly."

Similarly, President Kennedy rejected direct American participation in the 1961 Bay of Pigs invasion of Cuba because he felt it would be very awkward to justify after he had pledged abstinence from such a conflict. (This decision meant that air cover for the invasion would be inadequate, which contributed to the failure of the mission.) Likewise, in the Cuban missile crisis of 1962, the Kennedy administration ruled out a surprise air strike on the missile silos in part because it felt it could not construct a compelling rationalization for such an air strike. Kennedy opted instead for the more defensible naval blockade of Cuba. These examples illustrate what Snyder, Bruck, & Sapin (1962, p. 183) call "the continual interaction between considerations of what to do, and what to say.... Statecraft, from this point of view, is the art of combining the desirable and the justifiable."

Do ordinary people also try to calculate the defensibility of alternative courses of action before deciding how to behave? Although there is not a great deal of evidence, what evidence we have is certainly consistent with this hypothesis. Snyder, Kleck, Strenta, & Mentzer (1979) have provided perhaps the most convincing experimental support. They hypothesized that people generally desire to avoid the handicapped but are reluctant to admit it. People are willing to act on socially undesirable motives (e.g., avoiding the handicapped) only when they can plausibly argue that they had acted for some other reason. To test this idea, they had subjects make one of two different choices: (a) sitting next to a handicapped or a normal person and (b) choosing between two movies, one which required sitting next to a handicapped person, the other which required sitting next to a normal person. Only in the latter case, when avoidance of the handicapped person could be attributed to a movie preference, did subjects reveal their aversion to the handicapped.

Other, less direct, research support is also available. Many experimental manipulations that increase people's willingness to perform socially undesirable acts may do so by increasing plausibility of "good accounts" for the behavior. For instance, it was easier for subjects in Milgram's experiments on obedience to excuse their willingness to administer severe electric shocks if the experimenter explicitly accepted responsibility for the well-being of the individual receiving the shocks (Milgram, 1974). It is easier to excuse one's failure to help in an emergency when one believes that many others are also in earshot of the emergency (Latané & Darley, 1970, on diffusion of responsibility). And it is easier to justify refusing to donate to charity if the individuals in need of help are somehow responsible for their own plight (Schwartz, 1977). Exploring the interrelationships between attributional and behavioral decision making is a promising area for future development within the intuitive-politician research program. It may also serve the valuable function of linking up otherwise isolated bodies of social-psychological theory on such topics as decision making, helping, obedience, and aggression.

Where Will the Research Program Lead Us?

I stated earlier that the intuitive-politician research program is still in an early stage of development. In previous sections, I have sketched only some of the major directions in which the program seems likely to develop as researchers pursue the theoretical implications of thinking about people as intuitive politicians. In concluding, I would like to speculate on what form a mature version of the research program might take.

One crucial issue is whether it is realistic to expect the emergence of theories of the intuitive politician that have substantial cross-cultural and historical generality. The skeptic might well argue that it is not. The types of personal and social identities people strive to create, and the types of attributional strategies people use to protect or further those identities, may vary widely from one cultural-historical setting to another. Perhaps C. Wright Mills (1940) makes this point most effectively. When people leave groups and join new ones, they must learn new vocabularies of motives—rules for generating socially acceptable explanations of behavior. What serves as a plausible and identity-enhancing explanation in one group may make a highly negative impression on another group. In Mills' (1940) words:

> Motives are of no value apart from the delimited societal situations for which they are appropriate vocabularies. They must be situated. . . . Motives vary in content and structure with historical epochs and social structures.

Must advocates of the intuitive-politician research program be content with simply documenting the vocabularies of motives that prevail in particular times and places? Is this branch of social psychology, like other branches, "merely" a form of social history? (Cf. Gergen, 1973.) I do not believe so. The generality of psychological theories across cultural-historical settings depends crucially on the level of abstraction of the theory (Triandis, 1978). "Low-level" or concrete theories of the intuitive politician—which specify particular attributional tactics people employ to create particular impressions on others—are not likely to hold up well across cultural-historical settings. For instance, the vast majority of "forced compliance experiments" have been performed on middle-class, twentieth-century, American college students. These subjects often try to justify their counterattitudinal behavior by changing their attitudes to be consistent with their behavior. It is by no means clear that other subject populations would respond to the predicament created by the forced compliance paradigm in the same way. Subjects from Thailand might experience no "identity threat" from acting in counterattitudinal ways at the request of a legitimate authority figure (Triandis, 1978). Subjects from other cultures might experience identity threat, but employ very different attributional tactics to resolve the predicament (e.g., by offering excuses for their conduct).

Higher-level or more abstract theories of the intuitive-politician have much less difficulty in assimilating data on cross-cultural and historical variability in behavior. Unfortunately, such theories do not, at this time, go much beyond specifying the underlying tactics and goals of intuitive politicians: People should explain their behavior in ways that are plausible and that protect their claims to desired personal or social identities. The first requirement, plausibility, is extremely general; it simply means that people should offer explanations consistent with the facts of the situation, with prevailing ideas concerning causality, and with rules of evidence and inference in the language community (Scott & Lyman, 1968). The proliferation of cognitive theories of attribution underscores the enormous variety of factors that affect plausibility judgments. The second requirement, effectiveness in protecting or furthering claims to personal or social identities, is equally general. As noted earlier, there is virtually no limit to the types of identities people may seek.

From this standpoint, universal processes do exist (processes that occur in some form in virtually all human communities). The universals are, however, extremely abstract and functional. People use attributions to achieve desired personal or social identities, and, if they are to do so successfully, they must select attributions that meet plausibility requirements. What vary are the identities people seek, and the acceptable attributional strategies for creating those identities.

Ultimately, it is crucial for the intuitive-politician research program to develop theoretical formulations that integrate highly abstract, cultural-general constructs and highly concrete, culture-specific ones. Both types of constructs, as Triandis (1978) notes, play a key role in advancing our understanding of social behavior. Highly abstract constructs (plausibility, and personal or social identity needs) apply to virtually all times and places. They can serve as anchors and provide guidelines for developing standard methods of operationalizing culture-specific constructs that do vary—sometimes dramatically—across time and space (e.g., What do particular individuals at a particular time regard as a plausible explanation for conduct? What types of personal or social identities do they seek?) The abstract constructs give theoretical coherence to what would otherwise be isolated historical and anthropological facts. The specific constructs give empirical content to what would otherwise be vacuously abstract assertions about social life.

A very interesting example of the approach I am advocating here is V. L. Hamilton's (1983) cross-cultural work on attribution of responsibility. Her work focuses on how people assess the degree to which individuals should be held responsible (and hence punishable) for misdeeds. Psychologists who have studied this topic have emphasized individualistic determinants of responsibility judgments: What the actor did, what the consequences of the act were, and whether the act was intentional (Heider, 1958). Anthropologists and sociologists who have studied this topic have emphasized social context and role determinants of responsibility judgments: Given the actor's location in the social system, what do people think the actor should have done? Hamilton argued that an adequate universal model of how human beings judge wrongdoing must include deed, consequence, and intention variables, and role-expectation variables. In a well-designed cross-cultural study, she demonstrated that Japanese and American respondents use both types of information in assessing responsibility, although the Japanese were more sensitive to the actor's role position and to the social context of the act than were the Americans. Basically the same model applied to both cultures; however, the members of the two cultures placed different importance on certain variables in the model.

Hamilton's findings obviously have important implications for understanding how people use attributions to protect or further their claims to desired identities. Developing the best possible strategies of identity maintenance and enhancement requires an understanding of how members of the culture assess an individual's responsibility for conduct. In America, one may be well advised to focus on changing observers' perceptions of one's behavior or of one's intentions. In Japan, one may be well advised to focus on changing observers' perceptions of one's role relationships to the other persons involved or observers' perceptions of the social context in which the behavior occurred.

Concluding Remarks

In some respects, we all are intuitive scientists. In other respects, we all are intuitive politicians. Both the scientist and politician metaphors are examples of what McGuire (1983) has called guiding-idea theories: "Partial views of the person, each of which exploits the provocative implications of a selective depiction of human nature" (p. 25). Social psychologists can advance their understanding of the attribution process by exploring the research implications of both images of human nature.[5] Highly specialized realms of human activity such as science and politics serve to magnify and reveal basic truths about ourselves. However, there is a serious price to be paid by adopting this strategy of theory construction. We may come to believe too literally in the underlying assumptions on which we have based our theories. We may attempt to squeeze too much of reality into the Procrustean bed of hard-core assumptions that give direction and purpose to our research efforts (Feyerabend, 1970).

Of course, the difficult question is, "How much is too much?" How can one tell whether one has pushed a particular research program too far? Unfortunately, there are no clear guidelines for assessing where the explanatory "ranges of convenience" (Kelly, 1955) of the intuitive scientist and politician research programs begin and end. As I have argued, each program sensitizes us to very different sets of issues and questions. Each program also possesses enormous flexibility in accounting for new data. One of the greatest theoretical challenges confronting us is the integration of these partly conplementary, partly contradictory ways of looking at attribution processes.

REFERENCES

Ajzen, I. & Fishbein, M. (1975). A Bayesian analysis of attribution processes. *Psychological Bulletin, 82,* 261–277.

---

[5]I should add here that the politician metaphor is by no means the only alternative to the scientist metaphor. Social psychologists have also noted the similarities between the lay attributor and the lawyer (Fincham & Jaspars, 1980; Hamilton, 1980) and the stage actor (Brissett & Edgley, 1975; Scott & Lyman, 1968). These perspectives have a good deal in common with the politician metaphor: All emphasize the social functions and consequences of attributions. They differ primarily in emphasis and in tone. For instance, the stage-actor metaphor implies that behavior is very much under the control of well-defined roles, and it also leaves little room for internalized standards to constrain the types of social identities people claim, or the types of tactics people use to claim those identities. The politician metaphor—some stereotypes notwithstanding—implies a more intricate interplay between personal standards and external pressures in shaping social-identity goals and tactics. Perhaps most important, though, the politician metaphor serves to highlight important continuities between the attribution process as it is observed in the laboratory and in the "real world" of conflicting social, economic, and moral values.

Alexander, C. N. & Rudd, J. (1981). Situated identities and response variables. In J. T. Tedeschi (Ed.), *Impression management theory and social psychological research*. New York: Academic Press.

Anderson, P. A. (1981). Justifications and precedents as constraints in foreign policy decision-making. *American Journal of Political Science, 25,* 738–761.

Arkin, R. M. (1981). Self-presentational styles. In J. T. Tedeschi (Ed.), *Impression management theory and social psychological research*. New York: Academic Press.

Arkin, R. M., Appelman, A. J., & Burger, J. M. (1980). Social anxiety, self-presentation, and the self-serving bias in causal attribution. *Journal of Personality and Social Psychology, 38,* 23–35.

Austin, J. L. (1961). *Philosophical papers* (1st ed.). New York: Oxford University Press.

Baumeister, R. (1982). A self-presentational view of social phenomena. *Psychological Bulletin, 91,* 3–26.

Beckman, L. (1973). Teachers' and observers' perceptions of causality for a child's performance. *Journal of Educational Psychology, 65,* 198–204.

Bem, D. J. (1972). Self-perception theory. In L. Berkowitz (Ed.), *Advances in experimental social psychology* (Vol. 6). New York: Academic Press.

Bennett, W. L. (1980). The paradox of public discourse: A framework for the analysis of political accounts. *Journal of Politics, 42,* 792–817.

Blumer, H. (1969). *Symbolic interactionism: Perspective and method*. Englewood Cliffs, NJ: Prentice-Hall.

Bradley, G. W. (1978). Self-serving biases in the attribution process: A re-examination of the fact or fiction question. *Journal of Personality and Social Psychology, 36,* 56–71.

Brissett, D. & Edgley, C. (1975). *Life as theater: A dramaturgical sourcebook.* Chicago: Aldine.

Buss, A. H. (1980). *Self-consciousness and social anxiety*. San Francisco: W. H. Freeman.

Calder, B. J., Ross, M., & Insko, C. (1973). Attitude change and attitude attribution: Effects of incentive, choice and consequences. *Journal of Personality and Social Psychology, 25,* 84–99.

Carlston, D. E. & Shovar, N. (1983). The effects of performance attributions on others' perceptions of the attributor. *Journal of Personality and Social Psychology, 44,* 515–525.

Carson, R. C. (1969). *Interaction concepts of personality*. Chicago: Adline.

Collins, B. E. & Hoyt, M. F. (1972). Personal responsibility-for-consequences: An integration and extension of the forced compliance literature. *Journal of Experimental Social Psychology, 8,* 558–593.

Crowne, D. P. & Marlowe, D. (1964). *The approval motive*. New York: Wiley.

Darley, J. M. & Goethals, G. R. (1981). A naive psychological analysis of the causes of ability-linked performance. In L. Berkowitz (Ed.), *Advances in experimental social psychology* (Vol. 13). New York: Academic Press.

Deutsch, M. & Krauss, R. (1965). *Theories in social psychology*. New York: Basic Books.

Feather, N. T. & Simon, J. G. (1971). Attribution of responsibility and valence of outcome in relation to initial confidence and success and failure of self and others. *Journal of Personality and Social Psychology, 18,* 173–188.

Feyerabend, P. K. (1970). How to be a good empiricist—A plea for tolerance in matters epistemological. In B. A. Brody (Ed.), *Readings in the philosophy of science*. Englewood Cliffs, NJ: Prentice-Hall.

Fincham, F. D. & Jaspars, J. M. (1980). Attribution of responsibility: From man the scientist to man as lawyer. In L. Berkowitz (Ed.), *Advances in experimental social psychology* (Vol. 13). New York: Academic Press.

Fischhoff, B. & Fulero, S. (1977). What makes a good explanation? Decision Research Reports 77–10, Eugene, Oregon: Decision Research.

Fitch, G. (1970). Effects of self-esteem, perceived performance, and choice on causal attributions. *Journal of Personality and Social Psychology, 16,* 311–315.

Forsyth, D. R. (1980). The functions of attributions. *Social Psychology Quarterly, 43,* 184–198.

Gaes, G. G., Kalle, R. J., & Tedeschi, J. T. (1978). Impression management in the forced compliance paradigm: Two studies using the bogus pipeline. *Journal of Experimental Social Psychology, 14,* 493–510.

Gergen, K. J. (1973). Social psychology as history. *Journal of Personality and Social Psychology, 26,* 309–320.

Gergen, K. J. & Taylor, M. G. (1969). Social expectancy and self-presentation in a status hierarchy. *Journal of Experimental Social Psychology, 5,* 79–92.

Goethals, G. R., Cooper, J., & Nafficy, A. (1979). Role of foreseen, foreseeable and unforeseeable behavioral consequences in the arousal of cognitive dissonance. *Journal of Personality and Social Psychology, 37,* 1175–1185.

Goldman, K. (1971). *International norms and war between states.* Stockholm: Laromedsforlagen.

Graber, D. (1976). *Verbal behavior and politics.* Urbana: University of Illinois Press.

Greenberg, J., Pyszczynski, T., & Solomon, S. (1982). The self-serving attribution bias: Beyond self-presentation. *Journal of Experimental Social Psychology, 18,* 56–67.

Hamilton, V. L. (1980). Intuitive psychologist or intuitive lawyer: Alternative models of the attribution process. *Journal of Personality and Social Psychology, 39,* 767–773.

Hamilton, V. L. (1983). Universals in judging wrong-doing: Japanese and Americans compared. *American Sociological Review, 48,* 199–211.

Hass, R. G. (1981). Presentational strategies and the social expression of attitudes: Impression management within limits. In J. T. Tedeschi (Ed.), *Impression management theory and social psychological research.* New York: Academic Press.

Heider, F. (1958). *The psychology of interpersonal relations.* New York: Wiley.

Hewitt, J. P. & Stokes, R. (1975). Disclaimers. *American Sociological Review, 40,* 1–11.

Jackson, S. E. (1981). Measurement of commitment to role identities. *Journal of Personality and Social Psychology, 40,* 138–146.

Jellison, J. M. & Gentry, K. W. (1978). A self-presentation interpretation of the seeking of social approval. *Personality and Social Psychological Bulletin, 4,* 227–230.

Jervis, R. (1976). *Perception and misperception in international relations.* Princeton: Princeton University Press.

Jones, E. E. & Davis, K. E. (1965). From acts to dispositions: The attribution process in person perception. In L. Berkowitz (Ed.), *Advances in experimental social psychology* (Vol. 2). New York: Academic Press.

Jones, E. E., Gergen, K. J., & Davis, K. E. (1962). Some determinants of reactions to being approved or disapproved as a person. *Psychological Monographs, 76* (2, Whole Number, 521).

Jones, E. E. & McGillis, D. (1976). Correspondent inference and the attribution cube: A comparative appraisal. In J. H. Harvey, W. J. Ickes, & R. F. Kidd (Eds.), *New directions in attribution research* (Vol. 1). Hillsdale, NJ: Erlbaum.

Jones, E. E. & Nisbett, R. E. (1971). *The actor and the observer: Divergent perceptions of the causes of behavior.* Morristown, NJ: General Learning Press.
Jones, E. E. & Pittman, T. (1981). Toward a general theory of strategic self-presentation, In J. Suls (Ed.), *Psychological perspectives on the self* (Vol. 1). Hillsdale, NJ: Erlbaum.
Jones, E. E., Riggs, J. M., & Quattrone, G. (1979). Observer bias in the attitude attribution paradigm: Effects of time and information order. *Journal of Personality and Social Psychology, 37,* 1230–1238.
Katz, D. (1960). The functional approach to the study of attitudes. *Public Opinion Quarterly, 24,* 163–204.
Kelley, H. H. (1952). Two functions of reference groups. In G. E. Swanson, T. M. Newcomb, & E. L. Hartley, (Eds.), *Readings in social psychology.* New York: Holt.
Kelley, H. H. (1967). Attribution theory in social psychology. In D. Levine (Ed.), *Nebraska symposium on motivation.* Lincoln: University of Nebraska Press.
Kelley, H. H. (1971). *Attribution in social interaction.* Morristown, NJ: General Learning Press.
Kelley, H. H. (1972). *Causal schemata and the attribution process.* Morristown, NJ: General Learning Press.
Kelley, H. H. & Michela, J. (1979). Attribution theory and research. In M. R. Rosenzweig & L. W. Porter (Eds.), *Annual review of psychology* (Vol. 31). Palo Alto: Annual Reviews Inc.
Kelly, G. A. (1955). *The psychology of personal constructs.* (2 Vols.) New York: Norton.
Kendler, H. H. (1981). *Psychology: A science in conflict.* New York: Oxford University Press.
Kuhn, T. (1970). *The structure of scientific revolutions.* Princeton, NJ: Princeton University Press.
Lakatos, I. (1970). Falsification and the methodology of scientific research programs. In I. Lakatos & A. Musgrave (Eds.), *Criticism and the growth of knowledge.* Cambridge: Cambridge University Press.
Langer, E. J. (1978). Rethinking the role of thought in social interaction. In J. H. Harvey, W. Ickes, & R. F. Kidd (Eds.), *New directions in attribution research.* (Vol. 2) Hillsdale, NJ: Erlbaum.
Latané, B. & Darley, J. (1970). *The unresponsive bystander: Why doesn't he help?* New York: Appleton-Century-Crofts.
Malkis, F. S., Kalle, R. J., & Tedeschi, J. T. (1981). Attitudinal politics in the forced compliance situation. *Journal of Social Psychology, 115,* 259–270.
Maracek, J. & Mettee, D. R. (1972). Avoidance of continued success as a function of self-esteem, level of esteem certainty, and responsibility for success. *Journal of Personality and Social Psychology, 22,* 98–107.
McGuire, W. J. (1983) A contextualist theory of knowledge: Its implications for innovation and reform in psychological research. In L. Berkowitz (Ed.), *Advances in experimental social psychology* (Vol. 16). New York: Academic Press.
Mead, G. H. (1934). *Mind, self, and society.* Chicago: University of Chicago Press.
Merelman, R. M. (1966). Learning and legitimacy. *American Political Science Review, 60,* 548–561.
Merton, R. K. (1957). *Social theory and social structure.* (Rev. ed.). Boston: Allyn & Bacon.
Milgram, S. (1974). *Obedience to authority.* New York: Basic Books.

Miller, D. T. (1976). Ego-involvement and attributions for success and failure. *Journal of Personality and Social Psychology, 34,* 901–906.

Mills, C. W. (1940). Situated actions and vocabularies of motives. *American Sociological Review, 5,* 904–913.

Nisbett, R. & Ross, L. (1980). *Human inference: Strategies and shortcomings of social judgment.* Englewood Cliffs, NJ: Prentice-Hall.

Orvis, B. K., Kelley, H. H., & Butler, D. (1976). Attributional conflict in young couples. In J. H. Harvey, W. J. Ickes, & R. F. Kidd (Eds.), *New directions in attribution research* (Vol. 1). Hillsdale, NJ: Erlbaum.

Reiss, M. & Schlenker, B. R. (1977). Attitude change and responsibility avoidance as modes of dilemma resolution in forced compliance settings. *Journal of Personality and Social Psychology, 35,* 21–30.

Ross, L. (1977). The intuitive psychologist and his shortcomings. In L. Berkowitz (Ed.), *Advances in experimental social psychology* (Vol. 11). New York: Academic Press.

Ross, L., Bierbrauer, G. & Polly, S. (1974). Attribution of educational outcomes by professional and nonprofessional instructors. *Journal of Personality and Social Psychology, 29,* 609–618.

Ross, L., Greene, D., & House, P. (1977). The false consensus effect: An egocentric bias in social perception and attribution processes. *Journal of Experimental Social Psychology, 13,* 279–301.

Royce, J. R. (1978). How can we best advance the construction of theory in psychology? *Canadian Psychological Review, 19,* 259–276.

Sackeim, H. A. (1981). Self-deception, self-esteem, and depression: The adaptive value of lying to oneself. In J. Masling (Ed.), *Empirical studies of psychoanalytic theory.* Hillsdale, NJ: Erlbaum.

Scheier, M. F. & Carver, C. S. (1980). Private and public self-attention, resistance to change, and dissonance reduction. *Journal of Personality and Social Psychology, 39,* 390–405.

Schelling, T. C. (1966). *Arms and influence.* New York: Oxford University Press.

Schlenker, B. R. (1980). *Impression management: The self-concept, social identity, and interpersonal relations.* Monterey, CA: Brooks-Cole.

Schlenker, B. R. (1982). Translating actions into attitudes: An identity-analytic approach to the explanation of social conduct. In L. Berkowitz (Ed.), *Advances in experimental social psychology* (Vol. 15). New York: Academic Press.

Schonbach, P. (1980). A category system for account phases. *European Journal of Social Psychology, 10,* 195–200.

Schwartz, S. (1977). Normative influences on altruism. In L. Berkowitz (Ed.), *Advances in experimental social psychology* (Vol. 10). New York: Academic Press.

Scott, M. & Lyman, S. (1968). Accounts. *American Sociological Review, 33,* 46–62.

Shaw, M. E. & Costanzo, P. R. (1982). *Theories of social psychology.* New York: McGraw-Hill.

Sicoly, F. & Ross, M. (1977). Facilitation of ego-biased attributions by means of self-serving observer feedback. *Journal of Personality and Social Psychology, 35,* 734–741.

Snyder, M. (1979). Self-monitoring processes. In L. Berkowitz (Ed.), *Advances in experimental social psychology* (Vol. 12). New York: Academic Press.

Snyder, M. L., Kleck, R. E., Strenta, A., & Mentzer, S. J. (1979). Avoidance of the handicapped: An attributional ambiguity analysis. *Journal of Personality and Social Psychology, 37,* 2297–2307.

Snyder, R. C., Bruck, H. W., & Sapin, B. M. (1962). *Foreign policy decision-making.* New York: Free Press.

Stephan, W. G. & Gollwitzer, P. M. (1981). Affect as a mediator of attributional egotism. *Journal of Experimental Social Psychology, 17,* 443–458.

Stryker, S. & Gottlieb, A. (1981). Attribution theory and symbolic interactionism: A comparison. In J. H. Harvey, W. J. Ickes, & R. F. Kidd (Eds.), *New directions in attribution research* (Vol. 3). Hillsdale, NJ: Erlbaum.

Sullivan, H. S. (1953). *Conceptions of modern psychiatry.* New York: Norton.

Swann, W. B. & Read, S. J. (1981). Self-verification processes: How we sustain our self-conceptions. *Journal of Experimental Social Psychology, 17,* 351–372.

Taylor, S. E. & Fiske, S. (1978). Salience, attention, and attribution: Top of the head phenomena. In L. Berkowitz (Ed.), *Advances in experimental social psychology* (Vol. 11). New York: Academic Press.

Tedeschi, J. T. (1981). *Impression management theory and social psychological research.* New York: Academic Press.

Tedeschi, J. T. & Riess, M. (1981). Predicaments and verbal tactics of impression management. In C. Antaki (Ed.), *Ordinary language explanations of social behavior.* London: Academic Press.

Tedeschi, J. T. & Riordan, C. A. (1981). Impression management and prosocial behavior following transgression. In J. T. Tedeschi (Ed.), *Impression management theory and social psychological research.* New York: Academic Press.

Tedeschi, J. T. & Rosenfeld, P. (1981). Impression management theory and the forced compliance situation. In J. T. Tedeschi (Ed.), *Impression management theory and social psychological research.* New York: Academic Press.

Tetlock, P. E. (1980). Explaining teacher explanations for pupil performance: An examination of the self-presentation position. *Social Psychology Quarterly, 43,* 283–290.

Tetlock, P. E. (1981). The influence of self-presentation goals on attributional reports. *Social Psychology Quarterly, 44,* 300–311.

Tetlock, P. E. & Fleisher, E. (1981). Self-schemata, audience expectations, and self-presentation. Paper presented at the 89th annual meeting of the American Psychological Association, Los Angeles.

Tetlock, P. E. & Levi, A. (1982). Attribution bias: On the inconclusiveness of the cognition-motivation debate. *Journal of Experimental Social Psychology, 18,* 68–88.

Tompkins, S. S. (1981). The quest for primary motives: Biography and autobiography of an idea. *Journal of Personality and Social Psychology, 41,* 306–329.

Triandis, H. C. (1978). Some universals of social behavior. *Personality and Social Psychological Bulletin, 4,* 1–16.

Weary, G. & Arkin, R. M. (1981). Attributional self-presentation and the regulation of self-evaluation. In J. H. Harvey, W. Ickes, & R. F. Kidd (Eds.), *New directions in attribution research* (Vol. 3). Hillsdale, NJ: Erlbaum.

Wicklund, R. & Brehm, J. W. (1976). *Perspectives on cognitive dissonance.* Hillsdale, NJ: Erlbaum.

Wortman, C. B., Costanzo, P. R., & Witt, T. R. (1973). Effects of anticipated performance on the attributions of causality to self and others. *Journal of Personality and Social Psychology, 27,* 372–381.

Zillmann, D. & Cantor, J. R. (1976). Effect of timing of information about mitigating circumstances on emotional responses to provocation and retaliatory behavior. *Journal of Experimental Social Psychology, 12,* 38–55.

Zuckerman, M. (1979). Attribution of success and failure revisited: The motivational bias is alive and well in attribution theory. *Journal of Personality, 47,* 245–287.

Zuckerman, M., DePaulo, B. M., & Rosenthal, R. (1981). Verbal and nonverbal detection of deception. In L. Berkowitz (Ed.), *Advances in experimental social psychology* (Vol. 14). New York: Academic Press.

CHAPTER 9

THE EXCUSE: AN AMAZING GRACE?

C. R. Snyder
The Graduate Training Program in Clinical Psychology
The University of Kansas, Lawrence

*Amazing grace! how sweet the sound,
That saved a wretch like me!*

Opening lyrics to "Amazing Grace"
by John Newton (1779)

INTRODUCTION

Excuses have a bad reputation. When we think of them, they may seem to be silly, transparent ploys on the part of people to cover their mistakes, misdeeds, and failures. Further, we may think of excuses as appearing in *other* people, and they may even afford us an occasional chuckle. Recall, for example, comedian Steve Martin's old routine in which he first committed a blunder. After a well-timed pause, and in straight-faced indignation, he uttered, "Well, Excuuuuuuuuuuuuuuse me!" At best, excuses are relegated to an almost trite, and certainly easily understood, status. At worst, they often carry a stigma.

The present chapter, however, offers a more balanced perspective on excuses. Although the ultimate conclusion will not be that excuses are all good, it will be argued that they are not all bad either. In the subsequent pages, the reader will undoubtedly notice that the definition of *excuses* is expanded so as to include activities that heretofore may not have been conceptualized as excuses. In this stretching of the excuse-making concept, the subtlety as well as the pervasiveness of excuses in one's daily existence may become more apparent. Further, it will be suggested that excuses play an integral role in most of our lives, and as such, they do not just apply to other people. A model of excuse making, along with supporting data, will be presented in order to accomplish the aforementioned goals.

IN PURSUIT OF A POSITIVE SELF-IMAGE

The underlying assumption in the present chapter is that excuses are driven by the person's attempt to maintain a positive self-image. To understand this assumption, it is first necessary to define what is meant by a self-image, and then to briefly document the motivation to preserve a positive one.

Self-Images

The self-image is a person's private mental picture of a personally relevant event along a continuum of identity dimensions. *Events* represent one's actions and their consequences. (See Schlenker, 1980, pp. 125–126.) In this context, a personally relevant event may include actions that the person perpetrated, or may include actions that the person is linked to but did not even perform (e.g., the weatherperson blamed for a blizzard, or the son blamed for the sins of his father). Unlike an actual recording that faithfully documents a person's words and deeds (say, a surreptitious motion picture taken of an individual), the self-image is a shortened, very personal cognitive encoding of the event. In this sense, only the bare essentials of the event may constitute the self-image. These abbreviated self-images operate on principles that are similar to the storing of any information in memory; thus, a complex set of information is "chunked" in memory in a shortened version. (See Neisser, 1967.)

Identity dimensions represent important areas in a person's life and include continuums of intellectual, athletic, interpersonal, or other activities (Markus, 1977). Most people have a variety of identity dimensions along which they form self-images, but probably form self-images along their important identity dimensions. In turn, the individual self-images, defined on the basis of a person's identity dimensions, may yield an overall appraisal of oneself. This amalgamation of the self-image building blocks may thus contribute to the person's "self-concept" (Schlenker, 1980; Snyder, Higgins, & Stucky, 1983).

Positive Self-Images

Self-images are constantly playing in the theater of one's mind, and the usual goal is to preserve the positiveness of these images. A multitude of writers have spoken of the motivation to maintain self-esteem. William James (1890) described this motive as the "fundamental instinctive impulse." After James, the list of writers who have advocated a self-esteem drive reads like a "Who's Who." Included on this list are Alfred Adler, Karen Horney, Harry Stack Sullivan, Erich Fromm, Gordon Allport, Carl Rogers, and Abraham Maslow, to name a few. Building on the work of these previous authors, modern writings on the self-concept notion have also implicitly assumed a self-esteem motive. (See Wells & Marwell, 1976, for review.)

Empirical research has supported the self-esteem motive. For example, self-esteem generating personal feedback is accepted more readily than esteem-damaging negative feedback. (See Snyder, Shenkel, & Lowery, 1977, for review.) Likewise, there is a wealth of social-psychological research, much of which will be discussed subsequently under various types of excuse making, showing that people attribute the good things to themselves and the bad things to other people or objects. (See Snyder et al., 1983; Weary Bradley, 1978, for reviews.) When it comes to self-images, therefore, a commonly held assumption is that most of us work to preserve positive ones.

REVOLVING SELF-IMAGES: INTERNAL AND EXTERNAL AUDIENCES

Self-images are often for both external and internal audiences. *External audience* refers to all of those people or critics who may "evaluate" a person's actions (e.g., parents, teachers, bosses, judges). This emphasis on the role of the external audience in guiding a person's behavior has often been described under the rubric of impression management. One assumption within the impression-management perspective is that maintaining a positive image enables the person to continue social interactions, to avoid punishments, and to garner tangible rewards. (See Goffman, 1971; Tedeschi, 1981.)

The *internal audience* reflects the individual's standards and values. Obviously, the internal audience often entails an incorporation of the standards of the external audience (e.g., parents and authorities). Symbolic interactionism (Cooley, 1922; Mead, 1934) captures this perspective by suggesting that we are constantly imagining how others would see us. Likewise, various conceptualizations of moral development describe the inculcation of external values (e.g., social-learning theory, Bandura, 1977; psychoanalytic theory, Freud, 1927; cognitive theory, Piaget, 1926; Kohlberg, 1963).

Although there are undoubtedly persons who attend primarily to either external or internal audiences (Greenwald, 1982; Hogan, 1982), and there are instances in which the external-audience concerns may predominate internal-audience concerns (Snyder et al., 1983), it is probably very common for a person to simultaneously attend to external and internal audiences. (See Schlenker, 1984, for related discussion.) In most daily dilemmas, the concerns may rotate from external to internal audiences so quickly that the two audiences are actually fused. This state is referred to as "revolving images" (Snyder et al., 1983).

THE SELF-IMAGE THREAT

Excuses come alive because of a threat to a person's self-image. A threatened self-image occurs when a person appears to be responsible for a negative performance of some sort. At this point it is appropriate to briefly examine the factors that contribute to a negative performance, and a sense of responsibility for that performance.

Issues Pertaining to the Negativity of the Performance

Generally, a negative performance represents any action (word or deed) that does not meet the standards established by the person and society. The further the performance falls below the standards, the more "negative" it should be perceived. Additionally, the negativity of the performance should be related to the subsequent issues raised in this section.

Clarity of Standard As the standards for a particular activity become increasingly clearer, then so too should the negativity of the performances that do not meet those standards (Jellison, 1977). Thus, the failure to meet a "final" deadline (say for a paper in school) is more negative than not meeting a "suggested" deadline.

Importance of Activity Activities that pertain to important identity dimensions for a person should potentially generate more negative performances. The sense of involvement that accompanies important activities makes the outcome, whether good or bad, impactful for that person (Greenwald & Ronis, 1978). For example, it is worse for a professional football player to repeatedly drop passes than it is for a recreational athlete to do so.

Intentionality If a person intends to act in a particular "negative" fashion, that behavior is judged more severely than when the person did not intend to act in the negative fashion (Darley & Zanna, 1982). Related research suggests that an intended negative activity is perceived as being more negative than an unintended one (Rotenberg, 1980). Children learn, for instance, that it is far more negative to hurt someone "on purpose" rather than "by accident."

Power of the Critic In those instances where part of the feedback obviously hinges on external sources, the intensity of the threat of negative feedback may be related to the expertise, status, and general power of the critic (Halperin, Snyder, Shenkel, & Houston, 1976; Snyder & Newburg, 1981). It would much more troublesome, as a case in point, to hear that one had "problems with anger" if this message were delivered by a well-respected psychotherapist as compared to the carry-out boy at the grocery store.

Issues Pertaining to the Responsibility for a Bad Performance

A threatened self-image demands first, a negative performance, and second, a sense of responsibility for that performance. Responsibility reflects any information suggesting that the person is accountable for the negative performance. In order to understand this responsibility notion, it is useful to provide a brief introduction to the attributional model of social psychologist Harold Kelley. Kelley's model focuses upon the causes that appear to covary with an effect over time. If a particular cause seems to covary with a given effect, then it is reasoned that the effect should be attributed to that cause. (See Kelley, 1967, 1971, 1973.) Kelley suggested that three kinds of information—consensus, consistency, and distinctiveness—help to determine whether a particular behavior should be attributed to dispositional factors within the person or to situational factors outside of the person. Although Kelley's model deals with the attribution of causality to external or internal origins, in the subsequent presentation it will be assumed that greater *responsibility* relates to attributions of a more internal origin. Additionally, in the following presentation, it should be emphasized that Kelley's theoretical ideas concerning consensus, consistency, and distinctiveness will be applied to the responsibility for a negative performance both in the eyes of oneself and others. (See Harvey & Smith, 1977; Stevens & Jones, 1976.)

Consensus Consensus information reflects the extent to which many people have behaved (may include perceptions, attitudes, and opinions) similarly in the same situation. A person is held as being more responsible for a behavior when other people have not behaved in a similar fashion in the same circumstances. Thus, *lower* consensus suggests greater personal responsibility. The student, for example, who fails a test when everyone else does well is seen as having low consensus, and by inference, high responsibility for the poor performance (in the sense that the performance is attributed to factors internal to the student).

Consistency Consistency represents the extent to which a person has acted (possibly including perceptions, attitudes, and opinions) in the same fashion in the same situation over time. A person is held more responsible for a behavior when he or she has repeatedly acted in the same manner in the particular situation. Therefore, *higher* consistency implies greater personal responsibility. Take our student as an example again. If the student has time and again done poorly on tests, then he or she may be held especially responsible.

Distinctiveness Distinctiveness taps the degree to which a person acts (may include perceptions, attitudes, and opinions) differently in a given situation relative to other situations. A person is held more responsible when his or her behavior in one situation is similar to behaviors in other situations. Thus, *lower* distinctiveness leads to greater perceived responsibility. If our student is failing in one course, and in other courses as well, then he or she is held as being very responsible for the bad performance.

Relevant research examining the responsibility attributions to the person generally supports the aforementioned predictions when consensus, consistency, and distinctiveness information are available (Major, 1980; McArthur, 1972; Orvis, Cunningham, & Kelley, 1975; Ruble & Feldman, 1976). Furthermore, when only one type of information is available (e.g., consensus, but not consistency and distinctiveness), people make responsibility attributions similar to those predicted when all three types of information are available (Kulik & Taylor, 1980; Major, 1980; Orvis et al., 1975; Wells & Harvey, 1977).

In summary, low-consensus, high-consistency, and low-distinctiveness information may all contribute to a heightened perception of responsibility for a bad performance. The greater the negativity of the performance and the greater the seeming responsibility of the person for that performance, then the more threatened the self-image should be. Under the conditions of extreme negativity of performance and high responsibility for that performance, the self-image should be truly shaken. Something has to be done by the person to deal with this self-image threat. This something often takes the form of an excuse.

HERE COME THE EXCUSES

Definition and Excuse-Making Model

"Excuses are explanations or actions that serve to lessen the negative implications of an actor's performance, thereby maintaining a positive image for oneself and others" (Snyder et al., 1983, p. 45). This definition should be considered within the context of the diagram in Figure 9-1.

This model has three components through which excuses may work: the apparent-responsibility link, the negative performance, and the transformed-responsibility link.

The first component, the apparent-responsibility link, represents information (often of a physical "evidence" nature) that connects the person to a bad performance. In a legal sense (see Fincham & Jaspars, 1980; Hamilton, 1980), the apparent-responsibility link reveals whether or not the person actually engaged in the bad performance. The apparent responsibility must be established before the subsequent appraisal can be made of the person's role in a "bad" performance. (D'Arcy [1963] describes this as a *qualifying circumstance*.) This apparent-responsibility link often represents the first line of attack for an excuse maker who is seeking to establish that he or she really had nothing to do with the bad performance. ("I didn't do it" innocence pleas may be heard.)

The second component, the negative performance, has already been described in the section on threat to self-image. If the excuse maker must admit his or her apparent responsibility ("Yes, I did it"), then the next strategy may be to lessen the negativity of the performance through a variety of maneuvers. In

FIGURE 9-1
Excuse components.

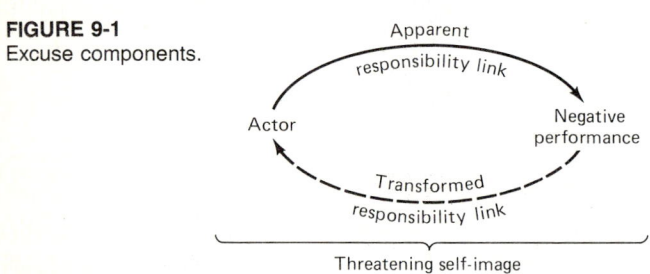

these reframing excuses the person implicitly argues, "It's really not so bad." This reframing or alteration of the appearance of the negative consequences has been referred to by others as *conventionalizations* (Backman, in this volume) or *justifications* (Backman, in this volume; Schlenker 1980; Scott & Lyman, 1968; Tetlock, in this volume).

The third component, the transformed-responsibility link, reflects additional information, often of a psychological nature, that modifies the degree to which the person should be perceived as being responsible for a bad performance. Thus, if the actor must admit that he or she "did it" (the apparent-responsibility link), as well as acknowledge that the performance is bad (the negative-performance component), then transformed-responsibility excuses will lessen the eventual sense of responsibility and personal and societal condemnation. The essence of the transformed-responsibility tactic is the assertion, "Yes, but . . ." Other writers have described this transformation of responsibility as *excuses* (Backman, in this volume; Schlenker, 1980; Scott & Lyman, 1968) or *quantifying circumstances* (D'Arcy, 1963).

Excuses that are aimed at lessening the apparent-responsibility link, reframing the negative performance, and lessening the transformed responsibility will be detailed in subsequent sections.

Lessening Apparent Responsibility ("I Didn't Do It")

This type of excuse attempts to sever the link between the bad performance and the person. Simple innocence strategies, and the somewhat more complicated blaming tactics, represent excuses that lessen the apparent responsibility.

Innocence: "It Wasn't Me." This type of excuse obviously has a counterpart in the legal system. (See Hart, 1968.) Beyond the verbal denial of having anything to do with the bad performance, the person may have an alibi to document his or her innocence. This tactic is strengthened when the person not only asserts that "It wasn't me," but can also point out "who it was."

Blaming: "It Was the . . ." There are many variations on this excuse strategy. If the person is in a group situation, for example, and the group fails, the individual will place the responsibility for the poor performance on other group members (Schlenker & Miller, 1977). "Some other dummy" in one's group gets the blame. This phenomenon is probably very familiar to anyone who has worked with people in group settings, where "buck passing" is legendary.

A slightly different blaming strategy involves "they lost" assertions. In situations where one may or may not associate with a group, for example, it appears that the person claims membership in a successful group and denounces membership in an unsuccessful one. Robert Cialdini and his colleagues (Cialdini, Borden, Thorne, Walker, Freeman, & Sloan, 1976) coined the term BIRGing as a reflection of the "Basking In Reflected Glory" process. In a series of studies, students at universities with powerful football teams (e.g., Arizona

State, Notre Dame, Michigan, Southern California) were found to wear more school-identifying apparel (jackets, t-shirts, buttons) on Mondays following a victory than on Mondays following a defeat. The reader can easily visualize the fans of championship teams who announce to the television camera "We're # 1." Interestingly, the same index finger that points to the sky after victories ("We're # 1") may point downward to the team in a blaming gesture after defeats ("They lost"). Elsewhere, in fact, it has been suggested that BIRGing needs to be yoked with a new corollary: CORFing ("Cutting Off Reflected Failure") (Snyder et al., 1983). CORFing could be documented by showing, for example, that there are fewer school insignias worn on days after the team loses as compared to days when the team doesn't play.

A blaming process similar to CORFing is "savage discovery" (Ryan, 1972). Here, the person blames the victim, and in doing so locates the cause of the problem in some underprivileged, strange, or different group.

> . . . Zero Mostel used to do a sketch in which he impersonated a Dixiecrat Senator conducting an investigation of the origins of World War II. At the climax of the sketch, the Senator boomed out, in an excruciating mixture of triumph and suspicion, "What was Pearl Harbor *doing* in the Pacific?" (Ryan, 1972, p. 3).

As a further example, consider the response of "humanistic" bureaucrats whose social programs have failed. They blame not the society more generally, nor the program; on the contrary, the "savage discovery" process locates the blame for the failure in "those people" (i.e., the recipients who didn't seem to profit from the program).

Reframing Performances ("It's Really Not So Bad")

Reframing excuse strategies share the common theme of diminishing the negativity of the bad performance. The general reframing subtypes treated in this section are subsequently described under the headings "See no evil, hear no evil," "Manipulating the standards for the bad performance," and "Derogating the sources of the negative feedback."

See No Evil, Hear No Evil This reframing excuse suggests that the person doesn't "comprehend" the negativity of his or her bad performance. As such, "See no evil, hear no evil" appears to reflect a perceptually linked tactic.

A first example of this type of excuse could be labeled the "No problem, no help" effect. In the Spring of 1964 in Queens, New York, Ms. Kitty Genovese was stabbed to death. Thirty-eight neighbors witnessed this murder, which took some 35 minutes, but they did not help or call the police. (See Rosenthal [1964] for an insightful analysis of this slaying and its repercussions.) This incident shocked American society, and ignited a series of studies aimed at showing why bystanders don't render aid. (See Latané & Darley, 1970.) These studies reveal that people in groups are less prone to render aid than people who are alone. What is relevant in the present excuse context, however, is what people say when they don't render aid. (This is the bad performance.) In one investigation known as the "lady in distress" study, research participants were led to believe that a female experimenter in a nearby room had fallen and seriously injured herself (a tape was played of her screaming). Among those who didn't help, typical responses were "I didn't think it was serious" and "I wasn't sure what happened" (Latané & Rodin, 1969). Evidently, a lot of things just aren't seen or heard, at least according to excuse makers.

Another "See no evil, . . ." reframing excuse involves situations where a person may cause a harm to another, and then argue that the damage isn't really very bad. This lessening of the damage is especially prevalent when the person has chosen to engage in the harmful activity. In this "choice-harm deescalator" effect (see Snyder et al., 1983), under higher choice conditions in which the person believes that he or she has willfully committed an action, the negativity of the action is especially lessened or downplayed. This has been found in studies where the action delivered to another person is an electric shock (Brock & Buss, 1962) or a verbal message (Riess & Schlenker, 1977). In our daily lives, this "choice-harm deescalator" may result in statements such as "It's not as bad as it looks" and "Oh come off it; it didn't hurt *that* much."

A third type of "See no evil, . . ." reframing excuse is similar to the "choice-harm deescalator," and is called the "victim derogation" effect. History recounts a rather sad list of victim derogations. The Jews killed by the Nazis were described as subhumans by their exterminators; the slaughtered North Vietnamese were portrayed as "Gooks" who didn't value human life; the victims of crimes are seen by the perpetrators as "deserving what they got," and so on. Indeed, the victim is often transformed into an object that is deserving of injury (Sykes & Matza, 1957). Related research suggests that "aggressors" do appear to derogate and dislike their "victims" (Cialdini, Kenrick, & Hoerig, 1976; Davis & Jones, 1960).

Manipulating Standards for Bad Performance This second general group of reframing strategies focuses on the standards that apply to the performance. The excuse maker attempts to rework the standards so as to provide a more charitable view of his or her particular bad performance.

A first way of manipulating the standards is to question their clarity. If the standards are fuzzy, how can we fail? The excuse maker may be heard to plead "There is no way to judge this sort of thing," or there is the classic student plea, "The test wasn't clear at all." A slight variant of this approach is the reframing tactic of lowering the standards. The idea here is to recalibrate the standards so that they are easier to attain. It is common for a newcomer, whether he or she is a young swimming coach or a just-elected President of the United States, to pronounce what a mess things are and how it will take a while to correct them.

If the standards can't be attacked for lacking clarity, or they can't be lowered, the excuse maker may try to change them to accommodate his or her performance. (See Jamous & Lemaine, 1962; Lemaine, 1966.) This is a customizing process of sorts. Contrary to the school-yard cliché that "It's not fair to change the rules after the game has started," the excuse maker may do so with considerable skill. In this vein, the reader may remember George Orwell's

(1946) book *Animal Farm*. After the animals had overthrown the cruel owner, their goal was to run the farm as a utopia. Commandments were written on the barn to signal such noble principles as "No animal shall sleep in a bed," "No animal shall drink alcohol," and so on. Eventually, the pigs take over the running of the farm and seemingly commit a multitude of transgressions. When the pigs began to drink alcoholic beverages, for example, the other animals protested and pointed to the relevant commandment. Mysteriously, it now read "No animal shall drink alcohol *to excess.*" As the story closes, and the farm becomes a prison for the animals, the pigs surplant all the commandments with one: "ALL ANIMALS ARE EQUAL, BUT SOME ARE MORE EQUAL THAN OTHERS." Although we don't live on Animal Farm, some of the following linguistic customizations will sound familiar (Hammond, 1972, p. 89).

> He is sneaky, you are crafty, I am subtle.
> His son is a bum, yours is a hippie, mine
>   is trying to find himself.
> She is a tramp, you are a flirt,
>   I have a warm, affectionate nature.
> She is childish, you are immature, I
>   am young at heart.

A final way of manipulating the standards involves the embedding (see Jellison, 1977) of a seemingly bad act into another context. This process may be called "exonerative moral reasoning." Here, for example, the killing of 100,000 people at Hiroshima is portrayed as an event that actually saved many more lives by shortening World War II. In the words of the bombardier of the plane that dropped the Hiroshima bomb, "I'm not proud of killing all those people, but I'm proud of saving all the lives we did" (*The Kansas City Star,* 1975, p. 4B). Other examples include parents who beat their children as a way of socializing them, physicians who withhold information from patients for their good, and researchers who temporarily deceive research participants in order to further science. Perhaps the reader may remember an instance in which a particular ill deed was neatly packaged as a necessary part of some larger virtuous act?

Derogating the Sources of Negative Feedback Yet another means of reframing involves attempts to discredit the sources of negative feedback. One target for derogation is the evaluative instrument that generated the negative feedback. Classic instrument derogations can be found after tests when students can be heard muttering "It was too picky," or "It was too long (or short or multiple choice)." Not surprisingly, teacher-evaluation research consistently shows that students who do poorly also give their exams low marks (e.g., Snyder & Clair, 1976). Research in the area of psychological feedback reveals a similar pattern of results: People who receive negative as compared to positive personal feedback are more prone to derogate the testing instruments (e.g., Snyder & Clair, 1977).

In addition to derogating the evaluative instruments, the excuse maker can derogate the evaluator who generates the negative feedback (Jones, 1973;

Mettee & Aronson, 1974). Again, the teacher evaluation area provides consistent support for the aforementioned type of excuse making. (See Anikeef, 1953; Clair & Snyder, 1979.) If one were to give total credibility to the comments of failing students, the obvious conclusion would be that it was because of "those lousy teachers." Further, it may be the case that this evaluator derogation may serve to lessen the emotional distress of failing students. Burish and Houston (1979) found, for example, that students who were allowed to derogate their test examiner evidenced lower levels of anxiety, depression, and hostility in comparison to students who were not allowed to engage in this derogation process.

Lessening the Transformed Responsibility ("Yes, but . . .")

The central notion in excuses that are aimed at the transformed responsibility link is that there are special extenuating circumstances relevant to the bad performance. The excuse-making person admits to having "done it," and admits that "it is bad," and then may launch into a series of "yes, but . . ." verbalizations.

Consensus Raising The idea inherent in consensus-raising excuses is that most people would behave in the same way as the person did in a particular situation. The individual's psychological responsibilty is thus lessened if it can be demonstrated that others would have done the same thing.

One excuse tactic is to appeal to task difficulty or luck as determining one's poor performance. If the task is sufficiently difficult, for example, the consensus-raising excuse maker can reason that anyone would do poorly on it. Luck, or lack thereof, can also engulf almost anyone. Research relevant to this topic reveals that after a failure experience, people tend to engage in excuse-like external attributions of task difficulty and luck, rather than internal attributions related to ability and effort. (See Zuckerman, 1979, for review.) This research is reminiscent of a *Peanuts* cartoon in which Lucy is talking to her teammate Charlie Brown after their baseball game. She asks Charlie who won, and what was the score. Charlie tells her that the other team won 68 to 0, whereupon Lucy turns to the opponents and screams, "LUCKY!" We laugh at Lucy, but it may be that she merely lacks finesse.

Another consensus-raising excuse involves the coercion-based notion that "I was merely following orders." There are extreme coercion based appeals such as the soldiers at the Mai Lai 4 killings who suggested that they were doing what their superiors ordered, or the Nazi executioner Adolf Eichmann, who pleaded at his trial that he was merely doing what he was told. At a less extreme level, we all may have heard (or used) such appeals as "He made me do it," or "Dad told me to do it." Coercion-based excuses raise consensus by implying that anyone in the same circumstances would behave in the same fashion.

Coercion pleas are inherent in the well-known Milgram (1974) studies of obedience. In these studies, research participants delivered electric shocks to "learners" as a means of facilitating their acquisition of information. Surprisingly, the research participants administered extremely high levels of shock (e.g., 450 volts). (Actually, although the research participants believed they were delivering shocks, no shocks were administered.) And how do research participants explain this "harmful" behavior? The answer is simple: "It's the experimenter's responsibility. He made me to do it." Interestingly, related research also suggests that the greater the perceived harm that is delivered to another person, the more the "responsible" person will assert that he or she had no choice (Brock & Buss, 1964; Harvey, Harris, & Barnes, 1975). This phenomenon has been called the "harm-choice deescalator," meaning that greater harm appears to generate less perceived choice on the part of the transgressing person (Snyder et al., 1983).

Perhaps the most obvious consensus-raising excuse involves the clinical term *projection*. Since Freud introduced projection as one of several defense mechanisms, it has generally been defined as the process whereby the person avoids a psychological threat by ascribing personal deficiencies and failings to other people. Relevant research reveals that ego-threatened as compared to nonthreatened people generate more negative ratings of other people (Holmes, 1978; Wills, 1981). Even more important, there are at least four studies that support the evidence for the stress reduction or self-image maintenance role of projection (Bennett & Holmes, 1975; Burish & Houston, 1979; Holmes & Houston, 1971; Zemore & Greenough, 1973). In these studies, projection appears to alleviate the stress that is related to a bad performance. Thus, not only do people appear to project their weaknesses onto others after a bad performance, but this may make them feel better. Examples of consensus-raising projection cut across socioeconomic and age boundaries.

> The young boy caught cheating on an exam moans, "But everyone was doing it"; the retired couple found shoplifting food plead, "Everyone in our boarding house has to do it." The poor woman who is distorting family information for welfare benefits argues, "A lot of others do the same thing"; the affluent businessman explains his tax evasion by asserting, "Most people cut corners on their taxes."
> (Snyder et al., 1983, p. 101)

Consistency Lowering The idea inherent in consistency lowering excuses is the supposed fact that the bad performance in a given situation is very unusual for the person. The excuse maker thus suggests that he or she should not be held as being totally responsible for this "one bad performance."

One of the ways to lower consistency is to assert that "I didn't mean to." This excuse employs the lack of intentionality argument. As noted previously, research suggests than intended actions, if they have negative outcomes, are perceived as being worse than unintended actions (Rotenberg, 1980). Likewise, people are held as being more accountable for negative actions that are foreseeable as compared to those actions that are unforeseeable (Shaw, 1968). Although one of the earliest childhood excuses may be the "I didn't mean to" one, it is also the case that unintentionality plays a role in the world of adult excuses. Certainly, the legal system places a good deal of weight on intentionality in determining the responsibility for a crime. Excuse makers may indirectly invoke by employing "drunkenness," "fit of rage," or insanity pleas (Tedeschi & Riess, 1981). This last tactic has become especially controversial since John Hinckley, Jr. was judged innocent of attempting to assassinate President Reagan because of temporary insanity.

A second consistency-lowering excuse relates to diminished effort: "I didn't try." Although attributions to external factors such as task difficulty and luck may serve as excuses (see previous section), the internal factor of effort may also serve an excuse function. By arguing for or exhibiting lowered effort, the excuse makers are suggesting that on future occasions they would do much better if they "really tried." Thus, it isn't that the person is incompetent, physically inadequate, or dumb (the truly threatening labels), but it is merely a matter of not trying. This is a case of where the lowered effort may heighten the ambiguity as to the real reason for the poor performance (Snyder & Wicklund, 1981). Research consistently shows that, after failure, people are prone to employ the lowered-effort type of excuse. (See Zuckerman, 1979, for review.) As an example of such research, Miller (1976) had college students initially take a social-perceptiveness test (actually a bogus test) and then told half of the subjects that they had succeeded and told the other half that they bad failed. When asked "How hard did you try on the test?," the failed students reported expending less effort than did the successful students.

A related process is inherent in self-handicapping theory, which posits that individuals may adopt a self-label that generates inconsistency-related excuses (Berglas & Jones, 1978; Jones & Berglas, 1978; Snyder & Smith, 1982). For example, in anticipation of potentially threatening evaluative arenas, research suggests the people may invoke the following inconsistency-raising self-handicaps: drug use (Berglas & Jones, 1978), alcohol consumption (Higgins & Harris, 1983; Tucker, Vuchinich, & Sobell, 1981), test-anxiety symptoms (Smith, Snyder, & Handelsman, 1982), poor health background (Smith, Snyder, & Perkins, 1983), shyness symptoms (Snyder, Smith, Augelli, & Ingram, in press), and history of traumatic life events (Degree & Snyder, in press). In all of the aforementioned studies, the person is shielded from the threatening arena by the inconsistency that is inherent in each of the self-handicaps.

Distinctiveness Raising A third general set of tactics related to lowering the transformed responsibility involves distinctiveness raising. As compared to consistency lowering where the excuse maker seeks to establish the fact that he or she would not repeatedly perform poorly in the *same* performance situation, in distinctiveness raising the excuse maker suggests that unlike the poor performance in one situation, there are *other* somewhat different performance arenas where he or she has performed well. By appealing to the other arenas where they have done well, the excuse makers are suggesting that their idiosyncrasy credits (see Hollander, 1958, 1976) should allow them to be held less responsible for a bad performance in one particular situation. By cashing in one's idiosyncrasy credits (i.e., the positive impressions that a person has attained in a variety of previous other situations), the person in a jam potentially increases the distinctiveness of the bad performance.

One way to increase distinctiveness is to divert the attention from the poor performance arena to those arenas where one has done better. Research related to this topic suggests that when people are shown to have a weakness in one area, they will compensate by presenting themselves positively in other areas (Baumeister & Jones, 1978). For example, the middle-aged, slow-pitch softball player who makes a fool of himself on the playing field, recounts to himself (and to whomever else will listen) that he has been more successful in other areas of his life such as his job and family.

Another related tactic for raising distinctiveness emphasizes the separation of the person who did poorly in a given situation from the "good" person who does well in a variety of other arenas. The "bad" person is split from the "good" one. In regard to this splitting process, Goffman (1971) suggests that apologies serve to separate the bad person who did something wrong from the contrite, overall "good" person. Likewise, if the transgressing person is full of remorse, he or she may be held less responsible for the ill deeds that have been committed (Darby & Schlenker, 1982; Schlenker & Darby, 1981). Relatedly, juries are more lenient on defendants when they express remorse (Austin, Walster, & Utne, 1976). Although apologies are often thought of as being only aimed at external audiences, in the context of the revolving-images notion used in the present excuse-making model, it may be the case that apologies also are aimed at convincing the internal audience of oneself.

In the previous discussion of consensus-raising, consistency-lowering, and distinctiveness-raising transformed-responsibility excuses, it may have occurred to the reader that an excuse may simultaneously achieve two or perhaps three of the consensus-raising, distinctiveness-raising, and consistency-lowering processes. When two transformed-responsibility factors are operative, a "double play" takes place. Often, the consistency and distinctiveness factors are connected. For example, the intentionality notion of "I didn't mean to" obviously lowers the consistency of the bad behavior for the particular situation, but it also raises the distinctiveness of the bad behavior from the other good performance situations. When all three processes operate at once, a "triple play" occurs. As an example, consider the soldier who harms an innocent civilian. His excuse was that he was ordered to do it; this coercion-based excuse raises consensus ("Any soldier would have followed the orders"), lowers consistency ("I haven't harmed civilians in this similar circumstance when I wasn't given an order to do so"), and raises distinctiveness ("I'm not an aggressive person in other arenas of my life").

In addition to those instances where several different processes may operate simultaneously in transformed-responsibility excuses, it should be emphasized that a reframing of the negative performance may occur along with a lessening of transformed responsibility. For example, by raising consensus through an "everyone was doing it" assertion, the person is lessening the transformed responsibility *and* is reframing the performance. In this vein, the negativity of an act should be diminished if that act is prevalent in the population (Snyder & Shenkel, 1976).

DIRTEing: Directing Internal Responsibility To External

The previous discussion of excuse strategies that are aimed at lessening the apparent responsibility, reframing the bad performance, and lessening the transformed responsibility highlights the usefulness of an attributional analysis of excuse making. Further, in many of the previous examples, a common process can be observed: The excuse-making person attempts to move the responsibility for the bad performance from himself or herself to outside factors. This *Directing* of *Internal Responsibility To External* sources (DIRTEing) is common to many excuses.

DIRTEing is rather obvious in the excuse strategies that are aimed at the apparent-responsibility link. In the spectrum of blaming tactics, the central goal is to deny personal responsibility by pinning it on someone or something.

DIRTEing also occurs in excuses that seek to reframe the bad performance. Derogation of evaluative instruments or people suggests that these external sources are really the ones responsible for the person's bad performance. Additionally, in many of the "See no evil, hear no evil" type of excuses, the person implicitly reasons that the victims were responsible and "deserved" what they got.

The third component of the excuse model, the lessening of the transformed responsibility, has several examples of DIRTEing excuses. By invoking task difficulty, the focus is placed squarely on the external situation. Likewise, by appealing to coercion, other people in the situation are given the responsibility. Finally, through projection-like excuses, the person suggests that the situation is driving the poor performances.

Although all excuses do not involve this DIRTEing process, it is likely that most people have these strategies in their excuse armamentarium. Further, the adroit excuse maker may be rather good at the DIRTEing process.

Boundaries: When Excuses Are Less Prevalent

Although excuse making is a common response to a "bad" performance, the reader may sense that there must be times when excuses are not as prevalent. Indeed, this is the case. In the present section, the situations that appear to dampen the excuse-making process will be explored, and then a discussion will be held regarding the type of people who are *not* as prone to excuse making.

Situations that Inhibit Excuse-Making ("When Modesty Is the Best Policy")

If a person's role expectations or the social norms suggest that it is appropriate to take responsibility for a failure, then excuse making should abate. Consider, for example, a teacher in a classroom situation. Here is an instance where a person (the teacher) is expected to take responsibility for failure (i.e., the student who is not doing well). In this vein, several studies do show that teachers appear to take responsibility for their students' failure. For example, Beckman (1973) found that teachers took increasingly more responsibility as their students' performed more poorly on a task; Ross, Bierbrauer, and Polly (1974) reported that teachers took responsibility for their students' failures on a spelling test; Ames (1975) suggested that teachers take responsibility even when they know that the student's probability of success in a task is going to be low. In regard to this seeming counterdefensive behavior of teachers, it has been argued that teachers intuitively know that an external audience will view them more favorably when they *accept* responsibility for failure (Weary & Arkin, 1981; Weary Bradley, 1978). Interestingly, Tetlock (1980) has found support for this proposition in that teachers who accept rather than externalize their students' failures are viewed more favorably.

Another situation where excuse making dissipates is one where the person knows that there is some source that may invalidate the excuse. A few examples may clarify this phenomenon. Arkin, Appelman, and Burger (1980, experiment 2) allowed people to make attributions following success and failures. The normal externalizing of failure occurred when people merely responded to a paper-and-pencil technique; however, when people were hooked up to a device that resembled a lie detector, the externalizing of failure was less pronounced. Presumably, the lie detector served to temper the excuse making. There are other "invalidation" sources in addition to a lie detector. For example, two studies show that the usual excuse-like attributional pattern is reduced when the person is under very intense scrutiny by an observer (Arkin, Gabrenya, Appelman, & Cochran, 1979; Wells, Petty, Harkins, Kagehiro, & Harvey, 1977).

The situations described in this section all suggest that it is sometimes more appropriate to preserve one's image by not making an excuse. Further, these studies emphasize the importance of a powerful and judging external audience. Thus, although the excuse model shown in this chapter stresses the interactive nature of internal and external audiences, this set of studies shows that there are occasions when concerns for the external audience may override concerns for the internal audience. While these studies certainly highlight the obvious point that certain situations may delimit excuse making, excuses are not necessarily eliminated. For example, the "invalidation" studies suggest that excuse making diminishes but does not disappear. Likewise, it has yet to be documented whether teachers privately engage in the usual excuse-making pattern after their students fail. Overall, there is a need to understand when and where excuses *won't* be made following failure. Key areas for future research will include the defensibility and perceived effectiveness of the excuse-making strategies (Schlenker, 1982; Schlenker & Leary, 1982; Snyder et al., 1983).

People Who Are Less Prone to Excuse Making Some people are not as prone to engage in excuse making after failure feedback. Who are these people? Because there are no individual-differences measures that directly measure excuse-making, the next best approach is to locate an individual-differences measure that taps the degree to which people take responsibility for their actions. (See Snyder et al., 1983, pp. 141–158 for a detailed discussion of individual differences in excuse making.) This is an easy task since one of the most popular individual-differences scales—*locus of control*—is based in the responsibility notion. That is, locus of control reflects the degree to which a person externalizes or internalizes responsibility for his or her actions. According to Rotter (1966; see also Lefcourt, 1981; Phares, 1976), some people report themselves as exerting control in their lives (internal locus of control), while others report outside forces as exerting the control in their lives (external locus of control). After the development of the Internal-External Locus of Control Scale (Rotter, 1966), there has been an enormous amount of research comparing the behaviors of internal to external locus of control persons (Phares, 1978). A very short summary of this research will follow.

People with an internal locus of control are less likely to engage in excuse-making behavior than those with an external locus of control. (See Snyder et al., 1983; Zuckerman, 1979, for reviews.) After failure on a test of "intellectual ability," for example, people with internal as compared to external locus of control were less likely to blame outside factors such as "The instructions weren't clear," "The test wasn't any good," "I was distracted" (Phares, Wilson, & Klyver, 1971). A second set of research findings indicates that internals prefer skill-determined tasks, whereas externals prefer chance-determined tasks with the implicit excuse of "I was unlucky" (Julian & Katz, 1968; Schneider, 1968). Relatedly, internals are less likely to select tasks with built-in rationalizations for failures (Phares & Lamiell, 1974). In another area of research on a phenomenon known as the "sour grapes" effect, internals were less likely than externals to devalue a test after failure feedback (Phares, 1971). Finally, research reveals that internals do not lower their reported effort expenditure to the degree that externals do in anticipation of a difficult task (the "I didn't try" excuse) (Ducette & Wolk, 1972).

In the aforementional studies it is important to emphasize that following failure, *both* external and internal locus of control people often made excuse-like responses, but the internals did so in a less marked fashion. Thus, although internal locus of control people are not as extreme in their propensity to make excuse-like responses, they (like the rest of us) do call upon excuses in a jam.

AN AMAZING GRACE?

Are Excuses Amazing?

Excuses are amazing for at least two reasons. First, their prevalence is almost astounding. Second, their subtlety is often rather surprising. The prevalence and subtlety of excuses are addressed next.

They Are Almost Everywhere As one leafs through the preceding pages and even includes the previous section on "Boundaries: When Excuses Are Less Prevalent," the overall conclusion is that excuse-making behaviors occur in a variety of situations. Likewise, the forms that the excuse making may take are extensive. Although many types of excuses have been presented in this chapter, it should be emphasized that there are two major bodies of excuse literature that have not been described because of space constraints. For example, in addition to the verbal or avowed excuses that have been presented in this chapter, it should be emphasized that physical deeds also can serve as excuses. As a brief taste of this point, imagine the inherent excuse power in injuries and other observable physical handicaps; moreover, imagine the drunk's behavioral repertoire of excuses. The list of physically apparent excuses goes on and on.

Yet another body of excuses not described in the present chapter is those that occur before, rather than after, failure situations. Although one typically thinks of excuses as retrospective strategies aimed at nullifying past bad performances, it is also the case that they occur in an anticipatory sense. For example, we may lessen the apparent responsibility by avoiding the bad performance arena (the "injured" athlete who will not run in a race that she may lose); we may reframe the upcoming bad performance by manipulating the standards or derogating the evaluative sources (the student who, prior to an exam, asserts that the teacher's questions are always tricky); or, we may lessen the anticipated transformed responsibility by suggesting in a consensus-raising fashion that anyone will do poorly on the upcoming task (the tennis player who asserts that his opponent is so good that anyone would lose to him). Although after-the-fact or retrospective excuses have received more attention, recent theoretical and empirical work has increasingly focused on before-the-fact or anticipatory excuses. (See Snyder & Smith, 1982; Snyder et al., 1983, for reviews.)

They Can Be Subtle We laugh at Steve Martin's "Excuuuuuuuuuuuuuuuse me" because it is outlandishly obvious. In the development of the present model of excuse making, however, it became increasingly apparent that many excuses are far from obvious. Further, because of the nature of the present model, it became necessary to envision many new and rather complex excuses. From this writer's perspective, therefore, the attempt to understand excuses has resulted in an increased belief in their subtlety.

The subtlety issue also emerges at the level of the excuse maker, who sometimes is and *sometimes is not* aware of his or her excuse making. Certainly, strategically employed excuses are at times within the awareness of the excuse maker. However, consider a self-image threat that occurs repeatedly in a person's life. In such instances, the excuse-making behavior may become rather automatic in nature. This process may be similar to the manner in which we learn many behaviors; initially we are very aware of the process (recall learning to ride a bike or drive a stick shift car), but over time the action may be performed out of habit. Like habits, therefore, over time excuses may fade from awareness.

In the previous discussion of excuses as habits, the person's lack of awareness is not a motivated process, i.e., as habits are formed they just naturally go out of awareness. Another view, however, is that excuse making and its attendant lack of awareness may be a purposefully motivated process. In this latter vein, excuse making may be similar to self-deception, which is the motivated lying to oneself. Both philosophers (e.g., Fingarette, 1969) and psychologists (e.g., Gur & Sackeim, 1979) have argued for the viability of the self-deception process. In terms of excuses, the motivated self-deception may occur because it is more psychologically satisfying to believe that one has not made an excuse than to believe that one has. Based on the author's informal interviewing of people regarding their responses when they have made a mistake, gotten themselves in a jam, or performed poorly, it is interesting to note that people say they have *reasons* for their "screwups." When they are asked to describe the responses of other people, however, the common answer is that others give *excuses* for their bad performances.

Before leaving this section on the subtlety of excuses, it is important to highlight the fact that the definition of excuses does not necessarily imply that they are always false. In many situations, for example, there is no objective yardstick for determining the "truthfulness" of one explanation over another. This is especially the case when the alternative explanations fit the facts equally well. As shown in the present chapter, people will prefer one explanation over another for purposes of their self-image. Therefore, although these excuse-based preferences are subjectively biased interpretations of events, they are not invariably errors. (For related discussions see Schlenker, in this volume; and Schlenker, Hallam, & McGown, 1983.)

Do Excuses Provide Grace?

The Merciless Excuse As excuses become more extreme and encompass most activities in a person's life, then they may become self-defeating. Although there are no readily available means of identifying the normal, adaptive excuse making from the more pathological forms, it is likely that there are some interrelated guideposts. First, there are undoubtedly situations where an external audience will expect the person *not* to engage in any excuse making. Recall, for example, the previous discussion of teachers and how they are expected to take responsibility for their students' failures. Thus, the person who makes an excuse in a situation where one is not supposed to may receive negative feedback from other people. Second, *extreme* excuse making may backfire socially. The person who constantly invokes excuses loses credibility as his or her strategies become more and more obvious. The subtlety is gone, and so too is the effectiveness. Third, as excuses become extreme or are given in clearcut situations where one is expected not to engage in excuse making, they may become very salient and as such may generate more personal distress than they preserve. In fact, a person who is highly aware of excuse making may experience a decrease in esteem. (See Mehlman & Snyder, 1984.) Fourth, excuse making may serve to limit the person's range of responses to the inevitable stressful events of life. In this sense, excuses may prohibit the person from psychological growth because they merely feed on themselves.

The Merciful Excuse While it is tempting to adopt the stereotypical view of excuse making as representing a sign of weakness, a more balanced view is probably justified. For most people, for example, excuses do not reach the extreme level described in the previous section. Likewise, there may be relatively few situations where it is expected that a person will not make an excuse after a bad performance. In the normal range, excuses may well be adaptive. Their sheer prevalence suggests that they must work. Further, the research that addresses the self-image or stress-reduction role of excuses indicates that they do "work." In the turmoil of our daily lives, therefore, excuses may serve *us* well. In the previous sentence, notice that the word *us* is emphasized. The point here is that it is likely that the reader has effectively used some of the excuses described in the previous pages. Thus, the fact that excuses are not just something that we observe in others may tend to reduce one's prejudicial attitudes about excuses as totally reflecting "weaknesses."

Upon careful analyses, it should come as no surprise that excuses are widely used and that they work. We teach our children to make excuses (see Schadler & Ayers-Nachamkin, 1983), and the use of excuses is part of the socialization process in general and school in particular. Parents, teachers, and "authorities" constantly demand explanations from children. And we also provide children with the clues as to what excuses will work. Mom is heard to say "I know you didn't mean to, but . . .", and the child is given a lesson in employing lack of intentionality. Or, Dad says, "You didn't do this, but tell me who did," and the child has a hint about blaming.

As children grow up, they find that they live in a society whose legal system also employs excuses. Laws represent the agreed-upon framework by which people live together in a society. Interestingly, embedded within the laws are excuse-like principles that determine the degree to which a person is held responsible for his or her actions. Given the integral role that excuses play in our everyday existence, it logically follows that excuses also should play a major role in the formal rules (i.e., laws) by which we live together.

Excuses are for ourself *and* other people. As such, they not only help to maintain the person's self-image, but also enable the person to continue interactions with other people. Excuses thus serve as a social lubricant. This point is revealed in a psychotherapy case of the present author. In this case, the client reported that he was very shy and uncomfortable at parties and had therefore stopped going to them. He also was becoming more uncomfortable interacting with people in a variety of other situations at college. As part of the treatment, the author asked him to go to a party and tell any new person that he met that he was rather shy and uncomfortable at parties. He agreed, and found this to be an excellent (and honest) ice-breaking way of initiating a conversation. He also reported that many people shared his feelings, and he felt better about himself. This is an instance where an excuse (shyness) served to facilitate personal and social gains.

Since we know that we can call on excuses in many of those inevitable moments when we will face psychological predicaments, excuses serve to provide some solace. The world of absolute responsibility for our bad actions is a terrifying possibility. Fortunately, we probably grant other people's excuses in many situations, and, of course, we grant our own excuses (which we probably call reasons) in an even greater number of situations. When you think about it, this is an amazing grace.

REFERENCES

Ames, R. (1975). Teacher's attributions of responsibility: Some unexpected counterdefensive effects. *Journal of Educational Psychology, 67,* 668–676.

Anikeef, A. M. (1953). Factors affecting student evaluation of college faculty members. *Journal of Applied Psychology, 37,* 458–460.

Arkin, R. M., Appelman, A. J., & Burger, J. M. (1980). Social anxiety, self-presentation, and the self-serving bias in causal attribution. *Journal of Personality and Social Psychology, 38,* 23–35.

Arkin, R. M., Gabrenya, W. K., Jr., Appelman, A. S., & Cochran, S. T. (1979). Self-presentation, self-monitoring, and self-serving bias in causal attribution. *Personality and Social Psychology Bulletin, 5,* 73–76.

Austin, W., Walster, E., & Utne, M. K. (1976). Equity and the law: The effect of a harmdoer's "suffering in the act" on liking and assigned punishment. In L. Berkowitz & E. Walster (Eds.), *Advances in experimental social psychology* (Vol. 9). New York: Academic Press.

Bandura, A. (1977). *Social learning theory.* Englewood Cliffs, NJ: Prentice-Hall.

Baumeister, R. F., & Jones, E. E. (1978). When self-presentation is constrained by the target's knowledge: Consistency and compensation. *Journal of Personality and Social Psychology, 36,* 608–618.

Beckman, L. (1973). Teachers' and observers' perceptions of causality for a child's performance. *Journal of Educational Psychology, 65,* 198–204.

Bennett, D. H., & Holmes, D. S. (1975). Influence of denial (situation redefinition) and projection on anxiety associated with a threat to self-esteem. *Journal of Personality and Social Psychology, 32,* 915–921.

Berglas, S., & Jones, E. E. (1978). Drug choice as a self-handicapping strategy in response to noncontingent success. *Journal of Personality and Social Psychology, 36,* 405–417.

Brock, T. C., & Buss, A. H. (1962). Dissonance, aggression and evaluation of pain. *Journal of Abnormal and Social Psychology, 65,* 197–202.

Brock, T. C., & Buss, A. H. (1964). Effects of justification for aggression and communication with the victim on postaggression dissonance. *Journal of Abnormal and Social Psychology, 68,* 404–412.

Burish, T. G., & Houston, B. K. (1979). Causal projection, similarity projection, and coping with threat to self-esteem. *Journal of Personality, 47,* 57–70.

Cialdini, R. B., Borden, R. J., Thorne, A., Walker, M. R., Freeman, S., & Sloan, L. R. (1976). Basking in reflected glory: Three (football) field studies. *Journal of Personality and Social Psychology, 34,* 366–375.

Cialdini, R. B., Kenrick, D. T., & Hoerig, J. H. (1976). Victim derogation in the Lerner paradigm: Just world or just justification? *Journal of Personality and Social Psychology, 33,* 719–724.

Clair, M. S., & Snyder, C. R. (1979). Effects of instructor-delivered sequential evaluative feedback upon students' subsequent classroom-related performance and instructor ratings. *Journal of Educational Psychology, 71,* 50–57.

Cooley, C. H. (1922). *Human nature and the social order* (rev. ed.). New York: Charles Scribner's Sons. (Original work published in 1902.)

Darby, B. W., & Schlenker, B. R. (1982). Children's reactions to apologies. *Journal of Personality and Social Psychology, 43,* 742–753.

Darley, J. M., & Zanna, M. P. (1982). Making moral judgments. *American Scientist, 70,* 515–521.

D'Arcy, E. (1963). *Human acts.* New York: Oxford University Press.
Davis, K. E., & Jones, E. E. (1960). Changes in interpersonal perception as a means of reducing cognitive dissonance. *Journal of Abnormal and Social Psychology, 61,* 402–410.
Degree, C. E., & Snyder, C. R. (in press). Adler's psychology (of use) today: Personal history of traumatic life events as a self-handicapping strategy. *Journal of Personality and Social Psychology.*
Ducette, J., & Wolk, S. (1972). Locus of control and extreme behavior. *Journal of Consulting and Clinical Psychology, 39,* 253–258.
Fincham, F. D., & Jaspars, J. M. (1980). Attribution of responsibility: From man the scientist to man as lawyer. In L. Berkowitz (Ed.), *Advances in experimental social psychology* (Vol. 13). New York: Academic Press.
Fingarette, H. (1969). *Self-deception.* London: Routlege & Kegan Paul.
Freud, S. (1927). *The ego and the id.* London: Hogarth.
Goffman, E. (1971). *Relations in public.* New York: Basic Books.
Greenwald, A. G. (1982). Ego task analysis: An integration of research on ego-involvement and self-awareness. In A. H. Hastorf & A. M. Isen (Ed.), *Cognitive social psychology.* New York: Elsevier North Holland.
Greenwald, A. G., & Ronis, D. L. (1978). Twenty years of cognitive dissonance: Case study of the evolution of a theory. *Psychological Review, 85,* 53–57.
Gur, R. C., & Sackeim, H. A. (1979). Self-deception: A concept in search of a phenomenon. *Journal of Personality and Social Psychology, 37,* 147–169.
Halperin, K., Snyder, C. R., Shenkel, R. J., & Houston, B. K. (1976). Effects of source status and message favorability on acceptance of personality feedback. *Journal of Applied Psychology, 61,* 85–88.
Hamilton, V. L. (1980). Intuitive psychologist or intuitive lawyer? Alternative models of the attribution process. *Journal of Personality and Social Psychology, 39,* 769–772.
Hammond, V. C. (Fall 1972). *The Saturday Evening Post, 244,* 89.
Hart, H. L. A. (1968). *Punishment and responsibility: Essays on the philosophy of law.* New York: Oxford University Press.
Harvey, J. H., Harris, B., & Barnes, R. D. (1975). Actor-observer differences in the perceptions of responsibility and freedom. *Journal of Personality and Social Psychology, 32,* 22–28.
Harvey, J. H., & Smith, W. P. (1977). *Social psychology: An attributional approach.* St. Louis: C. V. Mosby Company.
Higgins, R. L., & Harris, R. N. (1983). Strategic alcohol consumption: Drinking to maintain a positive image. Unpublished manuscript, University of Kansas.
Hogan, R. (1982). A socioanalytic theory of personality. In M. Page & R. Dienstbier (Eds.), *Nebraska Symposium on Motivation.* Lincoln, Neb.: University of Nebraska Press.
Hollander, E. P. (1958). Conformity, status, and idiosyncracy credit. *Psychological Review, 65,* 117–127.
Hollander, E. P. (1976). *Principles and methods of social psychology.* New York: Oxford University Press.
Holmes, D. S. (1978). Projection as a defense mechanism. *Psychological Bulletin, 85,* 677–688.
Holmes, D. S., & Houston, B. K. (1971). The defensive function of projection. *Journal of Personality and Social Psychology, 20,* 208–213.
James, W. (1890). *The principles of psychology* (Vols. 1 & 2). New York: Holt & Company.

Jamous, H., & Lemaine, G. (1962). Compétition entre group d'inéglae resources: Experience dans un cadre naturel. *French Psychologie, 7,* 216–222.
Jellison, J. M. (1977). *I'm sorry I didn't mean to and other lies we love to tell.* New York: Chatham Square Press.
Jones, E. E., & Berglas, S. (1978). Control of attributions about the self through self-handicapping strategies: The appeal of alcohol and the role of underachievement. *Personality and Social Psychology Bulletin, 4,* 200–206.
Jones, S. C. (1973). Self and interpersonal evaluations: Esteem theories versus consistency theories. *Psychological Bulletin, 79,* 185–199.
Julian, J. W., & Katz, S. B. (1968). Internal versus external control and value of reinforcement. *Journal of Personality and Social Psychology, 8,* 89–94.
Kansas City Star, August 3, 1975, p. 4B.
Kelley, H. H. (1967). Attribution theory in social psychology. In D. Levine (Ed.), *Nebraska Symposium on Motivation* (Vol. 15). Lincoln, Neb.: University of Nebraska Press.
Kelley, H. H. (1971). *Attribution in social interaction.* New York: General Learning Press.
Kelley, H. H. (1973). The process of causal attribution. *American Psychologist, 28,* 107–128.
Kohlberg, L. (1963). Moral development and identification. In H. Stevenson (Ed.), *Child psychology* (62nd. yearbook of the National Society for the Study of Education). Chicago: University of Chicago Press.
Kulik, J. A., & Taylor, S. E. (1980). Premature consensus on consensus? Effects of sample-based versus self-based consensus information. *Journal of Personality and Social Psychology, 38,* 871–878.
Latané, B., & Darley, J. M. (1970). *The unresponsive bystander: Why doesn't he help?* New York: Appleton-Century-Crofts.
Latané, B., & Rodin, J. (1969). A lady in distress: Inhibiting effects of friends and strangers on bystander intervention. *Journal of Experimental Social Psychology, 5,* 189–202.
Lefcourt, H. M. (1980). *Research with the locus of control construct* (Vol. 1) (Assessment Methods). New York: Academic Press.
Lemaine, G. (1966). Inégalité, comparaison et incomparabilité: Esquise d'une théorie de l'originalité sociale. *Bulletin Psychologie, 20,* 24–32.
Major, B. (1980). Information acquisition and attribution processes. *Journal of Personality and Social Psychology, 39,* 1010–1023.
Markus, H. (1977). Self-schemata and processing information about the self. *Journal of Personality and Social Psychology, 35,* 63–78.
McArthur, L. A. (1972). The how and what of why: Some determinants of consequences of causal attributions. *Journal of Personality and Social Psychology, 22,* 171–193.
Mead, G. H. (1934). *Mind, self, and society.* Chicago: University of Chicago Press.
Mehlman, R. C., & Snyder, C. R. (1984). Excuse theory: A test of the self-protective role of attribution. Unpublished manuscript, The University of Kansas.
Mettee, D. R., & Aronson, E. (1974). Affective reactions to appraisal from others. In T. L. Huston (Ed.), *Foundations of interpersonal attractions.* New York: Academic Press.
Milgram, S. (1974). *Obedience to authority.* New York: Harper & Row.
Miller, D. T. (1976). Ego involvement and attributions for success and failure. *Journal of Personality and Social Psychology, 34,* 901–906.
Neisser, U. (1967). *Cognitive psychology.* New York: Appleton-Century-Crofts.

Newton, J. (1779). Grace of Faith's Review and Expectation. In *Olney hymns*. London: Printed and sold by W. Oliver, #12 Bartholomew Close, Hymn #41, Book i.

Orvis, B. R., Cunningham, J. D., & Kelley, H. H. (1975). A closer examination of causal inference: The role of consensus, distinctiveness, and consistency information. *Journal of Personality and Social Psychology, 32,* 604–616.

Orwell, G. (1946). *Animal farm*. New York: Harcourt Brace Jovanovich.

Phares, E. J. (1971). Internal-external control and the reduction of reinforcement value after failure. *Journal of Consulting and Clinical Psychology, 37,* 386–390.

Phares, E. J. (1976). *Locus of control in personality*. Morristown, NJ: General Learning Press.

Phares, E. J. (1978). Locus of control. In H. London & J. Exner, Jr. (Eds.), *Dimensions of personality*. New York: John Wiley and Sons.

Phares, E. J., & Lamiell, J. T. (1975). Relationship of internal-external control to defensive preferences. *Journal of Consulting and Clinical Psychology, 42,* 872–878.

Phares, E. J., Wilson, K. G., & Klyver, N. W. (1971). Internal-external control and the attribution of blame under neutral and distractive conditions. *Journal of Personality and Social Psychology, 18,* 285–288.

Piaget, J. (1926). *The language and thought of the child*. New York: Harcourt-Brace.

Riess, M., & Schlenker, B. R. (1977). Attitude change and responsibility avoidance as modes of dilemma resolution in forced-compliance situations. *Journal of Personality and Social Psychology, 35,* 21–30.

Rosenthal, A. M. (1964). *Thirty-eight witnesses*. New York: McGraw-Hill.

Ross, L., Bierbrauer, G., & Polly, S. (1974). Attribution of educational outcomes by professional and non-professional instructors. *Journal of Personality and Social Psychology, 29,* 609–618.

Rotenberg, K. (1980). Children's use of intentionality in judgments of character and disposition. *Child Development, 51,* 282–284.

Rotter, J. B. (1966). Generalized expectancies for internal versus external control of reinforcement. *Psychological Monographs, 80,* (Whole No. 609).

Ruble, D. N., & Feldman, N. S. (1976). Order of consensus, distinctiveness, and consistency of information and causal attributions. *Journal of Personality and Social Psychology, 34,* 930–937.

Ryan, W. (1972). *Blaming the victim*. New York: Vintage Books.

Schadler, M., & Ayers-Nachamkin, B. (1983). The development of excuse-making. In C. R. Snyder, R. L. Higgins, & R. J. Stucky, *Excuses: Masquerades in search of grace*. New York: Wiley-Interscience.

Schlenker, B. R. (1980). *Impression management: The self-concept, social identity, and interpersonal relations*. Monterey, CA: Brooks/Cole.

Schlenker, B. R. (1982). Translating actions into attitudes. An identity-analytic approach to the explanation of social conduct. In L. Berkowitz (Ed.), *Advances in experimental social psychology* (Vol. 15). New York: Academic Press.

Schlenker, B. R. (1984). Identities, identifications, and relationships. In V. Derlega (Ed.), *Communication, intimacy and close relationships*. New York: Academic Press.

Schlenker, B. R., & Darby, B. W. (1981). The use of apologies in social predicaments. *Social Psychology Quarterly, 44,* 271–278.

Schlenker, B. R., Hallam, J. R., & McCown, N. E. (1983). Motives and social evaluation: Actor-observer differences in the delineation of motives for a beneficial act. *Journal of Experimental Social Psychology, 19,* 254–278.

Schlenker, B. R., & Leary, M. R. (1982). Social anxiety and self-presentation. A conceptualization and model. *Psychological Bulletin, 92,* 641–669.

Schlenker, B. R., & Miller, R. S. (1977). Egocentrism in groups: Self-serving biases or logical information processing. *Journal of Personality and Social Psychology, 35,* 755–764.

Schneider, J. M. (1968). Skill versus chance activity preferences and locus of control. *Journal of Consulting and Clinical Psychology, 32,* 333–337.

Scott, M. B., & Lyman, S. M. (1968). Accounts. *American Sociological Review, 33,* 46–62.

Shaw, M. E. (1968). Attribution of responsibility by adolescents in two cultures. *Adolescence, 3,* 23–32.

Smith, T. W., Snyder, C. R., & Handelsman, M. M. (1982). On the self-serving function of an academic wooden leg: Test anxiety as a self-handicapping strategy. *Journal of Personality and Social Psychology, 42,* 314–321.

Smith, T. W., Snyder, C. R., & Perkins, S. (1983). The self-serving function of hypochondriacal complaints: Physical symptoms as self-handicapping strategies. *Journal of Personality and Social Psychology, 44,* 787–797.

Snyder, C. R., & Clair, M. (1976). Effects of expected and obtained grades on teacher evaluation and attribution of performance. *Journal of Educational Psychology, 68,* 75–82.

Snyder, C. R., & Clair, M. (1977). Does insecurity breed acceptance? Effects of trait and situational insecurity on acceptance of positive and negative feedback. *Journal of Consulting and Clinical Psychology, 45,* 843–850.

Snyder, C. R., Higgins, R. L., & Stucky, R. J. (1983). *Excuses: Masquerades in search of grace.* New York: Wiley-Interscience.

Snyder, C. R., & Newburg, C. L. (1981). The Barnum effect in groups. *Journal of Personality Assessment, 45,* 622–629.

Snyder, C. R., & Shenkel, R. J. (1976). Effects of "favorability," modality, and relevance upon acceptance of general personality feedback prior to and after receiving diagnostic feedback. *Journal of Consulting and Clinical Psychology, 44,* 34–41.

Snyder, C. R., Shenkel, R. J., & Lowery, C. R. (1977). Acceptance of personality interpretations: The "Barnum effect" and beyond. *Journal of Consulting and Clinical Psychology, 45,* 104–114.

Snyder, C. R., & Smith, T. W. (1982). Symptoms as self-handicapping strategies: The virtues of old wine in a new bottle. In G. Weary & H. L. Mirels (Eds.), *Integrations of clinical and social psychology.* New York: Oxford University Press.

Snyder, C. R., Smith, T. W., Augelli, R. W, & Ingram, R. E. (in press). On the self-serving function of social anxiety: Shyness as a self-handicapping strategy. *Journal of Personality and Social Psychology.*

Snyder, M. L., & Wicklund, R. A. (1981). Attribute ambiguity. In J. H. Harvey, W. Ickes, & R. R. Kidd (Eds.), *New directions in attribution research* (Vol. 3). Hillsdale, NJ: Lawrence Erlbaum Associates.

Stevens, L., & Jones, E. E. (1976). Defensive attribution and the Kelley cube. *Journal of Personality and Social Psychology, 34,* 809–820.

Sykes, G. M., & Matza, D. (1957). Techniques of neutralization: A theory of delinquency. *American Sociological Review, 22,* 664–670.

Tedeschi, J. T. (1981). *Impression management theory and social psychological research.* New York: Academic Press.

Tedeschi, J. T., & Riess, M. (1981). Predicaments and impression management. In C. Antaki (Ed.), *Ordinary explanations of social behavior.* London: Academic Press.

Tetlock, P. E. (1980). Explaining teacher explanations of pupil performance: A self-presentation interpretation. *Social Psychology Quarterly, 43,* 283–290.

Tucker, J. A., Vuchinich, R. E., & Sobell, M. B. (1981). Alcohol consumption as a self-handicapping strategy. *Journal of Abnormal Psychology, 90,* 220–230.

Weary Bradley, G. (1978). Self-serving bias in the attribution process: A reexamination of the fact or fiction question. *Journal of Personality and Social Psychology, 36,* 56–71.

Weary, G., & Arkin, R. M. (1981). Attributional self-presentation. In J. H. Harvey, W. C. Ickes, & R. F. Kidd (Eds.), *New directions in attribution research* (Vol. 3). Hillsdale, NJ: Lawrence Erlbaum Associates.

Wells, G. L., & Harvey, J. H. (1977). Do people use consensus information in making causal attributions? *Journal of Personality and Social Psychology, 35,* 279–293.

Wells, G. L., Petty, R. E., Harkins, S. G., Kagehiro, D., & Harvey, J. H. (1977). Anticipated discussion of interpretation eliminates actor-observer differences in the attribution of causality. *Sociometry, 40,* 247–253.

Wells, L. E., & Marwell, G. (1976). *Self-esteem: Its conceptualization and measurement.* Beverly Hills, CA: Sage Publications.

Wills, T. A. (1981). Downward social comparison principles in social psychology. *Psychological Bulletin, 90,* 245–271.

Zemore, R., & Greenough, T. (1973). Reduction of ego threat following attributive projection. *Proceedings of the 81st Annual Convention of the American Psychological Association, 8,* 343–344.

Zuckerman, M. (1979). Attribution of success and failure revisited, or: The motivational bias is alive and well in attribution theory. *Journal of Personality, 47,* 245–287.

CHAPTER 10

IDENTITY, SELF PRESENTATION, AND THE RESOLUTION OF MORAL DILEMMAS: TOWARDS A SOCIAL PSYCHOLOGICAL THEORY OF MORAL BEHAVIOR*

Carl W. Backman
University of Nevada Reno

INTRODUCTION

Those who specialize in the sociology of knowledge might interpret the increasing preoccupation of psychologists with the process and effects of self-presentation as being a manifestation of certain dominant social trends. However, the focus on self-presentation can be considered one of a number of developments that reflect the emergence of a new paradigm in social psychology. Elsewhere (1979), I have suggested that the elements in this new paradigm include a view of man as an active agent, an emphasis on the meaning of events and settings, and a concept of science in which the goal of social psychology is to generate and verify models of the structure of interaction. As Ginsburg (1979) described, people are now seen as "active agents, capable of making plans, of acting as well as reacting, of doing things for reasons as well as having been forced to do them by causes" (p. 2). This conception can easily lead to an appreciation of a facet of human motivation such as self-enhancement, which in particular has become a part of a social-psychological explanation of a wide variety of research findings (Hales, 1981). Similarly, this new emphasis on the meaning of behavior in the context of particular events and settings has led to increased awareness of how important these situationally derived meanings are in the social construction of definitions of self. Finally, the renewed interest in social interaction, and particularly in its underlying normative structure, has led to a new appreciation of the importance of the normative background—the

---
*A portion of this manuscript was completed while the writer was a visiting professor of social psychology at Catholic University, Nijmegen, The Netherlands. Part of the theory presented here was developed with the support of Grant GS 39750 from the National Science Foundation and a special research fellowship from the National Institute of Mental Health. This support from these sources is gratefully acknowledged.

shared rules, beliefs, and meanings which influence the construction, maintenance, or change in people's self-concepts. Much of this chapter reflects the influence of this paradigmatic shift.

These developments have resulted in a growing convergence between the psychological and sociological traditions in social psychology, primarily in the direction of sociology, where such paradigmatic elements have long been rooted (Backman, 1980). Not only has this convergence been reflected in an outpouring of articles concerned with the relationship between the two social psychologies (Backman, 1980, 1983; Blank, 1978; Quinn, Robinson & Balkwell, 1980; Stryker, 1977; Stryker & Gottlieb, 1981; Wilson & Shafer, 1978) but discussion of this and related issues became a series feature in the *Society for the Advancement of Social Psychology Newsletter*. In this chapter, I would like to push the treatment of self-presentation further in a sociological direction by discussing self-presentation and related processes in the context of moral judgment and behavior.

MORAL DILEMMAS

The focus of this approach is on how persons resolve moral dilemmas. The term *moral dilemmas* is used to emphasize that the concern here is on the mindful, and in varying degrees, painful resolution of a conflict between alternative responses in a manner which minimizes adverse consequences.

Moral dilemmas fall into the class of social dilemmas, with the distinguishing feature that one of the possible consequences of the manner in which they are resolved is to alter self-evaluation. They differ from others in this class in that the way in which a moral dilemma is resolved, whether persons conform to a moral rule or not, is believed to have important consequences for others. This difference parallels the classic distinction made by the early American sociologist Sumner (1907) between folkways—customs and social conventions whose violation brings mild rebuke—and mores—moral rules whose violation prompts more severe sanctions because such rules are believed to promote the welfare of others. While resolutions of moral dilemmas often become scripted or routinized in time (Abelson, 1976, 1981), and relatively mindless (Langer, 1978), they do so because of understandings within a particular cultural group that can be used in the initial social construction of these scripted solutions. Such shared understandings include, among other cultural elements, norms, rules for their application, and accounts.

NORMS, ACCOUNTS, AND DEFINITIONS OF THE SITUATION

Accounts are explanations of behavior—commonly referred to as excuses, justifications, or rationalizations—that relate situated identities and the anticipated evaluative reactions of self and others to the way a moral dilemma is resolved. The term *identity* refers to the dispositional imputations or character traits that others are likely to attribute to an actor on the basis of his or her actions in a particular social context (Alexander & Knight, 1971). Accounts, as a part of people's definitions of situations, have very much become a focus in the self-presentation literature in psychology, in connection with the way they minimize self-disenhancement or, as in the case of acclaiming tactics (Schlenker, 1980), contribute to self-enhancement. When the concept of accounts has been employed in this manner, the emphasis has been on how persons, after the fact, explain their behavior to themselves and, where the behavior is public, to others as well. While sociologists have recognized this function of accounts, they have also viewed accounts as part of people's definitions of situations that influence the development of a line of conduct, particularly in response to situations involving a moral dilemma.

W. I. Thomas (1928), an early figure in what later became labeled the symbolic-interactionist tradition in sociology, is generally credited with giving prominence to the idea that people's definitions of situations influence their behavior. He suggested that preliminary to any self-determined act of behavior, there was always a stage of examination or deliberations which he termed *the definition of the situation*. He conceived of such definitions in essentially the same fashion as current cognitive theorists in psychology employ the notion of plans and schemas. Thomas (1966) argued that because individuals do not find current situations exactly like past situations, they must consciously define every situation as being similar to past situations; that in order to control reality for their purposes they must develop not a series of uniform reactions, but general schemes of situations that they can use as guides for behaving. This view is not only consistent with symbolic interactionism and those theories of deviance that emphasize the influence of people's definitions of situations, but, as I will document later, is also consistent with both social-learning explanations of norm violations and similar explanations offered by some contemporary cognitive theorists.

Tactics of self-presentation, particularly the invoking of accounts, are invariably involved in the generation of solutions to dilemmas because of the very nature of a moral dilemma. As previously noted, all moral dilemmas involve behavior relative to important norms and values, which in varying degrees are shared and internalized by members of a group.[1] Moral norms or rules of conduct prescribe or proscribe behaviors thought to be related to the welfare of

---

[1] In research on moral judgment and behavior, two types of dilemmas are employed. The simpler one involves a choice between conforming to or violating a norm which either requires costly behaviors or the renunciation of rewards intrinsically or extrinsically related to relevant behaviors proscribed by a norm. When this is part of an experimental manipulation, the participants are expected to make the choice. When the choice is embedded in a vignette and presented in a testing or questionnaire format, participants may either be asked to indicate a hypothetical choice, or, as in the methodology employed by Kohlberg (1969), to simply reason about the situation. The second, more complex, type of dilemma presents the participants with a choice between responding to conflicting norms; conforming to the norms governing the role of good subject versus conforming to a norm that requires aiding another in distress, as in the case of some studies of bystander intervention, or norms that proscribe harming another as was the case for the Milgram (1963) paradigm. Since elements of both these types may be combined, and since one way in which the more simple dilemma may be solved is by transforming it into a dilemma of the second type by redefining the situation so that the behavior of the participants may be perceived as conforming to some more important norm, we will structure the discussion in terms of the first type. It should be emphasized that choice in either case involves identity implications that may force a change in self-evaluation.

others. Since such rules are thought to be related to important outcomes by group members, their violation, and the consequent reduction in the value of outcomes that others experience, leads those members to make internal or dispositional attributions (Braiker & Kelley, 1979), i.e., they view the behavior as indicating what kind of person the offender is. The threat of attribution of negatively valued identity characteristics is one horn of a moral dilemma. The other horn arises from the fact that, typically, those same behaviors required or prohibited by norms are intrinsically or extrinsically related to other important outcomes. The problem the actor faces is to construct a definition of the situation that facilitates the achievement of desirable outcomes or the avoidance of undesirable ones, and at the same time allows for the maintenance of a favorable situated identity; in sum, to have his cake and eat it too.

To illustrate, the person tempted by the opportunity to shoplift faces such a dilemma. On the one hand, such behavior contravenes the norm that forbids theft. The consideration of violating this norm leads to the anticipation of guilt and of the possibility of shame should such violation become public. On the other hand, the financial advantage of not paying for the stolen item may be compelling. One possible solution is to define the situation so that the potential thief can be viewed by himself or herself, and possibly others, in the most favorable light possible, through construction of an account as a part of the decision process leading to the theft. Thus the person may justify the behavior by including in his view the idea that any loss will be covered by the store's insurance, or depending on the situation, invoke some other type of account.

At this point, it is important to make explicit a number of assumptions widely accepted in sociology and increasingly accepted in psychology. First, that definitions of situations precede and influence, through persons' anticipations of the consequences of their acts, their behavior (Mills, 1940). Second, in accordance with symbolic-interactionist theory, it is assumed that definitions of situations are powerfully influenced by the goals of the actors. Further, consistent with exchange theory, the assumption is that persons faced with conflicting purposes or goals will attempt to maximize their outcomes. While the outcomes associated with a maximally favorable identity are powerful inducements, it is recognized that these may be outweighed at times by other inducements and lead to definitions and resultant behavioral choices that favor purposes and goals other than that of self-enhancement. Finally, it is assumed that situational definitions are usually jointly constructed by participants in interaction; that they reflect, depending on the outcome of social influence processes, all participants' goals and identity claims. Even when definitions are constructed privately (either in the imaginary rehearsal of an episode prior to its public enactment, or where the enactment occurs under conditions of anonymity), the imagined reactions of internalized audiences as well as one's own imagined reaction become a part of a process of internal negotiation. This, while differing in some respects, is similar to the interpersonal process of negotiation, as will be noted in some detail later.

In attempting to construct and negotiate a definition of a situation that facilitates the resolution of a moral dilemma, actors are faced with a variety of opportunities and constraints. These are related to characteristics, both personal and social, of the persons in the situation (including those of the actors), the target of their acts, and in many instances, third parties who have a stake in the emerging definitions. These opportunities and constraints are also related to the characteristics of possible acts in the situation, as well as characteristics of the setting such as its ambiguity or its public or private character.

These characteristics of persons, acts, and situations enter into the joint construction or negotiation of definitions of situations in two ways. First, they directly influence the strength of moral rules that are applied by external and internal audiences to actors' behaviors. This is reflected in the severity of sanctions applied to, or the degree of moral culpability attributed to, actors. Thus physical abuse of a child, by virtue of the characteristic of age, is regarded as a more serious breach of morality than similar abuse directed toward an adult. Second, these characteristics indirectly enter in as they affect the creation and acceptance of accounts. Accounts, as a part of the emerging definition of the situation, modify the strength of moral rules and the degree of culpability resulting from norm violation. Again using age as an example, a child may be excused on the grounds of not knowing any better for a norm infraction that would be sanctioned if committed by an adult.

As previously noted, accounts are shared beliefs that relate behavior to moral norms and other social expectations in the construction of favorable situated identities. While a number of typologies of accounts (Schlenker, 1980; Schonback, 1980; Tedeschi & Riess, 1981) have been developed and elaborated on since Scott and Lyman (1968) introduced this concept into the sociological literature, a simple typology will be employed here, one which follows a typology that I presented in another essay (Backman, 1976). It includes three categories: excuses, justifications, and conventionalizations.

Excuses involve defining an actor's behavior in a manner that mitigates or eliminates his responsibility. They include definitions of the person's acts as having occurred as a result of chance, accident, or mistake, as well as accounts based on lack of opportunity, or lack of capacity, to behave otherwise (Glover, 1970). Excuses acknowledge the wrongness of the act, but mitigate the actor's responsibility. Justifications, while conceding the actor's responsibility, deny or mitigate the pejorative quality of the actor's actions under the circumstances. Situations may be defined so that the harm is viewed as nonexistent, trifling, or justified, given the character or behavior of the victim. An act of petty theft from a large corporation is defined as having little harmful impact, given the massive assets of the corporation, or is said to be an instance of just retaliation, given the corporation's pricing policies or its unfair employment practices. Other justifications include defining an action as in accord with some overriding higher principle (e.g., self-defense in the case of an assault) or as not wrong because others do the same or even more harmful acts.

Conventionalizations, while similar to justifications in that they both eliminate or reduce the pejorative character of an act, do not alter the perceived situational context, but transform the perception of the act itself. Conventionalizations (Lofland, 1969) redefine acts and transform them from what they appear to be to something else that is not so wrong. Frequently, this involves a rhetorical transformation of the act, a label that mitigates or removes its pejorative character. Thus, an act of embezzlement may be described as "temporary borrowing."

Elsewhere (Backman, 1976), I have suggested in greater detail the possible ways in which features of persons, acts, and situations affect the degree of moral censure applied to normative violations. This happens either as these features influence the strength of the normative expectations or the construction of accounts. Characteristics of persons making the judgment, such as their personal values, were seen to modify their judgments of the moral culpability of others, both in how seriously they took the offense as well as how valid they considered the possible extenuating circumstances. Thus, in a study of attitudes toward violence (Blumenthal et al., 1972), the findings were that persons with attitudes more favorable toward police were more accepting of their resort to violence. This study also found that persons favorably disposed toward the idea of retributive justice and the right of self-defense were less prone to condemn police violence, presumably because such values supported a justification of the acts of police.

Similarly, it was suggested that the characteristics of the actors being judged helped to determine their moral culpability. Those characteristics were seen to either alter the strength of the moral obligation to behave in a certain way or to provide a basis for accounts to reduce the obligation. Thus, persons with enhanced capabilities for helping others may be under greater moral pressure from both themselves and others to help, and those with reduced capabilities may encounter less pressure. To illustrate, a doctor or nurse is under greater obligation to aid an injured person than are others without such training. At the same time, the research on bystander intervention by Piliavin, Rodin, and Piliavin (1969) suggests that where intervention in an emergency may require some physical effort or danger, women appear to be less obligated to intervene. In similar fashion, characteristics of the victim were seen to affect the degree of moral censure engendered by someone's failure to help them or by an act of harm directed toward them. Thus, pertinent attributes of victims that are thought to make them especially resistant to or particularly susceptible to harmful consequences of an act may change the perceived moral culpability of the perpetrator. Thus mugging an elderly victim is regarded as more serious than mugging a young adult.

Characteristics of acts and situations are also related to the severity of condemnation of perpetrators, both in the application of moral rules and in the construction and negotiation of extenuating accounts. To illustrate the latter, an act whose distribution is unknown or perhaps assumed to be widespread, such as income tax evasion, is more easily defended in terms of the justification that almost everyone engages in such a practice.

The above example underscores a characteristic of situations that also is implicated in the emergence of justifying accounts, namely, ambiguity. If a situation requiring moral action is ambiguous, definitional leeway is provided and persons are more free to construct and negotiate situational definitions to their advantage. This was well illustrated in the surprisingly low rates of bystander intervention in the types of situations employed by Latané and Darley (1968) and Darley and Latané (1968), in their investigation of bystander intervention in emergency situations. With respect to one situation (Latané and Rodin, 1969) where subjects heard but did not observe what seemed to be the fall of a person in an adjoining room, Warner (1976) was able to demonstrate that through decreasing the ambiguity in this situation, bystander intervention could be dramatically increased.

The likelihood that a cost-reducing definition of a situation will be successfully negotiated by persons encountering a moral dilemma depends not only on the features of the objective situation such as characteristics of the persons, their acts, those of victims and the situation, but on other factors as well. These encompass a number of intra-individual variables such as individual differences based on prior learning of accounting schemas, and differences in the strength of the motive to avoid costly actions or forego rewarding ones by conforming to the moral dictates in the situation. Other intra-individual factors include the sensitivity of the person to cues in the situation that would challenge or support particular definitions, as well as the skill the person has in convincing others that the presented definition is veridical.

Interpersonal factors are also important, particularly as they affect the various processes of social influence that determine the outcome of negotiation. These factors include the variables that determine the outcome of the various processes of social influence that enter into the negotiations. The variables include the motives of other participants as they are influenced by the implications of various definitional elements for their outcomes, including their own identities, their repertoire of accounting schemas, their negotiating skills, and any special sensitivities to various elements in the situation. They also include factors influencing the relative power of those involved. Finally, the successful production of an advantageous definition depends on the availability of relevant cultural resources, shared beliefs, and understandings about reality that relate objective features of an episode to crucial elements in the subjective definition of the situation. To illustrate, in a society whose cultural beliefs provide little basis for explanations of human conduct in terms of the supernatural, accounts in these terms are not likely to emerge.

Essentially, the negotiations in an episode involving the resolution of a moral dilemma parallels that outlined in theories of role negotiation (Backman, 1983; McCall and Simmons, 1978; Secord and Backman, 1974). This should not be surprising in view of the fact that the negotiation in both instances involves a compromise between conflicting identity claims and other conflicting goals of the participants.

It should be emphasized that negotiation may occur in the public arena with others in the actual situation, and in the private arena or inner forum, with various internalized audiences including the self. The reactions of internalized audiences may include the imagined anticipated responses of those actually in the situation, which occur during rehearsals prior to action or during further negotiation in the public arena, or they may consist of the reactions of other groups or persons toward whom the actor refers his conduct, even though they are not situational participants. The various perspectives, including that of the self, that are brought to bear on the actor's anticipated and ongoing conduct, must all be considered in understanding the construction of accounts. And, as we note later, a consideration of differences in the conditions under which negotiations occur between the public and private arenas explains in part the widespread divergence between public and private morality. This issue, along with a number of others that theorists who are concerned with the determinants of moral behavior have had to grapple with, will be the focus of the remainder of this chapter.

But first it might be well to briefly summarize these ideas and to examine the way this approach differs from other approaches to moral judgment and behavior. It has been argued that a moral dilemma involves a conflict between two tendencies or motive states, one to achieve some goal that is blocked by moral considerations and the other to maintain a favorable view of self. In attempting to fashion an optimum solution, persons attempt to negotiate a definition of the situation that allows the achievement of both. Such definitions serve to blunt the effects of anticipated censure from self and others, either by reducing the strength of the rules operating in the situation or by providing a basis for accounts or explanations of the rule violation that excuse, justify, or disguise the nature of the act. In constructing and negotiating these definitions, persons are confronted with a variety of constraints and opportunities. These are related to a variety of personal, interpersonal, and cultural factors, as well as features of the objective situation that influence the likelihood that such definitions will be offered and accepted by the person and others.

The most significant manner in which the above approach differs from that proposed either by social psychologists studying altruism or prosocial behavior, or developmental psychologists studying moral judgment and conduct, is the emphasis on viewing moral conduct as a product of interaction and of the joint construction of subjective reality. Acts and their morality emerge out of interaction in which both processes of conflict and accommodation or cooperation are involved. It should be noted that various processes of accommodation are also frequently employed in the resolution of moral dilemmas. In general, particularly where their own outcomes are not jeopardized by doing so, others tend to honor the accounts offered by actors and support their definition of the situation (Goffman, 1959).

Yet, the importance given to the egocentric motivation of persons as agents highlights processes of interpersonal conflict, which tend to be ignored in other formulations. The idea of negotiation in the private as well as the public sector, and of the influence of multiple internalized perspectives, also highlights the role of processes of both conflict and accommodation within the individual. While such processes are probably universally operative in the construction of situational definitions involved in the resolution of moral dilemmas, the cultural resources that persons draw on in such a construction can be expected to vary depending on the particular historical-cultural context.

This last consideration, of course, places the kinds of limitations on theories of moral behavior of this genre that Gergen (1973) and Sampson (1981) have alluded to in their discussions concerning the limits of current social psychological knowledge.[2] Yet an understanding of these cultural resources is necessary if we are to be able to explain concrete instances of morally relevant behavior, since these are always imbedded in a particular historical and socio-cultural context. However, before discussing this topic, the causal role of situational definitions requires some further comment.

ON THE ROLE OF SITUATIONAL DEFINITIONS IN THE GENERATION OF CONDUCT

We noted at the beginning of this chapter that psychologists have tended to view accounts as devices that persons employ in a remedial fashion after they have behaved in an untoward manner. In contrast, the emphasis here has been on the role of accounts prior to action as they become crucial elements in situational definitions, permitting acts that might not have occurred in their absence. In the wake of the cognitive revolution in psychology, it hardly seems necessary to defend the proposition that such internal mental events influence behavior. Yet, this notion (when combined with the idea of human agency), while widely held in sociology, is still not entirely accepted in many quarters of psychology. Nevertheless, the theoretical and empirical convergence in support of this view within psychology is impressive.

An examination of some of the recent writing on the role of scripts in the decision-making process in general (Abelson, 1976, 1981), and more particularly in the context of deciding to engage in prosocial behavior (Langer & Abelson, 1972), provides a distinct parallel to Thomas's conception of definitions of situations that was previously discussed. While using different terminology, Abelson and others employing the concept of script are talking about essentially the same internal events. Scripts are learned definitions of situations. They are learned vignettes that guide the behavior of persons in episodes of interaction. Some are particularly important for the moral identities of actors because elements in the script relate situational features to accounts in a manner that affects the attribution of moral culpability. The role of these mental events in the generation of conduct is also acknowledged by Abelson when he suggests that cognitively mediated social behavior depends on the joint occurrence of two

---

[2]Both these theorists maintain that generalizations, or scientific laws in social psychology are greatly influenced by current sociohistorical conditions and cannot be expected to be valid in the face of social change. For example, Gergen suggests that cognitive dissonance theory depends on the contemporary cultural assumption that people cannot tolerate contradictory cognitions. This assumption, he would argue, is a learned disposition common to people of our time and place and is not something characteristic of the species; that is, not genetically given for the species.

events: the selection of a particular script to represent a given social situation, and the taking of a role within that script.

Bandura's (1978) recent extension of social-learning theory places him in the same camp. In language very much like that of symbolic interactionists, he suggests that because of the human ability to use symbols, persons can use foresight to plan courses of action, react to these courses in terms of cognitive inducements (that is, in terms of self imposed rewards and punishments), and thus modify their own behavior. In fact he notes, in connection with the person's capacity to react to anticipatory self-censure, that such anticipatory censure may be avoided by various disengagement practices, which essentially involve the invocation of the types of accounts that have been previously described. The linkage suggested here between norms, accounts, and identity also finds support in the work of Duval and Wicklund (1972), as well as that of others described in more detail later, who have demonstrated that persons are particularly apt to conform to moral norms when attention is directed to the self. This line of thinking is also consistent with the theory of altruism proposed by Schwartz (1977) that emphasizes the role of personal norms or self-expectations, as well as with interpersonal-congruency theory (Secord & Backman, 1974) that views conformity to norms in terms of the maintenance of the person's self-concept.

While the empirical support for the suggested role of such internal mental processes is at times not as clear as might be desired, there is a convergence of a number of lines of evidence. An early study, which traced the sequence of events leading to either conformity or deviance, supported the reasoning outlined here. Cressey (1953) found that in every instance of embezzlement, the development of rationalizations for the act occurred prior to its occurrence. While admittedly this finding was based on interviews with convicted embezzlers and thus was necessarily retrospective, it is consistent with the results of two experiments reported by Bandura, Underwood, and Fromson (1975). In those experiments where participants as supervisors had an opportunity to act punitively by administering varying levels of shock to workers for their poor performance, they tended to increase their aggression under conditions where responsibility was diffused and the recipients of the shock were dehumanized by being described in undesirable terms. In a post-experimental questionnaire, where those in the role of supervisor had an opportunity to rate their "supervisees' " responsiveness to their "disciplinary" measures and to give their reactions to their own behavior, those who behaved punitively by escalating the shock levels gave a variety of accounts, including among others, derogation of the supervisees, denial of responsibility, and the minimization of harm. While again this evidence is retrospective, the causal sequence suggested finds support in the work of still others. Schwartz (1973, 1977) has argued that a causal relation does exist between norms and behavior, from the fact that the positive correlation between personal norms and behavior found in his research holds only for those who see their behavior as having consequences for others and who accept responsibility for their acts. His work in developing scales to measure both of these tendencies parallels that of a number of sociologists (Ball, 1966; Ball &

Lilly, 1971; Verlarde, 1978) who have developed scales to measure differences between delinquents and nondelinquents in the tendency to employ accounts that justify delinquent conduct. As will be discussed later in the section of this chapter on individual differences, both Schwartz's scales and those employed in these studies of delinquents consist of items whose content reflects the substance of various accounts. Finally, if one views norms as essentially attitudes toward various behaviors, then the recent research (Bentler & Speckart, 1981) employing structural equation analysis, which concludes that attitudes do play a causal role, provides another line of support for the position taken here. In sum, while accounts undoubtedly are employed after the fact to justify norm violation, the evidence suggests that they also play a role prior to the act in facilitating such conduct. In fact, both Kelman (1973) and Bandura, Underwood, and Fromson (1975) have suggested that underlying the escalation of aggression may be a circular process, in which initial conditions favoring accounts facilitate aggression, and the aggression, in turn, encourages the further use of accounts which support a process of escalation.

CULTURAL RESOURCES AND THE NEGOTIATION OF DEFINITIONS OF SITUATIONS

In the learning of scripts, both Abelson and Bandura emphasize the role of intra-individual processes, such as categorization and abstracting from categories of episodes the norms and the rules governing their application. While these intra-individual processes are certainly involved in the learning of norms and the rules for their applications, the type of interpersonal processes that underlie negotiations which are emphasized here are clearly evident in the recent work by Much and Shweder (1978). These investigators have analyzed patterns of speech behavior in naturally occurring situations of accountability. These situations are behavioral episodes, which carry the potential that persons will be called to account because their behavior can be interpreted as a violation of social expectations. Such microscopic moments in everyday life, they argue, are the occasion where cultural rules are continually tested, clarified, and negotiated rather than learned in a rote fashion. Children, when called to account for untoward behaviors, learn not only the appropriate norms relevant to their acts, but in the process of successfully or unsuccessfully defending themselves, they learn the personal and situational elements that make a given rule applicable or inapplicable in the judgment of their conduct. In this process of active negotiation, children learn both the rules and related cultural resources that can be used throughout their lives as they negotiate definitions of situations that allow them to maintain or enhance their views of self, and at the same time, achieve other goals of importance to them.

Much has yet to be learned concerning the cultural resources that persons employ in the social construction of situational definitions relevant to moral conduct. These cultural resources consist of a body of shared understandings and related feelings of appropriateness that exist at various levels of conscious articulation. Analagous to the distinction in linguistics between surface and deep structure (Chomsky, 1965), one can distinguish those cultural elements, such as rules of conduct and conventional accounts of behavior that even small children are able to verbalize, from deeper shared understandings concerning linguistic forms, folk beliefs about the causes and nature of human behavior, rules of logic, etc., which constitute the deep structure underlying the consensus among persons from a given culture concerning the intelligility and warrantability (Harré, 1977) of behavior in a given situation.

The ethnomethodologists (Cicourel, 1972; Garfinkel, 1964) and the closely allied ethogenic movement (Harré, 1977; Harré & Secord, 1972) informed by the work of the sociologist Schutz (1964), and the linguist Chomsky (1965), have greatly modified and increased our understanding of the complexity of the normative character of social life.

Both of these schools of thought view as their primary task the discovery of the normative rules and shared understandings that persons employ in the construction of their everyday activities and in their judgments of such behaviors as meaningful and normatively appropriate. Both schools rely heavily on methods of linguistic analysis to uncover from the accounts or explanations that persons give of their activities, the cultural base underlying the structural forms that characterize various episodes of interaction. The ethnomethodologists Schegloff and Sacks (1973) have studied the structure of conversations focusing on, for example, the rules persons employ in bringing about the close of a conversation. Following in the ethogenic tradition, Marsh, Rosser, and Harré (1978) have uncovered the rules governing the seemingly violent and erratic encounters between members of rival soccer fan clubs.

The body of shared understandings and rules—which Garfinkel (1964) calls background expectancies or common understandings, Schutz (1964) refers to as a common scheme of reference, and Cicourel (1972), following the terminology of generative transformational grammar, calls basic rules—exist at their most primitive level as assumptions that make the joint construction of reality and action in concert possible. Thus, Schutz's (1964) rule concerning the reciprocity of perspectives is basic to social interaction, since according to this rule, persons routinely assume that their mutual experiences of the interaction scene would be the same even if they were to change places; that any personal differences in the assignment of meaning to everyday activities can be disregarded for the purpose at hand. This type of rule is undoubtedly universal and makes it possible for persons to proceed in the joint construction of social action.

As Cicourel (1972) has suggested, the complexity of the operation of such basic assumptions and the manner in which this parallels the distinction between deep and surface structure drawn in transformational grammar is illustrated in Schutz's discussion about the routine assumption persons make concerning the reciprocity of perspectives. In this example, Schutz argues that the question-answer sequencing requires a rule whereby a person's question provides a basis (reason) for another person's answer, while the possibility of a future answer from the latter provides a basis (reason) for the former's question. When a person asks a question, he or she has intentions (a deep structure) or a more elaborated version in mind than what he or she actually asks. The "pruned" or deleted surface question, therefore, presumes a more elaborated version which it is assumed the answerer will "fill in" despite receiving only the surface message. The answerer's reply, therefore, is based on both the elaborated and surface elements of the question, and the questioner, in turn, "fills in the answer" so as to construct the answerer's elaborated intentions. It follows then that both participants presume that each will generate recognizable and intelligent utterances as a necessary condition for the interaction to even occur, and each must reconstruct the other's intentions (the deep structure) if coordinated social interaction is to proceed.

To illustrate, the question and answer sequence "Why did you do that?" "Because it was only fair," while somewhat cryptic, is quite understandable to the questioner and the answerer. The answerer fills in the intent of the questioner; that is, a request for a moral justification was made. The questioner, in turn, fills in the meaning of "fairness" in that particular instance.

Garfinkel (1972) has devised a procedure to demonstrate this filling-in process. He asks respondents to report common conversations that they have had with another by writing on the left side of a sheet what the parties actually said in a series of successive interchanges, and on the right side what they and their partners understood they were talking about. An examination and comparison of both sides of the sheet reveals, among other things, that there were many matters that the partners understood they were talking about which were not actually mentioned. At the same time, many matters that the partner understood were understood on the basis not only of what was said, but also on what was left unspoken. Finally, that which actually was said, the utterances exchanged, served to document, or point to, or to stand instead of, the matters that each assumed they were talking about. Without this type of filling-in process, the actual exchange of utterances would not be understandable. To illustrate, Garfinkel reproduced such an exercise involving a conversation between a husband and wife. It began with the husband reporting that their child, Dana, managed to put money in a parking meter without being picked up. The remark was correctly interpreted by the wife as a comment concerning the rapid growth of their child. The comment also indicated to the wife that they stopped on the way home from the child's nursery school, which in turn led to a series of exchanges as to where and why this stopoff occurred.

This filling-in process is similarly recognized by contemporary cognitive-oriented psychologists as basic in the operation of schemas (Abelson, 1976, 1981) and plans (Miller, Galanter, & Pribram, 1960) as they influence the behavior of actors, by providing general structures for interaction within a particular episode. While the filling-in process can be assumed to be a universal phenomenon in human interaction, what is filled in will depend on the shared meanings available among members of a given cultural group. A portion of such elements, according to Schutz (1964) includes a stock of preconstituted knowledge such as a network of typifications or definitions of categories of individuals in general, of typical human motivation, goals, and action patterns. Also included is the knowledge of expressive and interpretive schemes of objective sign systems and, in particular, of the vernacular language.

Using an analogy to the idea of deep structure in a discussion of the construction of moral meanings of situations, Douglas (1970) referred to deep moral meanings that are not generally a part of the conscious thoughts of persons, but serve to form the frame that delimits much of the conscious thought in the purposeful construction of definitions of situations. In American society, he noted, these deep moral meanings include what is often referred to as a sense of fair play, a sense of decency, being for the underdog, or being a nice guy. He adds that most Americans would find it difficult to define such terms; yet they would be able to tell when they are relevant to a given situation, and thus recognize appropriate instances of them, and they would have a feeling that is related to them, that a concrete situation is right or wrong, just as a native speaker can sense that a grammatical construction is right or wrong.

While not necessarily informed about the above perspective, a number of investigators, principally psychologists, but sociologists as well, have been uncovering these elements of deep structure. This has been the case for studies of concepts of justice, particularly those related to rules of just or fair allocation of resources. Kayser and Schwinger (1982) have recently demonstrated that, consistent with the work of Mikula (1980), Leventhal (1976), Lerner (1977) and others, which of various allocation rules is considered fair depends on the perceived type of social relationship existing between the recipients of a good to be allocated. Underlying such judgments of fairness are configurations which are central parts of laypersons' theories on the functioning of groups.

Hamilton and Sanders (1981) have similarly demonstrated that the character of the role relationship between perpetrators of misdeeds and their victims influences the operation of rules governing the judgments of moral responsibility. Thus, when perpetrators are in a position of authority vis-à-vis their victims, as in the case of such role relations as parent and child, or supervisor and employee, lower levels of intent or foreseeability are required to judge the perpetrators as morally responsible for their acts. Presumably, this occurs because persons in authority are seen as having more diffuse and pervasive role obligations toward those in their charge than would be the case between persons of equal power and status. In a more recent study, Hamilton and Sanders (1983) were able to demonstrate the cultural character of such background understandings. They found that the judgment of Japanese subjects was more influenced by the type of relationship between perpetrator and victim than had been the case for the earlier sample of Americans.

That persons are apt to apply norms differently depending on a host of only dimly recognized assumptions is demonstrated in a study by Alves and Rossi (1981). They studied judgments concerning the fairness of earnings for both single persons and married couples in the labor force. Those to be judged were described in terms of a number of different characteristics indicative of relative merit (occupational and educational levels) and need (marital status and number of children). Their analyses of the normative structure of earning fairness revealed the operation of two conflicting norms, those of need and merit,[3] in determining such judgments of fairness. It also showed that the characteristics of the earner, as well as of those making the judgments, influenced the application of these two principles in concrete cases. Further, these characteristics were weighted differently depending on the case. Occupational attainments counted for more than educational achievement, and husbands' characteristics counted more than those of wives, in determining the fairness of a couple's earnings. Finally, the characteristics of those making the judgment modified these effects. In particular, there were small but statistically significant social class differences, with higher-status persons viewing as fair higher earnings for additional increments of education and occupational attainment, and lower status respondents allowing as fair considerably more earnings for each child in the family. It should be emphasized that those findings are not based on interview responses in which persons articulated the reasons for making their judgment, but on a regression of fairness ratings on characteristics of computer-constructed vignettes, in which earnings were randomly associated with various household characteristics. Undoubtedly, most respondents could have articulated the allocation rules such as those based on need and merit if asked. However, the manner in which these conflicting allocation rules were combined, and the weights assigned to the indicators of need and merit in arriving at a judgment of fairness, undoubtedly reflected a variety of considerations that were not readily articulated, but part of the background expectancies that constitute elements of deep structure. The findings concerning class differences are also instructive because they illustrate how persons' definitions reflect the all-too-human tendency to construct definitions to one's own advantage. To the degree that such indicators of need as number of children are recognized as important in the determination of the fairness of earnings, lower-status respondents benefit; similarly, to the degree that such indicators of merit as educational or occupational achievements are recognized as important, upper-status respondents benefit.

Social-class differences in the judgments of the fairness of criminal penalties have also been reported by Hamilton and Rytina (1980). These investigators reported considerable overall agreement among respondents, both as to the relative seriousness of various crimes and the relative severity of various punishments. In addition, when subjects were asked to assign punishments to crimes, such assignments reflected considerable consensus on the norm of just deserts: the idea that the punishment should fit the crime, and that the more serious the offense the more severe the penalty. An analysis of the sources of lack of consensus in the overall sample revealed, however, that low-income and black respondents were less likely than others in the sample to consistently relate a crime's seriousness to severity of punishment. Further, these subgroups

---

[3]In accordance with Bouldings' (1962) analysis, the conflict of these two principles results in the development of a cultural concept of a social minimum, a level of resources below which no unit such as a household should fall, and shared considerations of deservingness based on ideas of merit which provide a justification for the allocation of shares to units that are above that minimum.

differed to a greater degree from the average than others in their assessment of a crime's seriousness, and punishment severity. One other finding of subcultural differences in the evaluation of the fairness of criminal sanctions deserves mention before an explanation is suggested for these differences within the theoretical approach to moral behavior and judgment advocated here. Shortly after the conviction of Lt. Calley for his participation in the My Lai massacre, Kelman and Lawrence (1972) were able to field a national survey of attitudes toward various issues surrounding this event. The most striking attitudinal difference between those who approved of the trial of Lt. Calley and those who disapproved was that the disapproving groups felt it unfair to place soldiers on trial for doing their duty, whereas the approving groups believed that the killing of defenseless civilians could not be justified. Underlying this difference were a number of demographic differences, the most important being socio-economic status and education. Those of lower socio-economic status and those reporting less education were more apt to accept the justification involving a denial of responsibility on the grounds of adherence to what they regarded as the higher principle of duty. Those of higher status and education were less apt to accept the justification.

As Hamilton (1978) as well as those authors suggested, the willingness of persons in subordinate statuses to accept such a justification may rest on an implicit contract between those in hierarchic relations, with subordinates agreeing to the obligations of their subordinate status in exchange for a lower-level of responsibility than that demanded of those in authority. Underlying this, of course, is the ethic of equity that pervades the deep structure of understandings and assumptions that persons draw upon, in our culture, at least, in making judgments concerning the morality of the conduct of others and in the construction of the morality of their own conduct.

Not only are comparative ratios of rights and obligations apparently subject to judgments in terms of equity, which in turn influence the use and acceptability of accounts such as those involving a denial of responsibility on the grounds of duty to authority, but also the validity of another frequently employed account rests ultimately on equity considerations. On the surface, at least, it might appear difficult to understand why the account that others commit the same or even worse offenses would justify a misdeed. Yet, if an additional element and an implicit conclusion are added to this defense of culpability, both of which are implied by the speaker, and implicitly understood or filled in by the listener, this defense is seen as a justifiable one. That is, both add that since these widely committed offenses escape sanctions, it is only equitable that the speakers' own misdeeds should receive equally generous treatment.

This admittedly sketchy review of some relevant empirical findings concerning moral judgment illustrates the complexity of the cultural base with which persons construct definitions of situations that are understood and accepted by themselves and others. Many of these shared, and in varying degrees articulated, understandings are not distributed evenly throughout the population, but, as the previously reported class differences suggest, are the product of the structurally imposed shared experiences of subgroups in a given society. Such shared experiences enter into the development of such elements of situational definitions as accounts and other relevant beliefs in two interrelated ways. First, socially structured experiences influence the acceptability of accounts. As the findings of Kelman and Lawrence (1972) suggest, those whose life experience has been largely one of following orders may find an account in terms of the requirements of duty acceptable in mitigating moral culpability. Second, the effects of the social structure on the experience of those in various subgroups in a population may influence motivational bases for the development of accounts and other elements of belief that enter into the negotiation of definitions of situations and related judgments. Thus, the emphasis that higher-status respondents place on criteria of merit in judging the fairness of earnings is matched by a similar self-serving emphasis on criteria of need by those of lower status.

MORAL JUDGMENT AND MORAL BEHAVIOR

From the pioneering work of Hartshorne and May (1928) until the present (Blasi, 1980), a persistent problem has been the rather slight and inconsistent relationship between measures of various elements of moral cognition and moral behavior. While no attempt will be made to settle this thorny issue, the approach to moral judgment and behavior advocated here provides a basis for exploring the reasons for such weak and inconsistent results. If the characteristics of the social situations that elicit samples of moral reasoning are different from those operating in situations when the morality of behavior is being assessed, these findings would be expected. Our approach would suggest a number of crucial ways in which these situations might differ. If, for instance, the situations employed differed in a manner that affected the strength and salience of the competing motives of self-enhancement and the achievement of the ill-gotten gains of norm violation, a discrepancy between moral reasoning and behavior would be expected.

Damon's (1977) work with children is instructive on this point. Not only did he find a much stronger tendency for children to unfairly reward themselves in an experimental condition in which they were allocating real candy bars compared to a control condition with only cardboard replicas, but they appeared to adjust their level of moral reasoning to their behavior. In the situation where their moral behavior was being assessed, and in which they unfairly rewarded themselves, they verbalized at a lower level than they had previously displayed in an interview designed as a test of their level of moral reasoning. As the work on social desirability over the years has demonstrated, the behavior of persons in testing situations is particularly influenced by the goal of self-enhancement.

The emphasis that has been placed here on the role of accounts in reducing the moral obligation to engage in costly conforming behavior would suggest a second way in which situational characteristics may help explain varying degrees of concordance between moral reasoning and moral behavior. Features of the situation that is employed to measure moral reasoning, including those built into the testing materials themselves, may encourage the use of certain accounts which may or may not be elicited by features of the situation employed to measure moral behavior. A study by Krebs and Rosenwald (1977) provides an illustration of this point. They found a significant positive relationship between level of moral reasoning measured by a short form of Kohlberg's test of moral development (Kohlberg, 1969) and moral behavior as indicated by the mailing back on time of a completed questionnaire for which the subjects had already been paid. In an attempt to further specify the relation between the moral reasoning displayed on the Kohlberg test and the carrying out of a moral obligation to return the questionnaire, they compared the reasoning displayed by those at various stages of moral development distinguished by Kohlberg. Only a small minority of those subjects scored at levels other than levels three and four in Kohlberg's six-level classification system. According to Kohlberg's theory, the reasoning of subjects at levels three and four reflects concern for the good opinion of others, with those subjects at level three more sensitive to censure from particular others, and those at level four more influenced by censure from an impersonal legitimate authority. The comparison between those at stage three, six out of fifteen of whom returned the questionnaire on time, with those at stage four, ten out of eleven of whom did so, is particularly revealing. When reasoning about the morality of the behavior of those in the Kohlberg vignette where a husband steals a drug to save the life of his wife, those at stage three were particularly more prone than those at stage four to invoke an account which justified a husband's obligation to his wife, and to similarly justify the failure of a friend to report on the husband's whereabouts when he escaped from jail on the grounds of what they regarded as the higher principle of conformity to the obligations of friendship.

To the degree that responses to these features of this particular vignette reflected individual differences in the tendency to invoke accounts of this sort, the difference in behavior of those scored at stage three and four is perhaps understandable. The ten out of eleven at stage four who conformed to the norm requiring that persons return a questionnaire having already been paid to do so may have been less willing to compromise such a principle by invoking some other consideration. Those at stage three, who tended to qualify general moral principles in terms of particular relationships with others, may have felt little obligation to conform to their contractual obligations in the relatively impersonal relationship with an experimenter. To summarize, the positive correlation between moral behavior and level of moral reasoning found in this study could be explained by the suggestion that in this instance the testing materials that measured differences in levels of moral reasoning also measured individual differences in accounting behavior, which in turn influenced the behavioral choices on the criterion employed as a measure of moral behavior.

A third way in which situations where moral reasoning is typically measured differ from situations where the morality of persons' behaviors are assessed is that in the former, persons are essentially in the role of observers reasoning about the behavior of hypothetical others, and in the latter, they are the actors.

A recent analysis by Watson (1982) suggests that actor-observer or self-other differences in causal attribution are largely accounted for by the tendency for persons, when rating the causes of their own behavior, to give greater weight to situational determinants than they give when they rate the determinants of the behavior of others. One explanation of this tendency, as Watson suggests, is that by viewing their own behavior in this fashion, actors can avoid a feeling of responsibility, a tactic underlying the type of account we have called excuses. This tendency could be expected to result in a greater use of accounts and result in a higher rate of norm violation in the situation where the morality of the participants' behavior is being measured than would be reflected in the moral reasoning they display in the typical testing situation, where they are asked to reason about or make predictions about the behavior of hypothetical others in story scenarios.

PUBLIC AND PRIVATE MORALITY

One pervasive feature of situations likely to influence the degree to which persons conform to moral rules is their public or private character. The literature on conformity consistently shows that compared to situations of anonymity, greater conformity occurs either where the behavior in question is immediately open to the surveillance of others or where it will eventually be known to others, particularly others with whom the person expects to interact at some time in the future. Just as the typical testing situation for assessing moral reasoning is apt to differ from the situation where moral conduct is being assessed in the relative salience of self-presentational concerns compared with self-serving motives, the same can be expected of public compared to private conditions of conformity. In particular, self-presentational concerns can be expected to be more salient in the public condition.

Schwartz and Gottlieb's (1980) work on bystander intervention in emergencies can be interpreted in these terms. When participants were in a condition where they thought that another bystander would not know whether they came to the aid of a victim, they were less apt to intervene than in a condition where the other bystander was aware of their behavior and where the situation was so structured as to lead them to believe that the other bystander believed that intervention was called for. In the public condition of their experiment, the concern for self-presentation or, as Schwartz and Gottlieb label it, evaluation apprehension, was sufficient to nullify other motives such as those related to the avoidance of possible harm to the self stemming from intervention.

Yet, in this study as well as in other studies of conformity to moral norms, persons conform, although often to a lesser degree, when their conformity is known only to themselves. This is consistent with the approach to moral behavior outlined here. Persons respond not only to external audiences, but to internal ones as well, and their behavior is likely to reflect the effects of both. Whether these effects of various perspectives are additive or to some degree cancel each other will depend on whether similar expectations are held by various audiences, and whether the reactions of these external and internal audiences become salient (Buss, 1980). The earlier work of Duval and Wicklund (1972) and Fenigstein, Scheier, and Buss (1975), and the later work of Reis and Burns (1982), Scheier and Carver (1981), and Greenberg (1983) provides considerable empirical support for this supposition, initially emphasized by Mead (1934) and later by others in the symbolic interactionist tradition.

The reader can refer to the chapter by Carver and Scheier in this volume for some supporting experimental evidence. Two experiments reported there are particularly relevant. These include the one by Froming and Walker. In that study, subjects who believed that punishment is an ineffective and inappropriate way to produce learning, but who also believed that most people held the opposite opinion, were induced to deliver electric shocks to an ostensible other subject as punishment for incorrect responses in a supposed learning experiment. They did so, either under the conditions designed to make salient their private views of themselves, private self-consciousness, or in a condition designed to increase their awareness of how they were viewed by an external audience, public self-consciousness. They found, as predicted, that the former condition reduced the tendency to shock the learner, in accordance with their privately held standards, while the latter condition increased this tendency, in accordance with the standards they attributed to others in general.

The second study (Scheier, Carver, & Gibbons, 1981) is also consistent with the position taken here, particularly as it demonstrates that at times motives other than the need to view oneself favorably may prevail. In that experiment, persons who were either high or low on the tendency to refer their conduct to themselves for judgment (high or low private self-consciousness) were led to believe that they would be receiving high or low levels of electric shock as participants in an experiment that would produce valuable medical knowledge. Those in the low fear condition, anticipating a gentle shock, who were characterized by a chronic level of high private self-consciousness compared to those whose habitual levels were low, more often chose to continue the experiment in conformity to internalized norms favoring participation in a study designed to advance medical knowledge. However, they were less apt to continue under the high-fear condition. The implication of these findings, the authors conclude, is to suggest that while private self-focused attention may increase the effect of behavioral standards on conduct, it may also increase the tendency for a person's standards to be overcome by a hedonistic orientation, because such self-focus increases the intensity of the experience of positive or negative emotion.

We have emphasized throughout this chapter that the resolution of a moral dilemma is typically a result of negotiation. While negotiation often occurs in public as in situations of accountability described by Much and Shweder (1972), more often it goes on in the private forum of the imagination. At times, the negotiation in the private or inner forum is in anticipation of later public negotiation, if the person expects that a particular resolution of a moral dilemma is apt to be challenged when embodied in overt public behavior. If persons do not anticipate challenge, as in the cases where their behavior is not subject to the scrutiny of others, the resolution may be accomplished in the inner forum. In the latter case, the results of the negotiation may well be different, since negotiation in the inner forum is apt to differ under these circumstances in a number of ways.

Mead (1934) suggested over half a century ago that when persons talk to themselves or carry on an internal conversation, they supply both sides of the conversation. This allows them to determine who will be the other party or parties in the conversation as well as the imagined audience before which the conversation takes place, and more important, what each says. With such freedom in the inner forum, unconstrained by any anticipated challenge, it is not surprising that persons can much more readily fashion a situational definition, including appropriate accounts, that allows for a resolution of a moral dilemma in a manner that maximizes their outcomes. Undoubtedly this kind of definitional leeway accounts for some of the differences between private and public morality. How much, we would suggest, will depend on a number of individual differences that this approach to moral behavior underscores. These differences, along with others, are the focus of the next section of this chapter.

PERSONALITY CORRELATES OF MORAL BEHAVIOR

The approach to moral judgment and behavior outlined here suggests that attention should be paid to a number of individual differences, which for the most part have received insufficient attention in studies of moral judgment and behavior. Our comments concerning negotiation in the inner forum suggest that differences between persons in conforming to moral rules are in part the result of differences in the perceived standards held by significant others and reference groups to whom different persons refer their behavior during internal conversations. Also, these differences in conformity may reflect the degree of freedom different persons have in selecting and interpreting the imagined responses of these audiences. The amount of leeway in these respects may be constrained by a number of factors whose operations are likely to be influenced by situational and personal characteristics. The possibility that the resolution of a moral dilemma in the inner forum may be challenged in the public one is one such situational limit. Affective ties that the individual has with others may make it difficult to select some audiences and ignore others, and the awareness of how other audiences will be likely to react may limit the ability of persons to create, in their imaginations, audience responses that support their preferred definitions. One group of individual differences that has received considerable attention in studies of harmdoing and altruism, and other behaviors relevant to moral rules, is the various forms of empathy and role or perspective taking. A review by Underwood and Moore (1982) of studies concerned with the relation between various types of perspective taking and altruism reports often weak and inconsistent results. However, the somewhat more consistent results for one type of perspective taking, social perspective taking (involving the ability to understand or predict other persons' thoughts and actions and to communicate with others in a nonegocentric manner) seem consistent with the line of argument pursued here. The findings that persons high on this ability conform more to norms prescribing altruistic behavior would be as expected if it were assumed that such persons would be less prone to distort the imagined reaction of others.

The work on individual differences in private and public self-consciousness touched on in the previous section and elsewhere in this volume suggests the importance of these personality traits for the understanding of moral behavior. At the same time, the theory proposed here would add that the implication of persons' normative behavior for their self-evaluation is mediated by accounts and other cultural understandings that relate characteristics of actors, their acts, those of the target of their acts, and the situation to experienced degrees of moral culpability. This suggests that individual differences in the learned tendency to invoke various accounts also should be regarded as an important dispositional variable in understanding conformity to norms. Sullivan (1953) recognized this several decades ago. The work of Redl and Wineman (1951), and Sykes and Matza (1957), on disturbed and delinquent children, suggests the importance of accounts in the generation of norm violations. In fact, the work of Sykes and Matza has led to a number of studies that have attempted to relate patterns of accounting to delinquency.

Sykes and Matza, consistent with the position taken here, argued that delinquents neutralize the effects of norms through their acceptance of a number of kinds of excuses and justifications, termed techniques of neutralization, that serve to counter the anticipation of guilt prior to norm violations. These techniques of neutralization include denial of responsibility, "I didn't mean it"; denial of injury, "I didn't really hurt anybody"; denial of the victim, "They had it coming"; condemnation of the condemners, "Others do worse things"; and appeal to higher loyalties, "I did it for a friend."

While the evidence is not entirely consistent (Minor, 1980), a number of investigators (Ball, 1966; Ball & Lilly, 1971; Verlarde, 1978) have found delinquents more accepting than nondelinquents of such accounts and even more prone to attribute such acceptance to their peers. While these studies are correlational in nature—hence it is impossible to know whether this acceptance of accounts preceeded or followed delinquency—our earlier discussion of the evidence for the influence of accounts on behavior provides some support for the arguments of these investigators and arguments of our own concerning the role of accounts. These investigations, concerned with techniques of neutralization, typically involved developing scales to measure individual differences in the acceptance of accounts. The early work of Schwartz (1969) on the determinants of altruism, while seemingly unrelated, involved essentially the same approach. He constructed measures of individual differences in the tendency for persons to be aware of the consequences of their behavior for others and in the tendency to accept or deny responsibility for their acts. Scores on both of these measures were related to altruistic behaviors, in both correlational studies and studies where the experimental design supported a causal interpretation of the role of norms and accounts. It is interesting to note in this context that the items in the scale that were developed to measure the tendency to accept or deny responsibility included not only those that are typically associated with the concept of responsibility such as intention or capability, but also those items that reflected the content of other accounts not related to this notion but included in the typology of accounts described earlier. For instance, one item justified a lack of consideration for the welfare of another person on the grounds that the person had behaved nastily, a justification in terms of just deserts. This research and the theory of altruism proposed by Schwartz (1977) is similar in a number of respects to the approach advocated here, and it suggests an additional difference that should influence moral behavior, namely, the organization of norms and values within each person's belief system (Bem, 1970). Following Rokeach (1973), Schwartz suggests that values are arranged in a hierarchy of importance to the self. As a result, persons differ in the degree to which an act relevant to a particular value and related norms will be experienced as self-enhancing or self-damaging.

Elsewhere (1976), I have argued that individual differences in values also affect the acceptability of accounts. As noted earlier, a study (Blumenthal et al., 1972) of the attitudes of American men toward violence found that those who were favorably disposed to the idea of retributive justice (an eye for an eye and a tooth for a tooth) and who gave high priority to the right of self-defense were more accepting of the resort to violence by police. Presumably they would be more willing to invoke an account in these terms to excuse their own violent behavior. I have also suggested in this connection that a more lenient moral stance might be taken by those who tend to attribute the causes of events externally to luck or fate than internally to effort and skills. While this supposition was based on research (Phares & Wilson, 1972) where persons judged the behavior of others, there is evidence (Phares, Wilson & Klyver, 1971) to suggest that this applies to persons' judgments of their own behavior as well.

Certainly the tendency for persons to attribute the causes of their behavior to external forces would support the invocation of accounts of the excuse variety. Considerable research effort in social psychology has been expended in attempts to understand individual differences in this respect. Also, a considerable amount of work has been expended by developmental psychologists on childrens' concepts of the role of intent in judging conduct, another individual difference bearing on the use of excuses. Much more needs to be done concerning the psychological, social, and cultural bases affecting the use of other types of accounts, including various types of justifications, and the accounting technique, conventionalization. Our own unpublished research, along with such studies as that of Much and Sweder (1978) previously described, suggests that children learn the basis for the use of such accounting at quite early ages, generally prior to their school years.

CONCLUSION

In this chapter we have presented an approach to moral behavior based on some theoretical notions drawn largely from the sociological tradition in social psychology that is quite similar to the research and theory of recent interest in a number of areas of psychology. This approach explains conformity to or deviation from moral norms in terms of personal, situational, and cultural factors that influence attempts by persons to construct definitions of situations requiring moral conduct. These definitions are designed by persons to maximize their outcomes in terms of maintaining a favorable view of themselves in their own eyes as well in the eyes of others, while at the same time to avoid the costs that conformity to moral rules often entails. Crucial to such definitions are accounts and underlying cultural beliefs that persons employ in the construction and negotiation of definitions, both in the inner forum and before external audiences.

While some progress has been made toward an understanding of the cultural resources that persons draw on in negotiating definitions of situations and the social structural determinants of the content and distribution of those resources, it has often been done without the benefit of a guiding, overarching theory that emphasizes these cultural and social structural influences. It is hoped that the ideas presented here will provide a basis for such a theory.

This way of viewing moral judgment and behavior shows some promise of providing fresh insights into a number of issues that have been of concern to researchers in this area of study. With respect to the first issue, the relation between moral behavior and measures of moral knowledge and judgment, and a second issue, the relation between public and private morality, it was suggested that situational differences, as they affect the relative importance of self-presentational concerns compared to other motives, and the salience and content of the anticipated responses of various audiences may explain instances where moral judgment and behavior are disparate, as well as the ubiquitous differences between public and private morality. With respect to a third issue, the relationship of individual differences to moral conduct, this approach suggests the importance of variables that affect the linkage between the self and conduct in general, and in particular, individual differences in the tendency to employ various accounts. While our review of the literature concerning this topic indicates that a start has been made in this direction, much has yet to be done.

REFERENCES

Abelson, R. P. (1976). Script processing in attitude formation and decision making. In J. S. Carrol & J. W. Payne (Eds.), *Cognition and social behavior*. Hillsdale, NJ: Erlbaum, 33–45.

Abelson, R. P. (1981). Psychological status of the script concept. *American Psychologist, 36,* 715–729.

Alexander, C. N., & Knight, G. (1971). Situated identities and social psychological experimentation. *Sociometry, 34,* 65–82.

Alves, W. M., & Rossi, P. H. (1978). Who should get what? Fairness judgments of the distribution of earnings. *American Journal of Sociology, 34,* 541–564.

Backman, C. W. (1976). Explorations in psycho-ethics: The warranting of judgments. In R. Harré (Ed.), *Life sentences: Aspects of the social role of language.* London: Wiley, 98–108.

Backman, C. W. (1979). Epilogue: A new paradigm. In G. P. Ginsburg (Ed.), *Emerging strategies in social psychological research.* London: Wiley, 289–303.

Backman, C. W. (1980). The premature abandonment of promising research. In R. Gilmore & S. Duck (Eds.), *The development of social psychology.* London: Academic Press, 163–179.

Backman, C. W. (1983). Toward an interdisciplinary social psychology. In L. Berkowitz (Ed.), *Advances in experimental social psychology* (Vol. 16). New York: Academic Press.

Ball, R. A. (1966). An empirical exploration of neutralization theory. *Criminologica,* 22–32.

Ball, R. A., & Lilly, J. R. (1971). Juvenile delinquency in an urban county. *Criminology, 9,* 69–85.

Bandura, A. (1977). *Social learning theory.* Englewood Cliffs, NJ: Prentice-Hall.

Bandura, A. (1978). The self system in reciprocal determinism. *American Psychologist, 33,* 334–358.

Bandura, A., Underwood, B., & Fromson, M. E. (1975). Disinhibition of aggression through diffusion of responsibility and dehumanization of victims. *Journal of Research in Personality, 9,* 253–269.

Bem, D. (1970). *Beliefs, attitudes and human affairs.* Belmont, CA: Brooks/Cole.

Bentler, P. M., & Speckart, G. (1981). Attitudes "cause" behaviors: A structural equation analysis. *Journal of Personality and Social Psychology, 40,* 226–238.

Blank, T. O. (1978). Two social psychologies: Is segregation inevitable or acceptable? *Personality and Social Psychology Bulletin, 4,* 553–556.

Blasi, A. (1980). Bridging moral cognition and moral action: A critical review of the literature. *Psychological Bulletin, 88,* 1–45.

Blumenthal, M. D., Kahn, R. L., Andrews, F. M., & Head, K. B. (1972). *Justifying violence: The attitudes of American men.* Ann Arbor, MI: Institute for Social Research.

Boulding, K. E. (1962). Social justice in social dynamics. In R. B. Brandt (Ed.), *Social justice.* Englewood Cliffs, NJ: Prentice-Hall, 73–92.

Braiker, H. B., & Kelley, H. H. (1979). Conflict in the development of close relationships. In R. L. Burgess & T. L. Huston (Eds.), *Social exchange in developing relationships.* New York: Academic Press, 135–168.

Buss, A. H. (1980). *Self-consciousness and social anxiety.* San Francisco: Freeman.

Chomsky, N. (1965). *Aspects of a theory of syntax.* Cambridge, MA: MIT Press.

Cicourel, A. V. (1972). Basic and normative rules in the negotiation of status and role. In D. Sudnow (Ed.), *Studies in social interaction.* New York: Free Press, 229–258.

Cressey, D. R. (1953). *Other people's money.* Glencoe, Ill.: Free Press.

Damon, W. (1977). *The social world of the child.* San Francisco: Jossey-Bass.

Darley, J. M., & Latané, B. (1968). Bystander intervention in emergencies: Diffusion of responsibility. *Journal of Personality and Social Psychology, 8,* 377–383.

Douglas, J. D. (1970). Deviance and respectability: The social construction of moral meanings. In J. D. Douglas (Ed.), *Deviance and respectability.* New York: Basic Books, 3–30.

Duval, S., & Wicklund, R. A. (1972). *A theory of objective self awareness*. New York: Academic Press.

Fenigstein, A., Scheier, M. F., & Buss, A. H. (1975). Public and private self-consciousness: Assessment and theory. *Journal of Consulting and Clinical Psychology, 43*, 522–527.

Garfinkel, J. (1964). Studies of the routine grounds of everyday activities. *Social Problems, 11*, 225–250.

Gergen, K. (1973). Social psychology as history. *Journal of Personality and Social Psychology, 26*, 309–320.

Ginsburg, G. P. (Ed.), (1979). *Emerging strategies in social psychological research*. London: Wiley.

Glover, J. (1970). *Responsibility*. London: Routledge and Kegan Paul.

Goffman, E. (1959). *The presentation of self in everyday life*. Garden City, NY: Doubleday and Company, Inc.

Greenberg, J. (1983). Self-image versus impression management in adherence to distributive justice standards. The influence of self-awareness and self-consciousness. *Journal of Personality and Social Psychology, 44*, 5–19.

Hales, S. (1981). The inadvertent rediscovery of "self" in social psychology. Paper presented at the American Psychological Association Meetings, Los Angeles.

Hamilton, V. L. (1978). Who is responsible? Toward a social psychology of responsibility attribution. *Social Psychology, 41*, 316–328.

Hamilton, V. L., & Rytina, S. (1980). Social consensus in norms of justice: Should the punishment fit the crime? *American Journal of Sociology, 85*, 1117–1144.

Hamilton, V. L., & Sanders, J. (1981). The effect of roles and deeds on responsibility judgments: The normative structure of wrongdoing. *Social Psychology Quarterly, 44*, 237–254.

Hamilton, V. L., & Sanders, J. (1983). Universals in judging wrongdoings: Japanese and Americans compared. *American Sociological Review, 48*, 199–211.

Harré, R. (1977). The ethogenic approach: Theory and practice. In L. Berkowitz (Ed.), *Advances in experimental social psychology*. (Vol. 10). New York: Academic Press, 284–314.

Harré, R., & Secord, P. F. (1972). *The explanation of social behavior*. Oxford: Blackwell.

Hartshorne, H., & May, N. A. (1928). *Studies in the nature of character, Volume I: Studies in deceit*. New York: Macmillian.

Kayser, E., & Schwinger, T. (1981). A theoretical analysis of the relationship among individual justice concepts. Layman's psychology and distribution decisions. *Journal for the Theory of Social Behavior, 12*, 47–51.

Kelman, H. C. (1975). Violence without moral restraint: Reflections on the dehumanization of victims and victimizer. *Journal of Social Issues, 29*, 25–61.

Kelman, H. C., & Lawrence, L. H. (1972). Assignment of responsibility in the case of Lt. Calley: Preliminary report on a national survey. *Journal of Social Issues, 28*(1), 177–212.

Kohlberg, L. (1969). Stage and sequence: The cognitive-developmental approach to socialization. In D. Goslin (Ed.), *Handbook of socialization theory and research*. Chicago: Rand McNally, 347–480.

Krebs, D., & Rosenwald, A. (1977). Moral reasoning and moral behavior in conventional adults. *Merrill-Palmer Quarterly, 23*, 77–87.

Langer, E. J. (1978). Rethinking the role of thought in social interaction. In J. H. Harvey, W. Ickes, & P. F. Kidd (Eds.), *New directions in attribution research* (Vol. 2). Hillsdale, NJ: Erlbaum, 36–58.

Langer, E. J., & Abelson, R. P. (1972). The semantics of asking a favor: How to succeed in getting help without dying. *Journal of Personality and Social Psychology, 24,* 26–32.

Latané, B., & Darley, J. M. (1968). Group inhibition of bystander intervention in emergencies. *Journal of Personality and Social Psychology, 10,* 215–221.

Latané, B., & Rodin, J. (1969). A lady in distress: Inhibiting effects of friends and strangers in bystander intervention. *Journal of Experimental Social Psychology, 5,* 189–202.

Lerner, M. J. (1977). The justice motive: Some hypotheses as to its origin and forms. *Journal of Personality, 45,* 1–52.

Leventhal, G. S. (1976). Fairness in social relations. In J. W. Thibaut, J. T. Spence, & R. C. Carson (Eds.), *Contemporary topics in social psychology.* Morristown, NJ: General Learning Press.

Lofland, J. (1969). *Identities and deviance.* Englewood Cliffs, NJ: Prentice-Hall.

Marsh, P., Rosser, E., & Harré R. (1978). *The rules of disorder.* London: Routledge and Kegan Paul.

McCall, G. J., & Simmons, J. L. (1978). *Identities and interactions* (2nd ed.). New York: Free Press.

Mead, G. H. (1934). *Mind, self and society: From the standpoint of a social behaviorist.* Edited with introduction by C. W. Morris. Chicago: University of Chicago Press.

Mikula, G. (1980). On the role of justice in allocation decisions. In G. Mikula (Ed.), *Justice and social interaction.* Bern: Huber, 127–166.

Milgram, S. (1963). Behavioral study of obedience. *Journal of Abnormal and Social Psychology, 67,* 371–378.

Miller, G. A., Galanter, E., & Pribram, K. H. (1960). *Plans and the structure of behavior.* New York: Henry Holt.

Mills, C. W. (1940). Situated actions and the vocabularies of motives. *American Journal of Sociology, 5,* 904–913.

Minor, W. W. (1980). The neutralization of criminal offense. *Criminology, 18,* 103–120.

Much, N., & Shweder, R. A. (1978). Speaking of rules: The analysis of culture in the breach. In W. Damon (Ed.), *New directions for child development* (Vol. 2): *Moral Development.* San Francisco: Jossey-Bass, 19–39.

Phares, E. J., & Wilson, K. G. (1972). Responsibility attribution: Role of outcome severity, situational ambiguity and internal-external control. *Journal of Personality, 40,* 392–406.

Phares, E. J., Wilson, K. G., & Klyver, N. W. (1971). Internal-external control and the attribution of blame under neutral and destructive conditions. *Journal of Personality and Social Psychology, 18,* 285–288.

Piliavin, I. M., Rodin, J., & Piliavin, J. A. (1969). Good samaritanism: An underground phenomenon? *Journal of Personality and Social Psychology, 13,* 289–299.

Quinn, C. O., Robinson, J. E., & Balkwell, J. W. (1980). A synthesis of two social psychologies. *Symbolic Interaction, 3,* 59–88.

Redl, F., & Wineman, D. (1951). *Children who hate.* Glencoe, Ill.: Free Press.

Reis, H. T., & Burns, L. B. (1982). The salience of the self in response to inequity. *Journal of Experimental Social Psychology, 18,* 464–475.

Rokeach, M. (1973). *The nature of human values.* New York: Free Press.

Sampson, E. E. (1981). Cognitive psychology as ideology. *American Psychologist, 36,* 730–743.

Schegloff, E. A., & Sacks, H. (1973). Openings up closings. *Semiotica, 8,* 289–327.

Scheier, M. F., & Carver, C. S. (1981). Private and public aspects of self. In L. Wheeler (Ed.), *Review of Personality and Social Psychology* (Vol. 2). Beverly Hills, CA: Sage Publications, 189–216.

Scheier, M. F., Carver, C. S., & Gibbons, F. X. (1981). Self-focused attention and reaction to fear. *Journal of Research in Personality, 15,* 1–15.

Schlenker, B. R. (1980). *Impression management: The self-concept, social identity, and interpersonal relations.* Monterey, CA: Brooks/Cole.

Schonbach, P. (1980). A category system for account phrases. *European Journal of Social Psychology, 10,* 195–200.

Schutz, A. (1964). *Collected papers II.* (Edited by A. Broderson). The Hague: Nijhoff.

Schwartz, S. H. (1968). Words, deeds and the perception of consequences and responsibilities in action situations. *Journal of Personality and Social Psychology, 10,* 232–242.

Schwartz, S. H. (1973). Normative explanations of helping behavior: A critique, proposal, and empirical test. *Journal of Experimental Social Psychology, 9,* 349–364.

Schwartz, S. H. (1977). Normative influences on altruism. In L. Berkowitz (Ed.), *Advances in experimental social psychology* (Vol. 10). New York: Academic Press.

Schwartz, S. H., & Gottlieb, A. (1980). Bystander anonymity and reactions to emergencies. *Journal of Personality and Social Psychology, 39,* 418–430.

Scott, M. B., & Lyman, S. M. (1968). Accounts. *American Sociological Review, 33,* 46–62.

Secord, P. F., & Backman, C. W. (1974). *Social psychology* (2nd ed.). New York: McGraw-Hill.

Stryker, S. (1977). Developments in two social psychologies: Toward an appreciation of mutual relevance. *Sociometry, 40,* 145–160.

Stryker, S., & Gottleib, A. (1981). Attribution theory and symbolic interactionism: A comparison. In J. H. Harvey, W. Ickes, & R. F. Kidd (Eds.), *New directions in attribution research* (Vol. 3). Hillsdale, NJ: Erlbaum, 425–458.

Sullivan, H. S. (1953). *The interpersonal theory of psychiatry.* New York: Norton.

Summer, W. G. (1907). *Folkways.* New York: Ginn and Company.

Sykes, G. M., & Matza, D. (1957). Techniques of neutralization: A theory of delinquency. *American Sociological Review, 22,* 640–670.

Tedeschi, J. T., & Riess, M. (1981). Verbal strategies in impression management. In C. Antake (Ed.), *The psychology of ordinary explanations of social behavior.* London: Academic Press, 271–309.

Thomas, W. I. (1928). *The unadjusted girl.* Boston: Little Brown.

Thomas, W. I. (1966). Situational analysis: The behavior pattern and the situation. In M. Janowitz (Ed.), *W. I. Thomas on social organization and social personality.* Chicago: University of Chicago Press.

Underwood, B., & Moore, B. (1982). Perspective taking and altruism. *Psychological Bulletin, 91,* 143–173.

Verlarde, O. J. (1978). Do delinquents really drift? *British Journal of Criminology, 18,* 23–29.

Warner, D. B. (1976). Determinants of bystander intervention: The effects of verbal cues of victims and others present. Unpublished doctoral dissertation. Reno: University of Nevada, Reno.

Watson, D. (1982). The actor and the observer: How are their perceptions of causality divergent? *Psychological Bulletin, 92,* 682–700.

Wilson, D. W., & Schafer, R. B. (1975). Is social psychology interdisciplinary? *Personality and Social Psychology Bulletin, 4,* 548–552.

PART THREE

THE SELF AND SOCIAL POWER

The final section takes a closer look at the strategic use of self-presentation as a means of gaining power and exercising influence in relationships. The concept of power evokes images of politicians and businesspersons vying with one another for the control of important resources, using whatever devices are available to secure their goals. Although such examples make the concept of power salient, it is a fact of human existence that everyone confronts the task of exercising influence in order to achieve valued goals. In 1651, the English philosopher Thomas Hobbes (1952) wrote, "I put forth a general inclination of all mankind a perpetual and restless desire for power after power, that ceaseth only in death" (p. 76). For Hobbes, power meant the ability to obtain valued outcomes. To satisfy one's goals in life, be they to obtain love or friendship, possessions, respect, security, and even self-satisfaction (it is difficult to be satisfied when one has no friends, no job, no possessions, no respect, and lives in fear of others), one must influence the opinions that others have about oneself. It is not necessary to influence all others, of course, but the opinions of significant others, such as those who are attractive, esteemed, powerful, or close associates determine the extent to which one can satisfy one's own goals. Similarly, Bertrand Russell (1938) argued that the "love of power is the chief motive producing the changes which social science has to study" (p. 15). Clearly, the self that is presented to others serves as a base for the acquisition of power and the exercise of influence.

In Chapter 11, James Tedeschi and Nancy Norman examine the integral relationship between social power, self-presentation, and the self. They postulate that a basic motive of human social behavior is the desire to maximize one's influence potential (i.e., social power). Since the identities people project to audiences serve as a foundation for the actions of others toward them, securing valued identities through self-presentational behaviors provides a means to influence others and achieve valued goals. In their analysis of the types and functions of self-presentational activities, Tedeschi and Norman present a taxonomy for the relevant literature. They distinguish between strategic impression management, which pertains to achieving long-term objectives through the construction and maintenance of identities, and tactical impression management, which pertains to achieving short-term objectives in immediate situations. Crosscutting this distinction, impression management can be either assertive, designed to procure valued identities, or defensive, designed to maintain valued identities. After reviewing the pertinent literature, Tedeschi and Norman discuss the self-concept and self-esteem from the perspective of how these are affected by the power motive. They suggest (among many other provocative ideas) that the motive to maintain self-esteem is predicated on the satisfaction that accompanies the elevation of one's social power. Most of the Chapters in Part One emphasized (a) the relative autonomy of the private self once it has developed through socialization, and (b) the existence of several possible goals for public self-presentation. In contrast, Tedeschi and Norman emphasize (a) the continual potency of the public self, and (b) power as the central human motive from which virtually all other goals derive.

In Chapter 12, Bella DePaulo, Julie Stone, and Daniel Lassiter examine deception in social life. In people's quests to achieve their goals, they are often confronted with the temptation and opportunity to deceive others, a combination that sometimes results in lies or gross distortions. In turn, audiences always must make some attribution (consciously or unconsciously) about the sincerity or deceptiveness of the information they are provided by others. DePaulo, Stone, and Lassiter take a panoramic look at ideas and research on deceiving and detecting deceit. They consider the development of impression management and deception skills in children, the development of the ability to detect deception, people's accuracy in detecting deceit, the cues that are used by audiences to determine if others are lying, and even the personal and interpersonal consequences of detecting and telling lies. The chapter provides an informative analysis of the "darker side" of interpersonal behavior.

REFERENCES

Hobbes, T. (1952). *Leviathan*. Chicago: Encyclopaedia Britannica Publishers. (Original work published 1651.)

Russell, B. (1938). *Power*. New York: Norton.

CHAPTER 11

SOCIAL POWER, SELF-PRESENTATION, AND THE SELF

James T. Tedeschi
Nancy Norman
State University of New York at Albany

INTRODUCTION

Historically, the self has been viewed as a motivating, regulating, and evaluative force within the individual. The focus has been on the intrapsychic processes assumed to be associated with or affected by the self (however conceptualized). More recently, attention has been given to self-presentation, a set of behaviors designed by an actor to establish particular identities in the eyes of various audiences. Self-presentations may be sincere in terms of the actor's own self-image or may represent dissembling.

The present view is that self-presentations are influence tactics used to control the course of social interactions. Self-presentations are attempts to influence others to perceive the actor as having a particular identity. Actors aspire to attain identities that serve to facilitate the effectiveness of more direct forms of influence, such as persuasion, threats, and promises. This chain of events, including self-presentations, the establishment of identities, and the subsequent effects of those identities on the social influence process, places impression management firmly in the realm of social power.

Recognition that self-presentation is an important aspect of interpersonal relations raises questions concerning how the self functions in this interactive process. We will propose that the ideal self motivates persons to present identities which will maximize their social power, while self-esteem indicates the degree to which ideal identities and associated power potential are realized. This chapter will examine the relationships between social power, self-presentations, and the self.

SOCIAL POWER AND SELF-PRESENTATION

Tedeschi and his colleagues (cf. Tedeschi, 1972, 1974a, 1974b, 1983; Tedeschi & Lindskold, 1976) have consistently viewed the individual as primarily concerned with social power and influence. They postulated that a basic motive of human social behavior is a desire to maximize one's potential for influencing others (i.e., social power).

Many phenomena accepted as intrapsychic in nature may be reinterpreted in terms of their functions in social interactions. Data generated in support of cognitive dissonance theory have been reinterpreted in terms of impression management (cf. Tedeschi & Rosenfeld, 1981; Tedeschi, Schlenker & Bonoma, 1971). The transgression-compliance relationship alleged to reflect guilt (Freedman, 1970) or negative affect (Cialdini, Darby, & Vincent, 1973) has been reinterpreted as defensive self-presentation (Tedeschi & Riordan, 1981), emotions and humor can be viewed as influence tactics (Kane, Suls, & Tedeschi, 1976; Schwartz et al., 1978), interpersonal attraction has been conceived as a power resource (Tedeschi, 1974a), and aggression was interpreted as the antinormative use of coercive power (Tedeschi, 1983). However, there has been no systematic attempt to theoretically integrate a loose set of ideas regarding impression-management behaviors and social influence theory.[1] One goal of the present chapter is to provide a framework for such an integration.

Identities and Social Power

A power perspective is essentially a reinforcement view of human behavior. It assumes that people are interdependent for their rewards. People have few goals which do not require the aid or mediation of others. If for purposes of illustration we accept Maslow's (1954) view of human motivation, it would be assumed that people want food, shelter, sexual satisfaction, security, and self-actualization. In modern society, obtaining food requires that the buyer has money to give to a retailer in exchange for the commodity desired. The money, in turn, has to be acquired from someone. Similarly, if people want love, respect, status, or esteem, they must do something to get others to react to them in these ways.

Since just about all of the rewards we seek must be obtained through interaction with others, and since these others are not simply waiting to provide what we want, it is necessary to assert ourselves and try to be effective in influencing others to do what we need them to do so we can have what we want. If actors have those characteristics, attributes, or identities that facilitate various forms of influence, they should experience greater success and obtain more rewards than people who do not possess them. French and Raven (1959) have

---

[1] The terms self-presentation and impression management will be used interchangeably throughout this chapter.

proposed a set of such identities and referred to them as power resources. Among these resources are status, expertise, attractiveness, reward power, information power, and coercive power.

Social power has been defined as the potential to influence others (Dekadt, 1965; Simon, 1957). This potential typically consists of resources that can facilitate social influence and may include the dispositional characteristics of the actor or possession of material, social, or symbolic resources. Skill or style in utilizing various modes of influence may also enhance the effectiveness of the actor's influence attempts. For example, actors may make threats more effective by the way they phrase demands (cf. Fisher, 1969).

Self-presentations are attempts to control the identities attributed to the actor by an audience and thus may be viewed as influence attempts. Goffman (1959) discussed the strategies and structural aspects of self-presentations, while exchange theorists focused on the motivation behind these behaviors (Schneider, 1981). Goffman postulated that identities help to define the nature of the social situation, including the rules of conduct appropriate to the situation. Thus, a person can indirectly control another person's behavior by establishing the identities appropriate to each in that situation.

Social control, the motivation behind self-presentational behaviors, has clearly been the focus of Jones's (1964) work on ingratiation. Persons are viewed as making themselves agreeable or likeable to a status superior for the ulterior purpose of gaining some advantage for themselves. In general, self-presentations are meant to establish a particular image of some personal characteristic or relationship in the eyes of another person. Such behaviors may also affect the reputation, ideals, self-concept, and self-esteem of the actor.

Defensive and Assertive Impression Management

Tedeschi and Lindskold (1976), Schlenker (1980), and Arkin (1981) have distinguished between defensive and assertive impression management. Defensive impression management typically occurs when the actor experiences or anticipates a predicament. Any situation in which actors believe others may attribute some negative or undesirable quality or identity to them is experienced as a predicament (Schlenker, 1980). Actions taken to restore a positive identity or to remove or avoid negative typifications (or to transcend them) may be considered defensive impression management and are sometimes referred to as face work (Goffman, 1967). Defensive self-presentations are reactions by the actor seeking to mend a potentially or actually spoiled identity.

Assertive impression management refers to those behaviors initiated by the actor to establish particular identities or attributes in the eyes of another. Such behaviors are essentially offensive or acquisitive in nature and are not undertaken merely to defend some image of self in the eyes of others. For example, a person may wish to establish an identity as an intellectual and may engage in behaviors such as citing authors or quoting poetry in order to impress others with his or her knowledge. Assertive self-presentations can be risky and may, if they backfire, produce a predicament for the actor, who may then become more concerned with defensive self-presentation.

Tactical and Strategic Impression Management

A second distinction proposed by Tedeschi and Melburg (1984) is between tactical and strategic impression-management behaviors. This distinction parallels a similar one made by military theorists. For the military, tactics are actions taken for limited short-term goals, while strategic actions are directed to an overall or long-term goal. Actions taken to win a local battle or cut losses are considered tactical, whereas those planned to further the overall goal of winning the war (even if it means losing the battle) are strategic in nature.

With regard to impression management, a number of factors distinguish tactical from strategic behaviors. Tactical impression-management behaviors have short-term objectives and strategic impression management behaviors have long-range consequences over time and situations. For example, a person who promotes self in an employment interview is oriented to the short-term goal of obtaining a job offer. The specificity of the goal and the audience, as well as its short-term nature, characterize a self-presentation as tactical.

Strategic impression-management behaviors may also help the actor achieve short-run goals, but the significance of the tactical outcome is far outweighed by the long-term identities acquired by the person as a consequence of performing the behavior. The reputations of actors have significance (in attributional terms) for many situations, over a long period of time, and for many audiences. A reputation as an expert at some problem-solving activity will affect interactions with an unknown number of other people in unplanned ways over an indefinite period of time.

Seldom will a person gain an enduring reputation from a single self-presentation. Strategic impression management typically involves a variety of tactical behaviors cumulatively directed toward establishing a particular identity in the eyes of others. Strategic outcomes may be associated with repeated or habitual use of impression-management tactics. That is, behaviors directed towards tactical outcomes may inadvertently have strategic implications for long-term identities. Sometimes these identities will be unwanted, such as when a person is perceived as an alcoholic or as mentally ill.

Undesired long-term identities are typically the result of a consistent pattern of defensive tactical actions by the person. In such instances the tactical actions become self-defeating. While they may continue to solve short-run problems, tactical self-presentations may have such negative strategic import as to prevent the individual from attaining positive long-range goals. Defensive, strategic impression management behaviors tend to lock the person into a life style characterized by defensive, avoidance, and escape reactions at the expense of assertive, approach, and acquisitive patterns of behavior.

Assertive strategic forms of impression management involve self-construction and are undertaken to establish some long-term reputation or identity for the individual. These identities (sometimes referred to as motives, dispositions, traits, character, or personality) serve as power resources in that they facilitate the effectiveness of various forms of influence tactics. These reputational characteristics are typically functional for multiple audiences (or targets), are effective across various situations, and may also facilitate the effectiveness of many types of influence tactics. Indeed, actors may be generally aware that it would be desirable to possess particular reputational characteristics and may incur costs to achieve them, but might not have any immediate purposes or goals for influencing in mind. For example, a person might want to establish some form of expertise for a vague goal, such as "earning a decent income." For such people identity as an expert is a passport to a world in which they would have more control over events and other people.

TAXONOMY OF IMPRESSION-MANAGEMENT BEHAVIORS

The classification of impression-management behaviors into defensive-assertive and tactical-strategic categories forms a typology which can be represented by a 2 × 2 matrix. A taxonomy of impression-management behaviors can be partitioned within the context of this classification scheme. We will examine the specific behaviors or identities that are partitioned to each quadrant, and note the functions that they have for social interaction and influence.

Defensive Impression-Management Tactics

When events cast doubts or aspersions on some identity desired by actors, they experience embarrassment or shame. Embarrassment is an emotion caused by a predicament (Modigliani, 1971). Goffman (1967) states that "embarrassment occurs whenever the facts at hand threaten to discredit the assumptions a participant finds he has projected about his identity" (pp. 107–108). The ability to extricate oneself from predicaments through various kinds of defensive impression management tactics is a valued social skill. Among such tactics used to mend a spoiled identity are accounts, self-handicapping, apologies, and prosocial behavior.

Accounts When actors behave in ways that appear to break social rules or generate negative consequences, they may engage in motive talk (Mills, 1940). That is, when actors are faced with predicaments, where something they have done appears strange, crazy, untoward, immoral, or inexplicable, the actors may offer explanations for their behavior. Scott and Lyman (1968) suggest that such accounts are offered by actors so they can escape the negative typifications or attributions that audiences may make. Among the most important kinds of accounts are excuses, justifications, and disclaimers.

Excuses are verbal statements denying responsibility for negative events. They may take the form of denying intention for negative consequences, such as in the case of accident, mistake, or inadvertance. Or, the actor may attempt to dissociate from negative events by offering volitional excuses, alleging that the action was caused by forces the actor could not be expected to control, such as mental illness, physical disability, or pharmaceutical addictions. There is the problem for the actor, however, that if volitional excuses are used to escape responsibility or mitigate retribution for a specific action, a side effect might be that a negative reputational characteristic is created, which may reduce the individual's effectiveness in influencing others for a long time afterwards. For example, manifestations of symptoms of mental illness may prevent one from being convicted of a crime, but the stigma of being considered "crazy" may be a cost of using such a defensive tactic.

Justifications are verbal statements providing the reasons for considering apparent negative behavior as legitimate, justified, moral, and even good. By offering justifications actors try to associate their actions with various norms, values, and rules believed to be supported by the target audience. If the audience accepts the justification, the actor avoids the negative typifications but not the responsibility for performing the action in question. Justifications, like appeals to higher courts, provide the basis for a change in judgment by observers. Indeed, observers may draw correspondent inferences (Jones & Davis, 1967) regarding the actor's motives on the basis of the type of justification offered (Tedeschi, Riordan, Gaes, & Kane, 1983). The actor can retrospectively reconstruct events so as to avoid negative repercussions.

Accounts (excuses and justifications) are usually provided after the actor experiences a predicament. However, explanations can be given prior to a potentially embarrassing action. Stokes and Hewitt (1976) refer to such anticipatory explanations as disclaimers. They define a disclaimer as "a verbal device employed to ward off and defeat in advance doubts and negative typifications which may result from intended conduct" (p. 3). Of course disclaimers can take the form of excuses and justifications.

Self-Handicapping People may set up hurdles to make it difficult or impossible to succeed at solving tasks. This self-handicapping behavior provides the person with a ready-made excuse for poor performance and provides a defense against possible attributions by observers about lack of ability (Jones & Berglas, 1978).

Berglas and Jones (1978) demonstrated self-handicapping in a laboratory study. Between two tests of intellectual abilities, subjects were given a choice between taking a drug that would facilitate performance and a drug that would inhibit performance. In fact, the alleged drugs were placebos. All subjects had performed well on the first test, but half of them could not have understood how they succeeded (noncontingent success). Considered from an impression-management point of view this choice placed subjects in a predicament. If they took the inhibiting pill, they were likely to perform poorly on the experimental task, but if they took the facilitating pill, they might succeed but not gain credit for it.

Subjects who experienced contingent success on the first test tended to choose the facilitating pill, but male subjects who experienced noncontingent success on the first test and hence could not be confident about performance on the second test tended to choose the inhibiting pill. The latter subjects apparently decided that they could escape responsibility for failure, since the pill would serve as an excuse, but should they succeed, they would create a very positive impression because their personal characteristics would have overcome a significant handicap. Thus, taking the inhibiting pill was an action, implying an excuse for probable failure with some chance of gaining credit for success.

Jones and Berglas view self-handicapping as a type of ego defense, protecting the actor from negative information regarding his or her own abilities. However, we have interpreted self-handicapping as a behavior providing a ready-made excuse for failure that functions interpersonally in much the same way as disclaimers. Kolditz and Arkin (1982) have tested the ego-defense and impression-management views of self-handicapping. They found that subjects who experienced noncontingent success on the first test chose the inhibiting drug only when the experimenter who scored the second test would know which drug they had chosen. When the choice of drug was carried out privately so the experimenter would not know which one had been chosen, self-handicapping did not occur. Kolditz and Arkin concluded that subjects were more concerned about public identity than private self-esteem.

Apologies Another subset of defensive-tactical impression management behaviors has been referred to as *apologies*. According to Goffman (1971), apologies are confessions of responsibility for negative events which include some expression of remorse. Apologies may imply a desire to make restitution to any victims and constitute promises to behave appropriately in the future. As with justifications, apologies seek to align the individual with the standards of the audience. The interpersonal goal of apologies is to gain the actor a pardon or to gain the actor a more positive identity so that there will be a mitigation of any retributive actions taken by others. Research has shown that apologies are effective in achieving these goals (Schwartz, Kane, Joseph, and Tedeschi, 1978; Wood & Mitchell, 1981).

The degree of predicament experienced by actors affects the types of apologies offered by them. Schlenker and Darby (1981) demonstrated that as the consequences to the victim became more severe and as the responsibility of the actor increased, apologies changed from a simple "pardon me" to self-castigation and explicit requests for forgiveness. Since self-perception should parallel perceptions by external observers, those who make apologies should perceive themselves more positively than persons who refuse to apologize for transgressions.

Prosocial Behavior Actors may engage in prosocial actions when experiencing a predicament as a way of proving themselves as deserving of positive identities. Prosocial actions may emphasize the sincerity of an apology. Research has reliably established that prosocial behavior often follows transgressions (cf., Tedeschi & Riordan, 1981). For example, subjects who caused a table to collapse, tossing neatly arranged index cards on the floor, were more likely to comply to a subsequent request to aid in an experiment (Freedman, 1970). Violating norms or rules projects an identity of the actor as an immoral and bad person. By conspicuously engaging in behaviors that benefit others, actors may compensate for the apparent transgression and convince others that they really are good people.

Assertive Impression-Management Tactics

Actors may present identities that are directed at gaining specific and rather immediate rewards. These assertive impression-management tactics are emitted rather than elicited, and are meant to arouse some emotion in the target audience, such as liking, fear, respect, or sympathy. These emotions are expected to motivate the target to do something beneficial for the initiating actor. Assertive impression-management tactics include ingratiation, exemplification, intimidation, supplication, self-promotion, entitlements, and enhancements.

Ingratiation Tactics Ingratiation consists of a class of "behaviors illicitly designed to influence a particular other person concerning the attractiveness of one's personal qualities" (Jones, 1964). The goal of ingratiation tactics is to gain the approval and liking of an audience that controls significant rewards for the actor. Such rewards are foreseeable and rather imminent.

According to Jones and Wortman (1973), ingratiation includes four kinds of behavior: self-enhancing communications, flattery, opinion conformity, and doing favors. Self-enhancing communications are verbal statements which draw attention to one's positive characteristics and imply that one is worthy or deserving of liking. Flattery consists of positive referents made by actors about others in the hope of gaining the other's liking. Opinion conformity is similar to flattery in that actors agree with the opinions of others according to the premise that similarity breeds attraction. Favor doing is performed by an actor as an instrumental behavior to gain the other's liking, since the favor provides positive reinforcement to the target (Tedeschi & Riess, 1981).

Ingratiating behaviors are assertive in that the actor is not in a predicament and undertakes the behavior not as a reaction to some negative event, but in pursuit of the interpersonal incentives that may be obtained. Of course there are risks associated with ingratiation tactics, but the actor may attempt to avoid costs by the subtle or indirect way the relevant behaviors are performed (cf. Schlenker, 1980).

Other Assertive Tactics Jones and Pittman (1982) have proposed four other assertive tactics of impression management: self-promotion, exemplification, intimidation, and supplication. What characterizes each of these tactics, as described by Jones and Pittman, is that the actor engages in the tactic as a way of manipulating others and achieving some foreseeable, short-term rewards (or avoiding punishments). The use of these tactics may also have implications for long-term identities, especially if their use becomes habitual.

Exemplification Exemplification is behavior which presents the actor as morally worthy and may also have the goal of eliciting imitation by others. Such imitation presumably produces some advantage or reward for the model. For example, a supervisor may always arrive at work on time, never take more than one hour for lunch, and never exceed the time allowed for coffee breaks. The supervisor, by acting in such an exemplary fashion, may project an identity to superiors as committed to excellent performance and may induce subordinates to experience guilt over their idleness and perhaps to imitate the desired behaviors, thereby increasing productivity. The ultimate goal of the supervisor may be a positive job evaluation and a subsequent salary increase.

Intimidation Intimidation tactics are meant to induce fear in an audience which, in turn, makes the use of various forms of coercion more effective. Intimidation may cause the target audience to attribute resolve or malevolence to the threatener, thereby increasing the believability of threats, and also increasing the probability of deterrence or compliance by a target. For example, a threat may be accompanied by loud shouts or epiphets or by the brandishing of a weapon. The effectiveness of intimidation may be quite restricted, however. There is considerable evidence that the use of coercion tends to lead to conflict spirals and additional costs to all parties (cf. Tedeschi, Schlenker & Bonoma, 1973). Nevertheless, there are subcultures where intimidation is a frequent tactic in gaining advantage over others (Wolfgang & Ferracuti, 1967).

Supplication Supplication consists of behaviors meant to induce nurturant, prosocial, or socially responsible behavior from others. The actor presents an identity as a weak, needy, vulnerable, or dependent person. The failing or dependency must not be attributed to personal responsibility, but rather to uncontrollable factors (Barnes, Ickes, & Kidd, 1979). The goal of the actor is to gain some interpersonal advantage by invoking, directly or indirectly, a norm of social responsibility. Most social groups have norms that prescribe that able persons provide help for dependent others, such as children, the sick and the indigent.

Self-Promotion Self-promotion is similar to the ingratiation tactic of self-enhancing communications. However, instead of inducing liking, self-promotion usually involves ambitions for competence, such as intelligence, knowledge, skills, or athletic prowess. A job applicant will typically present self as having ability, experience, and motivation to do a good job. The self-promotor may credential self by displaying high school diplomas, certificates of achievement, or letters of recommendation. These tactics are usually employed for some immediate objective, such as obtaining a job. When an audience already has an image of the actor as competent, the actor may promote the self modestly (Ackerman & Schlenker, 1975). Self-promotion, like other impression management behaviors, may represent sincere communications, or they may involve deception.

Entitlements and Enhancements Two additional assertive-tactical impression-management behaviors have been identified: entitlements and enhancements (D'Arcy, 1963; Schlenker, 1980). These tactics may be viewed as forms of self-promotion. Entitlements are the opposite of excuses. Whereas excuses are attempts to absolve self of responsibility for negative events, entitlements seek to associate self with positive events. People are assertive in making such claims for credit. The goal is to gain the approbation and rewards provided for such positive behavior.

Enhancements are attempts to persuade others that the positive effects of behavior are perhaps even more positive than they were at first thought. If one is entitled to credit for positive outcomes, the greater the value of the outcome, the more credit and rewards there should be. Once attribution of cause and responsibility have been made to an actor for a positive event, he or she could try to enhance the value of the event and increase his or her own rewards.

Given that actors are not unbiased observers of the effects of their own behavior, it could be expected that they would perceive themselves as entitled to more credit than noncommitted observers. While entitlements and enhancements may be self-serving and exaggerated from the perspective of observers, they tend to be sincere.

Defensive Impression-Management Strategies

The use of a defensive impression-management tactic to avoid responsibility for negative events or to avoid undesired attributions by others may be effective. If so, the actor is encouraged to use that tactic again when placed in a predicament. Habitual use of particular tactics across situations and time may as a secondary impression (Schneider, 1981) project undesired identities to observers. When such identities emerge from tactical behavior, the behavior is considered strategic in its implications. Among the identities created as secondary impressions by defensive tactics are mental illness, addiction, alcoholism, helplessness, and debilitating anxiety. These diagnostic categories represent strategic forms of self-handicapping and serve the function of excusing almost any kind of untoward conduct by the actor. While the actor may actively resist the labels associated with the secondary impressions, the "symptoms" in the form of defensive impression management tactics may persist.

Mental Illness The idea that the symptoms of mental illness serve a self-protective function is not a new one. Adler (1913) regarded symptoms as excuses for past and future failures which threaten self-esteem. Snyder and Smith (1981) have placed Adler's notion into an interaction context and proposed that symptoms function to lower the expectations of others regarding self, externalize the causes of negative outcomes, and maximize positive attributions.

Haley (1963) interpreted neurotic and psychotic symptoms as forms of social power or influence. He described a case where a woman developed a compulsion, like Lady Macbeth, for washing her hands. The woman's affliction prevented her from cooking, washing dishes, cleaning house, going out to places chosen by her husband, and so on. According to Haley, the woman's neurotic compulsion served the very useful function of gaining control over her traditional European husband so that he ended up doing all those things she did not like doing. The identity of a compulsive neurotic, though perhaps a negative identity in some respects, served to gain numerous interpersonal objectives for this woman.

The habitual use of particular defensive impression-management tactics may be solidified as a strategic form of behavior when audiences, and particularly professional audiences, such as psychiatrists and psychologists, provide labels to apply to the actors. While at first actors may resist being labeled in terms of some diagnostic category (as being "ill") the identity may be incorporated into the self-concept. When the actor accepts the label, the strategic behavior which might have been terminated, compensated for, or channeled may become more stabilized (Scheff, 1974). That is, people who accept that they are mentally ill may act in ways consistent with such an identity.

Braginsky, Braginsky, and Ring (1969) carried out pioneering research showing that patients in mental hospitals manifested symptoms of illness when it was useful to do so, and presented themselves as more healthy when that identity served their purposes. Fontana and Klein (1968) found that the so-called schizophrenic deficit in performance occurred only when competent performance threatened the patients' goals. More recent studies have shown that subjects displayed symptoms of hypochondriasis (Smith, Snyder & Perkins, 1981) only when the symptoms could offer an excuse for incompetent performance. The low levels of energy, interest, and effort associated with both depression and learned helplessness suggests that these diagnostic categories may also be labels for strategic impression management behaviors.

Addictions Jones and Berglas (1978) suggested that alcoholism might be a defensive impression-management strategy. Persons who have strong fear of failing might begin drinking or taking drugs so they can attribute any failure to the interference of these chemical substances with proper physiological and psychological functioning. Thus, addictions may be interpreted as strategic forms of self-handicapping.

The current belief that alcoholism and drug addiction are illnesses requiring treatment and not behavior patterns deserving of punishment, reinforces their effectiveness as self-handicapping strategies. The addict is perceived as a person who has lost control over the chemical consuming behaviors that provide a ready-made excuse for irresponsible and reckless actions.

Social Anxiety and Shyness According to Leary and Schlenker (1981), shyness serves a defensive and strategic function for the individual. A lack of confidence in various social situations generates shyness (or social anxiety), and the individual tends to avoid or withdraw from such situations. Shyness serves a protective function for actors by providing them with an excuse for avoiding situations which are likely to make them look bad. Performance-related anxieties (e.g., speech anxiety, test anxiety, social anxiety) can serve as explanations for inadequate performance because of their acknowledged debilitating effects on performance. Smith, Snyder, and Handelsman (1981) have shown that people with high test anxiety manifest symptoms only when the debilitating effects of anxiety on performance are explicitly or implicitly acknowledged by the relevant audience.

Assertive Impression-Management Strategies

There has been a general failure by impression-management theorists to consider what kinds of identities persons seek to establish for themselves. Often, theorists merely state that persons seek to present a positive image of self to others and to avoid transmitting negative identities (e.g., Arkin, 1981; Jellison, 1981; Schneider, 1981). Generally, positive is taken to mean having attributes such as competence and likability. A power-oriented view of impression management behavior defines as *positive* any identity possessing the potential to influence others, even if such an identity brings about a negative evaluation by an audience. Actors try to establish identities that will facilitate, influence and maintain, or increase their power over other people.

It has often been observed that characteristics of the individual function as power resources in interactions with others (cf. French & Raven, 1959; Lasswell & Kaplan, 1950). Parsons (1967) has likened such characteristics to money. Just as actors make investments of time, energy, capital, and risk in order to make long-term profits, they also invest to acquire reputational characteristics that yield long-term effectiveness in influencing others.

People may use a variety of impression-management behaviors over time, situations, and audiences. When these behaviors are directed toward reputation building rather than used instrumentally to gain short-term advantages in social interaction, the behaviors may be considered strategic.

The identities people strive to attain are those which increase their social power. An integration of impression management and social influence theories allows us to specifically say what identities are involved.

Source Characteristics and Social Influence Tedeschi and his colleagues (cf. Tedeschi, 1972) proposed an influence theory including source characteristics, perceptions of the source's identities by a target, and how these latter perceptions affect the responses of the target to specific forms of influence attempted by the source. A schematic of the theory is shown in Figure 11-1.

The source's characteristics are shown on the far left of the schematic and represent objective and measurable factors (at least in some respects). These

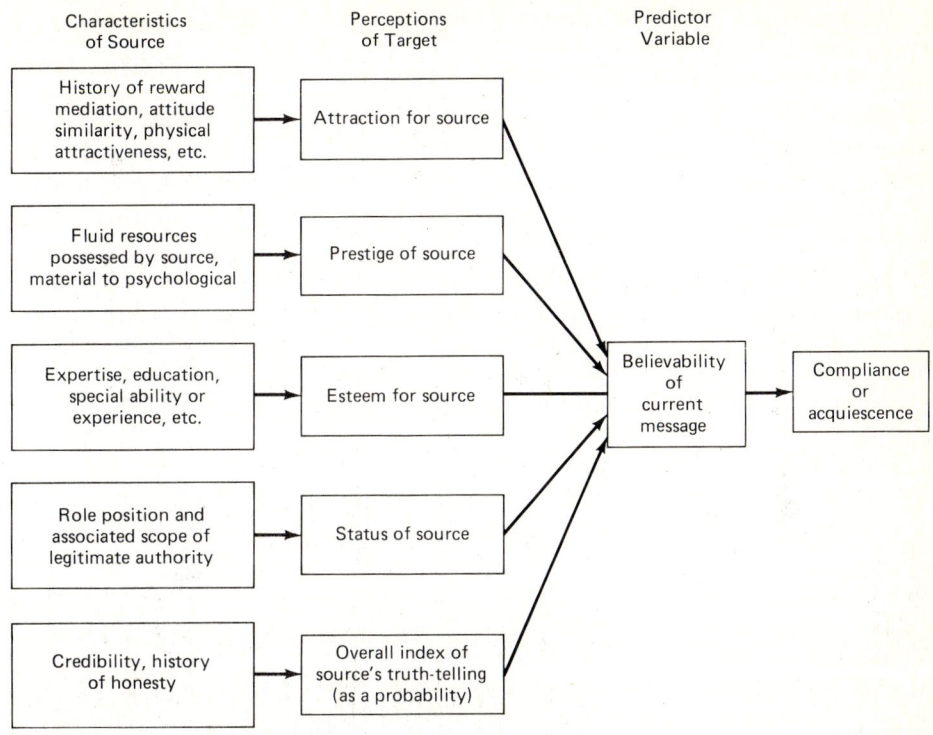

FIGURE 11-1
A schematic of influence theory.

characteristics are frequently manipulated in laboratory experiments. However, the target must perceive these characteristics if they are to affect the influence process. Just because a source has special abilities or expertise does not mean that a target will have an image of the source as competent.

The second column of variables refers to the target's perceptions of the source. Generally, these second-order variables would be expected to have specific functions with the objective characteristics of the source. For instance, the more expert a source actually is, the more he or she will be esteemed by the target. The source's characteristics and the target's perceptions of them are given different names so that the objective-subjective distinction is kept salient. Expertise represents the objective factor and esteem is the target's perception of the source's expertise.

There are occasions when the target gives the source low esteem even when the source is an expert, such as when there is value incongruency between the two parties (Weiss, 1957). It sometimes happens that the target highly esteems a source lacking in expertise, as when a con artist misrepresents self to others. People often have opportunities to make assertive self-presentations in a way to maximize the probability they will be perceived as having the reputational characteristics that will facilitate influence.

The theory depicted in Figure 11-1 proposes that the first-order variables are functionally related to target perceptions of the source, which in turn are related to the believability of the source's communications. Holding all else constant, the more believable the source's communications, the more success the source will have in influencing the target. The relevant identities to be established by the source for a target audience include trustworthiness, credibility, attraction, esteem, prestige, and status. While the theory does not explicitly indicate a more defuse quality of being morally good or bad, such an overall evaluative dimension is probably important in the reactions of individuals to each other (cf. Osgood, 1964).

Identities as Trustworthy and Credible Hovland, Janis, and Kelley (1953) defined trustworthiness in terms of an honest effort by a source to tell the truth and without any goal of exploiting the target. Essentially, someone who is honest and has no ax to grind is perceived as trustworthy. A person with such an identity is more effective in influencing others (Powell & Miller, 1967). We would expect, therefore, that persons may expend some effort to acquire a reputation for being trustworthy. An irony from the present point of view is that persons who wish to be perceived as trustworthy may desire such a reputation so they can gain advantage in social interactions. Concern about one's reputation for trustworthiness might very well prevent a person from using deception or directly exploiting others. In other words, even a Machiavillian disregard for the moral order in the pursuit of self-interest may lead the person to act in identity-consistent ways, bringing about short-term disadvantages. When a source has an identity as trustworthy, influence may take more open forms, typically the use of persuasive communications and explicit contracts.

There is some confusion in the distinction between the concepts of trustworthiness and credibility. While trustworthiness involves an attribution by a target that a source intends to send a valid message without exploitative interest, credibility in the present use refers to the relationship between the source's words and subsequent confirming or disconfirming events. For example, the credibility of a source's promises would be calculated by a count of how many times after making promises the source provided targets the rewards promised. In general, people are concerned that they present an identity to others as honest or credible. They often incur some costs to maintain credibility. There would be temptation to renege on promises if the source was not concerned about future reputation for credibility. That is, the concern about the effectiveness of future influence is an important reason for the consistency of the source in backing up words with corresponding deeds and provides for a certain consistency in behavior across situations.

Attraction, Expertise, Status, and Prestige Attraction is a complex power resource. It is established by a number of antecedent conditions, including attitude similarity, value congruence, mediation and expectation of rewards, need complementarity, and other factors. According to Tedeschi (1974a), people like to be liked because liking yields many benefits. People trust those they like and hence are more apt to be influenced by attractive sources. Usually, people benefit and do not hurt those they like. People are apt to justify untoward behavior performed by an attractive person. These are substantial benefits. It is no wonder that people devote so much time and effort to become attractive to others.

Prestige is the perception that a person possesses or has access to resources that can be used for purposes of social influence. People may engage in many self-presentational behaviors to establish that they can wield important resources in interpersonal interactions. Deceit and secrecy are frequently associated with establishing prestige. If others do not have direct access to measuring resources, actors may more easily manipulate information regarding the kinds and amounts of resources they have available and their willingness to use them. In such a context bluffing can be an effective strategy. For example, actors may claim alliances or coalitions that are not extant to intimidate others. The more prestige possessed by a source, the more effective any influence attempt is likely to be. Prestige is one of the more obvious factors involved in social influence and many people are motivated to acquire the resources that will yield an identity of high prestige.

Esteem is the perception that a person has special abilities or competencies. One of the more tried-and-true methods for acquiring an identity of high esteem is to acquire knowledge and skills and to display to others certain symbols of achievement, such as diplomas or ostentatious speech habits. Esteem is important in the influencing process, especially when the target is dependent on the superior information or skills of the source. There are many studies showing that experts are more persuasive than nonexperts (cf. Tedeschi & Lindskold, 1976, Ch. 8).

Status is the perception that a person has legitimate authority of a particular scope. This attribution is usually based on the role position of the person in some group or organizational setting and the values held by the observer. A person might hold a high role position in a group but not be given high status by a recalcitrant and unhappy group member, who has revolutionary aspirations. On the other hand, a person might not formally hold a high role position in a group but be given informal status by group members. Symbols are important in projecting legitimacy. For example, a person may have a special parking space, a big office, and a private secretary as indications of status. Generally, status is positively related to effective influence. This accounts for why people are so highly motivated to acquire status.

Summary of Taxonomy

Figure 11-2 presents a summary of the classification of impression-management behaviors described above. The behaviors appear in most instances to unambiguously fit into the 2 × 2 classification scheme. However, there are behaviors that fit into more than one category. For instance, we have noted that self-handicapping may be categorized as a tactical or strategic defensive behavior.

	Tactical	**Strategic**
Defensive	Accounts Excuses Justifications Disclaimers Self-handicapping Apologies Restitution Prosocial Behavior	Alcoholism Drug Abuse Phobias Hypochondria Mental Illness Learned Helplessness
Assertive	Entitlements Enhancements Ingratiation Intimidation Exemplification Self-promotion Supplication	Attraction Esteem Prestige Status Credibility Trustworthiness

FIGURE 11-2
A taxonomy of impression management behaviors.

We also have noted that some behaviors, like supplication, intimidation, exemplification, and self-promotion may develop into automated behaviors after becoming incorporated into one's overall personality and hence may not fit unambiguously into either the tactical or strategic category.

With the establishment of identities as the main ingredient involved in self-presentational behaviors, we are now led to address the role of the self and self-esteem in this interactional process.

THE SELF, SELF-ESTEEM, AND SOCIAL POWER

The self is a complex theoretical construct which has been given many different meanings. One aspect of self that all agree on is that it refers to the person's concept (or theory) regarding his or her own identities (cf. Epstein, 1973). Here, the self refers to the phenomenological composite of the many "selves" or identities that are projected in social interaction (Schlenker, 1984). Another aspect of self is an evaluative process whereby the individual compares various actions and the identities they imply against internal standards. The result is typically an evaluative judgment of good and bad. Judgments may be moral in the sense of right and wrong, but also may be amoral in the sense of judging standards of performance that have little or no moral implications, as when a person kicks a football a certain distance and then evaluates whether it was a good kick.

We propose that the self-system, including ideal self, real self, and the evaluative process, serves the power interests of actors because it guides and motivates them to achieve identities that facilitate more explicit forms of influence. Without some notion of self, people would not connect tactical behaviors and associated identities in one situation with self-presentations in other situations. The unity and consistency of behavior can be developed and maintained only by some organizing system, such as the self. Thus assertive impression-management strategies would be impossible without the regulation, guidance, motivation, and evaluation provided by the self-system.

Self-Esteem and Impression Management

William James (1890) interpreted the evaluative judgment of the social self as self-esteem. According to James, how you judge yourself will depend on the degree to which your actual successes coincide with the goals and aspirations you have set for yourself. One's actual successes reflect the real self while one's aspirations reflect the ideal self. A judgment that reflects a small discrepancy between real and ideal selves represents positive self-esteem and a large discrepancy reflects negative self-esteem. Most theories of self-esteem assume that the person is strongly motivated to maintain positive self-esteem (e.g., Cohen, 1968). Such a master motive presumably leads actors to act in a manner consistent with internal standards. When the actor acts inconsistently with these standards, this master motive lowers self-esteem and motivates the person to take some action to restore positive self-esteem. If the person is unable to restore positive self-esteem, some psychic dysfunction, such as experienced guilt, self-punishment, withdrawal and depression, may occur.

Self-esteem and impression-management theories have often been viewed as competing theories. For example, Weary (1978), Weary and Arkin (1982), and Zuckerman (1979) have posed competing predictions by the two theories in self-serving bias research. When people work at ambiguous tasks and receive feedback that they did well, they tend to attribute the success to internal factors such as ability and effort. However, when they are told they did poorly, they tend to attribute the failure to external factors such as bad luck or the difficulty of the task. This effect of outcomes on attributions, referred to as the self-serving bias, may be based on the person's need to maintain positive self-esteem (an internal reason), or on an impression-management concern for maintaining an identity of competence in the eyes of others (an external reason).

The two theories appear to present opposing sources for the person's behavior. Impression-management theory imbeds the individual into social interaction and views the behavior of the person as directed towards controlling interpersonal relations. That is, the motivation of behavior is viewed as external, caused by a desire to impress an audience with a certain identity. During interactions actors may have specific goals they want to achieve depending on the specific audience they are attempting to influence (Schlenker, 1982). Audiences control rewards, and obtaining these rewards is a goal of interaction. Familiarity with a particular audience secures knowledge of the specific identity that will be rewarded. This explains why individuals act differently when interacting with different audiences, such as with peers, parents, or employers.

Self-esteem theory focuses on cognitions (and their dynamics), and views the basic motivation of the individual as directed towards satisfying inner needs. The actor is viewed as behaving consistently with internal standards and not with the expectations of an audience. Thus, self-esteem and self-presentation motives are conceived as often in conflict with one another in governing the person's behavior. Baumeister (1982) suggested that in the presence of an evaluative audience an actor may engage in self-presentations, but that when audience salience and importance are absent, the person will engage in behaviors governed by self-esteem. We prefer the view that both processes serve the power interests of the individual and therefore are not in conflict.

Self-Esteem and Social Power

A person wants to experience positive self-esteem, not for some mysterious, inner-psychic reasons, but because it is a generalized reinforcer which is associated in an indirect way with the facilitation of social influence and the attainment of rewards. Increases in self-esteem signify the approximation of an ideal attribute or identity, which in turn, provides a power resource in future (perhaps yet unplanned) interactions with other people. A lowering of self-esteem signifies an increase in the discrepancy beween ideal and real self, suggesting that the person has suffered a decrement in social power and will be less effective in influencing others.

Our proposal is essentially a two-step process. Actors present themselves as having power-related identities, such as trustworthiness or expertise. If audiences confirm the identity presented, the real self closely approximates the ideal self and self-evaluation indicates positive self-esteem. The established identity also increases the effectiveness of the actor's influence attempts, thereby leading to desired outcomes in interaction with others. Thus, positive self-esteem is associated in a chain of events with rewards. Audience feedback that an undesired identity has been conveyed indicates a discrepancy from the ideal self (and a loss of power), and is experienced as lowered self-esteem.

An interpretation of the self as a system that serves a mediating function for the person whose primary concern is to become socially effective is consistent with the view that the self is an interaction concept. Ossorio and Davis (1968) suggested that the concept of a person was developed to distinguish one person from another and to focus responsibility for action. Structural concepts, such as traits, status, and motives, provide attributes along which persons differ.

Inherent in the concept "person" is a multitude of identities an actor presents to various audiences depending on how the actor wants to be viewed at a particular time. The presentation of a specific identity defines characteristics of an actor, such as goals, motives, intelligence and values, which define how an actor is perceived, regarded, and treated (Schlenker, 1980). Logically, then, the self must be conceived as essentially a system guiding the interactions of the individual. This perspective helps to avoid the booby trap of viewing the self as some sort of humunculus whereby the outer person somehow serves to satisfy the needs of some inner person.

Changes of Self-Esteem

The real self may be inferior to the ideal self for many reasons. The person may have genetic infirmities or characteristics associated with appearance or physical attractiveness. The person may lack skills or training because of environmental handicaps and lack of opportunity. Some people have abundant resources available to them through the chance of being born into wealthy families. Discrepancies in ideal and real self can be due to high ideals or a poor self-concept (or both). One can reduce the discrepancy by lowering ideals or raising self-concept. A person's conception of real self is drawn from comparative and reflective appraisals and self-perceptions (Bem, 1971; Festinger, 1954). Most people are embedded in rather stable social groups for long periods of time and self-concepts, rooted as they are in these groups, are not apt to change much over the short run. On the other hand, a highly mobile person who frequently shifts affiliations may not have a very stable self-concept. While significant changes in lifestyle were a rare occurrence among the serfs of eighteenth-century Europe, radical changes are not infrequent among twentieth-century Americans. Changes in social groups may affect changes in self-concept with an accompanying rise or lowering of self-esteem.

Lowering one's aspirations (ideal self) may be easier than changing one's self-concept. Ideal self is abstract and often not well articulated and hence can be changed without lowered self-esteem. Lowering ideals may even increase self-esteem if the individual believes the original ideal was set too high and could not possibly be obtained. A lowered ideal may be both necessary and beneficial to the person's psychological well-being.

There are occasions when the actor uses tactics that may have the side effect of bringing about negative evaluations by others. Such actions will not, however, have any impact on self-esteem, unless the actor changes ideal or real self. As long as the actor can justify to self that the behavior was necessary, correct, moral, or due to extenuating circumstances (due to external causes in the language of attribution theory), there will be no change in the self-system. The individual must often choose between tactics to gain an immediate reward or a strategic investment in longer-term self-construction at some cost now. An individual who refrains from going to an end of the year "beer bash" to study for finals may risk being labeled "uncool" for the sake of a long-term identity as a doctor. In many instances tactical and strategic behaviors are consistent with one another, as when ingratiation helps to establish the actor as a friendly, likable, and trustworthy person.

The individual must consider the probability and value of immediate reinforcements of tactical self-presentations against the probability and value of strategic outcomes of self-construction. Of course the probability and value of costs associated with the outcome for each choice must also be considered. The person will choose so as to minimize costs and maximize gains (the minimax principle). In the above example, the cost of missing a social event may be outweighed by the desire of obtaining the high grade-point average needed to get into medical school and eventually becoming a doctor.

Development of Ideal Self

Assuming that self-esteem is essentially an evaluation by the person comparing real to ideal self, a basic question is how the ideal self is formulated and what function it serves. Psychoanalytic theory proposed that a child develops an ego ideal during passage through various life stages and as a function of important experiences at each stage of development. Freud considered identification to be a critical process in the development of the ego ideal (cf. Brenner, 1955). Identification is essentially a defensive reaction to unacceptable id impulses and focuses on attributes and values of the parents. Identifications with people other than parents take place only to the degree that these others have parental-like attributes or authority. For Freud, the ego ideal served an important social-control function in civilizing the human animal.

Bandura's (1977) social-learning theory proposes that models who are reinforced for their behavior tend to be imitated by observers. Some characteristics of models are associated with more imitation by observers. For instance, Bandura and Huston (1961) have proposed a status-envy hypothesis. Observers will tend to more frequently imitate a rewarded model if that model also controls significant reinforcements. Furthermore, social-learning theory states that more nurturant models will be frequently imitated.

We postulate that the individual's ideal self is composed of identifications with or imitations of models (abstract or real) who possess identities, such as expertise, status, attractiveness, that make them effective in interacting with others. It is further postulated that self-esteem is a modulator system which directs the individual toward acquisition of greater power and records the gain or loss of power. Increases in self-esteem indicate that there has been a decrease in distance between real and ideal self, and hence that some attribute has changed in a direction of providing the person with greater power. For example, people may experience positive self-esteem following prosocial behavior because the behavior promotes an identity as helpful, cooperative, and attractive.

The ideal self may be considered a collage of characteristics possessed, or believed to be possessed, by models who have been successful in achieving interpersonal objectives. Which ideal identities the person will introject depends on a complex set of factors, including available models, own biological attributes, environmental opportunities or impediments, and learning experiences. The level of aspiration research of the 1940s suggests that the individual adjusts his ideals to his successes and failures. As Rosenberg (1968) concluded. "Most people tend to set goals that they interpret as falling within reasonable range of their potential accomplishments" (pp. 186). Thus, people continually adjust their ideal and real selves as a function of their unique experiences.

People may feel they can no longer adequately function with the reputations they have developed in the eyes of significant others. Sometimes, as Schlenker (1980) has noted, the actor may attempt to dissociate from an old self and convey a notion of a reconstructed self. For example, Charles Colson and John

Erlichman, convicted of criminal actions during the Watergate years of the Nixon administration, have become born-again Christians and devote much of their time to charitable causes. These reconstructions of self, involving a consistent use of prosocial tactics, may be interpreted as strategic in nature. While the reconstruction may originate from a predicament and thus begins as defensive behavior, the identities established are positive in nature. On the other hand, if the person develops functional amnesia or experiences a fugue state, the behavior would be better classified as a defensive strategy to escape from an unwanted identity.

Self and Identities

Self-presentation and the self-system are integrally related. The identities presented by actors may be based on ideal self, real self, the ideals of the audience, or the actors' concepts of how audiences perceive them. Usually, the actor's ideal self and the ideals of the audience will be similar since they commonly share the same culture. The ideals for both are those identities that serve as important power resources in that particular social group.

Stryker (1972) has noted that certain identities are more central (e.g., important) for the individual than others. Which identity is most salient at any given time may be dependent on the social situation. For example, in a hostile quarrel it is doubtful that expertise in computer programming would be an important identity to promote, although showing courage, strength, and determination might be quite effective.

A person's identities may be bound up with other people. For example, having a relationship with someone of the opposite sex or being the progeny of an important person in the community has important implications for self. It must be important to a person's self-concept to be a Rockefeller or Kennedy in America. Simply having the name provides access to power regardless of the attributes of the individual. Attractiveness of a female companion has been shown to be an important resource for a male. Audiences perceive a male as more socially desirable when the woman he is with is attractive rather than unattractive (Sigall & Landy, 1973).

It is important for the social functioning of the individual that the self-system be integrally related to social interactions. Should the self-system become functionally autonomous from the interpersonal context, many problems could ensue. For example, a person who has a strong ideal of possessing great resources and being a very famous person could acquire delusions of grandeur. Acute schizophrenia may represent a tendency by the individual to repress, ignore, or deny any identity that would make any sense to anyone else. People who believe that they are completely lacking in any ideal identity, and hence believe that others perceive them negatively, may withdraw from attempts at influencing others altogether.

Impression Management and Self-Esteem

The use of impression-management behaviors is related to the maintenance of self-esteem. Assertive impression-management strategies are used by actors to establish long-term identities which approximate the ideal self. The more successful the actor is in establishing these identities the more the real self will reflect ideal self, and a higher level of self-esteem will be maintained. Assertive impression-management tactics often have the effect of improving the image of an actor in front of an audience for the purpose of obtaining a specific reward for the actor. For example, through ingratiation or self-promotion tactics, actors may succeed in getting others to like them. This positive feedback may lead the actor to perceive self as more attractive, narrowing a discrepancy with ideal self, and hence increasing self-esteem.

Defensive impression-management tactics may be effective in excusing or justifying untoward behavior which would reflect an identity not indicative of the ideal self. These behaviors may prevent an increase in distance between real self and ideal self, and therefore serve to maintain self-esteem as well as public identities. When strategic forms of self-handicapping are successful in allowing actors to avoid responsibility for their negative behaviors, judgments cannot be made regarding the approximation of real to ideal self. The implication is that if these handicapped people did not suffer from alcoholism, anxiety, depression, or other strategic disorders, they could live up to the ideal standards of their social groups. The handicap prevents a clear evaluation of the actor's abilities and competence, and thus allows the individual's real self to remain ambiguous. Of course, self-esteem is not increased through the use of defensive strategies, although it may be prevented from decreasing.

The self can be conceived of as an integrator of behavior, discriminating when certain tactics or strategies would be most effective in producing desired results. That is, when is it most conducive to claim responsibility for success and deny responsibility for failure? The integration of attribution theory with impression management theory addresses such issues.

ATTRIBUTIONS AND IMPRESSION MANAGEMENT

A taxonomy of impression-management behaviors provides a basis of relationship to attribution theory. According to attribution theory (Heider, 1958), observers assign cause to the person or the environment. The classification into defensive and assertive impression management is clearly associated with internal and external attributions. Defensive behaviors, such as excuses that deny intentions or volition, are clearly meant to convince audiences that behavior (or the effects thereof) were not under the actor's control, and hence external attributions should be made. Even in the case of justifications, where the actor takes responsibility for consequences, the thrust is to explain the behavior in terms of norms, standards, and rules that "required" the behavior in question. A justification claims the actor had no choice but to perform the action, implies anyone else in an identical position would have done the same thing, and thus denies internal causation. Indeed, Scott and Lyman (1968) proposed that the normativity of the justification is the most important factor in its acceptance. Riordan, Marlin, and Kellogg (1983) have obtained evidence in support of the normativity hypothesis.

Assertive impression-management behaviors have the purpose of convincing observers that the internal attributions for environmental effects should be assigned to the actor. Entitlements are most directly designed to accomplish the objective of getting others to attribute cause to the actor. Impression-management behaviors designed to achieve identities that yield power potential would of course fail if others attributed them to environmental factors.

Buss (1978) has noted a distinction between reasons and causal attributions. Reasons refer to personal and social factors that serve to explain behavior, while causes are invariant associations between physical events. When asked to make attributions regarding behavior, people typically offer reasons. People may dissemble when asked to attribute cause for their own behavior, or they may be sincere. Similarly, an audience is motivated to allow others to save face and hence may provide explanations for an actor's behavior that are at variance with private perceptions. Hence, persons often provide reasons for their own or for other's behavior based on the implications the reason has for the actor's identity, and not on private beliefs. The issue of when insincere self-presentations lead to changes in self-concept will require a great deal more work in distinguishing between public and private attributions.

MOTIVES, PERSONALITY, AND IMPRESSION MANAGEMENT

Peters (1958) has distinguished between intentions and motives in terms of reasons. Intentions are explanations of specific goals of behavior, while motives attempt to explain behavior on a deeper level. Similarly, Schutz (1967) has referred to intentions as in-order-to reasons and motives as because-of reasons. Intentions are reasons that refer to the specific effects brought about or desired by the actor's contemplated or actual behavior. To state that one wrote a counterattitudinal essay in order to gain an incentive of $5.00 would be to state an intention. But it could be asked why the actor wanted $5.00. This deeper explanation ("because of") is referred to as a motive.

The type of explanation offered by an actor may affect the attributions of observers. Intentional reasons tend to focus on outcomes or environmental causes, and motivational explanations are of course associated with internal attributions. For example, in forced-compliance experiments large incentives are considered to be sufficient justification for counterattitudinal behaviors, but small incentives are considered to require internal reasons for the behavior because the external justification is insufficient.

According to Heider (1958), observers attempt to organize impressions of others in order to be able to predict behavior and assume some control over interaction. It can be suggested that the traits used in implicit-personality theories correspond to those identities making up the ideal self and serving as power resources. It is interesting to examine the major motives postulated by psychologists and note such correspondences.

The assumption that the acquisition, maintenance, and exercise of social power is a master motive of human behavior suggests that dimensions of personality will reflect repetitive use of particular tactics of influence, the kinds of identities the actor wishes to establish, and the social skills and sensitivities of the actor. There is space here to give only some sketchy ideas regarding this approach to personality. We will consider fear-of-failure and need-achievement motivation, needs for affiliation and approval, internal-external control orientation, and self-monitoring.

Fear-of-Failure and Need-Achievement Motivation

Fear of failure and need for achievement are conceived as social motives; that is, they are postulated as inner states of the person which account for recurrent behavior patterns across a number of situations. If we simply note the consistent pattern of behavior without reference to any internal states, we might reinterpret these "motives" as personality traits reflecting habitual impression management behaviors. For example, high fear-of-failure behavior typically follows either a very conservative pattern or a very risky one. One cannot fail if one tries to do only those things that are easy to do, but if one tries to do very risky things where almost everyone would fail, then failure is not very negative and success, if improbably achieved, would convey a very positive image. Very risky behavior, like the inhibiting pill in the self-handicapping research, provides an excuse for failure and some chance for a very positive outcome.

Achievement motivation represents a desire to acquire competence in specific areas of performance. In the present framework a person with high motivation for achievement is someone who devotes considerable time and resources to an assertive impression-management strategy directed toward establishing an identity for expertise, an important power resource.

Needs for Affiliation and Approval

People who have a high need for approval prove the point that motivation and skill are not always coincident with one another. These people tend to be conformists and are especially responsive to social reinforcers (Crowne & Marlowe, 1964). Yet, they tend to be nontalkative, not very friendly, and social isolates. While they desire approval from others, they are not assertive or skilled in getting it.

Strong affiliative motivation is manifested by assertive presentation of self as friendly and likable. People with high affiliative motivation do not like being alone and tend to be strongly influenced by others (McGhee & Teevan, 1967; Stang, 1972). Thus, they have both the need for approval from others, and the skill for gaining it.

Internal-External Control Orientation

We have noted that external attributions tend to function as defensive tactics, and that internal attributions serve as entitlements to responsibility and credit. As might be expected, people oriented toward internal control are assertive in describing themselves as competent and strong (Hersch & Scheibe, 1967), and they claim to have control over environmental contingencies (Lefcourt, 1972). People oriented toward external control appear to habitually use self-handicapping tactics. For example, they display ineffective problem-solving behavior and symptoms of debilitating test anxiety (Butterfield, 1964). Furthermore, as compared to internals, externals display more neurotic symptoms, are more apt to be schizophrenic, and they set unrealistic levels of aspiration in achievement situations (Hersch & Scheibe, 1967). Thus, internals behave in an assertive style, while the actions of externals are characteristically defensive.

Self-Monitoring

People who are concerned about appropriate self-presentations are sensitive to the expectations and evaluations of others, and are flexible in adapting to different audiences have been identified as scoring high on a scale of self-monitoring (Snyder, 1974, Snyder & Monson, 1965). Low self-monitors appear to be less reactive to the momentary expectations of others and devote more of their behavior to self-construction (McCown, 1978, Snyder & Swann, 1976, Snyder & Tanke, 1976). We suggest that low self-monitors are more concerned with establishing long-term identities, such as trustworthiness, emotional stability, and credibility, while high self-monitors are more concerned with the tactical maneuvers that will allow them immediate situational advantages. That is, low self-monitors tend to focus on strategic impression management, and high self-monitors are tactically oriented.

A systematic examination of social motives and personality dimensions in the context of social power, self-esteem, and impression management would be quite heuristic and would more clearly imbed such concepts into social interaction. Viewing these factors in terms of their interactional functions (viz, in terms of social power) offers a possibility of theoretical integration of important social-psychological concepts.

CONCLUSION

The present chapter has examined self-esteem and impression management in terms of their functions in interpersonal relations. Self-esteem can be viewed as a barometer (and generalized reinforcer) of potential power derived from evaluations of self against ideal identities. Impression management is concerned with public displays of identities, sincere or not, which may be designed to obtain immediate rewards or to establish identities that yield power potential. A taxonomy of impression-management behaviors provides suggestions for relationships with attribution, motivational, and personality processes and dispositions. An assertive style of behavior attempts to convince audiences that the actor's behavior is internally controlled, and a defensive style suggests that it is externally controlled. Tactical and strategic behaviors appear to provide a bridge between the short-term interactions studied by social psychologists and cross-situational consistency studied by personality theorists.

A number of hypotheses can be derived from the loose formulations provided herein. For example, a cost-benefit analysis would suggest that tactical self-presentations leading to lowered self-esteem would be undertaken only if the expected value of the immediate reward is believed to be greater than the expected value of preserving or enhancing one's reputation (and self-esteem). A reputation for a particular identity may have yielded a great many rewards, and the person might be quite protective of it, thus giving up many tangible available benefits or absorbing great punishment to save face.

The various associations between self theory, impression management, attributions, motivations, and personality suggest the possibility of developing an integrating theory. The present perspective suggests that such an integrating theory would be based on concepts of power and influence.

REFERENCES

Ackerman, B., & Schlenker, B. R. (1975, September). Self-presentation: Attributes of the actor and audience. Paper presented at the 83rd Annual Meeting of the American Psychological Association, Chicago.

Adler, A. (1913). Individual Psyhologische behandlung der neurosen. In D. Sarason (Ed.) *Jabreskurse fur arztliche fortbildung.* Munich: Lehnmann.

Arkin, R. M. (1981). Self-presentation styles. In J. T. Tedeschi (Ed.), *Impression management theory and social psychological research.* New York: Academic Press.

Bandura, A. (1977). *Social-learning theory.* Englewood Cliffs, NJ: Prentice-Hall.

Bandura, A., & Huston, A. C. (1961). Identifications as a process of incidental learning. *Journal of Abnormal and Social Psychology, 63,* 311–318.

Barnes, R., Ickes, W., & Kidd, R. (1979). Effects of the perceived intentionality and stability of another's dependency on helping behavior. *Personality and Social Psychology Bulletin, 5,* 367–372.

Baumeister, R. F. (1982). A self-presentational view of social phenomena. *Psychological Bulletin, 91,* 3–26.

Bem, D. J. (1972). Self-perception theory. In L. Berkowitz (Ed.), *Advances in experimental social psychology* (Vol. 6). New York: Academic Press.

Berglas, S., & Jones, E. E. (1978). Drug choice as a self-handicapping strategy in response to noncontingent success. *Journal of Personality and Social Psychology, 36,* 405–417.

Braginsky, D., Braginsky, B., & Ring, K. (1969). *Methods of madness: The mental hospital as a last resort.* New York: Holt, Rinehart and Winston.

Brenner, C. (1955). *An elementary textbook of psychoanalysis.* New York: Doubleday.

Buss, A. R. (1978). Causes and reasons in attribution theory: A conceptual critique. *Journal of Personality and Social Psychology, 36,* 1311–1321.

Butterfield, E. (1964). Locus of control, test anxiety, reactions to frustration, and achievement attitudes. *Journal of Personality, 32,* 355–370.

Cialdini, R. B., Darby, B. L., & Vincent, J. E. (1973). Transgression and altruism: A case for hedonism. *Journal of Experimental Social Psychology, 9,* 502–516.

Cohen, A. R. (1968). Some implications of self-esteem for social influence. In C. Gordon & K. J. Gergen (Eds.), *The self in social interaction.* New York: John Wiley.

Crowne, D., & Marlow, D. (1964). *The approval motive.* New York: Wiley.

D'Arcy, E. (1963). *Human acts: An essay in their moral evaluation.* Oxford, England: Clarendon Press.

DeKadt, E. J. (1965). Conflict and power in society. *International Social Science Journal, 17,* 454–471.

DeMonbreun, B., & Craighead, W. (1977). Distortion of perception and recall of positive and neutral feedback in depression. *Cognitive Therapy and Research, 1,* 311–329.

Epstein, S. (1973). The self-concept revisited: Or a theory of a theory. *American Psychologist, 28,* 404–416.

Fenigstein, A., Scheier, M., & Buss, A. (1975). Public and private self-consciousness: Assessment and theory. *Journal of Consulting and Clinical Psychology, 43,* 522–527.

Festinger, L. (1954). A theory of social comparison processes. *Human Relations, 7,* 117–140.

Fisher, R. (1969). *International conflict for beginners.* New York: Harper & Row.

Fontana, A., & Klein, E. (1968). Self-presentation and the schizophrenic "deficit." *Journal of Consulting and Clinical Psychology, 32,* 250–256.

Freedman, J. L. (1970). Transgression, compliance, and guilt. In J. R. Macaulay & L. Berkowitz (Eds.), *Altruism and Helping Behavior.* New York: Academic Press.

French, J. R., & Raven, B. (1959). The bases of social power. In D. Cartwright (Ed.), *Studies in Social Power.* Ann Arbor: University of Michigan Press.

Goffman, E. (1959). *The presentation of self in everyday life.* Garden City, NY: Doubleday.

Goffman, E. (1967). *Interaction ritual.* Garden City, NY: Doubleday Anchor.

Goffman, E. (1971). *Relations in public.* New York: Basic Books.

Haley, J. (1963). *Strategies of psychotherapy.* New York: Grune & Stratton.

Heider, F. (1958). *The psychology of interpersonal relations.* New York: Wiley.

Hersch, P., & Scheibe, K. (1967). Reliability and validity of internal-external control as a personality dimension. *Journal of Consulting Psychology, 31,* 609–613.

Hovland, C. T., Janis, I. L., & Kelley, H. H. (1953). *Communication and persuasion.* New Haven, CT: Yale University Press.

James, W. J. (1890). *The principles of psychology.* New York: Holt.

Jellison, J. M. (1981). Reconsidering the attitude concept: A behavioristic self-presentation formulation. In J. T. Tedeschi (Ed.), *Impression management theory and social psychological research.* New York: Academic Press.

Jones, E. E. (1964). *Ingratiation: A social psychological analysis.* New York: Appleton-Century-Crofts.

Jones, E. E., & Berglas, S. (1978). Control of attributions about the self through self-handicapping strategies: The appeal of alcohol and the role of underachievement. *Personality and Social Psychology Bulletin, 4,* 200–206.

Jones, E. E., & Davis, K. E. (1965). From acts to dispositions: The attribution process in person perception. In L. Berkowitz (Ed.), *Advances in experimental social psychology* (Vol. 2). New York: Academic Press.

Jones, E. E., & Pittman, T. S. (1982). Toward a general theory of strategic self-presentation. In J. Suls (Ed.), *Psychological perspectives on the self*. Hillsdale, NJ: Erlbaum.

Jones, E. E., & Wortman, C. (1973). *Ingratiation: An attributional approach*. Morristown, NJ: General Learning Press.

Kane, T. R., Suls, J. M., & Tedeschi, J. T. (1976). Humor as a social tool. In A. J. Chapman & H. C. Foot (Eds.), *Humor and laughter: Theory, research, and applications*. New York: Wiley.

Kraut, R., & Price, J. (1976). Machiavellianism in parents and their children. *Journal of Personality and Social Psychology, 33*, 782–786.

Kolditz, T., & Arkin, R. (1982). An impression management interpretation of the self-handicapping strategy. *Journal of Personality and Social Psychology, 43*, 492–502.

Lasswell, H. D., & Kaplan, A. (1950). *Power and society*. New Haven, CT: Yale University Press.

Leary, M. R., & Schlenker, B. R. (1981). The social psychology of shyness: A self-presentation model. In J. T. Tedeschi (Ed.), *Impression management theory and social psychological research*. New York: Academic Press.

Lefcourt, H. (1982). Recent developments in the study of locus of control. In B. A. Maher (Ed.), *Progress in experimental personality research* (Vol. 6). New York: Academic Press.

McCown, N. E. (1978). The effects of self-monitoring on self-presentation. Master's thesis, University of Florida.

Maslow, A. H. (1954). *Motivation and personality*. New York: Harper.

McGhee, P., & Teevan, R. (1967). Conformity behavior and need for affiliation. *Journal of Social Psychology, 72*, 117–121.

Mehrabian, A. (1970). The development and validation of measures of affiliative tendency and sensitivity to rejection. *Educational and Psychological Measurement, 30*, 417–428.

Mills, C. W. (1940). Situated actions and vocabularies of motive. *American Sociological Review, 5*, 904–915.

Modigliani, A. (1971). Embarrassment, face-work and eye-contact: Testing a theory of embarrassment. *Journal of Personality and Social Psychology, 17*, 15–24.

Osgood, C. E. (1964). Semantic differential technique in the comparative study of cultures. *American Psychologist. 66*, 171–200.

Ossorio, P. G., & Davis, K. E. (1968). The self, intentionality, and reactions to evaluations of the self. In C. Gordon & K. J. Gergen (Eds.), *The self in social interaction*. New York: Wiley.

Parsons, T. (1967). *Sociological theory and modern society*. New York: Free Press.

Peters, R. S. (1958). *The concept of motivation*. London: Routledge and Kegan Paul.

Powell, F. A., & Miller, G. R. (1967). Social approval and disapproval cues in anxiety arousing communications. *Speech Monographs, 34*, 152–159.

Riordan, C. A., Marlin, N. A., & Kellogg, R. T. (1983). The effectiveness of accounts following transgression. *Social Psychology Quarterly, 46*, 213–219.

Rosenberg, M. (1968). Psychological selectivity in self-esteem formation. In C. Gordon & K. J. Gergen (Eds.), *The self in social interaction*. New York: Wiley.

Scheff, T. J. (1974). The labeling theory of mental illness. *American Sociological Review, 39*, 444–452.

Schlenker, B. R. (1980). *Impression management: The self-concept, social identity, and interpersonal relations*. Belmont, CA: Brooks/Cole.

Schlenker, B. R. (1984). Identities, identifications, and relationships. In V. Derlega (Ed.), *Communication, intimacy and close relationships.* New York: Academic Press.

Schlenker, B. R., & Darby, B. W. (1981). The use of apologies in social predicaments. *Social Psychology Quarterly, 44,* 271–278.

Schneider, D. J. (1981). Tactical self-presentations: Toward a broader conception. In J. T. Tedeschi (Ed.), *Impression management theory and social psychological research.* New York: Academic Press.

Schutz, A. (1967). *The phenomenology of the social world.* Evanston, Ill.: Northwestern University Press.

Schwartz, G., Kane, T., Joseph, J., & Tedeschi, J. T. (1978). The effects of remorse on reactions to a harm-doer. *British Journal of Social and Clinical Psychology, 17,* 293–297.

Scott, M. R., & Lyman, S. M. (1968). Accounts. *American Sociological Review, 33,* 46–62.

Sigall, H., & Landy, D. (1973). Radiating beauty: The effects of having an attractive partner on person perception. *Journal of Personality and Social Psychology, 28,* 218–224.

Simon, H. A. (1957). *Models of man: Social and rational.* New York: Wiley.

Smith, T. W., Snyder, C. R., & Handelsman, M. M. (1982). On the self-serving function of an academic wooden leg: Test anxiety as a self-handicapping strategy. *Journal of Personality and Social Psychology: 42,* 314–321.

Smith, T. W., Snyder, C. R., & Perkins, S. (1983). On the self-serving function of hypochondria: Physical symptoms as self-handicapping strategies. *Journal of Personality and Social Psychology, 44,* 787–797.

Snyder, C., & Smith, T. (1981). Symptoms as self-handicapping strategies: The virtues of old wine in a new bottle. In G. Weary & H. L. Mirels (Eds.), *Integrations of clinical and social psychology,* New York: Oxford University Press.

Snyder, M., & Monson, T. C. (1975). Persons, situations, and the control of social behavior. *Journal of Personality and Social Psychology, 32,* 637–644.

Snyder, M., & Swann, W. (1976). When actions reflect attitudes: The politics of impression management. *Journal of Personality and Social Psychology, 34,* 1034–1042.

Snyder, M., & Tanke, E. D. (1976). Behavior and attitude: Some people are more consistent than others. *Journal of Personality, 44,* 510–517.

Stang, D. (1972). Conformity, ability, and self-esteem. *Representative Research in Social Psychology, 3,* 97–103.

Stokes, R., & Hewitt, J. P. (1976). Aligning actions. *American Sociological Review, 41,* 838–849.

Stryker, S. (1972). Symbolic interaction theory: A review and some suggestions for comparative family research. *Journal of Comparative Family Studies, 3,* 17–32.

Tedeschi, J. T. (1974a). Attributions, liking, and power. In T. Huston (Ed.), *Foundations of interpersonal attraction.* New York: Academic Press.

Tedeschi, J. T. (Ed.). (1974b). *Perspectives on social power.* Chicago: Aldine.

Tedeschi, J. T. (1983). Social influence theory and aggression. In R. Geen & E. Donnerstein (Eds.), *Aggression: Theoretical and empirical reviews.* New York: Academic Press.

Tedeschi, J. T., Bonoma, T. V., & Schlenker, B. R. (1972). Influence, decision, and compliance. In J. T. Tedeschi (Ed.), *The social influence process.* Chicago: Aldine.

Tedeschi, J. T., & Lindskold, S. (1976). *Social psychology: Interdependence, interaction, and influence.* New York: Wiley.

Tedeschi, J. T., & Melburg, V. (1984). Impression management and influence in the organization. In S. B. Bacharach & E. J. Lawler (Eds.), *Perspectives in organizational psychology: Theory and research.* Greenwich, Conn.: JAI Press, Inc.

Tedeschi, J. T., & Riess, M. (1981). Identities, the phenomenal self, and laboratory research. In J. T. Tedeschi (Ed.) *Impression management theory and social psychological research.* New York: Academic Press.

Tedeschi, J. T., & Riordan, C. (1981). Impression management and the transgression-prosocial behavior relationship. In J. T. Tedeschi (Ed.), *Impression management theory and social psychological research.* New York: Academic Press.

Tedeschi, J. T., Riordan, C. A., Gaes, G. G., & Kane, T. (1983). Verbal accounts and attributions of social motives. *Journal of Research in Personality, 17,* 218–225.

Tedeschi, J. T., & Rosenfeld, P. (1981). Impression management theory and the forced compliance situation. In J. T. Tedeschi (Ed.), *Impression management theory and social psychological research.* New York: Academic Press.

Tedeschi, J. T., Schlenker, B. R., & Bonoma, T. V. (1971). Cognitive dissonance: Private ratiocination or public spectacle? *American Psychologist, 26,* 685–695.

Tedeschi, J. T., Schlenker, B. R., & Bonoma, T. V. (1973). *Conflict, power, and games.* Chicago: Aldine.

Weary Bradley, G. (1978). Self-serving biases in the attribution process: A re-examination of the fact or fiction question. *Journal of Personality and Social Psychology, 36,* 56–71.

Weary, G., & Arkin, R. M. (1982). Attributional self-presentation. In J. H. Harvey, W. J. Ickes & R. F. Kidd (Eds.), *New directions in attribution research* (Vol. 3). New York: Erlbaum.

Weiss, W. (1957). Opinion congruence with a negative source of one issue as factor influencing aggreement on another issue. *Journal of Abnormal and Social Psychology, 54,* 180–186.

Wolfgang, M. E., & Ferracuti, F. (1967). *The subculture of violence.* London: Tavistock.

Wood, R. E., & Mitchell, T. R. (1981). Manager behavior in a social context: The impact of impression management on attributions and disciplinary actions. *Organizational Behavior and Human Performance, 28,* 356–378.

Zillman, D., & Cantar, J. (1976). Effect of timing of information about mitigating circumstances on emotional responses to provocation and retaliatory behavior. *Journal of Experimental Social Psychology, 12,* 38–55.

Zuckerman, M. (1979). Attribution of success and failure revisited, or: The motivational bias is alive and well in attribution theory. *Journal of Personality, 47,* 245–287.

CHAPTER 12

DECEIVING AND DETECTING DECEIT

Bella M. DePaulo
Julie I. Stone
G. Daniel Lassiter
University of Virginia

When a person deliberately tries to foster in others a belief or understanding which he or she considers to be untrue, that person is engaging in deception (Krauss, 1981). There are those who would defend deceit. Anatole France, for example (cited in Cabot, 1938), warned that "without falsehood, humanity would perish of despair and ennui" (p. 180). Even more enthusiastically, Oscar Wilde declared, "the aim of the liar is simply to charm, to delight, to give pleasure. He is the very basis of civilized society. . . ." (1891/1969, p. 305). Still, these few voices need to shout loudly to be heard over the vociferous condemnation of falsehood that has dominated discussions of deception for centuries. "Falsehood," Aristotle insisted, "is in itself base and reprehensible, and truth noble and praiseworthy" (1934, p. 241). A contemporary philosopher, Sissela Bok, agrees; she describes deceit and violence in the same breath as "two forms of deliberate assault on human beings" (1978, p. 19). Typically, people who are perceived as deceptive are also perceived as lacking in trustworthiness, credibility, and dignity. (See, for example, Bok, 1978; Kant, 1964.) Because of this "moral conspiracy against lying" (Ludwig, 1965, p. vii), people may be reluctant to tell outright lies.

It is likely that, whenever possible, people hedge, evade, exaggerate the truth, or tell only part of the truth rather than stating something that is clearly and completely dishonest. These strategies presumably make it easier for people, if challenged, to convince others (and maybe even themselves) that they really are not guilty of deceit (cf. Turner, Edgley, & Olmstead, 1975). The inherently ambiguous nature of many lies and truths—particularly those con-

---

*Preparation of this chapter was supported in part by a grant from the National Academy of Education to the first author.

cerning attitudes, feelings, and other internal states, rather than more objective facts—is also helpful to the deceiver in much the same way. That is, since there is no single description of any given attitude or affect that is the one and only accurate one, different aspects of a feeling state can be emphasized, and different interpretations can be defended as truthful. (See Schlenker, this volume.) Even after a deceptive statement has been made, initial attitudes can be reinterpreted retrospectively to be less discrepant with the stated attitudes than they might otherwise appear. (See Schlenker, 1982, for a review.)

The would-be deceiver's best strategy, though, is never to be suspected at all. Of all the impressions of themselves that people try to convey in their interpersonal interactions (e.g., impression of kindness, altruism, intelligence, or wit), perhaps the most important is that of honesty and truthfulness. In fact, in a study in which subjects rated the desirability of 555 personality traits, four of the six traits judged to be most likable were those of truthfulness (Anderson, 1968).

One of the many manifestations of honesty in interpersonal interactions is in the claims that people make about themselves and their performances. The value of truthfulness in these kinds of self-presentations has been empirically documented: People who are accurate and honest in the claims that they make are liked more and evaluated more favorably by others along a variety of dimensions than are those who are either unjustifiably boastful or overly modest (Schlenker & Leary, 1982a). Communicators *must* effectively establish their truthfulness to their target persons, for if they cannot do so, then all of their attempts to convey more specific impressions and to exert social influence are potentially imperiled. Without credibility, would-be persuaders may find that their arguments are ineffective, intimidators may find that their threats have been sapped of their sting, and ingratiators may discover that they have been compromised in their attempts to elicit liking (cf. Jones & Pittman, 1982).

To the targets of impression-management attempts, issues of sincerity are equally critical. Such targets ponder innumerable questions about the specific content of the messages being conveyed (e.g., What attitude is the communicator trying to advocate? What emotion is he or she trying to convey?). While considering each of these specific questions, perceivers must come to terms with one general overriding question—the question of whether to *believe* the content of the conveyed message, whatever that content may be. If the answer to this question is negative—that is, if the perceiver is suspicious of the communicator's sincerity—then another question immediately arises: If the overt content of the message is not to be believed, then what *should* be believed? What is the communicator's "true" attitude or feeling or disposition? What are the facts?

Rarely can the truth be confidently discerned merely by taking the opposite of what the liar has said. For, as Montaigne has lamented, often "the reverse of truth has a hundred thousand faces" (1962, p. 33). Suppose, for example, that a communicator expresses positive sentiments about a target person's friend. The target person, however, doubts the communicator's sincerity. If the expressed positive sentiments are not the truth, what is? Perhaps the communicator's sentiments are actually quite negative; or maybe they are in fact positive, but not quite as positive as those overtly expressed; or maybe they are highly ambivalent; or perhaps they are indifferent. How is the perceiver to tell?

Given ample time and sufficient opportunities, potential targets of deceit can use a variety of strategies in their attempts to uncover the truth. Persons who suspect their spouse of infidelity, for example, might compare notes with others (e.g., experienced or sympathetic friends), look for relevant evidence (e.g., whether the spouse's car is parked in a suspicious place at a suspicious time), and remain alert for inconsistencies over time in the spouse's stories. Sometimes, however, time is not ample and the only opportunity to detect the deceit is the present one. In such instances, the lie-detector's only source of information may be the verbal and nonverbal cues of the suspected deceiver. In this chapter, we examine the lie detector's skills and strategies used in detecting deceit (and the deceiver's skills and strategies used in perpetrating deceit) in these very challenging situations.

Research and theory on the verbal and nonverbal communication of deception have examined a variety of questions. For example: How successful are perceivers at recognizing when deception is or is not occurring, and at discerning the feelings or facts that the deceiver is trying to hide? Are certain sources or "channels" of communication—such as words or facial expressions or tone of voice cues—more revealing than others? Are there specific behaviors, such as gaze aversion or fidgeting, that tip off the fact that deception is occurring? Are there other behaviors that convey to target persons an impression of sincerity? Are behaviors that are interpreted as indicative of sincerity the same behaviors that really do occur more frequently when people are telling the truth than when they are lying? What kinds of strategies and experiences might contribute to success at deceiving and detecting deceit? How do children learn to tell lies and detect them? And, what are the personal and interpersonal consequences of skill at deceiving and detecting deceit—for both children and adults? These issues and others will be addressed in this chapter.

ACCURACY AT DETECTING DECEPTION AND READING LEAKED CUES

To illustrate the task of the perceiver attempting to make sense of various truthful and deceptive communications, we will return to the example of the person who is listening to a communicator (or "sender") describe another person in glowing terms. How is the perceiver to interpret this very positive description? Ordinarily, people assume truthfulness, and the overt content of messages is taken at face value. Those who speak kindly of another person are assumed to like that person, those who allude to an extroverted lifestyle are assumed to be extroverted, and those who say that they are proabortion are assumed to mean it. That speakers try to convey messages that are truthful, clear, unambiguous, and relevant is a fundamental assumption of social discourse (Grice, 1975).

There are times, though, when perceivers have reason to be skeptical about the overt content of a communication. Perhaps the speaker has said something which is implausible, or inconsistent with known facts. Or perhaps the speaker is in a situation in which misrepresentation is thought to be commonplace (e.g., a job interview). Will the perceiver then interpret the speaker's remarks differently?

Goffman (1959), writing from a dramaturgical perspective, suggests that even when people do harbor suspicions, they often keep those suspicions to themselves. To facilitate the smooth flow of social interaction, people do not challenge each others' communications or their assumed identities. Instead, under ordinary circumstances, they play along with the "lines" that others enact. (See also Schlenker, 1980.)

An attributional analysis suggests that perceivers should discount the overt content of communications when those communications were a product of external demands. For example, if subjects in an experiment were subtly pressured into writing an essay in support of a particular position, readers of the essay should not assume that the advocated position is the writer's true position on the issue. Research has demonstrated that perceivers do adjust their attributions in a way that suggests that they have taken situational constraints into consideration—but not sufficiently. Generally, perceivers assume that people's publicly expressed attitudes are more correspondent with their privately held beliefs than they really are (Jones, 1979; Ross, 1977). The implication for lie detection is that perceivers may still place some faith in the content of a sender's messages, even when they suspect that the sender is lying.

Perceivers, then, may conclude that the overt content of a communication should be believed, even when they are motivated to see through to the sender's "true" feelings or attitudes. In some situations, however, perceivers are not so highly motivated to get to the truth. Instead, they would much prefer to believe exactly what the sender conveys. If, for example, the person described kindly by the sender were the perceiver's close friend, then the perceiver might want very much to believe that the sender's effusiveness was genuine (cf. Gergen, 1965; Jones, Stires, Shaver, & Harris, 1968; Jones & Wortman, 1973).

Taken together, these various theoretical positions suggest that perceivers will generally believe in other peoples' truthfulness and accept the content of their communications at face value. When deception is in fact occurring, perceivers may infer that the senders' actual position is not quite as extreme as their expressed position, but rarely will they conclude that the true position is radically different from the one expressed.

Numerous paradigms have been used to study the communication of deceptive and truthful messages. For example, in some of Ekman's research, nurses attempt to convince an interviewer that the film they just saw (either pleasant or grotesque) was actually quite pleasant (e.g., Ekman & Friesen, 1974; Ekman, Friesen, O'Sullivan, & Scherer, 1980; Ekman, Friesen, & Scherer, 1976). Feldman has used a paradigm in which teachers give positive feedback to students who have performed well or poorly (e.g., Feldman, 1976; Feldman,

Devin-Sheehan, & Allen, 1978). In other studies, people are asked to describe truthfully someone they really do like and someone they really do dislike, and, in a parallel set of deceptive descriptions, they pretend to like the disliked person and they also pretend to dislike the liked person (e.g., DePaulo, Lassiter & Stone, 1982; DePaulo & Rosenthal, 1979b; DePaulo, Rosenthal, Green & Rosenkrantz, 1982; DePaulo, Rosenthal, Rosenkrantz & Green, 1982). In still other research, people dissemble about their personalities; for example, people who really are either introverts or extraverts may try to portray themselves as either extraverts or introverts (e.g., Lippa, 1976; Toris & DePaulo, in press). The lie detectors, for their part, are often asked to judge both the deceptiveness of the speakers, and the speakers' underlying affects or dispositions (e.g., How much does the speaker *really* like the person described? Is the speaker really an extravert or an introvert?).

One compelling conclusion that emerges from all of these studies is that perceivers do indeed tend to give senders the benefit of the doubt. First, they tend to believe whatever affect or disposition the sender is claiming, even when they know that the senders may be deceiving. Thus, perceivers believe that senders claiming to like someone really do like that person, and they also perceive as truly extraverted senders who are only pretending to be extraverts. Second, when making judgments of truthfulness and deception, perceivers report that most of the messages are truthful, even when lies and truths in fact occur equally often. (For reviews, see DePaulo, Zuckerman & Rosenthal, 1980c; Zuckerman, DePaulo & Rosenthal, 1981.)

Similar findings have been reported in other kinds of studies, too. For example, in a study of perceivers' reactions to modest, boastful, and accurate claims about performances, Schlenker and Leary (1982a) found that when perceivers had no other information about the performances, they tended to view all claims as sincere. In the dating domain, there is evidence to suggest that people whose invitations are rejected tend to believe the reasons given for the rejection more often than they should (Folkes, 1982). Since the fabricated reasons that rejected persons believe tend to be more positive than the true (but unstated) reasons for rejection, it appears that rejected suitors, like targets of ingratiation, are often "trapped by their own vanity" (Jones & Pittman, 1982, p. 258).

The second major conclusion is that perceivers—while giving senders the benefit of the doubt—still show evidence of successfully discriminating truths from lies. Thus, while perceivers do tend to judge most communications as truthful, they quite consistently perceive deceptive messages as somewhat less truthful than truthful messages. This differentiation between truth and deceit is usually referred to as *deception* accuracy (cf. Ekman & Friesen, 1969). Across dozens of studies, deception accuracy usually exceeds chance, although rarely by an impressive margin (DePaulo, Zuckerman & Rosenthal, 1980b, 1980c; Knapp & Comadena, 1979; Kraut, 1980). For example, in studies in which lies and truths occur equally often and a chance level of accuracy would be 50 percent, overall accuracy usually ranges from 45 to 60 percent (Kraut, 1980).

Perceivers can also discriminate truths from lies by their judgments of the content of senders' underlying feelings or attitudes. For example, when listening to senders who are pretending to like someone, perceivers tend to believe that the senders really do like the person; however, they also seem to realize that the intensity of the senders' liking is somewhat less than that expressed by senders who are truthfully describing people they really do like (e.g., DePaulo, Jordan, Irvine & Laser, 1982; Zuckerman et al., 1981; see also Jones & Harris, 1967).

INFORMATIVENESS OF VERBAL AND NONVERBAL CUES IN THE COMMUNICATION OF DECEPTION

The degree to which perceivers are able to discriminate truth from deception may depend importantly on the kinds of cues that are available to them. One popular assumption has been that nonverbal cues—more so than verbal cues—will "leak" the information that a person is trying to hide. Freud may have been suggesting that when he said, "He who has eyes to see and ears to hear may convince himself that no mortal can keep a secret. If his lips are silent, he chatters with his finger-tips; betrayal oozes out of him at every pore (1959, p. 94)." It was Ekman and Friesen, however (Ekman, 1981; Ekman & Friesen, 1969), who first provided a theoretical rationale for predicting that certain types of cues might be more revealing than others.

Two of the key predictor variables in Ekman and Friesen's formulations are automaticity and controllability. Ekman describes the automaticity principle in the following way:

> When emotion is aroused certain changes occur in face, body, and voice which can be considered *automatic,* and in this way different from the changes in the content of speech. By automatic I mean that the changes occur quickly, without deliberate choice, and at least initially go unnoticed by the person showing them. . . . When fear is aroused, for example, there is no pressure which impels a set of words to pop out of the mouth, tantamount to the backwards jerk of the torso, or a facial muscular contraction (1981, p. 271–272).

When people try to control their nonverbal behaviors in emotionally involving deceptive situations, then, they should have an especially hard time because they have to override this direct and automatic link between the emotion and the nonverbal behavior. Words are not that problematic, because there is no such automatic process that needs to be kept in check.

As Ekman (1981) has noted, there are many ways in which emotions might be involved in deceptive situations. For example, deceivers might feel emotional about the fact that they are trying to hide something. Usually that emotion is guilt. Deceivers may also feel eager to succeed in their deceit, or apprehensive about the possibility of not succeeding. Some deceivers may also experience "duping delight"—a kind of gleeful relishing of the experience of fooling other people. (See also Stebbins, 1975.) In these kinds of situations, in which some kind of emotion or motivation is involved, nonverbal cues should become especially revealing of deceit.

The verbal channel can be more effectively controlled than the various nonverbal channels in part because it is a channel that does not automatically change with changes in motivation or emotion. But the absence of automaticity is not the only factor that accounts for the controllability of verbal behavior. The verbal channel is also characterized by a greater "sending capacity" than the various nonverbal channels—that is, it can convey a large number of different kinds of messages, and it can convey most of them quite precisely. Further, it is a channel that senders have a great deal of practice attempting to control. Because words are very salient to others—i.e., because other people attend to senders' words, react to them, and hold senders accountable for them—the verbal channel may be monitored more routinely and more effectively than are the nonverbal channels.

Still another reason why it should be easier to control verbal behavior than nonverbal behavior is because people seem to be more consciously aware of verbal behavior. That is, senders are probably more aware of the particular words they are saying than of what their facial expressions look like to others or what their voice tones sound like. This greater awareness of their verbal behavior should help them to control that behavior more effectively.

Of the several varieties of nonverbal cues, some are more likely to be controlled than others. Theoretically, the face should be one of the most readily controlled sources of nonverbal information. For a variety of reasons, people should be motivated to monitor their facial expressions and quite skilled at doing so. The face is a highly visible channel, it can send many different kinds of messages and it can send them quite rapidly, and it is a channel that other people attend to, react to, and hold senders accountable for. The body fares less well than the face along all of these dimensions.

Like the face, the voice can send a variety of different messages, it is highly salient, and it is a channel that other persons comment on and react to. Therefore, it, too, should be a controllable channel. In fact, however, for reasons that are not entirely clear, tone of voice cues are much more difficult for senders to control than either words or facial expressions (Ekman, 1981; Zuckerman, Larrance, Spiegel & Klorman, 1981). Thus, in the communication of deception, tone of voice cues function more as body cues do than as facial cues or words do. In summary, senders who are trying to deceive others should be most successful in so doing when using words (since verbal behavior is readily controlled and is not automatically triggered by emotion), next most successful when using facial expressions, and least successful when using body movements and tone of voice cues.

Data relevant to these predictions come from studies in which judges attempted to detect deception from single channels—only the face, only the body, only tone of voice cues,[1] or only words, or from certain channel

---

[1]Tone of voice cues can be presented to judges apart from words by means of procedures such as content-filtering, in which certain frequencies are removed from the recorded voice (Starkweather, 1956). This procedure renders the words unintelligible, but most vocal characteristics remain (e.g., tempo, pacing, volume).

combinations—e.g., face plus body, or words plus tone. The results of more than thirty such studies are summarized in Table 12-1. The entries in the table are mean detectability scores. Deception has been successfully detected when lies are rated as more deceptive than truths. Higher numbers indicate that the judges were more successful at detecting deception (and, conversely, that the deceivers were less successful at fooling others). Since different studies used different scales (e.g., some used seven-point scales, others used nine-point scales), the entries in the table are standardized difference scores (expressed in standard deviation units) rather than raw difference scores. An entry of zero would indicate that the judges could not discriminate truth from deception at all—i.e., the deceptiveness rating that they assigned to the lies was exactly the same as the deceptiveness rating that they assigned to the truthful messages.

The detectability score earned by judges who were trying to detect deception from facial cues alone was nearly zero. In contrast, the detectability score earned by judges who had full audiovisual access to the senders—i.e., those who could observe senders' words, tone of voice cues, and body cues, as well as their face cues—was nearly a fully standard deviation higher. The increment in success at detecting deception that occurs when words, tone of voice cues, and body cues are added to face cues is equivalent to improving nearly 15 IQ points on an IQ test that has a mean of 100 and a standard deviation of 15.

The results in Table 12-1 are consistent with Ekman and Friesen's suggestion that senders generally are successful at controlling their facial expressions so as to fool perceivers. The only condition in which judges did not do better than chance at detecting deceit was the one in which they had access only to senders' facial expressions. Further, when all of the conditions in which facial cues were available to judges (alone or in combination with other cues) are compared to

TABLE 12-1
ACCURACY OF DETECTING DECEPTION

	Visual cues				
	Face		No face		
Auditory cues	Body	No body	Body	No body	Means
Speech (words plus tone of voice cues)	1.00(21)	.99(9)	1.49(3)	1.09(12)	1.14
No Speech	.35(6)	.05(7)	.43(4)	.00[a]	.21
Means	.68	.52	.96	.54	.68
		.60		.75	

Transcript Only: .70(6)
Tone Only: .20(4)

Note: All means are in standard deviation units (Cohen, 1977). The numbers in parentheses indicate the number of studies upon which the mean was based. Except for the face-only score (and the score in the empty cell), all accuracy scores are significantly greater than chance.
[a]Theoretical accuracy.
Source: Zuckerman, DePaulo, & Rosenthal, 1981.

the conditions in which facial cues were not available, it is apparent that judges actually did somewhat *worse* at detecting deception when facial cues were available ($M = .60$) than when they were not ($M = .75$). Facial cues, then, are indeed faking cues. In comparison, both body cues and tone of voice cues were more revealing of deception than facial cues.

Theoretically, judges should have had the most trouble detecting deception from senders' verbal cues. In direct contrast to this prediction, however, the results show that the verbal cues were highly informative and revealing. This is apparent both from the significant degree of deception accuracy that occurred in the words-only (transcript) condition, and from the striking jump in accuracy that occurs when words are added to tone of voice cues (compare the tone-only mean to the speech mean).

Why is it that the highly salient verbal channel, for which senders are held highly accountable, and which is characterized by such an impressive sending capacity, was not more successfully controlled by the senders? Why is it that judges could tell so easily, on the basis of a transcript alone, that the deceptive messages were in fact more deceptive than the truthful messages? One possibility is that the tremendous sending capacity of the verbal channel can in some ways be a liability to senders who are trying to convey a particular impression. The sending capacity of the verbal channel is attributable to the awesome number of words available to senders, with their many different shades of meaning, and the infinite number of ways that those words can be put together to convey meanings. Although this richness offers senders much potential for controlling the precise meanings that are conveyed, it also brings with it greater risk of *not* conveying the exact meaning that was intended. For example, when a sender is trying to feign liking for a disliked other, the perceiver will probably realize immmediately that liking is the attitude that the sender wants to be conveyed. However, something about the specific words or verbal devices that are chosen to simulate liking might alert the perceiver to the possibility that the expressions of liking are not genuine. In order to control successfully the many levels of meaning that can potentially be conveyed verbally (especially when deception is attempted), senders may need to devote more than routine amounts of attention and effort to the communication task. To succeed at picking and choosing just the right words, senders may need to be especially motivated to get away with their lies. In the next section, two studies are described which examined the effects of increases in motivation on verbal and nonverbal deceptive success.

RAISING THE STAKES: EFFECTS OF MOTIVATION ON DECEPTIVE SUCCESS

Discussions of deception often inspire scenarios brimming with excitement, intrigue, anxiety, or even danger. The liars who leap most readily to mind include the seamy defendants in Perry Mason type of murder trials, high-level governmental officials attempting to deceive whole nations full of human lie detectors, eerily charming psychopaths, and spouses faced by stinging accusations of infidelity. Although the lies that are perpetrated in these contexts are indeed exciting, arousing, and involving, these are not the deceptions of everyday life (cf. DePaulo, Zuckerman, & Rosenthal, 1980a). The garden variety of lies is much more likely to include such humdrum deceptions as telling dear Aunt Esther that her unsightly hairstyle is just lovely, feigning sincere interest in a soporific discourse, and agreeing amicably to a burdensome request for help. In fact, unlike murder suspects, everyday deceivers sometimes would not be terribly upset if they were caught in their lies. Relatively low levels of motivation to succeed might characterize the lies of embellishment that are told in order to make a tedious story more interesting, the dissimulations of disagreement forwarded for the sake of argument, the fanciful tales told in jest, the succinct lies proffered in place of the full-blown accounts that may not seem worth the time they would take to tell, the weak excuses offered by departing guests when a social event is already winding down, and the many courtesy lies that are more remarkable when they are not told than when they are (e.g., "I'm fine, thank you.").

When senders are not very highly motivated to lie successfully, should their lies be easier or harder to detect than when they are highly motivated to succeed? Earlier we argued that senders may need to be highly motivated to lie successfully in order to control effectively all of the many possible revealing nuances of their verbal communications. In the verbal channel, then, deceptive success might increase as motivation increases.

For nonverbal behaviors, however, just the opposite prediction might be made. When motivation to lie successfully is low, emotional involvement (e.g., detection apprehension) may also be low. In such situations in which emotional reactions do not automatically occur, successful control of nonverbal behaviors should be easier to achieve (Ekman, 1981). As motivation increases, however, it should become harder for senders successfully to squelch and mask the behavioral concomitants of such motivation that may appear in the face, body, and tone of voice. With increases in motivation, then, deception should become more detectable from channels that include nonverbal cues.

To clarify the role of verbal and nonverbal cues in different types of deceptive situations, we conducted a pair of studies in which we systematically manipulated, in conceptually distinct ways, senders' motivation to lie successfully. We predicted that highly motivated senders would try harder to control their self-presentations, but this extra effort would result in greater success at deceiving only in the verbal channel. Thus, the lies of the highly motivated liars (compared to those of the less highly motivated liars) should be more readily detected whenever judges had access to any nonverbal cues, but less readily detected whenever judges had access only to the senders' words.

In the first study (DePaulo, Lanier & Davis, 1983), senders were videotaped while they lied and told the truth in front of a panel of six of their peers. For senders in the *high motivation* condition, the study was described as one in which they would be "on trial" in front of a panel of their peers who would be carefully scrutinizing their behavior and evaluating their truthfulness. They were reminded of how important the ability to lie successfully can sometimes be, and they were told that psychological research had convincingly demonstrated that deceptive abilities are linked to professional success. Finally, it was added that videotapes and audiotapes of their performance would be made, and replayed for new groups of judges, so that their behavior could be examined even more carefully in the future.

In the *low motivation* condition, the study was described as a game in which some of the participants would lie and tell the truth while the others would try to guess when the senders were lying and when they were telling the truth. It was added that "in real life, too, lying is often like a little game." Examples of innocuous lies were given. It was explained that videotapes would be made just in case they might be of use at some later date, but that at the present, the expectation was that they would not be used again.

Judges were then recruited to rate (on a seven-point scale) the deceptiveness of each response on the basis of one of four different sources of information: (1) *verbal*—judges rated a verbatim, typed transcript of the senders' messages, (2) *audio*—judges heard an audiotape of the messages (verbal plus vocal cues), with no accompanying visual cues, (3) *visual*—judges saw only the head and chest of the senders, with no accompanying verbal or vocal cues, and (4) *audiovisual*—judges saw the visual cues and heard the accompanying sound track.

Table 12-2 shows that when the senders were not highly motivated to lie successfully, their lies were most easily detected by the judges in the three conditions in which verbal cues were available. Complacent deceivers, then, are betrayed by their own words. However, when senders are highly motivated to lie successfully, judges cannot make any reliable discriminations at all between truth and deception if all they have access to is the senders' words (i.e., only a transcript). Judges of highly motivated senders are successful, though, in both conditions in which they have access to the senders' tone of voice cues (audio and audiovisual).

TABLE 12-2
DETECTABILITY OF DECEPTION IN VERBAL AND NONVERBAL CHANNELS UNDER CONDITIONS OF LOW AND HIGH MOTIVATION TO LIE SUCCESSFULLY

	Channel			
Motivation	Verbal	Audio	Visual	Audiovisual
High	-.02	.38	.03	.48
Low	.22	.32	-.23	.19
High minus Low	-.24	.06	.26	.29

Note: Scores were computed by subtracting deceptiveness ratings of the truthful responses from the deceptiveness ratings of the deceptive responses. Thus, higher numbers indicate that the lies were more readily detected by the judges.

The difference in detectability between the highly motivated senders and less highly motivated senders is summarized in the bottom row of the table. (Positive numbers indicate that the lies of the highly motivated liars were more easily detected). As predicted, these results show that the highly motivated senders were especially successful at concealing their lies with their words; compared to the less highly motivated senders, they "talked a good game." However, these senders who were highly motivated not to get caught actually did get caught more often than less highly motivated senders whenever judges had access to any of their nonverbal cues. It seems, then, that in deceptive contexts in which senders' nonverbal cues are showing, the harder senders try to get away with their lies, the less successful they will be.

In the study just described, we badgered deceivers into trying hard to succeed in a context which had many of the trappings of a trial by jury. While jury settings are important contexts for the study of deceit, there are other settings that are more important for more of the people more of the time. These are the everyday, interpersonal contexts in which people might lie to make a good impression, to ingratiate themselves, or to keep the social machinery running smoothly. The currency in these contexts is not number of years in prison, but feelings of liking and trusting.

In the second study that we conducted (DePaulo, Stone & Lassiter, in press), we told the senders explicitly that their task was to make a good impression on the other person in the study. They were told that at all times, they should come across as a very sincere and very likeable person. We explained that we were studying their ability to present themselves favorably under several very challenging conditions. For example, they would not be able to see their partner, and thus they would receive no immediate feedback on the success of their self-presentational attempts. Also, they would be asked to lie about some of their opinions, and also to endorse certain opinions that were different from the other person's.

Subjects were given a photograph of their partner, who purportedly was watching and listening from behind a one-way mirror. (In fact, however, only the experimenter was behind the mirror, videotaping their performances.) The photograph depicted either a male or a female who was either attractive or unattractive. Subjects were also given their partner's answers to four attitude items. The answers were manipulated so that the partner appeared to agree with the subject on two of the items, and to disagree on the other two. The subjects' task was to express genuine agreement on one issue and genuine disagreement on another. Those were the truthful communications. They were also instructed to pretend to agree with their partner on another issue, even though they really disagreed—those were the ingratiating lies—and to pretend to disagree on the other.

Inherent in this design, we thought, were four interpersonal motivators. First, we thought that senders who had a partner of the opposite sex would be more highly motivated to lie successfully than senders who had a partner of the same sex. (See, for example, Lefebvre, cited in Jones & Wortman, 1973, for evidence in support of this assumption.) Second, we thought that senders who had attractive partners would be more highly motivated than senders who had unattractive partners (cf. Schlenker & Leary, 1982b). Third, we believed that women—who tend to score higher than men on a scale measuring the need for social approval (Crowne & Marlowe, 1964)—might be more highly motivated to lie successfully than males. And finally, we thought that senders would be more highly motivated to get away with their lies when they were pretending to agree with their partners (compared to when they were pretending to disagree), since lies of agreement are more often used in the service of ingratiation. As in the first study, judges rated the sincerity of the responses based on verbal, audio, visual, or audiovisual cues.

Table 12-3a shows that lies told to persons of the same sex as the deceiver were barely detectable in any condition. However, when senders were talking to persons of the opposite sex (and presumably, were more highly motivated to lie successfully), their efforts were actually less successful when judges had access to any of their nonverbal cues. The difference between senders addressing same-sex others and senders addressing opposite-sex others, then, paralleled the difference between the low- and high-motivation conditions in the first study: When senders are highly motivated, it is easier for judges (who have access to their nonverbal cues) to tell when they are lying and when they are telling the truth.

Table 12-3b shows a similar effect for lies of agreement and lies of disagreement. Lies of disagreement are difficult to detect from any kind of information. Lies of agreement, though—ingratiating lies that senders might be especially embarrassed to be caught telling—were detectable in both conditions that included visual nonverbal cues.

The pattern of detectability scores for lies told by males versus lies told by females is almost identical to the pattern for lies of disagreement versus lies of agreement. Specifically, the lies told by males were indiscernible in every condition. In both conditions that included visual nonverbal cues, however, lies told by females did tend to be detected by the judges. (See Table 12-3c.)

Contrary to predictions, lies told to attractive others (compared to those told to unattractive others) were not any more detectable from nonverbal than from

TABLE 12-3A
DETECTABILITY OF LIES TOLD TO PERSONS OF THE SAME SEX AND OPPOSITE SEX

Sex of Listener	Channel			
	Verbal	Audio	Visual	Audiovisual
Opposite Sex	-.04	.32	.25	.20
Same Sex	.04	-.10	.01	.02
Opposite minus Same	-.08	.42	.24	.18

TABLE 12-3B
DECTECTABILITY OF LIES OF AGREEMENT AND LIES OF DISAGREEMENT

Type of Lie	Channel			
	Verbal	Audio	Visual	Audiovisual
Feigned Agreement	.01	.12	.39	.30
Feigned Disagreement	-.00	.10	-.13	-.08
Agreement minus Disagreement	.01	.02	.52	.38

verbal cues. However, the attractiveness of the listener did have marked effects on senders' self-presentations. Across all channels and all types of messages (lies, truths, agreements, disagreements), senders talking to attractive others appeared to the judges to be *less* sincere than the senders talking to unattractive others. This finding is especially noteworthy since the judges had no idea who the senders were talking to—nor even that the listeners differed in any systematic way. The difference in the sincerity conveyed to attractive and unattractive others did vary by channel, and in the same way that detectability scores were predicted to vary. In the verbal condition, the senders seemed no less sincere when their partners were attractive than when they were unattractive. In all three conditions that included nonverbal cues, however, senders did seem less sincere when talking to attractive listeners.

In summary, people seem to be betrayed by their nonverbal cues in many of those situations in which they are most motivated *not* to be betrayed. Verbal cues, on the other hand, seem to be more tractable. When people care enough to put on a good show, they generally can concoct a lie that reads as though it is just as sincere and honest as any similarly conconcted truth.

It is unlikely that high levels of motivation will always disrupt nonverbal communicative success. For senders who are especially confident, skilled, or experienced at performing in situations in which success is particularly important, the effect of an increase in motivation may be to enhance the senders' communicative effectiveness.

TABLE 12-3C
DETECTABILITY OF LIES TOLD BY MALES AND FEMALES

Sex of sender	Channel			
	Verbal	Audio	Visual	Audiovisual
Female	.03	.08	.25	.34
Male	-.03	.14	.01	-.12
Female minus Male	.06	-.06	.24	.46

Since in both of the studies just described, other persons were watching the senders (or were believed to be watching them), the senders probably did not leave any of their behaviors completely unmonitored in any of the conditions. What might happen if senders were led to believe that certain of their nonverbal behaviors would not be observed by anyone? If, for example, a person were telling a lie over the phone, could that lie be detected by a roomate who—unbeknownst to the liar—was observing the liar's face?

Research indicates that completely unregulated facial expressions can reveal deception. In a study conducted by Krauss and his colleagues (see Krauss, 1981), senders were surreptitiously videotaped while they communicated to their partner either face to face or over an intercom. Judges who viewed the tapes were most successful at detecting deception when they had access only to the facial expressions (and not the speech cues) of senders communicating by intercom. The intercom senders probably tried most diligently to control their speech; their facial expressions, which they believed to be unmonitored, were left unguarded and hence were highly legible to judges attempting to detect deceit. In trying to spot deception, then, perceivers might do well to pay particular attention to those channels which the senders believe to be unobserved.

CUES TO DECEPTION

Actual Cues to Deception

So far, in discussing the role of verbal and nonverbal cues in the communication of deception, we have referred only to general sources of cues—e.g., the face, the body, or the tone of voice. However, many researchers have tried to pinpoint very specific kinds of behaviors that might occur differentially when people are lying, compared to when they are telling the truth. The particular verbal and nonverbal behaviors that researchers have chosen to study have generally grown out of certain hypotheses about the psychological processes and states that may be more likely to occur during deception than during truth-telling.

First, most people presumably tell lies much less frequently than they tell the truth. Because of this asymmetry in the amount of practice that people have at lie telling versus truth telling, people may feel less confident, more insecure, and more self-conscious when they are attempting to deceive. While people may take it for granted that they will be believed when they are telling the truth, they may be less likely to assume the same when they are lying. One possible consequence of this is that people may try harder and more deliberately to control their verbal and nonverbal behaviors when they are lying than when they are telling the truth. These attempts at control can result in presentations that appear to be a bit too smooth or too forced. Further, if senders are unsuccessful at controlling all channels equally well, then interchannel discrepancies may occur (cf. Zuckerman, DePaulo, & Rosenthal, 1981).

Second, lie telling is generally considered to be a morally dubious act. Consequently, those who engage in deceit may feel guilty about their behavior, and they may also experience heightened concern about whether or not they are successfully conveying the desired impression of honesty and sincerity.

Many specific behaviors have been demonstrated (or hypothesized) to characterize those persons who are concerned about making a particular impression on others, but insecure about their ability to do so (Schlenker & Leary, 1982b). These behaviors include *nervous responses,* such as fidgeting, stuttering, and stammering; *disaffiliative behaviors,* such as longer silences, longer latencies (time elapsed between a question and a response), decreased eye contact, and reduced participation in conversations; and *image-protecting behaviors,* which include innocuous conversational behaviors such as nodding, smiling, and refraining from interrupting. If we are correct in assuming that lie tellers are often anxious about their ability to convey a desired impression, then nervous behaviors, disaffiliative behaviors, and image-protecting behaviors may be reliable indicators of deception.

In that guilt and anxiety are both negative emotions, behaviors indicative of negativity may also be clues to deceit. For example, liars (compared to truth tellers) may make more negative statements, and their tone of voice and facial expressions may be more negative.

One strategy that deceivers may use to deal with their guilt is to try to dissociate themselves from their behavior by becoming distant, withdrawn, and evasive. For example, they might face the targets of their deceit less directly, sit farther away from them, and avoid eye contact. Also, their speech may be speckled with distancing devices called verbal nonimmediacy behaviors (Wiener & Mehrabian, 1968). Verbal nonimmediacy is used by speakers to distance themselves from the person addressed, from the content of their communications, or from the act of communicating those contents. Speakers who use passive rather than active forms, and who hedge their statements with qualifiers, are using some of the many categories of verbal nonimmediacy.

A third characteristic of lie telling is its cognitive complexity. Presumably it is more difficult to fabricate a plausible and convincing lie that is consistent with everything the target knows or might find out than it is to tell the truth. There is evidence to suggest that people engaging in cognitively complex tasks take longer to begin their response, speak more hesitantly once they do begin speaking (Goldman-Eisler, 1968), use fewer "illustrators" (hand movements which accentuate or qualify the accompanying verbal message) (Ekman & Friesen, 1972), and have pupils that are more dilated (e.g., Kahneman, 1973). If lie telling is in fact cognitively demanding, then these behaviors should occur especially often during deceit.

Finally, the literature on psychophysiological aspects of deception indicates that lie telling can be more arousing than truth telling (e.g., Lykken, 1974; Podlesny & Raskin, 1977; Raskin, 1982; Waid & Orne, 1981). The arousal that occurs during deception may be a product or concomitant of a number of different processes, including several that have already been described (concern about evaluation, fear of getting caught, performance of a cognitively challenging task). Behaviors that have been shown to be associated with increases in arousal include increases in pupil dilation, eyeblinks, pitch (voice fundamental frequency), speech errors, and speech hesitations.

Research on the behaviors that actually do occur during deception is summarized in the left-hand columns in Table 12-4. The table includes specific behaviors that have been examined in at least two different studies. A positive number indicates that the behavior is more likely to occur during deceptive responses than during truthful ones; a negative number indicates that the behavior is more likely to occur during truthful responses than during deception ones.

The table shows that some of our favorite cultural stereotypes about liars do not withstand the test provided by the existing empirical data. For example, the studies that have been conducted so far do not support the notion that liars have shifty eyes—nor even shifty bodies; neither glances nor shifts in posture occur significantly more often when people are lying compared to when they are telling the truth. Other indices fare much better, however. For example, liars blink their eyes more often, they have pupils that are more dilated, and they exhibit more adaptors (self-manipulating gestures, such as rubbing or scratching). They also give shorter, higher-pitched, and more hesitant answers that are cluttered with grammatical errors, repetitions, slips of the tongue, and other disfluencies. Liars also make more negative statements, more irrelevant statements, and more overgeneralized statements ("leveling"), and they tend to speak in a less "immediate" (i.e., more distancing) way. Senders who are about to tell a lie take more time to plan their performance than do those who are about to tell the truth. Perhaps they do so partly to try to produce performances that seem spontaneous and natural, and internally consistent. Instead, however, the communications of liars include more interchannel discrepancies and seem more rehearsed than the communications of truth tellers.

How do these findings accord with the hypotheses that lie tellers may be more insecure, more concerned about the impression they are making, more guilty or anxious, more cognitively challenged, or more aroused than truth tellers? The results provide some evidence in support of all of these hypotheses. (Because many of the behaviors are consistent with more than one interpretation, however, we will not try to argue too strongly for the superiority of certain hypotheses over others.)

First, as might be expected from senders who are insecure about their prospects of succeeding at conveying a desired impression, deceivers do appear to try hard—perhaps too hard—to control their self-presentations. Senders who are preparing to deceive someone take more time to plan their performances than do those who are preparing to tell the truth, and they are more likely to take advantage of an opportunity to find out more about the targets of their communications, at some cost to themselves (Elliott, 1979). The messages that they convey, however, appear overly rehearsed and lacking in spontaneity, and they are also marred by interchannel discrepancies. There are certain nervous

TABLE 12-4
CUES TO ACTUAL DECEPTION AND TO PERCEIVED DECEPTION

	Associated with Actual Deception	Associated with Perceived Deception
	Verbal	
Negative statements (5,0)	5.34***	
Irrelevant information (6,0)	2.17*	
Leveling (4,0)	2.16*	
Self-references (4,0)	- .38	
Immediacy (2,0)	-3.37***	
	Vocal/Paralinguistic	
Speech hesitations (11,2)	4.06***	3.17**
Pitch (4,2)	2.26*	2.82**
Speech errors (12,4)	2.14*	2.00**
Latency (15,5)	.28	3.61***
Speech rate (12,2)	-1.36	-2.84**
Response length (17,4)	-1.98*	- .61
	Visual	
Pupil dilation (5,0)	6.82***	
Adaptors (14,3)	3.50***	.51
Blinking (8,0)	1.96*	
Shrugs (4,0)	1.81	
Gaze (18,4)	.13	-3.25**
Gestures (12,0)	- .19	
Foot and leg movements (9,0)	- .22	
Postural shifts (11,2)	- .88	3.00**
Head movements (10,0)	-1.20	
Smiling (19,5)	-1.67	-2.97**
	Miscellaneous	
Discrepancy (4,0)	4.31***	
Planning time (2,0)	3.40***	
Responses seem rehearsed (2,0)	3.12**	

Note: The entries in the columns are Z statistics, computed according to the method for combining Zs. (See Rosenthal, 1978.) The numbers in parentheses indicate the number of studies on which the statistics are based. The first number indicates the number of studies of actual cues to deception; the second indicates the number of studies of perceived cues to deception. This table is an updated and modified version of tables presented earlier in Zuckerman, DePaulo, and Rosenthal (1981) and Zuckerman and Driver (in press).
*$p<.05$
**$p<.01$
***$p<.001$

behaviors that characterize lie tellers, too. For example, the occurrences of adaptors, speech errors, and speech hesitations are consistent with the notion that senders may feel anxious about their deceptive behavior. Converging evidence for this hypothesis comes from the reports made by the senders themselves after the lies (or truths) have been told. Senders indicated that they felt more nervous (DePaulo et al., 1983) and more insecure about their performances (Elliott, 1979) when they had been dishonest than when they had been honest. The evidence for disaffiliative behaviors is more mixed. Liars do not avert their eyes any more than truth tellers do, and they do not exhibit longer response latencies, but they do give terser responses.

We also suggested that, because of the guilt and anxiety that deceivers might feel, their behavior and demeanor might become more negative. The findings that liars make more negative statements than truth tellers directly supports this suggestion. The occurrence of lower levels of immediacy in deceptive messages than truthful ones is also relevant, since nonimmediacy has been linked to negativity, as well as to distancing. Further, DePaulo, Rosenthal, Green, & Rosenkrantz (1982) found that liars sounded more negative than did truth tellers to judges who could only hear the tone of voice of the messages; this was true even when the content of the messages (which the judges could not hear) was positive.

The hypothesis that deceivers may be reluctant to commit themselves to their lies receives solid support. Liars have less to say in response to any given question than do truth tellers, and the responses they do give are distancing, overgeneralized, and filled with irrelevancies, hesitations, and errors. Also consistent with this "noncommittal" interpretation are several studies that have assessed judges' global impressions of people who are lying or telling the truth. In those studies, the liars sounded more indifferent, more ambivalent (DePaulo, Rosenthal, Green, & Rosenkrantz, 1982), and less involved in what they had to say (Zuckerman, DeFrank, Hall, Larrance, & Rosenthal, 1979).

The hesitancy in liars' speech and the dilation of their pupils are consistent with the suggestion that lying may be a cognitively demanding task. That liars take longer to prepare their responses (before entering the situation in which their message is to be conveyed) is also consistent with this conceptualization; however, liars do not seem to need any more time than truth tellers to begin answering a question, once it is asked. Elliott (1979) asked his subjects directly, after they had attempted to convey an accurate or inaccurate impression, how easy their task had been. Consistent with the cognitive complexity hypothesis, those who had just told the truth claimed that their task was much easier than those who had told a lie.

Finally, the suggestion that lying might be arousing also receives strong support. The predicted increases, during deception, in pupil dilation, blinking, pitch, speech hesitations, and speech errors are all significant.

Table 12-4 is a summary of past research, and as such, it averages across many different kinds of deceivers and many different kinds of deceptive situations. Lurking beneath the generalities that the table so blithely offers may be some intriguingly divergent patterns. One example of this comes from the research on machiavellianism (Christie & Geis, 1970). High "machs" believe that other people are manipulable, and they seem to practice manipulative acts with an aura of emotional detachment. In a study of the behaviors of low and high machs during deception, Exline and his colleagues (Exline, Thibaut, Hickey, & Gumpert, 1970) found that high machs, when rightfully accused of cheating, fabricate a plausible denial and look their accusers in the eye while delivering it. Low machs, on the other hand, fabricate lies that are less convincing, and they are more likely to avert their eyes from their accusers while telling their lies. The high machs' strategies may be more effective than the lows', since highs tend to be more successful at perpetrating their lies (DePaulo & Rosenthal, 1979b; Geis & Moon, 1981).[2] In fact, on the basis of a large-scale program of research, Christie and Geis (1970) have concluded that low machs distinguish themselves from highs not so much by any morally grounded unwillingness to deceive, but rather by the ineptness of their deceptive attempts. Looking again at Table 12-4, one might surmise, on the basis of the Exline findings, that the null result for "glances" really results from the fact that different types of people use very different patterns of looking while telling lies.

Even results that are significant for the set of studies as a whole may in fact be more characteristic of certain types of persons. For example, DePaulo, Rosenthal, Rosenkrantz, and Green (1982) have shown that lies that are especially evasive and noncommittal are more likely to have been spoken by women than by men. Further, certain types of people show patterns of behavior that are exactly the opposite of those shown in the table. For example, although Table 12-4 indicates that most senders exhibit more nervous behaviors when lying than when telling the truth, senders who ordinarily may tend to be very expressive (e.g., extraverts; people who think of themselves as good actors) seem to adopt a strategy of overcontrol when lying: They engage in *fewer* nervous behaviors when lying than when telling the truth (Riggio & Friedman, 1983).

One of the most important moderators of cues to deception may be the senders' motivation to lie successfully (cf. Ekman, 1981; Kraut, 1980). To determine whether people betray themselves in different ways when they are especially motivated to lie successfully, the studies in Table 12-4 were divided into low- and high-motivation groups (Zuckerman et al., 1981). In the studies in which senders were more highly motivated to lie successfully (compared to those in which senders were less highly motivated), deceptive responses were shorter, slower, more negative, and more highly pitched than truthful responses, and they were accompanied by less gazing, less blinking, fewer head movements, fewer postural shifts, and somewhat fewer adaptors. Taken together, these data suggest that highly motivated liars exhibit more behavioral inhibition and rigidity, and perhaps also more negativity, than deceivers who are less highly motivated to get away with their lies. Perhaps the inhibition and rigidity are behavioral consequences of a "play-safe" strategy used by liars who are trying especially hard not to get caught. That is, deceivers might believe that "not doing" (e.g., not moving, not shifting around, not gazing, not fidgeting, not talking so much, and not even blinking) is less revealing—or at least, less clearly revealing—than doing. Unfortunately for the deceivers, however, this strategy probably does not work. As noted earlier, whenever perceivers can observe

[2]It should be noted, however, that the findings that high machs maintain more eye contact than lows, and are more successful at their deception attempts, have not always been replicated (see Knapp, Hart, & Dennis, 1974; O'Hair, Cody, & McLaughlin, 1981; Zuckerman et al., 1981).

liars' nonverbal behaviors, it is easier for them to tell when deception is occurring when the liars are highly motivated not to get caught than when they are not so highly motivated.

In general, it is unreasonable to expect any one cue or set of cues to be associated in a perfectly consistent way with every type of liar and every type of lie. Deceptive contexts vary considerably in the emotions, motivations, and expectations that they engender in the deceivers, and they also impose different cognitive processing demands. As these and other important dimensions of deceptive contexts vary, so, too, may the specific behaviors that distinguish lies from truths.

Perceived Cues to Deception

If people were perfect lie detectors, their judgments of deceptiveness would be influenced only by those cues that really do distinguish lies from truths. As we have already seen, however, people are imperfect detectors. Sometimes the cues that they should be using (e.g., pupil dilation) are cues that they do not even notice. Other cues that might potentially be quite informative may be noticed, but regarded as insignificant and therefore ignored, or—worse, yet—used in exactly the wrong ways. (See also Riggio & Friedman, 1983.)

The results of research on cues that influence people's *perceptions* of deceptiveness are summarized in the right-hand column of Table 12-4. A positive number indicates that the behavior was more likely to be interpreted as a cue to deception than as a cue to truth; a negative number indicates that the occurrence of the behavior was interpreted as a sign of truthfulness.

The table indicates that when senders gaze less, smile less, shift their posture more, speak more slowly, and take longer to answer a question, they are perceived by judges as more deceptive. A quick glance over to the analogous entries in the "actual" column shows that none of these behaviors really does distinguish truth from deceit to a statistically significant degree. Also, the occurrence of adaptors did not substantially influence perceivers' judgments, even though it should have. However, perceivers quite appropriately rated as more deceptive those senders whose utterances were hesitant, filled with errors, and highly pitched.

This less-than-perfect correspondence between cues that really are indicative of deception (actual cues) and cues that are believed to be indicative of deception (perceived cues) has important implications for self-presentation. For instance, it suggests that in order to be perceived as sincere, it may not always be sufficient simply to tell the truth. If a completely innocent truth teller happens to engage in behaviors that others *perceive* as signs of deception (even though they are not), that person risks being labeled as a liar. Both for liars who want their lies to go undetected, and for truth tellers who want their sincerity to be evident, it is more important to know about the cues that people *interpret* as signs of deceptiveness and truth than it is to know about the cues that really are signs of deceit.

For detectors of deception, of course, the actual cues are more important, for it is the actual cues that really do distinguish truth from deception. The discrepancies between actual cues and perceived cues might also be useful to human lie detectors by alerting them to commonly made judgmental errors. For example, while many perceivers are apparently tempted to infer from a person's shift in posture that deception might be occurring, they might in fact be better off assuming that the person's posture simply became uncomfortable.

As was true for the summary of actual cues to deception, conclusions based on the combined results of studies of perceptions of deceptiveness should not be overstated. For example, it is possible that the exact same behavior will be interpreted as indicative of deception in one context and of truth in another (Kraut, 1978). Because the results presented in Table 12-4 were computed by averaging across many different deceptive contexts, such context-dependent relationships cannot be discerned on the basis of Table 12-4 alone.

In discussing actual cues to deception, we noted that there are important individual differences in the cues that people use when deceiving. It seems, though, that there is much more consistency in the cues that influence people's *perceptions* of deceit. For example, Kraut and Poe (1980), in a study of detection of deception among customs officials and laypersons, have found that very similar "search" rules are used by the officials and the laypersons, and by the more and the less experienced officials. Also, DePaulo, Rosenthal, Rosenkrantz, and Green (1983) found substantial agreement between male and female perceivers in the cues they used in their judgments about deceit, and they also found a significant degree of consistency in the cues used in judging lies of liking compared to lies of disliking. In general, it is much more difficult to predict the cues that people will use when deceiving than it is to predict the cues they will use when trying to detect deceit.

Why should it be more difficult to find reliable and consistent cues to actual deception than to perceived deception? Senders vary markedly in their expressive skills and styles, and hence they may tell lies in many different ways. Further, even as they are telling the lie, their lie-telling behavior might change with changes in the reactions of the target person. For example, if the target person starts to show signs of apparent suspiciousness, the deceiver might try a different lie-telling strategy.

Perceivers, on the other hand, do not seem to show much variability in the rules they use to detect deception, perhaps because there are cultural stereotypes about deception that are known and accepted by almost all perceivers in the culture. The cues that perceivers rely on to detect deceit—as summarized in Table 12-4—do seem to describe the stereotypical liars who hem and haw, shift around in their seats, and have shifty (or avoidant) eyes. As already noted, not all of the cues that perceivers use are cues that they should be using. However, detectors have little hope of learning this through their own experiences. It is probably relatively rare for perceivers to come upon definitive evidence that indicates that a sender is in fact telling a lie. Even when such feedback is available to perceivers, they still may selectively attend to and remember only those sender behaviors that are consistent with their theory (which they share with most other perceivers) of how people act when they are lying. (See, for example, Anderson, Lepper, & Ross, 1980, and Lord, Ross, & Lepper, 1979.) Not only will the theory then remain unchanged, but perceivers' confidence in it may actually increase!

THE ROLE OF STRATEGIES AND EXPERIENCE IN SUCCESS AT DECEIVING AND DETECTING DECEIT

Success at Detecting Deceit

Experience at Detecting Deception: Customs Inspectors and Police Detectives
If we are right in assuming that perceivers often get only paltry and unsystematic feedback on their lie-detection attempts, and if they tend to see in that feedback only evidence which seems to support their initial (and sometimes erroneous) theories about deception, then perhaps even persons who have a great deal of experience at trying to detect deception are not remarkably successful. Consider, for example, customs inspectors, who as part of their jobs have perhaps hundreds of experiences daily at trying to detect deceit. What kind of feedback do they get? From the many travelers whom they decide not to search, they get virtually no feedback at all. Some of those persons may in fact be smugglers, but once the inspectors let them pass unsearched, they will almost never find out that they made a mistake. Even when inspectors do decide to search travelers who are in fact smuggling illegal goods, they may not always find those goods. In those instances, the inspectors would classify the travelers as nonsmugglers, when in fact they are smugglers. Consistent with this dim view, Kraut and Poe (1980) found that customs inspectors were no more successful than laypersons at deciding, on the basis of verbal and nonverbal cues, which travelers to search. Also, the successful inspectors (those who had made an impressive number of seizures the previous year) were no more accurate at the task than the less successful ones. Similarly, in a study in which police detectives and undergraduates observed interrogations of students who had or had not committed a particular mock crime, the detectives were no more accurate than the undergraduates in their judgments of guilt and innocence (Hendershot & Hess, 1982).

Even acknowledging that the feedback available to both customs inspectors and police detectives is imperfect, one might still find these results surprising. After years of deciding when to search someone, for example, shouldn't customs inspectors develop some sense of the kinds of persons who are likely to be worth their while to search? It is possible that inspectors *do* develop somewhat accurate search rules, but that these rules are based not on subtle verbal and nonverbal cues, but on other, more blatant cues, such as age, sex, and style of dress. In the Kraut and Poe study (and also in Hendershot & Hess), these cues could not have been useful, because the travelers who participated in their study were randomly assigned to the role of smuggler or nonsmuggler. Thus, the distribution of age, sex, and so forth in the smuggler group would be very similar to the distribution in the nonsmuggler group, even though it may not be the same in the inspectors' actual job experiences. What these studies show, then, is that on-the-job experience apparently does not enhance inspectors' or detectives' skill at detecting deception from verbal and nonverbal cues alone. It is still possible, however, that experience does improve their ability to use effectively other sorts of information. We do not want to suggest that on-the-job experience will never enhance skill at detecting deception from verbal and nonverbal cues; as yet, however, there is no evidence that it does.

Strategies for Detecting Deceit If a cynic were to review the data presented in this chapter, she or he might suggest that the reason people are not better lie detectors is that they are too naive and trusting. If only people were more wary of the fact that deception might be occurring at any time, then perhaps they would be more successful at detecting deception. In contrast, the assumption that lie detectors use theories that are (at least partly) erroneous implies a different answer to the question of the effect of wariness: Perhaps if perceivers were led to be more suspicious of deception than they are ordinarily, they would simply rely even more strongly on their imperfect theories. Hence, an increment in deceptive success would not necessarily occur. Data reported by Toris and DePaulo (in press) support the latter conceptualization. In their study, involving a simulated job interview, interviewers either were or were not warned that the applicants might be misrepresenting themselves. The warned interviewers were not any more accurate than the naive ones at detecting deception, and they were actually slightly worse at discerning the applicants' true characteristics. Heightened suspiciousness, however, did have other effects: The interviewers who were led to be more suspicious were less confident about their judgments, and they tended to perceive all applicants as more deceptive than did the naive interviewers. Further, applicants who were interviewed by warned (compared to naive) interviewers felt somewhat less successful in their attempts to portray their intended impressions—even though they were *not* less successful, and they perceived their interviewers as more manipulative. Increased suspiciousness, then, seems to serve only to decrease confidence and trust, without at the same time increasing the accuracy of interpersonal perceptions.

In the Toris and DePaulo study, perceivers were told, in effect, to become more alert to signs of deception, but they were given no clues at all as to what those signs might be. To help perceivers become better lie detectors, perhaps it is necessary to direct their attention to particularly revealing sources of information—sources that they might otherwise pay less attention to than they should (cf. Ekman et al., 1980). Suggestive evidence for this hypothesis was provided by a study conducted by Streeter and her colleagues (Streeter, Krauss, Geller, Olson, & Apple, 1977). In that study, which used an interview format, applicants' pitch was higher when they were lying than when they were telling the truth. When perceivers listened to tape recordings of the applicants' responses, they did not rely on pitch to decide whether or not deception was occurring. However, when the content of those tapes was filtered (i.e., the words were rendered unintelligible) so that pitch presumably became a more salient cue, perceivers did use it in their judgments of deceptiveness.

A study by DePaulo, Lassiter, and Stone (1982) directly tested the hypothesis that lie-detection success would be improved if perceivers' attention were directed to potentially revealing sources of cues, such as tone of voice cues. Before the lie-detection task, one-quarter of the subjects read an instruction booklet that suggested that they pay particular attention to the tone of voice of the speakers. Another quarter were told to pay particular attention to the words, and still others were told to pay particular attention to speakers' visual cues. A control group was given no special attentional instructions. All subjects then watched videotapes (with sound) of senders who were lying and telling the truth. Consistent with predictions, the attend-to-tone subjects did significantly better than the control group at discriminating truth from deceit. The attend-to-words group performed almost as well as the tone group, while the attend-to-visual subjects did no better than the controls. This study suggests that paying special attention to tone can improve lie-detection success, and that perceivers do not ordinarily take advantage of the information inherent in vocal cues without special prompting.

Another strategy that might facilitate lie-detection success is for perceivers to place more faith in their judgments of deceiver qualities that might be related to deceptiveness—qualities such as ambivalence, indifference, and tension. Like the strategy of attending to tone, this is a more directed and specific strategy than simply telling perceivers to be more alert to the possibility that deception might be occurring. There is evidence that perceivers can discriminate truth from deception not only by their ratings of deceptiveness, but also by their ratings of discrepancy, ambivalence, indifference, and tension (DePaulo, Rosenthal, Green, & Rosenkrantz, 1982). In fact, their discriminations along the ambivalence dimension may be even stronger than their discriminations based on ratings of deceptiveness. One possible interpretation of this is that perceivers may be more willing to label others as ambivalent than as deceptive, since attributions of ambivalence—unlike attributions of deceptiveness—are morally neutral. Perhaps, then, if perceivers were urged to use their intuitions about ambivalence to inform their judgments about deceit, their deception-detection success would be improved. This hypothesis has not yet been tested directly.

Success at Deceiving

Experience at Deceiving: Nurses and Presidents Do senders receive any more feedback from their attempts to deceive than perceivers do from their attempts to detect deceit? We cannot be sure of our answer to this question, but we believe that they do. We think that senders are often alert for signs that their lies might be arousing suspicion, and we think that the targets of deceit often convey evidence of the success of the senders' attempts. At the most inelegant extreme, targets may simply express directly their incredulousness. More often, however, the feedback is more subtle. For example, nurses who are disgusted by the sight of a patient's mutilated body may try to conceal this emotional reaction; if unsuccessful, they may learn of their lack of success immediately simply by observing the patient's reaction to their own reaction! If this analysis is correct, then it may follow that experience in a profession which involves practice at deceiving will result in an increment in deceptive success.

Evidence from two studies is supportive of the experiental hypothesis. In the first study (Ekman & Friesen, 1974), student nurses were filmed as they tried to convince an interviewer that the films they had seen were really quite pleasant (when one, in fact, was extremely unpleasant). A year later, the authors collected supervisors' ratings of the quality of the nurses' work with their patients. Results showed that those nurses who were especially skilled facial deceivers were rated by their supervisors as especially effective at their job. This suggests that deceptive abilities might contribute to success at nursing, and it also raises the possibility (which is more relevant to the present discussion) that skill and experience at nursing might enhance a person's deceptive abilities.

In the second study, Alker (1976) studied another job that sometimes involves the practice of deception—the job of President. Alker analyzed the speech of Nixon, Johnson, and Kennedy in press conferences during which they were known to have been lying, and compared these conferences to more innocuous press conferences in which no deception has ever been documented. For Nixon, the deceptive press conference was one in which he was denying any involvement in Watergate, for Kennedy it was a Bay of Pigs Conference, and for Johnson it was a Gulf of Tonkin conference.

Alker predicted that these conferences would be characterized by a high incidence of "mystification"—the presentation of some sort of myth as though it were objective reality. Mystification can manifest itself verbally in many ways. For example, a passive construction without an agent is a mystifying construction. An example is the phrase "it was decided . . .", which leaves the listener mystified as to who did the deciding. Another mystifying verbal form is the phrase "my fellow Americans," as used by presidents to put forward an assumed commonality in point of view which may also be a myth (Nixon's "fellow Americans" may not agree with him at all). Phrases such as "credible deterrent" or "valid argument" are likewise mystifying, leaving the listener baffled as to who thinks what is credible or valid.

Nonmystifying forms are very similar to the "verbal immediacy" constructions described previously, though they were generated independently of the immediacy scoring system. Nonimmediate forms (comparable to "mystifying" forms) have been shown to be actual cues to deceit in studies that were conducted primarily with college students. Thus, college students use less immediate and more mystifying forms when lying than when telling the truth. Further, when senders use nonimmediate, mystifying speech, perceivers judge them as more likely to be lying than when they use more immediate speech (DePaulo & Toris, 1984).

Alker examined six mystifying constructions, and found, exactly opposite to his predictions, that presidents tended to avoid these forms when they were telling their high-powered, highly consequential lies. When lying, presidents used a very nonmystifying style of speech—a style of speaking that tends to be most credible to most people. We cannot conclude definitively from the results of this study that on-the-job experience increased the Presidents' lie-telling abilities, but the evidence is not inconsistent with such an interpretation. Both the Ekman and Friesen and the Alker studies provide evidence for the experiential hypothesis that is at best only suggestive, but at the present time, suggestive evidence is all we have.

Strategies for Deceiving Senders who are intent on improving the success of their deceptive acts might, theoretically, do well to plan their lies (and truths) in advance. Planning might facilitate a smoother and more consistent performance and lighten the liar's cognitive processing burdens at the key moment when the deceit must be perpetrated.

In the study by DePaulo et al. (1983) described previously, senders were given in advance two of the four questions that they would be asked to answer in front of the panel of their peers. One of the questions that they were given was to be answered honestly, and the other was to be answered dishonestly. They had two minutes to plan both answers. The answers to the other two questions (one honest, one dishonest) had to be devised extemporaneously.

The lies that the senders had planned in advance were no more or less readily detectable than their unplanned lies. Furthermore, there were no indications that the lies were differentially detectable in different channels, depending on whether they were planned or spontaneous. The type of planning in this particular study might be somewhat analogous to that which occurs during conversations when the topic unexpectedly switches to a theme that one of the interactants would prefer to avoid. The interactant then has a limited amount of time to decide what to say (and how to say it). Other types of planning—for example, planning done much more carefully, further in advance, perhaps even involving overt rehearsal—might have a more pronounced effect on the detectability of deceit. (See Littlepage & Pineault, 1979, for some evidence consistent with this notion.) Also, planning might be especially effective only for certain types of people (Miller, deTurck, & Kalbfleisch, 1982).

Although the planning manipulation used in the DePaulo et al. (1983) study did not affect judges' accuracy at detecting deception, it did influence their perceptions. Responses that were planned, whether truthful or deceptive, were rated as more deceptive, more tense, and less spontaneous than responses that were not planned. Similarly, deceptive responses, whether planned or unplanned, were perceived as more deceptive and less spontaneous than truthful responses. While the deceptive responses in that study were, by design, just as often unplanned as planned, people who are not constrained by experimental design probably do plan their lies more carefully than their truths. Thus, perceivers' tendency to associate a lack of spontaneity with deceit may be justified in many instances.

In summary, unless it is done well in advance or by persons who are especially skilled impression managers, planning may not improve a deceiver's chance of fooling others. In fact, planning can backfire, making all responses (even truthful ones) seem more tense, more deceptive, and less spontaneous.

THE DEVELOPMENT OF DECEPTIVE ABILITIES

The abilities to deceive and to detect deceit may be among the most sophisticated skills in a person's communicative repertoire. In fact, deVilliers and deVilliers (1978) have suggested that the ability to lie successfully is the "ultimate achievement" in children's progressive mastery of the intricacies of discourse. In the following sections, we will review research and theory on the development of children's deceptive abilities.

Learning to Detect Lies

Understanding the Concept of Deception In order to detect deception, children must realize that people's overt expressions do not always correspond to their internal states. Appreciation of this communicative subtlety continues to develop over the course of the elementary-school years. During that time period, children show increasing awareness of the fact that other people sometimes express attitudes or affects other than those which they are really experiencing in order to ward off punishment, to prevent embarrassment or insult to oneself or others, and to maintain social norms (Saarni, 1979, 1982).

Astute deception detectors must also understand the defining features of a lie—that is, it is a message which the sender knows to be false, and it is designed to mislead. If these characteristics are not fully appreciated, lies may be confused with unintentional mistakes and with nonliteral linguistic forms such as irony, sarcasm, jokes, metaphors, fanciful stories, playful exaggerations, and games of make-believe (cf. Gardner, Kircher, Winner, & Perkins, 1975).

Piaget's Theory of the Development of Moral Judgments In his extensive analysis of the development of moral judgments, Piaget (1965) suggested that lies are defined and evaluated by different criteria at different ages. According to his theory, 5 to 7 year olds tend to be "moral realists"—to them, any moral fault committed by means of language qualifies as deceit. Issues of intentionality are not considered, and so innocent errors and even "naughty words" are labeled as lies.

Eventually, naughty words drop out of the list of verbalizations classified as lies, but for a time mistakes are still regarded as lies. This follows quite naturally from an objective assessment of lies as statements that are untrue. By this definition, a statement becomes more naughty as it deviates further from the truth. Thus, a child who claims to have seen a dog as big as a cow has told a very naughty lie since a cow is so much bigger than a dog could ever be. Similarly, a person who misjudges another person's age by 8 years has told a worse lie than someone whose estimate is off by only 4 years. There is even some evidence that longer or more complicated stories are judged to be worse lies than simpler, more straightforward tales. These three examples deal with the content of the deception. However, the material consequences of the deceit are important, too. One pair of stories that Piaget used to investigate the importance of consequences involved a traveler asking for directions. In one scenario, a child intentionally gives the wrong directions, but the traveler finds his way nonetheless. In the other story, the child tries to give the right directions, but the traveler gets lost. Before the age of about 8 or 10, Piaget argued, children will judge the second child as naughtier than the first, since the objective outcome was more undesirable in the latter case.

By around the age of 10 or 11, Piaget believed, children become sensitive to the importance of intent, and explicitly verbalize the adult definition of a lie. At this age, lies are evaluated subjectively, in terms of their goals. Mistakes are no longer regarded as deceitful, and lies that do succeed in misleading others are regarded as more morally despicable than lies that are found out. Whereas younger children refrain from lying out of a sense of duty and respect for still another set of adult prohibitions that they do not completely understand, these preadolescents, according to Piaget, have learned from their interactions with each other that truthfulness is a necessary foundation for social reciprocity, and mutual respect and trust.

In his naturalistic observations of children's "practical" moral reasoning (i.e., the reasoning they use in their day-to-day lives), Piaget found that children show some awareness of issues of intentionality as early as age 3. For example, in referring to one of their own behaviors, preschoolers might insist that it was "not on purpose." (See also Keasey, 1977.) Research conducted subsequently has also demonstrated that children can take other people's intentions into account at an earlier age than Piaget's story-paradigm findings had suggested. (See, for example, Darby & Schlenker, 1982; Nelson, 1980.) With age, though, the degree to which children weigh information about intentions in their judgments does tend to increase (e.g., Keasey, 1977), while the degree to which they weigh outcome information decreases (Surber, 1977).

Children seem to be better able to use information about intentions when information about outcomes has not been specified (Keasey, 1977); perhaps this is because young children often have difficulty dealing with several different pieces of information simultaneously (e.g., Gottlieb, Taylor, & Ruderman, 1977). Also, when judging ill-intended acts, children's moral reasoning appears to be more sophisticated than when judging accidental or well-intended acts (Karniol, 1978).

Newman (1982) has noted that it is not always necessary to consider issues of intent in order accurately to determine that a person is lying. To illustrate this point, Newman uses the example of a skit from Sesame Street. In the skit, Ernie comes home with a banana, and Bert indicates that he would like some of it. Ernie agrees, saying, "I'm going to divide this banana up so that both of us can have some." Ernie then turns away from Bert, gulps down the banana, then turns back to Bert, handing him the peel, and says, "See, I took the inside part, and here's the outside part for you." Subjects in grades one, three, six, and college watched the skit, and then were asked whether Ernie had told a lie when he said, "I'm going to divide this banana up." Almost all subjects indicated that what Ernie said was at least in part a lie. To identify Ernie's statements as deceptive, Newman argues, subjects need only recognize the inconsistency between the conventionally understood meaning of Ernie's statement (i.e., that dividing an edible object is understood to mean dividing the edible part) and the event that actually did transpire (Bert was given nothing edible). The youngest subjects seemed to recognize this discrepancy, and they labeled Ernie's statement as a lie. They did so without alluding to the mental states (e.g., motives, expectations) of either of the characters. The older subjects' understanding was more sophisticated. In discussing the skit, those subjects mentioned the inferences that Bert had made (e.g., that he expected to get some of the inside), and they sometimes also mentioned the fact that Ernie was intentionally trying to deceive Bert. These subjects understood the concept of literal truth; they claimed that Ernie's statement was partly the truth and partly a lie.

Finally, in a recent study of developmental changes in children's ideas about lying, Peterson, Peterson, and Seeto (1983) examined the evaluations made by children (ages 6, 8, 9, and 12) and adults of many of the same kinds of stories that Piaget had used. Their results were generally supportive of Piaget's original conclusions, with some qualifications. For example, younger children were—as Piaget had reported—especially likely to label exaggerations and mistaken guesses as lies. However, this confusion persisted at least until the age of 11, which is longer than Piaget had suggested.

Age Changes in Detecting Deception from Verbal and Nonverbal Cues

Earlier we argued that children need to understand the defining features of a lie in order to distinguish lies from nonliteral language forms such as metaphors and sarcasm. However, a theoretical understanding of the differences between nonliteral language and deceit is a necessary but not sufficient condition for the task of distinguishing the two forms when they occur naturally in the child's linguistic environment. Users of nonliteral language forms help perceivers accurately to identify their utterances by filling them with warnings of nonliteral intent (e.g., "dripping with sarcasm"). Often, these markers are tone of voice cues, but facial expressions, gestures, and contextual cues can be important, too. Although these nonsubtle markers presumably greatly facilitate the child's interpretive efforts, considerable difficulties still remain (cf. Kotsonis, 1980; Winner, Rosenstiel, & Gardner, 1976). Discrepancies between different components of a message (e.g., verbal versus nonverbal) are not always immediately apparent to children, and even when they are, the strategies used to resolve the inconsistencies are often markedly different from those used by adults (e.g., Blanck & Rosenthal, 1982; Bugental, Kaswan, Love, & Fox, 1970; DePaulo & Rosenthal, 1979a; Volkmar & Siegel, 1982). For example, when facial and vocal cues are very discrepant, preadolescents tend to pay relatively more attention to the facial cues, which may be less revealing of the senders' true feelings than are the vocal cues which adolescents and adults weigh more heavily.

The detection of deception is even more complex. Instead of purposefully marking their lies as such, deceivers usually try their best to mask the fact that deception is occurring. The communicative discrepancies that sometimes occur when senders try to neutralize their true feelings or simulate different feelings can serve to alert the perceiver to the fact that deception is occurring, but they can also lead to confusion as to whether the sender is really lying or simply honestly communicating genuine ambivalence. Further, the line between direct deception and exaggerations, omissions, or slight distortions is a blurry one even for adult perceivers—and perhaps also for the deceivers themselves.

Because of the complexity of the lie-detection task, and because many of the skills and understandings that may be essential to success at recognizing deception are still developing throughout the childhood years, the prognosis for the preadolescent lie detector is grim. However, during the adolescent years, the outlook brightens. There is evidence that throughout adolescence, perceivers are continually acquiring a diversity of skills, strategies, and experiences which should also facilitate their lie-detection success. The experiential factors are the most obvious ones. With age, perceivers bring to the deception detection task more and more cultural, social, and interpersonal knowledge; this knowledge may help them to realize that certain affects, events, or experiences described by another person are unlikely to occur or unlikely to be described in the way that the person is describing them. With age, perceivers also accumulate more direct experience with deceptive communications; this, too, should facilitate their lie-detection success. There is also evidence that during adolescence, perceivers approach their interpersonal worlds in ways that should continuously increase their sensitivity to issues of sincerity and deceit. For example, adolescents (compared to younger perceivers) are more likely spontaneously to try to infer another's feelings, to explain the qualities they perceive in others, and to reconcile any apparent inconsistencies in other people's behaviors and traits (e.g., Flavell, 1977; Peevers & Secord, 1973).

Empirical Evidence Research on children's understanding of deception has addressed some of the same basic questions as the research on adults' detection skills. These questions include: (a) Do children accept speakers' statements at face value, and (b) Can children differentiate truth from deception?

Most research on adults' acceptance of speakers' statements at face value has involved paradigms in which the only information available to the perceivers was the communication itself. On the basis of the verbal or nonverbal cues alone, perceivers were to determine whether to discount the meaning in the speaker's overtly conveyed message. Typically, little or no discounting occurs; rather, adult perceivers tend to accept speakers' statements at face value.

To study children's acceptance of overt meanings, it may be necessary to begin with the more basic question of whether children will discount overt statements when they are given clear information suggesting that they should.

This information might include not only the speaker's message, but also the objective "fact" with which the message conflicts, and a clear indication that the speaker was aware of the fact. In his research on this topic, Ackerman (1981) used a series of scenarios such as the following:

> Robert asked all of his friends to play baseball at 1:00. He wanted to have two complete teams. He counted up all that came, and it seemed they needed exactly two more for two teams. Then his younger brother came and asked to play, but Robert said, "Sorry, but we've got too many guys, so you can't play" (p. 480).

When given such a clear example of deception—one in which the speaker was aware of a fact, but made a statement which was inconsistent with that fact—most adults will immediately realize that Robert really did not want his little brother to play.

First graders, however, are not so sure. They are just as likely (or perhaps even more likely) to say that Robert really did want his brother to play than to say that he did not. Further, their answer to this question of intent is not dependent on whether they think that Robert was aware of the fact that two more players were needed. In this way, they are less sophisticated than third graders and adults, who do weigh speakers' awareness of the facts in their judgments of whether a speaker's use of a false utterance was intentional.

Although the first graders did not completely understand the issues involved in discerning intentionality, they did realize, for many of the scenarios, that the speaker's conveyed message was not to be believed. For example, when asked whether Robert had enough players for two teams, even first graders tended to say that he did not. With age, this tendency to discount the overt meaning became even stronger. Relative to older subjects, then, younger children were more likely to use a literal interpretive strategy.

Other kinds of studies, too, have shown that children are often biased toward making literal interpretations (e.g., Gardner, Winner, Bechhofer, & Wolf, 1978; Nelson & Nelson, 1978). Children's difficulty in integrating inconsistent cues (e.g., an utterance and a contradictory fact) has sometimes been attributed to their limited information-processing capacity. It may simply be too difficult for children to keep several items of information in mind simultaneously, and also try to compare, contrast, and integrate those items. Hence, they adopt the simpler strategy of interpreting utterances literally. Ackerman (1983), however, has demonstrated that children are in fact capable of detecting discrepancies between a speaker's statement and other information, and that they will contradict the speaker's statement under certain conditions—for example, when the speaker is a child. When children take literally statements made by adult speakers, they may do so because they believe adults to be informed and credible. Children, then, may be unwilling to look for information that is inconsistent with an adult's statement; or, if they do learn of such information, they may simply ignore it. Unsurprisingly, skepticism about the credibility of adults' statements increases with age (Ackerman, 1983; see also Ross, Campbell, Huston-Stein, & Wright, 1981, for evidence of increasing skepticism, with age, in children's interpretations of television commercials).

Several studies have examined children's interpretations of speakers' messages solely on the basis of the verbal or nonverbal cues that comprised those messages. In one study (Feldman et al., 1978), third graders observed tapes of the facial expressions of other third graders who were serving as tutors. The tutors always delivered praise to their tutees, regardless of the tutee's performance, which was sometimes excellent and sometimes poor. (The observers were unaware of the actual performance of the tutees.) The observers were able to distinguish between genuine and false praise, in that they rated the tutors of successful tutees as significantly happier with their students than the tutors of unsuccessful tutees. Similarly, in a study in which adults described a number of other people—for example, they truthfully described someone they really did like, and they pretended to like someone they really disliked—subjects at five different grade levels (sixth, eighth, tenth, twelfth, and college) accurately reported that the speakers feigning liking really did not feel as much liking as the speakers conveying genuine liking (DePaulo, Jordan, Irvine, & Laser, 1982). The most generous interpretation of these findings is that the perceivers recognized when deception was occurring, and then accordingly attributed less extreme positivity to the speakers than what was overtly expressed. The more likely interpretation, however, is that the positivity in the messages conveyed by the deceptive senders really was less extreme than the positivity conveyed by the truthful speakers, and the perceivers simply reported the degree of positivity that was overtly expressed. (See DePaulo & Jordan, 1982.)

The generous interpretation would gain plausibility if it could be shown that children can discriminate truth from deceit when asked specifically about senders' deceptiveness. The available evidence, however, is not encouraging. In the person description study described above (DePaulo, Jordan, Irvine, & Laser, 1982), only the twelfth graders and college students accurately rated the liars as more dishonest than the truth tellers. In another study (Morency & Krauss, 1982), first and fifth graders watched a series of pleasant and unpleasant slides, and tried to "deceive" while viewing half of them. That is, they tried to convey the impression that the pleasant slides were unpleasant and that the unpleasant slides were pleasant. Videotapes were made of the children's facial expressions, and rated by other first and fifth graders. Only a glimmer of lie-detection success was found. None of the children could detect the deception of the fifth graders, and the first graders' deception was discernible only when they were watching the pleasant stimuli. In summary, then, there is as yet no evidence that children can detect deception on the basis of message cues alone, except occasionally, when trying to detect the deception of other very young children. Since the accuracy achieved by adults at this task is only slightly better than chance, perhaps it should not be surprising to find that children have great difficulty, too.

Learning to Deceive

We do not know when children first begin to try to deceive others, but we suspect that some of the earliest forms of deception may include denials of wrongdoing to escape immanent punishment, and perhaps somewhat later, lies that are fabricated to obtain material rewards. Lies generated to secure social rewards perhaps occur later still, but not as late as truly altruistic lies (cf. Greenglass, 1972).

If there is an emotional concomitant to children's earliest lies, it is probably the fear of getting caught. Immature deceivers are not yet heavily burdened by the guilt, shame, or evaluation apprehension that older liars probably experience quite regularly (cf. Peterson et al., 1983). At the same time, however, they are not yet blessed with the fine muscular control, the cognitive and social skills, or the interpersonal experiences that can potentially contribute enormously to the success of their deceptive efforts. For example, it is only gradually that children come to appreciate fully that people are held responsible for their expressive behaviors, that those behaviors are ambiguous stimuli that are interpreted by others, and that such behaviors can therefore be manipulated so as to influence others.

Children's Management of Visual and Vocal Cues in Deceiving Like the research on children's detection of deception, most studies of children's skills and strategies in deceiving have focused on the use of visual nonverbal cues—usually facial cues. These studies document developmental increases in deceptive abilities throughout the childhood years.

In the slide-viewing study described earlier (Morency & Krauss, 1982), for example, first graders fooled their peers only when viewing the unpleasant slides; when viewing the pleasant slides, their peers were able accurately to determine when they were lying and when they were telling the truth. The fifth graders, in contrast, successfully deceived their peers on both types of trials. When the tapes were shown to the senders' parents, however, the children's deceptive skills seemed somewhat less impressive. The parents could detect the first graders' deception on both the pleasant and the unpleasant slides, and they could detect the fifth graders' deception when they were viewing the pleasant slides. There is evidence, though, that fourth and fifth graders can successfully deceive adults when the adults are strangers (Allen & Atkinson, 1978).

Because facial expressions are more readily controlled than body movements, one might expect that with age, children would become especially adept at controlling their facial expressions (cf. Ekman, Roper, & Hager, 1980; Yarczower, Kilbride, & Hill, 1979). Feldman and White (1980) tested this hypothesis with children ranging in age from 5 to 12 years old. The children sampled good- and bad-tasting drinks and for half of the trials tried to convince the experimenter that the good drink actually tasted bad or vice versa. One camera recorded subjects' facial expressions while another simultaneously recorded their body movements from the neck down. Undergraduate observers then judged the degree of deceptiveness of each clip. For girls, the results were exactly as predicted: With age, their facial expressions became less and less revealing of deception while their body communication became more transparent. Unexpectedly, the opposite pattern tended to occur for boys: Their deceptiveness became more and more obvious, with age, to observers who viewed their faces, while their bodily deceit tended to become somewhat better concealed.

In the Morency and Krauss (1982) and Feldman and White (1980) studies, judges rated the deceptiveness of the senders. In most other studies, judges rated the senders' affects or attitudes. These latter studies are particularly informative with regard to the strategies used by children at various ages in their attempts to deceive. Based on the literature, three strategies seem particularly important. The first strategy is perhaps no strategy at all. Its occurrence is indicated by a pattern of readability or leakage—when senders are pretending to feel a certain affect, their true affect "leaks" out, and the judges are not fooled. For example, children pretending to like a bad-tasting drink would be accurately perceived as liking the drink less than when they were actually sampling a good-tasting drink. A second strategy involves a naturalistic reproduction of the simulated affect. When this reproduction is utilized successfully, the senders would be perceived as liking the drink just as much when only pretending to like it as when they actually did like it. The last strategy might be called exaggeration, augmentation, or "hamming." When "hams" pretend to like a bad-tasting drink, they are perceived as liking the drink even more than when they actually do like it. This strategy tends to be very effective (DePaulo & Rosenthal, 1979b). Research has shown that the three strategies comprise a developmental progression (Feldman, Jenkins, & Popoola, 1979): First graders "leak" (see also Feldman et al., 1978), seventh graders use a naturalistic reproduction strategy, and college students are "hams."

Apparently, however, hamming is not a strategy used exclusively by adults, as Shennum and Bugental (1982) effectively demonstrated. In their study, 6- to 12-year-old subjects were instructed to assume the role of a famous movie star being interviewed by a talk-show host. The children were encouraged to show how well they could act. Specifically, on different questions, they were to pretend to like something they really disliked (substitute positive for negative), pretend to dislike something they really liked (substitute negative for positive), pretend to feel neutral about something they really disliked (inhibit negative), and pretend to feel neutral about something they really liked (inhibit positive). Truthful encodings were recorded in an interview conducted prior to the talk show simulation, in which the children honestly answered neutral questions and questions about their likes and dislikes. Separate recordings of subjects' facial expressions and their content-filtered voices were rated by adult judges on scales measuring affect (positive-negative) and deceptiveness.

When subjects' true feelings were negative, but they tried to inhibit those negative feelings, or substitute positive feelings for them, their facial and vocal expressions were extremely positive. In fact, children at all ages who were feigning positive affect looked and sounded more positive than they did when truthfully describing their likes. That is, at all ages, children who were trying to hide true negative feelings acted like hams. For facial expressions, hamming was less exaggerated for the older children, but for vocal expressions, the intensity of the hamming was constant across age levels. The elicitation of a hamming strategy at much younger ages in the Shennum and Bugental study (1982) than in the Feldman et al. (1979) study may have been a result of the explicit instructions to the children to act like famous movie stars.

Judges who were rating the voices on the scale of deceptiveness could detect the deception of the children at every age level equally well. When rating the children's faces, however, they were more often fooled by the older children. In keeping with Morency and Krauss's findings, and Feldman and White's findings for girls, children experiencing negative affect do become increasingly proficient at using their faces to deceive other people.

Also consistent with Morency and Krauss's research was the finding that children were less successful at deceiving when their true affect was positive than when it was negative. At every age level, children's lies designed to conceal positivity—whether communicated facially or vocally—were easily detected by the judges. When subjects were trying to neutralize (inhibit) their positive affect and when they were trying to substitute negative affect for it, their faces appeared just as positive as when the subjects were truthfully describing their likes. Thus, subjects' underlying feelings of positivity "leaked" through their faces. Surprisingly, no such leakage occurred through the voice. Subjects at all ages managed to sound neutral when trying to inhibit, and they also managed to sound negative when trying to substitute. The judges who successfully determined the degree of deceptiveness in these voices were apparently using cues other than the appropriateness of the degree of positivity that the children expressed.

Taken together, these studies seem to indicate that—unless they are encouraged to act like movie stars—first graders cannot successfully tell a lie. When they attempt to do so, their underlying affect leaks out, and the fact that they are lying is obvious to their peers. Third graders have trouble, too, in much the same way—their true feelings leak. There seems to be notable improvement by fourth and fifth grade. These children can fool their peers and adult strangers, and sometimes they can even fool their parents. There is some evidence that between the ages of five and 12, children become increasingly adept at hiding their deception facially. At all of these ages, however, children's voice tones readily reveal to others when they are lying and when they are telling the truth.

Children's Spontaneous Use of Impression-Management and Deception In the studies reviewed thus far, children were explicitly instructed to be deceptive. Such paradigms indicate whether children at different ages can potentially deceive successfully, but not whether they will try to deceive (or succeed at deceiving) when left to their own devices.

Saarni (1982) observed children's spontaneous use of impression management strategies in a study in which 9, 10, and 11 year olds were asked, in two different sessions, to evaluate workbooks for a market researcher. At the end of the first session, the researcher gave all subjects very appealing gifts as a reward for their help. Their responses to receiving these highly desirable items were videotaped. At the end of the second session, the children were given another festively wrapped package. Inside this one, however, was a highly unappealing, age-inappropriate toy.

For each of the two sessions, Saarni coded various verbal, vocal, and facial behaviors (indicative of positivity or negativity) exhibited by the children upon opening the gifts. The positivity of children's responses to the drab gift increased with age. As children grow older, Saarni suggested, they become increasingly willing (and able) to regulate their expressive behavior to accord with social conventions (such as the one that suggests that people should not reveal their displeasures at receiving an undesired gift). Comparison of the session-two reactions to the session-one reactions, however, showed that even the oldest children were not entirely successful at hiding their disappointment. Children at all three age levels showed more negative behaviors, and fewer positive behaviors, during the second session.

Verbally-Based Deceptive Strategies One of the few studies of children's verbally-based strategies for deceiving grew out of the research tradition on machiavellianism. In that study (Braginsky, 1970), an experimenter, presenting herself as a representative of a cracker company, gave children a taste of a cracker that had been dipped in a quinine solution. She then offered the children a nickel for every cracker they could convince an unsuspecting peer to eat.

The behaviors of the high and low mach children differed markedly. First, high machs were more successful than lows: They convinced their peers to eat many more of the quinine-dipped delicacies. Second, high machs engaged in more of all sorts of manipulative behaviors (omissive lies, commissive lies, bribery, two-sided arguments, blaming the experimenter) than did low machs, although the difference was significant only for omissive lies. Finally, the high machs sounded like little angels. Judges who listened to tape recordings of the transactions rated the high machs as sounding more innocent, honest, calm, and comfortable than the low machs. The judges also thought that the high machs used more effective arguments and were more likely to be successful in a sales position than the low machs.

Little girl machs told different kinds of lies than little boy machs. High-mach girls more often told omissive lies (they withheld information and evaded questions), while high-mach boys more often told commissive lies (they distorted information). In each case, the strategy was apparently effective: Frequency of omissive lies predicted manipulated success for girls but not for boys, while the reverse was true for commissive lies.

Training Grounds for the Development of Deceptive Abilities Where do children learn and practice their skills at deceiving and also at detecting deceit? There are many contexts, but here we will discuss just one. We propose that child's play, in many of its manifestations, functions as a training ground for the development and refinement of deceptive abilities. Probably every major category of play—for example, card games, board games, party games, and sports—includes numerous specific games that involve deceit. Many of these are popular games that fill countless childhood hours. For example, some sports, such as football and basketball, involve faking a pass or a throw in one direction but then actually tossing the ball in a different direction. This involves intricate coordination on the part of the ball handler, as well as sophisticated decoding strategies on the part of the defensive players. Card games that teach deceit include Old Maid and children's versions of poker. These games provide ample opportunity to practice concealment and dissimulation of both positive and negative affects. Board games such as checkers and party games such as "buttony button" (in which children try to determine who *really* has the button) train nonverbal skills especially. More complicated games, such as diplomatic or war-type simulations, sharpen children's skills at verbal deceit. Other games and ritual activities do not involve deception per se, but do allow for practice in the control of nonverbal behaviors (e.g., staring contests) and in the control of emotions (e.g., "the dozens").

If one were to design a program to teach deceptive skills, one might incorporate many of the special features that characterize game-type deceits. For example, one might like one's trainees to practice their developing skills guiltlessly, or perhaps even gleefully. In a communication task, it might help to have some familiarity with the other participants' expressive styles. This requirement is met quite adequately by involving friends as co-trainees. Further, in a training program, the phenomenon of interest is highly salient, and the examples of that phenomenon that are to be mastered at any given point in the program are held to a reasonable number. So, too, in games involving deceit, deception is often highly salient and the range of possible contents of the deceit is not unmanageably large. Finally, in many games and sports, feedback about the occurrence of deception is often direct, unambiguous, and immediate (e.g., the ball is or is not thrown in the direction of the ball handler's gaze). This feedback should improve children's deception abilities (cf. Zuckerman, Koestner, & Alton, 1984). Thus, while it may be true, as Piaget (1965) has claimed, that children learn from their interactions with their peers moral and interpersonal reasons for not lying, we would like to propose that children also learn and practice with their peers the skills necessary to tell lies, should they decide to do so.

THE AFTERMATH OF DECEPTION[3]

In discussing deception, we have primarily used the language of "abilities" and "skills" rather than "morals," "virtues," or "interpersonal respect and trust." At times, we may even seem to have implied that good liars and lie detectors should be commended for their talents. Was this really appropriate? Translated into an empirically testable issue, the question becomes: "What are the personal and interpersonal consequences of detecting lies and telling lies?"

---

[3]This section (and parts of the preceding section) was adapted from DePaulo and Jordan (1982).

We will tackle the detection question first. Let us assume that most of the time when people tell lies, they would prefer that their insincerity *not* be discovered. Observers who are skilled at detecting deceit, then, may suffer worse interpersonal consequences than those who are not blessed with this particular talent: For example, they may have fewer friends and feel less satisfied with the relationships that they do have.

Suggestive evidence supportive of this point of view comes from a series of studies of sex differences in the use of a "politeness" strategy in nonverbal communication (Rosenthal & DePaulo, 1979a, 1979b). The premise of the politeness research was that different sources of nonverbal cues or kinds of cues (e.g., face, body and tone of voice cues; discrepant cues) vary in "leakiness"—i.e., the degree to which they reveal affects that senders might be trying to hide. The major finding of this research program was a sex difference in the accuracy with which these various cues were decoded. While females tend to surpass men in their accuracy at understanding nonverbally communicated affects, their decoding advantage decreases as the cues become more leaky. Also, in decoding messages in which several different cues communicate conflicting emotions, females (more than males) trust the more overt and less "leaky" cues. It is as if females are politely refraining from reading just those cues that the senders would prefer to remain unnoticed. It is not yet clear whether women really do notice leaky cues, but then choose to ignore them, or whether they never notice them at all. The specific process that underlies the politeness phenomenon—whatever it may be—is one that seems to be learned over the course of socialization, for developmental studies have shown that with age, these sex differences in decoding become increasingly evident (Blanck, Rosenthal, Snodgrass, DePaulo, & Zuckerman, 1981).

More relevant to the present discussion is the evidence suggesting that there are social costs to reading unintended messages. In a sample of high-school students, both males and females who were especially skilled at reading covert cues were rated by their teachers as less popular and less socially sensitive than other students who showed the politeness pattern of superiority at reading overt (nonleaky) cues. This result was slightly more characteristic of the females than the males. For a sample of college students (though not for the high-school sample), similar findings were obtained based on self-ratings—that is, students who were especially skilled at reading unintended messages reported feeling less satisfied with the quality of their interpersonal relationships (Rosenthal & DePaulo, 1979a, 1979b).

The available evidence suggests that skill at uncovering deceit is at least in some sense not such a good thing. For one thing, it might cause social friction. A more naive approach to decoding deceit—namely, taking messages at face value—may have its advantages. This unsuspecting approach may in some circumstances be the easiest, quickest, and safest way to deal with the many complex and multileveled affective messages that people sometimes convey. Seeing only what you are supposed to see might be simpler not only cognitively but also emotionally. People who begin to doubt external appearances are first of all going to experience more uncertainty. They may also feel guilty about their suspiciousness and lack of trust, and further, they might find out something about another person's feelings toward them that they might be much happier not knowing (cf. DePaulo, 1981). Finally, perceivers who believe the overt messages that senders convey to them may find that such publicly expressed attitudes and affects provide a better guide to the way the senders will act toward them in the future than the views and feelings that senders keep to themselves (cf. Kiesler, 1971).

However, we do not deny that there are circumstances under which perceivers are much better off deciphering the truth—as for example, when the communicator might act in a way that will be harmful, insulting, or damaging, and knowledge of the communicator's true feelings can be used to prevent the harmful actions. We also believe that in certain professions, such as psychiatry and medicine, sensitivity to true, but covered-up, feelings might be especially beneficial.

Can we make a similar case that skill at deceiving is most often (though not always) socially hazardous? We think that predictions are less straightforward for this issue. (Also, there are fewer relevant data.) Consider, for example, the tale of the emperor's new clothes. This typifies the folklore of children as occasionally unselfconsciously and brutally honest. Children are especially notable not for the lies that they do tell, but for those that they do not tell. When children are young and cute enough, this forthrightness is usually excused as innocent or even "adorable." However, when children get old enough to be accountable for courtesy, parents and other authority figures begin to regard such frankness as socially embarrassing. At this point, it is costly for children *not* to tell lies.

Other kinds of lies are rewarded by peers rather than parents. For example, in delinquent gangs, a child who can fool a police officer earns status, prestige, and adoration. For this conniving child to reap such rewards, it is important not only that the lie be told, but that it be told well (i.e., convincingly). This is true for many categories of deceit, including lies told by adults—i.e., the interpersonal consequences depend on whether the lie is discovered.

The likely interpersonal ramifications of deceit might be conceptualized in terms of Lindskold and Walters' (1983) multiple classification of deceptive intents. Deceivers who are caught lying probably suffer negative interpersonal consequences if they intended to harm the target of the lie or if they were attempting to benefit themselves by their deceit. More positive social outcomes might accrue to the liar who was trying to help the target, particularly if the lie involved some possibility of risk or harm to the liar (cf. Peterson et al., 1983). Even in these instances, however, the consequences may not be entirely positive. The target of the lie might resent any dishonesty, even well-intended "white lies" or misrepresentations. Too, the recipient of a "helpful" lie might experience other negative affects that sometimes accompany the receipt of aid, such as an aversive state of indebtedness (cf. Greenberg & Westcott, 1983). Moreover, deceivers who are caught in their lies may lose the trust of the persons they have deceived; this trust may be difficult—or sometimes even impossible—to win back. Ironically, then, although deceivers may enjoy an increment of power as long as their lies go undetected (as, for example, when deceptive information leads a target person to make a decision that is in the deceiver's—but not the target's—best interest), this power differential may quickly be reversed once the lie has been discovered, and credibility and trust have been eroded. (See Bok, 1978.) In general, then, it is probably often socially beneficial *not* to get caught telling lies. (See also Schlenker & Leary, 1982a.)

In keeping with our discussion of the personal and interpersonal correlates of skill at detecting deceit, it is possible that skill at deceiving others carries different implications for females than for males. The one relevant empirical finding is consistent with this hypothesis: In Braginsky's (1970) study in which children were offered a nickel for each bitter cracker they could convince a peer to consume, the children who felt most uncomfortable after the interaction were the successful girls and the unsuccessful boys.

Other interpersonal consequences of deception are even more subtle. For example, recent research (Toris & DePaulo, in press) suggests that one effect of deception may be to undermine the degree to which two people are "in tune" with each other with respect to their perceptions of the tone of their interactions, and their feelings about each other. Ordinarily, liking is reciprocated: People are especially attracted to those persons who are especially attracted to them (Berscheid & Walster, 1978). Toris and DePaulo showed that such reciprocity does in fact occur when both persons in the relationship are telling the truth, but not when one of the persons is lying. Under conditions of deception, there is no correspondence at all between the degree to which A likes B, and the degree to which B likes A. Why is mutuality of liking destroyed during deceit? There is no empirically established answer to this question as yet, but the dynamics of the process might be as follows: In a dishonest relationship, A may feign greater liking for B than A really feels. B may accept A's positive sentiments at face value, and reciprocate them in full. B's liking for A, then, would exceed A's actual degree of liking for B.

Bok (1978) has described other effects that the practice of deception can have on the deceiver and on the social community. As a consequence of lying, she argues, deceivers may develop a dimmer view of themselves, and even of the targets of their lies. Further, once the first lies are told, others may follow more easily. "Psychological barriers wear down; lies seem more necessary, less reprehensible; the ability to make moral distinctions can coarsen; the liar's perception of his chances of being caught may warp (p. 27)." Still another risk inherent in telling the first lie is that it may in fact be necessary to tell more lies to keep the first one intact. In addition to the moral burdens of lying, the deceivers must then contend with the cognitive burdens of maintaining a mental record of the lies that have been told, the persons who were the targets of those lies, the persons with whom those targets might converse, the facts or anecdotes introduced into conversations that might prove inconsistent with the lies, and so forth.

Lies can foster more lies, not only by the deceiver, but also by the deceived. Children who are the targets of lies may tell lies in imitation, and adults may tell them in retaliation. As lies continue to multiply, Bok (1978) argues, the trust that exists at the level of the community begins to disintegrate, and ultimately, the society as a whole may suffer.

While few dispute the argument that some lies can have the deleterious consequences described by Bok, others (e.g., Bonhoeffer, 1955; Scheibe, 1980) have cautioned against the complete repudiation of all deceptive practices. For example, readily accepted social conventions such as courtesy, tact, and discretion often rely more heavily on deception than on truth. Thus, both truth telling and lie telling, they have argued, can be used in ways that are supportive of human dignity and trust, or in ways that are destructive of those same qualities.

REFERENCES

Ackerman, B. P. (1981). Young children's understanding of a speaker's intentional use of a false utterance. *Developmental Psychology, 17,* 472–480.

Ackerman, B. P. (1983). Speaker bias in children's evaluation of the external consistency of statements. *Journal of Experimental Child Psychology, 35,* 111–127.

Alker, H. A. (1976, September). *Mystification and deception in presidential press conferences.* Paper presented at the meeting of the American Psychological Association, Washington, D.C.

Allen, V. L. & Atkinson, M. L. (1978). Encoding of nonverbal behavior by high-achieving and low-achieving children. *Journal of Educational Psychology, 70,* 298–305.

Anderson, C. A., Lepper, M. R., & Ross, L. (1980). Perseverance of social theories: The role of explanation in the persistence of discredited information. *Journal of Personality and Social Psychology, 39,* 1037–1049.

Anderson, N. H. (1968). Likableness ratings of 555 personality-trait words. *Journal of Personality and Social Psychology, 9,* 272–279.

Aristotle. (1934). *Nicomachean ethics* (bk 4, chap. 7, pp. 189–251). (H. Rackham, Trans.). Cambridge, MA: Harvard University Press.

Berscheid, E. & Walster, E. H. (1978). *Interpersonal attraction* (2nd ed.). Reading, MA: Addison-Wesley.

Blanck, P. D., Rosenthal, R., Snodgrass, S. E., DePaulo, B. M., & Zuckerman, M. (1981). Sex differences in eavesdropping on nonverbal cues: Developmental changes. *Journal of Personality and Social Psychology, 41,* 391–396.

Blanck, P. D. & Rosenthal, R. (1982). Developing strategies for decoding "leaky" messages: On learning how and when to decode discrepant and consistent social communications. In R. S. Feldman (Ed.), *Development of nonverbal behavior in children* (pp. 203–229). New York: Springer-Verlag.

Bok, S. (1978). *Lying: Moral choice in public and private life.* New York: Pantheon.

Bonhoeffer, D. (1955). *Ethics.* New York: Macmillan.

Braginsky, D. D. (1970). Machiavellianism and manipulative interpersonal behavior in children. *Journal of Experimental Social Psychology, 6,* 77–99.

Bugental, D. E., Kaswan, J. W., Love, L. R., & Fox, M. N. (1970). Child versus adult perception of evaluative messages in verbal, vocal, and visual channels. *Developmental Psychology, 2,* 367–375.

Cabot, R. C. (1938). *Honesty.* New York: Macmillan.

Christie, R. & Geis, F. L. (1970). *Studies in machiavellianism.* New York: Academic Press.

Cohen, J. (1977). *Statistical power analysis for the behavioral sciences* (Revised edition). New York: Academic Press.

Crowne, D. P. & Marlowe, D. (1964). *The approval motive: Studies in evaluative dependence.* New York: Wiley.

Darby, B. W. & Schlenker, B. R. (1982). Children's reactions to apologies. *Journal of Personality and Social Psychology, 43,* 742–753.

DePaulo, B. M. (1981). Success at detecting deception: Liability or skill? *Annals of the New York Academy of Sciences, 364,* 245–255.

DePaulo, B. M. & Jordan, A. (1982). Age changes in deceiving and detecting deceit. In R. S. Feldman (Ed.), *Development of nonverbal behavior in children* (pp. 151–180). New York: Springer-Verlag.

DePaulo, B. M., Jordan, A., Irvine, A., & Laser, P. S. (1982). Age changes in the detection of deception. *Child Development, 53,* 701–709.

DePaulo, B. M., Lanier, K., & Davis, T. (1983). Detecting the deceit of the motivated liar. *Journal of Personality and Social Psychology, 45,* 1096–1103.

DePaulo, B. M., Lassiter, G. D., & Stone, J. I. (1982). Attentional determinants of success at detecting deception and truth. *Personality and Social Psychology Bulletin, 8,* 273–279.

DePaulo, B. M., & Rosenthal, R. (1979a). Ambivalence, discrepancy, and deception in nonverbal communication. In R. Rosenthal (Ed.), *Skill in nonverbal communication* (pp. 204–248). Cambridge, MA: Oelgeschlager, Gunn, & Hain.

DePaulo, B. M., & Rosenthal, R. (1979b). Telling lies. *Journal of Personality and Social Psychology, 37,* 1713–1722.

DePaulo, B. M., Rosenthal, R., Green, C. R., & Rosenkrantz, J. (1982). Diagnosing deceptive and mixed messages from verbal and nonverbal cues. *Journal of Experimental Social Psychology, 18,* 433–446.

DePaulo, B. M., Rosenthal, R., Rosenkrantz, J., & Green, C. R. (1982). Actual and perceived cues to deception: A closer look at speech. *Basic and Applied Social Psychology, 3,* 291–312.

DePaulo, B. M., Stone, J. I., & Lassiter, G. D. (in press). Telling ingratiating lies: Effects of target sex and target attractiveness on verbal and nonverbal deceptive success. *Journal of Personality and Social Psychology.*

DePaulo, B. M., & Toris, C. (1984). *Verbal nonimmediacy and its relationship to deception.* Manuscript in preparation, University of Virginia.

DePaulo, B. M., Zuckerman, M., & Rosenthal, R. (1980a). The deceptions of everyday life. *Journal of Communication, 30,* 216–218.

DePaulo, B. M., Zuckerman, M., & Rosenthal, R. (1980b). Detecting deception: Modality effects. In L. Wheeler (Ed.), *The review of personality and social psychology* (Vol. 1, pp. 125–162). Beverly Hills, CA: Sage.

DePaulo, B. M., Zuckerman, M., & Rosenthal, R. (1980c). Humans as lie detectors. *Journal of Communication, 30,* 129–139.

de Villiers, J. G., & de Villiers, P. A. (1978). *Language acquisition.* Cambridge, MA: Harvard University Press.

Ekman, P. (1981). Mistakes when deceiving. *Annals of the New York Academy of Sciences, 364,* 269–278.

Ekman, P. & Friesen, W. V. (1969). Nonverbal leakage and clues to deception. *Psychiatry, 32,* 88–106.

Ekman, P. & Friesen, W. V. (1972). Hand movements. *Journal of Communication, 22,* 353–374.

Ekman, P. & Friesen, W. V. (1974). Detecting deception from the body or face. *Journal of Personality and Social Psychology, 29,* 288–298.

Ekman, P., Friesen, W. V., O'Sullivan, M., & Scherer, K. (1980). Relative importance of face, body, and speech in judgments of personality and affect. *Journal of Personality and Social Psychology, 38,* 270–277.

Ekman, P., Friesen, W. V., & Scherer, K. R. (1976). Body movement and voice pitch in deceptive interaction. *Semiotica, 16,* 23–27.

Ekman, P., Roper, G., & Hager, J. C. (1980). Deliberate facial movement. *Child Development, 51,* 886–891.

Elliott, G. C. (1979). Some effects of deception and level of self-monitoring on planning and reacting to a self-presentation. *Journal of Personality and Social Psychology, 37,* 1282–1292.

Exline, R., Thibaut, J., Hickey, C., & Gumpert, P. (1970). Visual interaction in relation to machiavellianism and an unethical act. In R. Christie & F. Geis (Eds.), *Studies in machiavellianism* (pp. 53–75). New York: Academic Press.

Feldman, R. S. (1976). Nonverbal disclosure of teacher deception and interpersonal affect. *Journal of Educational Psychology, 68,* 807–816.

Feldman, R. S., Devin-Sheehan, L., & Allen, V. L. (1978). Nonverbal cues as indicators of verbal dissembling. *American Educational Research Journal, 15,* 217–231.

Feldman, R. S., Jenkins, L., & Popoola, O. (1979). Detection of deception in adults and children via facial expressions. *Child Development, 50,* 350–355.

Feldman, R. S. & White, J. B. (1980). Detecting deception in children. *Journal of Communication, 30,* 121–139.

Flavell, J. H. (1977). *Cognitive development.* Englewood Cliffs, NJ: Prentice-Hall.

Folkes, V. S. (1982). Communicating the reasons for social rejection. *Journal of Experimental Social Psychology, 18,* 235–252.

Freud, S. (1959). *Collected papers.* New York: Basic Books.

Gardner, H., Kircher, M., Winner, E., & Perkins, D. (1975). Children's metaphoric productions and preferences. *Journal of Child Language, 2,* 125–141.

Gardner, H., Winner, E., Bechhofer, R., & Wolf, D. (1978). The development of figurative language. In K. E. Nelson (Ed.), *Children's language* (Vol. 1, pp. 1–38). New York: Gardner Press.

Geis, F. L., & Moon, T. H. (1981). Machiavellianism and deception. *Journal of Personality and Social Psychology, 41,* 766–775.

Gergen, K. J. (1965). The effects of interaction goals and personalistic feedback on the presentation of self. *Journal of Personality and Social Psychology, 1,* 413–424.

Goffman, E. (1959). *The presentation of self in everyday life.* Garden City, New York: Doubleday.

Goldman-Eisler, F. (1968). *Psycholinguistics: Experiments in spontaneous speech.* New York: Academic Press.

Gottlieb, D. E., Taylor, S. E., & Ruderman, A. (1977). Cognitive bases of children's moral judgments. *Developmental Psychology, 13,* 547–556.

Greenberg, M. S. & Westcott, D. R. (1983). Indebtedness as a mediator of reactions to aid. In J. D. Fisher, A. Nadler, and B. M. DePaulo (Eds.), *New Directions in helping: Vol 1, Recipient reactions to aid* (pp. 85–112). New York: Academic Press.

Greenglass, E. R. (1972). Effects of age and prior help on "altruistic lying." *Journal of Genetic Psychology, 121,* 303–313.

Grice, H. P. (1975). Logic and conversation. In P. Cole & J. Morgan (Eds.), *Syntax and semantics: Vol. 3. Speech acts* (pp. 41–58). New York: Academic Press.

Hendershot, J., & Hess, A. K. (1982). *Detecting deception: The effects of training and socialization levels on verbal and nonverbal cue utilization and detection accuracy.* Unpublished manuscript, Auburn University.

Jones, E. E. (1979). The rocky road from acts to dispositions. *American Psychologist, 34,* 107–117.

Jones, E. E. & Harris, V. A. (1967). The attribution of attitudes. *Journal of Experimental Social Psychology, 3,* 1–24.

Jones, E. E. & Pittman, T. S. (1982). Toward a general theory of strategic self-presentation. In J. Suls (Ed.), *Psychological perspectives on the self* (Vol. 1, pp. 231–262). Hillsdale, NJ: Erlbaum.

Jones, E. E., Stires, L. K., Shaver, K. G., & Harris, V. A. (1968). Evaluation of an ingratiator by target persons and bystanders. *Journal of Personality, 36,* 349–385.

Jones, E. E. & Wortman, C. (1973). *Ingratiation: An attributional approach.* Morristown, NJ: General Learning Press.

Kahneman, D. (1973). *Attention and effort.* Englewood Cliffs, NJ: Prentice-Hall.

Kant, I. (1964). The doctrine of virtue. In *The metaphysics of morals* (Pt. 2, pp. 92–96). (M. Gregor, Trans.). New York: Harper & Row.

Karniol, R. (1978). Children's use of intention cues in evaluating behavior. *Psychological Bulletin, 85,* 76–85.

Keasey, C. B. (1977). Children's developing awareness and usage of intentionality and motives. In C. B. Keasey (Ed.), *Nebraska symposium on motivation 1977* (pp. 219–260). Lincoln: University of Nebraska Press.

Kiesler, C. A. (1971). *The psychology of commitment.* New York: Academic Press.

Kotsonis, M. (1980). *Children's interpretations of conversationally-implied meanings.* Unpublished doctoral dissertation, University of Virginia.

Knapp, M. L. & Comadena, M. E. (1979). Telling it like it isn't: A review of theory and research on deception communications. *Human Communication Research, 5,* 270–285.

Knapp, M. L., Hart, R. P., & Dennis, H. S. (1974). An exploration of deception as a communication construct. *Human Communication Research, 1,* 15–29.

Krauss, R. M. (1981). Impression formation, impression management, and nonverbal behaviors. In E. T. Higgins, C. P. Herman, & M. P. Zanna (Eds.), *Social cognition: The Ontario Symposium* (Vol. 1, pp. 323–341). Hillsdale, NJ: Erlbaum.

Kraut, R. E. (1978). Verbal and nonverbal cues in the perception of lying. *Journal of Personality and Social Psychology, 36,* 380–391.

Kraut, R. E. (1980). Humans as lie-detectors: Some second thoughts. *Journal of Communication, 30,* 209–216.

Kraut, R. E. & Poe, D. (1980). Behavioral roots of person perception: The deception judgments of customs inspectors and laymen. *Journal of Personality and Social Psychology, 39,* 784–798.

Lindskold, S. & Walters, P. S. (1983). Categories for acceptability of lies. *Journal of Social Psychology, 120,* 129–136.

Lippa, M. (1976). Expressive control and the leakage of dispositional introversion-extraversion during role-played teaching. *Journal of Personality, 44,* 541–559.

Littlepage, G. E., & Pineault, M. A. (1979, November). *Detection of deception of planned vs. spontaneous communications.* Paper presented at the meeting of the Psychonomic Society, Phoenix, Arizona.

Lord, C. G., Ross, L., & Lepper, M. R. (1979). Biased assimilation and attitude polarization: The effects of prior theories on subsequently considered evidence. *Journal of Personality and Social Psychology, 37,* 2098–2109.

Ludwig, A. (1965). *The importance of lying.* Springfield, IL: Charles C. Thomas.

Lykken, D. T. (1974). Psychology and the lie detector industry. *American Psychologist, 29,* 725–739.

Miller, G. R., de Turck, M. A., & Kalbfleisch, P. J. (1982). *Effects of self-monitoring and rehearsal on accuracy in detecting deception and behavioral correlates of deception.* Unpublished manuscript, Michigan State University.

Montaigne, M. Des menteurs. (1962). In M. Rat (Ed.), *Essais.* Editions Garnier Frères.

Morency, N. L. & Krauss, R. M. (1982). The nonverbal encoding and decoding of affect in first and fifth graders. In R. S. Feldman (Ed.), *Development of nonverbal behavioral skill* (pp. 181–199). New York: Springer-Verlag.

Nelson, K. E. & Nelson, K. (1978). Cognitive pendulums. In K. E. Nelson (Ed.), *Children's language* (Vol. 1, pp. 223–285). New York: Gardner Press.

Nelson, S. A. (1980). Factors influencing young children's use of motives and outcomes as moral criteria. *Child Development, 51,* 823–829.

Newman, D. (1982). Perspective-taking versus content in understanding lies. *Quarterly Newsletter of the Laboratory of Comparative Human Cognition, 4,* 26–29.

O'Hair, H. D., Cody, M. J., & McLaughlin, M. L. (1981). Prepared lies, spontaneous lies, machiavellianism, and nonverbal communication. *Human Communication Research, 7,* 325–339.

Peevers, B. H. & Secord, P. F. (1973). Developmental changes in attribution of descriptive concepts to persons. *Journal of Personality and Social Psychology, 27,* 120–128.

Peterson, C. C., Peterson, J. L., & Seeto, D. (1983). Developmental changes in ideas about lying. *Child Development, 54,* 1529–1535.

Piaget, J. (1965). *The moral judgment of the child.* New York: The Free Press.

Podlesny, J. A. & Raskin, D. C. (1977). Physiological measures and the detection of deception. *Psychological Bulletin, 84,* 782–791.

Raskin, D. C. (1982). The scientific basis of polygraph techniques and their use in the judicial process. In A. Trankell (Ed.), *Reconstructing the past: The role of psychologists in criminal trials* (pp. 317–371). Stockholm: Norstedt and Soners.

Riggio, R. E., & Friedman, H. S. (1983). Individual differences and cues to deception. *Journal of Personality and Social Psychology, 45,* 899–915.

Rosenthal, R. (1978). Combining results of independent studies. *Psychological Bulletin, 85,* 185–193.

Rosenthal, R., & DePaulo, B. M. (1979a). Sex differences in accommodation in nonverbal communication. In R. Rosenthal (Ed.), *Skill in nonverbal communication* (pp. 68–103). Cambridge, MA: Oelgeschlager, Gunn, & Hain.

Rosenthal, R., & DePaulo, B. M. (1979b). Sex differences in eavesdropping on nonverbal cues. *Journal of Personality and Social Psychology, 37,* 273–285.

Ross, L. (1977). The intuitive psychologist and his shortcomings: Distortions in the attribution process. In L. Berkowitz (Ed.), *Advances in experimental social psychology* (Vol. 10, pp. 173–220). New York: Academic Press.

Ross, R. P., Campbell, T., Huston-Stein, A., & Wright, J. C. (1981). Nutritional misinformation of children: A developmental and experimental analysis of the effects of televised food commercials. *Journal of Applied Developmental Psychology, 1,* 329–347.

Saarni, C. (1979). Children's understanding of display rules. *Developmental Psychology, 15,* 424–429.

Saarni, C. (1982). Social and affective functions of nonverbal behavior: Developmental concerns. In R. S. Feldman (Ed.), *Development of nonverbal behavior in children* (pp. 123–147). New York: Springer-Verlag.

Scheibe, K. E. (1980). In defense of lying: On the moral neutrality of misrepresentation. *Berkshire Review, 15,* 15–24.

Schlenker, B. R. (1980). *Impression management.* Monterey, CA: Brooks/Cole.

Schlenker, B. R. (1982). Translating actions into attitudes: An identity-analytic approach to the explanation of social conduct. In L. Berkowitz (Ed.) *Advances in experimental social psychology* (Vol. 15, pp. 193–247). New York: Academic Press.

Schlenker, B. R. & Leary, M. R. (1982a). Audiences' reactions to self-enhancing, self-denigrating, and accurate self-presentations. *Journal of Experimental Social Psychology, 18,* 89–104.

Schlenker, B. R. & Leary, M. R. (1982b). Social anxiety and self-presentation: A conceptualization and model. *Psychological Bulletin, 92,* 641–669.

Shennum, W. A. & Bugental, D. B. (1982). The development of control over affective expression in nonverbal behavior. In R. S. Feldman (Ed.), *Development of nonverbal behavior in children* (pp. 101–121). New York: Springer-Verlag.

Starkweather, J. (1956). Content-free speech as a source of information about the speaker. *Journal of Abnormal and Social Psychology, 52,* 394–402.

Stebbins, R. A. (1975). Putting people on: Deception of our fellow man in everyday life. *Sociology and Social Research, 59,* 189–200.

Streeter, L. A., Krauss, R. M., Geller, V., Olson, C., & Apple, W. (1977). Pitch changes during attempted deception. *Journal of Personality and Social Psychology, 35,* 345–350.

Surber, C. F. (1977). Developmental processes in social inference: Averaging of intentions and consequences in moral judgment. *Developmental Psychology, 13,* 654–665.

Toris, C., & DePaulo, B. M. (in press). Effects of actual deception and suspiciousness of deception on interpersonal perceptions. *Journal of Personality and Social Psychology.*

Turner, R. E., Edgley, C., & Olmstead, G. (1975). Information control in conversations: Honesty is not always the best policy. *Kansas Journal of Sociology, 11,* 69–89.

Volkmar, F. R. & Siegel, A. E. (1982). Responses to consistent and discrepant social communications. In R. S. Feldman (Ed.), *Development of nonverbal behavior in children* (pp. 231–255). New York: Springer-Verlag.

Waid, W. M. & Orne, M. T. (1981). Cognitive, social, and personality processes in the physiological detection of deception. In L. Berkowitz (Ed.), *Advances in experimental social psychology* (Vol. 14, pp. 61–106). New York: Academic Press.

Wiener, M., & Mehrabian, A. (1968). *Language within language.* New York: Appleton-Century-Crofts.

Wilde, O. (1969). The decay of lying. In R. Ellman (Ed.), *The artist as critic: Critical writings of Oscar Wilde* (pp. 290–320). New York: Random House.

Winner, E., Rosenstiel, A., & Gardner, H. (1976). The development of metaphoric understanding. *Developmental Psychology, 12,* 287–297.

Yarczower, M., Kilbride, J. E., & Hill, L. A. (1979). Imitation and inhibition of facial expression. *Developmental Psychology, 15,* 453–454.

Zuckerman, M., DeFrank, R. S., Hall, J. A., Larrance, D. T., & Rosenthal, R. (1979). Facial and vocal cues of honesty and deception. *Journal of Experimental Social Psychology, 15,* 378–396.

Zuckerman, M., DePaulo, B. M., & Rosenthal, R. (1981). Verbal and nonverbal communication of deception. In L. Berkowitz (Ed.), *Advances in experimental social psychology* (Vol. 14, pp. 1–59). New York: Academic Press.

Zuckerman, M. & Driver, R. E. (in press). Telling lies: Verbal and nonverbal correlates of deception. In A. W. Siegman & S. Feldstein (Eds.), *Nonverbal communication: An integrated perspective.* Hillsdale, NJ: Erlbaum.

Zuckerman, M., Koestner, R., & Alton, A. O. (1984). Learning to detect deception. *Journal of Personality and Social Psychology, 46,* 519–528.

Zuckerman, M., Larrance, D. T., Spiegel, N. H., & Klorman, R. (1981). Controlling nonverbal cues: Facial expressions and tone of voice. *Journal of Experimental Social Behavior, 17,* 506–524.

NAME INDEX

Abelson, R. P., 10, 25, 27, 76, 84, 98, 262, 269, 271, 273, 284, 287
Abramson, L. Y., 110, 111, 121, 124, 128, 141
Ackerman, B., 302, 318
Ackerman, B. P., 354, 364
Adelson, J., 36, 62
Adler, A., 110, 121, 236, 302, 318
Ajzen, I., 154, 171, 205, 228
Akert, R. M., 177, 195
Alba, J. W., 9–11, 14, 25
Aldwin, C., 111, 122
Alexander, C. N., Jr., 19, 25, 65, 68, 95, 210, 213, 229, 262, 284
Alker, H. A., 348–349, 364
Allen, J. G., 119, 122
Allen, V. L., 18, 27, 35, 48, 62, 64, 327, 355–357, 364, 366
Alloy, L. B., 110, 121, 127, 141
Allport, G. W., 13, 25, 182, 195, 236
Alton, A. O., 360, 370
Alvarez, M., 114, 122
Alves, W. M., 274, 285
Ames, R., 250, 255

Anderson, C. A., 345, 364
Anderson, N. H., 324, 364
Anderson, P. A., 224, 229
Andrews, F. M., 266, 283, 285
Anikeef, A. M., 245, 255
Apple, W., 346, 369
Appleman, A. J., 129, 141, 211, 218, 229, 250, 255
Appleman, A. S., 250, 255
Apter, M. J., 69, 95
Archer, D., 177, 195
Argyle, M., 31, 32
Aristotle, 2, 60, 62, 323, 364
Arkin, R. M., 14, 28, 90, 99, 129, 141, 176, 181, 195, 204, 211, 218, 222, 223, 229 , 233, 250, 255, 260, 295, 299, 304, 309, 318, 320, 322
Aronson, E., 244, 257
Asch, S. E., 135, 141, 154, 171, 177
Athay, M., 176, 181, 182, 195
Atkinson, J. W., 130, 133, 138, 143
Atkinson, M. L., 356, 364
Augelli, R. W., 247, 259
Augustine, 2

Austin, J. L., 199, 214, 201, 229
Austin, W., 248, 255
Ayers–Nachamkin, B., 254, 258

Backman, C. W., 15, 18, 23, 25, 27, 30, 32, 65, 68, 70, 71, 86, 89–91, 93, 95, 99, 101, 106, 117, 121, 124, 200, 241, 261, 262, 265–267, 270, 283, 285, 288
Baldwin, J. M., 16, 34, 36, 42–47, 49, 58, 62
Balkwell, J. W., 262, 287
Ball, R. A., 270, 282, 285
Ballen, P. G., 194, 198
Bandura, A., 35, 62, 65, 71, 78, 80, 84, 87, 95, 96, 130, 141, 237, 255, 270, 271, 285, 312, 318
Barkow, J. H., 184, 195
Barnes, R. D., 127, 143, 246, 256, 301, 318
Barron, F., 177, 195
Barton, R., 127, 143

NAME INDEX

Basham, R. B., 192, 198
Bateson, G., 111, 121, 187
Baumeister, R. F., 67, 83, 90, 96, 126, 141, 148, 171, 176, 195, 211, 229, 248, 255, 310, 318
Beavin, J. H., 103, 115, 125
Bechhofer, R., 354, 366
Becker, H. S., 120, 121
Beckman, L., 218, 229, 249, 255
Bell, R. Q., 185, 195
Bem, D. J., 101, 119, 121, 223, 229, 283, 285, 311, 318
Bennett, D. H., 246, 255
Bennett, W. L., 224, 229
Bentler, P. M., 271, 285
Berger, C. R., 139, 141
Berger, P., 176, 195
Berglas, S., 6, 26, 247, 255, 257, 298–299, 303, 318, 319
Berlyne, D., 102
Berne, E., 51, 62
Berscheid, E., 79, 80, 96, 363, 364
Biddle, B. J., 18, 25
Bierbrauer, G., 218, 221, 232, 249, 258
Blanck, P. D., 352, 361, 364
Blaney, P. H., 161, 171
Blank, T. O., 262, 285
Blascovich, J., 130, 143
Blasi, A., 277, 285
Blau, P., 72, 96
Blumberg, H. H., 108, 111, 121
Blumenthal, M. D., 266, 283, 285
Blumer, H., 208n., 229
Bok, S., 323, 363–364
Bonhoeffer, D., 364
Bonoma, T. V., 83, 99, 294, 301, 322
Borden, R. J., 127, 142, 241, 255
Boring, E. G., 42, 43, 62
Boulding, K. E., 275n., 285
Bradburn, N., 193, 195
Bradley, G. (see Weary, G.)
Braginsky, B., 303, 318
Braginsky, D. D., 303, 318, 359, 363, 364
Braiker, H. B., 264, 285

Breakwell, G. M., 69, 96
Breckler, S. J., 30, 31, 126, 129, 130, 168, 169
Brehm, J. W., 213, 215, 223, 233
Brennan, T., 193, 195
Brenner, C., 312, 318
Briggs, S. R., 170, 172, 182, 196
Brissett, D., 228n., 229
Brock, T. C., 243, 246, 255
Brockner, J., 162, 171
Bronowski, J., 29
Brooks, J., 185, 186, 197
Brown, I., 130, 142
Bruck, H. W., 224, 233
Bruner, J. S., 103, 121, 184, 187, 197
Buchwald, A. M., 110, 121
Bugental, D. B., 357–358, 369
Bugental, D. E., 352, 365
Burger, J. M., 129, 141, 211, 218, 229, 250, 255
Burgio, K. L., 162, 171
Burish, T. G., 245, 246, 255
Burke, K., 20, 25, 62
Burns, F., 19, 25
Burns, L. B., 280, 287
Buss, A. H., 31, 32, 35, 40, 62, 132n., 136, 137, 139, 142, 148–150, 172, 174, 177, 192, 193, 195, 196, 211, 229, 243, 246, 255, 280, 285, 286, 315, 318
Buss, D. M., 185, 195
Butler, D., 114, 124, 204, 232
Butterfield, E., 317, 319

Cabot, R. C., 323, 365
Calder, B. J., 215, 229
Calley, W., Lt., 276
Campbell, B. H., 138, 145
Campbell, J., 127, 145
Campbell, T., 354, 369
Cantor, J. R., 222, 234
Cantor, N., 10, 25, 70, 96
Cantril, H., 131, 135, 140, 144
Carlston, D. E., 221, 229
Carson, R. C., 5, 14, 25, 65, 70, 74, 76, 96, 208, 229
Carver, C. S., 31, 72, 79, 80, 87, 88, 96, 103, 121,

Carver, C. S. (*Cont.*):
136–138, 142–144, 146, 148, 150–152, 155, 157, 161–163, 168, 171–174, 223, 232, 280, 288
Caryle, T., 55
Castro, Fidel, 157–158
Cattell, J. M., 42
Cavert, C. W., 193, 197
Cervantes, Miguel de, 20
Chaplin, W., 127, 143
Cheek, J. M., 31, 55, 63, 70, 77, 91, 96, 97, 132n., 142, 168, 170, 172, 175, 177, 192, 193, 196
Chomsky, N., 272, 285
Christie, R., 341, 342, 365
Cialdini, R. B., 14, 27, 127, 142, 153, 172, 241, 243, 255, 294, 319
Cicourel, A. V., 188, 196, 272, 285
Clair, M. S., 244, 245, 255, 259
Clark, G. L., 105, 121
Clark, R. A., 130, 133, 138, 143
Cobb, S., 192, 196
Cochran, S. T., 250, 255
Cody, M. J., 342n., 368
Cohen, A. R., 309, 319
Cohen, J., 330n., 365
Collins, B. E., 215, 229
Colson, Charles, 312
Comadena, M. E., 327, 367
Condon, T. R., 41, 63
Cook, T. D., 135, 145
Cooley, C. H., 3, 16–18, 23, 25, 34, 36, 43–49, 53, 55, 56, 58, 63, 101, 116, 121, 147, 172, 237, 255
Cooper, J., 215, 230
Costa, P. T., Jr., 70, 98
Costanzo, P. R., 204, 218, 232, 233
Cox, C. L., 150, 173
Coyne, J. C., 111, 122, 124
Craighead, W. E., 110, 123
Cressey, D. R., 270, 285
Crocker, J., 9, 28
Crowne, D. P., 54, 63, 138, 142, 145, 211, 229, 316, 319, 335, 365
Crutchfield, R. A., 154, 172

Cunningham, J. D., 239, 240, 258
Cutrona, C. E., 193, 196, 197
Czerlinsky, T., 153, 173

Damon, W., 277, 285
Darby, B. L., 294, 319
Darby, B. W., 86, 96, 98, 248, 255, 258, 299, 321, 351, 365
D'Arcy, E., 240, 241, 256, 302, 319
Darley, J. M., 103, 122, 176, 181, 182, 195, 215, 216, 225, 229, 231, 238, 242, 255, 257, 267, 285, 287
Darwin, C., 44
Davis, D., 154, 171, 172
Davis, K. E., 203, 223, 230, 243, 256, 298, 310, 319, 320
Davis, S., Jr., 20
Davis, T., 332, 340, 349, 365
Deen, E., 159, 174
DeFrank, R. S., 341, 370
Degree, C. E., 247, 256
DeKadt, E. J., 295, 319
Dembo, T., 74, 91, 97
Dennis, H. S., 342n., 367
Dennis, N. F., 116, 122
DePaulo, B. M., 292, 323, 327, 328, 330n., 332, 334, 337, 340–342, 344, 347–349, 352, 355, 357, 360–365, 368–370
Dermer, M., 79, 80, 96
Derry, P. A., 110, 122, 130, 142
Descartes, R., 2, 4
de Turck, M. A., 349, 368
Deutsch, M., 159, 160, 172, 204, 229
de Villiers, J. G., 350, 366
de Villiers, P. A., 350, 366
Devin-Sheehan, L., 327, 355, 357, 366
Dewey, J., 3, 45, 73
Diener, C. I., 130, 142
Diener, E., 133, 142
Digman, J. M., 179, 196
Dipboye, R. L., 133, 142
Donne, J., 55
Dostoyevsky, F., 55

Douglas, J. D., 274, 285
Downs, A. C., 108, 123
Driver, R. E., 340n., 370
Ducette, J., 251, 256
Dunnette, M. D., 181, 196
Dutton, D. G., 90, 96, 119, 122
Duval, S., 31, 32, 35, 40, 63, 72, 96, 136, 142, 148, 157, 172, 174, 270, 280, 286
Dweck, C. S., 130, 142

Eagly, A. H., 117, 122
Edgley, C., 228n., 229, 323, 369
Eichmann, Adolf, 245
Ekman, P., 326–330, 332, 338, 342, 346, 348, 349, 356, 366
Ellenberger, H., 49, 63
Elliot, G. C., 339, 341, 366
Ely, R., 108, 117, 118, 125
Emerson, R. W., 45
Epstein, S., 8, 9, 25, 67, 96, 101, 107, 122, 308, 319
Eriksen, C. W., 152, 172
Erikson, E. H., 35, 63, 67, 96, 182
Erlichman, John, 313
Esterson, A., 114, 123
Evans, R. B., 42, 63
Evreinoff, N., 20, 26
Exline, R., 341, 342, 366

Fagot, B. I., 108, 122
Farina, A., 119, 122
Fazio, R. H., 103, 122
Feather, N. T., 130 142, 218, 229
Fein, G. G., 187, 188, 196
Feldman, N. S., 239, 258
Feldman, R. S., 326, 355–358, 366
Fenigstein, A., 31, 32, 80, 96, 137–139, 142, 148–150, 172, 174, 280, 286
Ferguson, M., 193, 197
Ferracuti, F., 301, 322
Festinger, L., 15, 26, 74, 91, 97, 101, 122, 311, 319
Feyerabend, P. K., 207, 228, 229

Field, P. B., 139
Fincham, F. D., 228n., 230, 240, 256
Fingarette, H., 252, 256
Fishbein, M., 154, 171, 205, 228
Fisher, R., 295, 319
Fiske, S., 203, 233
Fitch, G., 218, 230
Flavell, J. H., 353, 366
Fleisher, E., 211, 233
Folkes, V. S., 327, 366
Follansbee, D. J., 162, 171
Fontana, A., 303, 319
Foote, N. N., 65, 96
Forsyth, D. R., 204, 230
Fox, M. N., 352, 365
France, Anatole, 323
Freedman, J. L., 294, 300, 319
Freeman, J. A., 193, 194, 197
Freeman, S., 127, 142, 241, 255
French, J. R., 294, 304, 319
Freud, S., 34, 48–50, 52, 63, 110, 122, 176, 182, 237, 246, 256, 312, 328, 366
Frey, D., 90, 96, 129, 143
Friedman, H. S., 342, 343, 368
Friesen, W. V., 326–328, 330, 338, 346, 348, 349, 366
Frieze, I. H., 87, 88, 96
Froming, W. J., 138, 143, 155–157, 159, 168, 172, 280
Fromm, E., 20–21, 26, 236
Fromson, M. E., 270, 271, 285
Fry, W. F., Jr., 114, 115, 122

Gabrenya, W. K., Jr., 250, 255
Gaes, G. G., 223, 230, 298, 322
Galanter, E., 65, 76–77, 98, 273, 287
Gardner, H., 350, 352, 354, 366
Garfinkel, J., 272, 273, 286
Garner, W. R., 152, 172
Garvey, Steve, 66
Geis, F. L., 341, 342, 365, 366
Geller, V., 346, 369
Genovese, Kitty, 242
Gentry, K. W., 211, 230

NAME INDEX

Gergen, K. J., 33, 34, 61–63, 83, 96, 176, 183, 196, 211, 223, 226, 230, 269, 286, 326, 366
Gergen, M. M., 34, 62, 63, 183, 196
Gibbons, F. X., 150, 151, 155, 173, 174, 280, 288
Ginsburg, G. P., 154, 171, 172, 261, 286
Giuliano, T., 102, 113, 115, 125
Glass, D. C., 151, 171
Glixman, A. F., 127, 143
Glover, J., 265, 286
Goethals, G. R., 215, 216, 229, 230
Goethe, Johann Wolfgang von, 44, 55
Goffman, E., 19, 21–23, 26, 29, 34, 52, 53, 56–63, 72, 83, 85, 86, 96, 104, 105, 112, 122, 126, 143, 148, 173, 176, 179, 194, 196, 237, 248, 256, 268, 286, 295, 297, 299, 319, 326, 366
Golding, S. L., 114, 123
Goldman, H. J., 14, 27
Goldman, K., 224, 230
Goldman-Eisler, F., 338, 366
Gollwitzer, P. M., 166, 174, 204, 233
Gorkin, L., 119, 124
Goswick, R. A., 193, 194, 197
Gottlieb, A., 103, 124, 208n., 233, 262, 279, 288
Gottlieb, D. E., 351, 366
Gottlieb, I. H., 111, 122
Gough, H. G., 185, 196
Gouldner, A. W., 58, 63
Graber, D., 224, 230
Graziano, W., 79, 80, 96
Green, C. R., 327, 341, 342, 344, 347, 365
Greenberg, G., 129, 143
Greenberg, J., 159, 160, 173, 280, 286
Greenberg, M. S., 362, 366
Greene, D., 222, 232
Greenglass, E. R., 356, 367
Greenough, T., 246, 260
Greenwald, A. G., 7–8, 11–15, 26, 30, 31, 35, 63, 70, 90,

Greenwald, A. G. (*Cont.*): 97, 106, 122, 126, 127, 129–133, 135, 142, 143, 168, 169, 237, 238, 256
Gregory, R. L., 103, 122
Grice, H. P., 325, 367
Griffin, J. J., 108, 118, 125
Gruzen, J., 159, 160, 173
Gumpert, P., 341, 366
Gur, R. C., 252, 256

Hager, J. C., 356, 366
Hake, H. W., 152, 172
Hales, S., 261, 286
Haley, J., 111, 121, 303, 319
Hall, C. S., 53, 63, 72, 73, 97
Hall, G. S., 36
Hall, J. A., 58, 63, 341, 370
Hallam, J. R., 14, 27, 90, 98, 128, 144, 253, 258
Halperin, K., 238, 256
Hamilton, V. L., 227, 228n., 230, 240, 256, 274–276, 286
Hammond, V. C., 244, 256
Handelsman, M. M., 247, 259, 304, 321
Hansson, R. O., 194, 196
Harkins, S. G., 140, 143, 250, 260
Harré, R., 67, 71, 76, 97, 272, 286, 287
Harris, B., 127, 143, 246, 256
Harris, R. N., 247, 256
Harris, T., 51, 63
Harris, V. A., 326, 328, 367
Harrison, A. A., 101
Hart, H. L. A., 241, 256
Hart, R. P., 342n., 367
Hartshorne, H., 277, 286
Harvey, J. H., 114, 122, 127, 128, 143, 145, 239, 240, 246, 250, 256, 260
Harvey, O. J., 135, 140, 144
Hasher, L., 9–11, 14, 25
Hass, R. G., 222, 223, 230
Head, K. B., 266, 283, 285
Heidegger, M., 34, 63
Heider, F., 8, 15, 26, 35, 63, 203, 227, 230, 314, 315, 319
Heise, D. R., 103, 122
Heller, K., 192, 196

Helm, B., 194, 197
Hendershot, J., 345, 367
Henley, N., 178, 196
Herman, C. P., 153, 172
Hersch, P., 317, 319
Hess, A. K., 345, 367
Hewitt, J. P., 68, 86, 97, 222, 230, 298, 321
Hickey, C., 341, 366
Higgins, R. L., 66, 99, 126, 127, 144, 236, 237, 240, 242, 243, 246, 247, 250–252, 256, 259
Hill, C. A., 118, 119, 125
Hill, L. A., 356, 370
Hinckley, John, Jr., 247
Hobbes, T., 19, 26, 291, 292
Hobbs, S. A., 193, 197
Hobert, R., 181, 196
Hockenbury, D., 193, 197
Hoerig, J. H., 243, 255
Hoffman, M. L., 84, 97
Hogan, R., 2, 26, 31, 55, 63, 70, 77, 78, 91, 96, 97, 132n., 142, 168, 172, 175, 177, 178, 182, 186, 190, 196, 237, 256
Hogarth, R. M., 103, 122
Hollander, E. P., 247, 256
Holmes, D. S., 246, 255, 256
Holtgraves, T., 154, 171, 172
Homer, 2
Hood, W. R., 135, 140, 144
Hormuth, S. E., 120, 122, 151, 155, 173
Horney, K., 5, 72, 74, 97, 110, 123, 236
House, P., 222, 232
Houston, B. K., 238, 245, 246, 255, 256
Hovland, C. T., 139, 143, 306, 319
Howells, W., 190, 197
Hoyt, M. F., 215, 229
Hume, David, 2, 4
Humphries, C., 157, 168, 171
Huston, A. C., 312, 318
Huston-Stein, A., 354, 369
Hyman, H. H., 37, 63

Ickes, W., 151, 174, 301, 318
Indart, M., 193, 197
Ingram, R. E., 247, 259

NAME INDEX

Inouye, D. K., 130, 142
Insko, C. A., 215, 229
Irvine, A., 328, 355, 365

Jackson, D. D., 103, 111, 112, 115, 121, 123, 125
Jackson, S. E., 212, 230
Jacobson, L., 117, 124
James, W., 3–9, 13, 15, 26, 29, 31, 33–41, 43–49, 51–53, 57, 58, 62, 63, 65, 68, 72–74, 78, 97, 141, 143, 147, 173, 236, 256, 309, 319
Jamous, H., 243, 257
Janis, I. L., 79, 97, 139, 143, 306, 319
Jaspars, J. M., 228n., 230, 240, 256
Jellison, J. M., 211, 230, 237, 244, 257, 304, 319
Jenkins, L., 357, 358, 366
Jervis, R., 214, 230
Johnson, Lyndon B., 348
Johnson-Laird, P. N., 102
Johnston, W. A., 127, 143
Jones, E. E., 5–6, 26, 67, 72, 78, 83, 84, 90, 97, 126, 129, 143, 176, 195, 197, 203, 205, 210, 211, 222, 223, 230, 231, 239, 243, 247, 248, 255–257, 259, 295, 298–301, 303, 318–320, 324, 326–328, 334, 367
Jones, S. C., 14, 26, 74, 90, 97, 106, 109, 123, 244, 257
Jones, W. H., 31, 175, 192–194, 196, 197
Jordan, A., 328, 355, 360n., 365
Joseph, J., 294, 299, 321
Judd, C. M., 10, 26, 70, 97
Juhasz, J. B., 61–63
Julian, J. W., 251, 257
Jung, C. G., 34, 176–177

Kagehiro, D., 250, 260
Kahn, R. L., 266, 283, 285
Kahneman, D., 338, 367
Kalbfleisch, P. J., 349, 368

Kalle, R. J., 223, 230, 231
Kane, T. R., 294, 298, 299, 320–322
Kant, I., 4, 55, 60, 323, 367
Kaplan, A., 304, 320
Kaplan, H. B., 106, 123
Karniol, R., 351, 367
Kasmer, J., 154, 171, 172
Kaswan, J. W., 352, 365
Katz, D., 204, 231
Katz, S. B., 251, 257
Kayser, E., 274, 286
Keasey, C. B., 351, 367
Kelley, H. H., 35, 63, 74, 85, 97, 114, 117, 123, 124, 203, 205, 207, 212, 217, 231, 232, 239, 240, 257, 258, 264, 285, 306, 319
Kellogg, R. T., 315, 320
Kelly, G. A., 8, 26, 228, 231
Kelman, H. C., 271, 276–277, 286
Kendler, H. H., 204, 231
Kennedy, John F., 224, 348
Kenrick, D. T., 243, 255
Kernis, M., 159–160, 173
Kidd, R., 301, 318
Kierkegaard, S., 59, 60
Kiesler, C. A., 362, 367
Kilbride, J. E., 356, 370
Kircher, M., 350, 366
Kirker, W. S., 129, 144
Kleck, R. E., 225, 232
Klein, E., 303, 319
Klinger, E., 161, 173
Klorman, R., 329, 370
Klyver, N. W., 251, 258, 283, 287
Knapp, M. L., 327, 342n., 367
Knight, G., 262, 284
Knudson, R. M., 114, 123
Koestner, R., 360, 370
Koffka, K., 36
Kohlberg, L., 43, 237, 257, 263n., 278, 286
Kohler, W., 36
Kolditz, T., 299, 320
Kotsonis, M., 352, 367
Kozlowski, L. T., 153, 172
Krauss, R. M., 204, 229, 323, 337, 346, 355–358, 367–369
Kraut, R. E., 327, 342, 344, 345, 367

Krebs, D., 278, 286
Kuhn, T., 205, 206, 231
Kuiper, N. A., 11, 12, 26, 110, 122, 123, 129, 130, 142, 144
Kukla, A., 130, 145
Kulik, J. A., 10, 26, 70, 97, 240, 257

Laing, R. D., 114, 123
Lakatos, I., 205, 206, 231
Lake, R. A., 119, 122
Lamiell, J. T., 251, 258
Landy, D., 313, 321
Langer, E. J., 10, 26, 77, 79, 85, 97, 224, 231, 262, 269, 287
Langlois, J. H., 108, 123
Lanier, K., 332, 340, 349, 365
Larrance, D. T., 329, 341, 370
Laser, P. S., 328, 355, 365
Lassiter, G. D., 292, 323, 327, 334, 347, 365
Laswell, H. D., 304, 320
Latané, B., 140, 143, 225, 231, 242, 243, 257, 267, 285, 287
Lawrence, L. H., 276–277, 286
Lazarus, R. S., 111, 122, 124
Leary, M. R., 72, 79, 80, 82, 83, 87–90, 98, 162, 173, 174, 193, 198, 250, 258, 304, 320, 324, 327, 335, 338, 363, 369
Lecky, P., 8, 15, 26, 30, 32, 35, 63, 101, 105, 106, 108, 123
Lee, A. R., 114, 123
Lefcourt, H. M., 251, 257, 317, 320
Lefebvre, L. M., 334
Lemaine, G., 243, 257
Lepper, M. R., 345, 364, 368
Lerner, M. J., 274, 287
Leventhal, G. S., 159, 173, 274, 287
Levi, A., 90, 99, 206, 213, 233
Levine, H. M., 192, 198
Levine, M., 103, 123
Levy, A., 153, 172
Lewin, K., 74, 91, 97
Lewinsohn, P. M., 111, 125, 127, 143

Lewis, M., 185, 186, 197
Lieberman, A. F., 186, 197
Lilly, J. R., 271, 282, 285
Lindskold, S., 294, 295, 307, 321, 362, 367
Lindzey, G., 53, 63, 72, 73, 97
Lippa, M., 327, 367
Lishman, W. A., 110, 123
Littlepage, G. E., 349, 368
Lloyd, C. G., 110, 123
Locke, John, 3, 4
Loevinger, J., 132*n*., 143
Lofland, J., 266, 287
Lopata, H. Z., 193, 197
Lopyan, K. J., 156–157, 159, 172
Lord, C. G., 345, 368
Love, L. R., 352, 365
Lowell, E. L., 130, 133, 138, 143
Lowery, C. R., 237, 259
Ludwig, A., 323, 368
Lundgren, D. C., 94, 97
Lykken, D. T., 338, 368
Lyman, S. M., 204, 208, 214, 220*n*., 221, 226, 228*n*., 232, 241, 259, 265, 288, 297, 315, 321
Lynch, J., 192, 197
Lynch, M. D., 33, 63

McArthur, L. A., 239, 257
Macbeth, Lady, 303
McCall, G. J., 16, 17, 27, 65, 66, 68, 71, 74, 76, 98, 105, 123, 267, 287
McClelland, D. C., 130, 133, 138, 143
McCosh, J., 42
McCown, N. E., 14, 27, 90, 98, 128, 144, 253, 258, 317, 320
McCrae, R. R., 70, 98
McDonald, M. R., 110, 123
McFarlin, D. B., 130, 143
McGhee, P., 316, 320
McGillis, D., 205, 230
McGuire, W. J., 207*n*., 228, 231
MacIntyre, A., 60, 61, 63
McLaughlin, M. L., 342*n*., 368
Maddi, S. R., 175, 197

Maehr, M. L., 117, 123
Major, B., 239, 240, 257
Malkis, F. S., 223, 231
Mancuso, J. C., 34, 62, 64
Mandler, G., 7, 26
Manis, J. G., 34, 48, 64
Mann, L., 79, 97
Maracek, J., 83, 97, 108, 116, 123, 218, 231
Markus, H., 9, 10, 12, 26, 70, 97, 129, 143, 236, 257
Marlin, N. A., 315, 320
Marlowe, D., 54, 63, 138, 142, 211, 229, 316, 319, 335, 365
Marsh, P., 272, 287
Martin, Steve, 235, 252
Marwell, G., 237, 260
Maslach, C., 155, 173
Maslow, A. H., 236, 294, 320
Mason, Perry, 331
Matza, D., 282, 288
May, N. A., 277, 286
Mead, G. H., 13, 16, 18, 23, 27, 29, 31, 34, 36, 45–53, 56, 64, 65, 68, 98, 101, 116, 123, 147–148, 173, 181–182, 184, 185, 187, 197, 208, 231, 237, 257, 280, 281, 287
Mehlman, R. C., 253, 257
Mehrabian, A., 338, 369
Melburg, V., 90, 98, 129, 144, 296, 322
Meltzer, B. N., 16, 18, 27, 34, 48, 64
Meltzoff, A. N., 184, 197
Mencken, H. L., 84
Mensing, J., 117, 123
Mentzer, S. J., 225, 232
Merelman, R. M., 214, 231
Merluzzi, T. V., 162, 171
Merton, R. K., 210, 231
Mettee, D. R., 83, 97, 108, 116, 123, 218, 231, 244, 257
Michela, J., 207, 231
Mikula, G., 274, 287
Milgram, S., 225, 231, 245, 257, 263*n*., 287
Mill, J. S., 55
Miller, D. R., 37, 64
Miller, D. T., 127, 144, 247, 257

Miller, G. A., 65, 76–77, 98, 273, 287
Miller, G. R., 306, 320, 349, 368
Miller, L. C., 150, 173
Miller, R. S., 14, 27, 83, 90, 98, 127, 144, 241, 259
Mills, C. W., 85, 86, 98, 212, 216, 224, 226, 232, 264, 287, 297, 320
Minor, W. W., 282, 287
Minsky, M., 10, 27
Mischel, T., 33, 64
Mischel, W., 10, 25, 54, 64, 70, 96, 127, 143
Mitchell, T. R., 299, 322
Modigliani, A., 297, 320
Monson, T. C., 79, 80, 96, 317, 321
Montaigne, M., 324, 368
Moon, T. H., 342, 366
Moore, B., 281, 287
Moore, M. K., 184, 197
Morency, N. L., 355–358, 368
Morris, C., 49
Mostel, Zero, 242
Much, N., 271, 280, 283, 287
Mullahy, P., 50
Mullen, B., 101, 125

Nafficy, A., 215, 230
Nafzger, S., 117, 123
Nash, D. L., 101, 124
Nebergall, R., 131, 144
Neisser, U., 7, 9, 10, 27, 70, 98, 103, 123, 236, 257
Nelson, K., 354, 368
Nelson, K. E., 354, 368
Nelson, R. E., 110, 123
Nelson, S. A., 351, 368
Newburg, C. L., 238, 259
Newcomb, T. M., 157, 173
Newman, D., 351, 368
Newton, J., 235, 258
Newtson, D., 153, 173
Nietzsche, F., 55, 61
Nisbett, R. E., 7, 27, 203, 206, 207, 222, 231, 232
Nixon, Richard M., 213, 220*n*., 313, 348
Norem-Hebeisen, A. A., 33, 63
Norman, N., 5, 291–293

NAME INDEX

Odum, E. P., 105, 123
O'Hair, H. D., 342*n*., 368
Olmstead, G., 323, 369
Olson, C., 346, 369
Olson, C. T., 128, 145
Orne, M. T., 338, 369
Ortega y Gassett, J., 48, 64
Orvis, B. K., 114, 124, 204, 232
Orvis, B. R., 239, 240, 258
Orwell, George, 243, 258
Osgood, C. E., 306, 320
Ossorio, P. G., 310, 320
O'Sullivan, M., 326, 346, 366

Parish, E. A., 194, 198
Parsons, T., 304, 320
Paulhus, D., 150, 167, 174
Peake, P. K., 54, 64
Peevers, B. H., 353, 368
Peirce, C. S., 3, 73
Peplau, L. A., 193, 197
Perkins, D., 350, 366
Perkins, S., 247, 259, 303, 321
Perloff, R., 128, 145
Perry, H. S., 51, 53, 64
Peters, R. S., 315, 320
Peterson, C. C., 352, 356, 362, 368
Peterson, J. L., 352, 356, 362, 368
Peterson, L. M., 162, 171
Petras, J. W., 16, 27
Petty, R. E., 153, 172, 250, 260
Pfeutze, P. E., 50, 64
Phares, E. J., 251, 258, 283, 287
Phillipson, H., 114, 123
Piaget, J., 12, 27, 42–44, 237, 258, 350–352, 360, 368
Pierce, J., 117, 121
Piliavin, I. M., 266, 287
Piliavin, J. A., 266, 287
Pilkonis, P. A., 192, 193, 197
Pinault, M. A., 349, 368
Pittman, T. S., 5, 6, 26, 67, 72, 78, 84, 97, 126, 143, 210, 211, 231, 300–301, 320, 324, 327, 367
Plato, 2, 19
Plomin, R., 177, 192, 196, 197
Podlesny, J. A., 338, 368

Poe, D., 344, 345, 367
Polly, S., 218, 221, 232, 249, 258
Popoola, O., 357, 358, 366
Powell, F. A., 306, 320
Powers, W. T., 103, 124, 163–166, 173
Pratkanis, A. R., 7–8, 11–13, 26, 70, 97, 131*n*., 143
Pribram, K. H., 65, 76–77, 98, 273, 287
Pritchard, S., 128, 145
Pryor, J. B., 162, 171
Pyszczynski, T., 129, 143

Quattrone, G., 222, 231
Quigley-Fernandez, B., 129, 144
Quinn, C. O., 262, 287

Raskin, D. C., 338, 368
Rattner, M., 184, 197
Raven, B., 294, 304, 319
Read, S. J., 10, 28, 102, 103, 107, 125, 211, 233
Reagan, Ronald, 247
Redl, F., 282, 287
Rehm, L. P., 110, 124, 125
Reich, W., 51
Reis, H. T., 158–160, 173, 280, 287
Repucci, N. D., 130, 142
Reynolds, L. T., 16, 27
Rhodewalt, F., 6, 26
Richardson, K. D., 14, 27
Rieff, P., 44, 55, 64
Riess, M., 90, 98, 129, 144, 214, 222, 233, 243, 247, 258, 259, 265, 288, 300, 322
Riggio, R. E., 342, 343, 368
Riggs, J. M., 222, 231
Ring, K., 302, 318
Riordan, C. A., 213, 233, 294, 298, 300, 315, 320, 322
Robinson, 111, 122
Robinson, J. E., 262, 287
Rodin, J., 243, 257, 266, 267, 287
Rogers, C. R., 5, 73, 98, 110, 124, 236
Rogers, T. B., 11, 27, 129, 144
Rokeach, M., 77, 98, 283, 287

Ronis, D. L., 238, 256
Roper, G., 356, 366
Rorty, A., 73, 98
Rosen, S., 108, 111, 125
Rosenberg, M., 8, 11, 13, 27, 70, 72–74, 89–92, 98, 139, 144, 312, 320
Rosenberg, S. E., 130, 144
Rosenfeld, P., 90, 98, 129, 144, 223, 294, 322
Rosenfield, D., 14, 28, 90, 99
Rosenkrantz, J., 327, 341, 342, 344, 347, 365
Rosenstiel, A., 352, 370
Rosenthal, A. M., 242, 258
Rosenthal, R., 117, 124, 327, 328, 330*n*., 332, 337, 340–342, 344, 347, 352, 357, 361, 364, 365, 368, 370
Rosenwald, A., 278, 286
Rosenzweig, S., 127, 144
Rosoff, R., 110, 121
Ross, L., 203, 206, 207, 218, 221, 222, 232, 249, 258, 326, 345, 364, 368
Ross, M., 127, 144, 215, 229
Ross, R. P., 354, 369
Rosser, E., 272, 287
Rossi, P. H., 274, 285
Rotenberg, K., 238, 246, 258
Roth, D., 110, 124
Rotter, J. B., 251, 258
Rowe, D., 192, 197
Royce, Joshia, 3
Royce, J. R., 205, 210, 232
Rubin, K. H., 187, 188, 197
Ruble, D. N., 239, 258
Rudd, J., 210, 213, 229
Ruderman, A., 351, 366
Russell, B., 291, 292
Russell, D., 192, 193, 197
Ryan, W., 242, 258
Rytina, S., 275, 286

Saarni, C., 350, 358, 369
Sackeim, H. A., 222, 232, 252, 256
Sacks, H., 272, 288
Sampson, E. E., 140, 144, 269, 288
Sanders, J., 274, 286
Sansone, C., 194, 197

NAME INDEX

Santayana, G., 57
Santee, R. T., 155, 173
Sapin, B. M., 224, 233
Sarason, B. R. 192, 198
Sarason, I. G., 192, 198
Sarason, S., 36, 64
Sarbin, T. R., 18, 27, 33–35, 38, 48, 61, 64
Sartre, J. P., 60, 61
Saul, B., 119, 122
Schadler, M., 254, 258
Schank, R., 10, 27, 76, 84, 98
Scheff, T. J., 303, 320
Schegloff, E. A., 272, 288
Scheibe, K. E., 3, 5, 8, 16, 23, 29, 32, 33, 35, 59, 62, 64, 317, 319, 364, 369
Scheier, M. F., 31, 32, 103, 121, 137, 139, 142, 144, 146, 148–153, 155, 157, 161–163, 168, 171–174, 223, 232, 280, 286, 288
Schelling, T. C., 210, 232
Scherer, K., 326, 346, 366
Schlenker, B. R., 1, 11, 14, 15, 18, 27, 29–31, 33, 35, 64–67, 70–72, 74, 75, 77–94, 98, 99, 119, 120, 124, 126–128, 144, 162, 168, 173, 174, 193, 198, 204, 208, 210–218, 222, 223, 232, 236, 237, 241, 243, 248, 250, 253, 255, 258, 259, 263, 265, 288, 294, 295, 299–302, 304, 308–310, 312, 318, 320–322, 324, 326, 327, 335, 338, 351, 363, 365, 369
Schlenker, P. A., 14, 27
Schneider, D. J., 109, 123, 295, 302, 304, 321
Schneider, J. M., 251, 259
Schoeneman, T. J., 18, 28, 101, 119, 124
Schonbach, P., 214, 232, 265, 288
Schopenhauer, A., 33, 53
Schopler, J., 150, 174
Schutz, A., 272, 273, 288, 315, 321
Schwartz, G., 294, 299, 321
Schwartz, S. H., 225, 232, 270–271, 279, 282–283, 288

Schwieger, P., 128, 145
Schwinger, T., 274, 286
Scott, F. J. D., 42, 63
Scott, M. B., 204, 208, 214, 220n., 221, 226, 228n., 232, 241, 259, 265, 288
Scott, M. R., 297, 315, 321
Sears, P. S., 74, 91, 97
Secord, P. F., 15, 18, 27, 30, 32, 89–91, 99, 101, 106, 117, 121, 124, 267, 270, 272, 286, 288, 353, 368
Seeto, D., 352, 356, 362, 368
Seidman, J., 91, 99
Seinmel, A., 111, 124
Seligman, M. E. P., 111, 124
Seneca, 13
Sentis, K., 9, 26
Shaeffer, C., 111, 124
Shafer, R. B., 262, 289
Shakespeare, W., 19, 45, 55
Shapiro, E. G., 159, 174
Shaver, K. G., 326, 367
Shaw, George Bernard, 120
Shaw, M. E., 204, 232, 246, 259
Shenkel, R. J., 237, 238, 248, 256, 259
Shennum, W. A., 357–358, 369
Sherif, C. W., 131, 135, 140, 144
Sherif, M., 131, 135, 140, 144
Sherman, S. J., 119, 124
Shovar, N., 221, 229
Shrauger, J. S., 18, 28, 107, 109, 111, 119, 124, 130, 144
Shweder, R. A., 271, 280, 283, 287
Siegel, A. E., 352, 369
Sigall, H., 129, 143, 313, 321
Sillars, A. L., 114, 124
Simmons, J. L., 16, 17, 27, 65, 66, 68, 71, 74, 76, 98, 105, 123, 267, 287
Simon, H. A., 295, 321
Simon, J. G., 218, 229
Singer, E., 37, 63
Skelton, J. A., 6, 26
Sloan, L. R., 127, 142, 241, 255
Smith, Adam, 2–3
Smith, J., 9, 26
Smith, T. W., 247, 252, 259, 302–304, 321

Smith, W. P., 239, 256
Snodgrass, S. E., 361, 364
Snyder, C. R., 66, 69, 126, 127, 144, 200, 235–238, 240, 242–248, 250–253, 255–257, 259, 302–304, 321
Snyder, M., 102, 117, 124, 138, 144, 145, 176, 182, 194, 198, 211, 232, 317, 321
Snyder, M. L., 14, 28, 90, 99, 225, 232, 247, 259
Snyder, R. C., 224, 233
Sobell, M. B., 247, 260
Sobieszek, B. I., 117, 125
Solano, C. H., 194, 198
Solomon, M. R., 150, 174
Solomon, S., 129, 143
Sormon, P. B., 130, 144
Speckart, G., 271, 285
Spiegel, N. H., 329, 370
Stahelski, A. J., 117, 123
Stang, D., 316, 321
Starkweather, J., 329n., 369
Stebbins, R. A., 328, 369
Steele, C. M., 119, 124
Steensma, H., 159, 174
Stephan, W. G., 14, 28, 90, 99, 204, 233
Stern, D., 184, 198
Stevens, L., 239, 259
Stires, L. K., 326, 367
Stokes, R., 86, 97, 222, 230, 298, 321
Stone, G. P., 65, 67–68, 99
Stone, J. I., 292, 323, 327, 334, 347, 365
Strack, S., 111, 124
Strauss, A., 45–48, 64
Streeter, L. A., 346, 369
Strenta, A., 225, 233
Strickland, B. R., 138, 145
Stryker, S., 2, 3, 16, 17, 28, 65, 84, 99, 103, 124, 208n., 233, 262, 288, 313, 321
Stucky, R. J., 66, 99, 126, 127, 144, 236, 237, 240, 242, 243, 246, 250–252, 259
Sullivan, H. S., 5, 48–53, 58, 64, 110, 125, 208, 233, 236, 282, 288
Suls, J. M., 101, 125, 294, 320
Summers, A. A., 114, 123

Sumner, W. G., 262, 288
Surber, C. F., 351, 369
Swann, W. B., Jr., 10, 14, 15, 28, 30, 31, 70, 89–91, 99, 100, 102–108, 113, 115, 117–119, 125, 168, 174, 211, 233, 317, 321
Sykes, G. M., 282, 288

Tabor, L. E., 101, 124
Takemoto-Chock, N. R., 179, 196
Tanke, E. D., 317, 321
Tarde, M., 43
Taylor, M. G., 211, 230
Taylor, S. E., 9, 28, 203, 233, 240, 257, 351, 366
Tedeschi, J. T., 5, 67, 72, 78, 79, 90, 98, 99, 129, 144, 210, 213, 214, 222, 223, 230, 231, 233, 237, 247, 259, 265, 288, 291–296, 298–301, 304, 306, 307, 320–322
Teevan, R., 316, 320
Tesser, A., 10, 28, 108, 111, 125, 127, 145, 150, 165, 167, 174
Tetlock, P. E., 90, 99, 199–200, 203, 204, 206, 211, 213, 219–221, 233, 250, 259
Thibaut, J. W., 176, 197, 341, 366
Thomas, E. J., 18, 25
Thomas, W. I., 16, 28, 263, 269, 288
Thorne, A., 127, 142, 241, 255
Tobey, E. L., 151, 174
Tompkins, S. S., 207n., 233
Toris, C., 327, 346, 348, 363, 365, 369
Triandis, H. C., 226, 227, 233
Tucker, J. A., 247, 260
Tunnell, G., 151, 174
Turner, R. E., 323, 369
Turner, R. G., 151, 174
Turner, R. H., 8, 28, 73–75, 99
Tyler, L. E., 61, 64

Underwood, B., 270, 271, 281, 285, 287
Ungar, S., 83, 99
Utne, M. K., 248, 255

Vallacher, R. R., 101, 120, 125
Vandenberg, B., 187, 188, 198
Verlarde, O. J., 270, 282, 288
Videbeck, R., 117, 125
Vincent, J. E., 294, 319
Volkmar, F. R., 352, 369
von Baeyer, C., 111, 124
Von Grumbkow, J., 159, 174
Vuchinich, R. E., 247, 260
Vygotsky, 187

Waid, W. M., 338, 369
Walker, G. R., 156–157, 159, 172, 280
Walker, M. R., 127, 142, 241, 255
Walster, E. H., 248, 255, 363, 364
Walters, P. S., 362, 367
Warner, D. B., 267, 288
Wason, P. C., 102
Watson, D., 279, 289
Watzlawick, P., 103, 115, 125
Weakland, J., 111, 121
Weary, G. (Weary Bradley, G.), 14, 28, 90, 99, 127, 128, 141, 204, 213, 215, 218, 222, 229, 233, 237, 250, 260, 309, 322
Weber, S. J., 135, 145
Webster, M., 117, 125
Wegner, D. M., 101, 120, 125
Weiner, B., 130, 145
Weiner, M., 338, 369
Weiner, N., 103, 125
Weinstein, E. A., 17, 28
Weiss, W., 305, 322
Wells, G. L., 114, 122, 240, 250, 260
Wells, L. E., 237, 260
Wener, A., 110, 125
Wertheimer, M., 36
Westcott, D. R., 362, 366
White, B. J., 135, 140, 144

White, J. B., 356–358, 366
Wicklund, R. A., 31, 32, 35, 40, 63, 72, 96, 137n., 142, 148, 157, 166, 172, 174, 213, 215, 223, 233, 247, 259, 270, 280, 286
Wilde, Oscar, 323, 369
Wiley, M. G., 19, 25, 65, 68, 95
Wilke, H., 159, 174
Williams, K., 140, 143
Wills, T. A., 246, 260
Wilson, D. W., 262, 289
Wilson, K. G., 251, 258, 283, 287
Wilson, T. D., 7, 27
Wineman, D., 282, 287
Winner, E., 350, 352, 354, 366, 370
Witt, T. R., 218, 233
Wolf, D., 354, 366
Wolfgang, M. E., 301, 322
Wolk, S., 251, 256
Wood, R. E., 299, 322
Wortman, C. B., 5, 26, 127, 145, 218, 233, 300, 320, 326, 334, 367
Wright, J. C., 354, 369
Wundt, W., 42
Wyer, R. S., 70, 99
Wylie, R. C., 5, 28, 35, 53–55, 64, 73, 99, 110, 119, 125, 139, 145

Yarczower, M., 356, 370
Young, T. R., 58, 64
Youngren, M. A., 111, 125

Zajonc, R. B., 101, 109, 125
Zander, A., 74, 91, 99
Zanna, M. P., 238, 255
Zemore, R., 246, 260
Zillman, D., 222, 234
Zimbardo, P. G., 192, 198
Zuckerman, M., 204, 213, 215, 234, 245, 247, 251, 260, 309, 322, 327–330, 332, 337, 340–342, 360, 361, 364, 365, 370

SUBJECT INDEX

Abulia, 61
Acclamation, 86, 216
Accommodating self, 43
Accountability, 238–239, 246
Accounting, 86, 214–216, 262–284, 297–298
  acceptability of, 277, 283
  causal role of, 269–271
  cultural influences on, 271–277, 282
  defensibility of, 224–225
  as defensive impression management, 297–298
  developmental aspects of, 283
  disclaimers and, 222, 297–299
  honoring, 221, 268
  individual differences in acceptance of, 278, 282–283
  negotiation in, 220n.
  rehearsal of, 268
  in resolution of moral dilemmas, 262–284
  (*See also* Acclamation; Egotism; Excuse; Explanation; Justification)

Achievement:
  collective, 131, 133–136, 139–141
  of life goals, 180–181
  need for, 130, 138, 151, 316
  relationship to popularity, 191
Achievement motivation, 130, 138, 151, 316
Act, communicative, 47
Action identity, 120–121
Activity level, innate, 185–186
Adaptor, 339, 340, 343
Addiction as strategic impression management, 302, 303
Adjustment, personality, 179, 185, 188–194
Affect, 87–88, 107–110
Affiliation:
  need for, 178–179, 181, 185, 316
  selective, 89, 91, 105
  (*See also* Popularity; Sociability)
Agency of self (*see* Self, agency of)

Aggression:
  anticipatory account of, 270–271
  coercive power and, 294
  producing derogation of victim, 243
Alcohol:
  deindividuation and, 134
  self-handicapping and, 247, 302, 303, 314
Alienation, 191, 193
Altruism, 281–282
  (*See also* Helping; Prosocial behavior)
Ambiguity:
  of attributions, 247
  (*See also* Self-handicapping)
  shyness and, 192
  of situations, 267
Ambition, 179
  (*See also* Achievement)
Amnesia, 313
Analytic psychology, 34
Animal Farm (Orwell), 244
Anomie, 61
Anonymity:
  attitude change and, 223

381

Anonymity (*Cont.*):
  audiences and, 211
  conformity and, 279
  deindividuation and, 134
  diffuse self and, 136
Anticipatory attitude change, 152–153, 168
Anxiety:
  associated behavior, 88, 161–162, 338–341
  attribution and, 218
  consciousness of, 52
  toward depressives, 111
  expectations and, 23, 30, 73, 87–89
  goal importance and, 79, 88
  high standards and, 73
  about identity, 177
  lessened by excuses, 245
  locus of control and, 317
  loneliness and, 193
  as measured by Self-Consciousness Scale, 149*n*.
  as performance impediment, 161–162
  psychoanalytic view of, 50
  public self-esteem and, 139
  as self-handicapping, 247, 314
  in self-identification theory, 87–89
  self-presentational doubts and, 87–89, 162
  as strategic impression management, 302, 304
  Sullivanian view of, 51–52
  tailoring self-presentations and, 211
Apology, 86, 248, 297, 299–301
Approval:
  gaining by ingratiation, 300
  need for: conformity and, 316
    as ego involvement, 130
    public self and, 138
    self-consciousness and, 151
    social skill and, 316
    tailoring self-presentations and, 211

Approval (*Cont.*):
  pursuit of: as inherent tendency, 31, 180–181, 183, 188–191
    intuitive politician model and, 211, 218, 219, 222
    view of Scottish Moral Philosophers, 3
    (*See also* Affiliation; Popularity; Sociability)
"Armadillo" psychology, 175–176
Arousal from deceit, 338–341
Aspiration, level of, 74, 312, 317
Assertiveness:
  of impression management, 292, 295–296, 300–302, 304–307, 309, 314–318
  self-confirmation of, 102–103
Assessment in self-identification, 76–81, 84–89, 95
Assimilation:
  imitative, 43
  of information, 8–11, 14–15, 70, 106
Attachment toward parents, 186
Attention:
  to deception cues, 346–347
  focus of (*see* Focus of attention)
  selective, 89–90, 106, 169–171
  (*See also* Information processing)
Attention-seeking, 178–179, 183, 184, 190, 195
Attitude:
  toward authority, 185
  causal role of, 271
  derivation of word, 19
  as determinant of intentions, 154
  and fairness judgments, 276, 283
  inferring from statements, 326
  norms and, 271
  salience of, 154–156
Attitude change:
  anticipatory, 152–153, 168

Attitude change (*Cont.*):
  justificatory, 214–215, 223, 226
Attraction:
  as power resource, 294–295, 305–307
  reciprocity in, 363
Attractiveness:
  deception and, 334–336
  influencing by ingratiation, 300
  as power resource, 294–295, 305–307, 312, 313
Attribution:
  accounting and, 283
  (*See also* Accounting)
  actor-observer differences in, 127–129, 279
  anxiety and, 218
  assertive impression management and, 300–302
  availability heuristic in, 206
  belief perseverance in, 222
  (*See also* Cognitive conservatism)
  consensus information and, 217, 222, 239–240, 245–246, 248, 252
  consistency information and, 217, 239–240, 246–248
  constraints on, 216–219
  correspondence with behavior, 326
  counterdefensive, 90, 218, 219, 221
  cultural-historical context of, 215, 225–229
  (*See also* Accounting, cultural influences on)
  defensive, 212–216, 297
  (*See also* Egotism)
  depression and, 110–111
  distinctiveness information and, 217, 239–240, 247–248
  egotistical, 12–14, 85–86, 89–91, 127–130
  (*See also* Acclamation; Accounting; Egotism)
  false consensus effect in, 222
  goal importance and, 79

SUBJECT INDEX

Attribution (*Cont.*):
heightening ambiguity of, 247
(*See also* Self-handicapping)
impression management and, 314–315
impression-management value of, 219–220
to internal (dispositional) or external (situational) causes, 129, 217, 222, 245, 247
intuitive politician model of, 200, 204, 207–228
intuitive scientist model of, 200, 203–209, 217, 221, 228
logic of research programs on, 204–209
of moral culpability, 269
motivated biases in, 204, 206, 208–209, 213–228
(*See also* Egotism)
motive for, 204, 205, 208
offensive, 212, 216
persuasive impact of, 220, 222
plausibility of, 216–220, 223, 224, 226–227
(*See also* Believability)
in predicaments, 212–297
(*See also* Egotism)
private versus public, 220
rationality of, 200, 203–209, 217, 218
reinforcement of, 223
of responsibility, 14, 85–86, 90, 127, 221, 227–228
(*See also* Excuse; Responsibility)
self-certainty and, 108–109
self-critical, 90, 218, 219, 221
self-esteem and, 218
in self-presentation, 126
self-presentational success in, 219–222
self-serving, 12–14, 199–200, 204, 206, 208–209, 213–228, 297, 309
(*See also* Acclamation; Accounting; Egotism)

Attribution (*Cont.*):
shortcomings of, 221–222
sincerity of, 223
of status, 307
tactics of, 214–216
universal aspects of, 227–228
violation of norms and, 264
(*See also* Acclamation; Accounting; Excuse; Explanation)
Attribution theory, 203, 205, 314
Audiences:
external (outer), 44–45, 82, 126, 130–131, 207, 208, 211, 216–220, 237, 248, 250, 253, 265, 267, 279–280, 284
Goffman's view of, 23
internal (imagined), 30, 31, 44–45, 66, 82, 89, 126–131, 207, 208, 211, 219, 220, 237, 248, 250, 264, 265, 267, 268, 279–281, 284
similarities to external audiences, 44–45, 82
types of, 66, 82–84, 130–135, 180, 211–212, 237, 279–281
Augmentation principle, 205
Authoritarianism, 49
Authority:
accommodation to, 182, 185, 186
as power resource, 307
Authority figure, 182, 185, 186
Automaticity principle, 328–329
Autonomy, individual differences in, 177
(*See also* Self, agency of)
Availability heuristic in attribution, 206
Awareness:
of behavior during deception, 329
of excuses, 252, 253
of others, 186–187
(*See also* Self-Attention; Self-Awareness; Self-Consciousness)

Balance theory, 15, 35
Bargaining (*see* Negotiation)
Basking In Reflected Glory (BIRGing), 241–242
Bay of Pigs, 224, 348
Bayes' theorem, 203, 205
Behaviorism, 5, 36, 40, 43, 46–48, 54, 55
Belief, perseverance of, 222
(*See also* Cognitive conservatism)
Believability:
of identity images, 73–75, 82–84, 94
of impression management, 324
of influence attempts, 305–306
(*See also* Credibility; Honesty; Sincerity; Truthfulness)
Beneffectance, 12–14, 30–31, 127–130
(*See also* Egotism)
Beneficiality of identity images, 73–75, 82–84, 94
Bias:
beneffectance, 12–14, 30–31, 127–130
(*See also* Egotism)
cognitive conservatism, 12, 14–15, 70, 127, 222, 344–345
egocentricity, 12–13, 127, 187
egotism (*see* Egotism)
selectivity, 52, 89–91
in self-knowledge, 12–15, 30–31, 127–130
self-serving, 199–200, 204, 206, 208–209, 212–228, 297, 309
(*See also* Egotism)
shortcomings of attribution, 221–222
Bible, the, 44
Biogrammar, 178
Biology, foundations of self and, 175, 177–181, 183, 190–191, 195
Blame:
moral, 265, 266, 269, 276, 282

384 SUBJECT INDEX

Blame (*Cont.*):
  reduction of (*see* Accounting; Excuse; Justification)
Blaming tactics, 241–242, 249, 254
Bluffing, 307
Boastfulness, 324
  (*See also* Self-enhancement)
Bogus pipeline, 129, 223–224, 250
British Associationism, 3, 4
Bureaucracy, 184, 189
Bystander intervention, 263*n*., 267, 279
  (*See also* Altruism; Helping; Prosocial behavior)

California Personality Inventory, 185
Cause:
  compared to reason, 315
  inferences of, 203–205, 208, 314
    (*See also* Attribution)
  responsibility and, 239
    (*See also* Responsibility)
Centrality:
  of goals, 79
  of images, 69–70, 72, 77
Certainty of perceived self-images, 107–110, 117, 120
Character:
  as power resource, 297, 304
    (*See also* Disposition; Trait; Personality)
Cheating, machiavellianism and, 341–342
Choice in predicaments, 214, 215, 223, 246
  (*See also* Accounting; Excuses; Responsibility)
Choice-harm deescalator effect, 243
Class, social, 275–277
Clinical populations, self-verification and, 109–111
Coalition as power resource, 307
Coercive power, 295
  (*See also* Intimidation)
Cognition:
  anxiety and, 88

Cognition (*Cont.*):
  disorganized, 102
  motives and, 107–110
  social, 6–12
  (*See also* Information processing)
Cognitive complexity, 338, 341
Cognitive conservatism, 12, 14–15, 70, 127, 222, 344–345
Cognitive imperialism, 207*n*.
Cognitive script (*see* Script)
Collective self, 131, 133–136, 139–141
Committed image, 73
Communicative act, 47
Comparative appraisal, 101, 311
Comparison value, 103–104
Compensation in self-presentation, 248
Competence:
  as facet of positive self-image, 304
  as goal of self-promotion, 301
  locus of control and, 317
  socialization and, 181, 184–185, 187–189, 191–194
Compliance to influence attempts, 305
Computer:
  analogy to scripts and plans, 76–77
  analogy to self, 7–8
Condemnation of the condemners, 282
Confirmation bias, 14, 70, 102
  (*See also* Cognitive conservatism)
Conflict:
  as antecedent of negotiation, 268–269
  between goals, 264
  through group living, 178
  from intimidation, 301
  in moral dilemmas, 262, 268
  in values, 79
Conformity:
  approval need and, 316
  audiences and, 133, 135
  individual differences in, 177

Conformity (*Cont.*):
  as an ingratiation tactic, 300
  loneliness and, 194
  need for achievement and, 138
  to norms, 184, 270
  public-private differences in, 279
  reduced through accounts, 277, 278
  self-attention and, 148, 154–155, 168
  self-consciousness and, 137–138
Congruency theory, 89*n*., 270
Conscience, 84
Consciousness:
  of anxiety, 52
  of self (*see* Self-Attention; Self-Awareness; Self-Consciousness)
  stream of, 4, 7 8, 37–41, 62
Consensual agreement, perceptions of, 90
Consensual validation, 67–70
Consensus:
  false, 222
  as information for attributions, 217, 222, 239–240, 245–246, 248, 252
Conservatism, cognitive, 12, 14–15, 70, 127, 222, 344–345
Consistency:
  as information for attributions, 217, 239–240, 246–248
  between words and deeds, 306
  (*See also* Self-consistency)
Consistency theory, 35, 94, 106–107
Construction:
  of identity, 68, 183, 220*n*., 261
  of reality, 17, 24, 101, 188
  of situational definitions, 17, 200, 264–265, 267–268, 271–277, 280–281, 284
  of supportive environments for self, 30, 77, 89–92, 104–105

SUBJECT INDEX 385

Context:
  for behavior, 261, 262
  cultural-historical (see
    Cultural-historical context)
  for self-identification, 66–67, 75–81
Contextual epistemology, 207n.
Continuity of self, 2, 4, 8, 9, 14–15, 38–41, 52, 70–71
Control:
  locus of, 251, 283, 317
  need for, 191
  perceptions of, 110–111, 127–128
  self, 179, 184
  through self-presentation, 67, 293, 295, 297, 303
  through self-verification, 101–102, 115, 116
Control theory, 31, 163–167
Controllability of communication channels in deception, 328–329, 331, 332, 336, 337, 342, 356
Conventionalization, 241, 265, 266, 283
Conversation, structure of, 272–273
Cooperation as antecedent of negotiation, 268–269
Correspondent inference, 205, 298
Counterattitudinal behavior, 213–215, 223, 226
Courtesy, deception and, 362, 364
Covariation principle, 205
Credibility:
  of adults to children, 354
  deceit and, 323, 363
  as power resource, 305–306, 317, 324
  (See also Believability; Honesty; Sincerity; Truthfulness)
Crisis, midlife, 93
Cuban missile crisis, 224
Culpability:
  moral, 265, 266, 269, 276, 282

Culpability (Cont.):
  reduction of (see Accounting; Excuse; Justification)
Cultural-historical context:
  of attribution, 216, 225–229
  of explanations, 216, 225–229
  of moral dilemma resolution, 262, 271–277, 283–284
  of self, 34, 40–41, 59, 60
  of situational definitions, 267
  of social behavior, 24, 210, 216, 269
Curiosity, 102
Cutting Off Reflected Failure (CORFing), 242
Cybernetics, 103–104, 163–167

Darwinism, 45, 49
  (See also Evolution)
Deception:
  accuracy in detecting, 325–343, 361
  actual cues for detecting, 337–343
  age differences: in detection of, 351–355
    in use of, 355–359
  ambiguous nature of, 323–324, 353
  ambivalence and, 347, 353
  anxiety from, 338–341
  in attributions, 222–224
  for benefit of target, 362
  as cognitively demanding task, 338–339, 341, 343, 349
  commitment to, 341
  in communications, 323–364
  condemnation of, 323
  consequences of, 83, 360–364
  consequential, 348–349
  courtesy and, 362, 364
  cues to, 328–348, 352–353, 355–359, 361
  defense of, 323
  defined, 323
  detecting by content, 328
  development of abilities, 350–360

Deception (Cont.):
  development of moral judgment and, 350–352, 360
  experience at, 347–349, 356
  experience at detecting, 345–346, 353
  extemporaneity and, 349
  extraversion and, 342
  guilt from, 328, 338, 341
  insecurity in, 338–341
  intentionality in, 350–352, 354, 362
  justification of, 244
  learning to detect, 350–355
  machiavellianism and, 341–342, 359
  moral orientation and, 84
  morality of, 360–364
  motivation to engage in, 331–337, 342–343, 348–349
  mundane types of, 332
  negativity in, 341, 342
  nervousness from, 338–342
  versus nonliteral language forms, 350, 352
  nonverbal cues for detecting, 328–348, 352–353, 355–359, 361
  perceived cues for detecting, 343–345
  for personal gain, 362–363
  physiological arousal in, 338–341
  planning of, 349
  play, in development of, 359–360
  politeness strategy in detecting, 361
  prestige and, 307
  problems for deceiver, 362–364
  problems for perceiver by detecting, 361–362
  recognizing communications as, 350
  rehearsal of, 339
  in reporting attitudes, 223–224
  reputational constraints on, 306
  rigidity in behaviors during, 342
  self, 252–253

Deception (*Cont.*):
  sex differences in, 335–336, 342, 359, 363
  sex differences in detecting, 361
  social benefits from, 362, 364
  social costs of, 364
  spontaneity in, 349
  stereotypes about, 344–345
  strategies for, 349
    used by children, 357
  strategies for detecting, 325, 346–347
  success at, 347–349
  success at detecting, 345–347
  suspicions of, 326, 346–347
  verbal cues for detecting, 328–348, 352–353, 355–359
Deception accuracy, 327, 331
Defense of innocence, 214, 216, 240, 241
Defense mechanism, 49, 181, 246
Defensibility of explanations, 224–225
Defensiveness:
  in attribution, 219
  impression management and, 292, 295–300, 302–304, 313, 314, 317, 318
Definition of the situation, 11, 16, 17, 76, 200, 295
  causal role of, 269–271
  in moral dilemmas, 262–277, 280–281, 284
  success in politics and, 212
Dehumanization of victims, 270
Deindividuation, 133–135
Delinquency, 271, 282, 362
Delusion, self, 313
Democracy, 45, 49
Dependence, 114, 210, 301
  (*See also* Supplication)
Depression:
  absence of beneffectance in, 127–128, 130
  attribution and, 110–111
  lessened by excuses, 245
  loneliness and, 193

Depression (*Cont.*):
  maintaining symptoms of, 110–111
    as self-handicapping strategy, 314
  produced by lowered self-esteem, 309
  as strategic impression management, 303
Derogation:
  of evaluators, 244–245, 249, 252
  of negative feedback, 244, 249
  of victims, 243, 249, 270, 282
Descriptive explanation, 199
Desirable identity:
  anxiety and, 88–89
  believability of, 73–75, 94
  beneficiality of, 74–75, 94
  creating environments for, 89–92
  defined, 72–75
  distinguished from self-concept, 75
  influence of audiences on, 66
  mediating self-identification, 30, 75–84
  threats to, 85–89
  usefulness of, 73–75
Desirable image (*see* Desirable identity)
Desired identity (*see* Desirable identity)
Desired image (*see* Desirable identity)
Development:
  of deception abilities, 350–361
  mental, 42–43
  of moral judgment, 350–352, 360
  of morals, 43, 237
  of personality, 43, 44, 47, 49, 69–70, 175–191
  of self, 17–18, 42–47, 49–51, 175–191
  social, 43–47, 50
Deviance, 168, 190, 263, 270
Dialectic:
  of inner and outer self, 180

Dialectic (*Cont.*):
  of person and society, 43, 49–50
Diffuse self, 131–136, 139
Diffusion of responsibility, 225, 270
DIRTEing (Directing Internal Responsibility To External), 249
Disabilities as excuses, 298
Disaffiliative behavior, 87–88, 338, 341
Disclaimer, 222, 297–299
Discontinuity of self, 22, 29, 38–41
Discounting principle, 205
Disposition:
  as attributional cause, 217, 222
  biologically based, 179
  characteristics as power resource, 295
  imputation of, 262
  as power resource, 297
  (*See also* Character; Personality; Trait)
Dissonance theory, 15, 269n., 294
Distinctiveness:
  of identity, 69
  as information for attributions, 217, 239–240, 247–248
Distributive justice, 158–160
Dominance:
  as innate tendency, 178–179
  in relationships, 114
  self-verification of, 113, 118
  (*See also* Status)
Dominance orderings, 58
Double bind in schizophrenia, 111
Dramatism, 20
Dramatized performance, 22
Dramaturgy, 16, 19–23
  and accepting others "lines," 326
  criticisms of, 22–23, 176, 188
  socioanalytic theory and, 31, 176
Drugs, 136, 247
Drunkenness as excuse, 247
Duping delight, 328
Duty, 276–277, 351

SUBJECT INDEX

Ecological niche, 105
Efficacy, self, 35, 71
Effort:
   as consistency-lowering excuse, 247
   (*See also* Attribution)
Ego:
   acceptance of, 51
   as agency, 2
   alter and, 43
   biases of (*see* Egotism)
   defense through self-handicapping, 299
   ideal, 312
      (*See also* Ideal self)
   in psychoanalysis, 49
   pure, 38–39, 45
   threats to, 246
   totalitarian, 35, 127
   transcendent, 4
Ego involvement, 130–131, 135
Ego-involvement effect, 13
Ego-task analysis, 31, 130–141
Egocentricity, 12–13, 127, 268
   in children, 12–13, 187
   in pursuit of status, 191
Egotism, 12–14
   in attributions, 12–14, 85–86, 89–91, 127–130
   as beneffectance, 12–14, 30–31, 127–130
   depression and, 127–128, 130
   explanations and, 85–86
   image claims and, 83
   self-serving biases, 12–14, 199–200, 204, 206, 208–209, 212–228, 299, 309
Embarrassment, 22, 52, 297, 335, 350
Emotion:
   aroused in target by impression management, 300
   awareness of, 150, 151
   as influence tactic, 294
   intensified by private self-consciousness, 280
   revealed through nonverbal behavior, 328
Emotionality, self-confirmation of, 102–103
Emotivism, 60, 61

Empathy in resolving moral dilemmas, 281
Empirical self, 8, 34, 38, 43, 45, 53
Empiricism, 40
Enhancement as acclamation, 86, 90, 216, 300, 302
Entitlement as acclamation, 86, 90, 216, 300, 302, 315, 317
Environment:
   creating supportive, 30, 77, 89–92, 104–105
   obtaining cognitive mastery over, 203–204
Epistemology:
   contextualist, 207n.
   of research programs in attribution, 203, 205–210
Equality, 158–160
Equity, 158–160, 276
Esteem, 253, 305, 307
   (*See also* Self-esteem)
Ethnomethodology, 272
Ethogenics, 272
Evaluation:
   of role performance, 188
   of self, 308–314
Evaluation apprehension, 130, 279, 356
Evaluative orientation, 31, 137
Event, as action plus consequence, 236
Evolution:
   Darwinian influence on Mead, 45–46
   socioanalytic theory and, 175, 177–180, 190–191, 195
Exchange theory, 264, 295
Excuse, 86, 215–216, 226, 235–254
   anticipatory, 224–225, 252
   awareness of, 252, 253
   boundaries of, 249–251
   compared to entitlement, 86, 302
   compared to reasons, 253, 254
   consensus raising, 245–246, 248, 252
   consistency lowering, 246–248
   defensibility of, 250

Excuse (*Cont.*):
   as defensive impression management, 297–299, 302–304, 314, 316
   defined, 86, 240
   DIRTEing (Directing Internal Responsibility To External), 249
   distinctiveness raising, 247–248
   drunkenness as, 247
   as explanation to protect esteem, 200
   extreme, 253
   from failure to meet standards, 85–86, 90
   goal of, 236
   grace in, 251–254
   habitual nature of, 252
   in legal system, 254
   minimized by personality factors, 250–251
   minimized by situational factors, 249–250
   nonverbal, 252
   predicated by self-image threats, 237–238, 240
   prevalence of, 251–252
   projection as, 246–249
   in resolution of moral dilemmas, 262, 265, 268, 279, 282, 283
   self-deception and, 252–253
   socialization of, 254
   stigma of, 235
   strategies of, 241–248
   subtlety of, 252–253
   truthfulness of, 253
   types of, 241–248
Exemplification, 300, 301, 308
Expectancy:
   of performance, 161
   role, 176
   self-efficacy, 52–53
   in self-identification, 84–89
   self-verification and, 101–102
Expectancy-value model, 74, 217–219
Expertise as power resource, 295, 297, 305–307, 312, 316
Explanation:
   account as, 262–269, 272, 297

Explanation (*Cont.*):
  attributions in, 203–228
  cultural-historical context of, 215–216, 225–229
  defensibility of, 224–225
  descriptive, 199
  performative, 199
  plausibility of, 216–220, 223, 224, 226–227
  rationality of, 200, 203–209, 217, 218
  reasons in, 315
  satisficing, 206, 218
  in self-identification theory, 85–86
  self-serving, 12–14, 85–86, 89–91, 127–130, 199–200, 204, 206, 208–209, 212–228, 297, 309
Extraversion, 342

Face, 21–22, 57
Face work, 295
Failure, fear of, 303, 316
Fairness, judgments of, 274–277
Fantasy of desired identity, 93, 94
Favor-doing as an ingratiation tactic, 300
Fear:
  of failure, 303, 316
  induced by intimidation, 301
Fitness, as concept in evolutionary theory, 179–180
Fixed-action pattern, 183–184
Flattery, 300
Focus of attention:
  compared to evaluative orientation, 137, 169–171
  as determinant of behavior, 147–171
  individual differences in, 149–151
  manipulations of, 151–152
  (*See also* Self-attention; Self-awareness; Self-consciousness)
Folkways, 262
Forced compliance paradigm, 213–215, 223, 226

Foreseeability of behavioral consequences, 214, 215, 246–247
Frame theory, 10
Friendship, obligations of, 278
Front, 22, 57

"g" factor in human abilities, 182
Games:
  in development of deception ability, 359–360
  in personality development, 184–185, 187–189
  in ritualized interaction, 51–52
Generalized other, 47, 50, 148
Genetic psychology, 42
Gestalt school, 36
Globe Theatre, 19
Goal(s):
  achieved through identity, 72
  achieved through self-presentation, 291–292, 296
  as affects self-esteem, 309
  of apologies, 299
  beliefs and, 73
  centrality of, 79
  of changing self-concept, 110–111
  as channeling self-identification, 74–84
  control theory and, 163, 167
  in ego task analysis, 131–133, 135
  of exemplification, 301
  ideal images and, 72–73
  impediments to attainment of, 161–162
  importance of, 79, 82, 87, 88
  influence of audiences on, 66
  of ingratiation, 301
  for self, 30, 31, 65
  self-evaluation and, 169
  in self-identification, 75–81, 85, 95
  and self-identification types, 67
  self-presentation and, 82

Goal(s) (*Cont.*):
  self-verification and, 101, 120
  setting, 312
  situational definitions and, 264, 268
  in socioanalytic theory, 177, 182, 195
  superordinate, 135
  of supplication, 301
God, 38, 41
Grease (movie), 66
Group living, 175, 178, 179, 190–191
Guilt:
  countered by accounts, 282
  from deception, 328, 338, 341, 356
  defensive self-presentation and, 294
  induced by exemplification, 301
  produced by lowered self-esteem, 309
  psychoanalytic view of, 50
  over suspicions of others, 362
  from violation of norms, 264
Gulf of Tonkin, 348

Habit:
  customs and, 3
  of excuses, 252
  of impression management, 224, 302–303, 316
  in self-identification, 78, 81
  self-presentational, 191
Habitual self, 43
Hamming strategy in deception, 357–358
Harm-choice deescalator, 246
Harm-doing, moral dilemmas and, 263*n*., 281
Harm, mitigated by justifications, 265
Health, 192, 247
Hedonic satisfaction, 132, 139
Hedonism, 41, 280
Hellenistic drama, self in, 2
Helping:
  altruism, 281–282

Helping (Cont.):
  ambiguity of situation and, 267
  bystander intervention and, 263n., 267, 279
  moral dilemma of, 263n.
  obligations in, 266
  reduced by anonymity, 279
  responsibility for, 225
  (See also Prosocial behavior)
Helplessness, 302, 303
Heuristics in attribution process, 206
Hiroshima, 244
Historical-cultural context (see Cultural-historical context)
History, unpredictability of, 48
Honesty, 57, 306, 324, 338
  (See also Believability; Credibility; Sincerity; Truthfulness)
Hostility, 111, 193, 245
Humor as influence tactic, 294
Hypnotism, 41
Hypochondriasis, 303

I, 3, 38–41, 46–48, 147
Id, 49, 312
Ideal self, 72–75
  compared to real self, 72–73
  in control theory, 164–167
  development of, 312–313
  social power and, 293, 308, 310–315, 317
Idealized performance, 22
Ideals of the audience, 313
Identification:
  with culture, 50
  defined, 65
  of others, 65–66
  in psychoanalytic theory, 65–66, 312
  of self, 65–95
Identity:
  acceptance of other's, 326
  achieved through self-presentation, 292, 293
  "action identity," 120–121
  agency of, 61
  change in, 116–121

Identity (Cont.):
  conflicts in claims about, 267
  consensual agreement on, 67–70, 90, 112–113, 116
  construction of, 68, 183, 220n.
    (See also Definition of the situation)
  contents of, 68–70
  creating environments for, 89–92
  defined, 67–68
  deindividuation and, 133–134
  desirable (see Desirable identity)
  as determinant of information processing, 70–71
  dialectic of private and public, 180
  dimensions of, 236
  as dispositional imputation, 262
  embarrassment and, 297
  enhancement through attribution, 208–209, 212–228
  enhancing through assertive impression management, 295–296, 300–302, 304–307, 308
  in Erikson's work, 35
  evolved, 92–93
  facets of, 170
  functions of, 69–72
  ideal, 310–314
    (See also Ideal self)
  image: centrality of, 69–70, 72, 77, 313
    defined, 68
    desirability of (see Desirable identity)
    evaluative judgment and, 71–72
    functions of, 69–72
    goal achievement and, 72
    importance of, 69–70, 72, 77
    as interpretational filter, 71
    as prototype, 71
    as script or plan, 71
    usefulness of, 73–75

Identity (Cont.):
  as joint construction, 68–69
  maintaining through accounts, 264–265, 268, 270, 277
  maintaining through self-presentation, 175–177, 180–181, 186, 188–189
  moral, 269
  negotiation of, 183, 220n.
  occupational, 180
  as organizational structure, 69–70
  personal, 208–209, 215–217, 219, 222, 224, 226–227
  personal versus social specification of, 148
  power and, 304
  private, 93, 180
  versus private self-esteem, 299
  protecting through defensive impression management, 295–300, 302–304
  reference groups and, 37
  relation to self, 68–69
  satisfaction with, 93–94
  situated (see Situated identity)
  social, 208–209, 215–217, 219, 222, 224, 226–227
  social power and, 294–297, 303–315, 317–318
  socioanalytic view of, 175–176, 180–183, 188–189
  sociological view of, 24
  specification of, 65
  threats to, 212–216, 220, 223, 226
  types sought, 210–211
Identity image (see Identity, image)
Identity objectives, 211
Idiosyncrasy credit, 247
Illness, 192
  mental (see Mental illness)
Illusion of self, 52
Illustrator, 338
Image:
  committed, 73
  desirable (see Desirable identity)
  of irrationality, 210

Image (Cont.):
  revolving, 237, 248
  (See also Identity, image; Self; Self-image)
Imitation:
  of exemplifiers, 301
  ideal self and, 312
  as identification, 65–66
  of lies, 364
  loneliness and, 194
  rehearsal of roles and, 188
  in socioanalytic theory, 179
Immediacy of behavior, 338, 339, 341, 348
Implicit personality theory, 315
Importance:
  of goals, 79, 82, 87, 88
  of images, 69–70, 72, 77
  of performances, 238
Impression management:
  assertive, 292, 295–296, 300–302, 304–307, 309, 314–318
  attitude change and, 223–224
  attributions and, 314–315
  audiences for, 126–127, 130–131
  children's use of, 358–360
  deception in, 323–364
  defensive, 292, 295–300, 302–304, 313, 314, 317, 318
  depression and, 303
  differences in public-private behavior and, 211
  Goffman's view of, 23, 53, 58
  maintaining consistency of, 137–138
  morality of, 57–61
  versus private needs, 309–310
  in resource allocation, 159–160
  role of external audience in, 237
  self-esteem and, 309–314, 317–318
  sincerity in, 324
  as social esteem need, 208
  socioanalytic view of, 176–177, 180–181

Impression management (Cont.):
  strategic, 292, 296–297, 302–308, 317, 318
  tactical, 292, 296–302, 307, 309, 317, 318
  (See also Self-presentation)
Impression-management value of attribution, 219–220
Impression, secondary, 302
Incredible Hulk, 105
Inference:
  causal, 203–205, 208, 314
  (See also Attribution)
  correspondent, 205, 298
  direct forms, 293
  selective, 89, 91–92
  through self-presentation, 291, 293–297, 303, 304, 308–314
  value of truthfulness for, 324
  (See also Control; Impression management; Power; Self-presentation)
Information power, 295
Information processing:
  anxiety and, 88
  assimilation and, 8–11, 14–15, 70, 106
  attribution and, 203, 205–206
  biases in: beneffectance, 12–14, 30–31, 127–130
    cognitive conservatism, 14–15
    egocentricity, 12–13, 127, 187
    egotism, 12–14, 85–86, 89–91
    selectivity, 52, 89–91
    self-serving, 12–14, 199–200, 204, 206, 208–209, 212–228, 297, 309
  shortcomings of attributions, 221–222
  capacity of, in children, 354
  depressives and, 110–111
  as influenced by self, 8–15, 70–71
  nervous system and, 163
  selectivity in, 52, 89–91

Information processing (Cont.):
  self-verification and, 104–106
  tasks in, 205
Ingratiation, 5, 295, 300, 301, 311, 314, 324, 335
Inner-audience hypothesis, 126–130
  (See also Audience)
Inner orientation, 77
  (See also Self, private; Self-consciousness)
Innocence, defense of, 214, 216, 240, 241
Insanity as excuse, 247
Insecurity, 338–341
Instability of self, 6, 21
Instinct, 177, 183–186
Intelligence as personality trait, 179
Intention:
  deception and, 350–352, 354, 362
  explanation and, 315
  inferred in conversations, 273
  responsibility and, 227
  responsibility denial and, 238, 246, 248, 254, 283, 314
  self-attention and, 153–154, 170, 171
Interaction:
  need for, 178–179, 181, 185, 187
  normative background of, 261
  symbolic (see Symbolic interactionism)
Interaction sequence as unit of analysis, 182–183
Interdependence, 294
Internalized referent, 66, 82, 93
Interpersonal congruency theory, 15, 270
Interpersonal psychiatry, 51
Intimidation, 300, 301, 307, 308, 324
Introspection, 38
Intuitive politician model, 199–228
Intuitive scientist model, 8, 200, 203–209, 217, 221, 228
Irrationality, image of, 210

SUBJECT INDEX   391

Justice, 266, 274–277, 283
Justification, 14, 86, 90,
     214–216, 223, 241
   anticipatory, 224–225
   as defensive impression management, 297–299, 307,
     308, 314–315
   defined, 86, 265
   normativity of, 314–315
   in resolution of moral dilemmas, 262, 264–268, 271,
     273, 276, 278, 282, 283

Knowledge:
   limitations of, 269
   preconstituted, 273
   sociology of, 261

Language, 179, 272
Law, excuses in, 254
Legitimacy, 307
Level of aspiration, 74, 312,
     317
Lies (see Deception; Lying)
Life-as-theater analogy, 19
Life cycle as unit of analysis,
     192
Likeability, 179, 304, 324, 363
   (See also Attractiveness)
Linguistics, 272
Locus of control, 251, 283,
     317
Logical empiricism, 207n.
Loneliness, 88, 191, 193–194
Looking-glass self, 3, 18, 44,
     47, 147
Lying:
   by commission and omission, 359
   in forced compliance paradigm, 213–215, 223
   (See also Deception)

Machiavellianism, 341–342,
     359
Marital status, illness and, 192
Marketing personality, 20–21
Material self, 4, 38, 45
Materialism, 42

Maturity, psychological, 177
Me, 3, 37–39, 46–48, 65, 147
   (See also Self-as-known)
Meaning, 272, 274–277
   (See also Definition of the
     situation)
Mental illness:
   neurosis: as focus of traditional personality theories, 178
     locus of control and, 317
     in psychoanalysis, 50, 51
     in socioanalytic theory,
       190
     symptoms as forms of,
       303
     underachievement in, 181
     unrealistic standards and,
       72–74
   psychopathology: self-verification and,
     110–111
   socioanalytic view of, 189,
     190, 192–194
   symptoms as forms of,
     303
   schizophrenia: and denying
     acceptable identity, 313
     double bind, 111
     locus of control and, 317
     performance deficits in,
       303
     Sullivan's work and,
       50–51, 53
   as strategic impression management, 298, 302–303
Mentalism, 48
Mere exposure, 101–102
Metaplay, 186
Microanalysis, in work of
     Goffman, 56, 57
Midlife crisis, 93
Mind, 2, 46–48, 55
Modeling, 179, 194, 312
   (See also Imitation)
Modesty, 83, 90, 221, 302, 324
Montage, 39, 40
Moral judgment, 261–284
   development of, 43, 237,
     350–352, 360
   explanations of conduct
     and, 200–201
Moral realism, 350

Moral reasoning, 244,
     277–279, 351–352
Morality:
   alternative views of, 268
   cognition-behavior relationship, 272–279
   of deception, 360–364
   "deep" meanings of,
     274–276
   development of, 43, 237,
     350–352, 360
   dilemmas of, defined, 262
   exemplification and, 301
   judgments of, 261–284
   orientations toward, 84
   personality and, 281–283
   public versus private, 268,
     279–281
   realism and, 350
   reasoning about, 244,
     277–279, 351–352
   situational definitions and,
     262–271
   views of self and, 57–61
Mores, 262
Motive talk, 297
Motives:
   achievement, 130, 138, 151,
     316
   approval (see Approval,
     need for)
   for attribution, 204, 205,
     208
   conflict between, 268, 277
   consistency, 15
   in explanations, 315
   fear of failure, 303, 316
   for identity, 208–209,
     215–217, 219
   for identity claims, 211
   inferred from justification,
     298
   of participants in defining situations, 267
   power, 291–292, 294, 316
   as power resources, 297
   self-consistency, 106–111
   self-esteem (see Self-esteem)
   for self-presentation,
     309–310
   self-seeking, 41
   vocabulary of, 216, 226
My Lai, 245, 276
Mystification, 348

Naturalistic reproduction strategy in deception, 357
Need:
  for achievement, 130, 138, 151, 316
  for affiliation, 178–179, 181, 185, 316
  for approval: as ego involvement, 130
    public self and, 138
    self-consciousness and, 151
    social skill and, 316
    tailoring self-presentations and, 211
    (See also Affiliation; Popularity; Sociability)
  as determinant of image importance, 69–70
  identity, 208–209, 211, 215–217, 219
  as mediating self-identification, 77–81
  for order, 31
Negotiation:
  of identity, 183, 220n.
  of reality, 17, 24, 188
  of situational definitions, 17, 200, 264–265, 267–268, 271–277, 280–281, 284
Nervousness, 88–89, 338–342
Neurosis (see Mental illness, neurosis)
Neutralization, 282
Nonimmediacy of behavior, 338, 339, 341, 348
Normativity hypothesis, 315
Norms:
  as backgrounds for interaction, 261
  as behavioral attitudes, 271
  against conveying negative information, 108
  as determinants of intentions, 154
  development of conformity to, 184
  to discourage negative feedback, 111
  of distributive justice, 158–160
  excuses and, 249
  of just deserts, 275

Norms (Cont.):
  of merit, 274–275
  moral, 262–272, 282–284
  of need, 274–275
  for role performance, 182–183, 187
  salience of, 154–156
  and self-identification, 76–81
  of social minimum, 275n.
  of social responsibility, 301
  use of deception to maintain, 350
  violations of, 200, 262–269, 271, 277, 282, 300
Nurturance, 301

Obedience, 133, 225, 245–246
Obligations, 276–278, 351
Occupation, selection of, 91, 93, 180, 189
Oedipal crisis, 182
Opportunity structure, 103–105, 111, 112, 115, 120
Order, needs for, 31, 179, 195
Organization, social, 178–180, 183–184, 189, 191
Outer orientation, 77
  (See also Self-consciousness)

"Packaged" information, 68, 75, 78, 81, 94
Pecking order, 183
Performance:
  dramatized, 22
  Goffman's view of, 21–22, 57
  idealized, 22
  negative, 237–248, 252, 254
  reframing, 241–245, 248, 249, 252
  rehearsal of, 80
  socialization of, 23
Performance team, 22
Performative explanation, 199
Persona, 19
Personality:
  adjustment, 179, 185, 188–194
  correlates of moral behavior, 281–283

Personality (Cont.):
  defined, 179
  development of, 43, 44, 47, 49, 182–189
  development through stabilization of images, 69–70
  differences in self-consciousness, 149–151
  in ego-task analysis, 131, 137–139
  identity development and, 180–181
  impression management and, 315–317
  as mediating self-identification, 75–81
  as power resource, 297
  pragmatism and, 211
  as product of social interaction, 179, 188–189
  socioanalytic view of, 176–195
  as stable core, 177
  structures of, 179
  traditional theories of, 176–178
  traits in, 54–55
Perspective taking, 281
Persuasion, 136, 306–307
Phenomenology, 38
Plan:
  as characteristic of human activity, 76, 261
  compared to script, 76–77
  for deception, 349
  defined, 76–77
  as definition of the situation, 263
  goals and, 65
  identity images and, 71
  influence of audiences on, 66
  self-identification and, 30, 76–81, 85, 95
  self-verification and, 119
  in socioanalytic theory, 177
  as structure for interaction, 273
Play:
  in development of deception ability, 359–360
  and development of self, 18, 186–189
  and internalization of generalized other, 47

Pluralism, theoretical, 207
Politeness strategy in detecting deception, 361
Politicians, people as, 199–228
Popularity:
  decreased by deception-detection ability, 361
  pursuit of, 179–181, 188–191, 193, 194
Power:
  attractiveness as, 294–295, 305–307, 312, 313
  coercive, 295
  deception and, 363
  expertise as, 295, 297, 305–307, 312, 316
  ideal self and, 308, 310–315
  identity and, 294–297, 303–315, 317–318
  information as, 295
  need for, 191, 291–292, 294, 316
  reward, 295
  as self-direction, 2
  self-esteem and, 309–314, 317–318
  through self-presentation, 291–295, 303, 317–318
  source characteristics and, 304–307
  status as, 294–295, 305–307, 312
  symptoms as, 303
Power motive, 291–292, 294, 316
Pragmatic philosophy, 3–4
Pragmatism, 11, 16, 35, 45, 47, 53, 73
Praise, rejection of, 74
Predicament:
  attribution in, 212–216, 226, 254
  defensive impression management in, 295–300, 302, 313
Predictability of behavior, 179, 183, 184, 195
Prestige as power resource, 305–307
Pretensions, 74
Principle, in control theory, 165–167
Program, in control theory, 166–167

Projection, 246, 249
Promise, 293
Prosocial behavior:
  altruism, 281–282
  bystander intervention and, 263n., 267, 279
  as defensive impression management, 297, 300
  elicited by supplication, 301
  increased self-esteem from, 312, 313
  scripts and, 269
  (*See also* Helping)
Prototype, 11–12, 30, 71, 92
Psychoanalytic theory:
  accommodation to authority in, 182, 185
  advantage of therapist in, 59
  during changes in psychology, 36
  criticisms of, 43
  ideal self in, 72–73, 312
  identification in, 65
  and inculcation of values, 237
  intrapsychic focus of, 176
  neurosis and, 34
  and work of Erikson, 35
  and work of Sullivan, 49–51
Psychologist's advantage, 38, 52
Psychopathology (*see* Mental illness, psychopathology)
Pure ego, 38–39, 45
  (*See also* I)
Pure ego theories of self, 4, 8

Quantifying circumstances, 241

Rationality of explanations, 200, 203–209, 217, 218
Rationalization:
  compared to reason, 212
  of conduct, 224, 251
  in resolving moral dilemmas, 262, 270
  to sustain self, 104
  (*See also* Acclamation; Account; Excuse; Justification)
Real self as compared to ideal self, 72–73, 308–309

Reality, construction of, 17, 24, 188
  (*See also* Definition of the situation)
Reality-edited standards, 73
Reasons:
  compared to causes, 261, 315
  compared to excuses, 253, 254
Reciprocity, 272, 351, 363
Reference group:
  and conformity, 177
  in ego-task analysis, 131, 133–136, 139–141
  in resolving moral dilemmas, 281
  salience of, 147, 154–155, 157–158, 168
  and self-concept change, 120
  and value priorities, 212
Reference-group theory, 37
Reference value in control theory, 163–167, 169–170
Referent, internalized, 66, 82, 93
Reflected appraisal, 3, 17–18, 93–94, 101, 311
Reflectivity, 2, 16
Reflexivity, 17, 46, 147–149
  (*See also* Me; Self-as-known)
Reframing performance, 241–245, 248, 249, 252
Rehearsal:
  of accounts, 268
  of deceptive self-presentations, 339
  of performances, 80
Reinforcement:
  of attributions, 223
  from favor-doing, 300
  power and, 294
Rejection:
  of depressives, 111
  of explanations, 216–219
  self-consciousness and, 138
  sensitivity to, 150
Relationships:
  satisfaction with, 92–93
  self-verification in, 112–116
  socioanalytic theory of, 190–191
Religion, 42

Remedial behavior, 58, 269
Remorse as mitigating factor after transgressions, 248
Representativeness heuristic in attribution, 206
Repression, 50
Reproduction, social prerequisites for, 180–181
Reputation as power resource, 296–297, 304–307, 312–313, 318
Respect, pursuit of, 211, 219
Responsibility:
  acceptance of, 249–251, 270
  in apologies, 299
  apparent, 240–242, 249, 252
  attributions of, 14, 85–86, 90, 127, 200, 221, 227–228
  diffusion of, 225, 270
  egotism and, 90
  factors affecting, 238–240
  increasing by entitlements, 86, 90, 216, 300, 302, 315, 317
  locus of control and, 251
  minimizing by excuses, 85–86, 240–242, 245–248, 254, 265, 279, 282–283, 298, 299, 302, 303
  (See also Excuse)
  moral, 274–277
  for negative events, 213–215, 227
  person concept and, 310
  for positive events, 216
  and self-image threats, 237–242
  in status hierarchies, 276–277
  transformed, 240–241, 245–249, 252
  for transgressions, 227
Reticence, 88
Retributive justice, 266, 283
Revolving images, 237, 248
Reward power, 295
Ritual:
  as context for interaction, 178–179, 183, 191
  in games, 51
  Goffman's view of, 22–23, 57

Ritual (Cont.):
  as reflecting need for order, 31
  in self-identification, 76–81
  in socioanalytic theory, 183, 191
  in symbolic interaction approach, 17
  (See also Norms; Rule; Script)
Role:
  cultural-historical context of, 24
  defined, 18, 176
  derivation of, 19
  as determinant: of responsibility, 227–228
    of self, 148
  distance, 185, 187
  excuses and, 249
  expectations, 176, 182–183
  identity and, 68, 69, 176, 180, 182–184, 188–189, 195
  as information, 23
  "making," 84
  negotiation of, 267
  performances and, 11, 22
  pragmatism and, 3
  as reflecting needs for order, 31
  relation to self, in Goffman, 60
  responsibilities of, 274
  as script, 11, 19, 76–78, 176, 182–183
  in scripted actions, 270
  selection of, 31
  sex, 186–187
  socialization of, 117
  socioanalytic view of, 176, 180, 182–184, 186–189, 191, 195
  status and, 307
  structure, 183
  symbolic interactionism and, 17
  of therapist, 52–53
  in thought, 47
  unity of, 40
Role conflicts, 50
Role identities, 75
Role-playing, 18, 47, 181, 183–190

Role-taking, 3, 46–47, 181–184, 281–282
Role theory, 11, 18–19, 35, 48
Rotula, 19
Rousseau Institute, J. J., 42
Rule:
  in attribution, 203, 205–206, 216, 226
  as background for interaction, 262
  basic, 272
  changing, 91–92
  deep versus surface, 272–276
  as guide for behavior, 178–179, 182–184, 186, 191
  historical-cultural context of, 24
  and identity, 295
  moral, 57, 262–266, 271, 274, 279, 281
  and needs for order, 31
  in self-identification, 68, 75–81
  socialization and, 18
  in symbolic interactionism, 17–18
  view of Goffman, 22, 23, 57
  violations of, 297, 300
  (See also Norms; Ritual)
Rule-role theory, 183

Satisfaction with identity, 92–94
Satisficing, 206, 218
Savage discovery, 242
Schema:
  for accounting, 267
  as definition of the situation, 263
  identity and, 68
  as information, 23
  of self, 8–12
  sociological approach and, 24
  as structure for interaction, 273
  symbolic meaning and, 17
Schizophrenia (see Mental illness, schizophrenia)
Scientists, people as, 8, 200, 203–209, 217, 221, 228

Scottish Moral Philosophers,
  2–3, 16
Script:
  compared to plan, 76–77
  as context, 10–11, 17,
    76–78, 269–270
  defined, 10–11, 76–77
  identity images as, 71, 76–77
  as information, 23
  innate characteristics and,
    185
  processes in learning of, 271
  for resolving moral dilemmas, 262
  roles and, 11, 19, 76–78,
    176, 182–183
  self-identification and, 30,
    76–81, 85, 95
  as situational definition, 17,
    269–270
  social nature of, 11, 24,
    269–270
  in sociological analyses, 24
  symbolic meaning and, 17
  view of Goffman, 23
Script theory, 10–11, 76–77
Secondary impression, 302
Secrecy, 307
Security, 101, 294
Self:
  accommodating, 43
  accounting and, 264–265,
    268, 271, 277, 280, 284
    (*See also* Accounting)
  agency of, 1, 2, 17, 20, 24,
    29, 31, 43, 48, 59,
    61–62, 76, 89–92, 102–
    104, 148, 261, 268, 269
  in ancient philosophy, 2
  assessment problems, 54–55
  as audience, 66, 82, 89, 126,
    131, 237, 279–281, 288
    (*See also* Audiences, internal)
  autonomy of, 292
  biases in knowledge of:
    beneffectance, 12–
      14, 30–31, 127–130
    cognitive conservatism,
      12, 14–15, 70, 127, 222,
      344–345
    egocentricity, 12–13,
      127–187
    egotism, 14, 85–86, 89–91

Self (*Cont.*):
  biological foundations of,
    175, 177–181, 183,
    190–191, 195
  certainty of, 107–111
  collective, 131, 133–136,
    139–141
  computer metaphor for, 7–9
  consciousness of, 37–41
    (*See also* Self-attention;
    Self-awareness; Self-
    consciousness)
  consistency of, 70–71
  as content, 3–4, 7, 10,
    69–70, 147
    (*See also* Me)
  continuity of, 2, 4, 8, 9,
    14–15, 38–41, 52, 70–
    71
  creating environments for,
    77, 89–92, 104–105
  cultural-historical context
    of, 34, 40–41, 59, 60
  defined through self-
    presentation, 176,
    182–183
  delusion, 313
  development of, 17–18,
    42–47, 49–51, 175–191
    (*See also* Development)
  diffuse, 131–136, 139
  discontinuity of, 22, 29,
    38–41
  dramaturgical view of, 22,
    60
  embedded in society, 43–45,
    49–51, 60
  empirical, 3, 4, 8, 38, 43, 45
  enmity with society, 49
  evaluation of, 308–314
  facets of, in ego-task analysis, 130–141
  fragmentation of, 37, 53
  goals of, 30, 65
  habitual, 43
  hierarchical organization of,
    11
  historical-cultural context
    of, 34, 40–41, 59, 60
  ideal (*see* Ideal self)
  illusion of, 52
  as an improvisation, 61
  as imputation, in Goffman,
    22

Self (*Cont.*):
  information processing and
    (*see* Information processing)
  instability of, 6, 21
  as interaction concept, 310
  intrapsychic focus, 293
  introspective knowledge of,
    7
  as knower, 3, 4, 7, 8, 47,
    147
    (*See also* I)
  as known, 3, 4, 7, 8, 47, 147
    (*See also* Me)
  material, 4, 38, 45
  moral perspectives on,
    57–61
  motivational properties of,
    12–15, 41, 130–141
  multiple, 51
  negotiation of, 183, 220*n*.
  as object, 185, 188
    (*See also* Me)
  "packaged" information
    about, 68, 75, 78, 81, 94
  phenomenal, 6, 39
  philosophical approaches to,
    36
  plurality of, 37–39
  pragmatic philosophy and,
    3–4
  private, 131–134, 136–141,
    148–171
  as process, 3–4, 7, 10,
    69–72, 147
    (*See also* I)
  as prototype, 11–12
  public, 131–134, 136–141,
    148–171, 292
  pure ego, 3, 4, 8
    (*See also* I)
  real, as compared to ideal
    self, 72–73, 308–309
  reconstructed, 312–313
  relation to identity, 68–69
  relation to others, 18
  relation to society, 43–47,
    49–51
  as roles, 60
  schema of, 8–12
  in Scottish moral philosophy, 2–3
  social, 4, 6, 22, 37, 38, 43,
    45, 62, 141

Self (*Cont.*):
- social construction of, 68, 183, 220*n*., 261–262
- social power and, 291–318
- as soul, 2
- spiritual, 4, 38, 45
- stability of, 43, 54, 70–71, 113, 115
- stream of consciousness and, 37–41
- structure of, 7–12
- subjective versus objective, 7
- symbolic interactionism and, 16–18
- as system guide, 310
- as theory, 8–9, 67–68, 101, 308
- as "too good to be true," 127–130
- unified, 101
- uniqueness of, 48
- unity of, 2, 4, 5, 8, 9, 15, 39–41
- (*See also* Identity)

Self-acceptance, 51
Self-actualization, 294
Self-as-knower, 3, 4, 7, 8, 47
- (*See also* I)

Self-as-known, 3, 4, 7, 8, 47
- (*See also* Me)

Self-as-theory, 8–9, 67–68, 101, 308
Self-assessment, 54–55, 76–81, 84–89, 95
Self-attention, 146–171
- anticipatory attitude change and, 152–153, 168
- behavioral intentions and, 153–154, 171
- conformity and, 154–155, 168
- ego-task analysis and, 137–139
- goal importance and, 79–80
- individual differences in, 137–138, 149–151
- manipulation of, 136, 151–152
- moral behavior and, 270, 280
- norms and, 155–156
- private versus public, 31, 35, 137–138, 149–151

Self-attention (*Cont.*):
- reference groups and, 157–158, 168
- resource allocation and, 158–160
- stream of thought and, 40
- task perseverance and, 161–162
- (*See also* Self-awareness; Self-consciousness)

Self-awareness:
- anticipating reactions of others through, 208
- development of, 183–184, 186
- manipulations of, 136–137, 151–152
- of roles, 184
- (*See also* Self-attention; Self-consciousness)

Self-certainty, 107–111, 117, 120
Self-concept:
- as amalgamation of images, 236
- centrality and, 129–130
- certainty of, 107–111, 117, 120
- change in, 110–111, 115–121
- in clinical populations, 110–111
- as comparison value, 103–104
- congruence with behavior, 89*n*.
- defined, 8
- desirable images and, 75
- as determinant of behavior, 103–104
- formation of, 101–102
- functions of, 9
- Goffman's view of, 22
- ideal self and, 311
- real self and, 73–75
- information processing and (*see* Information processing)
- maintenance of, 270
- as mediating self-identification, 75–81
- negative, 100, 102, 106–112, 116
- power motive and, 292, 295

Self-concept (*Cont.*):
- preservation of, 101, 105 (*See also* Self-verification)
- reflected appraisal and, 18
- relation to identity, 68–69
- roles and, 19, 31, 176, 182–183, 187
- as schemata, 8–12
- social construction of, 68, 183, 220*n*., 261–262
- sources of information about, 101
- stability of, 43, 54, 70–71, 113, 115, 183, 311
- as theory, 8–9, 67–68, 101, 308
- verification of, 30, 100–121

Self-confirmation (*see* Self-verification)

Self-consciousness:
- anticipatory attitude change and, 153, 168
- aspects of, 31
- behavioral intentions and, 154
- conformity and, 155, 168
- deception and, 222, 237
- ego-task analysis and, 137–138
- external audiences and, 211
- facets of identity and, 170
- harm-doing and, 280
- measurement of, 137–138, 149–151
- moral behavior and, 280, 282
- norms and, 280
- purpose and, 168–169
- reference-group behavior and, 158, 168
- rejection and, 219
- resource allocation and, 158–160
- as role-taking ability, 183–185
- shyness and, 192
- (*See also* Self-attention; Self-awareness)

Self-Consciousness Scale, 137–139, 149–151
Self-consistency:
- absence in Mead's work, 46
- influenced by images, 70–71

SUBJECT INDEX

Self-consistency (*Cont.*):
  rationale for, 101–102
  in self-identification theory, 94
  theories of, 30, 31, 35, 106–107
  valuation of self and, 106
  (*See also* Self-verification)
Self-consistency motive, 15
Self-consistency theory, 106–107
Self-control, 179, 184
Self-criticism, 218, 219, 221
Self-deception, 222, 252–253
Self-disclosure, 30, 66, 67, 70, 75–81, 88
Self-efficacy, 35, 71
Self-enhancement:
  compared to self-verification, 94, 101, 106–111
  conflict with immediate gain, 277
  as element of human motivation, 261, 264
  explanation and, 263
  as ingratiation tactic, 300, 301
Self-esteem:
  ambiguity of measures of, 139, 140
  attribution and, 200, 208, 211, 213–219
  changes in, 111
  collective, 139, 140
  core levels of, 188
  as defined by James, 4
  ego-task analysis and, 139, 140
  as evaluative judgment, 4, 72
  excuses and, 302
  as generalized reinforcer, 310
  ideal self and, 73, 309–314, 317–318
  loneliness and, 193
  maintenance of, 165–166, 236–237, 253
  manipulations of, 109
  moral dilemmas and, 262, 263*n*., 277, 282, 283

Self-esteem (*Cont.*):
  need for, 13–14, 30, 31, 211, 261, 309–310
  compared to self-verification, 101, 106–111, 120
  self-identification and, 94
  as personality variable, 5, 23, 130, 139, 140
  power and, 292, 293, 295, 309–314, 317–318
  private, 139, 140, 299, 309–314, 317–318
  public, 139, 140, 299, 309–314, 317–318
  relation to ego involvement, 130
  relation to shyness, 192
  situated, 72
  social identity and, 180
  task performance and, 130, 162
Self-esteem motive, 13–14, 30, 31, 211, 261, 309–310
  compared to self-verification, 94, 101, 106–111, 120
  self-identification and, 94
Self-fulfilling prophecy, 117
Self-generation effect, 13
Self-handicapping, 247, 297–299, 302–303, 314, 315, 317
Self-identification:
  acclamations and, 85–86
  accounting and, 85–86
  anxiety and, 88–89
  assessment and, 78–81
  audiences and, 76–85, 94
  context for, 66–67, 75–84, 89
  defined, 65–66
  desirable images and, 39, 72–78
  ego-task analysis and, 31
  expectations and, 84–89
  explanations and, 85–86
  functions of images in, 69–72
  goals and, 67, 75–81, 85, 95
  impediments to, 84–89
  moral orientation and, 84
  plans and, 76–81, 85, 95

Self-identification (*Cont.*):
  scripts and, 76–81, 85, 95
  self-concept and, 75–81
  self-presentation and, 82–84
  situations and, 75–81
  unconsciousness of, 76–79, 83–84
  unrealistic, 73–75
Self-image:
  centrality of, 69–70, 72, 77
  excuses and, 236, 254
  explanations and, 204, 206, 208, 213–228
  importance of, 69–70, 72, 77
  influence on career choice, 189
  influence on self-presentations, 177, 195
  as information set, 236
  in socioanalytic theory, 177, 195
  threats to, 237–238, 240, 247, 252, 254
  (*See also* Identity; Image; Self)
Self-inquiry, 67
Self-knowledge:
  biases in, 12–15, 30–31, 127–130
  as desirable identity images, 75–81
  through games, 51
  through identity, 69
  limitations of, 47–48
Self-monitoring, 23, 80–81, 88, 138, 211, 317
  in anxiety, 88
  ego-task analysis and, 138
  impression management and, 317
  and presenting to external audiences, 211
  in self-identification, 80–81
Self-perception, 101, 103, 311
Self-preoccupation, 88
Self-presentation:
  appearance of truthfulness and, 324, 343
  attributional success in, 219–222
  audiences for, 82–83, 126–131, 237
  believability of, 82–84

Self-presentation (*Cont.*):
  beneficiality of, 82–84
  compensation in, 248
  consciousness of, 189, 191, 193, 194
  as cuticle, 57, 58
  deceit and, 34, 323–364
  defense mechanisms and, 181
  desirable images and, 70, 75–84
  ego-task analysis of, 31, 126–141
  focus of attention and, 146–171
  goal achievement and, 72
  goal importance and, 79
  issues raised by control theory, 167–169
  legitimacy of, 57
  marketing personality and, 21
  of modesty, 90
  moral dilemmas and, 261–263, 279, 284
  morality of, 34, 57–61, 323–324
  in resource allocation, 158–160
  self-identification and, 30, 66–67, 75–84
  self-monitoring and, 138
  skill in, 191–193
  social power and, 291–296, 310–314, 317–318
  socioanalytic theory and, 175–177, 180–181, 186, 188–189, 191, 193–195
  strategic, 5–6, 126, 291–318
  symbolic interactionism and, 18, 262–269
  taxonomy of, 292, 297–308
  "trying too hard" in, 339
  types of, 210–211
  unconscious aspects of, 83–84, 176–177, 189
  value of honesty in, 324, 343
  view of Goffman on, 21–23, 56–60
  (*See also* Impression management)
Self-preservation, 4, 14

Self-promotion, 300–302, 308, 314
Self-punishment, 309
Self-realization, 46
Self-recognition, 185
Self-reference effect, 13
Self-regulation:
  to achieve power, 308–309
  assessment and, 80–81
  control theory and, 162–171
  through identity, 68
  moral orientation and, 84
  self-attention and, 31, 162, 171
  self-identification theory and, 65, 66, 68, 80–81, 84, 94
  self-reflection and, 147–149
Self-reinforcement, 270
Self-satisfaction, 72, 93–94
Self-seeking, 4, 13, 41
Self-serving biases (*see* Egotism)
Self-serving explanation (*see* Explanation, self-serving)
Self-verification, 15, 30, 100–121
  as active search, 102–103
  approval and, 211
  control through, 101–102, 114–115
  defined, 101
  opportunity structures and, 103–105
  through perceptions, 89–91
  preference for confirmatory feedback, 102–103
  strategies of, 105–106
  (*See also* Self-consistency)
Sex roles, 186–187
Shame, 264, 297, 356
Shyness, 186, 192–193, 247, 254, 304
Similarity, attraction and, 300, 306
Sincerity:
  appearance of, 343
  assumption of, 325–327
  attribution and, 222–224, 292
  concern about, 338, 353

Situated identity, 19, 68–69
  accounts and, 200, 262, 264–265, 268
  face and, 22
  theory of, 19
Skepticism, 354
Skill, social, 181, 184–195
Sociability, 178–179, 181, 186
  (*See also* Affiliation; Popularity)
Social behaviorism, 46, 48
Social class, 275–277
Social cognition, 4–12
Social comparison, 158
Social Desirability Scale, 138
Social learning theory, 237, 263, 270, 312
Social perspective taking, 281
Social reality, construction of, 17, 24, 101, 188
Social self, 4, 6, 22, 37, 38, 43, 45, 62, 141
Socialization:
  adjustment and, 185, 188–189
  internalized audiences and, 17–18, 208n.
  of roles, 117
  socioanalytic approach to, 185–186
  symbolic interactionist view of, 17–18
  (*See also* Development)
Socioanalytic theory, 31, 55n., 175–195
Solipsism, 46n.
Soul, 2, 4, 5, 39, 46
"Sour grapes" effect, 251
Spiritual self, 4, 38, 45
Standards:
  assessment and, 80
  of the audience in apologies, 299
  clarity of, 238
  control theory and, 164
  desirable images and, 75–81
  ego-task analysis and, 132–133
  explanations and, 85–86
  falling short of, 84–89, 238
  ideal self and, 73, 308–310
  internalization of, 211, 237
  manipulating, 243–244, 252

Standards (*Cont.*):
  need for achievement and, 138
  power and, 308–310
  reality-edited, 73–74
  in resolving moral dilemmas, 280, 281
  selective adoption of, 91–92
  self-assessment and, 84–89
  self-attention and, 148, 164
  self-evaluation and, 84–89, 120, 308–310
  for self-identification, 65–67, 71–72
Status:
  of the audience, 211, 218
  children's perceptions of, 186–187
  concept of person and, 310
  obligations of, 276–277
  as power resource, 294–295, 305–307, 312
  pursuit of, 31, 178–181, 187–191, 193–195, 294–295
Status-envy hypothesis, 312
Status hierarchies, 178–179, 183
Stream of consciousness, 4, 7–8, 37–41, 62
Stress, 93, 246, 253
Structure:
  of conversations, 272–273
  of interaction, 261
  linguistic, 272–274
  pursuit of, 179, 183, 184, 195
  social, 178–179, 189
Sublimation, 49
Suez canal, 224
Superego, 49
Superordinate goal, 135
Supplication, 300, 301, 308
Symbiotic relationship, 115

Symbolic interactionism, 16–19
  development of, 34, 48
  dramaturgical approach and, 21, 22
  imagined reactions of audiences and, 17–18, 237, 280
  James' influence on, 5, 34, 48
  Scottish Moral Philosophers and, 3
  scripts and, 11, 269–270
  self and social needs and, 208*n*.
  self-regulation and, 270
  situational definitions and, 16–17, 263, 264
  socioanalytic theory and, 31, 175
Sympathy, 3
System concept, 164–167

Telos, 60–62
Temperament, 177, 185–186
Theatrical analogy, 19
Therapy, 110–111, 114, 116, 254
Thought:
  as active process, 37
  desirable images and, 75–81
  empirical self and, 45
  identity images and, 70–71
  social nature of, 18, 46–48
  stream of, 4, 7–8, 37–41, 62
Threat, 293, 294, 301, 324
Tonkin, Gulf of, 348
Totalitarian ego, 127
Toughness, image of, 210
Trait, 54–55, 179, 262, 297, 310
Transgression, prosocial behavior and, 294, 300

Trust, 307, 326–327, 346, 352, 362–364
Trustworthiness, 306, 317, 323
Truth, 73–74, 323–324, 351
Truthfulness, 323–327
Typification, 273

Uniqueness, 48, 69
Unity of self, 2, 4, 5, 8, 9, 15, 39–41
Unity principle, 15
Universalism, 45

Validation, consensual, 67–70
Vanity, 327
Values:
  of the audience, 211–212
  conflict between, 79
  in control theory, 164–167
  cultural, 186, 210
  ego involvement and, 131
  focus of attention and, 146–148
  hierarchy of, 283
  ideal images and, 72–73
  image importance and, 69–70
  integrity of, 105–106
  internalization of, 237, 312
  selectivity in, 89, 91–93
  self-identification and, 74–81
Victim derogation effect, 243, 249
Violence, 266, 283
Vocabulary of motives, 216, 226

Warranting, 272
Watergate, 213, 220*n*., 313, 348
Will, 2

HM 291 .S395 1985 c.1

The Self and social life

Saginaw Valley State College Library

DATE DUE

10/31 cam			
NOV 22 1989			
DEC 0 8 1989			
MAY 28 1992			
MY 04 '93			

DEMCO 38-297